*f***P**

Donna Rosenthal

Free Press

New York   London   Toronto   Sydney   Singapore

The
Israelis

Ordinary People in an Extraordinary Land

ƒP

FREE PRESS
A Division of Simon & Schuster, Inc.
1230 Avenue of the Americas
New York, NY 10020

For information about special discounts for bulk purchases,
please contact Simon & Schuster Special Sales:
1-800-456-6798 or business@simonandschuster.com

Designed by Jeanette Olender

Manufactured in the United States of America

1   3   5   7   9   10   8   6   4   2

Library of Congress Cataloging-in-Publication Data
Rosenthal, Donna, 1950–.
The Israelis: ordinary people in an extraordinary land / Donna Rosenthal.
    p.   cm.
Includes bibliographical references and index.
1. National characteristics, Israeli.   2. Israel—Social conditions.
3. Israel—Ethnic relations.   4. Orthodox Judaism—Relations—Nontraditional Jews.
I. Title.
DS113.3 .R67   2003   956.94—dc21   2003049229

ISBN 0-684-86972-1   ISBN 0-684-86973-X (Pbk)

To my cornea donor, who died on a day when Passover,
Easter, and Id al-Fatir coincided, and gave me the gift of sight.
A portion of the proceeds of this book will be donated to
the Israel National Center for Organ Transplants. Through
it, Israelis and Palestinians save each other's lives.

Contents

Acknowledgments ix

Introduction: Colliding Worlds 1

I Becoming Israeli

1. One of the World's Most Volatile Neighborhoods 7

2. Dating and Mating Israeli-style 23

3. A People's Army 47

4. Swords into Stock Shares 75

II One Nation, Many Tribes

5. The Ashkenazim: Israel's "WASPS" 97

6. The Mizrahim: The Other Israelis 113

7. The Russians: The New Exodus 130

8. Out of Africa: Ethiopian Israelis in the Promised Land 148

III Widening Fault Lines Between Jews and Jews

9. The Haredim: Jewish-Jewish-Jewish 173

10. The Orthodox: This Land Is Your Land? This Land Is
    My Land! 195

11. The Non-Orthodox: War of the Cheeseburgers 221

IV Schizophrenia: Non-Jews in a Jewish State

12. The Muslims: Abraham's Other Children   247

13. The Bedouin: Tribes, Tents, and Satellite Dishes   278

14. The Druze: Between Modernity and Tradition   292

15. The Christians: Uneasy in the Land of Jesus   305

V The Sexual Revolution

16. Marriage, Polygamy, Adultery, and Divorce Israeli-style   327

17. Oy! Gay?   357

18. Hookers and Hash in the Holy Land   370

Epilogue: Shalom/Salam   385

Notes   395

Bibliography   439

Index   451

Acknowledgments

This book has been a long time coming. I have many people to thank:

Bill Rosen, my editor at Free Press, who said, "Writing a book about Israel is rather like Lewis Carroll's Alice trying to play croquet with a flamingo: every time you get one leg pointing down, the other one springs up into the air." And the hardworking Andrea Au. Thanks to others at Free Press for believing in the book and delivering it to the finish line: Martha Levin, Dominick Anfuso, Elizabeth Stein, Carisa Hays, Sara Schneider, Elisa Rivlin, Edith Lewis, Lanie Shapiro, Stephanie Fairyington, Nana Geller, Wylie O'Sullivan, and Eric Fuentecilla.

Jan Lurie, the freelance editor whose wise guidance shaped the book from proposal to final manuscript. Your insights, patience, and perseverance helped me through the hardest parts of writing: cutting and making every word count.

Bonnie Solow, my literary agent and friend, who treated this book with tender loving care and gave me crucial advice along the way.

My friend, the late Jerry Landauer of *The Wall Street Journal*, for inspiring my career; Irv Leftovsky of the *Los Angeles Times*, a writer's dream editor; Jack Beatty of *The Atlantic* for encouraging me to write about the Ethiopian and Russian exoduses. And Pat King of *Newsweek* for helping make my previous book possible.

To those Israelis whose names are not in these pages for reasons of personal safety. And to those whose names are not in the book, but whose advice, arguments, and insights are in it: my friend Hassan Sayaad for showing me the land and the people over many years of horseback riding together, and Nadia, Nuha, Sami, Osama, and Walid. Frances Barrow, Ellen Rosenfeld, and Jane Falk for their invaluable research skills. Ralah, Yitzhak, and Meira (the best Russian translator) Gottesman. Orit, Noam, Ruth, and Shmuel Berger and Yitzhak Frankenthal— among the thousands of bereaved Israeli and Palestinian families. At Shatil: Rachel Liel, Avi Armoni, Naila Khouri, and Wende Akale. At Neve Shalom/ Wahat al-Salam: Shireen Najjar, Ahmad Hijazi, Ori Sonnenschein, Anwar Daoud; Diana Shalufi-Rizek and Daoud Boulos; Rabbi Boaz Cohen and Avi Dahan for opening doors to Shas. Phillip Kaldawi and Sarah Kreimer of the Center for Jewish-Arab Economic Cooperation; Yuval Rabin, Isabel Maxwell, and David Rubin for their observations on Israeli high-tech culture; Dafna Tsimhoni of the Technion for giving me her research on the Christians of the Holy Land; Wajeeh Nuseibeh and Abed Joudeh at the Church of the Holy Sepulcher; Gila Almagor, Yaacov Agmon, Eli Cohen, Dan Katzir, and Moshe Irgi for the directors' and actors' perspectives. The staffs of the International Sephardic Education Foundation and Jimena (Jews Indigenous to the Middle East). Avram Arbib and Hana Dayan, for introducing me to the Jews of Libya; Yossi Ohana, to the Berber Jews of Morocco; Yair Dalal for sharing the music of Iraqi Jews and Bedouin; and Moshe Pinker for your family stories of the Jews of India. The Sastiel family for welcoming me into the lives of the *samekh tet* Sephardim. The Israel Association for Ethiopian Jews, the Israel Women's Network, and the Brookdale Institute.

Thanks also to the reporters of *Ha'aretz,* especially Ori Nir, Lily Galili, Nitzan Horowitz, Danny Ben-Simon, and David Landau. David Horovitz, Hirsch Goodman, Isabel Kershner, Yossi Klein Halevy, and all the other talented reporters of the *Jerusalem Report;* Bret Stevens and his staff at *The Jerusalem Post;* and the journalists at Channels One and Two. Also, Donna and Arye Shahar; Gail Barzilay; Rina Segal; Nira Weiss; Abu Siam Salem; Gayle Hareven; Khalil Munir; Ra'ana Meridor; Arlene, David, and Efrat Chinitz; Shani and Merav Zefari; Dror Weiss; Tal Nevo; Hasiya Eytan; Basel Ghattas; Yitzhak Galnoor; Gideon Arad; Natan Shapiro; Zvi Rimalt; Judy Balint, Efrat Sharon; Galit Gunitz; David Ehrlich; Hava Contini; Danny Kaplan; Marie, Danny, and Yonathan Shek; Reda and Mona Mansour; Bruce Kashdan; Erella Hadar; Eran Etzion; Anna Azari; Danny Kiram; Amir Tal; Ekram Hiloul; Ilana and Sergio Lehrman; Yehuda Gradus; Laura Sachs; Annina Korati of Kibbutz Kfar Ruppin. I received much help from the late Dafna and Dov Izraeli, Zehara Schatz, and Ehud Sprinzak.

Also, Dr. Bezalel Shendowitz of Shaare Zedek Hospital for advising all of us members of the National Keratoconus Foundation.

And, most of all, to my wonderful family for putting up with me during this long journey. My parents for making me possible. My husband for loving an often distracted wife. Moriah, Daniel, Ari, and Elias, all under seven, for keeping me sane by playing with me—and reminding me that children are the biggest reason to continue the search for peace.

Introduction   Colliding Worlds

An international-news producer friend at CNN told me: "Our viewers are confused. We have footage of Jews who look like Arabs, Arabs who look like Jews. We have black Jews. Bearded sixteenth-century Jews, and sexy girls in tight jeans. Who are these people, anyway?"

Part of the answer, I hope, is in this book. Who are these Israelis who order Big Macs in the language of the Ten Commandments, believe that waiting in line is for sissies, and light up Marlboros under NO SMOKING signs? Their children, the world's biggest MTV fans, go to malls to get the latest Jennifer Lopez CDs . . . and gas masks. Most of these people are Jewish. Among Israel's Muslims, Christians, and Druze, many speak Hebrew and know more about the Bible and Jewish traditions than do most Jews in the Diaspora. But even including Arabs and Jews, there are only 6.7 million Israelis—not much more than the population of Baghdad—yet their country, smaller than New Jersey, captures the lion's share of the world's headlines.

This is a book about ordinary people trying to live normal lives during abnormal times. The Israelis in these pages are not politicians or generals or guests on *Nightline*. They are a disparate mix of radically modern and devoutly traditional. Despite the traumas of the second intifada, they fill symphony halls, dance in discos, and argue in cafés—most of which do not explode. Israelis are expert at living with a frequency of terrorist attacks no other people has endured for so long. They picnic at the Sea of Galilee and have all-night rave parties on the Red Sea. As a post-army rite, planeloads of Israelis celebrate a kosher Passover in Kathmandu. After traveling from Asia to South America, twenty thousand reunite near the ruins of Meggido (the Armageddon of the Book of Revelation)

1

to celebrate Rosh Hashanah, the Jewish New Year, Woodstock-style. Although the vast majority of Israeli Jews are secular, more than 98 percent of the country's synagogues are either Orthodox or ultra-Orthodox.

———————

In each chapter of this book, different types of Israelis tell their stories. Those stories celebrate diversity: Israelis wear army helmets, *kippot* (yarmulkes), *keffiyahs* (headdresses), wigs, and veils. They also wear baseball caps backwards and earphones connected to MP3 players.

Cross-cultural adventures between Jews and Jews abound. There's nothing like a "mixed marriage" where couscous meets gefilte fish. Ashkenazi Jews with origins in Europe and Mizrahi Jews whose families fled Islamic countries of the Middle East and North Africa struggle to bridge their differences. Tradition-bound Ethiopian Jewish mothers are shocked by the sight of strange, nearly naked white Jews tanning in "dental floss" bikinis. It's not easy for the teen wearing a knit *kippa* over his dreadlocks to tell his parents, in broken Amharic, that he's in love with a nonreligious white girl. Some highly observant Israelis design the world's most famous computer chips at Intel, where bomb shelters are frequently used—as synagogues, mosques, or meeting rooms. And in the cafeterias, Jews, Christians, and Muslims worry not only about fighting in Gaza, but also about the tumbling NASDAQ.

Some of the Digital Generation are former "dot commies" who left the Soviet Union after it crumbled. Since the 1990s, an avalanche of more than a million immigrants has given Israel the world's largest percentage of scientists, engineers, doctors, and musicians. But about half aren't Jews, and they've set up communities with churches, Christmas trees, and shops selling pork—which drives some Israelis crazy. Black-hatted politicians once had the clout to close down nonkosher eateries or malls on the Sabbath, but not since the 2003 elections brought a backlash against the ultra-Orthodox. Men on "modesty patrols," however, still check that ultra-Orthodox women bus passengers are "properly" dressed and sitting apart from men.

The modesty patrols can do nothing about the female soldiers. Israel is the only country that drafts (non-Orthodox Jewish) women. Fervently religious families face a new problem: teens who take off their black clothes and run away—some to join the army. That's where they come into contact with Arabic-speaking Israeli soldiers. Some are Bedouin or Christian. Most are Druze whose religious belief in reincarnation comes into play on the battlefield.

They spend more time in uniform that any national group, yet Israeli men have a life expectancy the third highest in the world. Those men come in all sizes, shapes . . . and sexual orientations. From army officers to El Al stewards, Israelis are flinging open the closets. So many thousands turn out for the annual gay pride parade in Tel Aviv that it's hard to hear rabbis, imams, and priests screaming "blasphemy." Israel's singing sensation is a gorgeous brunette. She was a "he" in the army. Other Israelis live in secret worlds—like a lesbian whose parents on an Orthodox West Bank settlement have no idea she has a girlfriend. Or Israeli Muslims who fear being labeled *luti* ("homosexual" in Arabic)—which can lead to death. While dramatic social transformations are occurring all over Israel, some ancient customs persist—including that of multiple wives. Yet in the Negev desert, a former Bedouin shepherdess who counsels women forced into polygamous marriages risked her own life to marry outside her tribe.

Because of the significant religious, historical, and cultural differences between and within Israel's various Arabic-speaking communities, four chapters of this book focus on Muslim, Bedouin, Druze, and Christian Israelis. That's where you'll find the story of a Muslim family that keeps the keys to Jerusalem's sacred Church of the Holy Sepulcher, and why a social worker in the ancient port of Jaffa calls herself a minority within a minority. Near the Basilica of the Annunciation in Nazareth, Jesus' turbulent hometown, Christian and Muslim Israeli teens sway to the rhythms of Arabic rap, ignoring tensions between their families. Half an hour away in Umm al-Fahm, a hotbed of Islamic fundamentalism, a housewife rarely misses daily prayers—or an episode of *The Young and the Restless*. A secular Muslim surgeon has an emotional breakdown after a suicide bomber kills one of her Jewish patients.

Israel's Arab Muslim citizens call themselves various names: Israelis, Arab Israelis, Palestinian Israelis, Palestinian citizens of Israel, Palestinians who live in Israel, Palestinians with Israeli passports, and the "stand-tall generation." The names they choose reflect their ages and/or political attitudes. This book uses neutral and less confusing terms: Arab Israelis or Muslim Israelis. A Muslim filmmaker describes his conflicting identities: "We're Israeli, but Jews treat us with distrust. We're Arabs, but Palestinians treat us with distrust." Since the second intifada, relations between Jewish and Muslim Israelis have deteriorated. Growing numbers of Muslims say the state's Jewish symbols alienate them: the flag with the Star of David; the national anthem that speaks of a "return to Zion"; and Independence Day, which many Muslims call "The Catastrophe." Then there are those who say they reject Israel's right to exist as a Jewish state, and wave Palestinian flags. Israel's 1.2 million Muslims have conflicting identities. A unique minority, they live in the world's only Jewish state in a region of 22 Arab states and 280 million Muslims. Many have Palestinian relatives in the West Bank, Gaza, Jordan, Lebanon, or Syria.

Where are the Palestinians in this book? Where are the words of Palestinian parents and children? Their lives, voices, and suffering are equally important and are not explored in depth here. They deserve their own book. For the most part only Israeli citizens tell their stories in *The Israelis*. In the epilogue, however, Jewish and Arab Israelis and Palestinians describe visions of a different tomorrow. They are like an estranged family forced to live separately together in the same house because no one will move. Will they continue to distrust and kill each other, or can they work together?

 Becoming Israeli

1

One of the World's Most Volatile Neighborhoods

It can be more difficult to cope with terrorism than with war. War is limited to geographical and time boundaries. Terrorism knows no boundaries. —Solly Dreman, clinical psychologist in the Department of Behavioral Sciences at Ben-Gurion University of the Negev

Rahamin Zidkiyahu, a fanatic soccer fan, tried convincing his boss to let him drive an earlier bus so he could get home in time to watch the World Cup match between Japan and Turkey. His boss refused. When the scheduled driver was late, Rahamin felt God was smiling on him. He eagerly volunteered to drive it. On the morning of June 18, 2002, Jerusalem's bus 32A was packed with schoolchildren and commuters: a boy with a *kippa* and a ponytail wearing a knapsack bigger than his back; the Israeli president's longtime maid; an engineer who left Russia after men beat her husband for daring to wear his kippa in public; Arab Israeli students on their way to a teachers college; Jews, Muslims, and Christians. Rahamin had driven this route for twenty-seven years and treated his passengers as friends. Many were. If they didn't have enough money for the fare, Rahamin, whose name in Hebrew means "compassion," lent it to them. When he saw people running to the bus stop, he'd wait.

Shiri Nagari missed the bus. To catch it, her mother sped to the next stop, so she wouldn't be late for her temporary bank job. The twenty-one-year-old with a blond braid that reached her legs was saving to pay for her Hebrew University tuition. She hoped to study medicine like her sister.

It was the last day of elementary school and Ethiopian-born Christian Galila Bugala couldn't wait. The eleven-year-old was so popular, her classmates chose her to be in charge of their fifth-grade "fun day."

As Shani Avi-Zedek boarded the bus, her mother reminded her to put on sunscreen. "The sun won't kill me," the fifteen-year-old responded, eager to join her ninth-grade class's swim party. She had busy days ahead: tutoring the child of a disabled veteran, dancing in a recital, then flying to Berlin as part of an Israeli-German youth exchange.

Raffi Berger kissed his wife goodbye and headed to catch the crowded bus to his chemistry lab at the Hebrew University. Orit was relieved Raffi had returned safely from emergency reserve duty. He was part of the military offensive that went into the West Bank to intercept would-be suicide bombers and destroy explosives labs. Before the newlyweds moved into their apartment, Raffi's brother, a statistician, suggested he borrow money to buy a car. "Are you kidding?" Raffi teased him. "It's safer to be a student in Jerusalem than a soldier in Jenin." Nevertheless, Raffi was a cautious bus passenger. He knew the statistics. The safest seats are near the driver.

At 7:50 A.M., Ayman Gazi, a student at the teachers college where Raffi's father instructs in math, got on the bus with a few of his Arab Israeli classmates. The last to board was a man with glasses and a red shirt. Before paying the bus driver, he took two steps forward. Seconds later, a tremendous ball of fire shot up, sending scorched schoolbags and legs flying. There was an eerie silence. Then screaming. The wailing of dozens of ambulances didn't drown out the moans.

Rahamin remained in his seat, his lifeless hands still on the steering wheel. Blood trickled down the steps of the front door. The blast destroyed the front half of the bus. The Palestinian's twenty-two-kilogram bomb killed Ayman, Raffi, Shani, Galila, Shiri, and fourteen other passengers. The bus was a blackened metal skeleton, so twisted that rescue workers had difficulty prying bodies from the wreckage. They placed them in black plastic bags in a line on the sidewalk. Outside the bags, the ownerless cell phones rang. And rang.

The grisly rain of explosives from the bomb aboard bus 32A showered nails and screws coated with lethal rat poison that lodged in brains and lungs and eyes. As the overexperienced medics, handguns strapped to their belts, loaded the seventy-four wounded into ambulances, they couldn't tell who were Jews, who were Arabs. Medical workers make no distinction. In maternity and emergency wards, Arabs and Jews lie next to each other. In morgues too.

Raffi Berger's wife, an elementary school music teacher, took a later bus. It suddenly veered onto an alternate route. The road's closed, her bus driver announced. A terrorist attack. Orit dialed Raffi's cell phone. No answer. She dialed again. And again. She phoned his lab at the Hebrew University. He hadn't arrived yet. She phoned his parents. They rushed from hospital to hospital. By noon, they decided to make the trip every Israeli dreads—to the national forensic institute in Tel Aviv. Bodies were so badly mangled it was impossible to identify him. The Bergers were shown charred shoes and wedding rings. A nurse took blood samples from Raffi's mother and father. Their DNA matched a slice of tissue. As fate would have it, Raffi was safer as a soldier searching for terrorists near Jenin than as a student sitting in the front of a Jerusalem bus.

———

The man in the red shirt who didn't pay his fare was Muhammad al-Ghoul, a graduate student of Islamic law at Al-Najah University in Nablus, where chemistry students have been caught running explosives labs, where signs on campus read "Israel has nuclear bombs, we have human bombs." On campus, recruiters for Hamas (an acronym for Islamic Resistance Movement, which in Arabic means "zeal" or "courage") successfully have enlisted a number of students willing to die fighting for an Islamic state that will include all of present-day Israel. Muhammad left his family a farewell note: "How beautiful it is to kill and to be killed . . . for the lives of the coming generation." At his family's home in a refugee camp near Nablus, visitors brought condolences and congratulations. "My brother is a hero. I'm not sad," his sister said. "I'm very happy he's a martyr," added his father. "Our sons want to die for our land, to get it back." A suicide bomber's family received at least $25,000 from Iraq and contributions from Saudi Arabian citizens. The family of a Palestinian killed by Israeli Defense Forces (IDF) while attempting to carry out a terrorist attack received $10,000. At the time of Muhammad's death, polls showed a majority of Palestinians approved of suicide bombings and supported the destruction of Israel.

Muhammad fit the profile of the "typical" martyr: a devout Muslim, single, male, and in his early twenties. During this intifada, however, new types of Palestinian suicide bombers have appeared: several young women, married men, and high school boys. Terrorists can look like anyone and be anywhere. They have disguised themselves in stolen Israeli army uniforms, as bearded Orthodox rabbis, even a sixteen-year-old punk rocker with hair dyed blond. The first female suicide bomber didn't need to disguise herself. The pretty twenty-seven-year-old looked like a typical Israeli. Not long after her cousin divorced her for being infertile, this Palestinian Red Crescent paramedic went to downtown Jerusalem and detonated. A terrorist willing to die is difficult to stop.

On June 27, 2002, a week after Muhammad al-Ghoul exploded bus 32A, Palestinian Television aired a "virgin" video. On it, a handsome Palestinian man saw Israeli soldiers. Then, out of a dreamy mist, gorgeous girls in billowy white robes, smiling enticingly, beckoned him. In the next scene, he killed the soldiers. As he fled, he was shot to death. The camera cut to a young woman in a white robe welcoming him to Paradise. In the last scene of the recruiting video, dozens of virgins gently caressed the smiling martyr. (Muslims who die killing as many Jews as possible receive the exalted title of *shahid,* "martyr of the Islamic Jihad.") Despite injunctions in the Koran against suicide, the pursuit of jihad, holy war, is considered sufficient license to take one's own life. From the first drop of blood the martyr spills on the ground, he goes to Paradise, where, the Koran teaches, "Seventy-two virgins await each martyr. . . . The women have doe eyes. They are like precious gems. They are so white, they are clear, and when they drink water you can see the water running down their throats." Dr. Adel Sadeq, chairman of the Arab Psychiatrists Association, had this to say about suicide bombers: "As a professional psychiatrist, I say that the height of bliss comes with the end of the countdown: ten, nine, eight, seven, six, five, four, three, two, one. When the martyr reaches 'one' and he explodes, he has a sense of himself flying, because he knows for certain that he is not dead. It is a transition to another, more beautiful, world. No one in the Western world sacrifices his life for his homeland. If his homeland is drowning, he is the first to jump ship. In our culture it is different . . . this is the only Arab weapon there is and anyone who says otherwise is a conspirator."

Yael Shafir awoke feeling euphoric. Outside her bedroom window, golden and pink light danced on the Judean desert. In the distance, Hebrew University and Hadassah Hospital on Mount Scopus. Hanging on her closet door, her white silk designer wedding dress. She knew he was the one the night they met at a Jerusalem disco. Although they've been living together for three years, Yael chose to spend her last unmarried night in her former bedroom in her parents' home in the comfortable Jerusalem neighborhood of French Hill. Shuffling into the kitchen for some Nescafé, she snapped out of her sleepy haze. Her parents and younger brother, Yair, were listening to a radio news alert. A suicide bomber. Bus 32A. "The first thing I thought was, 'Who do I know who takes that bus? Who lives in the area? Any of my kids?'" recalls Yael, a play therapist and reflexologist who works with severely retarded children. "I heard the details, then I couldn't handle it any more. Not on my wedding day. All I could think was, 'We've had a few days of calm. Why couldn't it last?'" Dorit, her mother, changed the radio dial. Stations were playing mournful Hebrew songs. After each terrorist attack, the same melancholy melodies.

Jerusalem was on red alert. At least four suicide bombers were on the loose. How many of the three hundred guests will cancel? A lot, Yael worried. Already, months earlier, an aunt from Tel Aviv phoned to say she was afraid to travel to Jerusalem. A cousin from Safed announced she was on edge, fearful about driving anywhere near a bus. The words "Extra Security" on Yael's wedding invitation weren't prophetic; they're standard in Israel. Yellow pages are filled with ads for guards equipped with Uzis or handguns. "Everyone has armed security guards for every celebration," Dorit says solemnly. "We hired eight."

Downtown Jerusalem was desolate. As Dorit, a curator at the Israel Museum, drove her daughter to the hairdresser, she noticed flags at half-mast mourning the bus passengers. While the stylist put white jasmine in

Yael's waist-length auburn hair, Dorit offered to get her lunch. "As I left, she said, 'Mom, please be careful. Look around. And don't stay too long. I love you.' That's how it is here. Before you go out to buy a sandwich, your kid gives you a loving speech in case you don't come back." When Dorit spotted a bumper sticker, "Live the Moment," she remembered that Yael and her fiancé were at Jerusalem's trendy Moment Café only one night before a suicide bomber snuffed out seventeen young lives. However, another engaged couple had been there that fateful night. Television news showed the bride-to-be's mother at her daughter's grave. Instead of a wreath, she placed a red bridal bouquet on it.

Yael's wedding was in Ein Hemed, a beautiful national park on the outskirts of Jerusalem, which the Crusaders named Aqua Bella for its bubbling streams. As guests drove up, guards checked each car. Each trunk. Each bag, each purse. They carefully inspected wallets, eyeliners, lipsticks. Israelis follow this familiar ritual before entering public places. They no longer view security guards with reluctant acceptance, but with profound gratitude. Near Crusader ruins guests crossed a stream and made their way to a natural outdoor amphitheater. From their seats they looked down on a stage made of stones. Instead of "Here Comes the Bride," Yael entered to a Blood, Sweat and Tears recording of "You've Made Me So Very Happy." As she walked from her past to her future at the *huppa,* the wedding canopy, she nervously glimpsed around, worried at how many guests had shown up. Relatives and friends had traveled from the Galilee, from the Golan Heights, from the Negev. Over three hundred and fifty guests, more than they'd invited. Despite the ongoing red alert, they refused to let terrorists terrorize. Such stubborn persistence has helped Israelis live in the world's most volatile neighborhood.

The family was delighted to set up extra dinner tables for the overflow crowd. Yael's new husband teaches drums and plays bass guitar in a band, so many guests were musicians. Because the couple wanted them to party, not play, they hired a DJ. The music was Israeli ethnic rock, American and British funk and punk, and Cuban and Brazilian music with a salsa twist. "Everyone was dancing, even my eighty-one-year-old grandfather. We partied and drank almost until dawn. Israelis know how to celebrate, how to grab life." Turning pensive, Yael adds, "We all know what's going on but at times we try very hard to disconnect from reality."

"It's a mitzvah to rejoice with the bride and groom on the happiest day of their lives. But surrounding me was a very black cloud," confesses Eli Ben-Eliezar, an executive with the Jewish Agency, which assists new and potential immigrants. Three hours before the wedding, Eli was weeping at a funeral. His cousin drove bus 32A. It's Jewish tradition to bury the dead as soon as possible to allow the soul to ascend to heaven, and Rahamin's soul started the ascent just nine hours after his final bus ride. A tremendous crowd gathered around his shell-shocked widow and four children. Theirs is a respected old Jerusalem family, Kurdish Jews originally from Iraq, who run an olive and pickle stall in the bustling open-air Mahane Yehuda market, a popular terrorist target. Among the mourners, his longtime passengers and fellow blue-shirted bus drivers, who are trained to identify would-be bombers. "Why Rahamin? The most loving, caring father?" Eli says despondently. "He was planning his son's bar mitzvah at the *kotel* [the Western Wall, Judaism's holiest site]. As a present, he bought tickets to EuroDisney Paris." There were several other funerals that afternoon at the rocky hillside graveyard, all passengers on bus 32A.

This was not the first time Eli had attended a funeral and a wedding on the same day. "For Yael's wedding, at least I had almost three hours. Last time, I had less than an hour. I kissed my best friend *mazel tov,* but I could stay at his wedding only fifteen minutes. I had to drive like mad to a one o'clock funeral. The boy was only eighteen, a few months younger than his murderer."

Before murderer Muhammad Farhat set off on his one-way mission for Allah, his mother fed him kebab and his favorite cucumber salad. He told her he'd dreamed about his reward: the virgins awaiting him in paradise. Mariam Farhat urged her son to go. Soon after, she received word that he had killed five teenagers and wounded twenty-three more Jews. "Only when I see all the Jews in Palestine killed will it be enough for me," she told al-Jazeera Television. "We love martyrdom as much as Israel loves the fantasy life it is leading." Hamas distributed the goodbye video, which showed her kissing her son and saying she wished she had "one hundred sons like him." Her husband, a policeman with the Palestinian Authority in Gaza, is paid to stop would-be terrorists.

Israelis live from one news report to the next. In this sliver of land smaller than New Jersey, most events are national. When Eli picked up the newspaper the day after Yael's wedding, the front page was filled with rows of photos of those killed on the bus: the beaming new mother, the ballet dancer, the grandfather. The dead aren't the only victims. Their parents, children, widows, siblings, and friends are maimed forever. Less than twenty-four hours after he'd buried his cousin, Eli heard about another suicide bombing near Yael's family on French Hill. He recognized one name, a young woman who worked for him. Another funeral after a wedding.

The powerful blast on French Hill jolted Yael's twelve-year-old brother. "I knew it was a real bad explosion by the sound," Yair reports matter-of-factly. Like many Israeli children, he is something of a ballistics expert. "Then I listen for the sirens. If I hear more than ten I know many people were hurt. This is one of the most bombed bus stops in the country. Already a few years ago, it had a plaque for the dead. Right away, Mom started dialing to see if everyone was okay." After every terrorist attack, Israelis follow this solemn, frantic phone ritual. If no one answers, people assume the worst. "Yael finally phoned. She was giving away her leftover wedding cake to the children at her school before taking off on her honeymoon in Paris." Yair has an uncanny resemblance to the boy wizard with thick glasses and brown hair. In fact, he got the nickname "the Israeli Harry Potter" when he cohosted a national television program about children's literature. On air, he answered questions preteens e-mailed him about *Winnie the Pooh* and *The Wizard of Oz* and other classics translated into Hebrew. Now, with his new contact lenses and spiked brown hair with reddish-blond tips, Yair's fans barely recognize him.

When her son is out of earshot, Dorit confides, "Yair sounds stoical, but he's very worried something will happen to us. He always asks 'Where are you going?' He has to know where everyone in the family is at all times. Until recently, he sometimes came to sleep with us." By age six many children have cell phones. Teachers receive special training to deal with traumatized children, how to explain the empty seat in the classroom. By law, Israeli schools have armed guards at the entrances. To beef up security, parents take turns guarding too. "Even going to his friends' bar and bat mitzvahs isn't simple. Guards inspect each child's invitation. If they forget to bring it, they can't enter. Right down the hill at a bar mitzvah, a terrorist shot eleven guests."

It's summer vacation. The basketball court on French Hill is empty; so is the soccer field. The neighborhood playground is closed. It used to be a lively place. When Arab children from the adjoining village of Isawiya came here, progressive Jewish parents were pleased. They hoped their children would play with the Muslim children. But fights broke out and the playground became a drug-dealing scene. Concerned Jewish parents collected money and built an even better playground in the village, so Arab children could have a place of their own. Even so, Arab children continued using the "Jewish" park. After some Jewish children were knifed, police closed the park—to everyone. Few Israelis in this formerly liberal-left neighborhood speak of peace and pluralism with much optimism.

"I used to hang out there with my friends. Now there's nowhere to play. Not much to do," grumbles Yair. "My friends from outside Jerusalem can't visit me because their parents say it's too dangerous here. I spend a lot of time at home, mostly at the computer." Cyber-friends from all over the country give Yair news alerts. He frequently knows the news ahead of his parents. He's at the keyboard at least three hours a day, discussing music, *Seinfeld,* and terrorism. Life on the edge has created a digital generation addicted to high drama. Some take part in Israeli-Palestinian hacker wars. In this "Inter-fada," the weapons are viruses and worms and words. An Israeli flag appeared on a Hezballah site. Porn replaced a Palestinian newspaper's home page. Israeli hacktivists have invaded Hamas and Islamic Jihad sites; Palestinian hacktivists have hit Israeli commercial and governmental websites. Cyber-friendships spring up in some chatrooms Yair visits. He's had a few friendly exchanges with a Palestinian boy. "Mostly, though, I chat with Israelis. Two years ago, I met a girl from Rishon Le Zion online. I wanted to visit her, but my parents wouldn't let me. Not until they met her parents. It happens whenever I want to get together with an Internet friend."

When Ofir met Sally, he bragged to his high school friends about their hot online relationship. The infatuated couple moved from chatrooms to emails and then talked on the phone. Sally told him she was twenty-five and Ofir liked the fact that she was so honest. The sixteen-year-old was excited about a possible affair with an older woman. And she was an American. A new immigrant living in Jerusalem. What she didn't tell him was that she frequented Internet cafés and struck up online flirtations with other Israeli men. Sally suggested Ofir take the bus from his home in Ashkelon, a port on the Mediterranean, and meet her at the Jerusalem Central Station.

Sally was charming, seductive. Now, they finally could be alone in her girlfriend's apartment. They took a taxi to her car near French Hill. They drove north. In minutes, they were in the West Bank. She stopped the car. Suddenly, two men armed with Kalashnikov rifles appeared and demanded that Ofir get out of the car. The boy refused. They put his bullet-ridden body in the trunk of their car.

Concerned that he hadn't come home, his parents reported him missing. Israeli officials traced the signals of his cell phone. They found Ofir Rachum near the Palestinian town of Ramallah. He had been shot by members of the Tanzim, the militia commanded by Marwan Barghouti, leader of Fatah's al-Aqsa Martyrs Brigade on the West Bank until Israeli police arrested him in 2002. A month later, Israeli soldiers posing as Arabs found and arrested a Palestinian named Amna Jawad Mouna who had selected Ofir as a "suitable" kidnap victim. She also was known as Sally.

———————

Unfortunately, I'm making good money. The more horrible it is, the busier I am," says freelance cameraman Kobi Yonatan. After each terrorist attack, his phone rings. ABC News, AP television, German or French or Japanese television asking him to shoot more slaughter scenes. "I stopped counting how many. More than thirty. Each one has its own special horror. Those pictures, especially the children, I can't erase out of my mind. To protect myself, I have a psychology tactic. I pretend what I'm seeing through my viewfinder isn't real. That I'm shooting a movie. I try to create a professional distance, like a doctor. It's a survival instinct." Kobi doesn't have to drive far to work because he lives in Jerusalem. No other Israeli city has had more attacks. Bus 32A begins its run in Gilo, his southern Jerusalem neighborhood. Seventeen of the dead passengers lived near his apartment. For nearly twelve years, his wife has taken bus 32A to her downtown travel agency. On the morning of June 18, her brother drove her to work.

Kobi keeps his flak jacket in his car so his three children won't see it. They don't understand what Daddy really shoots with his two Sony cameras. Maybe *A Bug's Life* or a *Power Rangers* video. He won't allow them to watch TV news or his documentaries. Four-year-old Gal deals in Pokemon cards. Seven-year-old Inbal loves Barbies. Ten-year-old Shani, an aspiring Doctor Doolittle, collects creatures. There's an aquarium in the living room. A baby alligator lives temporarily in the bathtub. On the balcony, there are two parrots in a cage. The glass containers in his bedroom hold lizards and beetles. "I really enjoy going to the wadi [dry river bed] with Shani," says soft-spoken Kobi. "Yesterday, we caught a snake and spiders. I wish I could spend my days finding turtles and crickets rather than shooting horror films."

Almost every night, the sounds of heavy machine-gun fire summoned him to work. Grabbing his flak jacket and camera, Kobi rushed to HaAnafa Street only three blocks from his apartment. His documentary *Street Under Fire* shows the lives of the working-class Israelis living there: religious and secular Mizrahi and Ashkenazi Jews, immigrants from the former Soviet Union and Ethiopia, and a few Muslim and Christian Arab Israelis. Sniper attacks from the Palestinian village of Beit Jala, not more than six hundred yards away, have scarred living room and bedroom walls. There are sandbags on balconies, metal shutters on windows. Kobi has videotaped armor-piercing bullets whizzing past terrified children and parents. Because peeking out a window could be deadly, families hunker down in the dark watching the shelling—live on TV news.

Beit Jala is a mostly Christian Arab village next to Bethlehem. It was a peaceful, prosperous place without borders. Israelis and its residents are friends and mingled freely. The intifada changed everything. Outside Islamic militants from the Tanzim entered, uninvited. They set up machine guns in Christian homes and churches. From this vantage point, it was easy to fire on the Israeli civilians of HaAnafa Street, provoking Israeli soldiers to retaliate against the heavy shelling. "That was the Tanzim's intention, to get cameramen to come to Beit Jala and get pictures of Israeli soldiers firing on Christian property," comments Kobi. The tactic worked. When Israeli soldiers shelled Beit Jala, the world saw TV footage of weeping families and homes damaged by Israeli bullets, often with close-ups of crucifixes. After seven months, in April 2001, Christian leaders of Beit Jala sent a letter to the Pope, church leaders, and UN Secretary General Kofi Annan pleading for help, accusing the Palestinian Authority of giving tacit approval to the "ethnic deportation" of Christians. Kobi adds that after the intifada began, Palestinian officials threatened to kill Israeli cameramen working in the West Bank and Gaza. Since then, most of the footage that international television outlets use is supplied either by Associated Press Television or Reuters, who employ mostly Palestinian or other Arab cameramen. Kobi goes on to say that nonprofessional Palestinians using their own video cameras also supply footage, sometimes shot to push their political agendas. "Rifles and tanks are weapons. So are cameras. In many ways, this is a media war. It's about creating images to influence world opinion."

The young artist gathers her brushes and paints. The city of Jerusalem has selected her to paint a fresco on a six-foot-high wall. She's putting on the finishing touches. It's a pastoral village scene in soft pastels: neat cream-colored stone houses, olive groves, and sheep wandering the light brown hills. A dreamy Beit Jala—without snipers. The mural covers the concrete barrier erected to protect the people of HaAnafa Street from the bullets of Beit Jala.

"We're directly in the line of fire. It usually goes on at night for hours. To be safe, my mother moved out of her bedroom," says high school student Oren Dagan, whose apartment faces Beit Jala. "In our parking lot, a bullet hit a soldier through his heart. I saw a cameraman trying to save him. Before I knew it, two army tanks were under my bedroom window. Each time their cannons fired, our chairs fell over. Days were usually safe. One day, after school, I was putting a snack in the oven. A shell hit the kitchen window, right next to me. If the government hadn't put in bulletproof glass, I'd be dead. I was afraid to go in the kitchen, but only for a few days. After almost two years of shooting, I got used to living in a war zone."

Many neighbors didn't. That's why his mother, a social worker whose Christian Israeli colleague lives in Beit Jala, volunteered to help. "Mom knows how to deal with panicky people. A guy in a wheelchair was in the street when shooting broke out. He was stranded. Then some soldiers drove him home in an armored car. Mom tried calming him. And another neighbor too. When bullets hit her refrigerator, she fainted. She was pregnant and lost her baby. I think I know why Mom stopped volunteering. I was at home studying. On her way home from work, she heard on the radio that Tanzim were shooting our street again. She couldn't get to me—there was a police barrier on our street. I called her cell phone and told her I smelled smoke. The mortars set fire to the brush outside. But I couldn't run out. It was too dangerous. Tanzim shot four of our neighbors. After three hours, it stopped. When Mom got home, she wanted us to get out of the neighborhood, to stay with friends, but I refused. I won't let terrorists force us to leave," he says defiantly.

"There's no normal day anywhere," continues Oren. "You put something in the oven, you can get shot. You travel to school, you might not arrive. My friend's uncle was guarding outside Supersol supermarket. He stopped a 'shopper' at the entrance. She set off a blast and killed him and a girl my age. And another friend is a waiter at a café. Around here, he's a big hero for being so alert. He wrestled a suicide bomber to the ground and saved everyone. And you know what? Café Caffit is more popular than ever. People wonder, 'Am I at the wrong place at the wrong time?' Sometimes you're at the wrong place at the right time. Like my classmate's father. He was late for work. If he'd been on time, he would have been driving bus 32A the morning it exploded. Do I still take it? Of course. It's the only bus we have."

Prague. Buenos Aires. Bangkok. The posters in Dalia Yonatan's travel agency are enticing. Unnecessarily so, because for Israelis, travel is no longer a treat, it's a psychological necessity. There are no elections in the summer because that's when most Israelis leave. Although record numbers of Israelis are buying tickets, the travel agency is almost empty. "Many of my customers are afraid to come downtown," explains Dalia. "So they order tickets by phone and we send a messenger to deliver them." There have been more than a dozen terror attacks near her office, which is in the notorious "triangle," bounded by Jaffa, Ben-Yehuda, and King George Streets. As soon as Dalia hears a blast, she phones Kobi, assures him she's okay, then tells him where to bring his camera. "They say I live and work in the two most dangerous places in Jerusalem. But now it doesn't matter where you are. It can happen anywhere."

Each morning, Dalia puts the children on a special bus for a short ride to summer camp at Kibbutz Ramat Rachel, named after Rachel, the biblical matriarch whose white-domed tomb is not far away. The olive groves near it have been in Kobi's mother's Sephardi family for nine generations. Children make pottery and take care of cows, chickens, and goats. They seem oblivious to the omnipresent Uzi-toting guards. Armed guards are not new. During its seventy-five-year history, the kibbutz has been destroyed and rebuilt four times.

At the Paradise Camp in Gaza run by Islamic Jihad, eight- to twelve-year-olds learn how to be suicide bombers. Campers are handed toy machine guns and sing songs about killing Jews with real ones. Youngsters dress up as suicide bombers and cover their hands with the "blood" of IDF soldiers. In August 2002, ten thousand children and parents in Gaza reveled and sang and distributed candies to celebrate the Hamas bombing of the Hebrew University cafeteria on Mount Scopus that killed eight and maimed eighty more.

"My schoolbag was half full of Pokemon cards, but I threw them all away because they're not important now. The pictures of martyrs are important. They're our idols," according to fourteen-year-old Saleh Attiti, who lives in the West Bank town of Nablus. He is swept up by the latest fad: collecting "martyr necklaces." Kids trade these necklaces with pictures of martyrs, as well as martyr medallions, plaques, and key chains.

Jerusalem's Malha Mall opened to great fanfare in 1993. It was one of the Middle East's biggest malls, with two hundred stores, a supermarket, two department stores, and parking for three thousand cars. (Israel now has more than thirty large malls.) Hopes were running high. The next year, Israel signed the peace treaty with Jordan, and King Hussein piloted his own helicopter from Amman to Tel Aviv. Soon, dozens of Arab states initiated commercial and diplomatic relations with Israel. The mall in Israel's capital, next to a high-tech park, the Teddy Soccer Stadium, and the Biblical Zoo, became a symbol of peace and plenty. Palestinians, Jordanians, Egyptians, and wealthy tourists from the Persian Gulf states and Saudi Arabia visited this shopping wonderland. Arabic-speaking customers were a welcome sign of normalcy. No longer was the world's only Hebrew-speaking country the Middle East's pariah state.

Today, Malha looks like any mall: kids race up the down escalators, listen to storytelling, watch puppet shows, and drag their parents into Toys 'R' Us. As in most malls, parents with strollers and lonely pensioners come to escape the heat, enjoy the air conditioning, and people-watch. Sports fans watch a match on television. But here, Malha is no longer any mall. Here, the TV screen is split: soccer on one side, on the other, body parts and medics. Israel television lets viewers choose their live realities. It's called the "routinization" of terror. Because many Israelis are cocooning in the safety of their homes, there's a sales boom for cappuccino machines and ice cream and bread makers. There's also a run on diet, detective, and spirituality books. Comedies and romances are popular at the Cineplex. Israelis are popping a lot of antidepressants during this home-front war of nerves, notes a pharmacist. He jokes darkly that no prescription is necessary for chocolate or Dial-a-Psalm.

On the mall's first floor, where shops sell designer sunglasses and Reeboks, a sign reads "Gas Mask Distribution Center." Young male and female soldiers assist anxious customers who come to "refresh" their out-of-date gas masks. They also pick up iodine capsules, an antidote to radioactive fallout, which doctors advise should be taken ten days after exposure. On the wall, an Army poster says "Gas Masks Are Part of Life." Tense Israelis ask how well the masks will protect against atomic, biological, and chemical attacks. There are also questions about the most effective antibiotics against anthrax and if smallpox vaccinations are safe for infants. Gas masks for children age one to three are on the shelves, next to those for three to eight. A female soldier calmly demonstrates how to place them on the children, to change the filters, to give injections of atropine, an antidote to nerve/poison gas. Dalia brings the children here for new masks each time they outgrow theirs. "They don't work unless they fit the face," she says knowingly. "Each time I gave birth, a soldier gave me a going-away present: a baby gas mask." Hospitals issue every newborn Israeli, Jew and Arab, an infant-size gas mask.

For those who need help from a higher source, there's a small synagogue on the mezzanine level. "My father would be horrified to see his grandchildren getting fitted for gas masks," adds Kobi. "It makes the unthinkable thinkable again." His Hungarian-born father lost all his family in Auschwitz. He died before thirty-nine Iraqi Scuds rained down on Israel. Frightened Israelis ran to special sealed rooms in their houses and donned their masks, praying they'd be protected from nerve gas made from German-manufactured chemicals. The special terror of poison gas makes victims even when it is only threatened. At Hadassah Hospital on Mount Scopus, where Kobi's three children were born, the rehabilitation ward is filled with victims of terror. A twenty-two-year-old student is in one room. Doctors can't remove the poison-soaked nail in his brain for fear it will cause more damage. In another, a severely depressed seventy-two-year-old Holocaust survivor, paralyzed from the waist down, is one of the "lucky" survivors of the Passover Massacre. She was at the Park Hotel in Netanya when a man wearing a woman's wig sneaked past a security guard and killed twenty-nine guests at a seder and injured 240 more. The Hamas bomber tried but failed to release lethal cyanide gas, the same chemical, the notorious Zyklon B, the Nazis used in the gas chambers.

"No one knows where the next big attack will come from. Lebanon Syria. Iran. Maybe al-Qaeda," says Kobi. He notes that the name Israel means "he who wrestles with God." "Our struggle is as old as Jewish history. Will it ever end?" Israelis are the only people who always have lived in fear of unconventional attacks. Israelis always have lived with air raid sirens and bomb shelters. Israelis are the only people who have been in a state of war or semiwar with at least half their neighbors. Israel is in the bull's eye of a region some call the "New Missile Middle East."

"This country is a giant laboratory for coping with every kind of pressure or anxiety. Just randomly pick any Israeli of any age and you'll have a great subject for research," observes educational psychologist Moshe Zeidner of Haifa University, who is an expert on stress. "People feel like they've won the lottery if their bus doesn't explode."

2

Dating and Mating
Israeli-style

*♡ How many calories does an American man spend
making love? Ten. English? Ten. An Israeli? One hundred—
ten to make love and ninety running to tell his friends.*
—*Popular joke about Israeli machismo*

*♡ Israelis tend to have a macho bravado in dating and
everyday life and reassure themselves that everything will be
fine even if it won't. This denial may also be a response to
the uncertainty of life here. On a deeper level, it may be a
response to our parents' or grandparents' helplessness in face
of the Holocaust.* —*Family therapist Rachel Biale*

"My parents let me go to clubs in Tel Aviv until three in the morning,"
says seventeen-year-old Ronit Heffetz. "They're afraid of terrorists, but
at my age, my grandparents were running guns for the underground and
soon I'm going in the army, so how can they say no? We have to go on
living and not be afraid." Even though the second intifada has brought
terrorism to the home front, it is still not uncommon to see fourteen-
year-old girls hitchhiking to a beach, twelve-year-olds walking home
from unsupervised parties at dawn, or an ten-year-old traveling alone on

a public bus. Parents know that if their child gets lost, any adult will help her get to her destination. In 2002, Israel had far less street crime involving kids than almost any major American city.

That's one reason Israeli kids are fiercely independent and exhibit more than their share of youthful bravado. Many Israeli parents are reluctant to set limits and encourage their children to be self-sufficient and resourceful, partly as preparation for the army and adulthood. But it's just one way to understand how Israelis develop their unique mating habits. As the world's only Jewish nation, Israel reflects a huge range of mores developed in two millennia of diaspora Judaism. A country with a population half the size of greater Los Angeles, with a shared history shorter than that of the United Nations, is nonetheless home to cultures that were formed in St. Petersburg, Baghdad, Brooklyn, and Bombay—with all the resulting chaos and richness in mating rituals.

And that's not all. In addition to the cultural conflicts within Israel are the even more dangerous conflicts between the Jewish state and its neighbors. Because of Israel's never-ending state of war, it is the only country that requires most of its eighteen-year-olds to leave home and serve with members of the opposite and equally hormonally charged sex. It makes for behavior that Israel's first prime minister, David Ben-Gurion, never dreamed of. Ronit's eldest brother Ori, a twenty-seven-year-old physics student, lives at home because there are few dorms at Tel Aviv University and renting an apartment is too expensive. He relates a typical Saturday morning scene: "I was in bed with a girlfriend. Ronit was in the army. My two brothers were on leave from the army and sleeping with their girlfriends. All three of our bedroom doors were closed. My mother's voice came over the intercom. 'I'm making brunch. Are you alone or do you have a guest?' Mom's realistic. She knows we're going to do it anyway. There's no game playing with Israeli parents, no bullshitting. They'd rather we do it here where it's safe, than sneaking off somewhere else."

Soon after Ori met his first serious girlfriend in high school, the 1991 Gulf War broke out. With Scuds hitting the Tel Aviv area, her family fled to a hotel in the Red Sea resort of Eilat. "We really missed each other. So she convinced her parents to let her stay with me and my family on weekends," he recounts. "Her mother made her promise she wouldn't sleep in my room. So each morning, she'd get out of bed and sleep in my sister's bedroom. One night we were coming very close to losing our virginity. At the most delicate time, we heard sirens. We grabbed our gas masks and ran down to the sealed room. We sat with my family, hearing the Scuds fall, guessing how close. When the radio announcer reported it was all clear, we returned to my bedroom and tried again. But we were too tense. The next time she slept over, we ignored the sirens. My mom pounded and pounded on the door. I told her we were coming down, but we didn't bother. And we didn't even bother putting on our gas masks. Six months later I went into the army. I wonder if the new improved [gas masks] are designed better to wear during sex?"

During a heightened alert period of the intifada, in August 2002, nearly two thousand mounted police, soldiers, and bomb disposal experts stood watch over Tel Aviv's Love March. No one expected the turnout: well over a quarter million revelers showed up for the weekend extravaganza. It resembled carnival in Rio, with nearly naked Israelis frolicking on the beaches, moving passionately to live music. At an all-night rave party, thousands were dancing away their despondency, kissing lovers, even strangers.

"We just want a sane life," explains Ori. "A few kilometers away in Gaza, Israeli soldiers and Palestinians are killing each other, but we let loose as if all that were continents away. We have what I call national Alzheimer's disease—no one wants to remember the morning's news." After seeing too many friends killed or wounded, Israelis have adopted the motto "Life is uncertain, so eat your dessert first." As with foreign travel, *carpe diem* isn't irresponsible, it's an escape from the pressure cooker. In this crisis-a-day country, the mood changes constantly, a roller coaster that ascends with each cease-fire and plunges with each new attack. Israelis have learned that fun, sometimes reckless fun, helps them feel as if these times are normal.

In the upper Galilee village of Metulla, on the nervous border with Lebanon, at a club inside a converted shoe factory, 2 A.M. is peak hour. The DJ ups the amps so no one can hear the Katyusha rockets. More than five hundred factory workers, students, kibbutzniks, and male and female soldiers are dancing wildly, as if Hezballah, the radical Islamic Party of Allah, didn't have thousands more rockets and missiles across the barbed wire fence. Even during these uncertain times, patrons aren't drinking much alcohol. (A recent study shows that drinking rates in Israel are lower than in North America and twenty-four European countries. There's so little boozing that Israel has few liquor stores and only in 2002 enacted drinking laws.) It's expensive: a bottle of Scotch that goes for $14 in France or the United States costs $35 in Israel. "We party, flirt a lot. No one has a long-term vision anymore," a student from Tel Hai College shouts above the din. "There are politicians who make me want to tear my hair out, but then I remember that this is a young country, a work-in-progress." His girlfriend flashes an alluring look. He stops in mid-thought and heads toward her.

On the beaches, no less than in the clubs, eroticism is out in the open. Teasing touches and rampant flirting are part of the (usually harmless) mating game, Israeli-style. People gesture dramatically, interrupting and challenging each other. The verbal pyrotechnics are not unusual; Israel is a lively open-air theater, a place for animated disagreements, a place for good arguments. Women make approving comments as they admire a well-built windsurfer wearing a postage-stamp-size Speedo. Men visually undress a redhead in tight shorts sitting alone. As she pulls out a Parliament, a man with little round French sunglasses leaps up and flips open a gold lighter. A female alone is never alone for long.

Maya is fourth-generation Sabra—Arabic and Hebrew for the local cactus fruit, a metaphor for native-born Israelis, who are said to have prickly exteriors but soft insides. Glancing at her watch, she notices that her boyfriend was due at this eating place at the Herzliya beach a half hour ago. According to Israeli time, he's not late. Many Israelis don't like being controlled by watches (as they are in the army) or planning too far in advance. Expressions like "lost time" or "saving time" rarely are heard outside the army. Maya's boyfriend, Noam, finally arrives and plants a kiss on her lips. He hands her an English-language version of *The Lonely Planet* guide to Peru. They discuss Ben-Gurion. Not Israel's white-maned founding father, but Ben-Gurion International Airport, where they'll head after her army discharge. Of course, they'll visit Machu Picchu, but thrill-seeking Israelis consider the lost Inca city tame. "We'll backpack in the Andes and visit tribes in the Amazon. Explore places not on a map. I want to have as many adventures as possible, taste everything," says Maya, glad to be out of the army, where she was a combat medic. "They say being around death teaches you to live. I don't know if it's true, but everyone in my unit wants to go to jungles in Laos or bungee jumping in New Zealand. My parents are less worried about me climbing the Andes than serving on the West Bank."

Noam, a twenty-six-year-old acupuncturist, says his parents convinced them not to go to Thailand. Since the day al-Qaeda bombed Israelis in a Mombassa, Kenya hotel and tried to take down an Israeli charter jet with two surface-to-air missiles, any place Israelis congregate abroad is not safe—especially Bangkok. Traveling Israelis are cautioned not to carry books in Hebrew or speak Hebrew in public. "My parents warned me not to visit any synagogues in Lima or Buenos Aires," says Noam. "The last time they were in synagogue was their wedding. For them, the army was the place to meet and mate. Mom was twenty-one, Dad twenty-three. By my age, they owned an apartment, had two kids and one on the way. Maya and me? We can afford a rented room and a good stereo. No one I know is in any rush to the altar—unless you want to have kids. You know why *Seinfeld* is popular? This is the scene here. It's about our lives. So is *Friends, Sex and the City,* and *Ally McBeal.* Only we lose the best years of our lives in the army. And if we don't start this trip soon, I'll be called to *miluim* [reserve duty]."

"So, you're on a diet?" the generously proportioned waiter eyes Maya's partially eaten tofu burger. She shakes her head no. "Then why are you eating like you're in Weight Watchers? You're not fat. If you were a little more *zaftik,* I'd go for you myself," he announces as he playfully pinches her arm. "Hey, things are different now," she says, annoyed. "Haven't you heard? The rules have changed." The waiter winks at Noam, who doesn't consider the waiter's behavior offensive; it's harmless flirting. And his comments aren't meddling, they're a sign of warmth, connectedness. Israelis often dish out advice to strangers as if they were members of a large extended, sometimes dysfunctional, family. The waiter returns with a decadently rich crème brûleé. No charge.

———

Rumors used to fly when an unmarried couple moved in together. No longer. Most cohabiting couples are young, educated, not very religious Ashkenazim. According to a recent survey, 26 percent of married Israelis lived with their spouse before marriage. (The rate is much lower among

Mizrahi Jews and Christian Arabs. It's practically nonexistent among ultra-Orthodox Jews, Muslim Arabs, and Druze.) Note the distinction "before marriage": in some Western countries, cohabitation is an alternative to marriage, but not in family-oriented Israel. It's a modern version of engagement, part of the route to the huppa, says Professor Yohanan Peres of the Department of Sociology and Anthropology at Tel Aviv University. "Israelis still have a strong belief that marriage protects the wife and children. Israelis perceive a wedding as an insurance policy, largely related to the sense of siege here. Because people feel danger, they want to be close to someone related by law."

Vered did. She also was sick of the questions. At least five times a day, taxi drivers, bank tellers, complete strangers asked if she was married. When she said no, they asked, Why not? She bought a fake gold ring, and whenever she was asked the dreaded question, she held it up. Then they asked how many children she has. She wondered if she ever would meet someone exciting. Close to her thirtieth birthday, she got to know Yossi, the contractor working on her apartment. Her brother wasn't thrilled. "He likes your blonde Ashkenazi hair. He's an *arse*." Her brother's crude comment, calling Yossi a stereotypical uneducated, uncultured Mizrahi, angered Vered. "I didn't care what my brother thinks. So Yossi didn't go to college. He's a self-made man. He's caring and attentive. And he comes from a loving Moroccan family. My last boyfriend gave my parents heart palpitations. He was Israeli, but not Jewish. An uncircumcised Russian. I'll never forget my mother's guilt-line: 'My family escaped Poland to build a Jewish homeland. And you want to give me non-Jewish grandchildren?' "

When Vered was promoted to part-time radio reporter, to celebrate Yossi took her to Eilat, one of the few towns in Israel still untouched by terrorism. Moses stopped here with the Children of Israel when they were looking for the Promised Land. During the time of King Solomon, ships arrived laden with gold, wood, and ivory. Eilat has gone from an Old Testament port to a playground for sun worshippers and water lovers. Relieved to escape the realities on land, Vered and Yossi donned masks and fins. Gliding along lacy coral canyons, they saw swirling schools of angelfish, blue-neon damsels, and clownfish playing on the reef. "It was an underwater jewel box. When I told Yossi there were as many tropical fish on the Great Barrier Reef, he was puzzled. I had to explain it's in Australia. 'Why did you go all the way there?' he asked. 'We have everything here.' "

As they walked hand-in-hand near the beach, they saw hair braiders, tattoo artists, body-piercing places. Yossi made fun of them. Vered swapped travelers' tales with kids selling trinkets from India and herbs from China. Her passport is filled with visas. He doesn't have a passport. "To Yossi, a trip to Eilat is going abroad. And he thinks the floating casinos are as good as Monaco. But he tried so hard to please me. Splurged on a swanky hotel, a biblical Disneyland with faux 'ancient' stone arches, but I didn't let him know it's not my taste. I'm the backpacker type. Last time I was in Eilat, I slept on the beach. His idea of a vacation is room service."

From their hotel balcony, they could see the lunar desert landscape and craggy mountains, which reminded Vered of a short story by Albert Camus. "Camus? Yossi never heard of him. And Camus lived in Algeria. But as he massaged me with coconut lotion, I didn't care." Afterward, the pillow talk turned serious. He owns a small plot near Jerusalem and wanted Vered to see some architectural plans. "His designs for a dream house—for us. I started trembling when I realized he was proposing. A huge-hearted guy. But the kind who thinks kitchens have windows so women can have a worldview. I told him I needed time. When he fell asleep, I kissed his face in apology. He'll make a very wonderful husband—for some other woman."

It wasn't until Vered broke up with Yossi that she started thinking she needed someone who didn't like bowling on weekends, someone cosmopolitan. After a few months, she met Yoel, a fascinating mix: a lover of theater, a successful lawyer with stimulating friends from the north Tel Aviv intellectual and artistic avant-garde, a gourmet, and a connoisseur of fine wine. He was also the son of a religiously observant Iraqi Jewish family, a family far more observant than Vered's own. Unlike two thirds of Israeli Jews, Yoel ate only kosher food. And, as if that weren't enough, Vered's secular parents, raised on bedrock socialist values, were taken aback to learn that she was dating an unabashed capitalist, and a successful one, who could afford to pay $300,000 for his one-bedroom condominium and $50,000 for his sports car (though, to be fair, half of that went to the taxes and tariffs on new cars). Never had the advice of Vered's sister seemed more appropriate: "Even rich men need wives."

As is often the case in matters of the heart, the differences that attract are the differences that make for friction. Because Yoel liked to approach life with an open mouth, Vered surprised him with a reservation at a candle-lit bistro overlooking the Tel Aviv port. He liked the sophisticated setting, but when he saw the penne pasta with Portobello mushrooms tossed with bacon bits and sweet cream sauce on the menu, he suggested they leave. He took her to an Italian restaurant that doesn't serve "anti-kosher cuisine." The wine list appealed to him, especially the Moscato from the Golan Heights Winery. (Not long ago, wine was used mostly for religious purposes, and Israelis assumed it should taste like year-old cherry juice.)

She felt a rush of anticipation when he invited her to a family *mangal* (Israeli barbecue). This was serious, so she went shopping for a special outfit. His parents live near Tel Aviv in Ramat Gan. Many Jews who fled Iraq in the early 1950s live in their neighborhood, perversely the recipient of four Iraqi Scuds during the six-week Gulf War. His mother, active in the Babylonian Jewish Heritage Center, researches family trees of the world's 310,000 Iraqi Jews, some of whom are planning tours of the many Jewish sites of post-Saddam Iraq. "When I stupidly said I didn't realize what a developed culture Iraqi Jews had, she made a biting comment. 'Only for three thousand years. When our art and literature were thriving, your Polish grandparents were living in shacks, eating stale bread.' I shot back, 'One out of seven Nobel prize winners are Jews. Are any Iraqi?' "

When Yoel informed her that he wants to "keep his options open," Vered knew his mother was speaking. "Not long after the mangal, I heard he was engaged. A much younger woman from the same Iraqi community, who never would eat pasta with bacon bits and sweet cream sauce."

———————

Some Israeli TV talk shows would be familiar to anyone who remembers the early days of Jerry Springer. Hosts and hot-tempered guests argue like siblings, shouting "Shut up" to one another. The pour-your-heart-out TV confessionals resemble a national village square, where a wacky mix of ordinary Israelis, celebrities, and astrologers tackle such issues as "A guy I just met has been called up for miluim in Gaza. He could be dead tomorrow. Should I sleep with him?" and "Why do so many teenage girls have eating disorders?" Tired of worrying about layoffs, a possible smallpox epidemic, or a Hamas cook poisoning restaurant food, audiences are turning to discussions about how to introduce your nonreligious girlfriend to your parents or the best Internet sites to find a mate: jdate, jcupid, or dosidate (for religious Jews). Radio also is an important outlet, says Tamar Katriel, professor of communications at Haifa University. "Israelis really bare their souls on late-night radio talk shows, because they can call in anonymously. Working-class Israelis use the radio therapeutically to talk about the most intimate subjects and the host acts as a kind of rabbi, advisor, miracle worker."

Romance is a hot topic in slick magazines and newspapers. Outspoken twenty-eight-year-old Karin Arad writes "Sex and the Big City," a column about love trysts for the Tel Aviv weekly *Ha'ir*. She got her journalistic break when she posted a funny, daring diatribe about men's sexual ineptitude on the Internet. Columnist Shira Agmon pens "City of Pleasures" for a competing weekly, *Zman*. The audacious twenty-six-year-old gives readers voyeuristic peeks into her bedroom with explicit details about what is or isn't going on beneath the sheets.

Secular Israelis looking for sex without commitment frequently rely on what U.S. college students call a "hookup." In Israel it's *yaziz*, slang for "a friend for casual sex." (*Yaziz* is a combination of *yedid*, Hebrew for "friend," and *lezayen*, a crude word for sex.) But any sort of physical affection is out for Orthodox Jews, until marriage. Because religious males and females often attend different schools, they're working from "different diskettes," observes one educator. Maybe that's why eyebrows were raised when an article in the right-wing *Makor Rishon*, a national weekly that runs an advice column for singles, profiled two religious women in their late thirties. Unable to find appealing mates, they gave up and, instead, chose to have children by artificial insemination. So many young religious women complain about disastrous dates with socially awkward students at *yeshivot* (religious academies) that a respected Jerusalem rabbi published an open letter in the weekly *Yerushalayim* scolding his students. Shower and brush your teeth, he admonished them. Instead of a taking a woman on a long, cheap walk, spend some money and take her to a café. Don't talk only about yourself or your Torah studies or ignore her while you speak on the cell phone, he warned. "And remember, a woman is a delicate creature, drive her home, . . . Don't drop her off at some dark and lonely bus stop. If you still don't understand that, you're a fool." His parting rabbinical advice: "Don't judge her by looks alone, and even if she's from the 'wrong' religious community or studies in university, don't dismiss her outright. Give her a chance."

My two brothers, they can bring girls home to sleep the night—but me? I can't," Avivit Betzalel says with a resigned shrug. She lives with them and her widowed mother in the same apartment her Iranian- and Afghanistan-born parents raised her and her seven older siblings. Growing up in this rundown Beersheva neighborhood of Mizrahi Jews who immigrated from the Middle East and North Africa in the 1950s and 1960s, Avivit refused to abide by her older brothers' overly protective rules. "When they were asleep I used to sneak out to meet my friends. One morning, my married brother came over and warned me: Don't do it again. He's really conservative; he won't even let his family have a TV in the house and he goes to synagogue every day." He's a black-hatted local leader of Shas (an acronym taken from Shomrei Torah Sephardim, or Sephardic Torah Guardians), a Mizrahi religious and political movement. "When I was drafted, he told me to ask for a religious exemption. He said, 'Guys and girls together are not acceptable. A girl belongs at home, not with guys.' But I think it's everyone's duty to serve." Her mother, who wears a headscarf, encouraged her to flout his warning.

"Liberating" is the word Avivit uses to describe life as a clerk on the military base deep in the Negev. "It was mind-opening. Four hundred soldiers from different worlds. Religious, antireligious," Avivit recalls, running her manicured nails through her dark brown hair. "I met all kinds of guys. A few made fun of me for not turning lights on during Shabbat. The officers hitting on [female] soldiers, that shocked me. Even though we had lessons on sexual harassment, some girls think officers are like rock stars. I didn't meet anyone special." After the army, Avivit returned to Beersheva, which, like much of Israel, is saturated with biblical history. Here, Abraham, the Jewish, Christian, and Muslim patriarch, at the urging of his wife, Sarah, cast out his concubine, Hagar, and their son, Ishmael, who became the father of the Arabs. Today, Israel's fourth-largest city is trying hard to become modern, but it's still a provincial place in Israel's backyard. "Not much to do. Only a few bars and restaurants and one really great club," says Avivit, who got a job as a legal secretary.

She met a guy who lives in Tel Aviv. The big city, ninety minutes away by bus, intrigued her more than he did. "For me, it's New York. So much to do, all kinds of restaurants and clubs that don't close." She was taken aback by Shenkin, a bohemian street in Tel Aviv, full of funky clothing designers, openly gay men, street guitarists, and Peace Now supporters. There were men taking vegetarian cooking classes and buying books like *Emotional Intelligence* and women who weren't afraid to ask them on dates. "Honestly, I was a bit afraid. I didn't know anybody there. My whole family, everyone I know lives in Beersheva." And the boyfriend? She'd never dated an Ashkenazi Jew or known anyone who laughs during Woody Allen movies. In her world, no one has ever heard Yiddish or cares if there is a Hebrew word for *angst*. Her illiterate mother speaks Farsi and faltering Hebrew. Avivit felt cross-cultural battle fatigue. "I decided I click better with Mizrahi guys. We have the same humor, like the same music. It feels more natural. We understand each other. We don't need to explain things."

Her religious married sister, who works in a Beersheva insurance office, told her about a client who said, "I want a woman like you. Do you know anyone?" Avivit agreed to meet him. "He was outgoing, full of life. And from my neighborhood, so we had a lot in common. I'm not so religious anymore, but I still keep kosher and light Sabbath candles. And I want a guy who has faith in his heart. The next date, he drove me to his apartment. As we watched a video, he pulled me close. 'I love your eyes, they're like the ocean.' He touched my hand and said, 'I like your skin, it feels like silk.' He's not a poet, but it was hard not to fall for his words. Okay. I'm not naïve. He was flattering me, even though he didn't know me. But I liked it. I could feel myself falling for him. By our next date, I tried watching the video, but couldn't concentrate. In no time, we were kissing, really deeply. He wanted more. I controlled myself and I said, 'No. We have to go step by step.' After that night, everything felt right. When he told me he believes in the Cinderella slipper story, a woman who is the perfect fit, my fantasies went into action. I could tell he was ready to settle down. He's already twenty-seven. And my family is pushing me."

When he didn't call, Avivit was confounded. She was tempted, but avoided passing his small grocery store. Trying to console herself, she listened to romantic Mizrahi songs of pain and longing. Then a girlfriend insisted they go dancing at the Forum Club. "Both floors were really crowded. My girlfriend saw a gorgeous guy, and as she made her move, I saw it was him. When the heart breaks, it doesn't make a sound. Enough with blind dates. There's a tradition that God sets the number of people you have to meet before finding your soul mate, that every one brings you closer to finding the right one. I believe everything has its season. A time for war, a time for peace, a time for love," she says, paraphrasing words of Ecclesiastes. "Who knows? Maybe this is my season."

Two years later, Avivit decided to find an apartment near Shenkin Street in Tel Aviv. Wandering into a coffee shop, she asked the manager if he needed a waitress. He gave her the job and became her first serious boyfriend. He's brought her to the vegetable stall where his Baghdad-born father works. His parents like her enough to include some religious traditions in their Sabbath dinners together.

North of the mountain town of Safed, the spiritual capital of the school of Jewish mysticism known as kabbalah, a winding Galilee road leads to a ravine fragrant with almond and peach blossoms. Single men and women from all over the country come on pilgrimages to a modest stone shrine, the tomb of Rabbi Yonatan ben Uziel, a *tzaddik,* or saintly man, who lived more than two thousand years ago. His religious thinking was so lofty, it is said that when he studied Torah, the spiritual heat would singe birds overhead. The sage died without ever having married. Tradition holds that when he got to heaven, the Lord asked him what favors He could bestow. The bachelor rabbi declared that what he wanted most was to help others enjoy what he had missed in life. That's why inside the shrine, men and women, separated by a screen, are praying for a match made in heaven. Sometimes, from the women's side, one can hear weeping sounds. Men and women reach out to touch the tomb from opposite sides of the divider. Some purposely forget their prayer books—with information about themselves and phone numbers inside. Others post "seeking a soul mate" messages on the walls with their email addresses.

A tree outside Rabbi Uziel's first-century tomb is festooned with dozens of multicolored scarves, headkerchiefs, and strips of cloth. To enhance their chances, women leave them as lucky charms, to remain connected with the place. At a makeshift stall near a creek, an entrepreneur sells amulets and holy books and dispenses advice to despairing singles. According to Jewish tradition, during the ten days of repentance between Rosh Hashana and Yom Kippur, God is especially close to the people of Israel and at this critical time answers prayers. People tell stories of those who searched for love in all the wrong places—until they prayed here and found the right mate. "I want a home, and children. The Jewish calendar revolves around the family. Judaism isn't for single people. God says it's not good to be alone," says a twenty-three-year-old on an outing organized by Shas for religious Mizrahi women longing for a husband. "My sister, she poured her heart out to God here. In only two weeks, she met her *basherte,*" Hebrew for beloved, partner, intended, or soul mate.

Not all supplicants are as religious. The manager of a spa relates how she tripped at a gravesite and literally fell into a man's arms. A lightning-quick romance led almost immediately to marriage. The secular cynic no longer was a disbeliever. So why is she back? "Time for a replacement," the divorcée explains. Fashion models, singers, and actors come here on the great spousal search. A gossip columnist broke the story of a Tel Aviv hairstylist who flew several of her single high-powered husband-hunting clients on a chartered plane to this shrine. Ex-hippies, New Age enthusiasts, social gadflies also believe the place is a pipeline to God. A physician whose patients include many scientists from the Weizmann Institute came to pour out hopes for her daughter. "It worked for my eldest. I'm about to be a grandmother." Each year, a quarter of a million divorced, widowed, and never-married Israelis visit, even in the middle of the night.

Dating strategies for the desperate run from ancient to New Age. Some Israelis enhance their chances by rearranging bedrooms using Feng Shui principles; others boost theirs by taking guided imagery seminars or transcendental meditation. Nearly 60 percent of Israelis are interested in mysticism, astrology, numerology, and the supernatural, according to a recent Gallup-Israel survey. Most devotées are women between eighteen and twenty-four years old. Bookstores sell *101 Israeli Mystics,* many of whom apparently work miracles for clients' love lives. There's Malka-Haya, who is in touch with Maimonides, and a deceased "kabbalist Yehiel," who speaks through his granddaughter. The angel Raphael communicates with a parapsychologist named Limor. A master medium who lives near the sprawling Intel Pentium 4 chip plant in Kiryat Gat says his waiting room is filled with people seeking romantic counseling. Practitioners often are divided by ethnic origin: astrology is primarily an Ashkenazi profession; experts in practical kabbalah and reading coffee grinds are mostly Mizrahim.

The first convention for professional Israeli matchmakers took place in Jerusalem in 1998 and was attended by several thousand mostly religious women. Since then, their numbers have been rising steadily. For ultra-Orthodox Israelis, it's something out of *Fiddler on the Roof:* "Matchmaker, matchmaker, make me a match . . ." Other Israelis, out of the army and universities and fed up with the sex-for-fun party scene, who want to find someone serious also are turning to matchmakers. "They go to advisors for everything," explains one matchmaker. "They use personal trainers, investment counselors, and head-hunters. Why should dating be any different?"

Liaura Zacharie considers matchmaking a Zionist mission. She was shocked to discover the soaring single Sabra rate: more than a third of adult Jewish Israelis are unmarried. She got into the profession by accident: "I went crazy seeing young, professional, idealistic immigrant friends losing hope of finding mates, ready to leave the country. Judaism revolves around family life. Being religious and single here is difficult. So my husband and I organized a party for them. Instead of thirty singles, more than a hundred showed up. And most were Sabras. I didn't realize there were so many singles in terrible trouble." After that party, she set up a dating service, Eden 2000, which has helped almost twenty thousand Israelis, from yuppie Orthodox to the not-so-religious, on their quest for love, running a web dating service, organizing hikes, ski trips, and kosher safaris to Kenya—before the al-Qaeda bombing of an Israeli-owned hotel in Mombassa. Most of her clients are in their childbearing years, which makes her happy: more than 30 percent of Jewish men age twenty-five to forty-four and a quarter of women of that age are unmarried. It's a very serious national problem, she continues. For a strong Israel, Jews need to marry and multiply. The country can't afford the singles rate of France or the United States because it's under "demographic siege." The government has given Zacharie a seat on the National Council of Demographic Planning, which is concerned that Israeli Jews are losing the "war of the wombs." Twenty percent of Israeli citizens are Muslim; it's estimated that by 2025, 33 percent will be Muslim. "Israelis are more marriage-oriented than people in other Western countries, but they're slowly changing. Jewish, Druze, and Christian Arab marriage rates are declining and people are marrying later," notes Professor Sergio Della Pergola, a demographer at the Hebrew University. "But not Israeli Muslims. They're marrying earlier. They've turned against modernism and moved back to traditional patterns."

And, sometimes, not so traditional.

———————

After the doctor bumped into a car in the hospital parking lot, he left a note on the windshield. The unusually polite, apologetic note impressed the nurse. They met in the cafeteria to discuss the damages. For almost a year, they continued meeting. It seemed platonic. Both in their thirties, they were cautious. Neither want their real names used. Adil is a Muslim Arab widower whose wife had died in a car accident. Yaffa had upset her religious Jewish parents by breaking off her engagement to a man they liked. She brought Adil home. Her grandparents speak Syrian Arabic. He speaks Galilee Arabic. Over dinner, everyone spoke Hebrew. Her family was cordial. But behind the scenes, there was pleading.

Adil invited her to his all-Muslim village in the Galilee, which is more than half Arab Israeli. His parents and other relatives were very hospitable. After she left, his mother said she would find him a suitable woman from the *hamula,* the extended family. He wasn't interested. Some of his cousins had broken with tradition and chosen Muslim spouses without family involvement. Why couldn't he?

Soon after Yaffa moved into Adil's apartment, they discovered his friendly Jewish neighbors were no longer welcoming. She found another note on her car's windshield. This one warned: "You're screwing an Arab." After someone sprayed "You're a traitor" on their front door, they searched for another apartment. At first, landlords assumed he was a Mizrahi Jew who looked like a young Omar Sharif. When they heard his Arabic-accented Hebrew, they found excuses. Renting was especially tough, with suicide bombings in Jerusalem fanning suspicions. Finally, they found a place. Jerusalem has two geographies: the one you can find on the map, the geography of place, and the one hidden in people's minds. Before this intifada, it was easier to ignore Jerusalem's darker map. Now they couldn't. They discovered a new geography—the geography of fear.

When the couple announced they wanted to marry, the reaction, in their words, was *"Romeo and Juliet* gone nuclear." Adil's father and brothers forbade him from entering the village again; they threatened to kill him. Only his mother continued to talk to him. Yaffa's family and friends begged her to leave him. It was the first time she had seen her father cry. They thought their love could transcend the escalating hatreds of the intifada. Nothing is simple in Jerusalem anymore. Not even love. After two years, they didn't have to tell each other what they knew: the perpetual tribal conflict had beaten them down. They retreated into their separate worlds. Love can't thrive in a situation without a solution.

———————

In a country with one Muslim Montague for every four Jewish Capulets, not many Muslim-Jewish Israeli couples live together openly. One love story became a national sensation. It was born on September 13, 1993, the day Yasser Arafat and Yitzhak Rabin signed the Declaration of Principles on the White House lawn. A Palestinian and an Israeli director signed an agreement to stage an Israeli-Palestinian coproduction of *Romeo and Juliet.* The setting for Shakespeare's tragedy of familial feuds was west Jerusalem, not Verona. The Montagues were Arab Israelis and Palestinians; the Capulets, Israeli Jews. When Romeo wooed his Juliet in the garden, he spoke Arabic; she answered in Hebrew. The tale of great passions and great hatred between two noble families became a metaphor for the tale of two nations unable to live together or separately. "The Arabic-speaking Montagues and Hebrew-speaking Capulets are here to stay—same as us," the Israeli director Eran Baniel said somberly. "The only alternative to peace is death."

Not long after *Romeo and Juliet* finished its tour in Israel, France, and Germany, *Forbidden Marriages in the Holy Land* was released. In this Arabic-Hebrew documentary, eight Montague/Capulet couples caught up in the conflict tell their stories. There is a Jewish Israeli who converted to Islam to live with her Palestinian husband in Gaza and a Jew who is married to a fiery Muslim Israeli whose brothers threaten to kill her. According to the Nazareth-born film director, Michel Khleifi, "Thousands of other mixed-faith couples live together in the Holy Land, most of them secretly."

Gil Shelef calls the mixed Arab-Jewish port of Haifa his "pocket of peace." He resembles a white Rastafarian with dark dreadlocks concealing his eyes. But when he met Natalie at a friend's party, he could see clearly. "Exotic looking. Not really dark skin. Sexy pout and the right amount of angst." They live in the same neighborhood, but their backgrounds are dissimilar. He speaks Hebrew, Arabic, English, and Spanish and reads Chekhov in Russian; his parents moved to Haifa in 1971 from St. Petersburg. She is part Ashkenazi, one of the founding families of Haifa, and part Egyptian Jew. "I liked that Natalie doesn't care about status, doesn't have those phony Tel Aviv values." To illustrate his point, Gil tells what happened with another woman when serving in the prestigious Navy Seals, the Special Forces unit famous for capturing the *Karine-A,* a cargo ship smuggling fifty tons of Iranian weapons to the Palestinian Authority. "It was a blind date and right away, she was coming on to me. I didn't know why, until she started asking about my job. I told her that I'd been transferred to an unimportant desk job because I injured my knee and, poof, her spark went out. If you don't have a fancy title, Tel Aviv women run in the opposite direction. Natalie didn't mind at all that I'm a bartender, a part-time bartender with no career goals."

Gil invited Natalie to the bar-café where he works, a cozy watering hole where friends, lovers, and bohemians discuss politics, recite their latest verses, and listen to the three-pack-a-day voice of singer Tom Waits. "I love the place, it's like my living room." They had drinks with some of his friends: a Muslim-Jewish student couple from the Technion, the son of an Arab member of the Knesset (Arabs make up 10 percent of the Knesset), and a staunchly secular Muslim engineer unhappily engaged to a religious woman from Umm al-Fahm, an all-Arab town run by the Israeli Islamicists who prohibit alcohol. "It made me happy that Natalie was enjoying the chill-out music and the scene—it's one of the few binational bars where Arabs and Jews hang out. I went to fix her a salad. When I returned, I assumed she was in the toilet, but she didn't come back. Finally, I found her outside. She said it was too crowded and smoky. It took a while until she opened up. 'I don't feel comfortable with Arabs. Is it okay if we leave?' I said, 'It's okay if *you* leave. Let's end it now.' In Israel, politics touches everything, even dating."

Not all soldiers live on bases. For those who commute from home, it's the life of a civilian when they're not in uniform. Twenty-three-year-old army intelligence officer Roi rarely puts on his khakis when he drives from his family's suburban duplex to the late-night shift on a secret base near Tel Aviv. "It's away from the front. No sense of war. A room, just computers and telephones. Very few people, just a skeleton staff of nineteen-year-olds. I'm in charge of computer systems, answering phone calls if people have problems. Usually, there's nothing to do. Our main job is staying awake. We listen to cool music on Galel Zahal (the army radio station). Conversations are mostly sex, drugs, and rock and roll. Military police can't enter because it's a classified area, so we wear T-shirts, sandals, and army pants. If nothing is happening, you can take a nap on one of the mattresses. Sometimes we don't nap."

He recalls a hot summer night. "I wandered around wondering, 'Will tonight be exciting or not?' If you're looking for it, you can find it. I saw a cute girl, just out of basic training. Normally, she wouldn't even dare look an officer like me in the eye, not one with my [high-ranking] insignia. But I was wearing a T-shirt and acting really macho, like the Marlboro guy. And it was very late. Everyone was gone. Just a guy and a girl and the rules, well, they don't apply."

They entered a restricted room lined with computers. On the wall, a few maps. And for comic relief, Iraqi and Syrian flags and photos of Saddam, Arafat, and Assad. He locked the door. They were undressed, breathing heavily, when an officer knocked and demanded, "Open up, I need to use the [secure] phone."

"Come back later," Roi tossed back.

"It's important!"

"Just give me two minutes. No one starts wars in the middle of the night."

There was no term in Hebrew for sexual harassment until Israel passed the world's most far-reaching law against it. "This legislation does more than protect women from unwanted advances. It changes the very meanings of masculinity and femininity in Israeli society," states Hebrew University Law School's Dr. Orit Kamir, who coauthored the groundbreaking legislation that the Knesset passed in 1998 after extensive lobbying from Israeli women's groups. The law targets sexual harassment in the workplace, the army, schools, and restaurants, on the streets—everywhere. It also forbids gay bashing. It allows flirting, off-color jokes, and consensual affairs. However, consensual sex between superiors and subordinates is forbidden. If the man is a woman's superior, she can lodge a complaint against him for sexual harassment or sexual attack, even if she agreed at the time to have sex. "It's not that we're trying to regulate sexual relations or to prevent romance," explains attorney Rivka Shaked, who represents women in the civil service, which is Israel's largest employer. "We are trying to prevent men from abusing their authority. When the man has power and the woman is a subordinate, you can never tell: Did she really agree? Or did she give in because she was afraid that she would lose her job if she didn't?"

The law, which is tougher than that of any other country, bewilders and angers some men. Some complain it puts them in sexual straitjackets, threatening Israeli romance. Under the law, flirting is legal, but sexual harassment isn't—and it's not just in Israel where the line between the two is confusing. "When I was young, we used to tell women, 'Your eyes are like two cups of Turkish coffee.' I agreed to vote for the bill only after I became convinced that this still will go on, that it wouldn't put an end to romance," said Ruby Rivlin, now speaker of the Knesset. A reporter for *Ha'aretz* wrote that "the law takes away an important male freedom of expression, the freedom to flirt." Israel is roughly ten years behind the United States in the evolution of the public discussion of sexual harassment. What some Israeli men consider normal may be shocking in Manhattan but not in the Mediterranean. Many Israeli men have difficulty believing that an admiring look at a woman's exposed legs, a playful pat on the buttocks, or a remark about her breast size is offensive. An army officer complains, "We've reached a stage where I can't kiss a woman soldier on the cheek when she's discharged." Women's groups are trying to educate men about inappropriate sexual comments and unwanted physical contact. As Yael Dayan, who, until the 2003 election, was a member of the Knesset heading the Committee on the Advancement of the Status of Women, puts it, "It's not to create a situation where there's no courting in the workplace or where every touch leads to a police complaint. But when a woman says no, she means no" (a word her late father, General Moshe Dayan, a notorious philanderer, ignored—or, possibly, rarely heard). "Israel is a place of contradictions," adds Shulamit Aloni, a veteran civil rights activist, former minister of education, and founder of the left-wing Meretz political party. "On one hand, the sky is the limit for women in civilian life, but we also live in a patriarchal and macho society—patriarchal because the rabbinate, which is very backward, controls marriage and divorce, and macho because of the army."

Women in the military often are viewed as men's helpmates, according to the late sociologist Dafna Izraeli of Bar-Ilan University's Gender Studies Program. "Traditionally, the military has had an aura of permissive license. A prevailing attitude is that men serve the nation and the women serve the men. It's no secret that the Israeli military is a hothouse of exploitative sexual relationships. Commanding officers often get 'the first pick' of female recruits. It's still not uncommon for pretty young female soldiers to become their 'trophies.'" In Israel's world-renowned air force, men regularly said, "The best men go to the pilots' course. The best women go to the pilots."

Although army regulations have prohibited sexual relations between superiors and subordinates for decades, they rarely were enforced. If a young female recruit complained about a senior officer harassing her, little happened. Even in cases of confirmed rape, officers quietly have been discharged, often with full pensions and privileges. Israelis realized the country had changed when, in 1999, the Supreme Court blocked the promotion of Brigadier General Nir Galili after a nineteen-year-old soldier on his base accused him of having sexual relations with her.

"Dozens of other cases like Galili's are never reported," says Nitzan Arbib, a soldier in the Education Corps, who, among her other duties, arranges mandatory sexual harassment lectures every few months for the five hundred men and eighteen women in her combat unit in the West Bank. "If I'm lucky, three or four show up and yawn in my face." She also sets up separate classes for their male commanders. "I sent a bullet-proof jeep to bring a guest speaker, a social worker, to our base. At least thirty officers promised to attend. I checked and double-checked and they all assured me they were coming. When I brought the speaker to the room, it was empty. We waited and waited. I made phone calls and got comments like this: 'Another lecture on sexual harassment? It's so boring.' 'I'm too tired, I was out fighting.' 'I've got chores to do, I forgot.' The commanders need the course more than their soldiers; some of them act like fifteen-year-olds. One guy said, 'The girls are crazy about me. They're here to sleep with guys, why else would they volunteer for a combat unit?' "

When Chen Nardi, commander of a basic training camp for combat soldiers, was promoted to lieutenant colonel, a fellow officer asked him, How are the girls? "When I reminded him that I'm a senior officer, that the women under my command are my subordinates, and that I'm married, he called me a *freier* [sucker]. After all, he said, 'having fun with the women is just part of the deal.' " Nardi, who now runs the Movement for a New Manhood and offers workshops in male-female relationships, observes that "changes in Israeli military and civilian society are revolutionary. Laws are challenging our definitions of masculinity and femininity. Women are demanding their rights and men are learning to treat them as equals. But some men don't realize the rules of the game have changed. They just don't get it. Men in high positions in the workplace, academia, and the military find it hard to stop their sexist, macho rituals and still think they have the privilege to make lewd sexual comments or demand sexual favors from women subordinates." He emphasizes that the army, by nature, "is a hierarchical, macho institution, where senior military brass can treat young, attractive recruits as perks. Because our survival is threatened, the warrior who defends our country has a particularly esteemed position. The general is like a great father to us all—he will protect us. Is it any wonder that Mordechai committed the crimes he did?"

He's referring to the spectacular fall from glory of veteran army general Yitzhak Mordechai. It was Israel's most publicized sexual harassment trial. In March 2000, the former defense minister and political leader, who aspired to run for prime minister in 1999, was convicted of sexual assault against two women. Despite the severity of his crimes,

Mordechai received an eighteen-month suspended sentence. Some women called the punishment a slap on the wrist; others called his conviction a victory for women's rights. The trial has spurred women to come forward to tell stories of improper advances to newspapers and on talk shows. Before the law was passed, as many as half of all Israeli women said they had been harassed, and three-quarters were afraid to complain or convinced it would do no good. Since then, the number of women reporting cases has risen sharply. At least fifty officers found guilty of sexual harassment have been dismissed. Still, according to an army spokesperson, only one in three victims files a complaint.

Then there are those who wish their superiors *would* make an improper advance. A strong-willed woman who worked in army intelligence complained about not being able to make a formal grievance. "I prayed he'd make a sexual move, so I could file a complaint. Unfortunately, he never did. My commander was the kind who goes mad and punishes you if your shoes are dirty. He didn't know what to do with an intelligent, left-wing girl," recalls Efrat. "If I made even a slight mistake in the difficult translation work he gave me, people heard him yelling at me through the window."

One day, a high-ranking officer visited her top-secret base in the Galilee to train her and a few other select soldiers in advanced Arabic translation. "He was so handsome. Very tall, light blue eyes. A part of the attraction was his insignia. It's an aphrodisiac. But his sexiness was much more than that. I really wanted him and planned my moves very carefully, trying to be witty and cute, running my hands through my hair. Three weeks later, 'Ami' left without even noticing me. But I couldn't stop thinking about him."

After seven months, the nineteen-year-old thought she had a valid reason to call the twenty-two-year-old officer. "My commander still was making my life hell and I was desperate for help." Efrat phoned Ami at headquarters in Tel Aviv and asked for a meeting. "He said no, that everyone in the army whines. I insisted it's really serious, that my commander was torturing me. He didn't believe me, but finally agreed to see me when I was in Tel Aviv on leave. After I told him my horror stories, I convinced him to help get me a transfer. As I left, I don't know why, I just blurted out, 'There's something else. I'm really in love with you.' He was shocked, didn't know what to do. He said very formally, 'I'm your commanding officer. Any relationship is forbidden.' Even if he were interested, he follows the rules, so it means I'd have to wait more than two years until my discharge.

"For two days, I was embarrassed, a zombie. On my last night of leave, he called and said, 'I've thought about it and we're going out.' We went to a movie in a mall. As we were walking out, a girl from the base spotted me and yelled out, 'Efrat! What are you doing here?' When she saw Ami, her eyes got wide. We hadn't even held hands, but by morning we were the talk of the base. In the army, a secret is something you tell to one person at a time."

Israel is one of the world's most densely populated countries. It's nearly impossible to remain anonymous. One soldier asked the phone operator for the number of a woman he'd met in a bookstore. "Forget it," she said. "Why?" he demanded. "She's back with her boyfriend." Israelis wear skimpy bathing suits, but women don't go topless as in France or Italy. Just think who might be on the next beach towel—your teacher, your dentist, your neighbor. Israelis don't crave solitude. Put Israeli strangers on a long stretch of beach and within minutes, they'll be close together gossiping. Try dozing on an airline with Israeli passengers. Even before takeoff, strangers are in the aisle talking noisily. Closeness promotes cohesion, but it also means that people know the intimate details of each other's lives. It's a group-oriented society; people often have difficulty understanding the exotic Western concept of "private space." From kindergarten, Israelis are taught the importance of belonging to a *hevreh,* a close-knit group of friends from school or scouts or the army that stay together for life. It's in the army that the most lasting friendships are forged. It's also a powerful matchmaker.

So, how did Efrat's romance with her commanding officer go? "Wonderfully. Intense. After I got out, I broke up with him. I want to experience lots of men. My mother married her officer. She and my dad are divorced. When they dated, the army songs were about women waiting for the brave soldier to return from battle. I like today's songs. About daring women going off to explore the world on their own."

Unlike Efrat, whose base has over eight hundred men and women soldiers and a disco three nights a week, Ilana was the sole woman soldier among ninety male combat soldiers. Her job was sorting mail. "I'll never be a beauty queen, but they treated me like a rare orchid. There's a saying: 'In the desert, every thistle is a flower.' I had a boyfriend back home and they respected me. Not one of them made a pass. I was like a psychiatrist to this broken hearts unit, hearing stories about girls who dumped them. These guys are lucky if they get home twice a month. They sit in the mud. Then in the broiling heat. Guarding. Going after terrorists. Their guns are part of their bodies. I saw a sign that describes their lives: 'America: 9/11. Israel 24/7.' "

Now Ilana is a junior marketing executive. "The atmosphere in our office is relaxed, friendly, and fun," she says. "Men aren't shy in blurting out what they feel. If a guy thinks my blouse looks sexy, he'll say so. Israeli men have a healthy respect for sexuality. It's not like when I visited England. You could be naked and they'd pretend not to notice. Here, when I'm in a meeting, it's like it was on the base. A man might stroke my arm and say, 'Your smile is so beautiful.' To me it's a compliment, not sexually suggestive. My boss calls me *motik* [sweetheart]. To him, it's affectionate. Sometimes I use innocent flirting to soften him up. And I've gotten him to give me assignments that guys working above my level can't get. After a meeting, he might give me a friendly hug. It's not threatening. If we got upset every time men squeezed our hands or made flirty comments, we'd never get any work done. We'd be too busy filing complaints."

The IDF is not, despite all the stories above, a dating service. It has a somewhat more serious purpose, as is seen in the next chapter.

3

A People's Army

🕉 *Even when the lion lies down with the lamb, it's still better for us to be the lion.* —Popular IDF saying

🕉 *The ideal is no longer peace, but the absence of war.* —The late poet Yehuda Amichai

Barely out of high school, Liron Heffetz was driving his tank in the Gaza Strip along the Israeli border, accompanying a bulldozer as it flattened tall stalks of wheat, taking down bushes potentially sheltering terrorists intent on infiltrating Israel. "I looked out and saw an old Palestinian farmer and his wife. I'll never forget the expression on their faces. Fear and despair. And anger. We were destroying their fields, their livelihood," recalls the nineteen-year-old soldier. "We were faced with a terrible choice: ruin their crops or let Hamas use the field to murder civilians. I decided that Israeli lives are worth more than a field."

On his way home in his khaki uniform, his M-16 slung over his shoulder, Liron stops at Tower Records. Because of Israel's small size, soldiers often travel from the front to home, a commute that rarely is more than two hours. All over Israel, male and female soldiers mingle freely with civilians. Most Jewish and Druze families have a full-time soldier or one in the reserves. At an age when Americans are leaving home and separating from their parents, Israeli soldiers' emotional dependence on their family increases. Those families arrive at military bases each Saturday armed with gefilte fish, spicy Moroccan couscous, Russian *piroshki*, and Ethiopian *wat* for their children who can't get weekend leave.

As Liron enters his parents' two-story house in a sleepy town near Tel Aviv, he deposits a heap of dirty laundry. "My parents treat me like a king. Mom makes my favorite foods. I sleep past noon and spend a lot of time playing piano and reading." A contemplative guy, he's been perusing the writings of David Ben-Gurion, Israel's first prime minister, who stressed that whereas imperialists might employ a professional army, an egalitarian nation requires a people's army.

Over Shabbat dinners Liron has been asking about Ben-Gurion. His grandfather, from a Syrian and Egyptian family that moved to Jerusalem eight generations ago, knew most of the founders of the state. He helped found both the Israeli Air Force and El Al Airlines. "When I volunteered for a combat unit, he was proud. I know he's afraid for me, so I don't tell him or my parents everything," says Liron, who already has lost five army buddies. While soldiers at a checkpoint were trying to intercept potential terrorists from entering Israel, a Palestinian opened fire. When Liron's friend David rushed to help a wounded soldier, he was shot dead. "We don't abandon our soldiers," Liron declares emphatically. "Soldiers will risk their lives to bring back a wounded guy."

Isn't it a relief to be on a two-day leave? Liron pauses before answering. "It's not like I'm going home to another world. You can't get away from this war." Israel today is a crazy mix of home and front with no clear-cut distinctions between enemy and friend. Liron's voice breaks as he talks about a fellow tanker who went home to visit his family in Gilo. Moments after ordering a drink at a downtown café on Ben-Yehuda Street, he was blown away by a suicide bomber. "Sometimes the front is minutes from home." He hesitates before noting the ironic twist of fate that happened to the family two houses away. After their son was discharged from the air force, he studied in the United States. When he graduated, his family urged him to stay there, safe from the intifada. He was working on the 103rd floor of the World Trade Center on September 11, the day al-Qaeda came to America.

One of Liron's older brothers, Tamir, has spent the day racing his Kawasaki motorcycle in the Negev, a last adventure before packing his duffle bag once again. A free spirit, sporting a blond ponytail and an earring—the IDF is a little short on spit and polish—he is not happy to be returning to reserve duty. Even though front-line soldiers like Tamir and Liron face the toughest role in the IDF, with the fewest leaves and more reserve duty than other soldiers, they share the national commitment to defense. Polls consistently show that a majority of Israelis would volunteer for service even if it were not compulsory. "We know that without the army, there wouldn't be an Israel. We can't afford to lose even one war or we'd lose our country," avows Tamir. "For me, being an Israeli means defending the country. But how many more call-ups can we have?"

Army service is the rite of passage for Israelis, no less profound for being common. Compulsory service starts at age eighteen. Jewish and Druze men serve three years, and Jewish women—Israel is the only country in the world that drafts women—serve at least two years. Israel has "only" about 140,000 full-time troops, a significant portion of its population, but its real military strength lies in the 400,000 reserve soldiers who serve four to six weeks a year. Former Chief of Staff Yigal Yadin once said, "Every Israeli citizen is a soldier on eleven months annual leave." Jewish and Druze men and some women are called up for reserve duty until their early forties.

Nothing unites this contentious country more than a belief in the importance of the army. After a wave of suicide bombings, including the Passover Massacre on March 29, 2002, the government sent troops into the West Bank and Gaza, areas granted to the Palestinian Authority as part of the Oslo peace process. The responses to the emergency call-up were astounding: 95 percent of reservists reported for duty. Thousands more, who did not get orders because they were too old, also volunteered. Optometrists, physicists, and plumbers left homes and jobs to climb into jeeps, armored personnel carriers, and helicopters. In the reserves, it's not unusual for a car owner to be under the command of his mechanic, a professor under his barber, a lawyer under a clerk.

The intifada has stretched the IDF to its limits, taking its biggest toll on reservists who leave jobs and families. Quite a few of the self-employed face bankruptcy. Wives are left alone to juggle jobs and children. University students miss classes. As the intifada drags on, many reservists like Tamir serve forty-two days at a stretch on missions like searching for hidden arms caches. Those who entered the West Bank city of Nablus saw walls papered with posters of Palestinian suicide bombers and discovered a three-hour videotape on which a masked Hamas instructor demonstrated how to construct a belt of explosives and where to stand on a bus to kill the most Israelis.

Israelis have always lived in a state of war, or semiwar, in a country that has never had permanent borders. Israel has the world's highest percentage of veterans, with most Jewish and Druze men having fought in two or three wars. During Memorial Day, the names of the more than twenty thousand Israelis killed in military conflicts scroll slowly on television screens: the War of Independence (1947–48); the Suez Campaign (1956); the 1967 Six-Day War; the War of Attrition (1968–70); the 1973 Yom Kippur War; the Lebanon War (1982–2000, and could re-erupt anytime). In less than sixty years, Israeli armed forces have accumulated a huge number of battle honors. The ragtag Jewish army of 1948, self-taught fighters in mismatched uniforms armed with cast-off antiquated weapons, World War I–era rifles, homemade submachine guns and mortars, driving "tanks" that were trucks with steel plate and concrete in between, won the first Jewish military victory in over two thousand years. The assault on Sinai in 1956, with French and British troops, ended short of victory by U.S. and Soviet intervention. The lightning six-day victory of 1967 destroyed the Egyptian air force on the ground in hours, conquered the West Bank, Sinai, and the Golan Heights, taking the Old City of Jerusalem and the Western Wall, barred to Jewish worship since independence. The 1973 Yom Kippur War began with Israel spectacularly unprepared for the surprise simultaneous Egyptian and Syrian attacks and ended with the IDF encircling the Third Egyptian Army and advancing to within 101 kilometers of Cairo and within artillery range of Damascus.

If the 1973 War, with its more than two thousand dead and five thousand wounded, compromised the myth of Israeli invincibility, the invasion and occupation of southern Lebanon—"Operation Peace for Galilee"—shattered it. The first intifada, which in Arabic means "uprising" or "shaking off," lasted from 1985 to 1992, but, in the judgment of many Israelis, the conflict that broke out in September 2000 is a direct consequence of Israel's ignominious departure from Lebanon, which convinced Israel's enemies that Israelis would no longer allow casualties—that they had gone soft. This war without a name—many Israelis simply call it "the Situation"—is different. Unlike the first intifada, a popular uprising in which unarmed Palestinians fought mostly with rocks, this conflict is fought with suicide bombers and sophisticated explosives. It is financed and equipped mostly by Iran, Syria, Saudi Arabia, and until Saddam's downfall, Iraq. Many Palestinians call it the "al-Aqsa intifada," which Islamicizes the conflict and connects it to the world's 1.2 billion Muslims who believe al-Aqsa Mosque on Jerusalem's Temple Mount/Haram al-Sharif is Islam's third-holiest place. Other Palestinians call it the "War of Annihilation," because they want Palestine to include all of Israel. In a conflict that is also fought on the pages of Arab schoolbooks, which include maps that omit Israel and call Jerusalem al-Quds, giving the conflict a neutral name is difficult. In this book, it is called the "second intifada," as of this writing the latest war that engages the entire nation of Israel.

Almost the entire nation. In 2002, the Knesset bowed to pressure from ultra-Orthodox politicians and passed the Tal Law legalizing the divisive practice of granting military exemptions to ultra-Orthodox men enrolled in yeshivot (religious schools). "They're draft evaders. It's disgusting, unfair," Tamir declares vehemently. "We feel betrayed. Instead of 'One People, One Draft,' we carry their load, protecting and supporting them and their enormous families. They refuse to shed their blood and we pay with our lives. If they don't want to share the burden, they should leave the country." In this politically heated country, this issue generates boiling resentment. That's the main reason voters made the anti–ultra-Orthodox Shinui the second-largest party in the 2003 Knesset. Big changes are in store.

The discriminatory draft started in 1954 when Prime Minister Ben-Gurion gave military exemptions to four hundred young Torah scholars. Today, more than thirty thousand army-age men receive military exemptions simply by enrolling in (and sometimes not even attending) government-subsidized yeshivas. Some men "find religion" shortly before they're drafted. A sarcastic story expresses the pervasive bitterness: When a reservist's father stopped to give a hitchhiking soldier a lift, an ultra-Orthodox yeshiva student also tried to get into the car. "Sorry, I only give rides to Israelis who serve in the army," the father told him. "But I serve in the army of God," the ultra-Orthodox student said. "Good," the father answered. "So ask God for a ride."

Yeshiva students aren't the only recruiting problem faced by the IDF. In February 2002, fifty-four soldiers signed a controversial Soldiers' Letter saying they refuse to serve beyond the 1967 borders; by 2003, the letter had more than 550 signatures. These reservists, some of whom are highly decorated officers with distinguished combat records, believe their fellow soldiers will be safer defending themselves from inside Israel than from the alleys of Jenin and Nablus. They call this conflict the "War of the Settlements" and want most settlers evacuated from the West Bank and from all of Gaza. Those six days in 1967 during which the IDF defeated the combined armies of Egypt, Jordan, and Syria did more than breed a myth of invincibility; it also tripled the size of the country. And, by the law of unintended consequences, it made Israel into an occupier and opened the door for the settlers.

The aftershocks reverberate today in these dissenting reserve soldiers who say they refuse to be called on to perform actions they believe violate the human rights of Palestinians, such as demolishing homes, uprooting orchards where terrorists may hide, or endangering civilians by using weapons in densely populated areas. Some have served time in military jail; a few cases have been heard before Israel's Supreme Court. Some of their fellow soldiers call them courageous. Most, however, argue that no democracy allows its soldiers selective refusal, that the army must follow what the elected government instructs it to do, which means stopping terrorists in Gaza and the West Bank before they strike. Some charge that these "refuseniks" give Palestinians the impression that terror succeeds, that more attacks will make other soldiers lose heart. Even left-wing soldiers are critical, saying they're not fighting to maintain the settlements; they're fighting terrorism. In a recent poll, 60 percent of Israelis said they're fighting for their survival; 20 percent said that the war is being fought to determine the borders between Israel and a future Palestinian state; only 11 percent believed the war is being fought over the settlements. "Almost everyone I know thinks settlements like the ones in Gaza and Hebron and those illegal outposts dotted through the West Bank are lunacy. We hate that our soldiers die guarding them," says Tamir, who, along with a large majority of Israelis, favors a Palestinian state and removing most settlements in the West Bank and Gaza—but only as part of a diplomatic peace agreement. "We won't have the security we want without a peaceful Palestinian state next to us. But the Palestinians won't get the state they want without deciding to live in peace with us. I'm a peacenik, not a pacifist," he says, paraphrasing the words of Israeli author Amos Oz.

Ronit Heffetz geared up for the army the same way her three older brothers did. "Scouts prepared them to serve and that's what it's done for me. We did everything together: hiked all over the country, pitched tents, learned to take care of each other." They go on night maneuvers, recreating battles of the underground, and crawl on their stomachs. If they get cut, they're told, "A little blood won't hurt you." Israeli youth movements, which range from non-Orthodox to Orthodox, right-wing to left-wing, teach behaviors valued by the army: camaraderie, resourcefulness, and group cohesion.

Attachment to the army is instilled early. Jewish children learn songs and stories of valor from the Maccabees to Masada to the daring rescue of Air France hostages at Entebbe that riveted the world on July 4, 1976. Remembrance is a key part of Israeli education. In the process of studying Jewish history—centuries of pogroms, massacres, and inquisitions—children learn the importance of selflessness and Jewish interconnectedness. As they observe holidays, they are introduced to a changing cast of characters who tried to wipe out the Jews: the Egyptians on Passover, the Greeks on Hanukkah, the Persians on Purim, the Romans on Lag b'Omer, and on Independence Day, the Arabs. On Independence Day, Jewish schools are decorated with the flags of the various military corps and children climb on Israeli-made Merkava 4 tanks. Questions about the army even appear in fifth-grade math books. Soldiers speak to sixth-graders about the importance of "refreshing" their gas mask kits. Children send gift packages and letters to soldiers. To make itself more relevant to career-oriented, technologically savvy recruits, the IDF sometimes sends soldiers to their former high schools to motivate students. Some go to prearmy training programs where they sample life on a base and see live fire exercises or get pep talks from soldiers turned high-tech successes.

It's impossible to avoid the army's influence. Streets are named after wars and military heroes. Even an ad for Tnuva cheese invokes the names of famous combat units: "Fifty percent Paratroopers, fifty percent Golani Brigade, one hundred percent family." Colloquial expressions offer a revealing insight about a people's preoccupations. French abounds with food expressions: "It's not end of the string beans" (it's not the end of the world); "the carrots are cooked" (it's all over). American English is replete with baseball terms: strike out, hardball, home run. Hebrew slang is filled with military terms: "She's a bomb" (she's sexy); "you're a cannon" (you excel); "like a military operation" (praising something done well); "we're going to send you on a missile" (we're going to fire you or kick your ass); "to urinate" (light artillery); "to defecate" (heavy artillery). Army service is such a key part of civilian society that even driver's license applications have spaces for one's military ID and profile number.

Field trips to historic sites are part of every Israeli's schooling. Jewish youngsters and recruits visit the Galilee grave of Yosef Trumpeldor, the spiritual father of the IDF. Trumpeldor, the most decorated Jewish officer in the czar's army for his service during the Russo-Japanese War of 1905, persuaded many Jewish youth to emigrate to Palestine, later starting Jewish military units in Palestine during the First World War and serving as deputy commander of the Zion Mule Corps, a unit of the British army, during the Gallipoli campaign. In 1920, when Arabs attacked a Jewish farming settlement called Tel Hai (Hill of Life), seven Jewish men and women led by Trumpeldor were killed in its defense. This national hero's last words are legendary: "It is good to die for our country." (Some historians, however, believe he probably died cursing in Russian.) Myth or not, the death of the one-armed Trumpeldor prompted both the creation of the right-wing youth organization Betar (from the acronym *brit* Trumpeldor) and the founding of the Hagana, the underground army that is the forerunner of the IDF.

Students and new recruits also visit Jerusalem's Mount Herzl Military Cemetery, named after Theodor Herzl, the father of modern Zionism. Near his simple black granite tomb are the graves of prime ministers Golda Meir, Levi Eshkol, and Yitzhak Rabin. Within walking distance of Mount Herzl is the Mount of Remembrance, site of the Holocaust Memorial Yad VaShem ("a memorial and a name," taken from Isaiah

56:5). Students and recruits come here to learn about the genocide that wiped out a third of the world's Jews. Since the early 1990s, the Ministry of Education has been sending thousands of high school students each year to Poland to visit concentration camps. They conduct memorial ceremonies in gas chambers, often clinging to one another, crying and proudly holding Israeli flags. "Never forget—that's what I learned when I was seventeen and visited Auschwitz. I stood where my grandfather Aaron last saw his parents, first wife, and baby before they were sent to the gas chamber. He didn't even get to say goodbye. He survived slave labor and arrived here with only one dream: to live in peace," says Dor Shapira, a university student. A major in the reserves, he's leaving class to join his infantry unit. "Maybe one day, my grandfather Aaron's dream will come true."

On September 13, 1993, PLO leader Yasser Arafat and Israeli Prime Minister Yitzhak Rabin shook hands as they ratified a Declaration of Principles on Interim Self-Government Arrangements while President Bill Clinton looked on. The Oslo Accords, as they are better known, nurtured a belief among many Israelis and Palestinians in Gaza and the West Bank that peace might finally be at hand. As the Oslo peace process continued, many Israelis started to behave as if they no longer faced any real external threat. Israeli soldiers and Palestinians went on joint patrols. Cars with Palestinian license plates drove through Tel Aviv. Many hundreds of Palestinians studied at Israeli universities. Israelis gambled in Jericho and listened to jazz in Ramallah. Elton John's and Madonna's concerts in Israel were sold out and "Material Girl" was a hit. The idealistic "we," a prevalent theme in Israeli songs and literature, was replaced by the individualistic "me." Consumerism and capitalism were in; self-sacrifice and socialism were out.

Army brass worried that the "cappuccino generation" was going soft. Combat units and officers schools had fewer volunteers. Many draftees wanted jobs clicking a mouse, not a trigger. Why be a foot soldier when you can get a free education in the best technical school in the world, the IDF? Many soldiers had dreams of being high-tech entrepreneurs. Others didn't want to put on a uniform at all. Motivation to serve plummeted. In 1988, 90 percent of eighteen-year-olds were drafted; by 1999, their numbers plunged to only 55 percent. That year, a third of eighteen-year-olds said they either didn't want to serve at all or not for the full three years. During the 1990s, because of the post-1973 baby boom and a glut of army-age newcomers from the former Soviet Union and Ethiopia, the IDF had more recruits than it needed. Receiving a military exemption became easier. Many soldiers were sent home from the army early, some for medical reasons, others because they were deemed "unsuited for service." One draftee recalls, "I asked to see a mental health officer and told him I was depressed. After ten minutes he said he didn't think I'd be enlisting. Then I went before the medical board. They asked me a few questions and wished me luck." Once upon a time, a blank in the military record required on Israeli job applications prompted questions about the candidate's reliability, not to say patriotism. Not during the booming 1990s.

Rock star–composer Aviv Geffen, nephew of hero-general Moshe Dayan, boasted of having avoided military service with a medical deferment. His provocative, politically loaded lyrics spoke to young Israelis, criticizing cherished Israeli values from collectivism to unquestioning patriotism. (He mocked Trumpledor's legendary exit line with this controversial lyric: "Is it good to die for the country?") The *enfant terrible*'s popularity was at its peak when peace with the Palestinians seemed within reach. Among the leaders of the peace movements were former high-ranking military officers; many were there on November 4, 1995, when Geffen sang at the largest peace rally in Israel's history. Prime Minister Rabin, warmaker turned peacemaker, embraced him moments before Rabin was killed by a twenty-six-year-old right-wing law student named Yigal Amir.

In spite of the national trauma of the assassination, the peace process limped on. Defense spending, about 25 percent of GDP in the mid-1980s, was slashed to less than 8 percent. (The United States and Britain spend about 3 percent of GDP on defense.) There was a new prosperity; foreign investments were pouring into the Israeli and Palestinian economies. Wall Street bankers and venture capitalists competed to hand out money to the latest Israeli IPO; soldiers admired the former air force pilot and army intelligence officer who excited investors with a robot lawn mover. Then came the July 2000 Camp David II summit. It ended when President Yasser Arafat rejected President Clinton's and Prime Minister Ehud Barak's proposal for a Palestinian state, offering 85 to 97 percent of the West Bank and Gaza, a shared Jerusalem, and a promise to seek a solution for control of the Temple Mount.

Several Palestinian leaders, including PA Communications Minister Imad al-Faluji, are on record saying that after Arafat walked out on the Camp David talks, Palestinians planned a major escalation of violence and that then-opposition leader Ariel Sharon's provocative visit to Jerusalem's Temple Mount on September 28, 2000 was a pretext to launch the planned violence. The ensuing intifada and rash of suicide bombings made young Israelis, and their idol, Aviv Geffen, realize the cappuccino years were over. With every Israeli man, woman, and child as potential targets, motivation to serve soared. Combat units were inundated with volunteers, unprecedented since the start of the Oslo peace process. "I should write a letter of thanks to Yasser Arafat," one top-ranking officer remarked dryly. Israelis are arguably more prepared to fight for their country than at any time since the 1973 Yom Kippur War.

Nothing, however, quite prepares them for the rigors of Israeli basic training.

———————

Sergeant Eli Rosenfeld wears the brown beret of the celebrated Golani Infantry Brigade, the most highly decorated infantry unit in the IDF. Limited in resources, the IDF has survived by giving enormous responsibility to young noncommissioned officers like the twenty-one-year-old Eli. He describes serving in the IDF as living in a "giant melting pot," a cauldron of cultures, a place where soldiers confront prejudices and stereotypes. Eli has gone on patrols on the Lebanese border, in the West Bank, and in Gaza with left-wingers, right-wingers, guys wearing knitted *kippot,* and soldiers who believe God is just a figment of the imagination. "Before I only knew Rehovot, my town. Now I'm learning about the people of my country. Our lives depend on guys like Muhammad [a Bedouin volunteer from a Galilee village, a grenade launcher] and Ahmad [an Arab Christian from Upper Nazareth]. And we really like the Russians. Especially the ones who volunteer for guard duty on Jewish holidays, so we can get off. And we volunteer for duty on Christian ones, so they can go home." For immigrants—and nearly 30 percent of Israel's population are foreign-born—serving in the IDF is a crash course on becoming Israeli. It's where an Ethiopian-born soldier confides to his Brazilian-born and

Druze tent mates about his family's financial problems and fears about his mortality.

Eli is an Ashkenazi, whose parents both have doctorates, train Jewish and Arab teachers, and come from a place fourteen times larger than Israel: California. Most of the soldiers in Eli's platoon are Mizrahim from working-class families who fled Arab countries. "When they first met me, some called me Snow White," the six-footer says, referring to his pale skin, reddish blond hair, and sky-blue eyes. Attitudes changed when they realized this karate expert speaks the latest Mizrahi slang and can please their palates. An amateur chef, Eli sometimes takes over the kitchen to prepare North African and Middle Eastern dishes for forty. Not only does he eat with his soldiers, but sometimes he stands guard duty with them and sleeps in the same cramped armored personnel carrier. "It's symbolic. Soldiers will follow you if you do what they're doing," he says, explaining the IDF ethos of officers leading soldiers into battle.

But despite the authority given both noncommissioned and commissioned officers, the IDF is as informal as it is formidable. The chain of command is lean, loosely structured, and goal-oriented. Soldiers rarely use military titles; they call their officers by their first name or nickname, though, during the six weeks of basic training, Eli's soldiers called him "Sir" and wondered if he was human. All military organizations rely on suppressing, at least temporarily, each recruit's individuality, and this is both more challenging and more important with a people famously used to ignoring "no smoking" and "no parking" signs. During grueling five-, ten-, and then sixteen-hour forced marches in sweltering heat or driving rain, soldiers carry at least thirty pounds: rifle, ammunition, water bottles, and the "wounded" on stretchers. The concept of never abandoning soldiers has enormous psychological import. In this people's army, the return of soldiers and bodies is sacrosanct. (As a result, Israel's enemies have exacted exorbitant prices in lopsided prisoner exchanges.) Sometimes they break an ankle, throw up, or collapse from exhaustion, says Eli, mentioning a well-known IDF expression: "Hard training makes easy combat." Sometimes, though, soldiers are driven beyond endurance. (In September 2002, two soldiers in the ultrasecret Duvdevan unit died during fitness-training exercises, one while running in full battle equipment, the other from dehydration.)

At the end, each soldier receives in one hand a rifle and in the other, their religious book—the Hebrew Bible, the Christian Bible, or the Koran. Because their book is secret, Druze soldiers are sworn in on a notebook with a picture of the tomb of Jethro, Moses' father-in-law, on the cover. Some parents compare the experience to the dramatic scene in which Abraham, following God's command, goes to sacrifice his son Isaac (Yitzhak) on Mount Moriah. Isaac was spared, but Israeli families are aware that one day there might be a knock on the door, uniformed officers telling them they have made the ultimate sacrifice.

Making life-and-death decisions places an enormous burden on eighteen-year-old soldiers who are expected to be philosophers, politicians, and very mature. And maturity and soldiering usually don't go together. That's one reason the IDF has an Education Corps. "More than teaching the best ways to kill, we teach them to ask: 'Is it necessary to kill?' " explains Nitzan Arbib, a soldier in the mostly all-female Education Corps, who teaches combat soldiers like the ones in Eli's unit. Her father was born in Libya, her mother in Poland. "I don't think of myself as half Ashkenazi and half Mizrahi," she says firmly. "I'm a regular Israeli." One of her responsibilities is setting up programs in which combat officers and their soldiers talk about moral dilemmas they might face. She is sifting through news reports, researching cases for officers to discuss with their soldiers about when a soldier should and shouldn't shoot. They're taught to fire only if their lives or those of innocent civilians are in clear and immediate danger and learn guidelines about preserving humanistic values in combat. "We teach them that a soldier holding a gun has some of God's power, the power to take a life. Soldiers are taught that they must avoid harming civilians even if it means they have to risk their own lives. That's why we call this the defense force." During basic training soldiers are instructed always to carry a card on which the Code of Ethics of the Israeli Soldier are written: 1. Devotion to the Mission, 2. Responsibility, 3. Reliability, 4. Personal Example, 5. Human Life, 6. The Purity of Arms, 7. Professionalism, 8. Discipline, 9. Loyalty, 10. Worthiness to Represent Israel, 11. Comradeship.

Why did Eli decide to be a combat soldier? "To be in the infantry, to defend my country, that's what I was educated for. At home and at my [religious] school, I learned about our deep connection to this land and to love it. My father taught me that to live in Israel is to be afraid you will be killed and to be afraid you might have to kill. I grew up learning to value Jewish ethics, like the sanctity of life. I try to make sure my soldiers do too. If a twelve-year-old Arab kid throws rocks and shouts 'Coward!' I want my soldiers to say 'Coward? Okay. That's who I am' and not shoot." Eli no longer keeps kosher or wears a knitted kippa, but many soldiers in his unit do. Although they are less than 20 percent of Israeli Jews, religious soldiers make up more than 40 percent of the combat soldiers—and the backbone of the officers corps, especially ground forces and special units. "Whether you wear a kippa or not, unfortunately this is a religious war. And throughout history, religious wars are always the most brutal. I wish we didn't need an army. If the Arabs put down their weapons today, there'd be no more violence. But if we put down our weapons today, there'd be no more Israel."

Eli's unit spent six long months patrolling the border with Lebanon after Prime Minister Barak withdrew the troops from the security zone in southern Lebanon in May 2000, ending a controversial twenty-two-year occupation in which Israel lost more than one thousand soldiers. The Islamic world hailed Hezballah, the radical Islamic Shiites, for defeating the mighty Israeli army and driving them out. Top Israeli military officials believe Lebanon was the model for the intifada that erupted four months later, that Hezballah and the Palestinians were convinced that Israelis had lost their will to fight and could no longer stomach more casualties and would make a similarly chaotic retreat from the West Bank and Gaza.

The area heated up while Eli was there: Iran and the Syrians (who control most of Lebanon) supply Hezballah with heavy arms, including thousands of long-range missiles capable of hitting Haifa and other Israeli towns. Hezballah also has tight links with Hamas, Palestinian Islamic Jihad, and the PLO. Eli calls it a border that never sleeps. "We scan the area through night vision infrared scopes. For example, if a soldier sees three silhouettes carrying weapons in a restricted area, he knows they're not shepherds or picnickers trying to slip across. If a soldier identifies them and has no reasonable doubt, then he must still get a clearance from his commanding officer before shooting. The soldier doesn't see faces or bodies. Just three nameless figures, terrorists trying to kill Israelis. It's a fast decision. Impersonal."

One night, Hezballah got very personal. They fired a rocket that injured three of Eli's soldiers and killed his radio operator. "We loved Elad so much. I didn't know how to tell the guys. No one trained me to deal with this," Eli recalls, his voice breaking. The next day, he and fourteen depressed soldiers went to the funeral in Ashdod. They asked Eli to write the eulogy. Before entering the military cemetery, he sat in a restaurant. "I was numb. I forgot how to write. There are no words to say goodbye to a brother." Hours later, Eli and his unit were back at the front. "No psychologist. No counseling. They expect us to be tough even though we're falling apart."

Duty in the West Bank and Gaza is a "worse hell" than on the Lebanese border, says Eli, "because it's urban fighting and we see faces up close. Everywhere we see Palestinians. They hate us, but most are innocent. The terrorists hide among hundreds of thousands of civilians who look just like them." Eli verbalizes a typical Israeli soldier's internal moral monologue: " 'Is that figure behind that boulder a man or a woman? It's a boy. He looks like an innocent sixteen-year-old. But a sixteen-year-old just blew up a candy store. He looks unarmed. But wait! Is something bulky under his sweater?' You study how he's dressed, but you must decide in seconds. If you shoot too quickly, you may kill an innocent boy. If you hesitate too long, you and others may be killed."

Eli is counting the weeks until his release. "I've learned that I don't hate Palestinians, but I hate the leaders who encourage them to hate. I hate that there is no Israel in Hamas's manifesto. I hate that there is no Israel on maps in Palestinian schoolbooks." Eli turns pensive as he describes how he's changed. "My parents say I went in a boy and came out a man. That being a soldier made me serious, mature. Well, I'd rather be immature and happy. I've lost three years of my life. I envy eighteen-year-olds in America who are worrying about college instead of about remaining alive."

When you have four army-age children, you don't get much sleep," says Liron and Tamir's mother, Reli. She describes sitting in a bomb shelter in

1973 with her newborn first son when her husband rushed off to war. Then she recites a line of a song popular after that bloody victory: "I promise you, my little one, that this will be the last war." With sadness she says, "It's thirty years later and still, I can't promise that to my kids." Reli served two years in military intelligence; her husband was a reserve officer until he was fifty. "I was a lot calmer when Liron was just a tank driver. As a sergeant, he has his head out of the tank. I'm relieved that soon he's transferring to tank repair. For now, I try not to think about it, to keep busy with work and friends." She is more worried about her sons traveling by bus to their bases than after they arrive: Sunday morning is the preferred time for terrorists to blow up buses, when they are filled with soldiers returning from weekend leave. "I ask my boys to call a lot. It's not that I need to speak with them. I just need to hear them say, 'Everything's okay.' Living like this isn't new for us. It's not like we've been living all our lives in Switzerland. But we wouldn't live anywhere else."

Now her daughter, Ronit, is anticipating high school graduation and induction into the army. While her mother worries about her seventeen-year-old spending an evening at a disco that might explode at any time, Ronit and her friends worry about which unit to serve in. "I can be a *jobnik* [work at a desk] anytime in civilian life," says Ronit. "I want to train combat soldiers, do something important."

Ronit is not alone in her ambition. Since the second intifada, 70 percent of new female recruits say they want to serve in combat units. This enthusiasm is a throwback to the prestate days, when the stereotype of the brave, busty Sabra with a rifle was partly based on reality. Women guarded agriculture settlements from attack by Arabs and served with men in underground organizations fighting the British, sometimes hiding grenades and pistols under their clothes in places where British soldiers were too polite to search. During the 1948 War, the army was the world's most integrated. Women soldiers guarded borders and fought in dangerous field operations. When Arabs attacked a mixed patrol in the Negev and mutilated corpses of women soldiers were found, the Haganah (the predecessor to the IDF) ordered women out of combat units.

Since then, most women have served in "combat-support roles," doing clerical and administrative work (often disguised by fancy titles). Others are social workers, medics, and radar operators. Women serve in observation units along the Lebanese, Jordanian, and Egyptian borders and do highly sensitive intelligence. Seventy percent of shooting instructors are women. Since 1974, women have been training men to drive tanks. Women also teach combat pilots on flight-simulation machines. But if it weren't for Alice Miller, that's as close as women would probably have gotten to combat.

A South African immigrant with a degree in aeronautical engineering and a civilian pilot's license, Miller wanted to try out for the prestigious pilot training course, but the air force refused. When she asked then-President Ezer Weitzman, the former commander of the air force, why, he responded, "*Meidele* [little doll, in Yiddish], have you ever heard of a man knitting socks?" In 1994, Israeli women's organizations helped her file a petition against the Ministry of Defense challenging male domination in the military. Miller won the landmark case and the Supreme Court ordered the air force and most units, except those engaged in direct combat, such as infantry, tanks, and paratroops, to admit women. Miller failed the air force entry exam, but seven other women passed. Though most either dropped out or flunked out, most observers agree that it wasn't because of gender discrimination: 90 percent of men fail the pilots' course as well.

The border patrol, a police unit not formally part of the IDF in 1995, was the first combat service to accept women. For years, the males of this famously macho bastion had made them the butt of jokes, but since the intifada, they are truly front-line defense units. In uniforms or disguised in jeans and sandals, they roam open air markets, rock concerts, and art fairs, vigilantly scanning faces, obliged to make life-and-death decisions virtually every day. Nowhere in Israel is the cliché "hair-trigger response" more appropriate: Is the baggy jacket worn by a teenager a fashion statement or a disguise for a belt filled with explosives? Is the wire dangling from a pocket a Walkman or a detonating device? Should the subject be tackled, shot, or asked for an identity card . . . at which point most terrorists detonate. And, most important, will caution result in more dead Israelis? One afternoon, Etti Rehavi of the border patrol was guarding a bus stop on French Hill in Jerusalem when a man stepped off the sidewalk and began strafing a bus filled with junior high school students. The nineteen-year-old cocked her M-16, raced to the front of the bus, and yelled "Get down!" to the passengers. She and her partner shot the terrorist, who'd already killed two teens and wounded dozens more. Six months later, in June 2002, a border patrol guarding the same area spotted a man getting out of a car and running to the bus stop. Unsure whether it was simply someone late for his bus, instead of firing they chased him. The man from Tanzim's al-Aqsa Martyrs Brigade exploded, killing seven, including a toddler, and wounding dozens more.

Hundreds of women serve with men on stakeouts, ambushes, and roadblocks. In just one area, nicknamed Givat HaShabahim, the Hill of Illegal Entry, between Taibe in Israel and Tulkarm in the West Bank, mixed border patrols stop about four hundred Palestinians trying to enter Israel illegally every day. Most are looking for work. Not all. The IDF says it arrests an average of seventy Palestinians a month planning attacks inside Israel.

All Palestinians detest the military roadblocks. They mean long, frustrating waits, often hours, while jittery, sometimes rude and inexperienced soldiers ask people to show identification. Frequently men are told to get out of cars, lift their shirts, and lower their pants to show they're not wired, that there is no grenade hidden in a pocket. Men feel humiliated, especially in front of children. In 2003, female soldiers began checking suspicious-looking female Palestinians, because there have been so many female suicide bombers and men disguised as women. When asked why IDF soldiers sometimes question other soldiers, Education Petty Officer Nitzan Arbib rattles off examples of "soldiers" who completed "successful" missions wearing stolen IDF uniforms. What about news reports charging that IDF soldiers detain ambulances with sick people? They do. Nitzan tells a story about soldiers who searched a Palestinian Red Crescent ambulance transporting a very ill child south of Ramallah. Under his stretcher they found an explosives belt with nearly fifty pounds of explosives. (The Passover seder bomber carried four pounds.) Soldiers are also on the lookout for Israeli ambulances; two have disappeared and would be first-rate for smuggling arms or being turned into car bombs.

A French fashion magazine ran a splashy color spread of an Israeli officer. It's hard to believe that Corporal Hani Abramov, lying in a hospital bed, her face grotesquely wounded, was that pretty woman in uniform. When the nineteen-year-old was on a jeep patrol near a kibbutz on Israel's border with the West Bank, a Tanzim gunman shot her in the face. After she gets out? "I'm returning to the field," she vowed on Israel Television. While she was recovering, IDF soldiers in the West Bank town of Qalqilyya captured two Palestinians who led them to a pickup truck packed with one and a half tons of explosives. Its destination: the Azrieli Towers, twin skyscrapers in Tel Aviv. The plot was modeled after the 1993 attack on the World Trade Center. Israeli intelligence says about 90 percent of terrorist attacks are stopped before they reach their targets. The corollary, of course, is that 10 percent are not.

Ya'ala, banot [Come on, girls]," commands a large woman with a short-barrel M-16. No one can pull a fast one on this twenty-three-year-old second lieutenant, who is intent on transforming her fifty women in khaki into battle-ready officers. During a lesson in hand-to-hand combat, the soldiers use rifle butts to hit the "enemy." They improve sharpshooting skills and take apart and reassemble Uzis blindfolded. This is Company Jasmine, the prestigious but punishing IDF Field Officers School for Women. To be selected for this rather new course for combat officers is difficult. These soldiers excelled. Some were paratroop instructors, others operated Patriot missiles. Efrat, the strong-willed daughter of a colonel, was an instructor in a snipers unit. Funny and slightly spoiled, Tal didn't want to serve coffee, so she served in Gaza. Then there is Sivan, who dropped out of air force pilot training and felt like a failure. To get close to combat, she joined the armored division. Yafit was stationed in all the "hot spots" and is determined to be the first Ethiopian woman field officer.

It's very early morning. These officers-in-the-making don't notice the wild flowers or pine trees. They've stopped discussing politics, perfumes, and men. They can barely breathe. It's an excruciating uphill march in a biting dust storm. They hate carrying the "wounded" woman on a stretcher. They have blisters. They're sweaty. It's unbearable, but the forced marches their male officer counterparts take are worse. They encourage each other, give each other shoulder massages. One cadet breaks down, but the others try to cheer her up. It's a test of strength, stamina, and sisterhood. Afterward, a cadet asks to meet with the commander and tells her the pressure is too much. She can't cope. She drops out.

Women's Training Base 12 hasn't had a face-lift since the British built it during World War II. With twenty women per room, there's no privacy. Whose turn is it to do kitchen duty? Guard the armory? These aspiring future colonels and brigadier generals squabble like sisters. They hate the strict discipline, the tight schedule, the nonstop training and fearing they will be the next one court-martialed. They bite nails, complain in diaries, and attack the vending machines. They eat to relieve stress. They eat to relax. They eat to fight fatigue.

There are enjoyable moments. During the all-female Purim party on the base, three hundred soldiers and their officers dance with guns, their dog tags dangling. The fun lasts only an hour. At 10 P.M., the cadets must go to sleep: early-morning march. Most wonder if they can survive the four months.

Home on Sabbath leave, a soldier listens to her mother worry that she's losing her femininity. She has "militaristic mannerisms," a swagger, and "tough" facial expressions. Putting on a slinky tie-dyed dress, the soldier-daughter assures her mother she's not morphing into a man. Over Shabbat dinner, another soldier's father reveals his great fear: "What happens if, God forbid, you're captured in action and abused or raped?" A female prisoner of war. She's willing to pay this price for equal opportunity.

Back at the base, there are lots of lectures. During one, a female colonel asks rhetorically, "How many women mayors are there? How many women members of Knesset?" In 2003, there were eighteen, a record. But Israel's parliament, with 15 percent women, is in fifty-sixth place between Andorra and Slovakia (the number might be higher if Israel's ultra-Orthodox and Arab parties had women representatives; the United States is forty-third). The colonel urges these cadets to shatter the military glass ceiling. "If women advance in the army, they'll advance in society. Be assertive officers. Get ahead. Prove women can do it." The list of ex-military officers who have "parachuted into politics" without much civilian experience is long. And all male. Israelis call it a "government of generals."

For the more arduous, advanced part of the course, the cadets of Company Jasmine are bused to a place close to nowhere in the Negev. They're the only women on this armor corps base. It's air-conditioned, but unbearable outside, over 104 degrees F (40 degrees C) in the shade. During a gas mask drill, because some women don't help each other, the commander punishes them with a teamwork exercise: build a camouflage tent, take it down, build it again—without speaking.

Later, they join male cadets for an armored personnel carrier course. The relentless training pushes some women beyond their physical and mental limits. There are tears when more cadets are thrown out of the course. The remaining women speculate who will be next.

At the heavy machine gun range, the women lie on their stomachs and fire round after round. A deafening barrage. Noa Feingold, their fellow cadet and teacher, admits, "As an artillery instructor, I want my troops to hit their targets. But thinking about it before I go to sleep, I say to myself, 'I'm teaching them to kill. What am I doing?' But in our situation, they have to learn to hit the target."

Some training is done without guns or olive-green uniforms. Wearing red, yellow, and pink bikinis, the cadets go through a strenuous workout in the base swimming pool. It is interrupted by loud rumbling. Tanks approach the pool area. Men open the turrets and enjoy the view. They know the name of each swimmer. Days before the course ends, a male officer cautions the women, "It's hard today. It's hard tomorrow. It will be harder the day after. As officers you won't share responsibility—it's yours alone."

It's closing inspection. They've cleaned their weapons, polished their boots, and washed floors. A sergeant major arrives. He's exacting about cleanliness. He notices a soiled window sill, a streaky mirror. Unacceptable. Fear and fatigue make a cadet laugh. The other women in the room lose control and laugh too. The sergeant major chews them out as if they're kindergartners.

They celebrate their last night on the base at a karaoke party with a regiment of male armor cadets. They sing and dance to a well-known song: "I was born for peace. I want so much to live in peace." Suddenly, a few men strip to their underwear and jump into the swimming pool. In prefeminist days, women would have ignored them. No longer. These officers-to-be pick up their guns and leave.

When Corporal Etti Elimelech leaves her base, people stare. She wears a man's uniform, shoes, and the gray beret of the Engineering Corps. In 2001, she and other women convinced IDF brass that women should wear the same uniforms as their male colleagues. "It's natural," she asserts. "We do the same jobs, same missions, and same training as men fighters. It contributes to our feelings of equality. Perhaps it's just symbolic, but the more such symbols we have, the more it helps." Since she won her battle, the IDF has been making a big push to expand women's roles. She serves in the special atomic, biological, and chemical warfare unit. There's a new battle. During a course on how to put on protective suits against chemical and biological attacks, some Orthodox soldiers walked our rather than train with women. Their rabbis had declared that the army's integration program violates *halakha*, or Jewish religious laws on modesty, and instructed their followers to refuse to serve in units with women soldiers. During a training exercise in the pilots' course, a religious soldier refused to carry a stretcher with a woman pilot on it.

When IDF soldiers entered Yasser Arafat's Ramallah compound in March 2002, they confiscated weapons and dozens of boxes of top-secret files. Those documents were the strongest evidence yet that the supposedly homegrown Palestinian uprising may be an uprising but is emphatically not homegrown. Israeli intelligence found a paper trail of violence planned, funded, and directed mostly from Iran and Iraq. They had written proof that Iraq was infiltrating operatives and weapons into Israel for "megaterrorism," that Saddam Hussein used Palestinian Authority officials as middlemen to smuggle oil, giving them millions of dollars in kickback money used to buy weapons, including rockets, land mines, machine guns, guided missiles, and tons of notorious C-4 explosives. In one of the Mideast's regular perversities, Iraqi oil money bought weapons from Iraq's sworn enemies in Iran, which also trains members of its proxies, Palestinian Islamic Jihad and Hezballah, to plan and carry out suicide attacks inside Israel.

Days after the documents were captured, on April 3, 2002, Israeli troops, tanks, armored personnel carriers, and bulldozers followed the evidentiary trail into the Jenin refugee camp, located twenty-six miles north of Nablus and the training ground for dozens of "successful" suicide bombers. The IDF was going after armed men from Hamas, Islamic Jihad, the al-Aqsa Martyrs Brigade, and Tanzim hiding among civilians. In six days of ferocious fighting, soldiers went house to house, smashing holes in connecting walls to avoid exposure to Palestinian gunmen in the streets. They uncovered enormous quantities of ammunition and explosives as well as dozens of bomb labs. Charges were widespread and damning: Israeli soldiers butchered innocent civilians.

The Palestinian news agency Wafa reported that soldiers had committed the "massacre of the 21st century." The Palestinian mayor of Jenin stated, "I just can't understand how human beings are capable of committing nefarious crimes as such. . . . Decomposed bodies of children and old people were scattered everywhere and two thirds of the camp has been reduced to rubble." Nasser al-Kidwa, the Palestinian representative to the United Nations, said on CNN, "Helicopter gun ships are throwing missiles at one square kilometer packed with almost fifteen thousand people in a refugee camp. . . . This is a clear war crime, witnessed by the whole world, preventing ambulances, preventing people from being buried . . . an all-out assault against the whole population." Palestinian officials described how the IDF "buried dozens of Palestinian bodies . . . in a ditch and used bulldozers to cover them." Palestinian minister Saeb Erekat said Israelis killed three thousand Palestinians, then lowered the number to five hundred. UN Special Envoy to the Middle East Terje Larsen of Norway said, "Combating terrorism does not give a blank check to kill civilians . . . the means used here are illegitimate and morally repugnant."

Headlines in the Middle East and Europe screamed: "War Crimes," "Atrocities," "Genocide." *The Guardian* reported that Israel's actions in Jenin were "every bit as repellent" as Osama bin Laden's attack on New York on September 11. A *London Times* correspondent compared the "deliberate destruction" in Jenin to what she's seen in Bosnia, Chechnya, Kosovo, and Sierra Leone. The *Daily Telegraph* reported that "hundreds of victims were buried by bulldozer in a mass grave." *The Independent*'s Phil Reeves called it a "monstrous war crime that Israel has tried to cover up." Reeves, like journalists at the *Times* and the *Telegraph*, all quoted the same man, Kamal Anis, who said that he "saw the Israeli soldiers pile thirty bodies beneath a half-wrecked house. When the pile was complete, they bulldozed the building, bringing its ruins down on the corpses. Then they flattened the area with a tank."

"I went to Jenin to find out what happened," says former IDF sergeant Daniel Gordon, an author and screenwriter who describes an encounter between a CNN reporter and Dr. David Zangen, a major in the reserves and medical officer in the Jenin camp. He told her that when the fighting was over, soldiers found photos of children who would be the next group of suicide killers, with notations indicating when each would be ready. "Perhaps you should ask yourself why," she said.

"I do," Dr. Zangen replied. "I can't imagine sending one's child out to be a mass murderer who commits suicide to kill women and children."

"Well, I can explain it," said the reporter. "For me it all comes down to one word, 'occupation.' "

"But," the doctor responded, "Jenin hasn't been occupied for nine years."

Dr. Zangen was the medical officer of the paratroop unit that bore the brunt of the fighting and saw close up what happened. "Some people say what we did was a massacre. The only thing massacred was the truth. Our soldiers went house to house to get people to leave so they wouldn't get hurt. When our soldiers and medics tried to reach the dead and wounded, Palestinian gunmen shot them. Others were killed when they moved booby-trapped bodies." What about charges that IDF soldiers prevented medical and humanitarian workers from entering the Jenin camp, that soldiers entered Jenin hospital? "Our soldiers never entered the hospital, although we knew terrorists were hiding inside. We let in every ambulance, but checked them." He tells of a patient inside an ambulance with an intravenous needle taped to his shirt, not inserted in his vein. Soldiers discovered he was a wanted senior terrorist.

There were many reports of a "stench of death" in the Jenin refugee camp. IDF officials claim that it came from animal carcasses and the exhumed corpses brought from nearby cemeteries and buried in a mass grave. A camera inside an Israeli intelligence drone flying above captured pictures of a funeral procession. The "corpse" fell off the stretcher and then got back on. The IDF said the mock funeral was staged to increase the body count for the United Nations committee investigating the massacre.

Four months later, the United Nations, which runs the Jenin camp, issued a report that found no evidence of a massacre. There were fifty-two Palestinians dead, thirty-eight armed fighters. Israel lost twenty-three soldiers. The report accused Palestinian militants of deliberately stockpiling weapons and putting its fighters among civilians in the densely populated Jenin camp, which is a violation of international law. The UN report questioned the reports of extensive destruction of homes and buildings in the camp. Witnesses and satellite photography showed the town of Jenin was untouched and most of the refugee camp was, at most, lightly damaged. The center of the camp, an area slightly larger than a football stadium, where intense house-to-house fighting took place, was extensively damaged. Many of the buildings were rigged with explosives and would have killed soldiers if they had not been destroyed. A senior Palestinian military officer informed *Time* magazine that some Palestinians who died were killed by rubble from the exploding booby traps with which Palestinian fighters had honeycombed the camp.

While on a routine training mission above the Negev Desert, a pilot in an F-15 Falcon going about 620 miles per hour collides with three migrating white storks. Two of them strike the jet's body and the third is sucked into the engine. Each six-pound stork hits with a force of about forty tons. Within seconds, the $50 million fighter jet erupts in flames, inverts, and crashes, killing the pilot and the navigator.

Israeli pilots flying at high speeds and low altitudes face much greater chances of colliding with migrating birds than being hit by hostile Arab fire. On March 2, 2003, Israel almost lost its chief of staff, Moshe Ayalon. His low-flying Blackhawk helicopter was nearly downed when a six-kilo crane hit it, shattering three windows and destroying the fuel tank. Israel has the world's highest concentration of birds and fighter aircraft. For Israeli air force (IAF) pilots, this juxtaposition can be fatal. In fact, the IAF has lost more planes to bird strikes than to the combined might of Arab pilots and missiles. Because Israel is at the junction of three continents—Europe, Asia, and Africa, the site of a geographical bird bottleneck—chances of bird-plane collisions are the highest in the world. During the spring and fall migrations, more than half a billion birds fly across this tiny nation. Over three thousand years ago, Jewish sages noticed the "miraculous" avian passage over the Holy Land, more than 280 different species. Only recently, however, have people found a way to keep birds from downing planes.

Enter the "bird soldiers," the women the IAF turns to for a vital task: routing planes away from the birds. Using scanning radar that can detect large squadrons of eagles, pelicans, and storks from fifty miles away, they give real-time warning to IAF pilots, keeping them and the migrating birds alive and saving the IAF untold millions of dollars in lost aircraft.

They're doing this life-saving work because of one of the air force's most ingenious weapons: an ornithologist. Yossi Leshem pilots the only aircraft the IAF permits to fly wherever it wants. In his motorized glider, he flies wingtip to wingtip with migrating birds, recording their behavior and precise flight paths. His strategy is simple: to avoid bird strikes, planes shouldn't fly in the same air space as the birds. "Birds know no political borders," says this animated man in a knit kippa who advised the U.S. Air Force during the 1991 Gulf War. His maps detail the mass migrations over Iraq, Syria, and Turkey during the 2003 Iraq War. Because of his innovative ideas—including the use of bird soldiers—bird strikes have fallen drastically. (Birds and Israeli military craft have collided more than twenty-six hundred times since 1972. In most cases, the pilots and planes managed to survive. The birds didn't.) His findings are the air force's flight bible.

———————————

IAF pilots are renowned for their amazing dogfights and aerial raids. During one mock air battle between the Israeli and U.S. air forces over the Negev, Israeli pilots "shot down" 220 American fighter jets and lost just 20 of their own. The IAF was on high alert throughout the Iraq War. With Saddam gone, combat pilots in F-16s are streaking across the skies training for the next, unknown mission. One of them is Roni Zukerman, kibbutznik and granddaughter of two leaders of the Warsaw Ghetto uprising. When she became Israel's first female fighter pilot in 2001, the media went wild. Pilots are such stars that *Wings*, a TV drama about them, has high ratings. One line from the show was taken from a morning Shabbat prayer: "May salvation come from the skies."

The Air Force is Israel's first line of defense, renowned for its skill and aggressiveness. IAF pilots have played a pivotal role in all of Israel's wars, never more than during the 1967 Six-Day War, when they destroyed the Egyptian, Syrian, and Jordanian air forces. On June 5, 160 fighter jets flew at an altitude of only thirty feet to avoid detection, pulling up for the attack only when they were almost over their targets. They cratered Egyptian runways to prevent any aircraft from taking off and then, in minutes, destroyed nearly half the Egyptian air force, 187 aircraft. The IAF lost eight aircraft, mostly from ground fire. Minutes later, in the second attack wave, the IAF destroyed ninety-four more Egyptian aircraft, as well as more air bases, command centers, and radar and electronic warfare equipment. Overall, the IAF destroyed 391 enemy planes on the ground and sixty more in dogfights, while losing only forty-six planes.

On June 17, 1981, the IAF put its enormous reputation on the line in one of the most difficult missions in its history. Eight pilots flew their F-16s for two hours over eleven hundred kilometers of enemy territory until they reached their target: a dome gleaming in the late afternoon sunlight. In one minute and twenty seconds, the French-built Osirak nuclear reactor near Baghdad lay in ruins. Twenty-seven-year-old Ilan Ramon volunteered to pilot the last plane, the most likely to draw Iraqi fire. "If I can prevent a second Holocaust, I'm ready to sacrifice my life," this son of an Auschwitz survivor said. If it were not for him and the seven other still-anonymous fighter pilots who flew in tight formation to send off a radar signal resembling that of a commercial airliner, Iraq would be armed with nuclear weapons.

Twenty-two years later, on January 16, 2003, the liftoff of the *Columbia* space shuttle was carried live on Israeli television stations and then the tape of the historic event was played again and again because Israel's first astronaut, Air Force Colonel Ilan Ramon, was on board. He brought a drawing by a fourteen-year-old boy killed in Auschwitz, of the Earth as seen from the moon, and a wallet-size Torah scroll that survived Bergen-Belsen along with its owner, his Tel Aviv University physics professor, who oversaw one of his space shuttle experiments. For sixteen days, Israelis had a mental respite from the intifada. On Saturday evening, February 1, Jerusalem time, Israelis watching television for the triumphant touchdown learned to their collective horror that instead of a hero's welcome, there would be seven funerals. Along with his remains, searchers found remnants of the Star of David insignia from his space suit. At the hilltop ceremony in the Galilee, his fifteen-year-old son, who wore a blue flight jacket, said he wants to follow in his father's footsteps. As it ended, mourners heard a roar in the sky: four pilots flying F-16s in a final goodbye.

"Today's threats," points out former IAF chief Major General Eitan Ben-Eliahu, "come from many directions and distances." Now that Iraq is no longer a threat, the IAF, like the rest of Israel, is concerned about the Tehran-Damascus-Hezballah axis and is nervously eyeing the northern borders with Lebanon and Syria. Syria has the largest chemical weapons stocks in the Middle East and long-range missiles to deliver them. Many intelligence analysts consider Hezballah, based in Syrian-controlled territory in Lebanon and largely supplied and run by Iran, the terrorist "A Team" and a greater danger than al-Qaeda.

Iran is a growing nightmare. Its Shabib 3 missiles (developed with North Korean aid) and chemical weapons (supplied by Chinese companies) can strike Israel. In development is the intercontinental Shahab 5, which will bring all of Europe and possibly the United States into range. By 2005, Iran is expected to be capable of producing enough enriched uranium and plutonium for several nuclear bombs. Iran is publicly committed to the destruction of Israel: its fundamentalist Shiite leaders encourage Hamas, arm the PLO, and were behind the Buenos Aires bombings of the Israeli Embassy in 1992 and the Jewish Center in 1994, in which eighty-five people were killed. Israelis take seriously this threat that Iran's former president, Ali Akbar Hashemi-Rafsanjani, made on Tehran Radio: "One atomic bomb would wipe out Israel without a trace while the Islamic world would only be damaged rather than destroyed by Israeli nuclear retaliation." They also take seriously this warning from Uzi Rubin, who as former head of Israel's Arrow antidefense program spent fourteen years developing the world's most advanced anti-missile missile system, designed to intercept incoming ballistic missiles such as Iranian Shahabs: "Iran has passed the point of no return. The Iranians cannot be stopped anymore. They have their indigenous capability now and they will continue their programs regardless of what the international community thinks."

On the heavily guarded Palmachim Air Force Base south of Tel Aviv, men and women wearing gas masks and protective suits practice reloading Arrow missile launchers in an environment "contaminated" with chemical and biological agents. Israel is the first nation to have such a defensive shield. Will it protect its 6.7 million citizens? The only real test will be during war.

It would be hard to find a soldier who doesn't prefer this low-tech idea of the late chief of staff of the Israel Defense Forces, Yitzhak Rabin: "There is only one radical means of preserving lives. Not tanks. Not planes. Only peace."

4

Swords into Stock Shares

☉ Israel and the Internet are a perfect match. They've waited 2,000 years for each other. —High-tech entrepreneur Dr. Yossi Vardi after his second $400 million sale of an Internet startup

☉ Israel makes more out of her brains than the Saudis out of their oil wells. —Former Prime Minister Shimon Peres

Minutes from the beautiful but brooding Old City of Jerusalem, Eli Barkat drives up to a hilltop industrial park and fast-forwards into the future. People here have more in common with people ten thousand miles away in Silicon Valley than with the ultra-Orthodox Jews and Muslims in synagogues and mosques down the road. Passing an Intel chip-making plant, Eli heads into an underground garage, which doubles as a bomb shelter. Quite a few cars are parked Israeli-style: on top of the white lines. Wearing the uniform of a high-tech CEO, jeans and a button-down shirt, Eli takes a black glass elevator up to BRM Technologies, the software and technology investment firm he and Nir, his older brother, founded with two friends. As the digital gold rush swept the Holy Land in the 1990s, they struck it rich making millions nurturing startups. Despite troubles on Nasdaq and in Nablus, high tech remains the piston driving Israel's economic engine.

Clocks in the lobby are set to the time zones of their spinoffs and clients in the United States, Europe, and Asia. Inside, sleep-deprived digerati are tapping away at keyboards, glassy eyed from staring at computer screens too long, trying to create the next killer application. Like Eli, they live and breathe the digital revolution and have a ferocious zeal to beat the competition. A stubbly bearded programmer and a software engineer are talking. Not long ago, they were twenty-two-year-olds in an IDF intelligence unit overseeing engineers working on cutting-edge projects. Now they are debating bits and bytes in Israeli "softwarespeak," a bit of English and Hebrew, the concise, three-thousand-five-hundred-year-old language in which the Ten Commandments and their emails are written. Their supervisor interrupts. "This isn't what I meant," he says. The programmer shoots back, "I know. My way works!" Such behavior seems insubordinate elsewhere in the world, but Israelis thrive on confrontations and solving problems by argument. "Because we say what we really think, we don't have to do any second guessing," the programmer explains, heading for the kitchenette, where coworkers cluster around the coffee pot shmoozing. Lines between personal and professional lives are thin, if not invisible. Gossip runs from hot dates to which Israeli company will next go public on Nasdaq. Then talk turns to why Nir Barkat wasn't elected mayor of Jerusalem.

More than any other group of Israelis, the Digital Generation has transformed this ancient land of prophets into a modern land of profits. One hundred and twenty Israeli companies, almost all high tech, are traded on the New York stock exchanges, more than any other country except the United States and Canada. "Wall Street is one place where Israelis are better known for our high tech than fighting wars," remarks Eli, who explains why Israel was ready for the Internet age before it arrived. "High tech suits the 'Israeli mentality,' because solving problems creatively is a way of life for us. We have a culture of innovation because we're used to improvising, making the impossible happen." During four years as a paratrooper, Eli learned to expect the unexpected and to make rapid life-and-death decisions based on little information. "In Lebanon, I remember we always had equipment shortages. The commander would say, 'Go innovate.' We discovered a place where terrorists hid equipment and found three broken jeeps. Soldiers took pieces from here and there. Within four hours, they were running. That's how we get things done."

Israelis love the story of a soldier whose tank was misfiring. Without the proper tools to fix it, he used the hairpin on his kippa.

Eli frequently uses his army skills to lead his "tech commandos" into business battle—and back from the brink. In the international high-tech industry the speed of getting a product to market can mean the difference between fortune and failure. Israelis have a reputation for bringing new products to the market quickly, explains thirty-nine-year-old Eli. "We think fast and thrive on speed. Something like a SWAT team. We've learned to survive by teamwork. The threat of war produces people who won't allow themselves to lose, who will go through walls for you to get what you want, who will work with gas masks on to meet a deadline. If our California office tells our Israeli engineers about a problem, by the next morning they have the solution. People who think the Internet moves quickly haven't seen combat. On the Internet it can take a month to see if you were right or wrong. In battle, it takes seconds. If you're wrong, you may not get a second chance.

"To Israelis, the word 'no' is a dare. For example, when I tell an Israeli entrepreneur 'The deal is dead,' he answers 'How dead? Is it still breathing?' There is no such thing as a dead deal. Israelis always try to find another way. You close the door on them and they jump in through the window."

Commuting among engineers in Israel, sales and marketing offices in Silicon Valley, and customers from Rome to Tokyo, Eli often lives out of his suitcase. "Israel is too tiny a local market for high tech, so Israelis must think globally and create international products." That's why many Israeli companies have research and development offices in Israel and sales and marketing offices abroad. Eli launched Back Web Technologies with $1.2 million in seed capital from BRM. Back Web sells software for laptops to the likes of Hewlett-Packard, Kodak, and IBM, whose traveling employees use it to access the Intranet when there's no Internet connection. Cisco called it "the Federal Express of the Internet." After going public on Nasdaq in 1999, it soared in value to $2 billion, wiped out competitors, and made millions. Since the tech meltdown, there have been layoffs, restructuring. "The tougher the business challenges, the calmer I am," Eli confides. "I believe in turning every problem into an opportunity. If it doesn't kill you, it strengthens you. High tech is about creating money and value. The military is about life and death."

Eli thinks seeing so many friends die on the battlefield gives him a more balanced perspective on what's important. But when he goes fishing in the Sea of Galilee, he forgets to relax. "I take it very seriously. It's war against the fish. I can't stand it when they don't bite," he jokes.

Back in 1988, Israel's most famous exports were Jaffa oranges. That was the year Eli, armed with degrees in math and computer science, teamed up with his ex-paratrooper brother Nir and a friend from the Hebrew University to start a garage operation designing software. "My parents' friends thought it was idiotic. An entrepreneur? That's a profession? Why can't I find a *real* job?" Eli lived with his mother, a folk dance teacher, and his father, an astrophysics professor, in a yellow limestone house on Sinai Desert Street. As business checks were bouncing, he held onto his dream of making it on Wall Street. Just when computer virus hysteria made headlines, the trio sold their antivirus product. "Suddenly, we had our first few millions. We had to decide whether to take the money and run or build something bigger." They chose to build high-tech businesses, including Check Point, which today is Israel's most successful high-tech company. "When I went to my father's sixty-seventh birthday party, his friends who'd treated me like a lunatic were all over me, handing me their grandchildren's résumés."

Their grandchildren and other young Israelis make pilgrimages to BRM's Jerusalem office pitching ideas and seeking seed money to launch startups. Quite a few get a hearing. Many dream of becoming the next Gil Shwed.

In 1993, Shwed, a computer whiz kid, arrived at the BRM office with an idea he'd cooked up in army intelligence: a firewall, a piece of security software that stops hackers from breaking into computers. It was risky; the Internet boom hadn't happened yet. Only large companies had Internet connections and cyber attacks weren't a worry. But the Barkat brothers shared Shwed's vision. BRM gave him technical and business assistance and about $500,000 for half of Check Point Software Technologies. It was quite an investment. Check Point is the world's leader in Internet security, the most valuable Israeli firm listed on the Nasdaq. Once Israeli role models were military heroes, now they're entrepreneurs. Guys like Gil Shwed.

———————

Gil Shwed's headquarters are in a skyscraper in the Tel Aviv suburb of Ramat Gan on land where the Barkats' grandfather, a bus driver, once grew tomatoes. Nicknamed "Gil Bates," this Israeli Bill Gates has built Check Point into a company that reached $20 billion stock market value in 2001. In 2002, he was featured on a *Forbes* cover as one of the world's few self-made billionaires under thirty-five (though since then, Forbes estimates his net worth at "only" $375 million). His twenty-fourth-floor office is decorated with abstract art, including a painting by a homeless San Francisco artist. A boyish-looking bachelor with cropped hair and John Lennon glasses, Gil explains his fondness for one blurry photo. "From far away, it looks very unfocused. From up close, it looks like a tree or whatever you want to see. That's why I like it. Because you can see what no one else can." That's what happened when people told him that his firewall idea wouldn't make money. "We knew that businesses all over the world were going to need Internet security. We saw things people didn't see. That's how it works in business. Maybe that's how it will work for peace. Answers will come from the unexpected." More than one hundred million software customers, including many governments and nearly all Fortune 500 companies, use Check Point's firewalls to protect them from cyber snoops. The popularity of broadband, always-on high-speed connections to the Internet through cable modems and DSL phone hook-ups, is making the computers of casual web surfers vulnerable to intruders. Analysts estimate the firewall market could reach $6 billion by 2005.

Check Point is a global company with an Israeli character and Gil is determined to keep it that way. "We love unorthodox experimentation and don't take things for granted. If someone says 'Do it this way,' we double check to see if we can make it better. Doing things in unusual ways is a way of life in Israel. We don't do things by the book and we're willing to challenge the rules and experiment, which can be an advantage." An American software CEO who has Israeli R&D offices made this observation: "When I tell an Israeli the shortest distance between two dots is a straight line, he'll try to find a shorter way." Gil concurs and describes his ten-minute commute from his Tel Aviv apartment. "I always try a different route to get here faster. If I see a red light, I turn right. I'm very impatient. I can't stand waiting."

Gil's impatience is not unusual in Israel. If the light turns green and you don't floor the gas pedal, Israeli drivers honk or yell out the window. They tailgate because they can't bear to have anyone cut ahead of them. Those painted lines in the middle of the road? Merely a suggestion. When an Israeli cop stops a driver, he is prepared for an argument that the law is stupid and should be changed. When asked why Israelis are such terrible drivers, Jerusalem's former mayor Teddy Kollek answered that when you have to fight a war every few years, safe driving becomes the farthest thing from your mind. "It's much more dangerous to drive in Israel than to travel in space," astronaut Ilan Ramon assured his family before leaving on his fateful mission. Israeli road warriors and high-tech entrepreneurs alike are known for taking risks and finding shortcuts. These behaviors create carnage on the roads, but they helped put Israel onto the fast lane of the information superhighway. Only the United States has more high-tech startups.

Gil thinks of Israel as a startup nation. "We managed to create a country from zero. Brought in immigrants. Fed them. Created a legal system. Built cities. Set up farms in the desert. Invented techniques like drip irrigation." He adds that innovative researchers have developed disease-free potatoes, wilt-resistant tomato plants, and new ways to boost the nutritional value of wheat and have made many types of crops resistant to viruses and fungi. Israel's most famous startupnik comes from a family of kibbutzniks. His mother, who grew up on Kibbutz Ramat Rachel near Jerusalem, lost her father during the 1948 War. (Gil's father's German family perished in the Holocaust.) This offspring of socialist dreamers is a practical realist, yet tries to blend the old kibbutz group cooperative spirit he admires into his office culture. "I want everyone to feel good together. Work is more than coming in the morning and leaving in the afternoon. I try finding creative ways to let people know I value them. The trick is to be unconventional." He just flew fifteen hundred staff and their partners for a group vacation in Sun City, South Africa; another year, it was Cancún, Mexico. Even lunch is a cross between a commune and a yuppie experience. Gil, a food aficionado, has twenty different local restaurants email menus to the staff. In the dining room, the custom is to share—a taste of Thai noodles, a bite of an enchilada. Near his office there's a cappuccino machine and yoga and aerobics classes. He joins his staff twice a week for a spinning class on stationary bikes—when he's stationary himself. He just returned from a trip around the world in eight days. Wherever he goes, black clothes are his trademark. Not to look cool, he explains. "Black is very practical. Sweaters. Socks. Everything matches."

Young Israelis, however, consider him cool, even in Lod, a downtrodden Jewish-Muslim town next to Ben-Gurion International Airport, where Gil spent the morning meeting former dropouts who are mentored by volunteers from Check Point. With yawning gaps between the mega- and minipaychecks and national unemployment about 10 percent, these are tough economic times. In 2000, before the intifada, the GDP grew by 7.4 percent. By 2002, it shrank by about 3 percent, a dramatic reversal.

Gil himself was a uninterested student. He credits his late mother, an elementary school teacher, for taking him on learning adventures. "We went around the country," he recalls. "She'd see a dairy and stop and ask, 'Can my kid watch how you milk cows?' She knocked on the door of *Ha'aretz* and asked, 'Can my kid see how you print the newspaper?' She had curiosity and chutzpah." The most memorable outing was to his father's office at the Ministry of Finance back in 1972. He was only five. "I saw a huge computer, like in the old movies. For a kid, it was very impressive. At nine, I signed myself up for an afternoon computer class in a religious community center. I was one of the only non-Orthodox children." By the time he was twelve, Gil had a summer job coding for a language-translation software company. By fourteen, the boy wonder was writing software programs for a computer company. While in high school, Gil was allowed to take computer science classes at the Hebrew University. He went to a few. Didn't have time. He left.

When the seventeen-year-old computer prodigy was drafted, he qualified for the army's special training programs for gifted students but turned them down. "It meant I'd have to go to university for three years and the army for six. I didn't want to commit myself for the next ten years. They didn't know what to do with me. They even sent me to learn Arabic." Gil ended up in a secret electronic intelligence unit doing a job he is not permitted to discuss. It probably was stringing together military computer networks to allow some users access to classified materials and denying it to others. The IDF was not intended to be a high-tech incubator; it was founded to defend the state. Nonetheless, it is impossible to imagine Israel's high-tech boom without the army. A huge percentage of

Israel's high-tech leaders served in elite intelligence units working brutal hours in highly motivated teams designing the state-of-the-art technologies that give the IDF its tactical edge. When they get out, they help power civilian high tech.

After his four-year army stint, Gil skipped college. He became a software consultant and shared his army idea with two friends, Shlomo Kramer, an alumnus of the same hush-hush intelligence unit, and Marius Nacht of the air force. "We started about two hundred meters from here," Gil says, referring to the apartment that belonged to Nacht's ninety-year-old grandmother, where the trio spent six months working on borrowed computers. "We worked until 1 A.M., then ate Japanese food or went for a drink on the beach." They unveiled their product at a computer show in Las Vegas in 1994. They didn't have flashy promotional materials. "Reporters wanted a press release. We were so naïve, we didn't really know what a press release was, but we wrote one anyway. Even though we didn't have any business training, we were good at guerrilla marketing." Judges gave their product the best software award. They called it FireWall. Today, it is a generic name throughout the computer world.

One of the first persons they hired was Dorit Dor, who also served in a classified military intelligence unit. Unlike Gil, she holds a diploma or three, including a doctorate in computer science from Tel Aviv University. Today, she's vice president in charge of product R&D. When told a current Israeli joke—Why is it great to have a female boss? Because you know you'll always make more than she does—Gil says, "It's not true here" and calls attention to the high number of women he has in senior management, and that more employees are out on maternity leave than in miluim (reserve duty). An American customer asks him why everyone is fighting and yelling. "They're just talking," he explains. The lack of difference in status among bosses, managers, and underlings stuns non-Israelis. Instead of hierarchical leadership, many Israelis prefer leadership by "natural authority."

Dorit describes a typical meeting: "Everyone speaks at the same time, interrupts in midsentence. Silence means you're not interested." It's not only at Check Point, it's the way Israelis communicate. If they don't interrupt or ask questions, it could mean you're not capturing their interest. The more interruptions, the better the conversation. If three or four

Israelis talk at once, that's a good sign. If they get excited and shout, they're probably quite interested. If someone starts pounding the table, you're making your point.

Many Israelis are inept at small talk; it's one of the inheritances of the founding generation, whose social skills, or lack thereof, were formed by a powerfully egalitarian collectivism. Social graces were considered superficial, insincere, or artificially formal. And a waste of time. To this day, Israelis like talking *dugri,* an Arabic/Turkish word that means talking straight and honestly. When Israelis talk dugri, there's little posturing or gamesmanship. Talking dugri is the opposite of subtle; it means speaking in a thorny Sabra style. Talking dugri means you know where you stand. Whereas some cultures tolerate or encourage uncertainty and ambiguity, most Israelis don't. A tactful expression such as "This proposal sounds interesting" confuses Israelis. Israeli style is blunt: "This proposal won't work." Rarely do Israelis soften sentences with phrases like "Perhaps you might consider . . ." or "If you wouldn't mind." Instead, they might say "You're wrong." Hebrew itself is extremely concise; a four-word Hebrew proverb becomes sixteen words when translated into English. Israelis often speak English like their Hebrew: terse, economical, and explicit. Although many English speakers admired the eloquent speeches the late Abba Eban made when he was Israeli UN ambassador, many Israelis criticized his rhetorical flair and "high-sounding" language. He was, of course, educated at Cambridge rather than at the Technion.

What about the ultra-Orthodox Jewish man on Dorit's team? Aren't there different conversational styles? "Not really," answers Dorit, who is the daughter of Argentine immigrants. The world of high tech is a relatively idealized version of Israel. No one cares if the person at the next computer is ultra-Orthodox or secular, right or left wing, born in Tel Aviv, Tehran, or Moscow. Dorit just discovered that one long-time staffer is an Arab Christian. How? "The Santa Claus doll on his desk."

It's nearly 10 P.M. Christmas eve. Gil is ready for a favorite nocturnal pastime: the great epicurean search. Maybe some *capellini alla pomodoro?* "Almost every night, I try a new restaurant with friends. Despite the security situation, Tel Aviv is very lively, more fun than Silicon Valley." Nowadays, most Israelis select restaurants by the quality of their security; he chooses them by the quality of the cuisine. As in the dining room at Check Point, dinner with Gil follows unconventional directives.

"Everyone has to order a different dish and share it. And business talk is not allowed. I try hard to keep fun and work separate. At home, I refuse to have a desktop computer or take conference calls." He phones a restaurant, but the place is full. He had asked for a table for "Gil"; if instead he had mentioned his celebrated last name, he could have had any table. The name Shwed carries nearly as much clout as the name of a general or prime minister. The sons of Yitzhak Rabin and Shimon Peres and the daughter of Ehud Barak didn't follow in their fathers' footsteps. Yuval Rabin, Chemie Peres, and Michal Barak also are high-tech entrepreneurs, members of the new Israeli digital elite.

Lights! Camera! Swallow! The patient pops a pill, except this isn't a pill; there's a blinking white light at one end. The camera-in-a-capsule travels painlessly through her gastrointestinal tract, continuously transmitting color pictures by radio frequency to sensors on a belt she wears. She goes home and excretes the pill naturally. After she gives her doctor the belt sensors, a device roughly the size of a Sony Walkman, he uploads the images to a computer and watches a speeded-up version of the footage, scouting for problems. The disposable video camera's swim through her small intestine recalls the 1966 sci-fi movie *Fantastic Voyage,* in which a miniaturized Raquel Welch and friends sail through a human body in a boat.

This "gut cam" brings good news to millions of people suffering from undiagnosed disorders and illnesses, including tumors, ulcers, irritable bowel syndrome, and Crohn's disease. Since patients around the world started swallowing it in 2001, doctors have detected scores of potentially fatal diseases in patients, from a three-year-old Norwegian with undiagnosed bleeding to a seventy-year-old New Yorker who had cancerous tumors removed. The M2A (for "mouth to anus") capsules, which cost $450 apiece, are saving patients from batteries of unreliable and often painful, invasive tests. They're also saving health systems enormous sums of money. The M2A currently is the only player in an international market worth billions of dollars a year.

This ingenious invention is the brainchild of a dogged missile scientist with a wild imagination. Gavriel Iddan is a fast-thinking, fun-loving former merchant seaman with a doctorate from the Technion and twenty-five patents under his expansive belt (including a tiny thermal imaging camera that can detect blocked blood vessels during cardiac bypass surgery). He describes the day in 1981 when he first thought about a camera-in-a-capsule. A friend, a gastroenterologist and professor at Tel Aviv Medical School, complained about the problems diagnosing gastrointestinal tract disorders accurately. "He told me, 'If you're such a smart scientist, why don't you find a solution?' 'Just give me a few days,' I joked. I didn't have a solution, but I couldn't get the idea out of my mind."

Gavriel knew nothing about the complexities of peering inside the small intestine, the coiled fifteen feet between the stomach and the large intestine. He is former chief electro-optical engineer at Rafael, which does research and development for the Israeli Ministry of Defense. At Rafael, one of his jobs was developing the seeker, or the "eye" of the missile, which captures a target and guides the missile. He thought, Why not design an ingestible guided missile with an electrical-optical camera that would send real-time pictures as it navigates the intestines? Only problem: crucial technology hadn't been invented. "Ten years later, we discussed the idea again. I made a long list of problems. It still was utterly hopeless. Batteries lasted ten minutes and we needed one that would last ten hours. And even if it did, what doctor would stay next to a patient for eight hours, watching a monitor while the capsule moves through?"

Gavriel wouldn't quit. When he told his bosses at Rafael, they thought his far-fetched idea was good for a Hollywood movie, not the Israeli military. "They said, 'We're in the business of missiles, not endoscopes.' They let me use the labs but weren't interested in investing in it," he remembers. In time, a series of technological breakthroughs made it possible. He and his colleagues built a small transmitter and tested it in a defrosted chicken. A friend invented a video camera a third the size of a dime. By chance in 1993, Gavriel read about a tiny new camera chip. The NASA scientist who'd designed it wasn't interested in Gavriel's mad concept until, during a phone call, he announced that in memory of his father, who'd died from an undiagnosed gastrointestinal tumor, he would design the chip. "I decided to make a little capsule and start some experiments," recollects Gavriel. A colleague ingested a capsule and compared the experience to swallowing a missile that doesn't explode.

In 1994, Gavriel applied for U.S. and Israeli patents. His investors set the first IPO after the FDA approved the M2A capsule in August 2001. Then came September 11. "I thought the IPO was all over, that we didn't stand a chance, but our CEO pressed on," says Gavriel, describing the jittery financial and political climate. Two weeks later, Given Imaging was the first company to go public on Nasdaq after the terrorist attacks. It raised $60 million. "After those tragic deaths, my big hope is that our pill will save many thousands of lives. That it will be what the Bible calls beating swords into ploughshares."

Given Imaging's world headquarters are a rural industrial park outside Yokenam, a small town between Haifa and Megiddo (Armageddon). More than ninety employees do research and manufacture the capsules here. (In case of missile attacks, there's a backup factory in Minnesota and emergency inventories in European warehouses.) The company has patents pending for other types of video camera capsules. In this new era of noninvasive medicine, doctors may be able to explore the insides of patients virtually instead of carving them up. In other buildings, there are more commercial spinoffs from Rafael's missile technology, for cryosurgery probes designed to destroy malignant prostate and kidney and liver tissue and ophthalmic digital imaging devices for the retina. One company makes video conferencing networking systems, another develops and manufactures lasers that can eliminate varicose veins, wrinkles, tattoos, body hair, and various skin cancers, and also lasers that treat glaucoma and cataracts, the two leading causes of blindness.

As with many high-tech concerns in Israel, Russian frequently is heard in the hallways and cubicles. Some of the more than one million former Soviets who have emigrated to Israel since the 1990s brought more than suitcases; they arrived with goldmines of research and data banks. One of them was mechanical engineer Gregory Pinchaski, who, soon after landing at Ben-Gurion in 1990, developed a stent, a spring-like coil used all over the world to hold open coronary arteries of patients who have undergone balloon therapy. A founding member of Medinol, he is a multimillionaire.

The Yokenam industrial park sits on the edge of a wadi, Arabic for dry riverbed. Gavriel Iddan was one of the first to coin the term "Silicon Wadi" for the hotbed of entrepreneurialism in the areas between Jerusalem, Tel Aviv, and Haifa. "The reasons I think we're leaders in world-class technology?" Gavriel launches into an hour-long lecture about the highly educated Jews who arrived in the decades before independence and founded top-ranking educational and research institutions. "And thanks to Hitler, we got a lot of world-class scientists. Professors the Nazis kicked out of German and other universities taught here."

It was also necessity, he continues. "Before the state, there was a total embargo on weapons. We either had to smuggle or manufacture them. We had to rely on ourselves; no one else would help. We had no choice. Improvise or die." There are those who thank French president Charles de Gaulle for forcing Israel to make itself an innovator in high tech. Israel fought the 1967 War mostly with French weapons. Afterward, France cut off all aircraft and missile shipments and increased exports to Israel's Arab neighbors. Israelis had to create their own aerospace industry and manufacture sophisticated communications and electronic equipment, optical instruments as well as upgraded aircraft, missiles, and tanks. They created the software to operate these systems. Products Israelis developed for the army flowed into the civilian market just in time for the communications revolution of the 1990s.

Since the days when Gavriel's parents immigrated to a semibarren Middle Eastern backwater controlled by the British, Israel has made a breathtaking leap from the Third to the First World. The economy has grown more than fiftyfold since 1948. Even as late as 1990, Israel's exports—70 percent agricultural—left mostly by container ships, not by FedEx or modem. Now, more than half of Israel's exports by monetary value are high-tech, meditech, and agritech, what Gavriel calls "modern-day versions of the old pioneering spirit. We don't have oil. We hardly have any water. The only national and natural resources we have are sand and brains. And with brains we're turning sand into silicon." He thumps his laptop computer. "What's inside? Microchips. They're made of silicon. And the software? It's made by brains."

In Haifa, modern glass offices tower over the Mediterranean. Microsoft, Sun Microsystems, GE, Motorola, IBM, and Hewlett-Packard run R&D centers from this city that reminds visitors of San Francisco. At Intel's Haifa design and development center, its first outside the United States, engineers designed the chips that helped spark the global personal computer revolution. They also did most of the work on the Pentium chips. And in 2003, they unveiled two new chips they'd secretly developed for notebook computers, the Centrino and Dotan, and a cell phone chip, the Manitoba.

Intel is the largest foreign investor in Israel. Dutch Holocaust survivor Dov Frohman, an Israeli electrical engineer, was part of the original group that founded Intel in the United States and invented the Electrically Programmable Read-Only Memory chip, or EPROM, a key building block of today's information technology industries, indispensable in telecommunications to automobiles. He then became general manager of Intel Israel and vice president of Intel Corporation.

The days of giddy growth ended when the global stock markets took a dive, but U.S., Japanese, German, Chinese, and other companies are actively prospecting in the Promised Land, snapping up products and firms. Bill Gates has famously said that Israel has developed the best high-tech culture outside the United States, which might explain why Microsoft's first international R&D center is located in Haifa's Matam technology park, next door to Intel and just up the Mediterranean coast from Cisco Systems and Motorola. Making a phone call? More than half the telephone calls in the United States go through Israeli-designed switches. Flying from Hong Kong to Washington, D.C.? An Israeli company installed the airports' traffic control systems. Enjoy *National Geographic*'s color photos? They were printed on a color system developed by Israelis. Want to listen to Christmas Mass from the Vatican over the Internet? Israeli whiz kids figured out how to broadcast it.

Between Haifa and Tel Aviv are the cafés where innovators and the hopeful gather. "My website is my identity," comments a twenty-five-year-old computer programmer formerly known as Tomer Karissi. "Last names are so archaic. Now that I've changed my name to Tomer.com, everyone knows that I'm a technological Israeli." The cafés host everyone, from the former fighter pilot who sells military flight-simulation software to train German, French, and Indian pilots, to a startup junkie with Skybot, a robot that cleans windows on skyscrapers. Then there are the entrepreneurs who designed the security fence surrounding Buckingham Palace using state-of the-art military technology and also designed the security systems at Chicago's O'Hare and other major international airports, and the former soldiers who developed the first software that allows people to make free voice calls using the Internet. Few Israelis even know that engineers at Motorola-Israel developed the first cell phone and that most of Windows NT was created at Microsoft-Israel.

I hawked canisters of Holy Land air and Holy Land earth to tourists visiting the Nazareth *souk* [market]," Imad Younis recounts with a chuckle. He also helped out at his father's leather shop next to the White Mosque, the oldest in Nazareth, built in 1821. After high school, he left the Galilee town where his family has lived since the sixteenth century, to study at the Technion. "I was one of ten Arab students in an electrical engineering department of nearly three hundred. The Jewish students got jobs quickly, but we had a hard time." Back in 1983, most high-tech companies made defense-related products, and Arab Israeli electrical engineers couldn't, and still don't, pass security clearances. Not until the Internet and the civilian electronics boom did jobs begin to open for Arab professionals. Technion's medical school hired Imad. "Those four years were great, designing research tools—from cardiac to neurology—every crazy idea the scientists had," he says, describing his job as head of technical support. Then, at a Haifa medical company, he helped develop blood pressure measuring and electrocardiogram systems. "I had the skills. I had the connections. I quit a good job, gave up a salary, and made a leap. I decided to follow my dream—to open the first Arab high-tech company. And I wanted it to have a Nazareth address."

In 1992, Imad moved back to Nazareth, Israel's largest Arab town. With his Nazarene wife, a civil engineer he met at the Technion, he set up a research lab in a cramped apartment on a narrow road not far from the largest Roman Catholic church in the Middle East. They worship at the Basilica of the Annunciation, which non-Orthodox Christians believe was the site of Mary's home, Joseph's carpentry shop, of the angel Gavriel's visit to Mary, and of the conception itself. Because his bank account was lower than the Dead Sea, the lowest spot on earth, Imad sold his VW Jetta to buy equipment. The Center for Jewish-Arab Economic Development, a nonprofit organization that assists fledgling Arab businesses, showed him how to write marketing plans and apply for government grants. University researchers hired him to design brain-mapping equipment and triggered his move to sell it for commercial use. He pressed on and moved to more spacious quarters.

There are no ultramodern skyscrapers or people plugged into the Internet via fiber-optic cable in the low-rent section of Upper Nazareth, where Alpha Omega Biomedical Engineering is sandwiched between a supermarket and a ceramic tile factory. Imad bicycles to work, "not because I can't afford a car, but this is the only way I can get in shape. Walking down airplane aisles doesn't give me much exercise." The determined CEO exports about $3 million worth of medical devices to eleven countries, from Germany to Japan to France. Neurosurgeons and brain researchers at the Mayo Clinic, Johns Hopkins, UCLA Medical Center, the National Institutes of Health, and two hundred more hospitals and labs use his tools, which cost between $10,000 and $100,000, to diagnose and treat movement disorders such as Parkinson's disease and to explore the brain's auditory, visual, and motor functions. "Our devices make it possible for surgeons to maneuver through the brain accurately and quickly, causing much less trauma to the patient. Brain surgery takes about eight hours. We're trying to shorten it to half an hour."

Alpha Omega Biomedical Engineering is open every day. On Christmas, on Id al-Adha (the Islamic Feast of the Sacrifice), on Yom Kippur. Someone is always around, explains Imad, because the staff celebrate different holidays—different Sabbaths, different Christmases and Easters, different New Years. On this day, some of the forty Muslims and Christian Arabs and Jews on staff are off in voting booths. The kaleidoscopic choice of thirty national parties reflects a fragmented society. "Politics and religion, we don't talk about that," Imad says with a sigh, reflecting weariness and wariness. "We have conflicts here, but not about that. Our fights are between our marketing and R&D departments. Right now we're battling against time—getting orders out." As his name suggests (in Arabic, Imad means "someone you can count on"), shipments can't be late.

Arab Israeli entrepreneurs frequently visit the country's first Arab Israeli high-tech company. Imad is too self-effacing to admit that in Jesus' boyhood home, he's considered a pioneer. "People come not to see me, but to see this place. It's like dropping a stone in a pool. And we're starting to make ripples." Another Arab Israeli man in the Galilee runs a company that makes a chemical compound that can lengthen the shelf life of fruits, vegetables, and flowers; another runs a startup that makes a vegetable compound aimed at lowering cholesterol. A Nazareth high-tech park is in the works.

But now it's time for a staff meeting. As always, Imad must decide: Arabic or Hebrew? Because the native Hebrew speakers are out of the office, he'll speak Arabic with simultaneous Russian translation. How many Russians work for Alpha Omega? "Don't call them Russians," he insists. "They're Israelis." To clarify what he means, he describes the annual staff bash at the Holy Land Restaurant near the souvenir stall where he once sold olive wood Nativity scenes. "Ramadan, Hanukkah, Christmas, and New Year's fell during the same period this year, so we held it before the Orthodox Christmas [January 7]." The people playing Arabic dance tunes on oud, burbek [drum], violin, and bass guitar were his software designers, computer programmers, and electric engineers—Arabs and Russian Jews.

"We're not just coworkers, we're friends. And it's not just at Alpha Omega, but with the scientists at labs in the Hebrew University, the Weizmann Institute, and the Technion we work with very closely, developing and testing new products together. Without them, my company wouldn't exist." And without Alpha Omega's cutting-edge equipment, the neuroscientists would be far less able to explore the brain, learn about memory and sensory impairments, and search for treatments for movement and mental disorders and chronic pain. "For thousands of years, we've had wars in the Middle East. In wars, we're very experienced. If people could see our labs, they'd see another reality: people working together not just for Israel or our bank accounts, but for humanity. It's a very inspiring picture of how life can be."

Almost monthly, it seems, Israeli researchers announce a biological breakthrough: a drug to prevent or treat juvenile diabetes, an antitumor vaccine, treatments to fight Parkinson's, multiple sclerosis, ovarian and prostate cancers, and malignant melanoma. Recent developments include artificial muscles that can move a human limb, a device for treatment of glaucoma, bioelectronic analysis that may help doctors treat AIDS patients, nano-size chips to detect chemical warfare toxins in water and air, and a strain of *E. coli* bacteria that kills mosquito larvae in standing water and then harmlessly dies out. And thanks to a female neuroimmunologist from the Weizmann Institute, spinal cord injuries may no longer be incurable. Israel has more engineers, scientists, life science researchers, and physicians per capita than any country in the world. After the United States, Britain, and Germany, Israel leads in the number of biotech, medical devices, and diagnostics startup companies.

Nava Swersky Sofer, a thirty-five-year-old venture capitalist, hunts for biomedical breakthroughs. "This is going to be the biotech century," she predicts from Columbine Ventures, the fund she started in Herzliya Pituah. A major partner is the Shamrock Group, the private investment arm of the Roy Disney family. Nava knows the field, moving across cultural barriers with ease, conducting tough negotiations in German, French, and English with American, European, and Asian pharmaceutical giants. At twenty-five, equipped with an MBA, she was the youngest member of the worldwide management group of Novaris. A former IDF captain, she also is the youngest Israeli to pass the bar and win legal disputes as a lawyer in army courts. "Israel is producing some truly fantastic biotechnologies," says this woman, who is busy concluding the nearly $200 million sale of an Israeli company that makes a revolutionary angioplasty device to Guidant, an American company that develops cardiovascular medical products. When asked about the Technion scientists who have discovered how to use DNA to construct a conductive wire a thousand times thinner than a human hair, a huge leap in the miniaturization of electrical devices, she grows animated. "It could lead to faster chips made of DNA for use in diagnostics, to say nothing of a new generation of computer chips. Despite Israel's minute size, we're a major innovator in medical devices and biotech." And part of the human genome revolution.

When Dr. Ariel Darvasi announced in October 2002 the discovery of a key gene linked to schizophrenia, the news made headlines throughout the world. His scientific detectives use a unique approach to unlock genetic secrets: they study Ashkenazi Jews.

Ashkenazim, who make up about 80 percent of world Jewry, are a classic "founder population," a term geneticists use to describe a modern population descended from a relatively small group of common ancestors who, over the centuries, have had minimal mixing with outside groups. The modern world's 10 million or so Ashkenazi Jews have a unique demographic history that can be traced to fifteen hundred families who lived in the Rhineland in Germany and Eastern Europe in the fourteenth century; Darvasi believes that "the original pool may be even smaller—maybe five hundred families." And their origins? After the Romans conquered Jerusalem in 70 C.E., their forebears left and scattered throughout Spain, France, Italy, and other Mediterranean basin countries. Over the centuries, they spread throughout Europe.

For religious and historical reasons, Ashkenazi Jews have, for the most part, married within the community, which shows up in their genetic uniformity. And because their rate of schizophrenia is similar to that of the world population—about 1 percent—the findings of the landmark study "are applicable to the entire human race," he says. Israel, with more than 2.5 million Ashkenazi Jews, is an ideal place to track down links between gene abnormalities and diseases.

The gene seekers at his three-year-old Jerusalem-based IDgene Pharmaceuticals study thousands of blood samples from Ashkenazi Jews in Israel suffering from schizophrenia; breast, prostate, and colon cancer; asthma, diabetes, Parkinson's, and Alzheimer's disease. Donors must have four biological grandparents of Ashkenazi heritage. Their genetic profiles, which are kept anonymous, are compared with those of healthy Ashkenazim in the hope of finding needles in the genetic haystack. They also look for genetic links to other illnesses, including multiple sclerosis, arteriosclerosis, hypertension, osteoporosis, and rheumatoid arthritis.

The ability to isolate a population of manageable size is a scientific boon for geneticists who must sift through 3 billion human DNA sequences and around forty thousand genes searching for genetic causes of common and often deadly diseases. A rival Icelandic firm is doing similar research, hurrying to make breakthroughs that could lead to new drugs. But according to Dr. Darvasi, former head of statistical genetics at pharmaceutical giant SmithKline Beecham, geneticists disagree over the degree of homogeneity of Iceland's population, which, according to some studies, includes people of Norwegian and Celtic descent. He believes that Ashkenazi Jews are more genetically homogeneous and emphasizes that Israel has a ten times larger gene pool; there are only a quarter of a million Icelanders. Iceland, however, has voluminous family records; not so Ashkenazi Jews. Because of the Holocaust, pogroms, and inquisitions and the fact that they scattered all over the world, many Ashkenazi Jews don't know details about the branches on their family trees. Homogeneity is a more powerful approach than genealogy, this Hebrew University professor of genetics believes. "The Ashkenazi gene pool is small enough to be studied intensively and big enough to contain significant variations." But it won't last, predicts Darvasi, an Ashkenazi married to a Yemenite Israeli. "Within a century, you won't find many full-blooded Ashkenazi Israelis."

So what's next? "Genes are the body's instruction manual, and understanding the blueprints are the first steps toward curing a disease. This is only the beginning," he cautions. Going from genetic discoveries to customized cures involves pharmaceutical companies, millions of dollars, and years of clinical testing. He and his forty scientific sleuths—geneticists, molecular biologists, and computer experts—are convinced that Ashkenazi genes will reveal many more medical mysteries.

As we will see in the next chapter, without the Ashkenazi Jews, there would be no modern Israel.

One Nation, Many Tribes

5

The Ashkenazim

Israel's "WASPS"

↺ In Israel, in order to be a realist you must believe in miracles. —Israel's first prime minister, David Ben-Gurion

Anat and Israel Peleg's high-rise apartment in Givat Shmuel (Hill of Samuel), built on former orange orchards, has a panoramic view of Tel Aviv's gleaming skyscrapers, sailboats gliding in the Mediterranean, and ultra-Orthodox Bnei Brak. In the distance, less than fifty miles away, lies the angry Gaza Strip. Their airy living room is filled with grandparents, cousins, uncles, and aunts gathered to celebrate Anat's mother's seventy-fifth birthday. They're doctors, poets, politicians, lawyers, and entrepreneurs, mostly secular, some very religious. They're left-leaning and right-wing, old-line socialists and New Economy capitalists. What they share is that they are all descendants of old Israeli Ashkenazi families, resolute European Jewish pioneers who built the country, revived the Hebrew language, and founded kibbutzim and Tel Aviv, the first modern Jewish city. Some Israelis call them WASPs: white Ashkenazi Sabras with *proteksia* (connections).

An elderly man brings up the day in 1993 when Yitzhak Rabin and Yasser Arafat made the historic handshake on the White House lawn, saying to a niece, "We built this country for you and you're destroying it." Even though they think differently, these opinionated Israelis steer clear of politics: they know each other's arguments and prefer to have a good time. "We're all looking for a solution; we just have different ideas of how to get there," observes Israel, who until 1996 was on the front lines of the predominantly Ashkenazi Labor Party, a Shimon Peres protégé. "I feel we and Palestinians have no choice but to find a way to live side by side. For me, Oslo is not a dirty word. It showed that psychological and economic barriers to peace can and must break down. We have to be realistic and find a way." Israel thought many of his neighbors in this bastion of leftist Ashkenazim still shared his views until his fifteen-year-old son canvassed forty of his peers. The right won by a landslide.

After years fighting for joint Jewish and Arab projects, for religious and educational pluralism, for making the increasingly multicultural country more compassionate, Israel decided to leave public service. Currently, he is vice president of the national lottery, an irony not lost on him. "Everyone feels like we're gambling on our lives," he says despondently. "I'm finding new ways to sell dreams: scratch cards. People say they can't think about peace because no one knows how each day will end. So much hopelessness, such frustration. This is not the country my parents built." In 1936, Israel's father emigrated from Poland to establish a kibbutz in British-controlled Palestine. He lost contact with his family, later learning that they, like almost all the Jews of Poland, perished in the Holocaust. When his second son was born in 1949, he named him Israel after his new family, the new state.

Anat, a soft-spoken, hard-nosed reporter, shares her husband's pessimism. She works for Kol Israel, the Voice of Israel radio network, which broadcasts in Hebrew and twelve other languages: Arabic, Moroccan Mughrabi Arabic, Farsi, Amharic, Russian, Ukrainian, Romanian, Hungarian, Spanish, Ladino, French, and English. When her beeper goes off, her children know that it usually means she must rush off to cover a suicide bombing or to interview hospital survivors. It seems lifetimes ago that her husband and children went to the fateful 1995 peace rally where three bullets killed Prime Minister Rabin. Anat was the first to break the news to the stunned nation that the assassin was a fanatically religious right-wing law student at Bar-Ilan University, which faces their apartment.

Glancing at her son and daughter, Anat continues with a sigh: "They grew up on rock and rap, I grew up on patriotic songs. These days, those songs about self-sacrifice are back on the radio. When I was their age, our country was isolated, claustrophobic, surrounded by enemies, disconnected from the world. We didn't have television. International movies came two years later. It really bothers me now to see my kids glued to the TV watching Israel at war. We were so happy to drive across the border and take them sightseeing in Jordan. For Ohad's eleventh birthday, we celebrated in a club in Amman and the waiters sang "Happy Birthday" to him in Arabic. When he got up and joined a belly dancer, the band broke into "Hava Nagila." Israel and I had tears in our eyes. I didn't think Ohad was crazy when he said his dream was to drive from Tel Aviv through Syria to Europe. Well, a few weeks ago, I was planning a surprise sixteenth birthday party for him at a Tel Aviv pub. I had to call it off—parents are too afraid to let their kids go to public places."

Anat is a second-generation Sabra, or what locals call "Israeli *Mayflower.*" Her great-grandparents built Tel Aviv out of sand dunes; her generation covered them with malls. Her fashion-mad daughter Re'ut ("friendship" in Hebrew) adores them. The thirteen-year-old, a delicate-looking carbon copy of her attractive mother, tries to convince her parents to let her go, assuring them that she'll shop only where it's "safe"—on the second floor. Suicide bombers, she reasons, usually detonate on the ground floor.

Like most Israeli schoolchildren, Re'ut has been assigned a "roots" project, but not many Israelis come from a family so intimately entwined with the history of Israel and the struggle to establish a Jewish state. "Don't be shy, ask a lot of questions," Anat urges her daughter. "What other person has so many answers?" Moving into reporter mode, Re'ut asks her spirited grandmother, who once headed WIZO, Israel's largest women's group, why her family left Russia.

"Jews were treated as aliens, an unwanted minority," her grandmother begins. "My mother and her parents survived the Kishinev pogrom in 1903. A Russian mob killed over fifty Jews on Easter, injured 500, and made thousands homeless." After that massacre, they decided to build a new life in a new Jewish nation. The Ismojik family were among the early pioneers who called themselves Zionists, after Zion, the traditional synonym for Jerusalem and Israel. They believed that after two millennia in exile, Jews needed the safety of a state of their own.

At the First Zionist Congress in Basel, Switzerland in 1897, Theodore Herzl said the Jewish people had the right to a national rebirth in their ancestral home. Herzl, a secular Budapest-born Jew, witnessed one of Europe's most famous outbreaks of virulent anti-Semitism when he was a journalist covering the Paris trial of French army captain Alfred Dreyfus, who was falsely accused of treason and sentenced to life in prison. He concluded that Zionism, a term coined in 1885 by Viennese socialist writer Nathan Birnbaum, was a truer path to security than assimilation. In Herzl's version, Zionism told Jews that they are one people, who could shed their diaspora minority mentality and ethnic divisions only in their own land, where they could create a modern Jewish state, where physical work, particularly agricultural, was valued. When the Zionist ideology was first conceived, the world's largest Jewish community was in czarist Russia's Pale of Settlement, where they lived with pogroms, no civil rights, and no access to academia and professions, while in Central and Western Europe, particularly in the famously multiethnic Austro-Hungarian Empire, Jews enjoyed historically high levels of emancipation, social mobility, and assimilation. Zionism was an ideology created in Western Europe that found its most attentive audience in Eastern Europe—and looked still further east for its realization, to Palestine, which for four centuries had been a province of the Ottoman Empire.

Government-inspired *pogroms* (a Russian word meaning "bloody mass attacks") and anti-Jewish laws drove the first organized emigration to Ottoman Palestine of young Jews, in the 1880s. It was called the First *Aliyah*, "going up," a word used interchangeably among Jews for both emigration to Israel and participation in Torah services. The Second Aliyah began in 1903, fueled by the pogrom in Kishinev, which Jews called the "city of slaughter."

"When my family set sail for Palestine in 1905, they were following Herzl's words, 'If you will it, it is not a dream.' See this?" her grandmother says, picking up a silver Hanukkah menorah on the living room mantle. "They had it with them when they arrived in Jaffa." This was the ancient port where early immigrants, Ashkenazi (Hebrew for "German") Jews fleeing persecution, pogroms, and poverty in Europe, landed.

"What was Jaffa like then?" asks Re'ut.

"Crowded and dirty, ruled by Turks. My mother's family and some other Russian and Polish families decided to move away. Together they bought land from Arabs north of Jaffa. In 1909, the sixty original families picked their plots by lottery and, in the sandy wilderness, built the first new Jewish town in two thousand years. They called it Tel Aviv [Hill of Spring]. They built small red-tile-roofed houses around a cultural center, which became the first Hebrew-language high school of modern times. My mother was one of the seventeen children who went to Gymnasia Herzliya," she proudly tells Re'ut. "She was one of the first children in Palestine who actually spoke Hebrew."

Re'ut looks surprised. "What did the Jews speak?"

"Mostly Yiddish, Russian, Polish, Romanian, or German," her grandmother replies. "My mother and her schoolmates used to go around Tel Aviv urging them to speak Hebrew." She helped bring this ancient language out of the synagogues and onto the streets. Even though Hebrew was not a spoken language, it has been in continuous use as a literary and religious language for Jews who were separated by centuries and continents. The sacred texts—the Bible, the Midrash, the Talmud—preserved this continuity. For eighteen centuries, Hebrew was not a living language. And that's where things might have stayed, except for Robinson Crusoe.

As a boy in nineteenth-century Czarist Russia, Eliezer Perlman, a Lithuanian Orthodox Jew turned secular, read a Hebrew translation of Daniel Defoe's classic of island survival and became convinced that this language of prayer should become a secular, spoken modern language, a vehicle that would unify Palestine's polyglot Jews. After sailing into Jaffa in 1881, he and his wife took the Hebrew name Ben-Yehuda, and he informed her they'd speak only Hebrew. He fanatically devoted his life to this idea. He educated his son at home in Jerusalem, keeping him isolated from other people so he'd hear only his parents speaking Hebrew. The boy didn't speak at all until age four. When he did, Ben-Zion (the Son of Zion) became the first Jew in two thousand years whose native language was Hebrew.

The challenges of re-creating a language required that sort of fanatic loyalty. Not only was Ben-Yehuda obliged to create new words from old roots—the biblical Hebrew word for chariot, *merkava*, was enlisted to create the modern Hebrew word for railroad, *rakevet*—but diaspora Hebrew lacked a uniform pronunciation. For the past two thousand years, Jews praying from Lithuania to Turkey to Iraq developed different dialects with several pronunciations of the same Hebrew spellings. Ben-Yehuda believed the Hebrew of Jerusalem's ancient Sephardi community had an authentic sound, closer to the biblical tongue than the Ashkenazi, which had changed more over the centuries. Many Ashkenazi immigrants, however, opposed him, charging that the Sephardi dialect sounded strange, coarse, masculine, and not Western. Ben-Yehuda persisted because he also felt that if all Jews adopted the Sephardi dialect, Sephardi/Mizrahi Jews would be brought closer to the increasingly powerful Ashkenazi establishment and help unify the different Jewish tribes. He also felt that adopting one Sephardi accent would lessen linguistic differences and rivalries among different Ashkenazi groups who had lived in different areas of Europe for centuries.

Jews fought bitter battles over Hebrew. When the Technion, Israel's preeminent technical college, opened in Haifa in 1913 with German as its official language, it took a violent student-faculty strike to get the administration to adopt Hebrew. Hebrew was a potent weapon in shaping an Israeli national identity. Zionism's central idea is that Jews are one people, exiles who should return to their ancestral homeland and shed their diaspora minority mentality and ethnic divisions to create a new Jewish society with a modern Jewish culture and language. Hebrew was, and is, the glue that binds together modern Israel.

Today, signs in Hebrew are everywhere, in trendy sushi bars, seedy strip clubs, the guard shelters at Re'ut's school. Nearly half of all Israelis now live in the sprawling Tel Aviv area, which is the center of Israeli business and culture. The old Gymnasia Herzliya is gone. In its place is the Shalom Tower, Israel's first skyscraper. The dirt streets where jackals once roamed at night are so congested that Israelis either double park or park on the sidewalks. Only after a bombing is parking no problem.

Re'ut's sixteen-year-old second cousin, Ongy Zisling, also is a descendant of the *Mayflower* generation. When he isn't tending calves on the kibbutz where he lives, he is studying or playing jazz on his sax. His grandfather founded one of the first kibbutzim, signed the Declaration of

Independence, and was Israel's first minister of agriculture. In 1921, Aaron Zisling fled anti-Jewish Arab riots in Jaffa, and with other young Russian and Polish Jews purchased land south of Nazareth from Arab landowners to build a collective farm. These idealistic pioneers called it Kibbutz Ein Harod, because it was near King Herod's spring. They lived in tents, drained swamps, and planted trees and crops, believing that hard physical labor would not only transform the country, it would transform them into new "Jews with muscles," unlike the frightened, persecuted Eastern European Jews who had been landless for centuries. Working the land symbolized the rebirth of the Jewish people; they liked to point out that the Hebrew word for man, *adam,* is derived from *adama,* Hebrew for land. They took Hebrew names like Barak (lightning), Tamir (towering), and Oz (strength) or agricultural names like Karmi (of the vineyard) and Dagan (corn); the new names were symbols of a personal and collective rebirth. They deliberately ate plain food prepared in communal workers' kitchens. Israel's first president, Chaim Weizmann, himself a nonsocialist "bourgeois" liberal impressed by their determination, observed, "To be a Zionist it is not necessary to be mad, but it helps." Despite their enthusiasm, life was grueling for these inexperienced farmers. The Jezreel Valley (God Will Sow Seeds) was infested with malaria and typhus; summers were scorching and winters, muddy quagmires. To guard against frequent Arab raids, they set up a watchtower. At early kibbutzim many suffered from severe emotional distress and homesickness for parents back in Europe. Cypress trees stand watch over Ein Harod's enormous cemetery. A few of the oldest gravestones are marked with the phrase: "Took His Own Life."

Still, these socialist visionaries persevered. Fervent about equality, they discouraged differences in income and rank. All property, except personal belongings, was owned communally. In the early years, antimaterialistic kibbutzniks shared clothes and shoes, ate all meals together, and decided many things by vote, sometimes even the names of their children. The goal was to create a new type of family in which everyone felt like brothers and sisters. Babies were separated from their parents at six weeks and raised in separate collective children's homes. In recent years, kibbutz life rapidly has become far less communal as members demand more privacy and autonomy in decision making. The children's houses, a symbol of traditional kibbutz life, were closed by 1984. Ongy and his younger brother were the first in the family to be raised at home. Although most of Ein Harod's five hundred members celebrate Passover, Shabbat, and other holidays together in the grant collective dining room, it is no longer the heart of this or most other kibbutzim. A few years ago, the Zislings enlarged their small house and added a kitchenette so they could eat dinners at home. Many of Israel's 275 kibbutzim now charge members for food, and some have even closed their dining rooms. In the 1970s, there was one television on the kibbutz. Today, like most kibbutzniks, the Zislings watch cable and satellite television at home.

Ongy's grandfather's generation were strictly informal (in this, at least, the new kibbutzniks haven't broken faith; Ongy never has owned a tie or a jacket); they looked down on jackets and dresses and even banned neckties, symbols of the hypocritical, decadent Europe they had fled. Rejecting artificially polite European "bourgeoisie" ways of speaking, they frowned on deferential forms of address. They were straight speaking, with an irreverent attitude toward authority. They were passionate about politics and argumentative. Ideological disputes at Ein Harod got so fierce that in 1953 the kibbutz split in two and some relatives didn't speak for years. Above all, kibbutzniks have been known as resourceful improvisers who enjoy creating their own rules. Other Israelis emulated these larger-than-life Jews. They were admired internationally and glorified in the late Leon Uris's best-selling book *Exodus* and the movie of the same name. Despite their small number—once 7 percent of the population; today, less than 3 percent—kibbutzniks have had a disproportionate degree of influence on the country. This group of Israelis has a distinguished military record and, not coincidentally, have been prominent leaders: five prime ministers—David Ben-Gurion, Levi Eshkol, Golda Meir, Shimon Peres, and Ehud Barak—are Ashkenazim who lived on kibbutzim. The kibbutz, philosopher Martin Buber once said, is the experiment that worked.

On the surface, it appears that way today. "The kibbutz is a great place to grow up, a big family," says Ongy. "No matter what happens, everybody is there for you. After the army, if I travel in Thailand or study music, they'll take care of it." All kibbutz members have cradle-to-grave housing, medical care, and education, including university. Ongy and his friends ride bikes past neat homes surrounded by manicured lawns. Graceful date trees and green corn stalks wave in the warm breeze;

bronzed kibbutzniks in shorts and sandals plow cotton fields and pick watermelons. Musicians from the former Soviet Union, a few of whom are new members of the kibbutz, practice in the concert hall. Volunteers from all over the world lounge around the enormous swimming pool. Israeli tourists visit the impressive art gallery where Ongy's grandfather's Judaica collection is on display and eat in the vegetarian restaurant his mother runs.

The enthusiasm for farming exhibited by Israel's first generation of immigrants is now matched by an equivalent expertise. Ein Harod's kibbutzniks have been raised in a literal land of milk and honey; their hives produce about one hundred tons of honey annually and the kibbutz manages a high-tech, thousand-cow dairy. Israelis are rightly proud of their agricultural performance. "Our dairy cows are world champions in milk production," reports Ongy's father, Ori Zisling. Five of his sons have worked in the dairy; one, an engineer, is developing milking robots. He boasts that Israeli chickens produce more eggs than anywhere in the world and their coops are monitored by home computer. Israeli cotton farmers hold the world record for most cotton produced per acre. The kibbutz's electronically controlled fish ponds produce enormous amounts of carp, bass, and St. Peter's fish. "These days, everything is electronic. People can sit at home and control irrigation by computer, making adjustments for wind, humidity, and temperature," notes Ori. Kibbutzniks use computerized drip irrigation/fertilization systems that make optimal use of scarce water. Innovative Israeli agricultural techniques are used all over the world. Experts in plant genetics are breeding new fruits and vegetables that thrive on brackish water. Kibbutzim produce half of Israel's agriculture, although most of their income no longer comes from toiling the land.

Suffocating from a socialist lifestyle in a country in love with materialism, kibbutzim have been in the throes of change since the mid-1980s. Struggling with outstanding loans, the offspring of socialist revolutionaries have been forced to read *The Wall Street Journal* and *Fortune* and bring in outside business managers. "We're becoming pragmatic realists, which means moving from citrus to chips and smart cards," explains Ori as he shows off Ein Harod's stainless steel factory that exports pasteurizing machines for dairy products, juice, and instant coffee. Blockbuster video stores buy Ein Harod's robotic video vending machines that dispense movies twenty-four hours a day. Hospital monitors, computers, and fax machines from Poland to Singapore use kibbutz-made thermal paper. Young technovisionaries run a kibbutz computer programming company. The Internet has liberated kibbutzniks and other Israelis from their biggest handicap: isolation from markets. Still, a physics professor and a physical therapist, along with more and more Ein Harod members, borrow the kibbutz cars to commute to jobs in neighboring towns. Their salaries, which are put in the communal pool, are a sizable source of Ein Harod's income. Other kibbutzim located closer to Tel Aviv or Haifa resemble bedroom communities, with members commuting to jobs at Intel and Motorola.

"It was natural to return to the kibbutz, get married, and be a dairyman after I got out of the paratroopers. Today, our children have other dreams." About 70 percent of Ein Harod's youth eventually leave the kibbutz. "It's even higher at other kibbutzim, a very, very serious problem," notes Ori, who unhappily acknowledges his own family's dilemma. One son, wounded by a Hezballah grenade during the Lebanon war, studies Chinese at the Hebrew University and will not return to the kibbutz. Another is a budding filmmaker at Tel Aviv University. The eldest, an engineer, lives in Philadelphia. "Even if my younger sons decide to stay, what happens if they marry women who don't? To survive, we're trying to figure out how to keep them or draw others back." Ein Harod's members are talking about letting their nonkibbutznik children build homes on the kibbutz. Ein Harod also is accepting new members; several immigrant Russian-speaking families have passed the three-year membership procedure. As lucrative jobs lure members away, about half of the country's kibbutzim have abandoned the egalitarian ethic and introduced competitive (differential) salaries. Ein Harod hasn't—not yet. "I still believe in equal pay, health care, housing, education, and old age security," declares Ori. "But we're surrounded by a capitalistic world. No one can say what will be. Let's face it, the idealism, self-sacrifice spirit of *halutziut* [pioneering]—when everything from money to meals to laundry was a communal effort—is ending. Today, we're doing a lot of soul searching about what a modern kibbutz means."

The founders never imagined that their children would be running vegan restaurants and renting out halls for yoga retreats and tai chi seminars, that debt-plagued kibbutzim would sell agricultural land to developers to turn into luxury homes for Israelis seeking a suburban life. A few kibbutzim have constructed malls that are open on Sabbath, when most Jewish Israeli retailers are closed. These shopping centers, complete with Home Depots and Toys 'R' Us, draw thousands of secular shoppers. A loophole in a 1951 law made this possible. A collective organization like a kibbutz or moshav cannot permit Jews to work on Shabbat "in a workshop, factory or agricultural fields," but there is no specific reference to retail stores like Ace Hardware and Pizza Hut, which didn't exist when the law was passed. The sale of valuable kibbutz land also means that citrus groves are disappearing, and cheaper competition from countries like Spain and Greece may cause Israel's famed Jaffa oranges to become a memory.

Not all Israelis are sympathetic to kibbutz woes. Ultra-Orthodox Jews have called the mostly secular kibbutzniks "antireligious pork eaters, profaners of the Sacred Name." Some religious right-wing Israelis have branded secular kibbutzniks "Arab-loving left-wingers." Bitter that past Labor governments partially subsidized them, granting them tax breaks, lucrative contracts, and other perks, some resentful Mizrahim from development towns and city slums have called the predominantly Ashkenazi kibbutzniks "elitists with swimming pools."

With the growth of Mizrahi power and the elections of several Likud-dominated governments since 1977, kibbutzniks and other Ashkenazim have lost their once near monopoly as political, military, cultural, religious, and economic leaders. Mizrahi-Ashkenazi differences are not an issue at Ein Harod, where nearly half the members were born in Iran, Iraq, Morocco, and Algeria. The critical problems are finding innovative ways to keep kibbutzim from closing, says Ori, who is studying the success of Kibbutz Shefayim, near Tel Aviv. Its members have built a popular water park and thriving shopping center. He likes the fact that most of the youth stay on the kibbutz, even though few get callused hands; only forty of the five hundred members work in the fields or dairies. "Working the land is losing its appeal," admits Ori. Once ideologically taboo, most kibbutzim hire outside labor; about three quarters of kibbutz agricultural workers are from Thailand or China. Not on Ein Harod. The only hired employees are forty Muslim and Christian Arabs from neighboring villages and Nazareth who for years have been working alongside kibbutzniks in the factories.

The Arab-Jewish bloodshed that raged in the area from 1936 to 1948 was a distant memory until Arab Israeli riots broke out nearby in September 2000, during the first week of the intifada. Ori insists that despite the intifada, Jewish friendships with local Arab Israelis continue. "People are surprised that we've hired even more Arabs. Why not? We still go to each other's births and weddings and funerals. Arabs and Jews who are not fundamentalists are good friends. Today, two Arab friends, an engineer and a contractor, were at my house and we discussed politics. I have lunch with friends in Nazareth [the largest Arab town in Israel, which is thirty minutes by bus]. Tensions are high, of course. I don't expect them to think the way I think. We're all humans, all hoping for other days. After the night comes the sun."

———————

Another different and significant group of Ashkenazim came to Israel after World War II carrying with them a heavy burden of painful memories. The children of these Holocaust survivors believe that the systematic destruction of European Jews, almost all Ashkenazim, is an unfathomable piece of Jewish history that continues to shape Israeli identity and feed old insecurities. "These days, when Mom turns on the TV and sees Jewish schools and synagogues burning in Europe, swastikas in cemeteries, and people shouting 'Jews to the gas chambers!' she bolts from the living room. She says it's the worst anti-Semitism since World War II and she doesn't want to remember," confides Gil Nevo, a thirty-three-year-old lawyer who grew up in Jerusalem, "a place where everyone remembers he's forgotten something, but doesn't remember what it is," as poet Yehuda Amichai once wrote. "When I was a kid, I asked her to help me with my 'roots' project. Do you know what she told me? 'It'll be fun to create a family tree. Use your imagination.' So, we invented relatives' names and professions and made up amazing stories." For years Haya, Gil's mother, always evaded questions. It wasn't until his older brother bought plane tickets to France for the whole family that she agreed to show her real roots. A few months before this intifada broke out, her four children rented a van and traveled through Haya's past, growing up on a family farm near Avignon in southern France.

Running along a promenade overlooking Jerusalem's Old City, the Mount of Olives, and the Garden of Gethsemane, Haya Nevo stops a moment to give her golden retriever some water. Impulsively she sets off into a meadow to pick sage and rosemary. "We actually found the stone house where I grew up. It was in ruins. We lived there until a neighbor turned my parents over to the Gestapo." French Resistance fighters hid her and her brother in the Alps. A French widow "adopted" Haya, giving her a necklace with a crucifix and a new Christian identity. "To this day," Haya recalls, "when I see one of those tourist manger scenes with baby Jesus, it looks strangely familiar." Her grandmother hid in Paris until the Nazis arrested her. Luckily, the war ended before she could be shipped to a death camp. Haya's parents weren't so lucky.

With the help of a Jewish relief agency, Haya's grandmother tracked down the two orphans. Her brother was in a displaced persons camp. "The world we knew had vanished," says Haya. Her grandmother wanted to leave the European graveyard and start a new life in Palestine but was forbidden from doing so by the British Mandate authorities. As Princeton historian Bernard Lewis writes, "In the 1930s, Nazi Germany's policies were the main cause of Jewish emigration to Palestine, then a British mandate, and the consequent reinforcement of the Jewish community there. The Nazis not only permitted this migration; they facilitated it until the outbreak of the war, whereas the British, in the somewhat forlorn hope of winning Arab goodwill, imposed and enforced restrictions. Nevertheless, the Palestinian leadership of the time, and many other Arab leaders, supported the Germans, who sent the Jews to Palestine, rather than the British, who tried to keep them out." Even so, since 1940, Jews had been running the British blockade, mostly by sea. In July 1947, the *Exodus,* a dilapidated steamboat with forty-five hundred refugees from DP camps on the island of Cyprus, including pregnant women and hundreds of infants, set sail for Palestine. As it neared the shores, four Royal Navy destroyers surrounded it. One rammed the hull and sailors machine-gunned it and threw grenades. When sailors boarded, passengers fought back with potatoes and cans of corned beef and bare fists. The sailors opened fire and clubbed women and children. In the battle, which lasted over two hours, four Jews died, including a day-old baby; nearly two hundred Jews were injured. Under guard, as the battered *Exodus* limped into Haifa, Jews packed onto the upper deck and sang "Hatikvah," the Hebrew hymn of hope. The would-be immigrants, who had survived the greatest genocide in recorded history, spent only minutes on the soil of the Holy Land. The British put these Jewish "hooligans" on three transport ships and deported them to the soil they hated: Germany. Once again, these Jews were fenced into camps (this time, British-controlled DP camps). The tragic odyssey of the *Exodus*—a huge public relations coup for the Zionists and a disaster for the British—helped persuade the world that Jews needed their own state.

On November 29, 1947, the UN General Assembly voted to partition Palestine into two states, one Jewish, the other Arab. The country was at the height of a bloody war when Prime Minister Ben-Gurion proclaimed the State of Israel on May 14, 1948. The next day, after British troops completed their departure, Egyptian planes bombed Tel Aviv and the Egyptian, Jordanian, Syrian, Iraqi, and Lebanese armies invaded. The war continued another six months. Six thousand died (in today's terms, the equivalent of the United States losing 2.5 million people).

Soon after the fighting ended, in February 1949, Haya, her brother, and grandmother left Marseilles in a boat crammed with more than a thousand survivors. "We slept in steerage," recalls Haya. "My brother and I played with the other kids. I'll never forget seeing grown-ups hide bread under their mattresses." The boat docked in Haifa, near the rotting hulk of the *Exodus*. Bewildered Europeans carrying battered suitcases, bundles, and babies disembarked into a country experiencing simultaneous death and birth pangs. Israel was in mourning for the war dead. Tens of thousands of demobilized soldiers were wounded, jobless, and homeless and there were severe food shortages. "Veteran" Israelis, former immigrants themselves, had to cope with a tidal wave of disoriented immigrants from more than seventy different countries. By the end of the year that Haya arrived, one out of three Israelis was a newcomer. Polish-born Ben-Gurion gave a pep talk to members of Israel's new governing body, the Knesset, 70 percent of whom were born in Eastern Europe: "To the best of my knowledge, there were neither houses nor jobs awaiting the six hundred thousand Children of Israel when they started the Exodus from Egypt, yet Moses did not hesitate a moment and delivered them from there."

Haya's first home was an abandoned British military camp in Haifa.

Then the three were moved to another camp jammed with thousands of refugee Jews. All over the country were hastily built *ma'abarot,* refugee shanty towns of tents or shacks with no running water, no electricity, no privacy. "Everything was rationed. We had coupon books, one egg a week, long lines," Haya continues. "I heard Boma [her grandmother's nickname] say that being in Israel made her feel that the entire world is not evil. That Israel gave Jews the strength to return to life after the Holocaust." Thousands of children were orphans like Haya who never learned what happened to their parents. Some didn't even know their own names or ages. Others had been in concentration camps and seen their parents shot or beaten. "Boma told me about one mother who still thought Nazis were after her. So she dyed her daughter's hair blonde so she could 'pass' as Aryan. Almost every night, we would hear people screaming in their sleep. The Holocaust was possible because Jews had no country of our own."

Before long they were moved to another immigrant camp, this time in Netanya, at the time a small town surrounded by orange groves, only seven miles from what was then the Jordanian border. They shared a tent with a French family, then were shifted to a wood shack with three other families, two Polish and one Italian. The European Jews didn't see themselves as an ethnic group, nor did they call themselves Ashkenazim; they were Belgians, Lithuanians, Hungarians, and Romanians, sometimes telling biting jokes about one another. "And there we were discovering that Jews weren't one people reunited in the Promised Land," Haya says a bit sarcastically. "Other neighbors wore North African robes, flowered kerchiefs, and spoke Arabic. Even among the Mizrahim there were tensions—there were Moroccans not liking Iraqis and Tunisians not liking Syrians. Yet, looking back, we were all refugees, victims of racism. The kids played together fine, we didn't see any differences, but adults pointed them out. When I was older, Boma saw me with a dark-skinned boy and said, 'Why are you dating a *schwarz* [Yiddish for "black"]?' He wasn't even Mizrahi, he was Polish. I ignored her. And so did my brother." (An astrophysicist at the Hebrew University, Haya's brother is married to a Yemenite Jew.)

At age twelve, Haya and her family moved into a small house in Netanya. At her school, which had many Mizrahim, Haya discovered another rift. "A few of the Ashkenazi Sabras looked down on us immigrant kids as foreigners. They laughed at my Hebrew accent and the way I was dressed. My grandmother wanted me to wear a dress and a hat, fine for Paris, not for Netanya. When I put on shorts and sandals and spoke better Hebrew, slowly I was accepted." To leave behind their past, many immigrants Hebraized their names. In Hebrew, Haya's name means "life." It used to be Claire. Her brother Issie became Yitzhak, "he who laughs." Haya hardly ever remembers seeing her grandmother laughing. "Until the end of her days she talked about my mother, her husband, all the family she lost. The only time she seemed happy was when she played *Carmen* on the phonograph. She played it over and over. Her friends were always melancholy too. The purple numbers tattooed on their arms were always there, a constant reminder why."

Though she has managed to transcend it, Haya Nevo is part of the generation of Ashkenazi immigrants whose worldview is dominated by the Holocaust, with the destruction of European Jewry. Earlier Ashkenazim arrived in Turkish Palestine carrying memories of pogroms in Odessa or Kishinev. Israel's great demographic transition since her arrival in 1949 has been a shift of focus to another group of diaspora Jews whose historical experience was fundamentally different: the Mizrahim.

6

The Mizrahim

The Other Israelis

❧ By the waters of Babylon there we sat and wept as we thought of Zion. —Psalm 137

❧ In Iraq we didn't know there were Ashkenazi Jews and Mizrahi Jews. We felt an innocent kinship with all Jews of the world. I was educated as an Iraqi Arab Jewish boy, just as a boy in Umm-al Fahm [Israel's largest all-Muslim town] is brought up as an Israeli Arab Muslim. . . . When I met with some Jewish and Palestinian intellectuals in Spain, the Palestinians described in touching words their longing for the land from which they had fled or were expelled. When it was my turn, I said that like them, I too am homesick, but in proud Israel, it is not proper for a Jew to miss his place of origin, not to mention that the ruling power in Baghdad was thirsty for my blood. —Sami Michael, one of Israel's leading novelists, who fled Baghdad in 1948

"When I was five, my aunt caught me sitting in an aluminum basin splashing myself with bleach. Terrified, she asked what was going on. I explained that I wanted to be white." Naomi Kehati, a clinical psychologist, grew up in a poor neighborhood in Tel Aviv. She was born in 1955 in a nearby immigrant tent camp where her parents lived after leaving Yemen in 1949. "My father was fifteen, my mother was twelve and already divorced from her uncle. My mother was illiterate. She cleaned houses and brought us used clothing from her employers." Naomi's deeply religious father had two jobs: as a scribe of holy Hebrew texts and as the janitor who swept the floors of her elementary school.

An outstanding student, Naomi was accepted at an academic high school in an Ashkenazi neighborhood in north Tel Aviv. "There was only one other Yemenite in my school," she recalls. "The transition was like an earthquake. I didn't fit in. I felt inadequate and lonely. The other students had well-developed political ideas and even argued with the teachers. When I went to their homes I was shocked. Only two children in a house and they had their own bedrooms. Books were everywhere. Their parents were the intellectuals of Israeli society. Then, one day, a boy in my class who had a crush on me suddenly appeared at our tiny house because we didn't have a phone. He saw the peeling paint and wall-to-wall people. My parents were eating with their hands, speaking Yemeni Arabic, and looking unkempt. I nearly died of shame. It was as if someone entered my intestine and saw the insides. I knew I hadn't done anything wrong, but I could tell in his eyes what he thought of our 'backwardness.' He had seen the 'Other Israel,' my Israel.

"Our schoolbooks were written from an Ashkenazi perspective. At home, nothing reflected what I had learned at school. We studied about the Jews of Europe, about the pogroms in Russia. The trauma of Holocaust overshadowed everything. I had terrible dreams about children in hiding, children in the camps. I was losing myself in their world. I learned about the heroic pioneers, all Ashkenazim, who established a new state and the kibbutzim, but not the stories of the other half of our people— people like me, the poor Mizrahim, the Arab Jews. I wanted to belong, but my story was not in the books. Our culture didn't seem to count."

The Jewish community of Yemen prides itself on origins as far back as biblical times, though their earliest records are "only" about seventeen hundred years old. When Yemen adopted Islam in the seventh century, Jews became second-class citizens, forbidden, for example, to ride a donkey lest they be higher than a Muslim pedestrian. Jews were forced by law to clean public latrines, and Jewish orphans were forcibly converted to Islam. With the birth of Israel, almost all sixty thousand Jews of Yemen trekked for weeks to an airstrip in the British protectorate of Aden. Thousands, like Naomi's grandfather, died en route. The survivors, more than fifty thousand, were flown to Israel in Operation Magic Carpet, more than four hundred flights on war surplus C-47s.

The story of Mizrahi (which means "east" in Hebrew) Jews is a seldom told part of modern Jewish history. With the rise of Arab and Islamic nationalism in the 1940s, anti-Jewish violence swept through parts of the Middle East and North Africa, where Jews had lived with alternating periods of peace and persecution for more than twenty centuries. Synagogues, homes, shops, and schools were burned or looted, Jewish property confiscated. Thousands of Jews were arrested and killed. From 1948 through the 1960s, 870,000 Mizrahi Jews fled Yemen, Iraq, Egypt, Syria, Lebanon, Morocco, Algeria, Tunisia, Libya, Iran, and Afghanistan; more than six hundred thousand refugees came to Israel. Some left huts, others left villas. Silversmiths left shops in Casablanca; doctors left hospitals in Damascus; entrepreneurs closed movie theaters in Cairo. Writers, scholars, political and judicial leaders also gave up careers. But whatever their circumstances in the indigenous Jewish communities they left behind—many of which predate by more than a thousand years the seventh-century C.E. Arab Muslim conquest—most arrived in Israel destitute. (Today, small Jewish communities remain in Iran, Morocco, Tunisia, Egypt, Iraq, and Lebanon).

By 1951, refugees in transit camps were overwhelmingly from the Middle East and North Africa. Most were religious and rarely had known secular Ashkenazim, especially shameless women who had naked legs and wore sleeveless dresses, who worked alongside men, even bossed them. They had crazy socialist ideas and ate unappetizing foods like schnitzel and black Russian bread. They had no taste for couscous or kubeh. Their accents didn't even sound like "real" Hebrew and their prayers and melodies sounded harsh and foreign. They didn't eat corn or rice on Passover. Even worse, most of these Ashkenazim did not observe the Sabbath.

Similarly, few Ashkenazim had ever met a Mizrahi Jew. Suddenly, here were Jews who resembled Arabs and shared their tastes in food and music. How could they listen to the Egyptian singer Umm Kulthum and not Mozart? There were cross-culturally insensitive officials who sought to transform them into models of themselves: secular, socialist Ashkenazi Israelis. Some adults were stripped of unpronounceable Arab and Persian names and given Hebrew names. To look more like secular Ashkenazim, some Yemenite children had their side locks cut off. Whether they spoke Kurdish or Farsi or Arabic, what many Mizrahi newcomers shared was being stereotyped and misunderstood. How could they be Jews if they didn't speak Yiddish, Golda Meir wondered in 1964. Like her, many "veteran" Israelis knew little about the newcomers' rich, varied cultures and religious traditions. According to author Tom Segev, "In the fifties, some Hebrew University professors were so worried about the 'ethnic problem,' they argued that the only way to rescue these Arab Jews from 'backwardness' was with a strong infusion of European cultural values."

"It was degrading for my family," recalls Sammy Smooha, an urbane, world-renowned sociologist at the University of Haifa, who spent his boyhood in a Jerusalem shantytown camp. "We were told not to speak Arabic, but we didn't know Hebrew. Everything was strange. My father went from being a railroad official in Baghdad to an unskilled nobody. We suffered a terrible loss of identity. Looking back, I'd call it cultural repression. Behind their lofty ideals of 'one people,' they were acting superior, paternalistic." The Smooha family was part of the oldest Jewish community in the world outside of Israel itself. Iraq, the Babylon of the Bible and the Talmud, was the Jews' first land of exile, after the destruction of the First Temple in 586 B.C.E. As in many Islamic countries, in Iraq Jews had held key roles in public and cultural life. There was a Jewish finance minister and Jewish deputy president of the Supreme Court until the pogrom of 1941, instigated by pro-Nazi Iraqis, in which 137 Jews were killed, hundreds injured, and thousands of homes and shops destroyed. Then, with the establishment of Israel, Zionism became a capital crime. In Baghdad, which was nearly a quarter Jewish, cheering crowds gathered to see Jews hanged in the central square. The Iraqi government nationalized Jewish property and jailed and killed hundreds of Jews.

Nearly all of Iraq's 150,000 Jews had escaped to Israel by 1951. Unlike many other Mizrahi Jews, refugees from Iraq soon made their way out of transit camps to Tel Aviv and other desirable towns in central Israel. "The junior high history textbooks used between 1948 until 1967 described Mizrahim as apathetic, primitive, and backward people who did not like to work," continues Professor Smooha, who is an expert on Israeli pluralism. The irony is that Mizrahi Jews largely were urban, from cities such as Baghdad, Damascus, Alexandria, Casablanca, Beirut, and Tehran, more sophisticated than desolate Eastern European *shtetls,* Yiddish for villages.

Speak to most any Jew from Iraq to Syria to Yemen and you will hear that Mizrahim are the oldest Jews of the diaspora, that they had established large and important communities a thousand years before the great Islamic conquest of the seventh century, before most of what today are called the Arab countries had any Arabs.

Jews have lived throughout the Fertile Crescent and Asia Minor for nearly three thousand years, but their spread was accelerated by the destruction of the first Jewish Temple in Jerusalem in 586 B.C.E. by the armies of Babylonia. The resulting diaspora created two spiritual centers for Judaism, an Aramaic-speaking one remaining in what is now Iraq and established during the Babylonian Captivity, and the other, after Persian King Cyrus the Great permitted Jews to return to the Mediterranean littoral, in Palestine. From both locations they established communities throughout the Middle East, including Arabia.

The Jews of Arabia exercised a great deal of economic power, engaging in viniculture, agriculture, and commerce in some key oases of the Hijaz, the Arabian Peninsula. Their ancient South Yemenite center ran the spice trade; stories of their legendary warrior king, Dhu Nuwas, a convert to Judaism in 520, are still part of Arabian oral tradition. Many pagan tribes in what is now Medina owed allegiance to the prosperous Jewish tribes of the area. The emergence of the Prophet Muhammad in 610 from the great tribe of Quraish in Mecca seemed to augur well for the Jews of Arabia. Muhammad, impressed with their biblical tradition, invited them to join his new community. Much of what they heard from him—compulsory fasts, almsgiving, praying in the direction of Jerusalem, strong principles of justice, and the absolute indivisibility and invisibility of God—was familiar. But his versions of biblical accounts seemed garbled to them. Jews refused to accept him as the last of the prophets sent by God. According to Jewish tradition, prophecy ceased centuries prior to Muhammad. Jews were castigated for their refusal to join Islam, while at the same time, both Judaism and Christianity were recognized as kindred, if inferior, faiths. As Muhammad built his new faith in the fledgling Muslim community of Medina, where he fled in 622, he produced increasingly heated polemics against the Jews. When the Jews rejected him, Muhammad subjugated some Jewish tribes and expelled others from Arabia. In some tribes all males were decapitated. The infidels who survived were required to submit to Muslim authority and pay tribute. In the Koran, Jews are vilified as corrupters and perverters of Scripture (Sura 4:44) and cursed by Allah for their "disbelief."

Islam's relative tolerance or intolerance of Jews and Christians fluctuated over the centuries and from place to place. The Prophet recognized the validity of both religions because they possessed written revelations, but classical Islamic legal theory holds that the possessors of Scripture should be opposed until they surrendered. In return for their adherence to special discriminatory regulation, such as taxes, they were offered protection (hence the term *dhimmis,* "protected peoples"). In the House of Islam, there was a niche for the so-called protected people of the Book, the Christians and Jews whose Scriptures and monotheism entitled them to some place in the world of Islam. Most of the Jews who occupied that place were Mizrahim.

Until the eleventh century, in fact, most of the world's Jews were Mizrahim. After that, Sephardim (from S'farad, Hebrew for Spain, where Jews first took up residence before the first century B.C.E.) took over as the dominant leaders of Jewry. (The word Sephardim often is inaccurately used to include Mizrahi Jews from North Africa and the Middle East who had no origins in the Iberian Peninsula.) The Sephardi Jews of Spain were Europe's largest Jewish community and its most accomplished, producing physicians, poets, mystics, and philosophers from Judah HaLevi to Solomon Ibn Gabriol. Its most famous son is probably the twelfth-century philosopher, physician, and jurist Moshe ben Maimon, better known to the West as Moses Maimonides, who grew up in Córdoba, at the time the most sophisticated city in the Islamic world. He lived briefly in Palestine and then settled near Cairo, where he was physician to the sultan's court and head of the Egyptian Jewish community.

The Inquisition, the expulsion of the Jews from Spain that started with the Castilian *reconquista* in 1492, was an epoch-making event in Jewish history. Sephardi Jews fled the Iberian Peninsula and scattered throughout the Mediterranean and Europe to Palestine, Greece, Turkey, Bulgaria, Yugoslavia, Italy, the Netherlands, and the New World (Columbus's crews included many secret Sephardi Jews). It was outside the Christian world, in the Ottoman Empire, that these Spanish and Portuguese exiles were most welcome. A number of Israeli Sephardim whose families arrived in Palestine after the expulsion today hold influential positions in Israeli society. They often distance themselves from Israeli Mizrahim, stressing their own cultural and linguistic heritage. Many older Sephardim still speak Ladino, the medieval Spanish spoken by the generation of the expulsion. In this chapter, and in Israel today, Mizrahi refers to descendants of Jews who left Islamic lands (though Turkish Jews are not included because most are Sephardim).

The economic and political decline of the Ottoman Empire was the turning point in the history of ethnic diversity within world Jewry. By the sixteenth century, Mizrahi and Sephardi Jews lost their cultural dominance and numerical majority to the Ashkenazim of Eastern Europe. By the end of the nineteenth century, Mizrahim made up only one tenth of the world's 10.5 million Jews, according to Sammy Smooha. At the outbreak of World War II, many of the world's Ashkenazim either had forgotten about the Mizrahim and Sephardim or considered them insignificant. The Holocaust forever changed Jewish demographics. Though Greece's Sephardi Jewish community was almost completely wiped out during the Holocaust and Sephardi Jews from Yugoslavia, Bulgaria, Romania, Italy, Libya, and Turkey also perished in the camps, nearly all of the 6 million murdered Jews were Ashkenazim.

When Mizrahim began arriving en masse in the 1950s, Ashkenazim, who then constituted more than 80 percent of Israeli Jews, were deeply entrenched in every aspect of political, cultural, and religious life. By the 1960s, however, the great Mizrahi migration had turned Israeli life upside down. The country now had a different complexion: 60 percent of Israelis were Mizrahim, mostly from North Africa. The new state desperately needed agricultural and factory workers and soldiers. Although few Mizrahim knew much about planting grapefruit or cucumbers, many were sent to work in kibbutz fields. Moroccans, Tunisians, Iraqis, and Yemenites started two hundred moshavim that helped protect dangerous border areas. Other Mizrahi extended families, accustomed to living in close-knit communities, were split up and sent to far-flung "development" towns in the Galilee, the Jordan Valley, or the arid Negev, where many got jobs in construction or textiles, food, and other low-tech factories. Israel's poor development towns and neglected urban areas are now home to their children and grandchildren—Israel's lower class.

———————

The grainy wind blowing in from the Negev Desert doesn't seem to bother the eleven-year-old boys in green shorts and bright yellow shirts heading to the soccer fields of Dalet, the poorest neighborhood in Beersheva. These boys live in cheerless concrete housing projects, which the government quickly built in the early 1960s when their families flooded in from North Africa. They're crowded: about twelve hundred people live in one apartment building, about the same number of people living on Kibbutz Ein Harod.

"*Ahlan, ahi* [Yo, Bro]," their coach greets them in Mizrahi Arabic slang. "It's kickoff time." Meir Bouskila, a husky man in blue jeans and T-shirt, is the Pied Piper of Dalet. For the past twenty years, this hyperkinetic man with smiling brown eyes has coached more than two thousand young Mizrahi soccer players, keeping them off the streets and out of gangs. Some parents stand on the sidelines rooting for their sons. "If it weren't for Meir, I'd have ended up in big trouble," says Itzak, a Tunisian-born truck driver who once played on his team. "My son looks up to him. Meir gives him discipline and yells at him if he doesn't do his homework." He also helps raise money for the kids' uniforms and textbooks. (Israeli schools require parents to buy their children's textbooks, a hardship for many Mizrahi families, who average about six children.) The boys need these donations. Half of Dalet's residents earn less than the minimum wage. Some even scrounge for bruised fruit and vegetables when the neighborhood markets close. Men and women with valid gun permits now easily find extra jobs as security guards.

"God gives me strength to help others," says Meir, who wears the knitted kippa of a religious Jew. He worries about his soccer players' future in this rough neighborhood plagued with drugs and joblessness, a world little known to Israel's more affluent Ashkenazim. Prime Minister David Ben-Gurion dreamed of reclaiming the Negev and turning it into one of the most vibrant, productive regions of Israel. Beersheva, the capital of the Negev, is home to a modern research hospital, two malls, and a few high-tech companies as well as the country's fastest growing university, named after Ben-Gurion. It's also home to some of Israel's most disadvantaged citizens. A former construction worker, Meir declares, "I'm not bitter. I'm a builder."

That's why he welcomes onto his teams children from Ethiopia and the former Soviet Union who live in a nearby new immigrants' absorption center. "I don't want these kids to feel like outsiders, like I did when we came," he says, remembering the six years his family spent living in a transit camp outside Beersheva. "Who cares if they barely speak Hebrew, as long as they want to play?" When a boy from Uzbekistan kicks a goal, his teammates cheer. "Hear that? That's the sound of Israeli children— Mizrahi, Ethiopian, Bedouin, and Russian. I want them all to feel 'blue and white.' I don't want any of my soccer players to feel left out of the game."

Meir and his parents emigrated from Morocco in 1963. By the next year, there were nearly three hundred thousand Moroccans, who made up Israel's largest single Jewish community until the former Soviets arrived during the 1990s. The more secular, urban, and educated Jews of Morocco, Tunisia, and Algeria tended to emigrate to France or Canada. The poorest and least educated came to Israel and had difficulties learning how to fight for their rights in the chaotic Israeli bureaucracy. "It took time, but we're getting our voice. When we face Arab threats, like now, everyone swallows their complaints," says Meir, a former combat medic. "It's sad that we're at our best when we're fighting. We need peace so the government can put its attention and money on cleaning up our problems right here." Nevertheless, he brags that his eldest son is rising quickly as a career army officer.

Mizrahim have risen to national prominence, especially in the military and politics, where educational qualifications and affluence are not entry requirements. Defense Minister Shaul Mofaz is Iranian-born. Foreign Minister Sivan Shalom left Tunisia as an infant. Former Foreign Ministers David Levy and Shlomo Ben-Ami and Interior Minister Eli Ishai are Moroccan-born, and former Defense Minister Yitzhak Mordechai is an Iraqi-born Kurdish Jew. In 2002, Iraqi-born Defense Minister General Benjamin Ben-Eliazar became the first Mizrahi elected to lead the Labor Party, though he was soon replaced by Amram Mitzna, mayor of Haifa. Meir considers Moshe Katsav, Israel's first Mizrahi president, a man with the common touch. "His story is ours." Katsav arrived from Iran at age six and grew up in a transit camp. The son of a meat plant worker, he appealed to the alienated have-nots of his poor Mizrahi development town, Kiryat Malachi. At age twenty-four, he was elected Israel's youngest mayor and then went on to join the Knesset. In 2000, when Likud selected him as their candidate for Israel's president, he declared: "I am not part of the aristocracy. I am not a nobleman." Katsav's surprise victory against the Labor Party candidate, Nobel prize winner Shimon Peres, the embodiment of the Ashkenazi elite, shocked the nation and symbolized a generational and ethnic shift in Israeli society. In his inaugural speech, President Katsav addressed Ethiopian immigrant children and all children of Israel's socioeconomic and geographic periphery with simple, powerful words of hope: "If I could do it, so can you." Meir says his soccer players identify with this unpretentious president with a kippa and Mizrahi Hebrew pronunciation. "They like seeing someone like him living in that huge President's House."

This full-time coach with a part-time salary lives near the soccer fields in a modest three-room house he built on HaTalmud Street, which he says is a palace compared to the wooden hut where he and his wife raised four children. Before entering, Meir reverently touches the silver mezuzah to the right of the door. Pungent smells of garlic and mint waft from the kitchen, where his wife is making Moroccan couscous and spicy fish with their daughter Dana, who has been looking for a job since finishing army service. They greet each other in a mix of Hebrew and Judeo-Moroccan (a distinct Arabic dialect). "Listen to this," prompts twenty-one-year-old Dana, as the ornate textured melodies of singer Zehava Ben fill the house. Palestinians, Jordanians, and Egyptians once packed concerts to hear this visiting Israeli singer belt out songs in Arabic and Hebrew. "She's our neighbor, her parents also are from Marrakesh. A Moroccan who made it. People used to call her the bridge for peace, but that was a billion years ago, when we thought peace was possible," says Dana. Ben also was a key figure in bringing Mizrahi music to the top of the Israeli charts. "Ashkenazim love our music. They used to call it 'cheap central bus station cassette music,' and that made me angry. Now it's all over the radio. On TV shows, it's so funny when Ashkenazim try to sound Mizrahi. My [Ashkenazi] friends wear *hamsas* [a hand-shaped Middle Eastern amulet meant to ward off the evil eye]. They hang them on their car mirrors for good luck. It's not just our food and music anymore; they've finally discovered other parts of our culture are cool."

There are framed photos of bearded Jewish Moroccan holy men like Abu Hasiera and Babi Sala on the dining room walls. "I believe in miracles," says Meir, who, like most Mizrahim, calls himself a "traditional" Jew. He also has a photo of Baghdad-born Rabbi Yitzhak Kadouri, the celebrated centenarian kabbalist. During elections, activists from the ultra-Orthodox Shas Party distributed hundreds of thousands of "magical" amulets blessed by Kadouri to attract Mizrahi supporters; vote Shas and you'll be blessed. Then in the 2003 elections Kadouri broke with Shas. Shas went from second- to third-largest party and, in an anti-ultra-Orthodox backlash, was excluded from the Sharon government. Unemployment and poverty fueled the popularity of Shas, Israel's most successful ethnic-based party, and with a surfeit of both, Dalet is an especially strong Shas stronghold. Bearded ultra-Orthodox men in black kippot speaking Mizrahi street talk go door to door enticing their neighbors to use its network of day care centers, kindergartens, schools, and yeshivas with free meals and free transportation. Formed in 1984, Shas is both an ethnic protest movement and a mainstream religious political party that grew with the rise of high-tech industry. It offers a mix of traditional Mizrahi values and a sense of belonging as an antidote to a deep sense of government neglect and social injustice. "They're everywhere, in all the development towns," says Meir, a devout Likud supporter and critic of Shas. But whether they support Shas or the Likud, many Mizrahim grew up despising the Ashkenazi-dominated Labor Party. "A lot of Mizrahim think of Labor as lefties, the antireligious elite who look down on people like us. They got here first and got the comfortable positions, but didn't do enough to help the weak," explains Meir. Although Shas leaders are ultra-Orthodox, most of their supporters are traditional, non-Orthodox Mizrahim, who, like Meir, practice a lenient form of Judaism. To them, belonging to Shas is a symbol of Mizrahi pride, a reminder of the Golden Age when their culture was exalted and they produced rabbis rather than most of Israel's Jewish criminals. When their leaders extol Maimonides as one of the greatest Jewish scholars, they are sending a message to Ashkenazim: we are not inferior.

Meir is upset that some of his players attend ultra-Orthodox Shas schools, a cloistered world of religious studies; hardly any arithmetic, science, history, or geography is taught. "How much Torah can they learn? You can't make these kids pray so much. My God is flexible and tolerant.

That means after I go to Sabbath services, I coach soccer. The kids need it, it boosts their self-image. They have goals and I've seen them achieve them. We Israelis fight well together, so why separate ourselves and fight each other? Why keep pushing the differences? We're all Israelis."

———————————

The Negev town of Kiryat Gat is due north of Beersheva, a ten-minute drive from the area where it is said David slew the Philistine Goliath. At a sleepy café near the bus station, chain-smoking men play backgammon and listen to the rich rhythms of North African Andalusian music. This is the twenty-eighth of the month, the day a third of the residents of this development town receive unemployment and welfare benefits from National Insurance. It's also the day the lines at the Mifal Hapayis lottery booth are the longest. "If I get a winning ticket, I'll leave," a young man says grimly, explaining that he lost his job making Sabbath and Hanukkah candles. He is a semiskilled worker in an increasingly digital country.

About a third of Kiryat Gat's residents are from the former Soviet Union. Like all new immigrants, they receive government grants and housing subsidies. "I hate the Russians, they get everything handed to them," Danny, an outspoken house painter, says contemptuously. "My parents got nothing when they were refugees [from Tripoli, Libya]. I'm just back from reserve duty. How do you think I feel seeing these Russians only here a few months and with money to buy the biggest apartment in my building? And a car tax-free. They're retired and we pay their pensions. We still rent and my wife takes the bus. The other day I yelled at their son. Do you know what he called me? An Arab."

In "mixed" towns like Beersheva and Kiryat Gat, election campaigns have become ethnic battles between Russian and Mizrahi candidates. Upset about losing their demographic and political clout, some Mizrahim derisively call the Russian speakers "turpentine" because they dilute Israel's "blackness" (i.e., the power of darker-skinned Mizrahim). Still, there are many Mizrahi Jews who are not bitter about the Russian-speaking immigrants. "I remember what it was like to be in their shoes. I'm better off, so why shouldn't I help them?" states a taxi driver, a Kurdish Jew who was born in Iraq. He rents his furnished four-bedroom apartment to two families from Ukraine. The fathers are security guards.

"They're educated, so I say, the faster they become Israelis, the better for Israel."

About three times more Mizrahim than Ashkenazim are unemployed, and Kiryat Gat has one of Israel's highest unemployment rates. The town's former main employer, Polgat Textiles, has closed two of its three factories. As in many development towns, hundreds of thousands of Mizrahim who operate looms, pack food, or process sugar are being thrown out of work. Manufacturing is being sent to countries like Turkey and Egypt and Jordan, where labor is cheaper. Other factories are hiring semilegal workers from countries ranging from Romania to Ghana, who earn even less than Israel's mostly Mizrahi blue-collar workers. Near some forlorn warehouses is Shalon Chemical Industries, where, before the Iraq War, employees were working around the clock producing NBC: nuclear, biological, and chemical "protective systems." Despite threats from Lebanon, Syria, and Iran, the workers making gas masks, decontamination powder, civilian respirators, and protective hoods now fear for their jobs.

Past some empty lots in the industrial zone, a concrete wall encloses another world—a silicon world. Intel, the world's largest computer chip maker, is inside. This enormous complex, set on seventy-five acres of desert, is Israel's biggest and most expensive factory. Inside its pink stone buildings with emerald windows tiny processors are creating a revolution. Intel Kiryat Gat has been producing more than $1 billion worth of the world's thinnest microchips yearly since it opened in 1999. In the lobby, a security guard sits near a glass display case with two ancient earthenware vases that construction workers uncovered. Appropriately enough, these 4,500-year-old vases were filled with sand—the raw material of Intel's silicon wafers.

The halls are filled with workers, most wearing the same passionately informal uniform: a badge, T-shirt, and jeans. A few in shorts head for the company gym, where they bounce to blasting rock music in an aerobics class. Elsewhere, in a conference room that doubles as a synagogue and bomb shelter, engineers and systems analysts discuss sales of the Israeli-designed Centrino chip. At lunch, people leave their cubicles and computer screens and proceed to the spacious cafeteria. There is no executive dining room for Intel's three thousand workers. Strict informality and diversity are the rules set by Dov Frohman, the founder and former president of Intel Israel, who is dubbed "the Herzl of High Tech." With his white beard, faded jeans, and sandals, he resembles an aging flower child, especially when he motorcycles from his home in Jerusalem.

Diners are a cross-section of Israelis: executives and technicians and van drivers. An electrical engineer with a long ponytail is eating pasta with a bearded Orthodox man in a knit kippa. At the salad bar, two women programmers chat in Russian. But the atmosphere of equality is not quite what it seems. "It's a secure job, but we know who gets the big paychecks," a woman serving grilled meat says in a thick Mizrahi accent. She's referring to the fault line that divides Israel's old economy—and its unemployed or unskilled workforce—from the new economy, with its mostly Ashkenazi engineers and other university graduates. In the mid-1960s, socialist Israel was the second most egalitarian society in the industrialized West, just behind Sweden. In today's free market economy, the disparity between the haves and have-nots is glaring. "Here we live in an air-conditioned world that is more Silicon Valley than the Middle East," says a twenty-four-year-old electrical engineer, one of the Jewish "gauchos" who emigrated from Buenos Aires. When he goes home to his trendy Tel Aviv neighborhood, he's in another Israel.

Although Intel gives employees generous cash incentives to relocate to Kiryat Gat, few of the technical staff take them. Of the two thousand workers employed directly by Intel and another two thousand working in jobs from catering to construction, only about six hundred actually live in Kiryat Gat, complains the deputy mayor. "The people who drive here from Jerusalem and Tel Aviv have the good jobs. Why would they want to live here?" grumbles a Tunisian-born security guard. "Why would they want their children to go to our schools? God forbid one of their daughters dates my son. In the army, I dated an Ashkenazi. She wanted me to tell her parents I was from Paris."

Mopping floors and working in the cafeteria are jobs mostly held by Mizrahim from Kiryat Gat and neighboring development towns. What can a huge high-tech company do to alleviate Kiryat Gat's chronically high unemployment problem, when only about two hundred of the town's fifty-five thousand residents are college graduates?

Problems start with Israel's two-tiered school system. Before 1995, no development town had an academic high school. Even today, nearly 40 percent of Mizrahi students attend trade schools, where they are poorly prepared to pass the high school matriculation exams that qualify them to go on to college or get a decent job. "Schools are failing these kids. This schooling for inequality reproduces the ethnic division, so how can we have real multiculturalism in Israel?" asks Yossi Ohana, project director for Mayanot le Haskila (Many Springs for Education). This group of Mizrahi educators work in Kiryat Gat and other development towns as well as blighted inner-city neighborhoods. They teach math and physics to disadvantaged children and train their teachers. They also counsel parents, often speaking to them in a mix of Hebrew and North African Arabic and quoting biblical passages that stress the importance of education. In the past three years, the percentage of Kiryat Gat students passing their matriculation exams has jumped from 44 to over 60 percent. "We're showing we can narrow the achievement gap. But no matter what we're doing to motivate them, we still live in an atmosphere that broadcasts that Mizrahim aren't capable. Just look at how the media covers us: ads with Mizrahi women selling detergent and Ashkenazi women selling fancy cars and laser eye surgery. Where are the TV and newspaper reporters with dark skin or Mizrahi accents? When we hear expressions like 'the neighborhoods' and 'development towns,' we know these are subtle code words for Mizrahi areas. People are careful not to use the word 'backward,' but kids are sharp. They understand expressions like 'he doesn't have our culture,' 'social problems in the development towns,' 'pockets of ethnicity,' and 'cultural poverty.' The message? The progressive Ashkenazim built this country. No wonder these kids don't have self-confidence. I can see myself in them," Yossi confides.

Yossi was six when his family left a small Berber village in southern Morocco and emigrated to Israel in 1969. "As a child I dreamed of looking like a 'real Sabra' with light skin. I was ashamed when people on the bus heard my parents talking Moroccan Arabic. Now I'm very ashamed of my shame." Sent to a vocational boarding school for mostly Mizrahi bad boys with "low intellectual capabilities," he received bad marks in math and English and thought he was stupid. "I didn't believe in myself, so I dropped out," he says. "When I was drafted, someone mistakenly wrote that I'd passed the matriculation exam for English, so I was sent to train as an intelligence officer. That's when I changed my name from Ohana to Hets to block out my Mizrahi identity. After the army, when I saw my soldiers going to university to study subjects like economics and law, I realized what education means. At twenty-four, I went back to high school." By age thirty, Yossi had his B.A. and M.A. degrees in history and political science. "My Mizrahi consciousness emerged slowly. About the time my fourth child was born, I changed my name back to Ohana. I did it even though giving my kids a Mizrahi name means they'll probably have a harder life. But I need to reclaim my Mizrahi identity. It's important that the kids I work with see that educated people also have Mizrahi names. Being Israeli does not mean being Ashkenazi. It took me a long time to learn that."

"The solution is to invest in education, show kids the job possibilities. Intel volunteers teach math, art, and technology to thousands of students and run science summer camps. We donate hundreds of computers to the schools and gave the municipal library a computerized system," reports Ahuva Marziano, a no-nonsense dynamo who runs Intel's community relations program in Kiryat Gat, which is trying to narrow the achievement gap. As a child, she immigrated to Israel from Iran with her parents. "My father is a truck driver and he pushed me to get an education." With the help of financial aid, Ahuva got an MBA from Ben-Gurion University. "Our influence will be felt in another few years. If people have the patience."

The hermetically sealed Clean Room, larger than two football fields, is the heart of Intel Kiryat Gat. It's fanatically sanitized, thousands of times cleaner than a hospital operating room, so no particle of dust can ruin the manufacture of the thin computer chips on top of silicon wafers, which are the "brains" of the world's computers. A group of wide-eyed local sixteen-year-olds and their teachers peer through a window, watching Clean Room technicians, who look like space aliens in airtight white "bunny suits," blue booties, and helmets, monitor each wafer. These mostly Mizrahi children, many of whose parents are high school dropouts, are face to face with a different Israel. "Wow! These technicians make American salaries?" asks a turned-on student, who wears his baseball cap backwards. "How do I get hired?"

"We need skilled workers," their Intel guide, the daughter of Yemenite immigrants, tells them. "If you study science and math and learn computers, your job possibilities will be exciting."

"Yeah, but exciting can't pay the rent," sniffs a girl with a nose ring.

"After my mother was fired from Polgat [the clothing factory], she couldn't get a job here." Intel has two hiring conditions that disqualify most of their parents: employees must have passed the high school matriculation exam and speak some English.

"We may not have a job for your mother," the guide says, "but maybe we'll have one for you."

7

The Russians

The New Exodus

⊘ Already not Russian, but not yet Israeli. —Actor in the bilingual Gesher Theater, composed of mostly Russian immigrants

⊘ Hebrew is the only language children teach their parents. —Israel's most famous poet, Ukrainian-born Hayim Bialik

When he was seventeen, the only Hebrew words Boris Katz knew were *shalom* and *masehot* (gas mask). That's how old he was when he, along with his parents, sister, and grandmother, escaped economic chaos in Ukraine to find a better life in Israel. Two months later, the 1991 Gulf War started. "What an introduction to Israel," says Boris. "Whenever we heard the air-raid alarms the five of us put on gas masks and huddled in the living room. We were really scared. We didn't know what was happening because the radio and TV news was only in Hebrew. We thought it was a nuclear bomb. Then one night, we heard an explosion down the street. It was an Iraqi Scud, and where was it made? In Russia!"

The burly six-footer now owns a much improved gas mask and has no shortage of news in Russian. With a flick of the remote, he and his wife can watch local Russian-language TV or cable news direct from

Moscow. He met Yonit while they were both students at a Hebrew University dorm. Their fifth-floor walkup near Tel Aviv is sparsely furnished with hand-me-downs from Boris's Israeli relatives. They entertain Russian-style with a lavish spread of calorie-laden dishes: cherry-filled blini, piroshki, and borscht crowned with sour cream. "People who waited in line for bread don't worry about calories," jokes Boris, who, with his gold earring, Palm Pilot, and Hebrew slang learned as a lieutenant in the IDF, looks and sounds like the Sabra software engineers he supervises at an Israeli cell phone company.

"At least Israelis don't cut in line because they're afraid the store will run out of food. They just cut in line because they're impatient," Yonit adds with a knowing smile. After emigrating from the Ural Mountains, she stopped using her first name, Yana, and switched to her Hebrew middle name, Yonit. In addition to studying industrial management, she works as a manicurist, painting the fingernails of a mostly Russian and Arab clientele. She'll soon quit; with a baby on the way, she doesn't want to inhale chemicals. "It's great living in a country with disposable diapers. When I went to look at cribs and baby clothes, there were so many choices. For me, the choice to make choices was difficult. We come from a place where there weren't many, where the government gave you a tiny apartment and told you what to do." Upon arrival in 1994, Yonit wandered through a twenty-four-hour supermarket staring at strange fruits called avocados and mangos. "I love the cheap vegetables. Where I grew up, they were so expensive, salads were for celebrations."

Boris and Yonit are part of the largest tidal wave of immigrants in Israeli history, one of the largest in the history of the world. After President Mikhail Gorbachev's easing of long-standing travel restrictions in 1989 and the ensuing breakup of the Soviet Union, more than one million emigrants headed for Israel. Not surprisingly, an aliyah representing some 20 percent of the entire nation has changed the face of Israel. From Upper Nazareth in the Galilee to Beersheva in the Negev, scores of shops display signs in Cyrillic script and Hebrew. Every fifth Israeli speaks Russian. One hears Russian in maternity and geriatric wards and voting booths. Russian names fill crime blotters, patient applications, and Ph.D. dissertations. More and more tombstones of soldiers, terror victims, and security guards are inscribed with Russian-sounding names. World-class athletes are winning medals for their adopted country. Talented musicians, filmmakers, and authors add to the rich mix of Israeli cultures. These newcomers have overturned Israel's delicate demographic and political balance. A massive political force, no other immigrant group has risen to power so quickly. Power brokers in the Knesset, they have held key positions in every cabinet since 1996. They're reshaping the country, making it more Ashkenazi, less religious, even more Christian.

A number of towns and neighborhoods resemble Moscow on the Mediterranean. Hundreds of nonkosher supermarkets sell pork sausages, Russian-style breads, Georgian wine, salted fish, and dozens of varieties of vodka. In restaurants and nightclubs in towns like Ashdod and Ashkelon, Russian is the national language, not Hebrew or Arabic. There are Russian-speaking psychologists, hairdressers, and hookers. For the nostalgic, travel agencies offer discount vacation tickets back to Uzbekistan and Ukraine. About three quarters of Russian Israelis watch four Russian cable TV stations with steaming soap operas, soccer matches, and much more news about the Kremlin than the Knesset. "When I came, we had one weekly Russian newspaper," recalls Boris. In his neighborhood kiosk vendors sell dozens of local Russian-language newspapers and magazines, including Russian *Vogue, Playboy,* and *Penthouse.* Israel's most avid readers, they patronize about four hundred Russian-language bookstores, some of which are popular hangouts for poetry readings.

The generic label "Russian" is grossly inaccurate. The majority come from the former European republics, especially Ukraine, Russia, and Belarus; others, the Central Asian states of the former Soviet Union. Immigrants range from a semiliterate airport porter from Georgia to an elegant divorcée from Russia's cultural capital, St. Petersburg, a stately city of palaces and museums. A Haifa bookstore cashier recalls that when she lived in St. Petersburg, she used to call Muscovites unsophisticated. "Here in Israel, I see all these 'blacks,' who barely speak Russian," she says scathingly, referring to darker-skinned Caucasian "Mountain Jews." They and other non-Ashkenazi Jews from Islamic Central Asian republics such as Uzbekistan, Azerbaijan, Tajikistan, Kazakhstan, and Chechnya tend to be very traditional and have larger families and less education than other immigrants from the former Soviet Union. "Israelis think we're all the same. We're not."

St. Petersburg alone has nearly as many residents as all of Israel. For those who left a vast land of eleven time zones, it is initially hard to grasp that train rides are no longer calculated in days, but in minutes. Ukraine is thirty times larger than Israel. "When I first stood on the beach at Eilat and saw Jordan, Saudi Arabia, and Egypt, I realized how small this country is," reports Boris. Living on a claustrophobic sliver of land surrounded by enemies was quite an adjustment. So is living in a cultural Cuisinart of hyphenated Jews—Iranian-Israelis, Italian-Israelis, even Indian-Israelis, sixty thousand of whom emigrated from southwest India, where they believe they arrived after the destruction of the Second Temple in 70 C.E.

What especially strikes Boris are the seemingly nonending verbal bullfights. "I see people arguing with traffic cops. On the bus, kids argue with the drivers. Parents encourage their kids to question authority. Parents even argue with teachers. In the Knesset, politicians curse and yell. They do in the Kremlin too, but at least they wait their turn. This is a culture of quarreling, but I've learned that it also is a culture of caring. An Israeli will knock you down with his car, but then he'll carry you on his back to the hospital."

Hospitals treat thousands from Ukraine and Belarus whose radiation-related illnesses were caused by fallout from Chernobyl's deadly plutonium. Israel has also inherited a gigantic geriatric population who come to spend their remaining years buffered by free medical care and social security benefits. But the ill and the infirm are the exception; thanks to these immigrants, Israel has the world's highest percentage of scientists, engineers, and physicians. Their brainpower has helped make high tech the fastest-growing sector of the economy. You can hear Russian from Motorola to Nokia to the Israeli phone company where Boris works with numerous former "dot.commies." More than one third of Israelis working in high tech and biotech are highly skilled ex-Soviets. "I guess you could say we're a new type of pioneer," says Boris, comparing his generation to that of his Ukrainian-born great-uncle, who helped start a kibbutz in the Galilee in 1932. "My uncle ploughed fields; we program computers and look under microscopes."

Israel already had deep Russian roots before the great immigration of the 1990s: most ideologists of Zionism and almost all prime ministers either were born in or had parents from areas annexed by the Soviet Union: Ben-Yehuda, Trumpledor, Jabotinsky, Ben-Gurion. Golda Meir, who emigrated to Israel from Milwaukee in 1921, was born in Kiev. Every Jewish Israeli town has streets named after Russian-speaking heroes. "On the bus, it's hilarious watching Israelis get tears in their eyes when the radio plays old patriotic Hebrew Zionist tunes about the brave soldiers and the beautiful land," says Boris. "They don't realize that many famous 'Israeli' melodies were Bolshevik or revolutionary socialist music." Unlike earlier Russians who came to "build and to be rebuilt" in a parched land, who greeted each other as comrade or *haver,* sang the "Internationale" and put on May Day workers' celebrations, most Russian-speaking newcomers are keen capitalists who detest socialism. When offered housing on kibbutzim, few accept. A kibbutz reminds them of a *kolkhoz,* the failed Soviet experiment in collective farming. These consumers crave condos in Haifa or Tel Aviv. Flights back to Kiev and Moscow are filled with briefcase-wielding Israeli Russians on the hunt for lucrative business deals.

Ex-Soviets also are the least Jewishly aware immigrants in Israel's history. Under the czars and then under the communist commissars, anti-Semitism was official government policy. During seven decades of militant official atheism, millions of families like Boris's were known as the "Jews of Silence." "We were afraid, we hid our Jewishness. I didn't even know my grandmother spoke fluent Yiddish until I heard her speak it on a bus in Tel Aviv." Upon arrival, not many even know what Passover is. "I knew almost nothing at my first Passover at my great-uncle's house," recalls Boris. "Passover was the birth of the Jewish nation and, in a way, my first seder was the birth of my Jewishness. It's an ancient festival of freedom. It was very meaningful when I tasted the bitter herbs [which are supposed to remind Jews of their lives as slaves in Egypt]. I thought of the bitterness my family went through. Jews never lived well in the Soviet Union and they still don't. They're still attacking Jews." Trying to conceal his anger, Boris describes a mob that in April 2002 marched down Kiev's main boulevard shouting "Kill the Jews!" and then beat up worshippers at the central synagogue.

The fact that most ex-Soviets have little knowledge about Judaism concerns Gregory Kotler, who is studying to be Israel's first Russian-speaking Reform rabbi. "Jews have to overcome decades of amnesia," declares Gregory, who has the rumpled look of a rabbinical student with his black beard and knitted kippa and tired brown eyes. "Not only did we know little about Judaism, we weren't taught that 2 million Soviet Jews were murdered during World War II. Who wants to teach that? A lot of Ukrainians, Lithuanians, and Latvians collaborated with the Nazis. Mostly what people know about Judaism are distortions and lies. I'll never forget when I asked a man from my town in Ukraine if he'd ever seen a Torah. He said, 'Yes, at the Museum of Atheism in Moscow, in a display that showed how primitive people once prayed.' "

Gregory, a former auto mechanic, is from Donetsk, the same coal-mining town where Natan (Anatoly) Sharansky, who spent nine years in a Moscow prison for being a Jewish activist, grew up. "I was like any Jewish child in the Soviet Union. All we knew about Judaism was that 'Jew' was written on our identity cards. Stalin closed our synagogue in 1937. The Jews that the Nazis and Stalin didn't wipe out physically, the communists did spiritually. I knew that my grandfather secretly was going to a neighbor's house to pray. I asked him to teach me about Judaism, but he didn't, he was too afraid about our safety." Jewish studies were forbidden in the Soviet Union until 1987. Gregory was drafted and spent two years in the army. "It was during Perestroika and soldiers were opening up, discussing their national identities. That's when I started thinking seriously about my own religion and God. When I got out of the army, I studied Hebrew with an old Polish man who had learned it as a boy. I fell in love with Hebrew; it awakened strong Jewish feelings inside me." Then, in 1990, an Israeli emissary arrived in Donetsk. "To see any foreigner was exciting, but he was the first Israeli," Gregory remembers. The next year, at age twenty-two, he left for Israel.

Stroking his beard thoughtfully, Gregory mentions that even after a few years in Israel, many immigrants don't even know the basics of Judaism: why Jews face Jerusalem when they pray, put mezuzahs on their doors, or what the dietary laws mean. He tells a story of a Russian woman who invited an Israeli-born colleague for tea. When she graciously offered him a platter laden with salami and cheese, he looked uncomfortable and didn't touch it. When she urged him to eat, he explained that he doesn't eat meat and milk together. She apologized profusely; she'd never heard of "kosher." So she went into the kitchen and set down two new platters, one with salami and the other with cheese, thinking she had solved the dietary dilemma. A Russian-speaking actor in Israel's internationally acclaimed Gesher Theater said it best: "Already not Russian, but not yet Israeli."

Gregory lives in a charmless section of Jerusalem with his wife and daughter. In the chilly, unheated living room, Marina lifts their three-year-old daughter and helps her light two Hanukkah candles. "We wanted to name her Tania after her grandma, but it's too Russian. And Toible is too Yiddish. So we gave her a modern Hebrew name, Talia [ewe], because we want her to fit in," Marina explains. They live in a drab apartment complex that was quickly built by the government in the 1950s to house Jewish refugees from Arab countries. "A lot of Russians are moving here because it is cheap," she says matter-of-factly, unaware that this blighted, mostly Mizrahi neighborhood called Katamonim was the birthplace of the Black Panther Movement. Back in the 1970s, the Panthers were angry young Mizrahim who protested what they called the favoritism Golda Meir's government showed to the two hundred thousand immigrants who managed to leave the Soviet Union. Some Mizrahim voice the same complaint—that today's new immigrants receive overly generous "Volvo-Villa" benefits: luxury housing plus luxury car. The Kotlers' "villa," a dreary two-room apartment, is lit only by bare lightbulbs. Their "Volvo" is the number 18 bus, which Hamas suicide bombers have blown up twice.

Marina works near the large Jerusalem mall, where, before this intifada, quite a few shoppers were Palestinians and Jordanians. In recent months, it seems security guards outnumber customers. At her company, which creates medical data banks, about a third of the workers are Russian speakers. With some amusement, Marina describes an office dispute: "Two Russians who share one job were quarreling bitterly over a work schedule, hiding their anger from their supervisor. It's not our custom to inform on others. We came here to escape authoritarianism. When the boss wasn't around, they settled their argument Russian-style—with a fistfight. Israelis yell at each other, even their bosses, but they don't hit each other." Because her coworkers speak tortured Hebrew, Marina says that their supervisors underestimate their abilities, which frustrates them. "Because my Hebrew is so bad, at work I say very little. For a long time I had a low-level job. They didn't think I was serious or clever." It took time, but her boss found out and promoted Marina, who has degrees in applied mathematics and computer science, to senior manager.

———————

When I arrived here in 1991, the joke was that if you weren't carrying a violin when you got off the plane from the Soviet Union, you were a doctor," recalls Dr. Baruch Persitz. This wave of immigrants has given Israel the world's highest ratio of physicians to patients. (More than 30 percent of Israeli doctors are from the former Soviet Union.) There are so many that some hospitals post signs warning Russian-speaking staff to speak Hebrew. "When doctors go on rounds talking to each other in Russian, we feel left out," complains a nurse at Soroka Hospital in Beersheva. "Sometimes I feel like I'm working in Moscow, not Israel. And when I'm with my patients, I need a translator. Most speak only Arabic." More than half the patients are Bedouin.

In Moscow, Dr. Persitz was a gastroenterologist. In Jerusalem, he's an acupuncturist and also has edited a Russian-language medical journal for Israeli doctors. "There are just too many of us," he reports. "It's part of the price we have to pay for starting over. For me, it's been worth it." Israelis are no longer startled to discover that the woman washing windows is a surgeon and the man pumping gas is an endocrinologist. After learning Hebrew, they need retraining to pass the stiff Israeli medical qualification exams. "Even if they pass, no matter how high their ranking was, they usually only get work as junior doctors," explains Dr. Persitz. "But at least here, hospitals have medicine and modern equipment. And doctors get paid. In a few days of work here, a doctor can earn what took a month in Russia."

The 40 percent unemployment rate during the peak of the immigration in the 1990s is over. Nonetheless, many of the overeducated are still underemployed. Between terrorist attacks, a string quartet plays on Jerusalem's outdoor Ben-Yehuda pedestrian mall. In Moscow, these virtuosos played in concert halls; now they play for a few shekels tossed into an open violin case. Some land jobs; more than a third of the Israeli Philharmonic's musicians are ex-Soviets. But the country has only a few dozen orchestras, so four hundred orchestra conductors and thousands of musicians have had to take a professional leap backward. Some live in development towns or outlying communities where rents are low and there is less competition for jobs. One concert pianist gives private lessons to Christian and Muslim Arab children in villages near Nazareth; a group of high school music teachers in Beersheva formed their own chamber ensemble, a welcome contribution to the Negev's barren musical scene. In the port town of Ashdod, the Andalusian Orchestra, a symbol of the Mizrahi cultural revolution, plays Middle Eastern music—but a Russian-born violist accompanies a Moroccan-born oud player in a group where many of the "Mizrahi" musicians are actually Russians.

There is no work in Israel for petroleum or mining or railway engineers and many are forced to change professions. At a Russian cultural club in Jerusalem, men sip tea, swap gossip, and play cards. "Israelis love immigration, but not immigrants," says a former forestry professor, who gripes about his job as a cashier at Pizza Hut. Then he admits that his income far surpasses the $78 a month he made in Minsk. A ballet teacher derisively describes his unkempt, undisciplined Sabra pupils. "Mismatched tutus and leotards. Their hair disheveled, wild. When they arrive late, do they apologize? They're so carefree, it makes me crazy." Yet this overbearing man with a commanding presence is afraid to open his own ballet school. He's baffled by Israel's free market economy. When asked the name of his former country, his answer is also baffling: "We lived in only one house in Chernivtsi. We never moved. Our house was in Ukraine. And the Soviet Union. And Romania. Poland, and before that Austria-Hungary."

At the Jerusalem club's packed career workshops, people learn how to search for jobs. In the former Soviet Union, where unemployment was a criminal offense, the government assigned people to jobs with little regard for their wishes. Counselors explain that they can no longer rely on bribes to land a job or get into a university or out of army service. Many must unlearn the popular Russian expression "If you don't oil [give a bribe], you cannot start your journey." They discover that jobs are advertised in newspapers, that eight-page résumés are unacceptable. "I didn't realize that here you have to 'sell yourself' to get a job," complains a physicist who held a prestigious post in Moscow. "When I went for a job interview at the Hebrew University, the department head asked me to describe my research. I didn't know what to say. We're not used to talking about ourselves. I thought it would sound like boasting. So I just said, 'All I've done is only a mere drop in the ocean.' " He didn't get the job.

Israelis admire risk takers and innovators. Nevertheless, some Russian speakers are afraid to show initiative because "they were taught if you make a mistake, you're punished," explains a job counselor who has observed widespread workplace miscommunication. "There's another problem. Sometimes they agree to do things they don't intend to do. Israelis interpret this as deceitful—they don't realize it's because we consider it rude to refuse a request." She goes on to describe the different work ethics of those who spent years in inept Russian workplaces where employees were treated callously, where the prevailing attitude was "They pretend they're paying me, so I'll pretend I'm working." And then there are those who disappear for hours to do errands because back home they had assured jobs and received salaries no matter how little they did. "We teach them that here they can't. There's a saying I like: 'We do not see things as they are, we see things as we are.' It takes time to learn to see life through Israeli eyes."

Gregory has other worries: the nearly half million Jews remaining in the republics of the former Soviet Union. "I grew up in an atheistic society where we were forbidden to practice our religion. We were Jews because the Gentiles treated us differently, not because we were religious. Repression isn't the big problem anymore. Assimilation is. It's the big threat to Jewish survival." Gregory has accepted a tempting job offer: to be the rabbi of Moscow's only Reform synagogue. "To leave will be really sad. Israel is our home. But if I don't go, who will?" Not many of Moscow's 250,000 Jews know much about their religion. Gregory thinks he can remedy that.

In fifty years, the majority of Israelis will be Orthodox—Russian Orthodox," David Chinitz, a religious Hebrew University professor says only half-jokingly. In some mostly Russian neighborhoods, it already seems he is right. In the early 1990s, a quarter of immigrants weren't Jewish; since 2000, in part because more than 80 percent of the Jews of Ukraine, Belarus, and Russia are married to non-Jews, rates have shot up to roughly two thirds, according to the Ministry of Interior. In late December, many Russian homes display fir trees decorated with lights and colored glass balls. Children welcome Ded Moroz, the Russian equivalent of Santa Claus. "When my neighbor saw me carrying a tree up the stairs, she hollered: 'If you want to celebrate Christmas, go back to Russia,' " says a thirty-year-old mathematician who lives in a Haifa suburb. "I told her, 'The tree isn't for Christmas, it's for the Russian New Year.' My husband is Jewish and all the Jews in Baku had trees for New Year's. Then she said, 'New Year here is Rosh Hashanah. January first is for Christians.' As soon as we have more money, I want to move from this building with leaking pipes and people who hate Russians to a 'European' neighborhood in Haifa." On Christmas (January 7 according to the Orthodox calendar, which follows the Gregorian calendar), Russian Orthodox churches are jammed. At Easter, churchgoers exchange the Russian greeting *Christos voskres* (Christ has risen). In most towns there are no Russian Orthodox churches, so a few Arab Greek Orthodox churches offer special services for Russian speakers. Some Russian-speaking Christians hold prayer meetings in their apartments. A number of other congregations, including Baptist, Seventh Day Adventist, and Messianic, are attracting Russian Christian converts.

"I was standing in line to get my driver's license and I saw a lot of people wearing crosses. What's going on?" an Orthodox Jewish teacher from Rishon LeZion asks rhetorically. Rishon LeZion, "First to Zion," was founded by Russian Zionists in 1882 who started the first successful agricultural settlement in prestate Palestine. This is where the first modern synagogue was built, where the first Israeli flag was unfurled, and where Romanian immigrant Naftali Imber wrote his poem "Hatikvah," now the words to Israel's national anthem. It also is where a Hamas suicide bomber killed sixteen Israelis in a pool hall on Sakharov Street in 2002. Because this city, the fastest growing in Israel, has so many Russian speakers, Rishon LeZion is nicknamed "Russians in Zion," the twenty-six-year-old teacher explains. "My great-grandparents escaped Christian pogroms in Russia to come here. If we keep letting in more Christians, it will be national suicide. This is the only Jewish homeland we have. We have to change the Law of Return."

The Law of Return grants every Jew the right to immigrate to Israel. In 1970, the Knesset amended it to include any person with just one Jewish grandparent. In other words, because of a man's long-dead Jewish grandparent, his Christian spouse and their Christian children and grandchildren are all eligible to receive free one-way tickets to Ben-Gurion Airport, financial benefits, and Israeli citizenship. When this amendment was made, Israel was a much poorer country surrounded by hostile neighbors and Jews were locked inside the Soviet Union. No one imagined that by the 1990s, the Soviet Union would disintegrate, Jews would be allowed to leave, and the average Israeli would earn almost $20,000 a year—quite an incentive for non-Jews to "discover" a Jewish grandparent, according to Hirsch Goodman, founding editor of *The Jerusalem Report*. High-jump Olympic contender Konstantin Matussevich was able to emigrate from Kiev because his wife had a Jewish grandfather. Even though they're now divorced, the six-foot seven-inch athlete continues vaulting for the Israelis because, as he explains, "Israel is the place where I belong." Many Israelis wish more such sports giants would somersault into the country; others wish the government would stop letting in those with such tenuous Jewish links.

Knesset member Avraham Ravitz, an ultra-Orthodox rabbi, spelled out his demographic concerns: "Twenty percent of our population is Arab, plus half a million non-Jewish Russian immigrants with another projected nine percent coming, plus 400,000 foreign workers. If you take all of this together, instead of having a Jewish state, already you have 40 percent who are not Jewish. Will Israel still be a Jewish country in a generation?" Former refuseniks who were jailed in the Soviet Union in the 1970s for teaching underground Hebrew and Torah classes have placed ads in the Russian-language and Hebrew press demanding a change in the Law of Return because it is destroying the Jewishness of the state. Newspapers in St. Petersburg are full of ads offering documents to "prove" that one is Jewish, warns Dr. Yuli Nudelman, a refusenik who immigrated in 1971. "Hundreds of thousands of non-Jews with no connection to the Jewish people are coming into Israel under false pretenses." Russian passports with Jewish-sounding names, altered to "prove" Jewish ancestry, are hot sellers on black markets in the former Soviet Union. Others are using forged birth and marriage certificates to "pass" as Jews.

Then there are the immigrants who consider themselves Jews, only to discover that the Israeli rabbinate does not. Under Jewish religious law, only persons with Jewish mothers—or converts—are considered Jews. In the former Soviet Union, it was the opposite. Under Soviet law, religion was determined through the father, not the mother. Because Soviet identity cards listed children by the father's nationality, many "non-Jews" suffered official anti-Semitism. When they became adults, children with one Jewish and one non-Jewish parent could choose their nationality. Thousands with Jewish fathers, who consider themselves Jews, immigrated to Israel. There they discover a new dilemma. As one IDF soldier describes it, "In Russia, they called me 'zhid'; here I'm a 'goy.' "

To avoid being killed by the Nazis, people who couldn't prove they were not Jews bribed Soviet authorities to change their identity card from "Jewish" to "Russian." Yonit's maternal grandmother probably saved her life by destroying her card. Sixty years later, when Yonit and Boris wanted to marry, it became a problem. She had no papers to convince the Orthodox rabbinate, which has a monopoly over Israeli Jewish weddings, that her mother is Jewish. The Orthodox rabbinate declared Yonit a non-Jew, and in Israel, Jews cannot marry non-Jews. So, like thousands of former Soviets, the couple flew to Cyprus to take their wedding vows. "I was taken aback," says Yonit. "Because my father proved he is Jewish, I'm Jewish enough to be an Israeli citizen, but not Jewish enough to marry a Jew here."

Shas, the ultra-Orthodox Mizrahi political party, has run radio ads calling Russian immigrants "churchgoers, counterfeiters, con men, and call girls." For Boris's family, these slurs became sharply personal. His parents live near Jerusalem in Beit Shemesh (House of the Sun), which has a religious Mizrahi majority and an expanding Russian-speaking minority. "It was very difficult for my parents to start new lives," he says. "For the first two years, the only jobs they could get were scrubbing stairs of apartment buildings. They didn't talk much, but I could tell they felt humiliated. A few times, I heard my mother crying. But they were determined to make a better life for me and my sister." His mother learned Hebrew and got her teaching credentials. Many of her high school English students are from North African families who support Shas. After his father passed the Israeli civil engineering exam, he received his contracting license and was ecstatic when a Shas rabbi hired him to be the construction engineer on a huge synagogue, school, and yeshiva complex. "It's funny because my dad didn't know anything about Judaism. I don't think he'd ever entered a synagogue. But he was so glad to have that job that when the rabbi gave him a poster of Rabbi Ovadia Yosef [Shas's spiritual leader], he hung it in the living room."

While his father was supervising the construction of the imposing stone religious complex, Shas staged a large anti-Russian rally against the local Russian-owned butcher shops, which sell pork. Shas leaders addressed the crowd, calling the non-Jewish Russian-speaking immigrants a "fifth column" of "pork, prostitution, impurity, and filth," who are "destroying the moral fiber of the nation." The head rabbi of the yeshiva said Israel is "awash with Gentiles who have no connection with Judaism and awash with abomination." "That demonstration devastated my father," Boris recalls gloomily. "He enjoyed working for them. Then they slapped him in the face with that ugly demonstration. We don't buy pork to rebel against Judaism, we do it because we've always eaten it and because it's cheap. Pork doesn't have any symbolism for us. Instead of stereotyping us, people should try to understand us. Why are so many blonde Russians called hookers? Why are guys with a lot of money called mafiosi? On the bus to work, I rarely read a Russian newspaper because it can be like holding up a red flag for someone to call me 'dirty Russian.'" (Now he has a Subaru and he reads Hebrew and Russian newspapers on the Internet.)

On October 17, 2000, at the outbreak of the second intifada, two IDF reserve soldiers took a wrong turn and ended up in Ramallah. That night, the nation watched chilling television footage as a Palestinian lynch mob gleefully threw a bloodied corpse from a police station window. It was Siberian-born Vadim Nozich. Just a week earlier, he had been under a wedding canopy taking his vows. That gruesome video abruptly changed Israeli attitudes. Vadim was everyone's husband, brother, and son.

"Compared to us, Israelis are very tolerant. Back home, racism is rampant. What's sad is that the children learn it from their parents. I did," says Hila Berl, a twenty-nine-year-old social activist. "We were raised to hate anyone who is not like us. We grew up with nationalistic slogans that we are the best. What did we know about immigrants? Who would immigrate to Ukraine? My father [a non-Jew] is a typical Ukrainian; he hates all foreigners, including Jews." Hila's family lives in Ashkelon, the mixed Russian-Mizrahi port with a Russian-born mayor. She heard her father, an elevator technician, say to someone, "Even though you're a Jew, you're nice." Each Saturday, he and his friends picnic in the park, singing Ukrainian and Russian songs and drinking. "They look down on Mizrahim. They hate the Arabs. I was like that until I went to the Hebrew University. And in this job, I meet so many progressive Israelis."

Hila works at the New Israel Fund, a national nonprofit organization dedicated to advancing Israeli pluralism, giving assistance and financial support to hundreds of grassroots groups, such as "disempowered" Mizrahim, Ethiopians, and Bedouin. She is involved with a project that helps newcomers from the former Soviet Union learn how democracy works in this obsessively political country. Many are surprised at the "auto sloganeering," the ubiquitous bumper stickers that declare people's opinions. "They're used to dictatorial rule, political chaos, and dysfunctional institutions, not dozens of choices at the ballot box," explains Hila. The former Soviets are relishing their adventures with democracy. Smart politicians know that if they want to survive, they have to court them. Left- and right-wing parties vie for their votes, sending Russian speakers to attract recruits, placing ads in Russian-language newspapers, running Russian subtitles in TV election campaign ads, and plastering the country with campaign posters in the Cyrillic alphabet. Whoever carries the Russian swing vote has won each election since 1992. And they like to vote out the incumbent. Their votes help put Yitzhak Rabin into office. Four years later, in 1996, they showed their anger at Shimon Peres's Labor-led government for not addressing their needs; their votes made Likud's Benjamin Netanyahu prime minister. Then in 1999, Ehud Barak hired Russian-speaking advisors who devised ways to enhance his appeal. They showed images of the former army chief in uniform and medals, emphasizing the daring operations that made Barak Israel's most decorated soldier. They portrayed this "warrior for peace" as a cultured intellectual with a degree from Stanford University. They even had this son of Lithuanian immigrants play classical piano to woo the ex-Soviets. It worked. They said *nyet* to Netanyahu. In May 2000, desperate to shore up failing Russian support, Prime Minister Barak called for a "civic revolution" against the religious parties, for civil marriage, buses on the Sabbath, and other secular changes that appeal to Russian voters. Then the intifada broke out. The former Soviets were part of the landslide that put Ariel Sharon, the son of Russian immigrants, into office in

2001 and again in 2003. One third voted for the anti–ultra-Orthodox Shinui Party.

Hila goes on to explain that *Vesti* (News), the largest circulation Russian-language newspaper, has a right-wing slant that reflects the "mentality of militarism and conquest we were raised on." Coming from a huge land, people don't understand why minuscule Israel would agree to return strategically significant lands, like the Golan Heights, to an avowed enemy like Syria. What about the children of Perestroika, who don't know much about the cold war, let alone Marx or Lenin? "If you want to find out how they think, read this," says Hila as she flips through *Vesti*'s youth supplement, *Teenager Plus*. In it, teens write about conflicting feelings about their Sabra classmates. "We have different interests, read different books, and listen to different music." "They call me names, so I stick with other immigrant kids." "What we learned in seventh-grade math, Israelis learn in tenth grade." "School is much freer in Israel. Back home, teachers were like prison guards. They did everything by the book and didn't praise us until we succeeded." "Israeli kids are so relaxed and a lot of fun because they live in the present. I want to be like that too."

Many are bicultural; they dance to the latest Hebrew rock yet know all the lyrics to the most recent Ukrainian rap. They speak far more Hebrew than their parents. What Israel's most famous poet, Ukrainian-born Hayim Nahman Bialik, wrote nearly one hundred years ago is still true today: "Hebrew is the only language children teach their parents." Some log onto Russian-language Internet chatrooms to "meet" other Russian Israeli kids; most, however, frequent Hebrew ones. At a chess club in Beersheva, children yell "*Yesh!*" (Hebrew slang for "Hurray!") as they watch a twelve-year-old girl play world chess champion Garry Kasparov to a draw in an Internet match. Immigrant players like her have moved Israel from mediocre to world class. "Chess was a Jewish profession in the Soviet Union; in Israel, it's a Russian profession," explains a lanky boy in slightly accented Hebrew.

At Shevah-Mofet High School in South Tel Aviv's industrial zone, a student complains that her mother pushes her to succeed: "She makes me take Russian so I can speak with my *babushka* [grandmother], and advanced physics too." In this school, commonly called the "Russian" school or "Harvard," the language of instruction is Hebrew, but in the halls and in the schoolyards one hears Russian. Most of the fourteen hundred students are children of Russian immigrants, who get up at dawn to take long bus rides to study engineering, robotics, mathematics, and literature. Many of their parents moved to Israel to give them a better future.

One balmy Sabbath evening in June 2001 many students decided to go dancing instead of studying for final exams. When eighteen-year-old Polena Vallis and her girlfriend arrived at a Tel Aviv beachfront disco, hundreds of mostly Russian-speaking teens were in line waiting to get into the Dolphinarium. "Suddenly a deafening noise," remembers Polena. "A boom and then a disgusting smell. Blood and bodies. I felt burning heat. Boys and girls were on fire. My legs were covered with blood. In the ambulance, I prayed I'd lose consciousness so I wouldn't have to hear the groans of the dying girl next to me." Doctors removed the shrapnel from Polena's leg and foot. Another teenager wasn't so lucky. Ilona Schwartof, who was wearing a T-shirt that said "Peace," dreamed of becoming a model. Today, her friends can't bear to look at her face. Nails and screws packed in the bomb lodged in her brain. After two years of therapy, there is improvement; she can speak about fifty words.

Most of the dead and 120 wounded were Russian-speaking teens. It was the worst collective tragedy the million-strong community has experienced. Strangely, many say it was a turning point, making them feel more accepted by Israeli society. It's evident at a stone memorial at the spot inscribed with names in both Hebrew and Cyrillic. Sabras of all ages and backgrounds stop to place flowers and notes.

The Islamic Jihad suicide bomber kept the promise he made in his video: "I will tear their bodies and their bones into pieces so they will taste death. To kill the Zionists, the occupiers, we will do this in honor of the martyrs, in honor of the Prophet." Hussein Mohammed Tawil's parents have shown journalists the letter of congratulations Yasser Arafat sent them. He called their son a "model of manhood. . . . To turn one's body into a bomb is the best example of willingness to make a sacrifice for Allah and the homeland." He enclosed a map of Palestine with the letter. It included all of Israel.

Ina Harp never will forget the night she lost six of her Sheva High School classmates at the Dolphinarium. Will she go to a disco again?

"Yes. I'm a teenager and I love to dance. If I don't go, then it's as if that lunatic who blew himself up won. So we have to continue our lives and dance."

———————

Metulla is Israel's northernmost village. Nestled between cypress and olive trees, with a view of Mount Hermon, it's on the volatile Lebanese border, a most unlikely place for Israel's only Olympic-size ice skating rink. Inside, soothing sounds of classical music cannot drown out the reverberating booms of anti-aircraft fire. Nonetheless, the dancing couples gliding effortlessly on the ice are perfecting routines for their next international competition. "Before I came here," says an instructor, "my friends warned me that figure skating in Israel was as popular as racing camels in Siberia."

They were wrong. Outside this rink in the Galilee, skaters with names like Sergei, Tatiana, Galina, and Vadim keep busy. They've flown from Tokyo to Minneapolis, winning medals for their adopted country. Although there's no modern Hebrew expression for ice skating (the closest verb means "slipping"), for the first time, Israelis can dream about the Winter Olympics.

8

Out of Africa

Ethiopian Israelis in the Promised Land

-ᴓ As a thirsty man goes to water, as a hungry man goes to food, that is how I came to Israel. —Menasie Menashe, an eighty-six-year-old kes, *or Ethiopian Jewish religious leader, addressing the Knesset soon after his arrival in 1991*

-ᴓ The first time my father saw a TV he flipped out and asked, "How did so many people get into that small box?" He was too shy to change his clothes in front of them in the living room. —Ethiopian Israeli comedian Yossi Vassa, twenty-eight, in his one-man show

For nine months he became James Bond, preparing for one of the biggest covert operations in history. The first Ethiopian Israeli officer in the Israeli air force, Solomon Ezra risked his life hundreds of times, bribing dozens of Ethiopian officials to smuggle thousands of his fellow Jews out of their remote mountain villages, where for centuries they had prayed to return to Jerusalem. Caught in the middle of a famine and a bloody civil war, they faced extinction. Their simple grass and mud huts and synagogues were destroyed, their husbands and sons murdered. Most fled by foot or hid in trucks on the arduous journey to Addis Ababa. They arrived there ill and destitute and had to wait in crowded hovels in the worst slums of the capital. Solomon assured them that they'd soon reach the Promised Land. They prayed that he was telling the truth.

Their prayers were answered on May 23, 1991. Just as rebel troops were closing in on Addis Ababa, unmarked aircraft supplied by the IAF and El Al arrived for the exodus. They had only a few hours to rescue Ethiopia's Jews before the encircling forces would prevent them from leaving. Solomon sent out the long-awaited news. Thousands of frantic Jews began flooding into a compound near the Israeli Embassy. Dressed in white flowing robes, they were barefoot and hobbling. Pregnant women carried babies strapped to their backs. Most of the Jews were children. The logistics were staggering. For thirty hours, Solomon and other Ethiopian Israeli officials questioned them and checked lists to confirm their identity. In a parting message they were told to leave behind all possessions because every bundle meant another Jew couldn't fit on the plane.

At 1:45 A.M. the Israeli government gave the green light. Bus convoys left for the airport guarded by Israeli soldiers disguised in civilian clothes, with Uzi submachine guns hidden in schoolbags. The apprehensive passengers boarded the big birds with metal wings, the first planes they had ever seen. In minutes, nearly three dozen jets were jammed with Ethiopian Jews. In some of the jets, seats had to be removed. "I asked the pilot how many passengers in his plane. He told me over one thousand. I warned him that it was impossible, the plane couldn't hold more than five hundred," recalls Solomon. "His answer? 'It's okay. I don't want to leave any of my people behind.' I never felt more proud to be an Israeli." (The *Guinness Book of World Records* lists it as the largest number of people in one plane.)

The long nightmare was over. As the displaced Ethiopian Jews left Africa, some cried, most were silent. They knew everything was about to change. During the 1,600-mile flight to Israel, Israeli doctors on board delivered seven babies. "It was a miracle," reminisces Solomon, who left on the last plane. "As we flew over the Red Sea, I felt like we were the children of Israel escaping Egypt." In thirty-six hours, Israelis smuggled 14,324 Ethiopian Jews aboard thirty-three jets. Called Operation Solomon, it was history's largest human airlift, unparalleled in scope and speed.

When they landed, many newcomers, overcome with joy, kneeled and kissed the ground. "The pilots were crying, the soldiers were crying, the bus drivers were crying. Seeing most of my people come home was my life's dream," says Solomon, a gentle, down-to-earth man who is a hero to many of Israel's one hundred thousand Ethiopians. "What other country would go through the danger of rescuing poor Africans? Never before have black people been brought out of Africa in dignity and immediately welcomed as lost brothers and sisters."

Israelis were electrified by the dramatic rescue of these "lost" brethren, who for centuries believed they were the world's last remaining Jews. These unassuming Ethiopian Jews charmed Israelis, who showered them with so many clothes, cribs, and toys that absorption officials had to ask them to stop. "Just when we Israelis were wondering what Zionism was all about, we saw it in action," said a Tel Aviv waitress with blue concentration camp numbers tattooed indelibly onto her arm. Like many Israelis, she "adopted" immigrants, tutoring them, helping them to maneuver through the bureaucracy. It's unusual for Israelis to share a consensus, but almost all agreed that the rescue of Ethiopia's Jews was one of the country's finest moments.

The three hour and twenty minute flight from Addis Ababa to Tel Aviv took illiterate villagers from one of the world's poorest countries to an urbanized, high-tech center. In a single weekend, they went from being a pariah Jewish minority in a black country to living in a land of nonblack Jews. They arrived during the peak of the massive Soviet immigration and were placed in absorption centers and converted hotels already bursting with Russian speakers, few of whom had ever met a black person. At the Shalom Hotel, a former luxury hotel in Jerusalem, former Soviets did not understand why some Ethiopian women were sleeping in the hallways; it was because there were no menstrual "blood huts" where they could be apart from their families to observe biblical purity laws. The Soviets also were not aware that their new neighbors didn't turn off lights or faucets because they feared the miraculous electricity and water wouldn't reappear. With only three elevators serving nearly one thousand Ethiopian and Soviet immigrants, a simple trip to the lobby could take more than fifteen minutes. Groups of giggling Ethiopian children would push into an already crowded elevator and press all sixteen buttons in the "moving black box." When the elevator stopped at each floor, they peeked out to look around. Russian-speaking passengers glared at them. "They're from another world, and I'm late for a job interview," was a typical comment. "Anyway, how can these blacks be Jews?"

"There are no two Jewish communities more disparate," according to one-time Soviet political prisoner Natan Sharansky, who flew to Addis Ababa as a journalist to witness the massive airlift. "Our immigrants were the most spiritually isolated from Judaism and these Ethiopians were the most isolated geographically. Back home we were almost completely assimilated, while the Ethiopians had preserved Judaism for centuries after being cut off. Ours had almost no idea of Jewish communal life, whereas Ethiopians' very survival and identity depended on close tribal communities. I was among the Israelis standing by the empty airplanes in Africa to bring them out. This journey was the moment I had come to Israel for."

In the hotel lobby, a puzzled newcomer struggled to open a can of Coke, unaware that the white sheet she was draped in toga-style was meant for her bed, not her body. A group of Ethiopians pondered how to use a pay phone. On a couch, an Ethiopian Israeli social worker reassured a woman frightened by the strange sound of a vacuum cleaner, and then showed her how to diaper her baby. Because there were no private cooking facilities, families ate in a huge dining room. A female Israeli soldier encouraged a man to eat with fork and knife instead of his hands, not realizing that Ethiopian men are not accustomed to taking orders from a younger person and certainly not a woman. They were served inedible unspicy foods like soft-boiled eggs, cheese, and olives. A man examined slices of turkey and wondered if this strange meat was kosher, slaughtered according to their strict biblical requirements.

In the playground of an immigrant absorption center, an Ethiopian youngster wearing a donated "Shop 'Til You Drop" T-shirt helped a Ukrainian boy build a sand castle. Nearby, a three-year-old girl sang a Russian song to her Barbie doll. When an Ethiopian boy started drumming on a plastic pail, a blonde child from Kiev jumped up to join her new Ethiopian friends in an ancient Amharic dance. Unlike their parents, these toddlers are color blind.

In a crowded basement clinic serving more than one thousand

Ethiopians living at Jerusalem's Diplomat Hotel, children and their parents sat on chairs and on the floor, waiting patiently and silently. For most, it was their first encounter with a Western doctor. An overworked pediatrician told a man that he had tuberculosis and then handed a teenage girl antibiotics for her intestinal parasite. A woman's face contorted in agony when the doctor explained she has trachoma, a potentially blinding eye disease. "We don't have enough translators, nurses, or eye doctors," explained Dr. Michael Harari, an Australian Israeli. A few patients gasped noisily. Asthma? he wondered. His Ethiopian Israeli nurse-translator grinned and explained that the gasping sound means yes in Amharic. When Dr. Harari told a woman to give her sick daughter a *nar*, the Ethiopian Israeli translator looked perplexed. She knew that *nar* means candle in Hebrew, but was unaware it also means suppository. When a bearded *kes,* or spiritual leader, in a white turban walked in complaining of a cough, the nurse respectfully asked, "Didn't you take a teaspoon of the medicine?" The kes didn't know what a spoon was, so he took his medicine with a ladle. "We're trying to deal with so many misunderstandings and cultural differences," explained Dr. Harari. "Many patients complain their hearts hurt. At first, some inexperienced doctors gave them nitroglycerin because they didn't realize that to Ethiopians, the heart is the source of all physical pain."

Still other Ethiopians were deeply depressed because family members never made it to Israel. Behaviors that Israeli mental health practitioners tended to interpret as posttraumatic shock syndrome, anxiety, or depression caused by the trauma of migration are believed by many Ethiopian immigrants to be spirit possession, or *zar*. In time, a number of Israeli doctors learned to refer patients for a "second opinion" to a traditional healer, or *balazar*. "All my life I knew war in Ethiopia. Finally I have peace," related twenty-two-year-old Malaku Mukonen as he caressed his infant daughter, Israela, born days after his arrival. He sat in his Jerusalem hotel room, listening to the news in Amharic. "I wish my parents could see her." Reluctantly, he recounted how his parents died of starvation during the civil war. He brightened as he told of his plans: "After I learn Hebrew, I want to go to school and become an airplane mechanic."

Even now, thousands more Ethiopians are arriving in Israel. They quickly shed their traditional cloth robes. In ill-fitting donated jeans and sneakers, they explore contemporary Israel. Entering computer shops, they watch Israeli kids play the latest games. These deeply religious East African Jews stare at nearly naked women lying on the beaches trying to darken their skin. They turn to veteran Ethiopian Israelis like Solomon to explain the mysteries of life among these *ferenji* (strange white Jews). "I understand their shock," says Solomon, a compassionate man with a steel backbone. "When I first saw people driving on the Sabbath, I wondered if this was really Israel. It felt as though I'd landed in the wrong country." That's why he likes taking newcomers to pray at the Western Wall in the Old City of Jerusalem, the last remnant of the Temple of Solomon, "where we know we're in the right place. The first time I touched these stones, it was like a bright sunrise after a long dark night."

An electrical engineer who designs Intel's next generation of computer chips, Solomon never used electricity or saw a phone until he was twelve. He grew up in a hut in a remote Jewish village in the craggy Ethiopian highlands where his father, a tenant wheat farmer, eked out a living. The devout Jews of the village meticulously observed the Sabbath and dietary laws and practiced ancient biblical rituals such as sacrificing goats for Passover. Solomon and his family prayed in a grass and mud synagogue every Friday night and Saturday and fasted every Yom Kippur. On Passover, women made matzah by hand, and at the seder, men sat with men, women with women, children with children. For twenty-five hundred years their songs and stories were filled with longing to return to the land of Zion.

Questions about when and how they adopted Judaism probably are unanswerable. Solomon, who comes from a long line of kessim, says some people believe Moses had a black wife from Kush, the biblical name for Ethiopia. Isaiah 11:11 strongly implies that there was an established Ethiopian Jewish community in the days of that prophet, approximately 740 B.C.E. Some scholars believe they are descendants of the lost tribe of Dan. Another theory is that they are descendants of Jews who left Israel after the Babylonians destroyed the Temple of Solomon in 586 B.C.E. According to the Ethiopian national founding story, Sheba, the queen of Ethiopia, and King Solomon conceived a son who was educated in the Jerusalem court. He became Menelik I, founder of the Ethiopian Solomonic dynasty. Both Jews and Amhara Coptic Christians claim they are descendants of indigenous people who intermarried with Jewish priests and attendants whom King Solomon had sent with Menelik I when he went to assume the kingship of Ethiopia. The only thing certain is that Judaism was widespread in Ethiopia before the Aksum dynasty converted to Christianity in the fourth century.

Whatever their origins, for centuries Ethiopian Jews worshipped according to ancient rituals laid down in the Five Books of Moses (Torah) and older parts of the Bible (Prophets and the first half of Writings), written in Geez, the ancient Semitic language of both Jewish and Christian scripture and liturgy writings. They didn't know of later Jewish books and laws. The Talmud (the Mishna or oral tradition and Gemara) were developed in Babylonia and Palestine beginning in 515 B.C.E., long after they lost contact with other Jews. In their isolation, Ethiopian Jews developed their own interpretations of Judaism. Historical literature describes more than a million Jews and a Jewish king and queen who ruled much of Ethiopia in the sixth century. After Jews lost their independence in the seventh century, Coptic Christians forbade them from owning land. Although Jews spoke the same language and physically were indistinguishable from their Christian landlords, they lived apart in their own villages. Their Christian neighbors despised and feared Jews, derisively calling them *falasha* (strangers) and accusing them of having *budda,* the "evil eye" or Satanic powers. Besides harvesting wheat and tending cattle, Jews were blacksmiths and potters, low-caste work that used fire, which is associated with witchcraft. It was a common belief that by day, Jews disguised themselves as humans and at night turned into hyenas, who could suck the blood of unwary victims. In addition to the hostility, contempt, and persecution, Jews sometimes were sold into slavery or massacred. Thousands converted to Christianity.

The outside world was not aware of the black Jews of Ethiopia until Scottish explorer James Bruce mentioned them in his 1790 book, *Travels to Discover the Source of the Nile.* Seventy-seven years later, the Alliance Israelite Universelle, a French Jewish philanthropy, learned that English missionaries were converting Jews and went into action. They sent Semitic scholar and linguist Joseph Halevy to Ethiopia to investigate if these people could possibly be the lost Jews of legend or the descendants of the lost tribe of Dan. When he arrived, Ethiopians suspected that this white man who claimed to be a Jew really was another Christian missionary. When Halevy spoke of Jerusalem, they got excited and asked,

"Do you come from the blessed city? Have you beheld with your own eyes Mount Zion, and the House of the Lord of Israel, the Holy Temple?" Halevy concluded that these African practitioners of biblical Judaism were indeed Jews. And they concluded that, indeed, Halevy was the first white Jew they ever had seen.

Halevy's student, Dr. Jacques Faitlovitch, moved to Ethiopia and dedicated his life to bringing them closer to mainstream Jews. Ethiopians revered this Orthodox Polish-born Jew who was responsible for their entry into Jewish consciousness. If it were not for him, they probably would have disappeared from the Jewish landscape. Dr. Faitlovitch opened a boarding school and a synagogue in Addis Ababa in 1923. He taught Jewish men to wear *tallit,* prayer shawls, and kippot and women to light Sabbath candles. They learned to pray in Hebrew, adopt the Star of David, bar mitzvah their sons, and observe holidays such as Hanukkah and Purim, which came into the Jewish calendar after the Ethiopians were cut off from other Jews. Dr. Faitlovitch sent gifted young Jews to Palestine for a Jewish and general education. They returned to their villages to teach and prepare Jews to emigrate. The highly respected Ashkenazi Chief Rabbi of Palestine, Abraham Isaac Kook, wrote a letter to world Jewry in 1921 urging them "to save our Falasha brethren from extinction and to rescue these holy souls from the House of Israel from oblivion and bring their young children to Jewish centers in Palestine."

History, however, interrupted their plans. The Italian fascists occupied Ethiopia in 1936 and closed synagogues and schools and harassed the Jews. After the Second World War, Dr. Faitlovitch again took up the cause. But European Jews, devastated by the Holocaust, were consumed with trying to build a state in Palestine.

By the 1950s, a few Israelis were teaching Judaism and Zionism in Ethiopian villages. They brought twenty-seven promising young Jews to Israel, including Solomon's eldest sister. Despite Dr. Faitlovitch's tireless efforts to convince Israeli rabbis to stop questioning their Jewishness and bring in more Jews, by the time he died in Tel Aviv in 1955, he hadn't. It wasn't until 1973 that Sephardi Chief Rabbi Ovadia Yosef (now the spiritual head of Shas) ruled that they are authentic Jews, descendants of the lost tribe of Dan, and urged they be brought to Israel immediately to fulfill the prophecy of Isaiah of bringing all scattered Jews back to their homeland. The timing was terrible. A few months later, the October Yom

Kippur War started and Ethiopia cut off relations with Israel. The next year, Emperor Haile Selassie, who had reigned for fifty-seven years, was overthrown in a military coup led by Afro-Stalinist dictator Mengistu Haile Mariam.

In 1975, Solomon Ezra was awarded a scholarship and left his village to study at a high school in Addis Ababa. One day, while sitting in his math class, "Suddenly, two undercover police entered. In front of everyone, they arrested me. They accused me of being a Zionist spy. My only crime was studying Judaism underground. They put me with ten men in a room the size of a bathroom. No window and once a day, bread and water. They beat me with electric wires. I prayed to die," he remembers with a shudder. "It would have been better than the torture." Six months later, an Israeli intelligence agent from Mossad managed to smuggle him out of prison.

"I was sixteen when I first stepped off that airplane onto the sacred soil of my true homeland," recalls Solomon, "and it was the happiest day of my life." At the time, there were only about a hundred other Ethiopian Jews in Israel. Solomon was alone and sent to live and study on a kibbutz. "I was surprised that when the teachers came into the classroom, Israeli students didn't stand and they called them by their first names. At first, I used to sit quietly in the back or looked up at the teachers when they were talking," he recalls. "They probably thought I wasn't paying attention or couldn't understand their Hebrew or had emotional problems. But we don't look into the eyes of elders, not even when we talk to our parents. And we're taught to keep our feelings inside." Solomon kept a lot inside. His parents and six brothers and sisters were stranded in the village. It would be twelve years before he would see them again. "My classmates were really wonderful. I helped them with their English and math and they helped me with my Hebrew homework. They taught me to argue and interrupt. I couldn't believe how direct Israelis are, how they let their emotions just spill out."

When he was drafted, the military decided that this soft-spoken teenager with scars on his legs had the right stuff. "They accepted me into the air force and I was so proud," Solomon says, grinning. At first, men in his unit assumed the pilot in the khaki air force uniform and blue beret was a Yemenite. None of them had ever seen an Ethiopian. "People treated me really well, except one officer. During training, he called me *kushi* [offensive Hebrew slang for black, which is derived from Kush, the biblical name for Ethiopia]. 'I'm insulted,' I yelled back at him. 'I'm a Jew, just like you.' He apologized. I never heard a racist comment again. Outside the base, I always got a lot of stares. One Rosh Hashana I went to a Hasidic synagogue. When people heard me praying in Hebrew, they looked at me, not their prayer books. That's one reason I was determined to be an officer. I wanted to show my family and all the Ethiopians still stuck in the villages that we can make it here."

During his six years in the air force, Solomon flew F-16 fighter jets on secret missions. He was decorated by President Chaim Herzog in 1984 as one of the IDF's most outstanding officers. "The air force is the School for Chutzpah. That's where I learned that there always is a way when there is no way." That attitude helped Solomon use ingenious ways to bring Ethiopian Jews to Israel clandestinely.

Driving to his family's apartment in Kiryat Gat, Solomon stops his car at a large black granite monument honoring the nearly five thousand Jews who died on the horrific trek from Ethiopia to the Sudan in the mid-1980s. Nearly every Ethiopian Israeli lost loved ones to starvation, disease, or murder by bandits on their journey across Ethiopia or in the miserable Sudanese refugee camps, where many were beaten or raped. Solomon lost an uncle and twenty cousins. But the dream of going to Israel kept even more Jews coming. Aware of a rising death toll in the refugee camps, the Israeli government bribed President Numeri of Sudan. In 1984–85, nearly eight thousand Ethiopian Jews were rescued in a series of airlifts code-named Operation Moses. When news of the secret deal leaked out, the Sudanese government halted the rescue. It was not long before Solomon headed for the Kenyan side of the Ethiopian border. Using phony European student visas and work permits, he smuggled nearly six thousand Jews into Israel from 1986 until 1990. Then came Operation Solomon. Completed in a weekend, it was the biggest, most dramatic secret airlift in history, named after King Solomon and partly masterminded by his namesake, Solomon Ezra. No other Ethiopian has helped rescue so many Jews.

Few Jews have sacrificed so much to emigrate. And no group has arrived with more handicaps: blacks in a white society, preindustrial villagers in an urbanized postindustrial country. The Israeli government invests roughly four times more for each Ethiopian than for other immigrants. As one Ministry of Absorption official put it, "Absorbing the Russians is a huge national challenge, but absorbing the Ethiopians is our national test of honor." Ethiopians receive free Hebrew classes, health coverage, counseling, and a range of other benefits. Because of government grants, all Ethiopians, except the latest arrivals, have been able to move out of absorption centers and trailers into their own apartments or public housing. They receive the highest housing subsidies of all immigrants, about four times more than ex-Soviets. Because of Israel's sky-high real estate prices, even a 90 percent grant on a $120,000 mortgage means most can afford only apartments in marginal neighborhoods or development towns. Nonetheless, studies show that most Ethiopians are satisfied with their apartments and are living near extended families.

Ethiopians who came as part of Operation Solomon joyfully reunited with relatives they hadn't seen in years. For some, the joy didn't last. One husband was distraught to discover the wife and children he hadn't seen for eight years had turned into strangers—brash, aggressive Israelis. "We married when I was fifteen," explains his forty-year-old wife, who last saw her husband in their isolated mountain village where she made clay pots, wove straw baskets, and raised three children. She now carries a Palm Pilot instead of water from the well. She no longer prepares the spongy pancake bread called *enjera* on an outdoor fire; she uses a gas oven. No longer a reserved woman in a white flowing robe, this confident dental hygienist much prefers her elegant sporty look. The three children no longer speak Amharic or avert their eyes to show respect when they speak to their fifty-five-year-old father. In the straw hut, he was the authority figure; in the apartment in Lod, near Ben-Gurion Airport, he is no longer the provider and educator. In Israel, his skills as a cattle herder who knew how to forge plowshares and knives are useless. He is unemployed with little to do while his wife earns and his children learn. Ethiopian wives, often from ten to twenty years younger than their husbands, usually adapt much more quickly. The unemployed husband–working wife phenomenon is common. When men grow depressed about lost prestige and control, tensions rise. Divorce among Ethiopians is about six times that of other Jewish Israelis.

In Ethiopia, children depended on their parents. In Israel, parents depend on their Hebrew-speaking children to help them deal with non-Ethiopians. "My father is really anxious nowadays," says his daughter, who is on a nursing scholarship. "He turns on the television and sees ambulances, a terrorist attack. People crying and blood. He doesn't understand what's going on. He panics and calls me or my mother." Few adult Ethiopians know Hebrew, which can be more than inconvenient; it can prove deadly. This was devastatingly illustrated near Upper Nazareth in 2002, when a bus driver noticed a suspicious man and ordered all passengers to evacuate. Everyone did except an eighty-five-year-old Ethiopian who didn't understand the warning. When the suicide bomber detonated, he was still in his seat. The only casualty, he was a victim of terror and his lack of Hebrew. No other group of Israelis is as cut off from information as the Ethiopians: only one and a half hours of radio is broadcast in Amharic daily and only a half hour of Amharic television on Friday afternoons. There are two small Amharic-language weeklies; three quarters of Ethiopian adults are illiterate. A hot line offers counseling in Amharic to parents and children. But not all Ethiopians understand Amharic; a number speak only Tigrinya, an Ethio-Semitic language largely confined to Eritrea and northern Ethiopia.

With her languid brown eyes and chiseled features, Ziona has the arresting looks and drive to realize her dreams of either emulating her cousin, a model for Israeli television and magazines ads, or becoming a television makeup artist. Right now, though, this high school student from Beersheva has Bible history and Hebrew literature homework to contend with. Her parents can't help. They can't read or write simple Hebrew. Most Ethiopians receive financial aid to pay for textbooks, lunches, and gym clothes, but with six children, her parents never have enough. Ethiopians are the poorest Jewish group in Israel; over two thirds of Ethiopian families depend on welfare and have five or more children. Ziona studies at a state religious school, as do most Ethiopian students. Her after-school tutor is trying to help her come up with money to join her classmates' Passover field trip to the Galilee. "It's not just the trip I want," she says. "It's freedom. At school they make all of us wear long skirts and long sleeves, but afterwards, my girlfriends dress as they want. Not me. My mother hates this," she says, indicating her cleavage-spilling blouse. "My parents say I'm not acting Ethiopian. Well, I'm not. I'm Israeli." Taught to be reserved and exercise emotional restraint, Ethiopian children are not supposed to say no to elders, to speak in the presence of adults without permission. In more traditional families, children do not eat until after their parents have eaten and greet a respected elder with a time-honored gesture: kissing the knees, the site of a man's strength. (In Amharic, a *gulbatam*, a knee person, is a brave, resilient man with physical stamina.) "I like going to my girlfriend's [a third-generation North African]. Her mother has the right attitude. She rents really cool videos. Mine only likes those [Amharic-language] romance videos."

"The second generation, children born in Israel or who came as toddlers, who barely speak Amharic or Tigrinya, have big problems. Their parents don't understand them and they're ashamed to be seen with their fathers because they wear white robes and walk with sticks," says Menberu Shimon, who counsels at-risk Ethiopian youth. "They're exploding with problems. Some have no bus money. Some have no parents." Menberu is one of many Ethiopians who arrived without parents. His mother died trying to escape through the Sudan. He arrived alone at age fourteen. At the time, it was government policy—because religious parties won a political battle—to place most Ethiopian children in religious vocational boarding schools. Most either had no family or no friends who could take care of them. The other students were troubled Mizrahim, often from malfunctioning families. "It was hard. I lost the most precious person in my life and the teachers didn't understand what I was going through," Menberu recalls. The boarding schools made the same mistakes they did with Mizrahim, he says, "making us ashamed of our culture, our religious traditions. They told us we don't practice Judaism properly. A few of my friends had parents. When they went home on Shabbat, they refused to eat their mother's food because we were taught it wasn't kosher enough. Our teachers said that real Jews put mezuzot on doors and don't sacrifice goats on Passover. Well, we are real Jews." Because teachers often underestimated their abilities and gave them culturally biased tests, Ethiopian children often were put in low-level classes. "It was ignorance, not racism," insists Menberu. "They see a shy boy who can barely speak Hebrew, so why not train him to be an electrician or a mechanic? A good-natured, pretty girl: well, she can take care of babies or old people. Because teachers stereotyped children, many intelligent ones lost the chance for a higher education. Our children are smart. They want to learn."

With most families reunited, the days of dead-end vocational boarding schools are ending. More than two thirds of Ethiopian children live at home and attend neighborhood schools. They're also integrating fairly well: 84 percent of Ethiopian children have Sabra friends. Recent studies show that when Ethiopian children are given enrichment courses and placed in good academic high schools, they match or surpass their Sabra peers. Teachers remark that their Ethiopian students often exhibit better memory skills, concentration, and patience than other students. "We come from a traditional African oral culture," explains Solomon. "Not only do children memorize the names of everyone in our extended family [from five hundred to twelve hundred members], we're expected to know our family members going back at least seven generations. We memorize all 150 psalms in the Book of Psalms and the hundreds of proverbs our parents taught us." Many, but not enough, children receive individualized tutoring and after-school courses in computers, Hebrew, and English. Thousands of Ethiopians attend free academic summer camps. As a result, the proportion of Ethiopian immigrant high school graduates eligible for matriculation certificates has quadrupled from about 7 percent in the early 1980s, the lowest figure of any ethnic group in Israel, to 28 percent in 2002. Quite an increase, but still, less than half the national average. More than half of Israel's Ethiopians are under age nineteen and, with a cash-strapped government, a significant number are falling though the cracks. "A lot desperately need more tutors, more mentors," insists Menberu. He knows because he works with Ethiopian youth like Yoni.

Yoni wears low-slung baggy jeans, adores Bob Marley and Rastafarian culture, and wears a knitted kippa atop his dreadlocks. Putting out a cigarette, he waits for friends outside Ethiopian Style, a hair salon on the fourth floor of Tel Aviv's Central Bus Station. Yoni is cutting class again from his religious school. "I thought about studying photography, but I'm doing lousy in school," he says in the latest Hebrew slang. "My teachers are really boring. All they do is give us homework and homework." More than half of Ethiopian children live in a single-parent family. Yoni lives with his father, an unemployed factory worker. Thursday afternoons, hundreds of Ethiopian teens hang out at the bus station. Some are disillusioned with school; many decide to cut class forever. Some visit the "drop-in center," two small rooms decorated with murals, nostalgic scenes of village life, white-robed Jews trekking to Israel and Ethiopians praying at Jerusalem's Western Wall. There are handwritten signs on the walls quoting rabbinic sages, like this one: "Nothing can stand in the way of the will." Kids sit on a worn couch and watch a *Star Wars* video; others meet with Ethiopian counselors who offer help to failing students and juvenile delinquents. Lately, few come. The Tel Aviv Central Bus Station is a prime target for terrorists. The terrorists aren't expected to disappear, and neither will another serious problem: Ethiopian children have almost double the high school dropout rate of Sabra children.

"In Ethiopia we didn't have a youth crisis. Everyone knew his role. The roles are not clearly defined here," says Batia Eyob, who interviewed hundreds of young Ethiopian Israelis for her master's thesis at the Hebrew University. "We had our traditional leaders and traditional extended families. The kessim were the religious authorities; here they have no role. Below them were the heads of families—elders, fathers. The system worked because of the village structure. Now that everyone is together in Israel we have leadership problems. This change has had painful effects on holding the community together." A serious graduate student who arrived in 1983 at age ten, Batia conducted some of the first research done on Ethiopian Jews in Israel by an Ethiopian Jew. To take the pulse of this geographically disparate group, she monitored Amharic-language call-in radio programs. "Most young people are trying to be as Israeli as possible. A lot find their 'Israeliness' in the army. It's not unusual for soldiers to hide medical problems so they can join the infantry, tank corps, and paratroopers. Many of them believe, 'The more front line, the more Israeli.' Others are trying to figure out who they are, struggling with mixed identities." In 1996, Tel Aviv University researchers placed two large maps on the floor, one of Israel and the other of Ethiopia. They asked two dozen former soldiers, all Ethiopian-born, to stand where they felt at home. A few hesitatingly stood on the Israeli map, a few on the Ethiopian map. Most chose the empty space in between. More than twenty thousand Ethiopians were born in Israel, and "a lot of them don't know much about Ethiopia," concedes Batia. They too are trying to figure out who they are.

In rap-and-reggae clubs like Soweto in Tel Aviv, Ethiopians in cool hip-hop clothes gyrate on the dance floor, imitating groups they watch on MTV. They are infatuated with African American rappers, actors, and basketball players. Some men wear gold chains and have adopted rapper nicknames like Ice-T and Puff Daddy. "I love rap. We call it a black person's CNN," says Devorah, a beautiful woman with long hair braided in cornrows and an emerald stud in her nostril. She and a girl-friend, who work at a Tel Aviv bank together, come here for late-night fun. "When my mother says stay home, I tell her this is a great place to meet [Ethiopian] guys. I know she wants me to meet one." Devorah goes on to explain that her family dislikes the "white guy" her sister married. Because of his color? "No," she says abruptly. Because he's a waiter? She admits that he doesn't have much ambition, but the big problem is "He's not religious. At the seder, he doesn't even know the prayers."

The government's most successful affirmative action initiative is in higher education. Ethiopian students in universities and colleges are fully subsidized, from tuition to housing. Ten years ago, there were only 145 Ethiopian college students, mostly in social work and education. Today, more than two thousand are studying social sciences, engineering, computer programming, nursing, and medicine. A girl Solomon rescued is now a diplomat with the Foreign Ministry, part of a burgeoning professional class that is serving as mentors in their own community. Shlomo Berihun is part of a new generation of Ethiopian university students: black and proud and Jewish—and playing parent to younger Ethiopians. Pointing to a group of high school students taking computer programming at an innovative science and math program at the Technion Institute in Haifa, he reports, "Most of their mothers and fathers have never been in a classroom. But once these kids get a taste of this, they want it." Shlomo holds a B.A. in psychology and a master's in management. "I get angry when people say Ethiopian kids aren't motivated. What about the barefoot children who walked from Ethiopia to try to get to Israel?" Shlomo himself survived a twenty-five-day trek from his village in northern Ethiopia to the Sudan in 1984. "On the way, we were robbed and left stranded in the desert." After eight months in a wretched Sudanese camp, Shlomo was airlifted to Israel. He was one of the lucky ones. Instead of being sent to a religious vocational boarding school, he studied at the Andover of Israeli boarding schools, which is about half Ethiopian. Shlomo credits the enlightened principal of Yemin Or Youth Village near Haifa for turning out high-achieving students. "We were

taught that if we want to be known for more than poverty and polite-
ness, higher education is the answer. We learned that we have a wonderful culture and must not lose it. Pride in our heritage is the basis for
self-pride. Without it, there's no success. Without a past, you don't have
a future."

Ethiopian soldiers have earned a reputation as highly patriotic and dis-
ciplined, with superb stamina and a fierce determination to excel. More
than 95 percent of eligible Ethiopian eighteen-year-old men serve in the
army, a higher percentage than any group of draftees. The first soldier to
die in the intifada was an Ethiopian, Yossi Tabjeh, flown to Israel when
he was eleven, shot by his Palestinian Authority partner while on a joint
patrol a few hours before Ariel Sharon made his provocative visit to the
Temple Mount. On September 4, 2001, Natan Sandaka also was on patrol with his Sabra partner. It was during morning rush hour on
Jerusalem's Street of the Prophets and Ethiopia Street. The soldiers spotted a young *haredi* with a beard, a long black coat, black kippa. His large
green backpack was suspicious. When Natan sprinted after him and ordered him to stop, the terrorist smirked and hit the switch. Natan took
the full force of the explosion. He was in a coma, severely burned, his
lungs punctured by shrapnel and not expected to live. "Natan saved my
life and the lives of many, many Israelis," his Sabra partner declares. "I
call him *hachi achi* [best brother]." Other members of his unit kept vigil
by his bed at Hadassah Hospital, as did President Moshe Katsav. Two
weeks later, Natan awoke to discover he was a national hero. "We work
hard to prove we're the best," said the disfigured Natan, who was a child
when he was rescued during Operation Solomon. "We want to return
something to Israel for what it has given us." His family of ten has sent
all its sons to combat units.

Because Ethiopian women come from religious families, they have the
option of serving in the regular army or performing national service in
jobs like teaching in after-school programs for Ethiopian children. Parents are no longer reluctant to let their daughters move onto mixed army
bases, and it is no longer remarkable to see Ethiopian women soldiers
barking orders at men during rifle and tank training. Bat-Chen Yalu escaped Ethiopia in 1985 with her parents and eight siblings, fleeing on

foot with only the clothes on their backs for a month-long trek into Sudan. In a daring raid into the Sudan desert, an Israeli Air Force rescue unit swooped the family into a C-130 and airlifted them and other Ethiopians to Israel. After she was drafted into an Air Force rescue unit, Bat-Chen discovered she was working with some of the same doctors and medics who rescued her when she was only five. "Destiny guided me to those who brought me to Israel," she says.

"We owe our Jewish brothers and sisters our education, our homes, and even our lives. But during the blood riots the whole country discovered we're not as patient and gentle as they thought." Solomon is talking about what the Ethiopians call the "big outrage." On January 24, 1996, *Ma'ariv* newspaper broke the story that for years, officials of the Magen David Adom blood bank had been secretly discarding blood donated by Ethiopians because of fear of HIV infection. When they discovered that blood they'd donated out of patriotism was being dumped, about fifteen thousand Ethiopians marched to the prime minister's office in Jerusalem. Some protesters pelted police with rocks and bottles filled with fake blood. Others held banners that read "Our blood is as red as yours" and "We are just as Jewish as you are!" "They deceived us by accepting our blood and then secretly throwing it out. Blood is very symbolic to us; it means the soul. So rejecting the substance that makes us and other Jews one family was very emotional," Solomon explains. "It felt like our fellow Jews had discarded us into garbage cans." The Ethiopian community's indignation evoked national sympathy. After the magnificent secret airlifts, people were saddened to see Ethiopians so disillusioned and wounded. Close to 70 percent of Israelis agreed with the protesters. Strangers stopped Ethiopians on the streets and congratulated them for speaking out. Prime Minister Shimon Peres apologized, calling the blood policy "irresponsible and stupid," and appointed a committee of inquiry. The findings: the covert blood dumping was not racism, it was an extreme case of misplaced paternalism. Medical officials justified their secrecy, claiming they didn't want to stigmatize Ethiopians, who had left a country where AIDS is prevalent. The demonstrations woke Israelis to other serious problems. Despite the government's affirmative action policies in housing, jobs, and university admissions, socioeconomic integration was not progressing as quickly as hoped.

Before the blood riots, Israelis rarely discussed racial discrimination, which, because of its connection to the Holocaust and anti-Semitism, is an emotionally loaded term. At Shalon High School in Kiryat Gat, which has a mix of Ethiopian, Mizrahi, and ex-Soviet students, a science teacher expresses a prevalent perspective: "Racism? It doesn't exist. We're all Jews. My Ethiopian students, especially those born here, think, talk, and act like everyone else." When Ethiopians complain of discrimination, a common response is "Welcome to the club," which means all immigrants, from Holocaust survivors to Indians to Georgians, experience prejudice based on ethnicity, economic class, and how long they have been in Israel. Known for their formal dress and behavior, German immigrants are nicknamed *yekke,* Yiddish for "jacket." Moroccan toughs are called "knives"; wealthy Russians are called mafiosi. And, as with everywhere on earth, homegrown ethnic "humor" can get rough: "What's the difference between a Hungarian and a Romanian? A Hungarian will sell his grandmother. A Romanian will too, but he won't deliver." But when Ethiopians hear Israelis joking "Why did we bring you to Israel? We needed spare parts for the Yemenites," they don't laugh.

"Ethiopians are especially sensitive to questions of color," says Batia, "because we never were a racial minority until we arrived in Israel. And lots of Israelis haven't had much contact with us. A student at Ben-Gurion University told me that when she entered an office for a job interview, the employer asked her straight, 'When we spoke on the phone, why didn't you tell me that you're Ethiopian?' " In Hebrew, there is no word for tact. In a recent poll, when asked to choose between equally qualified candidates for a job, Sabras much preferred Ethiopians to former Soviets. Ninety-five percent of Sabras said they would not mind having their child serve under an Ethiopian army officer, 89 percent said they would be happy to be treated by an Ethiopian doctor, and 71 percent do not consider Ethiopians a burden on the economy. However, 71 percent would consider it "a problem" for their children or grandchildren to marry an Ethiopian.

Although overt racial discrimination is rare, Solomon and other Ethiopian Israelis had to battle to let in about twenty thousand more people stranded in Ethiopia because some government and religious officials still question the authenticity of their Jewish roots. They are called Falash Mora, descendants of Jews who converted to Christianity. In the nineteenth century, European Protestant missionaries targeted Ethiopian

Jews for conversion, offering them food and education. Then the great famine of 1888–92 wiped out about two thirds of Ethiopian Jewry, including many kessim. The Ethiopian Coptic Christian Church owned much of the land and wouldn't let Jews own it unless they converted. Many became Christian to survive. "My uncle's family converted so they could own land," says Solomon. "His family secretly continued practicing Judaism. Their Christian neighbors considered them Jews." Solomon compares these conversions to the forced conversion of Spain's Jews during the Inquisition. Their detractors in the Israeli government and religious establishment argue that Israel must not open its gates to people whose ties to the Jewish people are tenuous, that if they let in the Falash Mora, untold thousands of impoverished Ethiopian Christians looking for a better life will try to enter Israel by pretending they are Falash Mora. Some already have used fraud and bribery and sham marriages. Each Easter and Christmas, they fill the Coptic church on Jerusalem's Ethiopia Street.

Supporters of Falash Mora emigration argue that unlike the more than thirty thousand Christian immigrants from the former Soviet Union, they have Jewish blood and Jewish roots and relatives in Israel. Thousands of ragged adults and children have moved from their villages to camps in Addis Ababa and Gondar, sleeping on fiber mats with barely enough to eat, awaiting permission from the Israeli Embassy to emigrate. Solomon, an expert on the lineage of Jewish Ethiopians, has returned to Ethiopia to help Israeli immigration authorities verify each person's Jewish ancestry. He also helps supervise schools where adults and children learn Hebrew and rabbinic Judaism. Children and adults there keep kosher, light Shabbat candles, and blow the shofar for Rosh Hashana. "They're living Orthodox Jewish lives," says Solomon. "When I saw a boy in the synagogue close his eyes when he was reciting the *Sh'ma* [Judaism's holiest prayer, 'Hear, O Israel, the Lord our God, the Lord is One'], I asked him, 'What do you see when you close your eyes?' 'Israel,' he told me." Ethiopian Israelis and groups like the North American Conference on Ethiopian Jewry are pressuring Israel to allow in the remaining twenty thousand Falash Mora. Once in Israel, some undergo a ceremonial return to Judaism.

Even for the vast majority of Ethiopian Israelis who have lived as devout Jews for centuries, in Israel religious life is not without its problems.

Because Ethiopian Judaism was based on the Bible, not the Talmud, the Israeli rabbinic establishment is ambivalent about their full Jewishness. The Chief Rabbinate insists they go through a symbolic conversion ceremony to remove all doubts about their Jewishness. The rabbis reason that during centuries of separation from the rest of world Jewry, Ethiopians didn't follow proper religious laws of divorce, remarriage, and conversion; thus, there was a significant mix of non-Jews. A few weeks after Solomon arrived in Israel, the Rabbinate sent the sixteen-year-old a note demanding he go through a symbolic conversion process, a ritual immersion in a *mikvah.* (This is an insulting request for Ethiopian Jews, who purified themselves in rivers and equate immersion in a ritual bath with the baptism Christian missionaries tried to force on them.) They also demanded he undergo a symbolic circumcision (taking a drop of blood from the penis in case the original circumcision had not been performed according to *halakha,* Jewish law). "When I read that note, I was so depressed. I went back to my room on the kibbutz and cried for hours," Solomon recalls. "How can I convert from Jewish to Jewish? I can't be more Jewish. I grew up Jewish, praying three times a day, always keeping strictly kosher. I refused to go though that humiliating process to be accepted as a full Israeli Jew. I was so angry, I threw off my kippa."

While he was serving in the air force during the Lebanon War, Solomon got time off to prepare for his wedding. Wearing his khaki officer's uniform, he went to the Chief Rabbinate's office in Jerusalem for a document that all Israeli Jews are required to have before they get married: proof that they are single and Jewish. A clerk asked him to show his certificate of conversion through ritual immersion. "I told him I'm a Jew. No matter how many times you put me in water, I can't become more Jewish than I am. I refuse to do it." After the clerk refused to give Solomon the document, he demanded to see the rabbi in charge. The clerk told Solomon that the rabbi was busy. Outraged, the air force officer stormed into the rabbi's office. When Solomon tried to clarify the situation, the rabbi, a bearded man wearing the black kippa of an ultra-Orthodox Jew, shook his head and said the conversion ruling applies to all Ethiopian Jews. "I was furious. I told him I've been fighting a war for four years. Then I said, 'You've never been in the army. How can you tell me I'm not Jewish enough to get married? I suffered to be a Jew in Ethiopia and now you're making me suffer here?' The rabbi still refused.

I told him that I wasn't going to leave his office until he signed the certificate. He reached for the phone and said he was going to call the police. I put my M-16 in his face and told him, 'If you dial that phone, I'll kill you. Sign the paper.' He did and I walked out."

The chutzpah Solomon and other young Ethiopian soldiers acquired taught them to speak out rather than be quiet and accepting. "We learned to stop sitting on our hands and to act like other Israelis when we had grievances," says Solomon. "We learned quickly the Israeli way of getting attention." Fuming Ethiopians held marches through the streets of Jerusalem and sit-down protests outside the Chief Rabbinate headquarters. Some threatened mass suicide unless the rabbis backed down on the humiliating demand that all Ethiopians go through symbolic conversion. Much of the press and secular Israelis supported their cause. Finally, the Chief Rabbinate ruled that the state accept Ethiopians as Jews.

The Rabbinate, however, refused to back down on another painful issue: they stripped away the religious authority of the kessim. The kes cannot conduct a wedding, a bar mitzvah, or a burial. When Solomon's seventy-three-year-old mother died in 1994, over thirty-five hundred Ethiopians traveled from all over Israel to the cemetery in Lod to pay their respects. Her father was the late Chief Kes of Ethiopia. Incongruously, an ultra-Orthodox rabbi with a black hat and black coat conducted the funeral ceremony. "There were fifteen learned kessim there and they all knew how to bury my mother according to our traditions, which are right out of the Five Books of Moses," Solomon remembers sadly. "But in Israel, none of them could."

III

Widening Fault Lines

Between Jews and Jews

9

The Haredim

Jewish-Jewish-Jewish

↺ There's Jewish. Then there's Jewish-Jewish. We're Jewish-Jewish-Jewish. —Moshe Stein, age thirteen

A sweltering desert wind known as a *hamsin* blows through Jerusalem. The airless bus is filled with female and male soldiers listening to the bus radio blaring out ominous intifada bulletins, interspersed with earsplitting rock songs. Two Hebrew University students in shorts and tank tops are in the back chatting, ignoring the rotund woman across the aisle, rocking as if she's in a trance. She's reading the Book of Psalms. When the bus nears Mea Sharim, the city's most populous ultra-Orthodox neighborhood, this woman, clothed in an old-fashioned long dress with long sleeves, black stockings, and a dark scarf, gets off along with other similarly attired women. Men in black coats, black pants, and black hats also disembark, disappearing into the bustling open-air market. These ultra-Orthodox Jews, or haredim, biblical Hebrew for "those who tremble before God," make up about a third of all Jerusalemites. Many look as though they belong in a nineteenth-century Polish or Russian shtetl. In many ways, they do: the calendar here always seems to read 1874, the year pious East European Jews built the first Jewish communities outside the Old City in nearby Mea Sharim. The area still resembles a walled

173

fortress; today, however, the walls are psychological. Living in a carefully constructed, self-contained world, haredim try to preserve centuries-old East European Jewish traditions. The air in this ultra-Orthodox area of Jerusalem "is saturated with prayers and dreams," as the late Israeli poet Yehuda Amichai wrote. "Like the air in industrial cities, it's hard to breathe."

There are as many ways to be ultra-Orthodox in Israel as there are to be Jewish. To the untrained eye, however, ultra-Orthodox Jews appear indistinguishable, like extras out of *Yentl* or *Fiddler on the Roof*. Subtle differences in their clothes and head coverings can reveal which rabbis, rituals, and politicians they follow. One group of haredi men wear sashes over long black coats and black pants tucked deep into black socks; others wear short pants that reveal white socks. All men wear black kippot and cover them with black hats. To the discerning eye, a hat broadcasts the wearer's religious beliefs. Each haredi group wears hats tilted at distinctively different angles. Some men push their brims up, others down. Some hats have three indentations, others two. Then there are men's *peyot,* the side curls. Some men wear theirs short, others dangle them below their ears.

Signs in this haredi neighborhood warn women to dress modestly, not to expose much skin. Blouses cover them from collarbone to wrists. Their long skirts barely reveal their opaque stockings or knee socks. Even young girls must wear long dresses, following Deuteronomy 22:5: "The woman shall not wear that which pertains to a man. All who do so are an abomination to the Lord." All married haredi women cover their hair, adhering to a Jewish law that says a "woman's hair is lust-provoking." Depending on their haredi group, women wear demure hats, scarves, or wigs. Religious Mizrahi women follow a ruling by Rabbi Ovadia Yosef, who forbids them to use wigs. In his eyes, orthodox Ashkenazi women who wear wigs violate the stricture that "the sight of a woman's hair is an impropriety." Even though all haredi groups believe Jewish laws must be followed strictly, they often disagree about how they should be interpreted. Members of different haredi groups rarely pray in each other's synagogues.

Though decimated during the Holocaust, Ashkenazi haredim are no longer a marginal minority as they were when Israel was founded. They have ballooned to almost half a million, largely due to their soaring birthrate and a renaissance of newly religious Jews. The baby boom is apparent; narrow streets are filled with pregnant women pushing baby carriages and children playing everywhere. On a jungle gym, girls in ankle-length dresses manage to perform acrobatics, while their friends jump rope and roller-skate. Wide-eyed boys admire a thirteen-year-old friend's bar mitzvah present, an almost new racing bike. They all wear black kippot and have white *tzitzit,* or ritual fringes, peeking out from under their shirts. No secular children are in sight. "My father wants me to have friends who believe like us," explains Moshe Stein, the bar mitzvah boy. "They [secular Jews] don't know what is *Shabbos* [Yiddish for Sabbath]. And they don't know what is kosher. There is Jewish. Then there's Jewish-Jewish. We're Jewish-Jewish-Jewish."

His father, Benjamin Stein, agreed to let his family be interviewed if their real names and identifying details were not used. A thoughtful, gaunt-looking man, he appears older than his thirty-five years. His hair, short peyot, and generous beard are peppered with gray. With ten children, the scene in their four-bedroom government-subsidized apartment is controlled chaos. "With children in the house, all corners are full," he remarks. When Benjamin was twenty, a professional matchmaker introduced him to sixteen-year-old Sarah. After two walks in the park, they decided to marry. Quickly and faithfully, they followed the commandment "Be fruitful and multiply" (Genesis 1:28). "Sweeter than honey is a house filled with children," he says in uncolloquial Hebrew. Benjamin is a fourth-generation Israeli, yet his Hebrew is stilted, a sign of his limited contact with the nonreligious world. Books on Jewish religious law, halakha, line the Steins' living room walls. One small section of the wall is intentionally bare and unpainted in memory of the destruction of the Temple. Hung prominently above the huge dining room table is a black-and-white photograph of a 103-year-old man with a flowing white beard and black hat: Rabbi Eliezar Menahem Schach, the leader of the non-Hasidic "Lithuanian" haredim, the religious group to which the Steins belong. (Although many followers do not have Lithuanian ancestry, the group named itself after the country where their style of Judaism once flourished, primarily in the city of Vilna, now Vilnius, once called "the Jerusalem of Europe.") Benjamin was among the hundreds of thousands of ultra-Orthodox male mourners who turned out for Rabbi Schach's funeral in Bnei Brak in 2001. From the beginning of the state, Rabbi

Schach pressured the government to make public institutions observe Jewish practices and give all ultra-Orthodox students military exemptions. He frequently angered the non-Orthodox majority by calling them "pork-eating idolaters," claiming they are not "real Jews." Even though haredi leaders rail against "godless" Israelis, secular politicians continue to court them. Until the 2003 elections, their political power could make or break government coalitions.

Secular Zionist leaders assumed religion would have little place in the new country. The once-illustrious haredi East European world of great Torah learning centers was wiped out during the Holocaust; about four fifths of the haredim were murdered in concentration camps, a higher proportion than any other group of Jewish victims. Soon after independence, Prime Minister Ben-Gurion agreed to Rabbi Schach's and other rabbis' requests to free haredi scholars of military obligation and let them try to rebuild their devastated community. When Ben-Gurion introduced military deferments in 1954, they applied to about four hundred students; in 2002, deferments were granted to over thirty thousand draft-age yeshiva students. Israeli leaders did not foresee the astounding explosion of draft-exempt religious scholars. Today, more Jews are studying in religious academies than in the entire Jewish world before the Holocaust.

The vast majority of haredi males, like Benjamin and his three sons, are full-time religious students. Benjamin spends most of his day studying in a *kollel*, an academy where married men study Judaism's holiest book, the Torah. (The school is subsidized by the government and donations from abroad.) The Torah, from the Hebrew verb meaning "to teach, to guide," refers to the first five books of the Bible, the Pentateuch or the Five Books of Moses. "The Torah is God's gift to us. It is God's blueprint, His book of laws." Benjamin goes on to add that for thousands of years "the Torah has kept Jews alive, telling us how to behave, how to be Jews. It is the bond for Jews scattered all over the globe." For haredim, the Torah is the word of God, dictated to Moses on Mt. Sinai. Haredi males also pore over the rest of the Jewish Bible: the T'nakh, an acronym of Torah (Law), Neviim (Prophets), and Ketuvim (Writings), and the Talmud, an encyclopedic work interpreting biblical laws and oral traditions and extensive commentaries. (Jews do not call their Bible the Old Testament, because they consider their Bible the *only* Testament.) Haredi men devote hours to memorizing, discussing, and disputing detailed commentaries that cover virtually every aspect of Jewish life, from medicine to marriage to menstruation.

Quite a few centuries-old observations written by rabbis who were psychologists of their day are still rich and relevant; others are totally arcane. "Study is my livelihood and Talmud is my profession," declares Benjamin, who doesn't work. The same is true for about 70 percent of Israeli haredi men. As he succinctly puts it, "The spiritual wealth of learning Talmud is worth more than any paycheck." His wife is the family's only wage earner. A plump, ebullient thirty-four-year-old, Sarah Stein wears a reddish wig, *sheitel* in Yiddish. It's smartly coifed, which is not surprising, as she styles and sells wigs imported from New York in the dingy apartment she leases near their apartment in Geula, which means "redemption" in Hebrew. Here ultrareligious women can escape from diapers, dishes, and dogma. In the straightlaced haredi world, where a married woman's duty is to be attractive only to her husband, wall posters sometimes criticize women who wear "too fashionable" wigs. Indeed, some haredi women deliberately wear frumpy synthetic wigs. But not Sarah's customers. They leave her salon in chic, even sexy-looking wigs. "Modesty is within, no matter what you wear. It's not bad to keep beautiful," Sarah insists. "No one tells us to be ugly. Otherwise, we would stand out in our neglectedness."

Sarah takes her grueling schedule, split between clients and children, in stride; she always has lived in a world where men learn and women work. Being married to a full-time Talmudic scholar means she is terminally tired but has a prized place in Israeli haredi society. "Back when Jews lived in shtetls and ghettoes, people were so poor they were busy just trying to find enough to eat. So how many men could afford a life of spiritual study? Very few, I tell you. To study Torah and Talmud is the ultimate *mitzvah*: everything is there. Everything. Laws, ethics, and history. And even psychology. It's like the ocean, so vast and deep. And to be a scholar like Benjamin? And right here in Jerusalem? The biggest honor." To stress her point, Sarah quotes a line from Isaiah (2:3): "For out of Zion shall go forth Torah and the Word of God from Jerusalem."

The Steins depend on government subsidies, including stipends for each child, free health services, municipal tax exemptions, and, of course, Sarah's earnings. Her wig business is doing well, but with ten children and slashes in government subsidies, buying meat or eating at the neighborhood *glatt* kosher pizzeria are infrequent treats. The children wear hand-me-downs. This Passover, Sarah hopes to have enough money to buy them new shoes. "What we don't have in money, we have in spirituality," she comments, quoting a religious teaching. "What we have is not poverty, it's living simply." In haredi neighborhoods, the un-adorned face of this "simple living" is especially evident during holidays, when people line up for free food parcels. Near the Steins' apartment, every Thursday afternoon at 5:30 P.M. a charity distributes Shabbat meals. Jerusalem has the highest poverty level of any Jewish city in Israel and the lowest per capita income. It is followed by the mostly haredi town of Bnei Brak. The average haredi family has more than seven children. More than half live below the poverty line, dependent on public money, supplemented by charity. Non-Orthodox Israelis are quick to point out that it is poverty by choice, as close to 60 percent of haredi men have tax exemptions and are not looking for work.

In haredi communities, where doors are often unlocked, families de-pend on mutual support. Neighbors baby-sit and lend each other cars, clothes, and cribs. "If anyone in the community needs help, everyone is there. You're never alone," confides Sarah, who holds up a fax of a prayer from a friend of a friend in Bnei Brak. The stranger has a sick baby and wants Sarah to take the piece of paper to the nearby Western Wall and slip it between the ancient stones. Neighbors frequently pop over to send a fax, use her washing machine, or borrow cassette tapes; the Steins' collection ranges from "haredi rock" to commentaries on the Torah. In what little free time Sarah has, she joins friends and customers in an all-woman choir.

Like almost all haredim, the Steins don't own a television and never have been to the cinema. "We're not against technology," Sarah declares, pointing to her flip-top cell phone and microwave. "But movies and tele-vision are full of temptations that poison family purity and give people *yatzir ha-ra* [the evil instinct]. I'd love to see haredi television. Maybe one day we'll have it. For now at least, we have plenty of good haredi talk radio." Although the Steins own a radio, the children are not allowed to touch the dials to avoid tuning in to nonharedi stations. "There's lots of good music. There's the matchmaker program. I listen to people calling rabbis with problems and the psychic rabbi. His soul is in such pure shape that he sees things right. He's been correct with my friends. And with me, when it was a tense time and I was not sure to import wigs or not. He told me that the door of success is marked push and pull. So I pushed and the women are buying. One just bought three wigs! And I love listening to the haredi horoscope program, too. Using your horoscope in a holy way is acceptable. Not only do the stars have meaning, in Judaism every number does too. I like number 6 because it represents the heaven and the earth and the four directions. The rabbi explained that Magen David [literally, Shield of David, the six-sided Jewish Star of David, which is a twentieth-century symbol of Judaism] means God is everywhere. So we listen to the radio. I've given up trying to convince Benjamin to buy the kids a computer. He won't hear of it." When the Steins fly to visit relatives in New York, they sit in El Al's movie-free "haredi section," where men can don their prayer shawls and phylacteries, *tallis* and *tefillin,* and pray in the aisles facing east toward the Western Wall without attracting stares. "Once when we flew," admits Sarah, who is a bit of a rebel, "I let the children move to where they could see *101 Dalmations*. And why not? My neighbor lets her kids watch *The Lion King* on CD on their laptop and nothing bad happens."

In the Steins' world, practically everything is divided into obligatory and forbidden. They strictly follow Jewish laws and thousands of rituals and rabbinical edicts that govern things from which shoe to tie first in the morning to which music they may listen to and whether software piracy falls under the biblical prohibition against stealing. Nonharedi Jews ignore most of these restrictive, ancient rules and traditions. Haredi Judaism places a heavy emphasis on ritual as a way of getting closer to God. Haredim think about how they perform nearly every act, from preparing food to washing hands before eating to making love on Friday night, because each act is a spiritual link to God. "We don't do things automatically," Benjamin explains. "There is meaning in every little part of life." In the Stein household, the Ten Commandments are just the beginning; religious Jews try to follow the Torah's 613 divine commandments or *mitzvot,* specific ethical and moral laws. "Our life is guided by the mitzvot," says Sarah, who strictly obeys *kashrut,* the biblical dietary laws meant to add sanctity and hygiene to Jewish lives and help Jews maintain their identity living among non-Jewish neighbors. The Steins also rigorously observe Shabbat, which in Hebrew means "to cease" as well as "to rest."

"From birth, we're raised on Shabbos," explains Sarah, using the Yiddish word for the sabbath. "It's the Queen of the Days. It means joy, no work—just praying and eating and relaxing with family and friends, doing things that really count." Shabbat has been compared to a sanctuary of time for the soul, time to feel the world of the sacred. It isn't just a day. It's a destination. The Hebrew words for the six other days are simply numbers counted down until Shabbat: Sunday is the "the first day" to Shabbat, Monday "the second day" to Shabbat, and so on, until the seventh day. Most Jewish shops and businesses in Israel are closed by noon on Fridays to give people time to leave the everyday world and prepare for the Shabbat, the only Jewish "holiday" that is one of the Ten Commandments. For more than three thousand years, as Jews have wandered around the world, they have carried Shabbat with them as a portable home, a movable tabernacle. Shabbat is the heart of Judaism. As poet Ahad Ha Am wrote, "More than the people of Israel have kept Shabbat, Shabbat has kept the people of Israel."

From sunset on Friday evening until three stars appear in the sky on Saturday evening, observant Jews will not do any work. They will not handle money, answer the phone, listen to the radio. They will not light cigarettes, turn on lights or the stove, or use any kind of electric appliances because "kindling a fire" means work. Religious kibbutzim use timing devices to activate the electric milking machines early Saturday morning and to turn them off after the milking is completed. Because observant Jews are not allowed to push elevator buttons on the Sabbath, the Knesset passed a law in 2001 stating that every new multistory public or private building, from hotels to hospitals, must have at least one "Shabbat elevator," which automatically stops at each floor. Haredim interpret work so strictly some will not even tear toilet paper and have a supply prepared in advance. Over the centuries, hundreds of pages of obtuse, esoteric minutiae have been written about types of work prohibited on the Sabbath, which include weaving, sewing, building, cooking, writing, plowing, and reaping. Riding a bus is forbidden, as it is the same as riding a horse, which was prohibited by the Talmud "in case he pulls a twig off a tree," because of the biblical injunction that forbids "reaping."

Driving is forbidden because it entails work, igniting an internal combustion engine. On Shabbat, haredim try to rule their roads, sometimes cursing or throwing stones at blasphemers who dare to drive through their neighborhoods.

To prepare for Friday night Shabbat dinner, Sarah and her daughters spend the day shopping, cleaning, and cooking. She bakes challa, a cakelike bread that Ashkenazim twist and braid as a reminder that Shabbat holiness must be intertwined with the secular days. Gefilte fish (Yiddish for "stuffed") is a family favorite (fish are a symbol of fertility, and on this night, married couples are required to make love). Sarah and the girls put on a white tablecloth and wear white Shabbat dresses; white is associated with purity. Forty minutes before sundown, Sarah ushers in the "divine presence" by lighting two Sabbath candles. One of the Shabbat rules prohibits lighting a fire, so the candles must be lit prior to the beginning of the Shabbat. One lit candle symbolizes the soul; lighting two mystically provides an "extra soul." One is in honor of the commandment to remember the Sabbath and keep it holy, and the other one represents guarding the Sabbath by not performing the forbidden labors. Women perform this sacred act "because home is even more important than *shul* [synagogue]. Here, God feels at home." Men must pray three times daily at particular hours; women are not required to participate in public prayer "because God wants us to do what's most important—be at home with our children," explains Sarah as she wipes spilled Coca-Cola from the kitchen floor. At twenty minutes before sundown, Benjamin and the boys walk to the nearby synagogue, where they read the same weekly Torah portion Jews all over the world are reading. Before eating, Benjamin and the boys sing King Solomon's love song (from Proverbs 31:10–31), extolling the virtues of "a woman of valor," showing appreciation for his exhausted wife. Then Benjamin recites a *kiddush,* a sanctification prayer over the wine and then over the challa.

They often invite friends to this festive, cholesterol-rich dinner. Sometimes when there are male guests, the little girls get fidgety, even unruly. At home, as in the synagogue, when they're among unrelated males, they are not allowed to pray and sing. Centuries ago, the Talmudists who wrote the Gemara decided that "a woman's voice is lewd" and hearing it will distract men from praying. That's why haredim follow a law called *kol ishah,* voice of the women, which prohibits them from hearing a woman singing or praying. In haredi and Orthodox synagogues, men and women sit apart so they will not be distracted from prayers. In haredi synagogues, women sit in balconies or behind curtains where men cannot sneak a peek at them. The proscription against men and women mixing in public worship is taken from Talmudic descriptions of a women's section in the ancient Temple of Jerusalem.

At haredi weddings and bar mitzvahs and other celebrations, men and women don't eat or dance together; they're separated by a partition, or *mechitzah*. "We went to the bar mitzvah of a neighbor boy who plays with Moshe. When they served the meat and chicken, it looked delicious, but we just ate the salads," recalls Sarah. "They're very religious Moroccans. Benjamin says we shouldn't eat because their food isn't kosher enough for us. When the women asked why I wasn't eating, I didn't want to embarrass them, so I said I had stomach flu. We joined the toast because their wine is okay for us. I have nothing against them or Persians or even Kurds, but their customs and halakha are not ours. Mizrahim even eat rice at Pesah [Passover]." Not only are there competing kashrut standards between Ashkenazi haredim and Mizrahim, but even within the Ashkenazi haredi world people sometimes won't eat in each other's homes. Some haredi groups operate their own ritual slaughter facilities because only their ultrastrict kosher label is "kosher" enough.

Whether it's chicken or detergent, Sarah buys only superscrupulously kosher products, with the "right" kind of kosher certificate, certified by her community's own strict inspectors. "For us, only *She 'erit Yisrael* [the certificate of kashrut observed by the Lithuanians] can be trusted," she explains. "Our inspectors never allow the tiniest trace of an unkosher substance to infiltrate." Their neighborhood, a mix of different haredi and Mizrahi groups, has markets with products sporting an array of kosher certificates. A few markets even have separate shopping hours for men and women. The manager of a nearby post office refuses to employ women; they might offend male customers. At public pools haredim frequent, men and women swim at alternating times. Some of Israel's state beaches are segregated into sections for haredi men and women. Haredi women usually sit apart from men on buses; when they walk, some even move aside when men are near so as not to contaminate them by "passing between two women." "Some people believe in this foolishness," says Sarah with a chuckle. "Down the block, there's a family of Gerer [Israel's largest Hasidic sect]. He's so strict like that with his wife. He won't let her walk in public with him, and he doesn't even call her by her first name." Although not nearly as rigid, Sarah and Benjamin dare not show any physical or verbal affection in public. Holding hands in front of strangers is immodest. It is forbidden lest it arouse lascivious thoughts, which in turn could result in wanton emission of semen, a halakhic offense. This is why haredi rabbis usually prohibit the use of condoms, birth control pills, and the IUD except for medical or psychological reasons. Haredim consult their rabbis for medical advice on matters from impotence to infertility to mammograms. Some haredi women are too modest to let their doctors touch their bodies. If the doctor discovers cancer or any other serious disease, women often keep it a secret. Such a stigma makes children less marriageable.

At home, too, haredim must observe rules of modesty. When Sarah's sixty-year-old secular friend visited from Tel Aviv, Benjamin refused to sit with her because unrelated people of the opposite sex should not be alone in the same room. The friend gave their seven-year-old daughter a "dental hygienist" Barbie doll. After she left, Benjamin put the Barbie back in the box, as uncomfortable with Barbie's shape as the most militant feminist. "He said that what secular girls know at seven, our girls must not know until seventeen," reports Sarah, who did not protest when her husband instructed her to exchange the curvaceous Barbie for a "proper" baby doll. "He knows more about everything that really matters. Just like a bus can have only one driver, in marriage there can be only one leader. The holy blessed Torah teaches us that if we treat our husbands as kings, they will treat us as queens." Occasionally, she chafes at his treatment. When Sarah brought home a popular Israeli woman's magazine to study the latest hairstyles, her husband spotted it and found the photos "morally polluted." Sarah took the "unkosher," unfit magazine out to the trash, even though she disagreed. Somehow, she has forgotten to discard the issues she keeps in her wig salon.

The haredi newspaper Benjamin reads has no photos of attractive models. It has no photos of women at all. Some female reporters use only their initials, and a typical wedding announcement runs only the bride's first name. (The paper also has listed Jerusalem shops and restaurants that dare to open on Shabbat and instructs readers to boycott them. Some have been vandalized or burned.) Benjamin occasionally buys a secular newspaper "to understand their thinking. It's very uncomfortable reading their press—it's controlled by haredi haters. They call us 'Khomeinists' and 'parasites,' " he says sadly, alluding to the widespread secular Israeli perception that haredim are fundamentalist draft dodgers living on government handouts. "Whenever I leave the neighborhood, I know what people are thinking when they see me. I can feel their hatred. When I went to the Passport Office, I heard a woman in line say, 'The only thing we have in common with those *dossim* is our passports.' " (Dossim, a derogatory word for haredim, is Yiddish-accented Hebrew for "religious.") He describes hiking in Ein Gedi near Masada and stopping at a gas station afterward. "I asked where is the men's room. The attendant said, 'It's over there, but it's for Israelis, not 'blacks' [a derisive term referring to his black haredi garb]. All the secular know about us are just ugly lies. They say they hate us even more than the Arabs. But ever since the Arabs started sending suicide bombers here, at least they've stopped saying that."

The Steins' eldest child, Leah, a sixteen-year-old with a long braid and braces, soon will be ready for the professional matchmaker. A young haredi woman's value is based on her looks and her family's religiosity, finances, and connections. Haredi children marry young—daughters usually by seventeen to twenty, sons by twenty to twenty-three—and the average haredi family will have eight children. So, by the time Sarah and Benjamin are in their fifties, they could be "blessed" with more than seventy grandchildren. "With small families, rumors go around that something is wrong," Sarah confides. "Still, I hope Leah doesn't have too many. Nowadays, who can afford a decent-size apartment? To find one, she'll probably have to move out of Jerusalem. Really cheap ones are out in the settlements. But what good is a big apartment if your [Palestinian] neighbors want you dead?"

A great catch for a "Torah-true" girl like Leah would be a "Torah-true [haredi scholar]" man. "I know The Holy One will help us find someone suitable." Would a Torah prodigy from a respected Hasidic family qualify? Sarah points out that her ultra-Orthodox group, the Lithuanians, also call themselves Mitnagdim, which means opponents. "That's because our rabbis were against the Hasidim. We still don't like the way they center their lives around their rabbis and let them run everything.

But compared to others in this country, the Hasidim are the closest thing we have to Jews."

Hasidism swept through destitute Jewish communities in Eastern Europe in the eighteenth century. The charismatic founder of this populist movement, Rabbi Yisrael Ben Eliezer, better known as the Baal Shem Tov (Master of the Good Name), challenged the traditional Lithuanian practices of Judaism. He taught that the way to God is through the heart, not the head, through fervent prayers, songs, and dance, not stuffy Talmudic study. Hasidic folksy teachings brought a spiritual uplift to downtrodden semiliterate Jews who never could be scholars or rabbis like the Lithuanians. His disciples stressed the joy of performing good deeds rather than the fear of disobeying minor Jewish laws. Hasidic embrace of kabbalah, the practice of Jewish mysticism, also attracted followers. Its magical, mysterious teachings about heaven, reincarnation, and the coming of the Messiah offered an escape from a miserable world of stark poverty and murderous Cossack and peasant pogroms.

The revolutionary Hasidic teachings became such a threat that the unofficial head of Lithuanian and Russian Jewry, the esteemed Vilna Gaon (the Genius of Vilna, Lithuania) Elijah Ben Solomon Zalman, excommunicated the Hasidic Jews, whose anti-intellectual attitudes and emotion-laden practices, in his view, distorted Judaism. The bitterness has lessened, but Lithuanians still consider themselves the "true guardians" of Talmudic law and traditions and believe Judaism survived through the centuries because Jews were attached to Torah study. They have no doubts that Judaism must not change with the times; rather, Judaism must change the times. Religious Ashkenazim divided into two groups: Lithuanians and Hasidim. The rift did not end there. Hasidic groups split and named themselves after their founding rabbis' pre-Holocaust East European hometowns, such as Ger, Breslov, Belz, Satmar, and Lubavitch. Almost two centuries later, Lithuanians and the various Hasidic groups are still at odds, but usually ally to vote against the non-Orthodox majority.

"Benjamin really wants Leah to marry a Torah-true boy, but on this, we agree like cat and dog," she confides. "I prefer her to marry a man who earns a real living, maybe working with computers." An obvious solution might be a computer-savvy Lubavitcher boy, as these Hasidim were the first religious Jewish group with their own website and some run their own high-tech companies. Sarah looks incredulous. "The way they revere that rabbi? It's close to idolization. We [Lithuanians] don't believe in a miracle-working *rebbe*. Our leaders called him a heretic." She's referring to the charismatic Rabbi Menachem Schneerson, who led the Lubavitchers/Habad for forty-four years from his home in New York's Crown Heights until he died in 1994 at age ninety-one. "They built an exact replica of his red brick Brooklyn headquarters right here in Israel and he never even visited. And when I was at the airport, I saw a huge billboard with his face. And you know what was written on it? 'We Want the Messiah, Now!' Some of them think he's the Messiah. This idea no Jew should accept."

More than any other religious group, the Lubavitchers/Habad have reached out to nonobservant Jews, believing they are the antidote to assimilation, that there are only two kinds of Jews, religious Jews and not-yet-religious Jews. Some "Habadniks" drive vans nicknamed "mitzvah tanks," handing out Sabbath candles and encouraging men to put on tefillin. They transformed a small community of Eastern European Hasidim into an international educational network. Many emissaries running their schools, children's camps, and classes in 109 countries are *ba'al teshuva*, newly religious or "born-again Jews." Many who attend are not haredim or even Orthodox.

Throughout Israel, the number of ba'al teshuva are growing fast. Some are joining various Hasidic groups, others the Lithuanians. "We welcome them, but it's really best they marry amongst themselves." Usually loquacious, Sarah falls silent, lest she commit the sin of *lashon hara*, the evil tongue or malicious talk. Jews are taught that the tongue separates man from beast and that speech is what makes them closest to God, who is as concerned with what comes out of the mouth as what goes into it: the laws of slander and gossip appear in the Bible next to lists of nonkosher foods. Among other things, a Lubavitcher boy, especially one from a newly religious family, wouldn't be an acceptable match for Leah because his mother did not go to a mikvah, or public ritual bath, before conception. Any child of a ritually unclean mother is "not kosher." Judaism associates purity of body with purity of soul. Sarah scrupulously obeys the sexual laws of purity. While she is menstruating, she does not touch her husband, and when her cycle ends, she immerses herself in a mikvah to restore her purity. For haredi and many Orthodox men and women, going to a mikvah for both physical and ritual purification is a crucial part of being a Jew. The Talmud calls the mikvah one of Judaism's ten key institutions.

While her parents worry about finding her a "kosher" match, Leah worries about homework. Her dark blue high school uniform almost hides her Nike shoes. The haredi educational system has ruled that women are not suited to arduous Torah study. "He who teaches his daughter Torah, it is as though he teaches her lewdness" (Mishna, Tractate Sotah 3:4). Boys and girls go to separate schools with different curricula. Haredi girls take distilled religious courses, where they learn Jewish religious law and the weekly Torah portion. From childhood, haredim strive to be righteous, performing an extraordinary amount of charitable work. Judaism places greater priority on helping people than worshipping God because God is never in need but people are. Giving charity (*tzadaka* in Hebrew literally means "justice" or "righteousness") is a religious obligation. Leah's classmates deliver kosher meals to the poor as well as working in an old-age home. Others volunteer at Yad Sarah, a charity that distributes free medical equipment such as wheelchairs and crutches to Jews and Arabs. The Lithuanian haredi Uri Lupolanski is Jerusalem's mayor.

The prohibitions on secular education for girls are far less stringent than those for their yeshiva-educated brothers. Some haredi girls learn art, math, English, and some science, though not biology. They can read Hebrew literature, but not books that might expose them to irreligious ideas. Rabbinical censors do not allow girls to read the works of acclaimed non-Orthodox Israeli authors like Amos Oz or A. B. Yehoshua or David Grossman that would challenge their beliefs. All curriculum is screened to ensure that it is free of "offensive content" that might slander religion or contradict Jewish law. Most important, it must not mention heretical ideas like Zionism. Many haredi schools are staunchly anti-Zionist. Leah knows nothing about Theodor Herzl, David Ben-Gurion, Moshe Dayan, or Golda Meir. She never has heard "Hatikvah," Israel's national anthem. When haredi politicians hear it being played in the Knesset, they sometimes remain seated or walk out along with some fellow anti-Zionists—most of their Arab colleagues.

Although their education is funded by the "Zionist" government, haredi students are taught that establishing the state was a modern Jewish catastrophe because only God is allowed to restore Israel to its land. They still do not forgive the founders for rebelling against divine destiny. Many haredi schools do not fly the Israeli flag; haredi children are encouraged to pray that one day Israel will become a theocracy, ruled by the laws of the Torah. Most haredim either ignore Independence Day or mourn on it. Rabidly anti-Zionist haredim fast on this day of "spiritual destruction." For Lubavitch/Habad Hasidim, however, Independence Day is a religious holiday because they believe the birth of Israel in 1948 marked the beginning of the messianic redemption. Haredi children do not commemorate the anniversary of Yitzhak Rabin's assassination. Sometimes on Lag b'Omer, a spring holiday when Israelis party around bonfires, television runs footage of haredi children throwing Israeli flags into the flames, enraging most viewers.

Most haredi girls' schools today are more concerned with turning out Torah-true girls who can combat crushing poverty than cheerleaders for their flag-burning brothers. Tellingly, Leah's high school brochure promises to groom girls "to take their honored places as Jewish mothers, while training them for a fulfilling career that will enable them to help support their families." Once popular haredi female fields—teaching, child care, and secretarial—are overcrowded and underpaid. Increasingly, haredi rabbis realize that girls need new skills if they are to extricate their families from poverty. Leah's school is undergoing a quiet revolution. At the computer lab, girls learn Microsoft Office 2000. Some dream of becoming programmers. However, the computers do not have modems—cyberspace scares haredi rabbis. A communiqué signed by leading haredi rabbis, posted in ultra-Orthodox neighborhoods, branded the Internet "a danger one thousand times greater than television," which could bring "ruin and destruction upon all of Israel . . . it incites and encourages sin and abomination of the worst kind." Most haredi rabbis ban only home Internet use. However, there are exceptions: "High-tech jobs are perfectly permissible; the Internet, on the other hand, is a problem. No one supervises it; there's nothing to protect someone from harmful influences," says a spokesman for Eidah HaHaredit, an umbrella group of hard-line haredim who forbid any link to the Internet because it is "a deadly poison which burns souls."

More than a third of all haredi families own computers. No one knows how many obey rabbinical orders to delete home Internet browsers. Benjamin Stein's synagogue is near the Torah Scholar Software shop. Such a shop doesn't flout rabbinical edicts, he explains, because there are volumes of answers to halakhic questions and no good index, so software makes things easier to find. Although he's in favor of scholars using computers to write about Talmudic subjects, to find obscure texts, he will not allow one in his home even though his wife and children wouldn't dare ask for a modem. What does he think of the Internet? He grimaces and with the wave of a hand pronounces it "terrible garbage. You have to supervise the children all the time; you never know what they could find." Yeshiva students have been caught using their cell phones to access erotic services on the Internet. In 2002, haredi rabbis threatened to boycott cell phone companies that sell their followers phones with Internet connections. Benjamin is seemingly unaware that only a few blocks away in the trendy Russian Compound lined with latte bars and late-night pubs, haredi men avidly web-surf at the Netcafé. Some shop online, join secular chatrooms, and even check out X-rated websites. With growing poverty and a secular backlash, more haredi men are searching job sites. They are beginning to combine Torah-true with high-tech.

The Haredi Center for Technological Studies is on a quiet street in Mea Sharim. Above the entrance, a plaque features a line from medieval Sephardi physician-philosopher Moses Maimonides: "The highest degree of charity is to help a person earn a livelihood, so that he needn't rely on others." Surprisingly, when the center opened in 1997, prominent haredi rabbis—Hasidic, Lithuanian, and Mizrahi—who rarely agree on anything, gave their blessing to this groundbreaking place. Since opening with thirty-five students, enrollment has exploded to more than two thousand students in five schools across Israel. In this "haredi atmosphere," women attend daytime classes; men attend at night. (Haredim are prohibited from studying in universities that have coed classes and are full of "unbelievers.") The center acts as a bridge between the insular haredi world and the fast-paced world of high tech. Haredi women generally pick up computer languages, technical writing, and engineering faster than yeshiva-trained men, because they've learned subjects such as English, algebra, and geometry. They study to be programmers, systems administrators, graphic artists, and computer repair technicians. Some opt to work at home, where they watch their children and stay out of the public eye. Others look for jobs with haredi companies, where they can work in all-female departments. Increasingly, some seek lucrative jobs in the high-tech world.

Pressured by poverty, a growing secular backlash, and cutbacks in state support, male enrollment is increasing. The transition is difficult. They come to the center knowing little of the world outside the yeshiva and synagogue and with few marketable skills. The typical haredi male studies full time at a religious seminary from age six until he is forty-two and past draft age. After bar mitzvah age, as in Shas schools, boys do not study science, history, math, and English because secular subjects are "*bitul* Torah," that is, wasting time that should be spent studying Torah. Some do not even know multiplication tables. Sometimes their Hebrew is so substandard it is difficult to understand what they are saying or writing. However, these "men of the Book" are used to rigorous studies, spending up to twelve hours a day figuring out complicated Talmudic logic and decoding conflicting rabbinical opinions. Talmud pages are filled with nonlinear, multiple conversations and different typefaces, like some ancient chatroom. Teachers find these men, trained to be analytical and intuitive and to break Talmudic problems into tiny parts, skilled at learning Java and other computer programming languages. "The Torah is actually the world's first hypertext," observes secular multimillionaire venture capitalist Yossi Vardi, who invested in a haredi software company because its owners are "very motivated and sharp-minded from years of studying the Talmud." The prestigious Technion supervises the center's courses and grants its haredi graduates a highly prized diploma. The Technion professor who oversees the programs sees the revolutionary potential of bringing haredim into the information age. "What we're doing is one of the most important missions in Israel today," he stresses. "We're integrating haredim into Israeli society."

Har Hotsfim, one of Jerusalem's two high-tech areas, is surrounded by new haredi apartment buildings. Haredi high-techies are joining companies like Intel. Dvora, a modest haredi woman in a Pentium 4 world, works for the world's largest chipmaker. Her large black beret hides her hair; she doesn't want her name used because "my working with men is a sensitive issue." During her first weeks at Intel, she felt like she was walking on eggshells. "I was trying to figure out how to act," she says,

using the latest Hebrew slang. "But these Intel people are very consider-
ate. I found I can work here without compromising on halakha. When I
heard a software engineer curse, I even had the courage to speak up and
ask her to stop. Because we're mingling with secular and even Orthodox,
we're helping them understand us. I became friendly with one girl in my
work group; she always asks me a lot of questions. It's good people are
curious. So I invited her to my house for Shabbos. They want to know
things like why we eat round matzah on Passover, why my husband lets
me work here. After that terrorist shot up the bus my daughters take to
school, she asked me how I managed to show up for work. I told her I'm
not afraid. Every bullet has an address."

The transition from Torah to high tech is not easy for some men. A
Hasid working in a cubicle keeps his black fedora atop his computer
monitor. He appears oblivious to his coworkers, some of whom wear
miniskirts and work on the Sabbath. However, they are not oblivious to
him. "When he started, he had never seen a Roman numeral, never heard
of Yahoo or Bill Gates," says a coworker. Each afternoon, he joins men
from different haredi groups for prayers in the bomb shelter–synagogue.
Because he is safely past draft age, he has given up his full-time Torah
studies to help feed his family. Most younger haredi men opt to remain
full-time religious scholars, which, for now, gives them military exemption.

On Memorial Day, when sirens blare across Israel, most Jewish Israelis
stand silently in honor of soldiers who died for their country. Most
haredim defiantly ignore the ceremony. Shocking television scenes of
yeshiva boys laughing or playing while the siren sounds infuriate most Israelis, who, for decades, have been accusing them of a massive draft
dodge. Israelis are increasingly angry that they or their loved ones are
putting on uniforms and risking their lives while able-bodied haredi men
study safely. They showed it on their ballots in 2003, when they made
the anti–ultra-Orthodox Shinui Party Israel's second largest party.

"I know they resent us," recounts Benjamin Stein. "I have an exemption. And I hope my sons will too. With soldiers fighting terrorists, what
I say to explain seems trite to the secular, but that's only because we're
talking two different languages. We believe our prayers can be as power-

ful as tanks and guns. By praying to protect the nation, we are doing them more of a favor than serving in the army. More of their sons would die if we didn't pray. We are soldiers in the service of the nation. God watches over them because of us." Such a response angers Israeli soldiers, who demand to know why haredi blood is more valuable than theirs.

In 1998, their questions were answered by the Israeli Supreme Court (including two Orthodox judges who endorsed the decisions) in a landmark decision outlawing army exemptions for draft-age ultra-Orthodox males. According to this unanimous decision, the exemptions have created a deep rift in Israeli society and a growing sense of inequality. They wrote: "The current situation has created an entire population that is not integrated into the labor market and is increasingly dependent on state stipends." The situation might change because black-hatted politicians—Ashkenazi and the Mizrahi Shas—are excluded from the Likud-Shinui coalition. No longer can their combined voting power cripple a government that tries to enforce the law. Will this be a new era in Israel, in which religion and politics are not inextricably mixed?

Even though their rabbis forbid them from doing so, a small yet growing number of haredi men who can't take the rigors of yeshiva study are enlisting. These young yeshiva dropouts with dangling peyot serve in a special all-haredi "holy battalion," where they have no contact with female soldiers and can observe Shabbat, take Talmud classes, and eat "proper" food. (By law, all IDF food is kosher, but not kosher enough to fit the stricter haredi kashrut standards.) These Ashkenazi and Mizrahi haredim get up early for prayers and then pick up their assault rifles; their infantry combat unit is one of those responsible for security in the Jordan Valley. Haredim don't apply for certain jobs such as air force pilots, because they can't fly on Shabbat and their beards interfere with oxygen masks. When these soldiers return home on leave, few dare enter their haredi neighborhoods in uniform.

"There is real brainwashing against the military," states a new recruit who could pass for a well-built California surfer. "Serving instead of studying is a defect for life. Put on a uniform and you lose all chance for a good *shidukh* [marriage partner]." This soldier in khaki should know. He is an ex-haredi.

To avoid bringing shame to his family, who live in a haredi community in Haifa, "Josh" requested that his real name not be used. It's difficult to imagine that only ten months earlier, he was a frightened twenty-one-year-old with peyot, a black coat, and a black kippa. His transformation started under the bedcovers, where he secretly wore a headset to listen to secular radio stations. At bar mitzvahs and weddings, if there were secular male guests, Josh was at their side. He saw a poster with a phone number. It took time, but he dialed it—a hot line run by volunteers from Hilel, an organization that assists haredi youth who have decided to become secular. It took enormous guts for haredi Josh to take a bus out of his neighborhood with no possessions, no money, and no nonharedi friends. At an arranged place, he met his foster family, who gave him his first peek at a strange new world. He cut off his peyot and removed his black coat and knickers. From his foster brother's closet, he picked out tight Levi's, a suede jacket, and sandals. He looked like a secular suburbanite. But he wasn't. Not on the inside. During his first days "out," Josh's foster brother took him to his first movie. Overwhelmed, Josh roamed through his first mall, kicked his first soccer ball, attended his first rock concert. "I didn't even know who Aviv Geffen was. I had never heard his songs. Someone told me that he's Moshe Dayan's nephew. I was a blank," he recalls. "Then people got up and men and women started dancing together—right in the aisles—it was a shock. On Shabbat someone gave me a cigarette. I took a puff and then hid it so God wouldn't see."

Leaving haredi life is daunting. Josh left a world of absolute answers for a world of continuous choices. No longer is everything in his life prescribed, from what he should wear and read to whom he should marry. He spent a lot of time exploring Tel Aviv, which he had been taught was the modern version of Sodom and Gomorrah. "A girl working at Ikea started flirting with him and he didn't know what to do," recalls his foster brother. "He asked me 'How do you date?' I told him to ask her out for coffee. The girl had no idea this cool-looking guy had absolutely no experience with women. He didn't even know how babies are born." Josh had spent his life studying in an all-male yeshiva. The only women he'd known were relatives.

A social worker counseled Josh and put him in a group with other former haredi youth. One trains horses on a secular kibbutz. Two former "runaways" are studying for the matriculation exam and hope to be admitted to university. Another studies at Bezalel Academy of Art in Jerusalem. After leaving the cloistered haredi world, all suffer similar adjustment problems—from loneliness to enormous guilt for "deserting" family and friends. Josh says he often feels like a traitor. "In the haredi world, it's better to have a child who is a criminal than one who has left religion," he remarks in a barely audible voice. "When I 'defected,' I disgraced my entire family." Even though he'd decided to leave, he waited a year until his two older sisters married. He says the stigma of his defection will spoil his younger siblings' "marriage value."

After a few days "out," Josh phoned home. His mother answered. "When she heard my voice, she started crying. I talked, but she didn't say anything. Not a word. Then I sent her a letter. Then another. I guess no answer is also an answer." A few months later, he called again. "This time, my father answered. When he heard my voice, he shouted, 'You no longer exist. I now have only eight children.' And then he hung up. Maybe they'll never let me visit them," Josh says forlornly. "But never will I be able to erase them from my life."

10

The Orthodox

This Land Is Your Land? This Land Is My Land!

↺ A Jewish man was shipwrecked on a deserted island. After many years, rescuers arrived and were stunned to see he'd built three Orthodox synagogues. Why three? "One synagogue is the one I pray in," he answered. "The others are the ones I'll never set foot in."

↺ A poor religious settler takes a job sitting outside the town where he will be the first to greet the Messiah. "Why did you accept such a low salary?" complains his wife. "It doesn't pay much," he agrees, "but at least it's long-term, steady work."

With its spacious stone houses, tennis and basketball courts, and children on scooters and skates, Alon Shvut resembles a bucolic Arizona suburb rather than an Orthodox West Bank settlement in the world's most famous war zone. Whether they're messianic fundamentalists or merely scrupulously observant, the six hundred families here consider themselves lucky to live in this spiritually rich spot in Israel's biblical heartland, only twelve miles south of Jerusalem. The residents—most of them Sabras, including laptop-toting civil servants, scientists, politicians, and high-tech executives—regard themselves as modern Orthodox Israelis showing the same idealistic, self-sacrificial spirit of the (mostly secular) Zionist pioneers who built the country. In fact, religious settlers are the most well-known of Israel's (mostly nonsettler) Orthodox population. They and their children have a flourishing religious life, but unlike the ultra-Orthodox haredim, are not isolated from secular Israelis. Along pathways shaded by pomegranate, olive, and date trees are four synagogues, ritual baths, and an abundant array of Torah-oriented activities. The most eye-catching building is the ultracontemporary Har Etzion Yeshiva, a renowned Talmudic academy. Among the male students immersing themselves in rabbinical texts are six hundred soldiers combining Judaic studies with compulsory military service. This hilltop settlement—between Hebron, the city of Abraham, and Bethlehem, the birthplace of David—is in an area biblically rich and emotionally charged, a place where scriptures, historical narratives, and nationalisms are tangled in a lethal embrace. Here, when a Jewish man says to a Muslim "Mine is longer than yours," they're talking about history.

The yeshiva's attractive campus is a short walk from the Zomet Institute, a theological think tank where rabbis research questions ranging from who is a Jew to the conscription of women and the ethics of organ transplants. (They encouraged the family of a yeshiva student killed in a Tel Aviv Hamas bus bombing to donate his organs. A Palestinian girl received his liver.) There's also a factory that produces rabbinically approved devices created by engineers who enlist technology to maintain necessary activities without obliging Jews to desecrate the day of rest by writing or using electricity. For observant farmers, there are automated greenhouses and milking and egg-handling systems. The factory manufactures special high-tech Shabbat devices such as special timers that switch on various electrical appliances. Engineers created Sabbath elevators preset to stop on every floor, obviating the need to press buttons, which is forbidden (using an electrical circuit is de facto "kindling" fire), and switches for electric wheelchairs. Israeli hospitals use their Shabbat nurse-signaling systems and medical equipment. For religious doctors, soldiers, police, and politicians there are Shabbat phones and, because rabbis permit temporary writing in emergencies, "Shabbatpens": the ink disappears after a few days. Kippa-wearing soldiers use Shabbat-friendly devices on their walkie-talkies, video surveillance systems, and jeeps.

Alon Shvut, the largest of the fourteen mostly Orthodox settlements in this part of the West Bank (known as Gush Etzion), has a bustling regional community center that offers aerobics, crafts, and religious classes. In one, Orthodox feminists debate how much hair a married woman must cover; in another, why the Supreme Court's 2003 ruling banned women from praying aloud, reading from the Torah scroll, and wearing prayer shawls and phylacteries (usually reserved for men) at the Western Wall. In the auditorium, amateur actresses rehearse *Queen Esther*, a play they perform for women-only audiences to raise money for orphans and widows, victims of terrorism. (They sold out even though after dark the roads between settlements are even more dangerous.) Not all settlers were born in Israel; for residents who speak English, Russian, French, or Amharic, there are intensive Hebrew lessons. Not all settlers were born Jewish; in summer 2002, Peruvian Indians left huts and were welcomed into new trailer homes in this Judean hills settlement. Although these former Christians have taken Hebrew names, they do not yet know the difference between Herzl and Hamas. The "Inca Jews" already have been taught the "holy trinity": the Torah, the People, the Land. And they call the West Bank of the Jordan River by its biblical names, Judea and Samaria. "We knew we were coming to a place called 'territories' because we know other Peruvians who immigrated earlier and are living in the settlements," said a kippa-wearing convert who carries a Spanish-Hebrew prayer book. "But I have no problem because I don't consider the territories to be occupied. You cannot conquer what has belonged to you since the time of the patriarch Abraham."

Swimmers in the community center's Olympic-size pool observe gender-segregated hours. Instead of doing laps, first-grade teacher Shlomit Katz jogs, with a skirt over her sweatpants because of "modesty. And women must not dress like men," she explains, heading back to the six-bedroom house where she raised seven children. "What better place to grow up than where the Jewish people were born. Right on the Path of the Patriarchs." Sounding part historian, part tour guide, she describes how Abraham passed through this pastoral part of Judea on his way to take Isaac to be sacrificed on Mount Moriah, now the Temple Mount. David was born in Bethlehem, tended sheep here, and then went on to proclaim his kingdom. Rachel's Tomb near Bethlehem is only a five-minute drive away: "And Rachel died, and she was buried on the way to

Efrat [a former name for Bethlehem]. And Jacob set up a pillar upon her grave; the same is the pillar upon Rachel's grave unto this day" (Genesis 35:16–20). Judaism's first holy site, the Tomb of the Patriarchs, is only seven minutes away. Both are heavily guarded. "Sometimes I pray there," says Shlomit. "And I'm not afraid to go. The soldiers protect us."

Shlomit and her husband are among the founding families of Alon Shvut, which means "return to the oak," referring to the eight-hundred-year-old tree that stands outside the electric security fence. Growing up, Shlomit gazed at this enormous tree from the Israeli side of the pre-1967 border. "For me, it symbolized my dream to return."

The four Orthodox kibbutzim of Gush Etzion had been destroyed by Arabs and rebuilt twice before the 1947 UN vote on partition of Britain's Palestine Mandate into Arab and Jewish states. During the battles that preceded Israel's Declaration of Independence, Jordan's British-trained Arab Legion attacked, and Shlomit and other babies were smuggled out; her mother escaped hidden in a truck transporting cows. During the five-month siege, most of the men and women were killed, the rest taken prisoners by the Jordanians. Gush Etzion was destroyed for the third time on May 13, 1948, only one day before Prime Minister David Ben-Gurion declared the independence of the Jewish state. At their memorial service, he eulogized the defenders of Gush Etzion, who prevented Egyptian troops from reaching Jerusalem: "I can think of no battle in the annals of the IDF which was more magnificent, more tragic or more heroic than the struggle for Gush Etzion. . . . If there is a Jewish Jerusalem today, the Jewish people owe their gratitude to the defenders of Gush Etzion."

"For nineteen years, we couldn't go back. The Jordanians controlled Judea and Samaria. Then the miracle." Shlomit believes God was smiling on the Jews during the 1967 Six-Day War, especially the third day, when her fiancé, Yaacov, and his paratroop unit entered the Old City of Jerusalem and tearfully prayed at the Western Wall. That day, June 7, IDF soldiers also reached the razed kibbutzim of Gush Etzion. Survivors and their children asked Prime Minister Levi Eshkol for permission to return. After carefully considering the enormous political implications of putting settlements in the newly conquered Jordanian territories, the Labor leader consented. In 1971, Shlomit and Yaacov and a few other families set up Alon Shvut, which was the first nonkibbutz settlement and became the prototype for other settlements. Her father founded a nearby settlement. What was once just a rocky hillside is today Efrat, an Orthodox community of seven thousand residents. Since 1967, every Israeli government, both Likud and Labor, has supported the settlers of Gush Etzion. In Ehud Barak's negotiations with Yasser Arafat and then in the Yossi Beilin–Abu Maazen plan, most of the fifteen Gush Etzion settlements were to be annexed to Israel.

Shlomit's children are the third generation of her family living in Gush Etzion. Her youngest son, Nevo, like his five brothers, is a reserve officer in a combat unit. "At home, my friends are religious and right-wing. In my unit, most of my friends are secular and leftist, except one. He's Bedouin," says the twenty-four-year-old budding documentary maker now back from Gaza. He explains that he didn't choose the religious film school in Jerusalem because "it's too conservative. All my life I studied in Orthodox places. It's enough. I'm religious but not closed off from the world. I want to meet other people and understand what's going on with them." With a laugh, he says his classmates at Hadassah College of Technology have nicknamed him The Settler. "I want to make documentaries to give secular people insights into our lives, to show what it's like studying in a yeshiva or dating if you're modern, Orthodox, and a settler like me. Most people have very distorted ideas about us. They think we're all crazed fundamentalists."

Nothing causes more heated debate among Israelis than the quarter of a million of their fellow citizens who live among three and a half million Palestinians. The 123 settlements dotted throughout the West Bank and seventeen in the Gaza Strip range from encampments of a few trailers to thriving towns of more than twenty-five thousand. More than half the Israelis living on settlements are not Orthodox, but were attracted to the other side of the 1967 borders by subsidized housing, tax breaks, and good schools. Orthodox settlers are all shades of right, from pragmatists who believe it is possible to coexist with their Arab neighbors to extremists who say "No Arabs = No Terror" and would like to see hostile Palestinians "transferred" out of the West Bank to Jordan.

No matter where they are on the ideological map, Orthodox settlers believe the 1948 establishment of the State of Israel and the ingathering of Jewish exiles from all over the world were no accident. In their eyes, the 1967 Six-Day War victory, when Israel captured the West Bank from Jordan and Gaza from Egypt, was a divine miracle that brought the cradle of Judaism back into the hands of the Jews. They believe in the signs first cited by the Prophets indicating the coming of the Messiah, that redemption will take place when Jews control the Land of Israel. For the first time since 1948, Jerusalem was reunited and Jews could worship at places such as the Western Wall in Jerusalem and Judaism's second-holiest and oldest site, the Tomb of the Patriarchs in Hebron. Religious Zionists took up their sacred cause, "reclaiming" lands they consider physically and spiritually inseparable from Judaism, lands they consider their biblical birthright, lands God promised to Abraham four thousand years ago. Palestinians call these lands occupied and are determined to make them their national home. The settlers' many Israeli critics call them an enormous obstacle to peace, a danger to the IDF soldiers who defend them, and a drain on the floundering economy. The settlers are a force that all Israeli governments have had to contend with since the 1967 War. They have enough political leverage and sympathetic ministers to threaten to bring down any government that tries to remove them from their sacred land.

However, there is enough infighting among bickering Orthodox settler factions to keep any observer dizzy. Some distrust Netanyahu even though most agree that a Palestinian state would be a "primary school for the world's suicide bombers." Others hate Sharon for "surrendering to terrorism" by calling for a Palestinian state and removing some settlement outposts. A number of Orthodox settlers are openly critical of extremist settler rabbis who preach that loyalty to the Torah is more important than loyalty to the state, and tell kippa-wearing soldiers to disobey their commanders' orders that they should remove settlers from tiny illegal outposts. (On the other hand, in 2003 settlers stopped some illegal outposts from being evacuated by buying the land from the cash-strapped Palestinian owners. In some cases, settlers reportedly paid to fly the Palestinian sellers out of the country to protect them from being harmed by agents of the Palestinian Authority.) Israeli security forces maintain tight surveillance over a small group of fanatics who dream of building the Third Temple. In 2001, Joseph Cedar, a religious former West Bank settler turned filmmaker, won six Israeli Academy Awards for his shocking *Time of Favor*, about followers of a charismatic settler rabbi (played by Moshe Dayan's son) who plot to blow up the Dome of the Rock so Jews can pray at the Temple Mount and prepare for the Messiah. "Some of that movie was real. It's very upsetting to think there are people like that," says Nevo, who describes the range of political outlooks not just among Orthodox settlers, but within families. "My two older brothers are more right-wing than me. I'm more like my father."

After reciting Shaharit (morning prayers) at the nearby synagogue, his father, Yaacov, drives to his senior-level job at the Ministry of Education in Jerusalem. The commute can take twenty minutes. Or hours. Sometimes the road is closed. The $41 million bypass Tunnel Road was built to speed Israeli settlers safely past Palestinian villages and refugee camps, yet despite the concrete barriers to protect drivers from snipers, there have been many attacks and deaths. Is his Mazda bulletproof? Yaacov shakes his head no. "Arabs throw stones at me. A few shots here and there. So far, no damage," he says nonchalantly. A woman who lives in another West Bank settlement complains she can afford to buy only one $1,500 bulletproof vest. When her six kids are in the car, she doesn't know which one to put it on. Faced with such an impossible choice, she does not give it to any of them. Does Yaacov wear a bulletproof vest? "No. They don't help. Everyone I know who was killed was shot in the head." So, how does he protect himself? "Before I start the car, I recite the Prayer for the Road: 'May it be your will O Lord our God and God of our ancestors to guide us and direct our steps in peace; to sustain us in peace and to lead us to our desired destiny in joy and peace and to bring us back home in peace.'"

Even though Palestinian gunmen have declared open season on settlers, residents of Gush Etzion continue taking this harrowing commute to Jerusalem. In fact, families are moving to Alon Shvut, not out, Yaacov stresses. "If people left because of the attacks, soon we'd end up losing Alon Shvut, then Jerusalem, then Tel Aviv, and then we'd end up in the sea." Not only are people moving to Judea and Samaria to fulfill a religious duty to expand the Jewish state to its biblical borders, but they feel the settlements are a security buffer. According to a poll taken during the third year of the intifada, 68 percent of Israeli Jews say that "regardless of the size or strength of a Palestinian state, if one is established it will constitute a threat to Israel"; only 9 percent believe a Palestinian Arab state will reduce the threat to Israel. This is a dramatic change: before the intifada broke out, barely 30 percent of Israelis called themselves right wing. Most, however, feel that an independent Palestinian state is both morally and politically necessary to end the struggle between two legitimate national movements and favor territorial concessions and dismantling many settlements.

"We want peace. But not at any price," continues Yaacov. Every morning he reads the left-wing *Ha'aretz* newspaper, which he says has more readers per capita in Alon Shvut than in any other Israeli community, in the settlements or in Israel proper, though most Orthodox settlers (and nonsettlers) espouse unflinchingly right-wing views. "We want to find out what the enemy [liberal journalists] thinks. The press all over the world call us all kinds of ugly names. Settlers are synonymous with monsters. Fanatics. Crazed zealots. Fascists. It's sad that people don't know who we really are or what we're about." What about charges that settlers are taking Palestinian land? "The only time Jews haven't lived here is between 1949 and 1967. The land where we live has belonged to Jews since the 1920s. Arabs sold it to Jews. Three years ago, we built a new neighborhood in Alon Shvut and not one meter was expropriated from Arabs. Under normal circumstances, many Arabs willingly sold us their land because they wanted the money. But today, the [Palestinian Authority] and terrorists intimidate them. We only build on land we can prove belongs to Jews. Morally and ethically, that is how it should be done."

More than one thousand Orthodox children attend the Gush Etzion regional school, at which Yaacov's wife, Shlomit, is a teacher. The school's maintenance chief, an Arab who has worked there for three decades supervising Jews and Arabs, was recently put on temporary leave with pay because of the children's fears of Arabs—even him. In May 2001, two boys from the remote settlement of Tekoa skipped school, probably to scout for a place to build a bonfire for the festival of Lag b'Omer. When Yosef Ishran, fourteen, and American-born Kobi Mandel, thirteen, didn't return, their parents assumed they were with friends demonstrating in Jerusalem that the government should get tougher on terrorists. By dark, though, they panicked. After an all-night hunt, searchers entered a cave and saw blood smeared on the walls. Under a pile of rocks, they discovered the boys' mutilated bodies, their skulls smashed. Thousands of children and parents from the settlements of Gush Etzion attended the double funerals. Afterward, residents of Tekoa went to the giant cave where the boys were found. They lit bonfires and chanted psalms that King David may have written when he sought shelter there.

At 7:30 A.M. on September 20, 2001 two armored schoolbuses leaving Tekoa stopped alongside a bullet-ridden car. Three toddlers inside were screaming: their mother was shot dead, their father bleeding. The bus drivers had to decide whether to risk a rescue, knowing terrorists might be readying another ambush, or rush their young passengers away. They sped off. When the children arrived at the Gush Etzion regional school, once again, trauma specialists were called in. When they asked them to sketch pictures of a safe place, one girl drew the school with tanks outside; a boy drew himself praying in a synagogue with a rifle in the next chair.

How can families raise children in this perilous place where parents bury their young, where armed residents patrol the surrounding road? Stubborn? Brave? Idealistic? Insane? "We have a real connection to the land, to our history and traditions. We believe this is where God and the Torah instruct us to live," says Shani Simkovitz, a divorced mother raising her five children in Tekoa. The wind-whipped hilltop settlement, home to 250 families, has a goat dairy and organic mushroom farm and six Ashkenazi and Mizrahi synagogues with different styles of Orthodox observance. To the north, Tekoa has vistas of the Mount of Olives in Jerusalem. The Judean Desert and the Dead Sea are to the east, and in the far distance, Mount Nebo in Jordan, where, according to Scripture, God allowed Moses to view, but not enter, the Promised Land. The Herodion, a mountain palace-fortress built by King Herod, is quite close. When Tekoa residents discovered the government planned to give it to the Palestinian Authority as part of the hated Oslo process, some became soldiers of God. They climbed up the mountain and held prayer and psalm sessions and refused to leave. Shani explains why Judea and Samaria are the parts of the Land of Israel most connected with the Bible and Jewish history: "Judah, one of the twelve tribes of Israel, lived here. From the name Judea [Yehuda in Hebrew], we got the name Jews. The Arabs use biblical names for places like Hebron, Bethlehem, and Jericho. Why don't they use the name Judea? Wouldn't they sound strange claiming we Jews stole Judea from the Arabs?" She argues that settlers didn't resurrect biblical names for these lands. The *Encyclopedia Britannica* and United Nations documents called the area Judea and Samaria until 1950. The term West Bank (of the Jordan River) came into use after the 1948 War during Jordan's nineteen-year rule. "There never was a land known as Palestine governed by Arabs. When the British and the Turks ruled here, Jews were Palestinians." She pulls out a crumpled paper. It is her grandmother's 1900 Ottoman Turkish birth certificate from the Old City of Jerusalem. It says "Palestina."

Because she doesn't know how to drive, Shani often hitchhikes from Tekoa to her office at Alon Shvut. She raises funds for the Gush Etzion settlements, mostly from Jews and Christians abroad. Projects include a retreat center for religious-secular dialogue and research labs that develop "green" (environmentally friendly) products. The fund-raising used to emphasize building schools; now it's on reinforcing them against mortars. The Gush Etzion settlements also have pressing needs for bulletproof vests for children, first-aid stations, night vision binoculars, and closed-circuit video systems. Surprisingly, a number of settlements still don't have security fences. "We absolutely don't want a fence," Shani makes clear. "A fence says here ends the Jewish community and stops our natural growth on legitimate Israeli government–owned land. Besides, we can't live fenced in like a ghetto. We had ghettos in Poland." Although Tekoa is unfenced, during outbreaks of shooting, soldiers sit in tanks outside the entrance and survey the area atop the Herodion. Why should secular left-wing soldiers risk their lives defending religious right-wing settlers? "The reason we are here is because this is an inseparable part of the country. We are a buffer zone. Without our important communities, the borderline would be in the lobby of the Hyatt Dead Sea or the Hyatt Hotel in Jerusalem. We are here to defend Israel." She then goes on to add that *many* soldiers from the settlements defend Israelis inside the 1967 borders. Her own soldier-daughter serves in Sderot, an impoverished town inside southern Israel that has been hit dozens of times by rockets from Gaza. "All of Israel is one battlefield. We're a little David surrounded by twenty-two Arab Goliaths. No matter how much land we offer them, it never will be enough. We know it isn't going to be easy, but we will prevail. We have to. Out of the Holocaust came the world's only

Jewish country. Jewish history repeats itself. It's full of tragedies and strength and miracles."

———————

Cake? More coffee?" Ruth Gillis, a jolly Orthodox woman with a hat covering her dark hair, asks soldiers gathered at a roadside kiosk for free home-cooked meals. Sometimes these soldiers, who protect the Gush Etzion settlements, leave thank-you notes, such as "Don't give in and don't give up. The tankers of the Yehuda Brigade." Ruth manages to find time to volunteer even though she's a single mother of five young children. It was her idea to set up this kiosk in honor of her late husband, a world-renowned hematologist and part-time cantor killed in a terrorist attack while driving from Hadassah Hospital to their settlement of ninety religious families. As his funeral cortege made its way to the cemetery in Gush Etzion, thousands of Palestinian and Jewish patients, doctors, and settlers lined the highway. After the funeral, one of Gillis's patients, a very close associate of Arafat, called the Hadassah Medical Center to apologize. "Instead of bringing Arafat here from exile in Tunis and arming his followers and letting them indoctrinate their people with hate, we should have invested in the Palestinians' quality of life," says the widow. "We should have given them textbooks and medicines and infrastructure, not thousands of guns. We chose the wrong option." A leaflet at the kiosk reads "Oslo = 1,300 Israelis murdered, 10,000 injured." Another, "Road Map = Map of Illusion."

When settlers are killed, new settlements sometimes are set up. (Since the start of the intifada, at least sixty-six outposts or fledgling settlements have sprouted up, according to Peace Now, an advocacy group that opposes Jewish settlements in the West Bank and Gaza.) After Dr. Gillis's funeral residents and the mayor of Gush Etzion vowed that a new settlement, Tzur Shalem, would be built in his memory. That's why ten families came to be living in trailers only a few hundred meters from the Gillis's settlement. While Dr. Gillis's family was still mourning, on June 5, 2002, two Palestinian men disguised in IDF uniforms armed with rifles and an ax entered Tzur Shalem. They killed a reserve soldier and a young settler couple; she was nine months pregnant.

Gush Etzion mayor Shaul Goldstein paid a condolence call to the reserve soldier's widow and two children, who are not religious and not settlers. The family doesn't blame the settlers, he says, dismissing critics who charge that settlements don't protect Israel, that soldiers protect the settlements. He also doesn't regret the decision to set up the outpost, which he calls a "neighborhood." Rather than "settlers," he prefers the word "residents," and instead of "settlement," he uses the word "community" or "town." "A settlement is temporary, a place where you don't belong. We belong here. This is our land." This young mayor, one of the up-and-coming right-wing religious settler leaders, grew up in Beersheva, in a left-leaning, secular family. Because he had a typical, nonreligious Israeli education, he says, his background helps him understand the reasons so many Israelis don't comprehend the religious settlers' determination to stay. "Many young Israelis know more about Hindu shrines than Jewish ones. They think our biblical places are just piles of old rocks, so they don't mind giving them to the Palestinians." While he was in the air force, he read about Christianity and Islam, dabbled in New Age religion, and wandered from one rabbi to another, until he "discovered the Bible isn't just a book on the shelf. I decided that if Jews have the right to live anywhere in France or the United States, why shouldn't we have the right to live anywhere in our historic homeland? After all, Abraham lived in Hebron, not Haifa. Bethlehem was the city of David, not Beersheva." He lives in Neve Daniel, a settlement ten minutes from Jerusalem, with his wife and six children. "For ten years I was optimistic. When I was elected mayor, delegations from Hebron and Arab villages came and hugged and kissed me. I really thought we and our Arab neighbors could live together. We visited each other's houses on Id al-Fitr, Id al-Adha, on Sukkot and Passover. We shared sadness over the death of a father, happiness on the birth of a child. Their kids played with computers at my house and played soccer with my kids. I thought that we, 'the people,' would succeed where government had failed; we would show that peace is not of the brave, but of simple neighbors. When I went into that cave and saw how evil men with stones murdered those two boys, my hopes were shattered." Since then, he can't count how many coffins he's seen lowered into the ground.

Hanging prominently in his sunny Alon Shvut office, which overlooks the wadi where David fought Goliath, is a Jordanian map dated 1951 on which Jewish-owned land in Gush Etzion is marked in red. To Mayor

Shaul Goldstein, the map proves that Jordanians officially recognized that Jews legally purchased the land from Arabs. Although he was only eight during the 1967 War, he can go on for hours about why Israel should not give up most of the lands they captured and give Palestinians an independent state. "And let them bring in Hezballah, al-Qaeda, Syrians, and missiles here? Palestinians say they're fighting against the Israeli 1967 'occupation' and that if we evacuate the settlements, they'll stop terrorism. But between independence and the 1967 War, Arabs infiltrated from Jordan, Egypt, Syria, and Lebanon and killed hundreds of Israeli civilians. When the PLO was founded in 1964 to liberate 'Palestine,' what Palestine were they trying to liberate? Jordan controlled the West Bank. No Jews were living here. The PLO was created to destroy Israel. In English, they tell the world they're fighting against the 1967 occupation, but in Arabic, they say they're fighting against the 1948 occupation of Palestine. I believe what they say in Arabic. In schools, their mosques, and the press. This war isn't against settlers. This is a religious war. And it will continue if Israel gives them a state."

On a Friday evening in November 2002, a group of Jewish settlers completed their regular Shabbat prayers at Hebron's Tomb of the Patriarchs. While returning to their homes, guarded by IDF soldiers, shots rang out. An Islamic Jihad ambush. Twelve soldiers and settlers were killed. It is dangerous protecting two of the most volatile settlements in the West Bank: Hebron and adjoining Kiryat Arba. A month later, on December 18, 2002, near the same spot, a nineteen-year-old border patrol soldier was ambushed. "Is it worth it—the tomb, the holy places—for my daughter and the other soldiers who died?" her grieving mother asked from her home inside Israel. "Every day I must face the fact that I buried my daughter. There isn't a piece of land worth these lives."

Hebron is an ancient town of deep, mutual hatreds and frequent bloodlettings. Nowhere else in the West Bank do Israelis and Palestinians live as close together and as far apart. Nowhere else are relations as poisonous and as deadly. The Muslims and Jews of the City of the Patriarchs are among the most devout and most radical—a volatile mix. The five hundred religious Jews—families and yeshiva students—live in heavily guarded enclaves in the heart of Hebron amid 130,000 Palestinians who hate them. As witness to their resolve to stay, that land is almost as important as lives, these settlers readily show fresh graves and bullet holes in their homes. Like the secular kibbutzniks of the 1950s, they talk about self-sacrifice and pioneering and settling the land, but their Zionism is something Herzl never dreamed of. Some cars with yellow Israeli license plates have "Hebron, Always and Forever" bumper stickers. Settlers are keen to explain that for Jews, only Jerusalem is more holy than Hebron.

The town of Hebron dates from around 1720 B.C.E., but the land around it has an even longer provenance—as with many places in the West Bank, a biblical provenance. According to the book of Genesis, Abraham purchased the field and the Cave of Machpelah as a family tomb from Ephron the Hittite for 400 silver shekels. Much is made by biblical commentators that Abraham insisted on buying the land rather than accepting the Hittite's offer of burial privileges without legal ownership. Much is also made of the purchase of Machpelah as the origin of the land of Israel, because according to Genesis, the patriarchs Abraham, Isaac, and Jacob, also known as Israel, are buried there, along with the matriarchs Sarah, Rebecca, and Leah. (The only one missing is Rachel, who died in childbirth in Bethlehem, where her tomb is also a shrine.) To many Jews, and most settlers, Jewish history *begins* in Hebron.

Subsequent books of the Bible record that after the exodus from Egypt, Joshua assigned Hebron to Caleb from the tribe of Judah (Joshua 14:13–14), who subsequently led his tribe in conquering the city and its environs (Judges 1:1–20). Following the death of King Saul, God instructed David to go to Hebron, where he was anointed king of Judea (II Samuel 2:1–4). Seven years later, in Hebron, David was anointed king over Israel (II Samuel 5:1–3). The city was part of the United Kingdom of Israel and, later, the Southern Kingdom of Judea until it fell to the Babylonians in 586 B.C.E. Jews continued to live in Hebron (Nehemiah 11:25) and the city was later incorporated into the (Jewish) Hasmonean kingdom. Beginning in the thirteenth century, when Palestine was ruled by the Muslim Mamelukes, Jews were barred from entering the Tomb of the Patriarchs and restricted to the seventh step of an exterior staircase, where they could pray and peer through a window at the tomb. The Tomb is sacred to all three monotheistic faiths because it is the burial place of their mutual father, Abraham. Jews built the original shrine; Byzantine Christians rebuilt it as a church; medieval Muslims built it as a mosque. Genesis describes Abraham's two eldest sons, Ishmael and Isaac, separated since boyhood and leaders of rival nations, coming together for the first time in almost seventy-five years to bury their father here.

During the 1948 War, Hebron was captured by the Arab Legion and annexed to Jordan. From 1948 until 1967, during which Jordanians and local residents razed Hebron's Jewish Quarter and desecrated the Jewish cemetery, Jews were not permitted to visit Jewish holy sites in Hebron and the rest of the West Bank and East Jerusalem. Then, less than a year after Israel captured the entire West Bank in the Six-Day War, a group masquerading as tourists went to Hebron's Park Hotel for Passover and refused to leave, announcing that they had come to reestablish Hebron's Jewish community, massacred in 1929. To defuse the crisis that would inevitably result from building a settlement in Hebron proper, Prime Minister Levi Eshkol's Labor-led government decided to build a settlement outside the town. Taking its name from the Book of Joshua— "Now the name of Hebron before was Kiryat Arba"—construction started in 1972. Today, the settlement of Kiryat Arba has six thousand religious and nonreligious residents.

Devoutly religious Baruch Goldstein often walked from his home in Kiryat Arba to pray at the Tomb. A former town council member and emergency physician, he treated Jewish settlers and Arabs in Hebron. After Israel signed the Oslo Accords with the PLO, the number of attacks on local settlers escalated, which kept the Brooklyn-born doctor busy trying, often unsuccessfully, to save lives. This long-time disciple of the assassinated Rabbi Meir Kahane and member of his radical right Kach Party blamed sacrilegious Yitzhak Rabin and his ministers for the settlers' deaths and for destroying the dream of redemption by giving away the Land of Israel to Palestinians. Early one morning, Dr. Goldstein put on his army reservist's uniform and went to Jewish prayer service in the Tomb of the Patriarchs. Afterward, he stepped into another hall, hid behind a pillar, and opened fire with his assault rifle in the cave's Ibrahimi Mosque, where approximately five hundred Muslims were kneeling in Ramadan prayers. In three minutes, he killed twenty-nine unarmed worshippers and wounded more than one hundred. Only after several Arabs bludgeoned him to death with iron bars did the shooting stop. The 1994 massacre sparked riots that lasted for days. Since then, Jews and Muslims no longer come together here; the Tomb has separate entrances for them. Israeli soldiers guard the sacred area, ready for the next battle between the offspring of Isaac and the offspring of Ishmael.

Most Israelis were repelled by the slaughter. Speaking before the Knesset, Prime Minister Rabin said he was ashamed of the massacre and in his worst nightmare could not imagine an Israeli perpetrating such a heinous crime. Some members of Rabin's cabinet called for an immediate evacuation of Hebron's Jewish settlers. The Israeli government outlawed the Kach Party for preaching anti-Arab violence. Some settler leaders privately said the ban was long overdue.

But even today, hard-core members of the extremist messianic right do not consider Baruch Goldstein a deranged doctor, but a hero for avenging the blood of settlers murdered by Palestinians and trying to derail the hated Oslo Accords. Geula Amir was one such hero worshipper, an Orthodox kindergarten teacher who made pilgrimages from her home in Herzliya to Baruch Goldstein's grave in central Kiryat Arba. Her twenty-five-year-old son is a Goldstein admirer too. He studied law and computers at Bar-Ilan, Israel's only religious university, and studied at the campus yeshiva, where he sometimes outperformed his Talmud teachers. In his free time, he brought fellow extreme right students for solidarity weekends with the radical settlers in Hebron, where they held Sabbath services and prayed at the Tomb of the Patriarchs. He also took part in settler confrontations with soldiers and demonstrated against the Rabin-Peres government for giving tens of thousands of guns to Arafat's "army of terrorists" (the Palestinian police), approving Palestinian autonomy in the West Bank and Gaza, and "selling out" the settlers (the final Israeli-Palestinian negotiations would be over the evacuation of the settlements). For those who believe in the redemption of Greater Israel and the coming of the Messiah, the Rabin-Peres Oslo "treason" caused a theological crisis because full redemption can take place only when the Jews control the biblical Land of Israel. At antigovernment demonstrations, posters appeared with Rabin wearing either an S.S. uniform or Arafat's keffiyah. And the word "Traitor."

On Saturday, November 4, 1995, Yigal Amir went to synagogue and prayed that this night God would let him save the nation. During the bus ride, he removed his knit kippa. Arriving at the Kings of Israel Square in Tel Aviv, he made his way to an ill-lit parking lot beneath the stage where

Prime Minister Rabin was speaking to the pro-peace rally about "violence eroding democracy." Convinced he was about to do God's will, Yigal Amir fired three bullets into Rabin's back, killing the hero of the 1967 War.

After the assassination, police searched Amir's room in his parents' house. They found a 550-page book, *Baruch, The Hero: A Memorial Volume for Dr. Baruch Goldstein, the Saint, May God Avenge His Blood*. Amir told his investigators he was certain God approved of the killing and hoped that it would stop the peace process.

———

Every spring during the festival of Lag b'Omer, more than one hundred thousand religious Israelis from all over the country and the settlements head to Mount Meron in the Galilee. A parade of pilgrims make their way up steep, winding paths to the tomb of Rabbi Shimon Bar Yochai, the second-century sage believed in folk tradition to be the author of the Zohar, the main literary work of the Jewish numerological and mystical tradition known as kabbalah. Many of those gathered here are traditional Mizrahi Jews whose families made similar journeys when they lived in North Africa or the Middle East. Praying at the tomb of a holy person on the anniversary of his or her death is an auspicious time, when prayers may be answered, sickness healed, and secrets of holy text revealed. This annual scene resembles a Jewish Woodstock more than a sacred assemblage; it's an outdoor spiritual supermarket mixing piety, picnicking, and partying. Vendors stand behind rows of stalls selling candles to light at Rabbi Shimon's tomb and copies of the Zohar. People also buy religious music and amulets supposedly blessed by Mizrahi kabbalists. Lines to purchase lottery tickets are especially long; a ticket blessed at the grave of this holy rabbi can be a big winner.

Friends warmly embrace, older ones often greeting each other in Judeo-Arabic dialects such as Moroccan Mughrabi. Colorful tents made of blankets and carpets cover the area in a bright mosaic. In the brutal sun, women set up multicourse feasts while men barbecue goats and sheep; meat kosher-slaughtered on Mount Meron is especially holy. This is a holiday of culinary overindulgence and free-flowing wine. To high-spirited live music and incessant drumming, people sing songs praising Rabbi Shimon and the mystical marriage of his soul with God. There are stories of stern Torah authorities who tried prohibiting these raucous, all-night celebrations, until Rabbi Shimon appeared to them in dreams, saying the anniversary of his death should be a time of rejoicing, not mourning. Many dance with abandon around huge bonfires, even throwing scarves and candles on them for good luck.

"The bonfires are in honor of the spiritual light Rabbi Shimon brought to the world. After all, his teachings are in the Zohar, which means 'shining light,' " explains an Ashkenazi woman fresh from a trip to India. A New Age Jew, she studies in a "yeshiva-ashram" in nearby Safed, the birthplace of kabbalah. Habad-Lubavitch women distribute literature about the Messiah while dancing nearby are Mizrahi men wearing white kippot, who are newly religious followers of Breslov, an Ashkenazi Hasidic group. The crowd is astoundingly heterogeneous.

Among these merrymakers are thousands of strait-laced haredim, who take different pilgrimage paths up the mountain, trying to avoid the "sacrilegious" Hasids and "superstitious" amulet-carrying Mizrahim. When worshippers reach a walled courtyard, differences disappear. They become an enormous wave, pushing to reach the tomb of the second-century mystic who is revered by everyone on Mount Meron. On Lag b'Omer, it's the custom of religious Mizrahim and Ashkenazim alike to cut a boy's hair when he turns three, the age when he first begins to learn Torah; everywhere women stand apart, watching boisterous men and boys singing and dancing in circles, celebrating as long-haired three-year-old boys get their first haircut. This Orthodox belief stems from a passage in the Zohar that compares man to a tree. The Torah also rules that it is prohibited to pick the fruits of trees during their first three years of growth; similarly, boys are left "unharvested" until age three, when they begin their religious education.

Outside the tomb, a Mizrahi teenager calls out *"Tisadou v'tevorhu* [Eat and be blessed]" as she hands out slices of roasted meat. On this special day, it's a mitzvah to share food, especially with the poor. She offers some to elderly haredi women who politely refuse, probably because they interpret the Jewish dietary laws differently from Mizrahim. Kashrut laws were meant to unite, not separate Jews, the teenager complains. "Aren't we the same religion? The same Jewish people?"

An olive-skinned man stands beside a giant poster of an octogenarian in a regal black robe with gold embroidery and a blue, turban-like hat:

Baghdad-born Rabbi Ovadia Yosef, the caustic-tongued spiritual leader of the Shas political party and symbol of a golden age when Mizrahi religious culture flourished. "Rav Yosef is responsible for my spiritual awakening, he's a great *gaon* [Talmudic genius]," says the man in passionate street Hebrew, inviting passersby to a Shas religious revivalist rally.

When Adi Rosenfeld first met Moti Lalou, she'd vaguely heard of Rabbi Ovadia Yosef; she had never dated a Mizrahi. She was in uniform, part of an Orthodox women's army unit tutoring Ethiopian and ex-Soviet children in a state religious school. Moti was a teacher at the same Orthodox elementary school in a blighted section of Netanya. Adi admired Moti for spending his free time bringing donations from bakeries to the cash-strapped in this seaside town, and admiration soon turned into attraction. "Even though we had a lot of common interests and our Hebrew accents are the same and we both love the spiritual sides of Judaism, Moti comes from a religious and cultural background that is different from mine," Adi says, with a toss of her waist-length brown braid.

Moti is the son of Orthodox Algerian Israelis who make pilgrimages to Rabbi Shimon's tomb on Mount Meron. (He got his first haircut there.) Adi is the daughter of Orthodox American Israelis who make pilgrimages to science fairs and museums. Her family emigrated in 1982 and live in a book-filled home near the Weizmann Institute of Science in Rehovot. Her parents, both educators, train Arab and Jewish teachers. After Moti's parents escaped anti-Jewish riots in Algeria in 1956, they were housed in a transit camp in Netanya, where they now live. Their unpretentious apartment is close to the market where they sell spices. "The heart of our foods lies in the spices," explains Moti, who enumerates some favorites: cinnamon, coriander, cayenne. Adi grew up believing "spices" meant either pepper or salt. The two families have different religious customs and political outlooks. The right-leaning Lalous voted for Netanyahu and Sharon and admire Rabbi Ovadia Yosef. They believe in swift retaliation for terrorist attacks and that settlements bring security. The left-leaning Rosenfelds voted for Rabin, Peres, Barak, and Mitzna. They believe in negotiating with enemies and dismantling many of the settlements. Although the two families are separated by a political and cultural chasm, the petite eighteen-year-old soldier and lanky twenty-five-year-old teacher knew their love would bridge it.

Adi and Moti set a wedding date. "As we prepared, I became aware of how very different our religious rituals are," confides Adi, who felt like she was on a *National Geographic* expedition, discovering customs of North African Jewry. She was the first Ashkenazi to join Moti's family; his six sisters married men from Algerian, Iraqi, and Moroccan backgrounds. Three nights before the wedding, she and her family were invited for dinner at Moti's family's apartment. Here, the large Lalou clan introduced the Rosenfeld family to the Night of the Henna, a traditional prewedding Mizrahi and Arab celebration. "I was stunned. It was very fancy, like a mini-wedding," says Adi, with exuberance. "And so warm and joyous." She was asked to put on a Lalou family heirloom, a green velvet Algerian caftan with intricate gold hand embroidery. Moti wore a white caftan and a red fez with a tassel. The ceremony began as Mrs. Lalou brought out a platter rimmed with crimson passion flowers. Dark-red henna paste—from the Song of Solomon: "My lover is to me a cluster of henna blossoms from the vineyards of Ein Gedi"—filled the center. With a gold coin, she scooped out the henna, helping Adi and Moti stain temporary tattoos on their palms, ancient symbols for long life and prosperity. Then the guests threw pastel-colored almond candies and rose water at the couple, wishing them *siman tov,* Hebrew for "good omen," and *mabruk,* Arabic for "good star." Toasting them with copious quantities of arak, members of Moti's family clapped and sang spirited Jewish Arabic songs. Moti's six sisters danced while delicately balancing heaping platters of delectable desserts.

As the rhythmic music and pounding of drums grew louder, the swaying of the undulating women intensified. "At first I was very bashful. I'd never danced like this before," recounts Adi. "And I had never seen men and women dancing in such a provocative, uninhibited way." "Nice" Orthodox Ashkenazi girls don't. But that night, Adi joined in the unrestrained dancing, as did her parents and three younger brothers. On this night, the bridge over the cultural chasm was colored henna red.

Moti and Adi live near her parents in Rehovot, a mixed city of blue-collar workers and professionals, both religious and secular. Many neighbors in their weathered-looking apartment building are Russian- or Amharic-speakers, like their former students. The couple keep kosher

Mizrahi-style and Adi is gamely trying to emulate her mother-in-law's cooking. "The magic in the foods brings magic to the religious celebrations," says Moti, whose eyes light up as he wistfully describes lamb laced with cumin, mouthwatering *tajines* (meat and vegetable stews), *bastila* (pigeon pie), and sumptuous spiced couscous. Herring, corned beef, and rye bread are not to his taste.

Selecting their new daughter's name also created a cross-cultural religious adventure. Mizrahim name babies after living relatives, and Moti hoped to bless the baby with his mother's name. But Ashkenazim believe that having the name of a living person could rob a baby of a full life. "We knew we would disappoint one side of the family because, in Judaism, names have a lot of meaning," explains Adi. "They're closely linked with the soul." She gave birth a week before Hanukkah, and they named their daughter Liora, Hebrew for "I have light," in memory of Adi's late grandmother. Moti's mother gave Liora a gold rectangular charm inscribed with the word *Shaddai* (Almighty), one of many Hebrew euphemisms for God. Two dolphins dangle from it; they symbolize good luck. From her mother-in-law Adi learned that "fish sleep with their eyes open, so the evil eye can't take over them."

When Moti has questions about Jewish law, he takes a book off the shelf and the book is most likely written by the firebrand spiritual leader of Shas, Rabbi Ovadia Yosef, Israel's chief Sephardi/Mizrahi rabbi from 1973 to 1983. This eminent Torah scholar has written more than thirty user-friendly books on Jewish law, and most Mizrahim own at least one. (His books rarely are found in Ashkenazi homes and are banned from Lithuanian yeshivot.) Israel has two chief rabbis—Ashkenazi and Sephard/Mizrahi—who administer affairs according to their own religious laws. The dual chief rabbinate has led to serious and sometimes absurd differences. The concept of the chief rabbinate and rabbinical courts are not part of Jewish tradition and law, and ultra-Orthodox Jewish groups do not recognize their authority. The Chief Rabbinate system was instituted by the Ottoman Empire and continued by the British. For hundreds of years, most Jews in the Holy Land were Mizrahi/Sephardi and the Ottomans recognized only the Sephardi Chief Rabbi. The Sephardim treated Ashkenazi immigrants condescendingly; in the eighteenth century, Ashkenazim constituted only 20 percent of the Jews of Palestine. In 1911, Sephardi rabbis unsuccessfully tried to unite the Jewish community in Palestine with one set of religious laws and customs. Under British rule, as Ashkenazi immigration increased, Mizrahim became an overlooked minority. After Independence, when the demographic patterns reversed and Mizrahi Jews again became the majority, the religious establishment remained Ashkenazi.

While Moti, a Hebrew University grad, studies for his CPA exams, Adi is finishing her master's degree in special education at Bar-Ilan University, where it is not unusual to see secular students dress as if they're going to the beach and religious ones who kiss the mezuzah before entering a classroom and write "With the Help of God" on exam papers. After the first year of marriage, Adi started wearing a hat and ankle-length skirts. "In tiny little steps, Moti and I are becoming more religious than our parents. I know it's hard for my family to accept, but I feel I'm representing the Orthodox by how I dress and act. We religious people are a minority and, in a way, I'm a symbol. I feel I have a mission to fulfill to be kind and generous. I want people to feel good about us Orthodox." Adi and Moti do not cook on Shabbat, turn on electricity, watch television, use the phone, or drive. They put Liora in a stroller and walk to a synagogue.

Many Israeli Mizrahim attend traditional Orthodox "ethnic" synagogues of people who left the same countries. "I'd never prayed at a Mizrahi synagogue, even though I grew up near this one," says Adi, who sits in the balcony with women and girls. She is the only Ashkenazi among mostly Moroccan, Algerian, and Tunisian worshippers. "It took me two years to feel comfortable with their traditions, melodies, and prayer book. My ears weren't used to the Arabic tunes, so different from any I had ever heard. They repeat these very emotional melodies over and over, very beautiful melodies that go back centuries. Everyone has memorized all the prayers and songs, even the little kids. It goes back to the time when some Jews couldn't read, so they had to memorize everything. There's so much more singing, bonding, such strong spirituality and love for our religion, it brings tears to my eyes. The [Ashkenazi] services I grew up with are so boring in comparison—people pray quietly and the *hazan* does most of the singing. Those who are very observant and those not so observant are united in prayer. I'm struck by how open-minded everyone is. After services, I saw a guy with an earring, his hair slicked with gel. He kissed the rabbi's hand very respectfully. Then, in front of the rabbi, he took off his kippa and turned on his cell phone. I saw him drive off, maybe to a disco or a party. What Orthodox Ashkenazi would do that on Shabbat, right in front of the rabbi?"

Most Mizrahim follow a lenient, flexible approach to Judaism and see nothing wrong with driving to the beach or soccer stadium after synagogue (most professional soccer matches are played on Saturday). It is said that no Mizrahi is emotionally severed from Judaism, only distanced from religious practice. Although Jews originally from Iraq to Morocco, Egypt to Yemen, follow slightly different religious practices, they are much more homogeneous than Ashkenazim and are not split into fractious religious camps. The baffling subdivisions of Ashkenazi Judaism—among various non-Orthodox, Orthodox, and ultra-Orthodox haredi and Hasidic groups—are alien to Sephardi and Mizrahi Jews. Judaism in the Mediterranean, North Africa, and the Middle East did not undergo the tremendous changes that transformed much of Ashkenazi Judaism.

Ashkenazi Jews were what modern Israelis would call Orthodox until medieval ghetto walls started crumbling and Jews no longer had to live in separate quarters or wear distinctive clothing or Jewish badges. During the "emancipation," roughly from 1789 to 1917, in most Western and Central European countries Jews were given more civil rights and religious freedom, even granted citizenship. ("Emancipation" in Eastern Europe was another matter. Half the world's Jews lived in Russia, where they were socially ostracized and largely untouched by the changes of the Emancipation, until hundreds of thousands of them fled westward in the 1880s.) Jews were allowed in many secondary schools, universities, and liberal professions. By the late nineteenth century, no longer unified by segregation, many Ashkenazi Jews gave up the very pious ways of their traditional parents. (Haredim continued to adhere strictly to the religious laws and maintain their communities and rabbis' courts.) By the end of the nineteenth century, most Western European and North American Jews were not Orthodox and either relaxed or abandoned key Orthodox observances such as Sabbath rest, dietary restrictions, daily prayers, and ritual baths. Assimilation often led either to questioning or a loss of Jewish identity. Intermarriage, once rare, became more common.

Today, "Orthodox" in Israel slowly is becoming redefined by how it differs with "non-Orthodox" trends, especially the Reform and Conservative movements. Jews like Adi and her family believe it is possible to combine Jewish traditions with a contemporary life.

Unlike Adi, her mother shows no outward sign that she is Orthodox. Outside the synagogue, Melodie has no problem wearing pants or leaving her hair uncovered. She lectures at a college near Beersheva where her students are mostly Jewish and Bedouin special education teachers. She's proud Adi is studying for a master's in special education and has a part-time teaching job at a progressive Orthodox girls' high school, where imparting a good education is more important than checking the length of skirts and sleeves. Teachers don't believe it is against Jewish law for girls to study Jewish texts, including the Torah. They encourage girls to think independently and stand up for themselves. Girls also learn humanistic Jewish values and the beauty of cultural and religious pluralism. Teachers stress that all forms of Judaism should feel welcome in Israel. Unlike many religious high schools, this one doesn't mix politics with education.

Melodie and Sherman Rosenfeld strongly believe in the separation of synagogue and state: the Beit Knesset and Knesset. Adi and Moti don't. "If we separate state and religion, what's the connective thing?" counters their spirited daughter. "Then Israel could become just like any other country. For centuries, our ancestors were persecuted or killed for keeping religious traditions—for praying, for keeping kosher—but they still did, even in hiding. Jews lit Shabbat candles in concentration camp latrines. I find it sad that many secular Ashkenazim don't realize Judaism means so much more than a seder or fasting on Yom Kippur." Both Adi and her parents are saddened that both her younger soldier brothers have taken off their kippot. The army often is an Orthodox Israeli's first experience of living intensely, living dangerously with secular Israelis. Kippa-wearing soldiers discover that they not only think differently, but they use different Hebrew expressions. The religious soldier may say "With God's help," while his secular jeep mate will say "Hope for the best." An observant soldier will say "Shabbat shalom," and her secular commander might respond, "Have a fun weekend." On Rosh Hashanah the secular soldier will say "Happy New Year" and her Orthodox boyfriend answer, "May you be inscribed for a blessing."

Whether they live in Israel or in settlements, many Orthodox families are grappling with the pain of children flirting with secularity. When the book *Generation of Discarded Kippot* came out about why so many young men are taking off their kippot and women "leaving the path," the author, educational psychologist Shraga Fisherman, expected to be denounced. Instead, parents and teachers have been inviting this dean of a religious Zionist college in the West Bank settlement of Elkanah to give lectures. Fisherman has found that "many teenagers say they're not allowed to ask questions at home or in the yeshiva. When a kid who studies Torah for twelve years tells me that the first powerful spiritual experience he ever had was in Goa (a beach town in India popular with post-army Israelis), we have to ask ourselves, God in Heaven, what's going on in the schools?" Although there are no reliable statistics about how many Orthodox youth, settlers and nonsettlers, are going secular, he cites one poll showing that as many as 23 percent are *datlashim,* the Hebrew acronym for "formerly religious." A poster illustrates the predicament: a knit kippa unraveling until nothing is left.

A strange, soup-bowl-size multicolored embroidered kippa covers Sherman Rosenfeld's brown hair. This designer of educational science programs at the Weizmann Institute also travels the country coaching Jewish, Christian, and Muslim Arab science teachers, who range from passionately religious to fervently antireligious. "I wear this 'nonpolitical' kippa because my Judaism is not about politics, it's about spirituality and social justice. The material, size, and color of a kippa in Israel can reveal a man's religious and political affiliation," he says, describing what he half-seriously dubs "Kippology." "A black velvet kippa can mean a haredi who doesn't recognize Israel. A loosely knit, white kippa is worn by Bratslav hasidim. The Habad hasidim have a different kippa. If Israelis see you wearing a small, closely knit kippa, they assume you have right-wing politics. I think Israeli Judaism has become overly politicized, stereotyped in one-dimensional ways. When someone gets blown up, we don't ask 'Knitted kippa, black kippa, modern Orthodox, or not religious?' We're all in this together, a peace-hungry society fighting for survival."

Although Sherman's unusual kippa, from Buchara, does not reveal his political beliefs, in Israel religion and politics are firmly knotted. He likes the perspective of Meimad, a small left-leaning party associated with Israel's once dominant, now declining Labor Party that is an Orthodox alternative to religious right-wing pro-settler parties. The settler movement, he believes, overemphasizes the holiness of the Land of Israel. "I know a lot of settlers who say 'This is our land and it was given to Abraham, promised to us by God. We can't give it back.' Meimad would say, 'Yes, that's true, but Judaism has other values, the values of compromise, of life and peace with our Arab neighbors. And these values are more important than land.' "

In Sherman's view, many settlements were a mistake. He's not alone; as part of a peace deal with the Palestinians, about three quarters of Israelis favor dismantling many of the settlements. In April 2003, Prime Minister Sharon said of the settlements, "I know we will have to part with some of these places." Sherman says, "Because of our coalition system, for years the strong settler political lobby has forced our governments to act in ways that are not in the best interests of the people. Some settlements are impossible to maintain, nondefensible, and cause more conflict with the Palestinians. I have a nuanced position. I think some so-called settlements within the national consensus should stay, like Gush Etzion and areas around Jerusalem."

The Rosenfelds have seen Orthodox Israelis squabbling over the Yitzhak Rabin Synagogue, which faces Adi and Moti's apartment. The only synagogue in Israel named after the late prime minister, it opened a year after he was assassinated. Some fellow Orthodox Jews keep their vows never to enter it because it is named after the secular Sabra whose politics they detest. When Rabin Synagogue announcements are put up, they sometimes are torn down. "Politics overshadowing spirituality. That shows we still have a lot of work to do." Sherman explains that naming the synagogue after Rabin makes a statement: "Look what happens when politics gets mixed up with religion. This tragedy is one of the unhealed wounds of Israeli society. It was not just one of the darkest moments of Israeli history, it was one of the darkest moments of Jewish history. Rabin's death showed we must tolerate other views. In today's politically charged environment, again people are finding it hard to listen to views that are not theirs. We need more dialogue among all Israelis, but also within the Orthodox communities. There's too much infighting and infighting doesn't bring us closer to God. We need to listen. It is a challenge not only in Israel, but throughout the Middle East."

11

The Non-Orthodox

War of the Cheeseburgers

⊘ Two men are sitting on a park bench in Jerusalem. After a long silence, one heaves a tremendous sigh: "Oy!" The other stands and hollers, "If you're going to talk about religion, I'm leaving." —Israeli joke about the hot-button issue of religious pluralism in Israel

⊘ What's the difference between Orthodox, Conservative, and Reform Jews? The mother of the Orthodox bride is pregnant. The Conservative bride is pregnant. The Reform rabbi is pregnant. —A doctor in an Israeli maternity ward

Sivan Meshulam has quit her job designing gas masks. While she searches for work illustrating books, the twenty-eight-year-old has moved back into her family's stone house in Jerusalem. Its garden, thick with fragrant jasmine and purple frangipani, is an oasis of calm, surrounded by weathered nineteenth-century Ottoman Turkish walls. Just outside the gate is another world: the bustling Street of the Prophets, which cuts through the heart of West Jerusalem. Here, non-Orthodox Jews like Sivan bump shoulders with ultra-Orthodox Jews on their way to pray at the Western Wall. In a neighborhood restaurant popular with students, writers, and disillusioned left-wing activists, a waitress with a navel ring serves "white steak" (a Hebrew euphemism for forbidden pork). Down the block, in a dry cleaning shop, exhausted-looking haredi women pick up their husbands' black suits. Nearby, Israelis sway to the hypnotic beats of a tango class led by a dancer with flamboyant orange hair. This city that religion built—and repeatedly destroyed—is home to the pious and the perplexed. "You can see all the different faces of Judaism right on our street," says Sivan, who, like most Israeli Jews, is neither rigorously Orthodox nor completely secular but somewhere near the middle. "We live close together and very far apart."

About 80 percent of Israeli Jews are non-Orthodox, a category with endless variations. Some eat milk and meat, but never on the Sabbath. Most are two-holiday Jews who pray in synagogue only on Rosh Hashana and Yom Kippur. Others pray in the soccer stadium, but only when their team is losing. Whether they are staunchly atheistic, agnostic, semiobservant, Reform, or Conservative, non-Orthodox Israelis lead Jewish lives. Almost all attend a Passover seder, light Hanukkah candles, and enjoy Sabbath dinners. Most Israeli Jews fast on Yom Kippur and observe at least some of the kosher dietary laws. They circumcise their sons and, thirteen years later, give them bar mitzvahs. Nearly all Jewish homes have a mezuzah on the doorpost. So do rooms in Israel's public buildings.

Israel is at once a secular state and a holy land. The state symbols are Jewish. The official emblem is the menorah; the seven-branched candelabra shaped like the ancient moriah plant was an important ritual object in King Solomon's Temple. The shekel was used as currency before the time of Abraham. The national anthem, "Hatikvah" ("The Hope"), an early Zionist hymn, describes the ancient "hope to be a free people in the land of Zion and Jerusalem." The blue-and-white national flag, with a Star of David in the center, is based on the *tallit* (prayer shawl), which symbolizes the importance of bringing the holy into daily life. The Hebrew dialogue in bodice-ripping movies would largely be understandable to the subjects of King David three thousand years ago. An Israeli who can read the Hebrew of modern literature, of comic books and newspapers, can also read fragments of the Dead Sea scrolls.

Israel runs on "Jewish time." It uses the solar-lunar Jewish calendar, which starts from the date God created Adam and Eve. (The solar Christian calendar starts with the birth of Jesus. The Muslim calendar is solar-lunar and begins with the escape of Muhammad from Mecca to Medina on June 16, 622.) Israel's national holidays are Jewish. Few Jewish Israelis work on Shabbat, the national day of rest; most Jewish businesses are closed, buses don't run (except in Haifa and Eilat), and El Al, the national airline, is grounded. Many Israelis head to the airport or beaches during the two New Year holidays, Passover (the birth of the Jewish people) and Rosh Hashanah (the birth of man). Even the most rabidly antireligious Israelis celebrate holidays few diaspora Jews do. Israelis wear costumes on Purim, plant trees on Tu b'Shvat, party around campfires on Lag b'Omer. And although the overwhelming majority of Israeli Jewish youth—about 75 percent—attend state secular schools, those secular schools have a strong Jewish orientation. In nursery school, children learn Jewish customs and Rosh Hashana, Hanukkah, and Passover songs. Second-graders study the Bible as history and literature and celebrate the beginning of their Bible studies with a *kabbalat Torah* (acceptance of the law) ceremony, usually at an Orthodox synagogue. During field trips, children see up close the Bible's connection with the land. They learn Jewish stories in stones as they wander amid tombs of prophets and kings, ruins of ancient synagogues and battlefields. Before graduating high school, they take a national matriculation exam that tests their biblical knowledge. The army regularly runs Bible contests, as do prisons. Bulletin boards in government offices list the three daily times for prayer. There are prayer books in doctors' and dentists' offices as well as in hospital waiting rooms. Even the doors in the Haifa subway are inscribed with the Torah's commandment to rise before old age and honor the elderly. The "secular" Israeli majority are much more traditional, more connected to Jewish life than most secular Jews in the diaspora.

On the way to do volunteer work assisting a wheelchair-bound sculptress, Sivan passes streets named for the first-century B.C.E. rabbi Hillel (who summed up Judaism as: "What is hateful to you, do not do unto others"), King David, and Rambam (Maimonides). "Judaism is everywhere you turn. Almost every street, it seems, has a synagogue," says Sivan, who, like most non-Orthodox Israeli Jews, believes in God and Jewish spirituality but is not interested in synagogue-based religiosity. Jerusalem has more than a thousand synagogues, and her architect father has designed two of them. "It's so ironic. The last time he attended services was my brother's bar mitzvah. He had to be taught what to do when the rabbi called him to the Torah. He never learned much about Judaism. He grew up in hiding when a million and a half Jewish children were killed." Her father was one of the lucky Jewish children in Nazi-occupied Europe: despite an alliance with the Third Reich, Bulgaria's King Boris II and the church refused to deliver most of the country's fifty thousand Sephardi Jews to the extermination camps. "In communist Bulgaria, Dad didn't learn much about religion. We had to teach him. I'll never forget when he picked up one of my elementary school books which explained Bible stories and was surprised that the stories are so incredibly human. Then he read my brother's high school Bible and fell in love with the poetry, the rich Hebrew, all the dramatic history."

In contrast, Sivan's mother was raised in a moderately religious home. Many Saturday mornings, she walked with her father to services at a Jerusalem Ashkenazi Orthodox synagogue. "There were only two kinds of synagogues—Orthodox and ultra-Orthodox," recalls Mira. "By high school, I decided to be like all my friends and go to no synagogue at all. And when I was in the army, to be really Sabra meant to be really secular. That's when liberal, humanist values became my religion. I taught my kids that you don't have to be religious to love our traditions, that Judaism is not just for those who wear black hats and wigs. We often have Shabbat dinner at my brother's—his wife cooks fantastic Moroccan food. We light the candles, say *kiddush* [the blessing] over the wine and *hamotzi* over the bread, and eat spicy fish. Afterwards, we used to go off and party. No more. Life has changed. We sit and talk. People really need each other. We're all feeling depressed. Everyone is searching for meaning in these terrible times. A tragedy on both sides. Some of the biggest agnostics are getting interested in religion. Going to synagogue. Studying kabbalah. An atheist friend was in a Jewish-Palestinian dialogue group. When the Palestinians stopped coming, the group decided to keep going—talking this time to Orthodox Jews, whom they rarely get to know. They discuss religious texts together and have philosophical talks."

Mira and Sivan live in Israel's ground zero. There have been dozens of grisly terrorist attacks within minutes of their house—even in front of it. One blast shattered the kitchen window; a head flew over the garden wall. A terrorist disguised as an Orthodox Jew had detonated himself. "How can there be God out there?" Mira wonders. "How can God let all this happen?" Sivan, who is painting a playful watercolor portrait, puts down her brush and interrupts. "Sometimes I stop at makeshift memorial shrines where people put candles and flowers. I don't know the proper way to pray, the rituals, but you don't have to be religious to pick up a psalm book. I think psalms are accepted no matter who says them. I appreciate the haredim who leave the psalm books at the shrines. And I appreciate them for cleaning up [body parts] after the bombings. They make no distinction if the person is Arab or Jew, religious or not. These are the haredim I respect. They volunteer with devotion. Why can't they show the same respect for all living Jews? When I think of some of our neighbors, I get angry. They believe there's only one way to be a Jew— their way."

Sivan vividly recalls walking home from elementary school through ultra-Orthodox Mea Sharim, which is around the corner from her house. "Some haredi children suddenly started yelling a strange word at me. I had no idea what that word meant. All I knew was I didn't look like them. When I got home, I asked my parents, but they didn't know that word. They said it wasn't Hebrew. Then someone told me that it was Yiddish for 'slut' "—and by implication, secular female. Haredi men on "modesty patrols" sometimes harass secular women with exposed arms or legs who enter their neighborhoods. They have thrown ink and cursed at dozens of women on the way to work at the Ministry of Education near a haredi neighborhood. Local bus shelters that have displayed sexually suggestive ads have been burned.

When Sivan was a teenager, a haredi neighbor asked her to come into her apartment and turn on the lights. "I did it and then I started thinking, If it's forbidden for a Jew to turn on lights on the Sabbath, why did she ask me, another Jew, to commit a sin? Just because I'm secular, I'm not a *real* Jew? She thought of me as a Shabbos goy [the Gentile who, on the Sabbath, helps religious Jews perform functions they are prohibited from on their day of rest]. I got upset and asked a rabbi and he explained that she was violating religious law. It really annoys me that there are narrow-minded haredim who think everything that deals with Judaism is theirs. They believe they have better values, that they're holier than us. We're also legitimate Jews. If not for the nonreligious Zionists who brought

Jews here, a lot of haredi families probably would have remained in Europe and been killed. Someone told me that almost half of all high school students say they hate haredim."

Most Israeli high school students read the science magazine Mira edited. It wasn't allowed in ultra-Orthodox schools. "They think science is for the seculars and the Bible is for them. Well, I tried to show my readers the Bible belongs to all of us," says Mira, who often put biblical quotations about nature in the magazine. "Judaism was one of the first great environmental religions and many ancient ecological themes in Jewish law and tradition are relevant today," she emphasizes. She quotes a line from Deuteronomy relevant to both the rash of Arab arsonist attacks on Israeli forests and fields and the IDF destruction of those Palestinian olive groves where terrorists hide: "Even if you are at war with a city . . . you must not destroy its trees" (Deuteronomy 20:19–20). Because of government cutbacks, the magazine folded, and Mira now runs a Jerusalem ecological educational center that tries to create "green" Arabs and Jews. She is also part of a volunteer group trying to preserve historic sites on the Street of the Prophets. The family's 150-year-old home, a symphony of curves with thick stone walls and high, vaulted ceilings, was one of the first houses built outside the Old City's walls. It's a national landmark, a treasure of Jerusalem's secular history.

The house was built in 1850 by the English painter William Homan Hunt, a founder of the pre-Raphaelite movement and an early Christian Zionist. In 1892, Ottoman Turkish soldiers took over the house, then the Russian Orthodox Church. In 1914, Dr. Helen Kagan, a twenty-four-year-old pediatrician from Tashkent, Uzbekistan, turned this house into a busy clinic which she ran with two American nurses from Hadassah. The one-named poet Rachel lived here in 1925 and wrote a famous poem, "Pear Tree," about a tree in the garden; later, Dr. Kagan's husband Emil Hauser, the world-famous violinist and founder of the Budapest Quartet, started Jerusalem's first music academy there, a center for musicians who had fled the Nazis.

Dr. Kagan was a nationalist who let members of the Jewish underground hide smuggled gold in the garden because she knew the Turks would not suspect her. She was one of the only doctors for Jerusalem's eighty thousand Jews, Muslims, and Christians—a third of whom were dying from cholera, malaria, typhus, or starvation. One patient this secular Zionist saved was a feverish haredi boy from neighboring Mea Sharim. Paradoxically, years later he founded Neturei Karta (Guardians of the City), a tiny ultra-ultra-Orthodox anti-Zionist sect.

Sivan remembers a balmy evening watching television in the living room with her mother. "We heard a noise outside, but didn't know what it was. It was scary. Then I noticed a boy staring through the open window. I was frightened; he looked strange. He had a black hat and long peyot. I thought he was staring at us until I realized he was watching our TV. We invited him to come in and watch. He was really shy. Awkward. He sat in front of the TV. He was very stiff. When I handed him the remote control, he got excited and kept pressing the button, jumping from program to program. A few minutes of a talk show, then *Who Wants to Be a Millionaire?* He kept staring at the screen like he was in a trance. It was really hot, sticky hot, but he never took off his heavy black coat. He wouldn't even drink our water. Maybe because our glasses aren't kosher enough for him. A few days later, we saw him standing at the window again. It was really bizarre. I told him to come to the door. He sat down and picked up the remote and, like last time, just kept jumping from channel to channel. I thought haredim call TV an evil abomination, but this kid sure loved it. He wouldn't tell us his name. He thought the 'modesty police' were following him because his father was a famous rabbi. He hardly looked at us; maybe he felt weird to be alone with two strange women wearing shorts. Our living room is full of 'forbidden' books that he can never read—books on biology, Greek art, even my *Catcher in the Rye,* which we're required to read in high school. In yeshivas, boys read only Torah. He came unannounced, always at night. After a few times, he stopped coming. We never saw him again. And he hardly said a word.

"Sometimes when I hear haredi boys speaking Yiddish in the neighborhood, I think of him," says Sivan. Around the corner is 11 Ethiopia Street, the former home of Eliezer Ben-Yehuda, the father of modern Hebrew. Yiddish-speaking haredim who believed the Holy Tongue should be used only in prayers and not defiled by everyday use pronounced a religious excommunication against this Hebrew-speaking heretic. The plaque outside the Ben-Yehuda house has been stolen so often that today it is unmarked. Another "secular heretic," Yitzhak Rabin, was born two houses away.

The Ben-Yehuda house is not far from Israel's best-known haredi–

secular battlefield, Bar Ilan Street, where haredi "Shabbat cops" lob vicious verbal assaults at blasphemous Shabbat drivers. Other times, they hurl rocks or dirty diapers. During demonstrations to keep the street open to Shabbat traffic, sometimes police erect barriers to separate the ultra-Orthodox from the non-Orthodox. On occasion, when violence erupted, they've used tear gas to stop Jews from attacking each other. Religious neighborhoods have the right to bar Shabbat traffic, but busy streets like Bar Ilan that run through both non-Orthodox and ultra-Orthodox neighborhoods have an ambiguous status. Israel's Supreme Court endorsed shutting Bar Ilan Street to traffic only during Shabbat services, and for now, most ultra-Orthodox accept this arrangement. "I was at a peaceful demonstration a few years ago. As I was walking home, suddenly, for no reason, a haredi man spit on me, and I was dressed respectfully," Sivan says angrily. "These 'black hats' have time to spit and throw rocks, but no time to work or serve in the army. They say they're too busy praying. Sometimes when I back the car out of the driveway, haredi men shout 'Shabbos!' 'Shabbos!' at me. Those religious fanatics have no right to impose their religious rules on us. They're fighting over a spiritual day that is supposed to be about peace?"

Bar Ilan Street is not the only site for Israel's secular–religious tug of war; so are the Golden Arches. When the first McDonald's opened in Jerusalem in 1995, non-Orthodox Jews eagerly lined up for milkshakes and cheeseburgers. Infuriated by this unkosher fast-food invasion into the Holy City, ultra-Orthodox Jews demonstrated. A few months later, an arsonist tried to burn down the restaurant. It was only the beginning. McDonald's has paid hefty fines—more than $20,000—for allowing Jewish teenagers to flip burgers on the Sabbath. It isn't permitted to sell the popular Egg McMuffin sandwich because it contains pork and must charge extra for its burgers because McDonald's Israel pays 40 percent more for its Argentinian and Uruguayan beef than its American counterparts; Israeli law prohibits the import of nonkosher meat.

The chain's problems were raised into high relief when McDonald's decided to open a branch in the city's new bus station in 2002. The haredi community threatened that if it wasn't kosher, they'd organize mass demonstrations. McDonald's agreed to make it kosher. That wasn't enough: Jerusalem's religious council demanded that McDonald's change the name of all its kosher branches to McKosher, arguing that otherwise it was deceiving the public by suggesting that the entire chain is kosher. When McDonald's said no, the city's religious council refused to issue it a kosher certificate, a necessity for any restaurant operating in the bus station. McDonald's lawyers went into action and the Jerusalem Magistrate Court accepted their arguments. Even without the kosher certificate the restaurant is thriving: near the golden arches a sign says "All the food is kosher and we're closed on Shabbat." Selling bread during Passover is forbidden; McDonald's gets around this by serving burgers on buns made of potato flour instead of wheat (unleavened grain). In other restaurants, religious fault lines were visible when ultra-Orthodox "Passover Police" went on patrol. If they spotted religious renegades eating forbidden foods like pizza or hot dogs on buns, they fined the errant restaurant owners. Non-Orthodox Jews protested by patronizing the rebel restaurants.

In 2003, with the ultra-Orthodox out of the national government, "Passover Police" disappeared. Nevertheless, kosher certification is very important; losing it means losing valuable customers. That's why most Israeli food manufacturers, schools, hospitals, hotels, and wedding halls pay kosher inspectors to certify that their kitchens adhere to religious dietary laws, that milk dishes, for example, are not placed on the meat side of the kitchen. Inspectors check to see that hotels do not desecrate the Sabbath; Friday parties must end at least two hours before Sabbath begins, and no Saturday night festivities can begin before Shabbat ends. Hotels that allow non-Jewish events such as Christmas or New Year's parties may lose their kosher certification. Modesty is considered important, too. A few wedding halls that have allowed scantily clad belly dancers to perform have had their kosher certification suspended. Being a "kosher cop" can be a lucrative business. Sometimes too lucrative: Orthodox and haredi kashrut inspectors have been caught demanding under-the-table fees to look the other way, even making outrageous demands such as telling restaurant owners to tune radios to Orthodox stations rather than secular army radio. Victims rarely protest lest they lose their kosher certificates.

"Sometimes it feels like it's them and us," says Sivan, describing the widening divisions between Jerusalem's non-Orthodox and ultra-Orthodox. "We hardly talk to each other. They despise our modern culture, they're repulsed by us." Some secular Israelis bitterly joke that there should be two Jewish capitals—Jerusalem for the Jews and Tel Aviv for the Israelis. In the past decade, tens of thousands of young non-Orthodox Jews have moved out. "I really love Jerusalem, and my family is here and this house where I was born," says Sivan. "A lot of my friends left for Tel Aviv. I might be next."

"I understand how she feels," says Mira as she licks the glue on a postage stamp (the glue on all Israeli stamps is certified kosher). She is mailing in a check for her city tax bill and she is irate. "What really makes me angry is that we're supporting them and look how they treat us." Despite being more than a third of Jerusalem's population, ultra-Orthodox pay less than 10 percent of the city's taxes. So few ultra-Orthodox families have a wage earner that each non-Orthodox taxpayer finances between one and three ultra-Orthodox families. "They're milking us, taking money from my pocket. My neighbors with ten kids don't even pay taxes or send their sons to the army. They think God intended us to work hard for them. They do the studying, we do hard work and fight the wars for them, and then the messiah will come. Why should men who refuse to join the army and refuse to work get tax exemptions? They're living off our backs. We've done our duties—I was a soldier, my ex-husband was in the Yom Kippur War and in the reserves, both my children were in the army during the Gulf War when Scuds were falling." Haredim in Jerusalem have a lot of political power, she points out. Not only do religious Jews make up the majority on the city council, but in 2003, Jerusalem had its first haredi mayor, the father of twelve children.

As for future voters, most of Jerusalem's Jewish children are haredim. The war of the wombs is evident down the street at Bikur Holim Hospital (Visit the Sick), where pregnant patients in the busy ob-gyn waiting room are mostly ultra-Orthodox or Muslim. "Soon we'll be outnumbered," says a secular obstetrician. "When I have to make a life-saving medical decision, my haredi patients won't agree unless they get their rabbi's approval. Imagine, in the twenty-first century, I need permission from a fundamentalist rabbi to save a life. When the rabbi doesn't answer in time, I've had to ask a [secular] judge for a court order to proceed."

Paradoxically, as the power and population of Jerusalem's ultra-Orthodox expand, secular life has became spiritually and culturally more diverse. Incense-filled New Age shops sell books on yoga and kabbalah and tarot cards. The capital has internationally acclaimed museums and vibrant film and music and book festivals. Street fairs are lively but interspersed with armed guards. There are health food shops and nonkosher restaurants. Until the second intifada, some clubs were so "in" that hip Tel Avivians drove to the capital to dance to technopop music until dawn. "It's true," notes Mira. "Paradoxically, Jerusalem has become more secular and more religious. When I was a kid, I swam in Jerusalem's first 'mixed' male and female pool. Haredim were so horrified when it opened. They called it Brika Hameriva [Pool of Dispute] and threw stones at us when we swam." Now, not only does Jerusalem have dozens of "mixed" public swimming pools, but it has a few "mixed" synagogues, where male and female worshippers sit together.

I don't mind that we're called the 'synagogue of the seculars.' I'm pleased that people are coming here who never have been involved with a congregation. The younger generation, the high-tech generation, have a tremendous thirst for an authentic Israeli form of liberal Judaism," declares Rabbi Meir Azari of Beit Daniel Synagogue. It is the only Reform synagogue in Tel Aviv, which is about 90 percent non-Orthodox. A new type of outspoken rabbi, Rabbi Azari has sparked debates about the role of religion in the world's only Jewish state. The Orthodox rabbinate has a monopoly on Jewish marriage, divorce, conversions, and funerals. Rabbi Azari has been urging the non-Orthodox majority to take back some religious rights their secular leaders and grandparents conceded when they founded Israel. "After Rabin's murder, people who are unwilling to enter an Orthodox synagogue started coming here. They didn't want to surrender their religion to Yigal Amir's right-wing Orthodox constituency." This intifada has brought an upsurge in attendance from previously nonobservant Israelis. Beit Daniel's religious services, preschools, youth and retiree groups, and Judaism classes for Russian-speaking immigrants are packed. Rabbi Azari and other Reform and Conservative rabbis are overwhelmed with Israelis seeking a spiritual alternative to secularism, asking them to conduct their weddings and bar and bat mitzvahs.

This is quite an accomplishment, as the state-sanctioned Orthodox Rabbinate considers them "illegitimate." They do not recognize any non-Orthodox forms of Judaism. Even though about 80 percent of Israeli Jews are non-Orthodox, almost all—98 percent—of the more than ten thousand synagogues in Israel are either Orthodox or ultra-Orthodox. "In their eyes, only Orthodox Judaism is kosher," charges Rabbi Azari. "They believe that recognizing us would undermine their monopoly as the Judaism of Israel. Israel is the only democracy in the Western world where Jews do not have freedom of religion, the only place where Jews deny religious freedom to Jews. What we're fighting for is the right for Israelis to have the freedom to choose how they want to be Jewish."

Reform and Conservative Jews have run joint national media blitzes in newspapers, billboards, buses, radio, and TV—in Russian as well as Hebrew. Rabbi Azari caused a national stir with this ad, which ran repeatedly on Israel Radio: "I want to tell you a secret: there is more than one way to be Jewish. Our community believes in Judaism according to the spirit of the time and place. In our congregations, men and women are equal. In our synagogues, men and women sit together, bat mitzvah girls are called to the Torah, and in our marriage ceremonies the woman also betroths the man. If you want to learn about this type of Judaism, call. You just have to choose." The Orthodox Chief Rabbinate countered with newspaper ads warning Israelis not to attend Reform or Conservative synagogues because their "prayers will not be heard by God." But Israelis responded. Rosh Hashana and Yom Kippur services at Reform and Conservative synagogues have standing room only.

Attacks on Reform and Conservative Jews continue. The Chief Rabbinate calls them "far more dangerous" than average "wayward" nonobservant Israeli Jews. "We never had a problem with the Jewishness of Jews who were not observant," former Ashkenazi Chief Rabbi Yisrael Lau said. "But I do have a problem with someone who comes and says, 'This we don't need, that is outmoded and the other is anachronistic.'" Before his term ended, Sephardi Chief Rabbi Eliahu Bakshi-Doron went so far as to warn that Reform and Conservative Judaism will lead to assimilation, which will be even more disastrous for Jews than the Holocaust. Shas's satellite and Internet broadcasts have called Conservative and Reform leaders "usurpers trying to destroy Judaism," who practice "Christianity without a cross." Jerusalem's former deputy mayor Haim Miller said, "Everyone to whom the integrity of the Jewish people matters must struggle to see that the Conservative Jews have no place in Israel." Some ultra-Orthodox newspapers ran such bellicose articles that the attorney general had to intervene and admonish editors and publishers for their "libelous provocations." Vandals even have attacked Reform and Conservative synagogues.

Despite these attacks—perhaps because of them—most Jewish Israelis are openly discontented with the Orthodox rabbinate's control over their lives. Recent polls show an overwhelming 79 percent of Israelis believe that *all* branches of Judaism should be given equal status in Israel. No longer do secular Israelis quip "The synagogue I don't attend is Orthodox." No longer do they call the Conservative and Reform movements "watered-down Judaism," American imports, or "Judaism lite." Israelis who have spent time in the United States or Europe have learned about non-Orthodox alternatives to Judaism followed by most Jews outside Israel. In America, only 6 percent of the Jewish population is Orthodox; 80 percent are either Reform or Conservative.

Non-Orthodox Israelis are also being swept up by what some call a "Jewish Renaissance." In Judaic study groups, non-Orthodox Israelis are learning the "Jewish bookshelf." From secular kibbutz dining rooms to tenement basements to yuppie beachfront condos, groups discuss Jewish philosophers such as Maimonides, read writers like Bialik, study the Zohar, and debate the weekly Torah portion. "I think it's great that we're taking Jewish books out of the closet, because these Jewish books are our heritage too," says Tamar Kriegel, who attends a Beit Daniel study group with thirty other young Israelis, ranging from a medical student to a mechanic. "Shul is cool. Everyone in my classes is finding something magical reading the Torah, the Talmud, and the Mishna in the original Hebrew. We're learning to read between the lines, finding meaningful connections with our lives." A twenty-seven-year-old counselor for autistic adults, Tamar is studying the women of the Bible. Her favorite is Michal, daughter of King Saul. "She was in love with David. And she did what Jewish women don't realize we're allowed to do—she put on tefillin." An iconoclast herself, Tamar wears a vibrantly colored embroidered Bukhara kippa A kippa-wearing woman attracts stares, she admits. "It makes people very curious. When they ask me about it, I just say 'I'm religious.' This confuses them even more because when most Israelis hear 'religious,' they still think either Orthodox or haredi. And I certainly don't look it," she says with a laugh, indicating her flirty skirt and cowboy boots. "Where is it written that women are forbidden from wearing kippot? Men wear them to show God is always above them. Isn't God always above women too? We're challenging some traditions of Judaism. Why shouldn't women pray with men?"

The prayer area in front of the Western Wall, Judaism's holiest site, has a partition separating men and women, as in Orthodox and ultra-Orthodox synagogues. When mixed groups of Conservative and Reform men and women dare to break tradition and pray together, violating "the division of roles that God assigned men and women," outraged ultra-Orthodox Jews sometimes shove, curse, or throw bags of chocolate milk at them. "The Wall belongs to all the Jewish people," declares Tamar. "Women are also legitimate Jews. We should have the right to pray the way we wish. To put on tefillin, kippot, and prayer shawls. And why shouldn't women be allowed to read out loud from the Torah?"

She raised a lot of questions at her grandfather's funeral. Tamar asked Rabbi Azari to officiate, but non-Orthodox rabbis are not allowed to conduct funerals in Orthodox cemeteries, and there are only a few Jewish secular cemeteries in Israel (except those on kibbutzim, where space is limited). "They said my rabbi isn't authentic. Treated him like a second-class Jew. Even though my family isn't religious, we had no choice. We had a 'black hat' [ultra-Orthodox rabbi]." Hundreds of mourners turned out for her grandfather's funeral; he was a renowned oil painter, a founder of Ein Hod, the famous artists' colony on Mt. Carmel near Haifa. At the graveside, Tamar began reciting the mourner's kaddish (the prayer for the dead) aloud, challenging the Orthodox tradition that prohibits a woman from praying in front of men. "The rabbi was horrified. A woman reciting kaddish? He made threatening faces, but I just ignored him. My mother whispered 'Stop' to me and my father was freaking out. People wanted to take me away, but I kept on praying." Then, Tamar picked up the shovel to put dirt on the grave, again breaking Orthodox tradition (only males are supposed to do this final act). "The rabbi threatened to leave. I know I upset people, but this was my last time with my grandfather, and I have every right to mourn my way, to show my love for him. I also wanted people to realize they shouldn't have a monopoly on Judaism. Who says our way of death has to be Orthodox? We should have the right to decide how we can bury our relatives. Maybe if the Orthodox would stop coercing us, my friends wouldn't feel so alienated. Maybe they'd come to synagogue Friday night instead of the pubs."

Israelis of all persuasions are debating the role religion should play in their democracy. The non-Orthodox majority compares itself to David facing the Orthodox and ultra-Orthodox Goliath. Non-Orthodox Israelis are upset that there is little separation between synagogue and state. Officially, Israel is a secular state with no state religion. But Israel has no formal constitution, partly because most non-Orthodox Jews want a constitution that guarantees more political, social, and religious freedoms. When David Ben-Gurion read the Proclamation of Independence in Tel Aviv on May 14, 1948, establishing the first Jewish state in two thousand years, the founders themselves did not know what a "Jewish state" meant. The Proclamation explicitly states that Israel "will guarantee freedom of religion." The majority of ultra-Orthodox Jews want a constitution based on traditional Judaic laws; in fact, a whopping 64 percent believe Israel should be a theocracy. The argument appears intractable.

Because no formal constitution defines the bounds of religious authority, governments often yield to the demands of Orthodox and/or ultra-Orthodox religious parties in their coalitions. This is the reason non-Orthodox Jews, specifically the Conservative and Reform movements, turn to the civil courts to challenge the Orthodox establishment's monopoly on religion. Their legal battles have been largely successful. The activist Supreme Court has made numerous groundbreaking rulings favoring religious pluralism. It has attacked unequal and sometimes illegal government subsidies to Orthodox and ultra-Orthodox schools and religious institutions. It has allowed kibbutz stores to open on the Sabbath. It has ordered Israel to recognize conversions to Judaism made by Reform and Conservative rabbis abroad. But when the Supreme Court outlawed army exemptions for draft-age ultra-Orthodox males, the decision was so explosive that outraged haredi rabbis called out their troops.

On a brilliantly sunny afternoon in February 1999 about half a million haredi men showed up near the Supreme Court. It was the largest antisecular demonstration in the history of Israel's vitriolic modern religious wars. Protesters carried banners with slogans such as "The antireligious Supreme Court is persecuting us" and "The Torah is holier than their laws." This "black hat" power rally united the frequently squabbling Hasids, Lithuanian haredim, and Shas supporters. Rabbi Ovadia Yosef, Shas's spiritual leader, called the Supreme Court a "wicked institution" and its nine male and three female justices "leftist judicial tyrants . . . enemies of Judaism . . . and the cause of all the world's torments." Rabbis led their followers in prayers. Chief Justice Aharon Barak received so many death threats—similar to those Prime Minister Rabin received before his assassination—that he had to get full-time bodyguards.

Near the Supreme Court, an estimated fifty thousand protestors showed up for an anti-haredi counterdemonstration. Convoys of buses from the Galilee to the Negev brought in students, professors, teenagers, kibbutzniks, and Russian-speaking immigrants. Some were militantly secular, others wore knitted kippot. All came to show support for the Supreme Court's decisions on religious pluralism. Some held placards that read "Take Judaism back from the haredim!" "Don't let them hijack Judaism!" "Put them in the army too." Rabbi Azari and dozens of other Reform and Conservative rabbis attacked the privileges of the ultra-Orthodox minority, from their military exemptions to the patronage system that supports their religious institutions and schools at taxpayer expense. Supporters sang "The Song of Peace" and distributed posters of a multicolor Star of David, a symbol of pluralistic Judaism. "We showed we're the majority and we're no longer willing to be silent. We're the Jews—they're the alternative," says Rabbi Azari, who describes how this demonstration helped ignite a religious revolution. In 2003, the anti-haredi Shinui—which means "change"—became the second-largest party in the government. For the first time in two decades, there were no ultra-Orthodox parties in the coalition. "I hope this victory will lead not to hatred, but to the rise of alternative Jewish voices. Already we're seeing dramatic changes in the spirit of Israel. This is not Iran anymore."

As a post-army rite of passage, tens of thousands of young Israelis travel to Asia or South America each year for a kaleidoscope of experiences. After six months motorcycling across India, Tamir Heffetz arrived at the "roof of the world." At Nepal's Buddhist monasteries and Hindu temples, he was taken aback to hear more Hebrew than Hindi. An even bigger surprise was Passover near the Israeli Embassy. "It looked like a scene from Exodus. Israelis wandering in from all over, dusty, barefoot, in sandals, in tie-dyed shirts and long scarves—everyone heading to this huge tent," he says, shaking his long blond ponytail. He was at the world's largest Passover seder. Tables were laden with matzah, wine, and gefilte fish—shipped in from Israel. For nearly a thousand young Israelis, it was kosher in Kathmandu. "Here I was, so far from home, and who was there? Guys I knew. Last time we were together we sang Passover songs in a tent too—but it was an army tent. We had our seder by candlelight, not to be romantic, but so Hezballah wouldn't fire at us. I had trouble eating. I was all screwed up; I'd just seen my officer get blown up. At least, in Kathmandu, no one was shooting at us."

Tamir and his older brother, Ori, spent months in Asia "cleaning heads" and doing "spiritual searching." When Ori landed in India, a favorite spiritual supermarket for the post-army set, he headed to New Delhi's main bazaar and checked in at the Rama guest house. "I was hanging out on the roof with a bunch of glassy-eyed Israelis, trading travel tips, hitting on girls. They were sharing ganja pipes. An Israeli Habad rabbi came up and sat with us and tried being part of our scene. When he asked what we were doing on Shabbat, one guy said, 'Who cares about Shabbat?' The rabbi was really cool, he won our trust without annoying us. He said, 'Why not come for Shabbat, we're cooking great kosher food.' Why not? Anything for a free meal. So we went. It was great food. What surprised me was that so many of these Israelis knew so little about Judaism. Some women lit Shabbat candles for the first time in their lives. Some guys put on tefillin for the first time. One guy told me he didn't know Shabbat could be so spiritual." Ori, who calls himself "semiobservant," often attends a multigenerational Shabbat dinner at the Tel Aviv apartment of his German-born grandmother and his grandfather, who is from an old Syrian and Egyptian family from Jerusalem.

"It's strange that so many Israelis have to leave the country to discover Judaism," continues Ori. During his travels in Thailand, he discovered that "wherever Israelis hang out, there's a Habad rabbi." He spent Rosh Hashana, Yom Kippur, and Sukkot along with other Israelis at the Habad House in Bangkok, where the kosher kitchen fed more than ninety thousand Israeli backpackers a year until warnings of a potential al-Qaeda attack lowered their numbers. "We sang songs, listened to the rabbi's stories about the Baal Shem Tov. Some had really positive Jewish experiences. I saw these rabbis turning some kids on to Judaism."

Like many Israelis, Ori discovered other mysteries. Under the palms on the beaches of islands in southern Thailand and in Goa, India, thousands of Israelis in skimpy bathing suits, non-Orthodox and Orthodox alike, dance to throbbing psychedelic Israeli trance music. "We give trance a chance. We break all the rules because we're out of the army, which is like getting out of jail. We're discovering life. And a lot of people discover people of other religions." Ori recalls meeting a fun-loving British woman near a Thai temple. "When she told me it was Easter Sunday, I asked what it means. She couldn't believe I didn't know what Easter is. What Israeli knows anything about Jesus? She was the first Christian I'd ever met. I think most of us have to leave Israel to meet Christians."

Far from volatile, fractious Israel, thousands of Israelis hungry for harmony head to Dharamsala in India, home of the Dalai Lama. (Many also join the annual Dharamsala seder.) Even the nephew of former Ashkenazi Chief Rabbi Yisrael Lau, a twenty-eight-year-old who had studied in a yeshiva, calls India his second spiritual home. Ori sat cross-legged and closed-eyed in a Krishna consciousness ashram in Bombay and the temple in Puna where the Beatles once meditated. "I have strong monotheistic Jewish beliefs," he says, emphasizing that he believes in one indivisible God. "Even though Hindu and Buddhist temple ceremonies involve idol worship, I got insights that opened my mind about Judaism. My new consciousness made me appreciate Judaism in new ways."

Back in the Holy Land, more and more Israelis are combining their romance with Asian mysticism with Jewish spirituality. At "yeshiva-ashrams," Orthodox Jews study Hasidism, kabbalah, and Asian mysticism. While studying physics at Tel Aviv University, Ori met many fellow "India graduates" in his Chinese and Indian philosophy classes. Some twenty thousand Israelis attend the annual Bereshit (Genesis) festival for three days in the Megiddo (Armageddon) forest each Rosh Hashana. It attracts Israeli flower children, out-of-uniform soldiers, and families. Jews study reiki and reflexology. There are tai chi, yoga, and shofar-blowing workshops. Near a meditation pyramid, the common greeting is "Are you from the East or South?" (i.e., Did you backpack in Asia or South America?). People share books about Tibetan Buddhism and kabbalah. Vendors make a bundle selling Jewish soul music, reggae, and fusion CDs.

During Rosh Hashana services, a new type of Israeli Judaism is evident in an enormous tent called the House of Love and Prayers. In this "synagogue" worshippers sing traditional Rosh Hashana prayers accompanied by drums and guitars. Children wander among worshippers offering traditional apples in honey. After the ecstatic singing and impassioned praying, they hold hands and embrace. The celebration ends with blasts from dozens of shofars (rams' horns).

At dozens of other Israeli Jewish spiritual gatherings there are Bibles. There also are bands. A favorite is Sheva, a group from the Galilee. Its musicians—Jews, Christians, and Muslims—started playing together at trance concerts in India for Israelis. Dressed in flowing Bedouin robes, they play sitar, Persian xylophone, and Moroccan drums, singing Hebrew and Muslim psalms. The audience dances with wild abandon to their well-known Hebrew-Arabic song "Shalom-Salam." They chant "Peace be on us, on everyone. Peace, on us and all over the world. Peace, Peace!" For the moment, these hypnotic, repetitive lines seem to drown out the high decibels of Israeli life.

An estimated two hundred thousand Israelis are involved in New Age Judaism. "It's a modern Israeli alternative to the need to find a tribe," says Dr. Yoav Ben-Dov of the Institute of Philosophy and the History of Science at Tel Aviv University, who has studied the young Israelis in India. "We're seeing a growing belief in things related to mysticism. A return to mystical experiences, an Israeli culture of exploration. Young Israelis are looking at Judaism and finding new ways of connecting with traditions. Middle- and upper-class kids are turning to all kinds of New Age versions of Judaism. But those from lower socioeconomic groups, who never were part of modern Israel, are returning to the Judaism their grandparents followed in places such as North Africa and reinventing it." They do not realize that the amulets their rabbis give them often are made in India.

The stars in the velvet sky above Netanya are so bright you can almost hear them twinkling. Yisraela Gratzyani is exhausted from pleading another divorce case. This tall brunette is glad to be spending Sukkot, the week-long celebration of the harvest (the Feast of Tabernacles), with her relatives at this seaside town. She admires the *sukkah,* a hut made of palm branches decorated with aromatic fruit, which her younger brother, Gidi, built in the backyard. All over Israel, Jewish families eat outside in sukkot, remembering the temporary dwellings ancient Israelites lived in after fleeing Egypt and wandering for forty years in the desert. "It's really fragile, like the fragility of life," Yisraela says, referring to all the lives cut short during intifada II. "It feels like we're living in a sukkah all the time, that at any time we suddenly could be blown away."

"We don't need permanent walls to feel secure, but we need faith in God," says Gidi, who has his sister's striking dark Mediterranean looks. "The sukkah is to remind us to step back and appreciate the simple gifts of the earth," he explains as he picks up an *etrog,* an aromatic lemon-like fruit, and a *lulav,* a cluster of date, palm, myrtle, and willow branches. "Each kind of branch represents a different type of Jew—those who study the Torah, those who perform kind acts, those who do both, and those who do neither. When we hold them together, we're a community: there is more uniting us than dividing us." Following Jewish tradition, Gidi waves the lulav in the four directions of the compass and then up and down, gestures symbolizing God's omnipresence.

When he finishes the ceremony, Yisraela helps her mother, who is a hairdresser, and her grandmother serve a lavish array of Sephardi foods: stuffed peppers and tomatoes, roasted eggplant salads (*salata de berenjena asada*), cheese-filled pastries (*borekas*), grape leaves stuffed with rice, nut-filled pastries (*travados*), and layered filo pastry (*baklava*)— proof that cooking kosher does not mean putting on a culinary straitjacket. The three women speak Ladino, fourteenth-century Spanish, the language of Sephardic Jews, the language of Cervantes (who according to the author's recent research was one of Spain's hidden Jews). Like the language and the tantalizing food, this family has Spanish, Turkish, Greek, and Italian influences.

Yisraela follows Jewish rituals selectively. After lighting candles each Sabbath, she loves to go dancing at friends' house parties. She keeps her kitchen pork-free, but outside, adores sweet-and-sour shrimp. "I'm a traditional Sephardi, which means I have strong emotional ties to Judaism, but I'm very open-minded." Some objects in her purse reveal her diverse sources of inspiration: a miniature book of psalms, an amulet blessed by a Kurdish rabbi, a hamsah, and a Pink Floyd and a Led Zeppelin CD. As a teenager she had hoped to be a rock singer, an Israeli Madonna, but ended up arguing for women's rights in the Knesset and Supreme Court. She sang lots of melodies and prayers in the Sephardi synagogue of the moshav that her grandfather and other Greek-Italian immigrants founded. Now that she lives in Tel Aviv, she occasionally goes to the closest synagogue. "I don't care what kind of synagogue it is. There's only one God and He hears our prayers wherever we are." When prodded, however, she admits, "When I go to [Ashkenazi] Orthodox, Conservative, or Reform synagogues, their prayer styles and melodies sound strange to me."

While the family eats in the sukkah, Yisraela's stepfather chides Gidi about his religious transformation. A former fashion model, he now sports a beard and a black kippa. Thousands of nonreligious Israelis are becoming *ba'alei teshuvah,* newly religious Jews. Gidi goes to synagogue daily. He loves the ecstatic worship, the fervent prayers and celebrations fueled by lively Hasidic dance and music. At home, he uses two sets of kosher dishes and cutlery for dairy and meat. Many non-Orthodox Israeli parents whose children have joined the return-to-religion movement ask the same worried questions: Is this metamorphosis a temporary escape from the demands of Israeli life, the round-the-clock grim news, reserve duty, bank overdrafts? Are you flirting with Orthodoxy or marrying it?

Gidi got interested in the Breslov Hasids, a once tiny, obscure group of Yiddish-speaking Jews that has become Israel's fastest-growing Hasidic group. Young Mizrahim and Sephardim discontented with what they call "empty secularism" are attracted to this Ashkenazi Hasidic movement started by Rabbi Nahman in Bratzlav, Ukraine, in 1802. Yisraela helped spark her nonobservant brother's religious transformation when she gave him some of Rabbi Nahman's writings. His enigmatic fables are some of the most spellbinding in Jewish literature. Said to have influenced authors Franz Kafka and S. Y. Agnon, they are studied in Israeli secular Hebrew literature classes. "They constitute a universe of their own in which dreamers go beyond their dreams, beyond their desires, swept away by their quest for imagination and salvation and an infinite craving for innocence and wonder," wrote Elie Wiesel. "They're full of simple wisdom, inspiration."

Gidi's unbendingly secular stepfather, a former kibbutznik who drives a taxi in Tel Aviv, comments about seeing these newly observant Jews "dancing around their vans with loudspeakers blasting Hasidic music. I see them handing out leaflets. All over, they have those stupid posters and bumper stickers." He's referring to the Hebrew slogan printed on them: "Uman, Uman, Rosh Hashana," urging Israelis to join the annual mass Rosh Hashana pilgrimage to Rabbi Nahman's grave in the Ukrainian town of Uman. "Religious nuts," he says, unable to conceal his annoyance.

"Serving God is not nutty," retorts Gidi, who is now studying with a Habad rabbi. "I'm just trying to be the Jew I should be, trying to help others." Trying to play mediator, Yisraela interrupts, using skills she learned as a family practice lawyer. "He and his friends serve in the army. They pay taxes. What's wrong with joyful prayer, faith in God? The whole country appreciates the work he's doing."

Gidi's work keeps him on permanent alert. He is one of the religious volunteers who rushes to the scene after a terrorist attack. Amid the stench of burned bodies, he gathers body parts for burial because Jewish law teaches that every piece of the body is holy. In an all-too-frequent grim ritual, he numbers every eye, every hand, every foot. He scrapes bits of flesh off buses, off walls and fruit and vegetable stands, and carefully places them in plastic bags for burial. Parts that they can't match with a corpse are taken to a forensic institute for DNA, X-ray, and fingerprint identification. Gidi and the men with whom he works are the world's most experienced experts at gathering and identifying body parts. Until September 11, no other country had such a group of volunteers.

He has nightmares. He can't eat meat. He can't touch anything red— tomatoes, cherries, strawberries. He continues with the work because "it's the biggest mitzvah a Jew can do. It's a pure deed because there is no way a dead person can repay. There is nothing you can get from him. What's important in my life is doing good deeds."

After an attack in the open-air market not far from Gidi's house, Israelis beat an Arab worker. He was innocent. "They should find out who did it and punish them and make them pay all his hospital bills. It's part of Judaism to be tolerant, not to hate," says Yisraela, reciting a proverb her grandmother taught her: "If you live to seek revenge, dig a grave for two." Her grandmother has reason to hate. Her Turkish Sephardi family lived in the holy city of Hebron for generations. In 1929, anti-Jewish riots broke out and Arabs killed more than sixty Jewish neighbors and children. At age six, her grandmother saw her father's Arab business partner stab him to death. "Even after that, she never lost her faith in God or hated Arabs." When Yisraela fell dangerously ill and needed an emergency transfusion, the only one with matching blood was an Arab who worked in her grandparents' orange groves. "He saved my life. He prays in Arabic, I pray in Hebrew." Has this intifada made her less tolerant? "Absolutely not. When a bomb goes off, I say 'Rotten terrorist.' I never say 'Rotten Arabs.'"

IV

Schizophrenia: Non-Jews

in a Jewish State

VI

12

The Muslims

Abraham's Other Children

🌣 *These days I see some small hope on the horizon. Maybe these last years of brutal madness for everybody will end. Here in Haifa, I see Jews and Arabs living together. What we need are models of coexistence, such as more good schools where Arab and Jewish children can learn about each other's cultures and to respect differences. I think the ideal age to begin is three, before the child is exposed to the surrounding tensions. This could be an important gift for the children of this conflicted land.* —Pediatrician Yasser Mansour, forty, part of a group of Arab and Jewish parents trying to create an Arab-Jewish preschool

🌣 *We are not Arab-Israeli or Muslim-Israeli. Those are divisive terms that ignore our identity and history. I'm an Arab Palestinian who lives in Israel, one of the indigenous people of this land.* —Suhad Hammoud, twenty-nine, human rights lawyer who defends Palestinians in Israel, the West Bank, and the Gaza Strip

While tanks and suicide bombers have been killing trust between Jews and Palestinian Arabs, pediatric pulmonologist Yasser Mansour, an Arab

Israeli Muslim, has been saving lives, from the newborn fighting for air to the toddler choking on a peanut. "I became a pediatrician because I want to help children. It doesn't matter to me if they are Arabs or Jews," Yasser declares with a conviction that is affirmed by many grateful Jewish and Arab parents. They express their appreciation in numerous ways: a Hasidic father gave him an amulet blessed by a rabbi; a mother wearing a white Islamic hair scarf brought pastries; a Shas politician demonstrated his trust by nailing a mezuzah on his clinic door. This tireless forty-year-old healer treats children at two Haifa clinics and at Rambam Hospital, where Jewish and Arab youngsters have adjoining beds in the pediatric ward. Throughout this hospital, Arab Israeli doctors care for wounded soldiers and Jewish victims of terrorism, and Jewish doctors treat terrorists and Arab Israeli victims of terrorism. Recently, in Haifa's first major terrorist attack, a passenger got on a bus crowded with Arab and Jewish passengers and detonated a nail-studded belt of explosives, killing fifteen. Within moments, Arabs and Jews alike rushed into the blood-soaked street to help the dozens of wounded. "That's why this town is special," says Yasser, who was at the bedside of the injured bus driver. "Haifa is an island of sanity."

Yet, in the hospital parking lot, a few cars have bumper stickers espousing anti-Arab sentiments, even illegal racist ones such as "Arabs Out." Asked how he feels about it, a look of dismay passes over his face. "As there are fingers on my hands, there are all kinds of Jews and all kinds of Arabs. When the children play together in the waiting room, they don't judge each other by names or religion. These differences mean nothing to them."

But those same differences mean a great deal to many adults. Yasser describes standing in line at Ben-Gurion International Airport with about thirty Jewish pulmonologists for a flight to a conference in Istanbul. Without a stethoscope and hospital whites, a six-foot-tall, olive-skinned, mustached man named Yasser is a red flag, and a wary airport security official pulled him aside. He presented his Israeli passport. He showed his Rambam Hospital staff identification. He pulled out his membership card in the Arab-Jewish Haifa Rotary Club. "Do you know how humiliating it is to be the only one singled out? In front of my colleagues?" he says, trying to remain calm as he recounts the painful ordeal that occurred before the second intifada. "One of my Jewish friends said next time I go to the airport, she's going to give me a T-shirt that says, 'I am not a terrorist. I am an Israeli.' Now when they question our loyalty, I see we aren't always trusted. I feel the conflict between the 'Israeli' and 'Palestinian Arab' parts of my identity. We have fractured identities." Welcome to the schizophrenic world of Israel's Muslim Arabs.

Yasser Mansour is a Sunni Muslim, as are more than one million other Arab Israelis, representing 87 percent of Israel's Islamic population. Muslims are the fastest-growing group of Israeli citizens, with a birthrate about double that of Israeli Jews. One out of every five Israelis is a Muslim Arab; within twenty years, the ratio is predicted to rise to one in three. Yasser, like most of the Arabic-speaking parents in his waiting room—the cleaning woman, the secretary, the unemployed steel worker—are the offspring of the group known as the Arabs of '48, who decided to stay put during Israel's 1947–48 War of Independence. For those who did not—most of the Arabs of Palestine—the consequences were calamitous. Roughly seven hundred thousand Arabs fled, mostly to Jordan and parts of Palestine, which Egypt and Jordan conquered during the 1948 War: respectively, Gaza and the West Bank. (Their numbers have grown to nearly 4 million registered refugees, with nearly one third living in UN-administered refugee camps.) How many Arabs fled and how many were pushed out remains a contentious topic among warring historians. The 160,000 Arabs of '48 who stayed were disoriented, poor, and mostly illiterate. They also were fragmented and leaderless; most of the upper and middle classes left, along with most of their religious leaders. The mass exodus destroyed almost all Arab political, social, and Islamic institutions created during the British Mandate. In the new state of Israel, Arabs suddenly were a minority and the Jews a majority—an unfamiliar situation to both groups.

Many Arabs of '48 were "internal refugees," displaced from homes and villages destroyed or abandoned during the fighting and from lands they traditionally farmed. The new government expropriated Yasser's parents' Galilee village because it was in a "militarily strategic" location. They had a lot of company; the new government of Israel confiscated roughly 40 percent of the land traditionally worked by Palestinian Arabs, for military or agricultural use. The family moved to Haifa, which was filled with houses abandoned by seventy thousand Arabs who had fled the country, again, under circumstances that remain an ongoing argument. Yasser's father, who left school at age fourteen to support his dislocated family, worked in the vegetable section of a Haifa supermarket for thirty years and put all five children through university. When Yasser was a pediatric resident, his father and a classmate from their former village introduced him to Jumana, who was studying to be a preschool teacher. It wasn't long before the families from the long-gone village were reunited at the couple's moderate-size wedding—only four hundred guests.

While their young sons play a Hebrew-language geography game on the computer, Yasser and Jumana relax on their apartment balcony, which overlooks the port and is next to the terraced Bahai gardens of this hillside Mediterranean town. "We only want them to play nonviolent games on the computer," says thirty-one-year-old Jumana. "On television, not a week goes by without fighting or funerals. When I catch them watching the news, I put on a Bugs Bunny video or *Harry Potter*." Yasser says almost all his patients are affected by the violence. "They're having trouble sleeping. They're hyperactive. Nervous. Restless. It's good that our schools have special programs to help them cope. So far, we're managing to keep our sons' minds on other things. And we have great news." Jumana is expecting a girl.

Yasser and Jumana are part of the expanding Muslim middle class. Doctors working in Israeli hospitals aren't rich; bus drivers can earn more. What seems like a fortune to the Russian émigré physicians is fairly modest by Israeli standards. In fact, to supplement his $1,500 monthly part-time hospital salary, Yasser rents space in a clinic in a mostly Jewish white-collar neighborhood with a urologist and a psychiatrist, both Russian immigrants. Yasser shares another clinic with a Christian Arab internist and a Jewish gynecologist in a blue-collar Jewish-Arab neighborhood. "Most of their parents are very right-wing Likudniks. Each time there's an attack, I expect to lose Jewish patients. But no matter how bad it gets, almost no one has stopped coming, which makes me happy."

In other "mixed" cities like Jerusalem, Acre, Lod, and Jaffa, "coexistence" means living together separately; in Haifa, it means "living together." "For Arabs, Haifa is the best place to live and work," notes Yasser, whose neighborhood and medical practice are a mix of Muslim and Christian Arabs, secular and haredi, Ashkenazi and Mizrahi Jews. "We still feel coexistence is possible." He credits Haifa's open-minded former mayor, Amram Mitzna, a retired IDF general who was in charge of the West Bank during the first intifada, with maintaining the unusually good Arab-Jewish relations in this polarized nation. (After ten years as mayor, Mitzna, who said he wanted to dismantle settlements unilaterally and negotiate with Palestinians despite ongoing terror attacks, was elected head of the Labor Party. He ran for prime minister against Sharon, who won in a landslide. On May 4, 2003, Mitzna resigned as Labor Party leader.) "He had strong relations with Arabs because he really cares about all his citizens. He knows we [Arabs] don't believe in words, only actions. That's why we respect him. He made us feel that we're all part of Haifa, that we all belong. We live everywhere. We buy apartments where we want, not like in other cities. He really tried hard to give us political, economic, and educational equality. And pushed for more Arab-Jewish projects." Yasser and Jumana and a group of other Arab and Jewish parents are trying to convince City Hall to back their idea for Haifa's first Arab-Jewish elementary school. "Why should our kids go to separate schools? More than ever, Arabs and Jews need models to show they can have good relations."

Bilingual and bicultural, Yasser and Jumana both speak fluent Hebrew with only a trace of an Arabic accent. They dress no differently from their secular Jewish friends. In fact, they know more about the Jewish religion and customs than some secular Jews. With a smile, Yasser recalls hearing a Jewish woman admire a little girl's long curls. "When I told her the child is a boy, she didn't know what I was talking about. After I explained that his parents are religious and won't cut his hair until he's three and probably not until Lag b'Omer, she teased me that I sounded like a rabbi." He and Jumana keep abreast of the juicy political gossip about Jewish and Arab Knesset members as well as the latest power struggles in the Palestinian Authority. They're omnivorous readers of the Arab and Hebrew press, especially the left-leaning *Ha'aretz* and Israel's largest circulation *Yediot Aharonot,* which strangely enough is read by more Arab Israelis than any Arabic-language newspaper. Cable and satellite television bring in a new wealth of Arabic-language news from the most popular, al-Jazeera, to stations in Saudi Arabia, Syria, and Hezballah's rabidly anti-Israel al-Manar, which broadcasts from Lebanon. Most of the time, Yasser and Jumana watch CNN and Hebrew-language television news, political satires, and documentaries. Jumana also is a fan of MTV from Lebanon.

"When our Arab and Jewish friends come over, we sometimes discuss how Haifa is becoming more Russian (it is a quarter Russian-speaking). A Russian arrives and, right away, has more rights than Arabs do. And a lot of them aren't even Jewish. We see them buying pork [at Arab Christian and Russian butchers] and everyone knows some pray to Jesus in churches. But nowadays, what we talk about is the *matsav* [the Situation]. You can't get away from it, not even at the dinner table." Yasser's use of the vague Hebrew word *matsav* reflects the confusion most Israelis have about the three years of bloodshed they do not call war. He paraphrases author Amos Oz: Will this be a Chekhovian tragedy where everybody ends up bitter and alienated and disaffected, or a Shakespearean tragedy where everybody ends up dead? "This is the worst time I've ever experienced. And for the Palestinians, the despair is beyond belief. My eighty-year-old cousin from Gaza got a permit to visit us. He says everyone is suffering. No work. The infrastructure is destroyed. Doctors can't visit. We need solutions, not victories. More than anything, we want Palestinians to have their state. But our aspirations are different. We have our state. This is our country. There is nowhere else I would live. My family was born here. We're Israeli citizens. This is our home. Jews and Arabs have to think seriously about what kind of future it will be because we're all going to be sharing it."

In Haifa, more than almost anywhere else in Israel, Jews and Arabs have a long history of mutual give and take. Religious divisions are not a burning issue. Partly because Moses, Jesus, and Muhammad never set foot here, there is room for all faiths. There are few ancient holy sites. At a famous one, Elijah's cave, a religious pilgrimage site known for its miraculous healing powers, Muslims, Christians, and Jews have been worshipping at the same time in the same place without problems for generations. Following Friday noon prayers, religious Muslims pour out of local mosques. In January 2003, Yasser's parents made the hajj to Mecca, one of the five pillars of Islam. Neither he nor Jumana often enters a mosque to worship. On school days she puts on conservative clothes and heads to a mosque with twin minarets and a grand white dome on Mount Carmel to teach toddlers who belong to a small Shiite sect of Islam, the Ahmadies.

Although Jumana and Yasser are not observant, sometimes they eat *halal* (Islamically permitted) meat that her uncle, a religious butcher from a nearby village, gives them. Not only do many Israeli Muslims eat *haram* (forbidden) foods, but some go to restaurants during the holy month of Ramadan, when eating, drinking, smoking, and sex are prohibited from sunrise to sunset. To Islamic fundamentalists, these actions are blasphemous, but in this tolerant town, fundamentalists are scarce.

Although alcohol, dancing, Western music, and immodest dress are haram, a number of Haifa pubs and nightclubs are full of Muslims who openly ignore these religious injunctions. "I don't plan to return to my village. It's too conservative," says a chain-smoking woman wearing a tangerine-colored tank top. Most Muslims live in all-Arab towns and villages in the Galilee and central Israel. "I don't like my relatives criticizing what I wear, telling me what man from what family I should marry. Here I can do as I like." (In Arabic, the concept of privacy often is associated with loneliness.) At Haifa University where she studies Arabic literature, about one in five students are Muslim, the highest ratio of any Israeli university. She plans to remain in Haifa. So do a number of her girlfriends. Haifa's Islamic clerics don't scream sacrilege and Haifa's haredim don't throw stones. On the Jewish Sabbath, Arabs and Jews fearlessly drive or take buses through haredi neighborhoods to the soccer stadium to root for Maccabi Haifa, whose Arab players are local heroes. She frequently goes to the beach—not the segregated one behind Rambam Hospital; that one is partitioned: one side for haredi men, the other for haredi women.

Among the students, children, and veterans in wheelchairs at Israel's biggest peace rally on November 4, 1995 were thousands of Arab Israelis. One was Yasser Mansour. "People don't realize so many of us were there, but we were. We were so full of hope," he says. "From a few hundred meters away, I could see Rabin standing on the platform. We loved him because he understood our struggle to be treated as full citizens. His courage made real change seem possible. He was creating a new Israeli reality." Prime Minister Rabin was the first Israeli leader to acknowledge that for decades, Labor and Likud governments alike had neglected Israel's Arab citizens. Arab voters were influential in Rabin's victory, and his Labor-Meretz coalition government was the first in Israeli history that depended on the support of Arab Knesset members.

Rabin's administration was the first government to start closing the enormous social and economic gaps between Israeli Muslim Arabs and Jews. It began to improve housing, pave roads, and build sewers in Arab towns and villages; it started to increase funds for Arab public schools and promised to put more Arab university graduates into governmental positions. Along with Rabin, the vast majority of Arab Israelis supported the Oslo Accords, hoping it would end generations of bloodshed and hatred between their fellow Palestinians and Jews and bring to an end a widespread Jewish perception of them as a hostile minority and security risk.

"The land of our birth was making peace with our Palestinian people," adds Yasser. "We believed that finally we would be treated as full, loyal citizens. As we sang 'The Song for Peace' with Rabin, I kept thinking this is the sane Israel, the best Israel. We felt like we belonged as never before. Looking back, it was the happiest time I remember." As Yasser and his friends pushed through the crowds, they heard rumors. "People were saying, 'Rabin was shot. Rabin was shot.' I couldn't believe it. No one could. All the way on the bus back to Haifa, we listened to the radio for news. We didn't know what had happened. When I got home around midnight, Jumana and I watched television, waiting and hoping it wasn't true. And then we heard the bulletin: Rabin was dead." Recalling the night nearly a decade later, Yasser's voice cracks and his large hands tremble. "Killed at a peace rally. Killed with 'The Song of Peace' still in our ears." Yasser falls silent and his eyes become teary.

When he has time to surf the Internet, Yasser reads what Israelis are writing on Walla!, a popular Hebrew-language cyber chatroom. After each terrorist attack, postings get particularly virulent, he notes. "When I read what some people write, I feel sick. I've never seen so many anti-Arab messages, so much terrible racism, as if all Arabs are bloodthirsty terrorists. When times are good, I feel Israeli, but when I read these ugly messages, I feel more Palestinian. It's an ongoing identity crisis. I want to believe the two parts of myself can live in peace. I can't believe we've sunk so low."

Israelis always have been suspicious of a package left on a bus, in a theater, or at a mall. With Palestinian men and women doubling as bombs, many Jews fear that any Arab, including an Israeli, could be a potentially lethal package. "Jumana and the boys hardly leave Haifa anymore. When I go to Tel Aviv or somewhere for a meeting, my big fear is a bomb goes off." Being an Arab in the wrong place at the wrong time can be dangerous. After a Palestinian suicide bomber killed two Jews in the outdoor market in Netanya, a few Jewish men spotted an Arab man running away and beat him so badly he was hospitalized. He was innocent, one of the tens of thousands of Palestinians from the West Bank, Gaza, and Jordan who live and work—legally and illegally—inside Israel. "Jumana and I used to shop there, but now what Arab would take such a risk? Lately, I feel more like a citizen of Haifa than of Israel. No one I know here treats me any differently since the intifada."

"Wait a minute," Jumana interrupts. "Even Haifa isn't the same as before. With strangers, the atmosphere has changed. When I take the children to play in the park, sometimes I call out to them in Hebrew, not Arabic." This hazel-eyed woman easily "passes" for a Jew. Many Arabs and Jews look alike.

According to the Book of Genesis and the Koran, Jews and Arabs are both the children of Abraham/Ibrahim, descendants of his sons Isaac and Ishmael. (Abraham in Hebrew is Avrohom, meaning "father of many nations.") Some recent Israeli discoveries indicate that the relationship isn't just in Genesis, but in genetics.

Research by Dr. Ariella Oppenheim of Hadassah Medical School has demonstrated that Jews and Arabs share a recent common ancestry. The number of mutations that appear in the Y chromosome—the sex-determining chromosome that passes, unchanged, from father to son—of Jewish and Arab men works as a kind of biological clock. Because mutations are assumed to appear at a constant rate, scientists can calculate how recently a branch diverged.

Dr. Oppenheim's team compared the Y chromosomes of 143 Israeli and Palestinian Muslim Arabs whose great-grandfathers were not related to those of 119 Ashkenazi and Mizrahi/Sephardi Israeli Jews. The results: Arabs and Jews had about 18 percent of all their chromosomes in common. The DNA examination showed that over 70 percent of the Jewish men and more than 50 percent of the Arab men inherited their Y chromosome from the same paternal ancestors, ancestors who lived in the Middle East in the late Stone Age, about nine thousand years ago. Another geneticist found that the Y chromosome in Middle Eastern

Arabs was almost indistinguishable from that of Jews. According to Professor Oppenheim, part, if not the majority, of Muslim Arabs in Israel are descendants of Christians and Jews who converted during the rise of Islam in the seventh century C.E. Those Jews and Christians, in turn, were descendants of a population that inhabited the area for several centuries, some dating back to prehistoric times. "Our findings are in good agreement with historical evidence and suggest genetic continuity in both populations, despite their long separation and the wide geographic dispersal of the Jews," Oppenheim reported.

Haifa long has felt far from the front lines, immune to terrorism. For eighteen years, an Arab Israeli family that has run a Haifa restaurant didn't bother to hire a security guard for their popular hangout. One Sunday afternoon in March 2002, a twenty-two-year-old entered. He wasn't interested in felafel and he didn't differentiate between Arabs and Jews. The tremendous blast destroyed the entire restaurant. Among the fifteen Israelis the Hamas suicide bomber killed were a young Arab father and a Jewish director of Beit Hagefen, a local Arab-Jewish cultural center that runs interreligious discussion groups, art exhibits, and a traveling Arabic-language theater. The day Matza Restaurant reopened, loyal Jewish and Arab customers packed in. "That's the spirit of Haifa," says Yasser. "I used to think that one day it would be the spirit of all Israel. We're still trying to show the way, that even bombs won't stop Jews and Arabs from living together." But with a note of caution, he adds, "The whole country is different now. If the killings and the suspicions continue, who knows what kind of together it will be?"

Suhad Hammoud is part of the new Arab generation. Like Yasser, she is not religious, but their political outlooks differ. Less moderate and more impatient, she does not want to be called an Arab Israeli. "Those words deny our identity and history," she insists. "I'm a Palestinian citizen of Israel." She's not alone. In a 2000 poll, nearly 70 percent of Arab Israelis identified themselves as Palestinians, and only 15 percent described themselves as either Israeli or Israeli Arab. A telegenic beauty with a face framed in long brunette curls and wearing a tight skirt and high leather boots, Suhad, an outspoken lawyer fighting for the civil rights of Arab Israelis, exudes a self-possession and assertiveness beyond her twenty-nine years. "The Arab minority in Israel is part of the Palestinian nation. Israel, for me, is a country that took our land and gave us passports. Israel is my home, but I didn't choose to be Israeli. I am a Palestinian and my parents are Palestinian. Do we want to move to a Palestinian state? Of course not. Our roots are here." She fully intends to remain an Israeli citizen, not out of love for Zion, but because this is her land. Many young Arab Israelis agree.

She goes on to describe how very different her "awakened" generation is from the "defeated" generation, people her parents' age, the roughly 8 percent of Israel's Arab population born before the birth of Israel. They saw the Jews of Palestine defeat five Arab armies and found themselves living within a Jewish state with an overwhelming fear of its hostile Muslim neighbors. Fearing they could turn into a dangerous "fifth column," the new government imposed military administration on Arab Israelis in 1948, and they began developing what Suhad calls "complexes of a subjugated mentality." Arab citizens of Israel have the right to vote, but at the time, their movements and political activities were restricted. During decades of hostilities against Israel, whether conducted by regular Arab armies or Palestinian terrorists, almost all Arab Israelis remained nonviolent, law-abiding citizens. With the exception of radio (Israel had no television until 1968), Arab Israelis were cut off from the surrounding Muslim world and people who shared their religion, language, and traditions. The Arab world perceived them as hostages or collaborators of the Jews. Sometimes they were labeled "whipped cream Arabs," derided for their easier lives and for not helping the anti-Israel struggle. Soon after the military administration was lifted, the 1967 War broke out and the defeated generation witnessed another defeat. In six days, Israeli forces took the Golan Heights from Syria, the West Bank and East Jerusalem from Jordan, and Gaza and the Sinai from Egypt. With borders open for the first time, Arab Israelis reestablished ties with friends and families and discovered that the financial and social gaps between them were enormous. During the ensuing years, the ease of contact began to have an impact on Arab Israelis' shaky identities. Many began developing a new Palestinian consciousness.

Suhad's generation wasn't even born when Egyptian, Syrian, and Jordanian forces staged a surprise Yom Kippur 1973 attack and a stunned Israel managed to hit back and humiliate the Arab world again. By the end of the 1970s, the Arab world was beginning to restore its trust in the "whipped cream" Arabs. Several former Arab Israelis represented them in the PLO. Even though it was a crime before the 1993 Oslo Accords, Arab and Jewish Israelis were meeting with Arafat. Ahmed Tibi, an Israeli citizen and Hebrew University graduate, was an official advisor to Arafat (he is now a member of the Knesset). During the first intifada, some Arab Israelis donated food, money, and medicine to their Palestinian brethren in the West Bank and Gaza. They staged nonviolent protests, including one in Nazareth in 1988, which, at the time, was the largest Arab Israeli demonstration in Israel's history. Some Israeli Jews began to ask: Can they be pro-Palestinian without being anti-Israel? Some Israeli Arabs began to ask: Can we be pro-Israel without being anti-Arab? Seeing the PLO transformed from a terrorist group into an internationally recognized organization in 1993 helped fuel Arab Israeli Palestinian nationalism. In the period between the 1993 Oslo agreement and the second intifada, some Arab Israeli schools played the Palestinian national anthem and invited Palestinian Authority officials to graduation ceremonies. "Whether we live here in Israel, in refugee camps in Gaza or Lebanon, or in America or anywhere in our diaspora," Suhad emphasizes, "we Palestinians are one people."

Suhad is from Acre, one of the world's oldest and most picturesque ports, on the bay north of Haifa. For four thousand years, Acre has been battered and bloodied by successive invaders, who have left Gothic archways, domed arcades, ancient synagogues, churches, and mosques inside the walled Old City as silent stone reminders. After the Christian Crusaders massacred most of the Muslims in 1104, they changed the name from Akko to St. Jeanne D'Acre and made it the capital of their Holy Land kingdom. In 1918, the British captured the city from the Ottoman Turks. They turned the palace of the notorious Turkish governor of the Galilee—his cruelty earned him the nickname al-Jazaar, "the Butcher" in Arabic—into the largest prison in Palestine. Today, it is a museum. The nearby al-Jazaar Mosque, which has a shrine with a few strands of hair said to be from Prophet Muhammad's beard, is the focal point for Acre's rapidly growing Muslim community. What was once the Islamic educational and spiritual center of the Galilee where judges used to study shari'a, Muslim religious law, is now a drug-dealing area. Governmental neglect, an uninspired local leadership, and the second intifada have left merchants strapped with unsold souvenirs. Once thriving Acre is a socio-economic mess.

Walking past a group of men puffing on bubbling water pipes to have lunch in an empty seafood restaurant, a fifty-year-old contractor describes the shifting scene in Acre. "We have fundamentalists trying to put Korans into our hands. And the 'sushi-eaters,' the educated ones, saying we should join the Palestinian struggle. What do they want, to make this place like [the Palestinian Authority]? Run by corrupt gangsters who shoot anyone who asks how they got rich? I'm part of the silent majority. We're fed up. Going bankrupt. Before, people got along. Arabs and Jews. We lived in the same apartment buildings, did business together. No more. Jews who can afford it are moving out." About a third of Acre's fifty thousand residents are Muslim. Demographic forecasters say that by about 2006, they will be the majority.

When Suhad was growing up, there were many more Jews in her neighborhood. At age eight, she and her friends attended a local summer camp. She was the only Arab. "We were all in groups named after army units," she recalls. "Mine was called Golani Brigade, just like the name of my street. It was during the Lebanon war when Israel invaded. I remember the counselor telling us how our army was strong and how our soldiers would defeat the Arabs. I heard some kids say, 'Arab dogs, go to hell.' After the class, the counselor saw me in the corner, crying. She apologized and said she didn't realize what she said hurt me. Even at that age I was aware that being an Arab in a Jewish state gives you the mentality of 'the Other.' All national holidays are Jewish. Everything is Jewish."

Suhad is no different from many mostly young Arab Israelis who want Israel to replace its national Jewish symbols—from "Hatikvah" to the blue-and-white flag with the Star of David—with symbols that are not "offensive." "Everything Zionist makes me feel it is the cause of my disaster. The flag is the symbol of the state that destroyed over four hundred of our villages inside Israel." She refuses to sing "Hatikvah," which describes the Jewish yearning for Zion. "I remember as a kid feeling fear mixed with hate when I heard it. I hate the words." In perfect Hebrew she recites the words *nefesh yehudi* (Jewish soul). "Do we have Jewish souls? And what about the words 'to be a free people in our land, the land of Zion and Jerusalem'? All the words exclude us." Israel Television goes off the air at midnight playing the national anthem. "Whenever I hear it, I rush to the TV to turn it off. At least now I have cable and satellite I don't have to hear it."

Suhad's parents sent her to all-Arab schools. "In high school, we sang patriotic Palestinian songs. And I remember when the PLO was in exile in Tunis and declared a Palestinian state, we really celebrated." She describes Yom Hazikaron, Memorial Day, hearing the wail of air raid sirens signaling the two minutes for Israelis to stand silently honoring fallen soldiers and victims of terrorism. Jewish students attend teary-eyed ceremonies with solemn music and listen to heart-wrenching stories of how graduates of their school died in combat. The scene at her high school, Suhad recalls, was not like that. "When we heard the sirens, none of us in class stood, except for one Druze guy. All of us laughed at him." Asked why, she responds, "He was betraying us Palestinians."

When the sirens signaling Yom Hashoah, Holocaust Day, are mentioned, Suhad pauses. She looks uncomfortable. "Actually, I'm sick of people analyzing who stands or who doesn't stand at attention. And, of course, only the 'good' Arabs stand, the 'bad' ones don't. I don't stand, but I don't have any bad feelings about it—Arabs can't ignore such a catastrophe. We learn about it in school." Students in other parts of the Middle East don't. Media in the Palestinian Authority, Egypt, Syria, Lebanon, and Saudi Arabia are filled with stories either denying the Holocaust or praising the Final Solution and Hitler. In 2003, Egyptian TV aired a hate-filled series based on the anti-Semitic forgery *The Protocols of the Elders of Zion,* and in 2002, the Egyptian government daily *Al-Akhbar* ran an article calling the Holocaust "a fabrication, a lie and a fraud . . . a huge Israeli plot. . . . Hitler, if only you had done it, brother, if only it had really happened, so that the world could sigh in relief." "It is okay to learn about the Holocaust, but I didn't learn my own Palestinian history," Suhad complains. "Our textbooks are developed by the government—we [Arabs] learn our history from the eyes of the other."

Israeli law provides for a separate, Arabic-speaking state school system with a different curriculum. From the third grade until the twelfth, Arab students are required to study Hebrew, usually taught by Arabic-speaking teachers. They study Hebrew grammar and read prose and poetry from the Bible, the Golden Age in Spain, and contemporary Hebrew literature. "I studied more Torah than Koran. I had to be examined in the matriculation exams on Judaism, not Islam. I must tell a personal story.

In the matriculation exam, we were asked to write about a person who had a special influence on us. Can you think who I chose? I, an Arab young woman, wrote about Rachel [Israel's most famous female Jewish poet]. I really liked her and have nothing against her, but still, this incident tells the whole story. Arabs aren't involved in the decision making about the curriculum. We read Zionist literature and poetry, not Arab Palestinian poetry which is studied throughout the Arab world, nothing about Arab authors except for the nonpolitical ones."

Conflicting versions of history become evident on Independence Day, when Jews throughout the country enjoy parades, parties, and picnics. Patriotism has been much on display since the second intifada: Israeli flags flutter from cars, from homes—some Jews drape themselves in huge ones. Suhad, like most other Arab Israelis, boycotts the celebrations and commemorates al Nakba, Arabic for "the disaster" or "catastrophe," which is the term used throughout the Arab world for the creation of Israel in 1948. They attend rallies where some people wave PLO or Hezballah flags. Others make pilgrimages to the ruins of pre-1948 Arab villages and memorials for Arabs killed in wars with Israel. On May 15, 2000, Arab Israelis stood silently for the first time, mourning the day Israel became a state and showing solidarity with intifada II. A survey of Arab Israelis by Professors Sammy Smooha and Assad Ganem of Haifa University reveals a dramatic rise in Arab Israeli feelings of alienation from the state and its institutions, coupled with intensifying criticism of the government. Arabs who said they were willing to fly an Israeli flag on their homes dropped from 43 percent in 1995 to 27 percent in 2001. Only 33 percent of the respondents said the word "Israeli" accurately describes their identity, as opposed to 63 percent who said so in 1995.

From Acre to Lod, young Palestinian men and women are launching a new musical style: Palestinian rap. One of the most popular rappers is twenty-four-year-old Tamer al-Naffar, who sets his social and political grievances to an insistent, relentless rhyming beat. His trio, DAM, plays to crowds as large as three thousand and also gives free concerts to peace groups made up of Arab and Jewish Israelis and Palestinians. In one of their most popular songs, "Who's the Terrorist?," the angry, alienated lyrics, a mix of Arabic and Hebrew, rail against Jews for fearing Arabs and their government for distrusting Arabs. "I'm the terrorist? You're the terrorist. How can I be a terrorist when I live in my country? Our blood is not the blood of dogs, but human blood, and it's valuable. I have Israeli citizenship, but it doesn't do anything for me. So I'm an Israeli citizen, but it doesn't say anything about me. At the end of the day, I decide who I am." "I'm just a Palestinian," says Tamer, "who happens to live in the war zone that's called Israel."

While her Jewish friends in Acre were being drafted into the army, Suhad was preparing to leave home to study at her lawyer father's alma mater, Tel Aviv University. With two Arab girlfriends, a fellow law student and an English literature major, she looked for an apartment to rent near campus in the liberal Ramat Aviv neighborhood. She recalls phoning landlords. "One woman asked me, 'So you're a student? Are you done with your military service?' When I told her I hadn't been in the army, she asked me, 'What kind of name is Suhad?' An Arab name, I told her. 'Ahh, an Arab name?' she said. 'Well, I have to ask the neighbors.' "

Another landlord she called detected Suhad's very slightly accented Hebrew. " 'Are you from Russia?' she asked me. When I told her I was born here, she asked, 'So, what are you? What are your origins?' I told her, 'I'm an Arab, a Palestinian,' and her voice changed. She said, 'Call again, tomorrow.' I called a lot of places and, finally, we went to a state mediator and he told us frankly that 'many people are sensitive that you are an Arab.' It was a humiliating process," she says with barely repressed anger. The three girls finally found an apartment near campus. Apartment hunting is now harder. Since intifada II, to more and more Jews the word "Palestinian" sounds more like "potential terrorist" than fellow citizen.

Suhad was one of ten Arab law students in a class of about two hundred Jews. "My [Jewish] classmates had a lot of misconceptions about Muslims," she reports. "They assumed that because I wore pants and didn't cover my hair, I must be a Christian Arab." (A few semesters later, students elected a Christian Arab woman as student body president of the law school.) "My Jewish classmates were liberal and we had a lot of political debates. Some visited me in Acre. I think it was the first time they'd been in an Arab home." Most Jewish students only have superficial contacts with Muslim Arab Israelis, in shops, buses, restaurants, and hospitals. Deeper encounters are rare. After graduating from law school in 1997, Suhad worked in a Haifa law firm run by Arab women for Arab women. At the same time, she hosted a daily radio show, *Law and Court,* interviewing Arab and Jewish Israeli lawyers and judges on government-run Israel Radio. Her program was discontinued after a controversial show on the rights of Arab political prisoners. Israel Television hired her to cohost *Arabesque,* a weekly bilingual program on Arab affairs. Then Suhad and a few Jewish Israeli lawyers spent a year studying civil rights law at American University in Washington, D.C. on scholarships largely financed by U.S. and Israeli Jews. "I told people I'm a Palestinian, part of a generation that is not afraid to challenge the goverment for treating us like second-class citizens. We're not afraid to speak out or fight for our rights. We demand equality with the Jewish majority, the rights of full citizens." She vowed that she would work to make Israel a "state for all its citizens" instead of a Jewish state.

This desire, which on the surface appeals to the principles of progressives around the world, is a threat to Israel's existence as a Jewish state. It also symbolizes a revolution in national identity for many Arab Israelis. Knesset member Azmi Bishara is a vociferous proponent of this idea. Bishara demands an end to the Law of Return. He wants to bar entry to Jews who want to immigrate and give Palestinian refugees (who with their offspring now number approximately 4 million) the right to return. His support for the Palestinian national struggle is not in doubt; his support for a Jewish Israel is. In June 2001, at a memorial ceremony in Syria for the late President Hafez al-Assad, Bishara stood alongside Israel's enemies, Hassan Nasrallah, head of Hezballah, and leaders of Hamas and other militant Islamic Palestinian organizations, and made a speech urging Arab countries and terrorist organizations to step up "resistance" against Israel. On Bishara's return to Israel, he said, "I am not an Israeli patriot; I am a Palestinian patriot." Outraged Jewish Knesset colleagues called him a traitor. Bishara has Arab Israeli detractors too who "accuse him of among other things intellectual dishonesty for waving the flag of democracy and minority rights in Israel while at the same time courting the dictatorial Syrian regime," writes Isabel Kershner of the *Jerusalem Report.* By then, Suhad already had joined Adalah, the Legal Center for Arab Minority Rights in Israel, which rushed to his defense.

"Our Knesset members like Bishara advance our struggle," says

Suhad, who like many university-educated Arab Israelis admires him. "Adalah ['justice' in Arabic] fights for Palestinian Israelis to achieve equality as citizens. We make use of all the tools of the law—legislation, litigation, the media—to achieve our goals." Suhad started this work at a historic time, October 2000, the first week of intifada II. Tens of thousands of Arab Israelis encouraged by Arafat and Arab Israeli leaders like Bishara demonstrated in solidarity with the Palestinians. Riots broke out in her hometown of Acre, in Jaffa, and throughout villages and towns in the Galilee and central Israel. There was an outpouring of anger and frustration about what they called empty promises from the government. Others were yelling for revenge for Sharon's provocative visit to Haram al-Sharif/the Temple Mount. A few young Arab Israeli men pulled Jews from cars and beat them. Some others set forest fires on hills near Jewish communities in the Galilee, stunning Jews and Arab neighbors who—except for these three days—had lived in peace since 1948. For three days, rioters closed certain roads in northern Israel. In the crazed atmosphere, some untrained, unprepared Israeli police (mostly Jewish, a few Christian, Bedouin, and Druze) were overwhelmed by crowds of angry demonstrators. They panicked and shot live ammunition, killing thirteen Muslim Israeli men and injuring hundreds more. These were the bloodiest internal Arab protests in modern Israeli history.

Suhad and a battery of other Arab Israeli lawyers working with Adalah investigated these killings and presented their findings at governmental hearings in the Supreme Court in Jerusalem. They placed a map with thirty-four purple dots, sites of major clashes between police and Arab Israelis, in the hearing room next to the judges' dais. Because she knows the Israeli media from the inside, Suhad was a temporary spokeswoman. "Part of our struggle as lawyers is to win public opinion," she says. "Our generation understands the Jews, knows how to talk to them in their own language." A *Ha'aretz* newspaper reporter at the hearings described the media savvy of Arab Israelis who were putting the state on trial:

They look like yuppies, dress in fancy suits, speak three languages fluently and always are available to reply to questions from the local or foreign press. . . . They are a far cry from the traditional image of the Arabs in the Hebrew press—as outsiders whose voices go unheard.

Whenever there is a break, the Adalah people, supported by three Arab Knesset members—Ahmed Tibi, Mohammed Barakeh and Azmi Bishara—who are just as experienced in dealing with the media, approach reporters, feed them reactions and interpretations about the testimonies they have just heard. . . . They monitor the reporting closely and have no hesitation about criticizing or correcting reporters if they think it's necessary. They're pros who know the importance of short sound-bites for the television cameras, how to give good quotes for the radio and get good newspaper headlines.

As police testified, Arab fury escalated. After an Arab father whose son had been killed rushed the witness stand and punched a police officer, a wall of bulletproof glass was set up. Police maintained that they were unprepared, undermanned, and shot live bullets in self-defense. "Why did police fire live ammunition? When Jews demonstrate, they never use live bullets," charges Suhad. "They were brutal. Since these police shootings, our feelings of discrimination have intensified and so has our solidarity with the intifada. Palestinian citizens of Israel feel more than ever that we are the 'illegitimate citizens of the state.' I want my baby son to grow up in a country where he feels he belongs completely." *Ha'aretz* reporter Ori Nir observed that the reinforced glass partition in the hearing room symbolized a growing distance and deepening alienation between Jews and Arabs, a poignant symbol of how the intifada has driven Arab Israelis and Jews further apart.

When Ehud Barak ran for prime minister in 1999, Arab Israelis, normally very divided communities, gave him almost all their votes, hoping his left-of-center government would bring about revolutionary change. In the national election in February 2001, they took out their anger on Prime Minister Barak for not apologizing promptly after the October shootings or delivering on promises to them. Almost all Arab Israelis either boycotted the elections or turned in blank ballots, contributing to Ariel Sharon's first record landslide victory.

Umm al-Fahm, the largest all-Muslim town in Israel, about a half hour southeast of Acre, is the "capital" of the Israeli Islamic Movement. There are walls spray-painted with slogans such as "Islam Is the Answer" and

"Death to the Jews," while others brandish angry Arabic graffiti, red swastikas, and faded posters of Saddam Hussein. Jews rarely venture here anymore, not to fix their cars cheaply, not to buy the famous olive oil, nor to teach at the Center for Science, Technology and Art. Not since the most violent riots in Israel broke out here at the start of intifada II. Not since a Jewish father driving his family home from a weekend at the Sea of Galilee was stopped by someone at the entrance to this hillside town who asked, "Where is Umm al-Fahm?" When the driver gave him directions in Hebrew, the man shot him and then disappeared into town. Not since several Palestinians and members of the Israeli Islamic Movement have been caught planning to launch terrorist attacks. And not since a March 2003 pro-Iraq rally in which residents called for Saddam Hussein to bomb Tel Aviv with chemical weapons. Umm al-Fahm is located in the "Triangle," the region in central Israel nearest to the West Bank towns of Jenin, Nablus, Qalqilyya, and Tulkarm, conservative Islamic centers and Hamas and Islamic Jihad strongholds. It is not difficult to find people here who think suicide bombers are martyrs, not murderers.

"What do people expect from us? There are Palestinians on both sides of the border who hate and even kill Jews, who think doing nothing is a kind of suicide. Most of us obey laws, and what does the government do? It neglects us. What Jews have, we Arabs should have," asserts Nabila, a housewife who points out that even though her extended family lives in a large, two-story house, "everyone in Umm al-Fahm is squeezed for space." There is a severe housing crunch in this former village; since 1948 its population has grown sevenfold, to more than forty thousand. It is the regional center for some twenty thousand Arabs from surrounding Israeli villages. The infrastructure is overburdened, from unpaved roads to underequipped schools. Unemployed men with little to do hang out on the streets, play backgammon in cafés, or go to the mosques. "The Islamic Movement takes care of the poor, gives them food and money, just like Shas does for the [Mizrahi] Jews. That's why we support it," says Nabila. The fast-growing Israeli Islamic Movement has won control of Arab communities from the Galilee to the Negev. Many credit its rapid growth to its extensive social services; it runs clinics, libraries, camps, schools, and the kindergarten where Nabila sends her son. He has the most common name for an Israeli boy, Muhammad.

"We named him after The Prophet. We believe there is no God but Allah [Al Lah is Arabic for 'The God'] and Muhammad was his messenger," explains Nabila, a devout Muslim who doesn't shake hands with male visitors and whose husband will not allow her to use their last name.

The white walls of their living room are decorated with framed verses from the Koran and a picture of Jerusalem's famous silver-domed al-Aqsa Mosque. When Nabila was born in 1980, there were only four mosques in Umm al-Fahm; now there are twenty-five. "Thanks to Allah, may His name be praised, I see more and more devoted people. Women everywhere dress like this," she says, referring to her long skirt and *hijab*, a white Islamic head covering. "The girls, even the little ones. And the teachers too. People show us respect and it's written in our holy Koran that women should be covered." Rising numbers of young women like Nabila are showing outward signs of Islamization; about 65 percent of Arab Israelis call themselves "religious." "Before I married, I dressed immodestly, but inside, always I had faith in God." Nabila, who attends weekly religious classes at a mosque, is much more pious than her parents, who, like many older Arab Israelis, were swept up by the secular struggle for Arab rights championed by the Arabs and Jews of the Israeli Communist Party (Hadash). Umm al-Fahm was a bastion of the Israeli Communist Party until 1989. That's when Sheik Ra'ed Salah, whose slogan is "Islam Is the Truth, Islam Is the Solution," was elected mayor. Since then, the Israeli Islamic Movement has been running City Hall.

Even the mayor's office has an adjoining private mosque, reports her husband, whose overalls are stained from painting cars. Also an ardent supporter of the Islamic Movement, he embraces Islam fervently. He is a *hajji*, an honorific title that means he made the *hajj*, the pilgrimage to the holiest city Mecca, where Muhammad was born in 570. Thousands of Israeli Muslims have made the journey, which all Muslims are commanded to do at least once in their lifetime. This afternoon, Nabila and her husband are watching the hajj live from Mecca on satellite television: 2 million pilgrims slowly circling the *kaaba*, the enormous black cube-shaped House of God which has a sacred black stone embedded inside. "When the children are older, I'll bring Nabila," he says. "People come from all over. From Iran. From Pakistan. From Indonesia." Only one in five of Islam's 1.3 billion followers is Arab; in fact, the world's six largest Islamic populations are in Indonesia, Pakistan, India, Bangladesh,

Turkey, and Iran. "Most wear white robes because in the sight of God, we are all equal. It doesn't matter if you're very rich from Kuwait or poor from Algeria, our Koran is the same Koran and our Prophet is the same Prophet. We recite the same prayers, we fast during Ramadan." And when the hajj is over, this family like Muslims everywhere celebrates Id al-Adha, the Feast of the Sacrifice. The three-day holiday, a time of prayer, rejoicing, and feasting with family and friends, commemorates God's command to Ibrahim/Abraham to sacrifice his son Ishmael on the kaaba in Mecca to test his faith, the Islamic version of the "binding of Isaac" in Genesis 22. Nabila's husband slaughters a sheep or goat and distributes the meat to the poor because Allah allowed Ibrahim to sacrifice a goat instead of Ishmael.

When asked about Islam's ancient Jewish roots, Nabila replies that the Prophet Muhammad taught that Arabs are the other children of Ibrahim through his first-born son, Ishmael, by Hagar (his Egyptian maid). Many Islamic ritual laws such as circumcision and prohibition against eating pork and nineteen of the twenty-five prophets in the Koran are from Jewish scripture. "We believe in the Torah," Nabila quickly points out. "But the Jews distorted it, falsified it. Our Koran corrects it. And it corrects the Christian Bible too." Muslims consider the Koran the literal word of God and that Islam is God's final revelation. "Muhammad was God's last Prophet. He completed the work of Moses and Jesus. It is written in our Koran that Islam is the true religion of Ibrahim. Islam is the true religion of Moses. And of Jesus too. And the Prophet Jesus," she adds, "was not crucified. A man who looked like him was substituted in his place on the cross because Allah would not allow such a thing to happen to one of His Prophets. One day, there will be only one religion left and it will be Islam."

Islam means "surrender" or "submission to the will of God," and Nabila and her husband dutifully submit. Five times a day—at dawn, midday, afternoon, evening, and night—when the muezzins call out from loudspeakers *Allahhu Akbar,* Allah is great, summoning the faithful to prayer, devout Muslims stop wherever they are, in fields and factories, shops and schools, take off their shoes, and face toward Mecca, bowing, prostrating, and then kneeling before God while reciting verses from the Koran. "Sometimes at home, I spread out my mat and pray. Even though women don't have to, some Fridays I go to the mosque," says Nabila, who prays in the upstairs women's gallery; the main floor is for men. Afterward, the imam, the prayer leader, gives a sermon. "Sometimes he talks about giving money to the poor or one of the other pillars." She's referring to the "five pillars of Islam": declaring the oneness of Allah and his messenger Muhammad, praying five times daily, fasting during Ramadan, giving charity, and making the hajj to Mecca at least once in a lifetime. There are Muslims who promote a sixth pillar, jihad, struggle or armed conflict in defense of Islam. "Last Friday, the imam warned against gambling, against drinking." Alcohol, which is forbidden in Islam, is not sold in Umm al-Fahm. However, the empty Maccabee beer and vodka bottles in olive groves and wheat fields indicate, as journalist Ori Nir points out, that drinking is a serious problem among Israeli Muslim youth. "He also tells us about dangers of permissive lifestyles. Boys and girls mingling is haram [forbidden]. We're conservative, but not fanatics. This isn't Saudi Arabia." With a half-smile, Nabila enthusiastically describes her addiction to *Lilac,* an Arabic Israeli magazine version of *Cosmo.*

For Arab Israelis, as for most of the Arabic-speaking world, the most popular station is al-Jazeera (the Peninsula), the CNN of the Arab world, which broadcasts pictures of the intifada from Arab perspectives, unifying Arabs behind the Palestinian struggle. On it they watch anti-Islamists and Arab journalists quiz Arab heads of state about government censorship and corruption. On hard-hitting talk shows, Arabs now dare discuss taboo subjects such as honor killings, homosexuality, and polygamy. Nabila's tone changes when asked about an Israeli guest on al-Jazeera, Jabara Hussniya, who was the first Muslim woman elected to the Knesset. "We don't like her. She's a Zionist sympathizer. She's in a Jewish political party [the leftist Jewish-Arab Meretz Party]. No Arab should be in the Knesset. Sheik Salah says it's illegal."

She's referring to Sheik Ra'ed Salah, the charismatic former mayor, who carries a bag with a Koran and a cell phone. A number of political analysts consider this tall, bearded fifty-year-old Israel's most important political and religious Muslim leader—and a sharp challenge to Israel. When the Islamic Movement decided to take part in Knesset elections in 1996, Sheik Salah split off and formed the Islamic Movement's militant northern wing, which he now runs. Sheik Salah's movement does not recognize Israel and does not take part in national elections. According to his swelling ranks of hard-line supporters, it is against Islamic law for any Muslim to take a loyalty oath to "the illegal Zionist entity." As Sheik Salah, whose late father and two brothers serve in the Israeli Police, put it, "Israel is illegal, built entirely on usurped holy Islamic land. The Knesset is against what Allah ordered and bequeathed to us. Israel is an alien state, against the goals of the *umma* [Islamic community]. The Islamic religious position toward the illegal Zionist entity is total rejection, continuous resistance and constant jihad. It has no right to exist." He believes an Islamic government must rule between the Jordan River and the Mediterranean Sea—which means over all of Israel.

After the 1967 War opened the borders with the West Bank and Gaza, thousands of Israeli Islamic students, including Sheik Salah, went there for religious training. After this devastating six-day defeat, Muslims were looking for new answers and Islamic fundamentalism was taking root. At the same time, Israel allowed Palestinian religious figures including Sheik Ahmad Yassin, founder and spiritual leader of Hamas, to preach and lead Friday prayers in Israeli mosques. The number of mosques in Israel more than quadrupled. By 1978 Saudi Arabia, which, like most Muslim states, had prohibited Israeli passport holders, including Muslims, from entering, agreed to allow Israeli Muslims to make the hajj to Mecca using Jordanian laissez-passer papers. Within a year, the Iranian revolution succeeded and Khomeni began exporting Islamic fundamentalism. Some Arab Israelis, swept up by radical Islam, linked up with generous donors from Iran, Saudi Arabia, Kuwait, and other oil-rich Persian Gulf emirates who funnel "charitable contributions" to Islamic groups that believe the Israeli-Palestinian conflict is a religious war.

Sheik Salah's supporters do. They actively promote Islam in Israel, from running youth clubs to building religious schools. Umm al-Fahm's Islamic Studies College is a sister school to the Islamic Law Faculty of Al-Najah University in the West Bank city of Nablus. Signs on campus read "Israel has nuclear bombs, we have human bombs." In September 2001, to celebrate the first anniversary of the intifada, thousands of students stepped on Israeli and U.S. flag doormats and then entered an exhibit in the school cafeteria celebrating suicide bombers. In a replica of the Jerusalem Sbarro pizzeria where a Hamas suicide bomber had killed fifteen Jews, a student reenacted the grisly bombing. There even were bloody plastic body parts dangling from the ceiling. In another section, mannequins were dressed as suicide bombers, each holding a Koran and an automatic rifle. In front of a mannequin of an ultra-Orthodox Jew with a black hat, black jacket, and black trousers was a large rock with a recording device embedded inside that called out "Oh believer, there is a Jew behind me. Come and kill him." Hamas's campus volunteers have recruited a number of suicide bombers and would-be bombers, including young Israeli men from Umm al-Fahm's Islamic Movement. In addition to Hamas, Hezballah, Islamic Jihad, and Fatah-Tanzim, Israeli intelligence reports that al-Qaeda has tried to recruit Israeli Muslim citizens, who can move easily inside Israel.

When asked about terrorists, Sheik Salah says he "understands their motivations and admires their technical prowess." He describes what *shahids* (martyrs) find in paradise. "It is written in the Koran and in the Suras [the traditions about the life of Muhammad] the shahid receives from Allah seventy virgins, no torment in the grave, and the choice of seventy members of his family and his confidants to enter paradise with him." Along with Islamic Movement and other Arab Israeli Knesset members, Sheik Salah has paid condolence calls on and given contributions to families of Hamas suicide bombers. (Until Saddam's downfall, the Iraqi government "rewarded" each suicide bomber's family with $25,000 and gave $1,000 to each Palestinian injured fighting Israelis.) A prolific poet and writer, Sheik Salah also believes in waging jihad through the media. An Israeli Islamist monthly publication published in Umm al-Fahm runs commentaries on the Koran along with his stridently anti-Israeli columns and biographies of Muslim "martyrs." In May 2002, Israeli police arrested Sheik Salah, who is suspected of funneling millions of dollars from Islamic groups abroad to Hamas-affiliated organizations in the West Bank and Gaza Strip.

In Umm al-Fahm, as in numerous Arab Israeli towns, walls are plastered with posters of Jerusalem's al-Aqsa Mosque and the incendiary warning "al-Aqsa is in danger," which is the rallying cry of the Islamic Movement. This mosque is Islam's third-holiest shrine and sits on the Temple Mount or, as Muslims call it, Haram al-Sharif, which means Noble Sanctuary. It is the world's most contested and potentially most explosive piece of real estate, sacred to the world's three major monotheistic religions. The Temple Mount is Judaism's holiest site, where Jews all over the world face when they pray. It is where the First and Second Holy

Temples stood. Below it is the Western Wall, the outer wall of King Herod's Second Temple. According to Christianity, Jesus as a child and again as an adult visited the Second Temple. And it is the spot from which Muhammad dreamed he ascended to heaven.

Jerusalem was a Christian city within the Byzantine Empire during Muhammad's lifetime. Six years after he died in Medina in 632, Jerusalem was captured by Muslims. Caliph Abd al-Malik built the magnificent Dome of the Rock on the Temple Mount/Haram al-Sharif. The world-famous shrine with the gold-topped dome dominates Jerusalem's skyline. It is built over an exposed rock, which, according to Jewish tradition, is where God asked Abraham to sacrifice his son Isaac in the ultimate test of his faith. Muslims believe that from this sacred rock, Muhammad rode al Buraq, his flying horse, which had the face of a woman and the tail of a peacock, on a night flight to the seventh heaven. There, Muhammad met all the Prophets who had preceded him and Allah, who was on a throne surrounded by angels. Arabic inscriptions inside the Dome of the Rock include ones commemorating the Islamic victory over Judaism and Christianity. About eighty years after Muhammad's death, the next caliph transformed the Byzantine Church of St. Mary that stood on the Temple Mount. He added an onion-like dome and converted it into a mosque. He named it al-Aqsa, after what the Koran calls *al-masjid al-aqsa,* the Farthest Mosque. It is where Muhammad went after leaving the Sacred Mosque in Mecca, though the Koran never mentions the actual location of al-Aqsa Mosque.

Jerusalem has been conquered thirty-seven times, controlled successively by Jews, Babylonians, Assyrians, Romans, Byzantines, Arabs, Crusaders, Ottomans, and, during World War I, the British. When the Jordanians seized the Old City and East Jerusalem in 1948, they expelled all Jewish residents, and for nineteen years, no Jews were allowed to visit the Western Wall or any religious sites and Christian residents were compelled to include Muslim teachings in their schools. During the 1967 War, Israel captured the Old City and East Jerusalem and opened Muslim, Christian, and Jewish sites to people of all faiths and gave custodianship of the Temple Mount/Haram al-Sharif to the Waqf, the Muslim Religious Trust. In 1993, Yasser Arafat removed the Jordanian-affiliated clergy and appointed the controversial Akram Sabri as mufti, chief Islamic cleric of Jerusalem, as well as imam of al-Aqsa Mosque. Five years later, the Waqf prohibited Jews and Christians from worshipping on the Temple Mount/Haram al-Sharif, ruling that the area is purely Muslim and that no Jewish Temple ever existed there. The influential mufti, whose sermons and radio and television broadcasts attract enormous audiences, has called Jews "sons of pigs and monkeys" and warned that if Jews "try to control our mosque it will be the end of Israel. . . . If they try to pray on our site it will mean massacres the magnitude of which only Allah knows."

He is not the only Muslim leader who believes that Jews have no historical connection to Jerusalem, though he is among the most outspoken. (Jerusalem, the Jewish capital for three thousand years, is mentioned in the Hebrew Bible 657 times. It is not mentioned in the Koran nor in Muslim prayers.) "The Bible tells about the Temple and the Temple Mount. We believe that the Bible was forged and it says so in the Koran. The issue of the Temple Mount and the Temple is not the only thing that was forged in the Bible," insists Sheik Salah. "The Jews do not have a right of any kind in the Temple Mount area or to so much as one stone of al-Aqsa Mosque. Researchers and archaeologists have already proved that. The al-Buraq Wall [the Islamic name for the Western Wall] is not the western wall of the Temple." Muslim academics and archaeologists have said on Palestinian Television that incidents described in the Hebrew Bible actually took place in Yemen. A number of PLO publications and Internet postings argue that "whatever Jewish temple might have existed" was in Nablus in the West Bank. By this reasoning, Jesus never was in Jerusalem, never was on the Temple Mount.

Sheik Salah is known throughout much of the Islamic world as head of the nonprofit al-Aqsa Foundation, which is funding numerous projects on the Temple Mount/Haram al-Sharif, partly intended, in the eyes of most Israelis, at destroying evidence of its Jewish past. Since 1999, it has been conducting extensive unauthorized construction work, "renovating" and expanding parts of the Temple Mount/Haram al-Sharif. With the approval of Mufti Sabri, Sheik Salah is often there, overseeing engineers and volunteers from the Israeli Islamic Movement who have been digging, excavating, and paving the site. Using bulldozers, stone-cutting machines, and power saws, they have turned the cavernous Solomon's Stables under the Temple Mount/Haram al-Sharif into the marble-pillared Marwani Mosque, which can hold fifteen thousand worshippers.

As underground excavations proceed, rich historical evidence proving Judeo-Christian connections to the Temple Mount is disappearing. In the thousands of tons of earth that have been dumped into the nearby Kidron Valley, archaeologists have found destroyed Jewish artifacts from the First Temple period and unique Christian relics from Byzantine and Crusader times. Fearing an international Islamic backlash, a succession of Israeli governments have not stopped the transformation of the Temple Mount. Demands by Israeli and international archaeologists, engineers, historians, and scholars to inspect the work have been refused. Non-Muslims are not permitted on the Temple Mount.

During the Camp David peace talks in 2000, Israeli and Palestinian negotiators bitterly contested sovereignty rights over the Temple Mount/ Haram al-Sharif. A month after the talks failed, on September 28, 2000, Ariel Sharon, then leader of the opposition Likud Party, visited the Temple Mount/Haram al-Sharif with a large police escort, saying that he was exercising his Jewish sovereign rights. (He went for political, not religious reasons, afraid that Benjamin Netanyahu would contest his bid to be Likud's candidate for prime minister.) The next day, following the Friday sermon, protests erupted. Seven Palestinians were killed in clashes with Israeli security forces. According to the findings of the Mitchell Committee, the Palestinian Authority made no effort to contain the demonstrations that spread to the West Bank and Gaza and a week later to Israel. Led by then mayor Sheik Salah and members of the City Council, hundreds of men from Umm al-Fahm burned symbols of the Jewish state—a bank, a post office, and a gas station (which happened to be owned by a Christian Arab)—and attacked a bus driver (who happened to be an Israeli Muslim Arab) and then burned his bus. They lobbed rocks and Molotov cocktails at police who battled unsuccessfully to keep a main highway open.

Intifada II frequently is dubbed the al-Aqsa intifada, to emphasize its Islamic connection. Two weeks before it broke out, about seventy thousand people filled Umm al-Fahm's soccer stadium for Mayor Sheik Salah's fifth annual "al-Aqsa Is in Danger" rally, which is also a fundraiser for his Temple Mount construction work. Men chanted "With blood and fire we will redeem Palestine"; some wore headbands with the slogan "Palestine from the river to the sea." The spotlight was on Sheik Salah, who was framed against a huge computer-enhanced picture of al-Aqsa Mosque. It was symbolically in chains, with a clenched fist arising from flames. A fiery speaker, Sheik Salah warned the crowd, "Israel's insistence on sovereignty over Haram al-Sharif is a declaration of war on the Muslim world. Only Muslims and Palestinian people are allowed authority over it. We will share not one stone or grain of sand with the Jews." Before the rally, Palestinian and other Arab television stations broadcast footage of a charred al-Aqsa Mosque, giving viewers the impression that Jews had destroyed it. But the footage wasn't live; it was shot in August 1969, after a deranged Australian Christian tourist set a fire and damaged part of the mosque.

Three days before Sheik Salah's next annual "al-Aqsa Is in Danger" rally, the world changed. Al-Qaeda terrorists flew hijacked airliners into the World Trade Center and the Pentagon. President George W. Bush vowed to avenge the attacks with a "crusade." Crusade is an explosive word for Muslims, because it evokes memories of the brutal Crusader wars, when "infidels" killed Muslims, defiled holy Muslim soil, and made Jerusalem capital of their kingdom from 1099 to 1187. The Israeli government asked Sheik Salah to cancel the rally in Umm al-Fahm's soccer stadium. He didn't. He addressed the crowd standing before an enormous new poster. It featured Yusuf ibn Ayub, the twelfth-century Muslim Kurdish warrior hero better known as Saladin, riding a white stallion into Jerusalem to throw out the Crusaders. In the background was al-Aqsa Mosque with the caption "We've returned to al-Aqsa." Sheik Salah warned the crowd, "We are the owners of al-Aqsa. Our right to it is a Muslim, Arab and Palestinian right totally." He went on to accuse the United States of waging a "crusade" against Islam and then called on President Bush to convert to Islam.

One of Sheik Salah's most loyal followers missed that rally. A few days earlier, Muhammad Shaker Habashi, a well-to-do, middle-aged merchant with two wives and ten children, went to a train station at Nahariya, about thirty minutes away. He was wearing jeans and carried a knapsack and a suspicious-looking cardboard box. When he detonated it, Habashi blew himself up and killed three bystanders and wounded eighty more Israelis, including three Arabs from his own Galilee village. Habashi made history: he was the first Arab Israeli citizen to carry out a "successful" suicide bombing. After the attack, Hamas released a video of the bearded Israeli citizen holding an M-16 and a Koran, which Israel

Television aired. "I am going to commit a religious self-sacrifice," Habashi coldly explained. "Allah gives me the honor of being a shahid." Hamas distributed a flyer gloating that Habashi proved they could recruit Arab Israelis to strike deep inside Israel.

Habashi's neighbors in the village of Abu Snan quickly condemned him; some demanded that his family be expelled, that his two homes be destroyed, and that his two widows not receive government stipends. In this mixed Muslim, Christian, and Druze village of ten thousand, children carry Spiderman and Pokemon backpacks, but their parents carry grudges. "This is a disaster. It hurts us [Muslims] even more than the Jews," fumes Tarik, a local watermelon and tobacco farmer. "When I heard someone bombed his store, I wasn't sad." He points out that Habashi, who frequently organized Islamic Movement marches, was related to Sheik Salah. "I wish Israel would redraw the border and push Umm al-Fahm over to Palestine. They yelled for Saddam to bomb Israel. They hate Israel, so let them become Palestinians. Do they want to? Of course not. They want to remain Israelis because they know life is better here. I would rather see my daughter marry a Jew than one of them."

Tarik is not the farmer's real name. During his interview he reconsidered his decision to speak on the record, saying grimly, "I could be killed." Seven of his neighbors are in jail, convicted in November 2000 of planning terror attacks inside Israel, including murdering fellow villagers who "collaborate" with Jews and trying to recruit other Arab Israelis to spy for Hezballah. "We're ashamed of them. Imagine, Habashi lived right near a Druze, and not just any Druze. A big shot—a major general. I'm sure a lot of the Druze and Christians in our village are wondering which of us [Muslims] could be the next 'enemy from within.' And then those Palestinians accuse us of being too Israeli and not willing to do more for them, not willing to die for them," he says, pouring another glass of Merlot. What if one of his fourteen religious brothers and sisters visit and see he's enjoying a bottle of wine? "I put it away. I respect them. My mother is a hajji. Nice, normal people go to the mosque too."

Putting on a Pink Floyd CD and draining his glass, he reveals fears about the growing split between moderate Muslim Israelis and those who don't think the state should exist. He hurls colorful Arabic insults at certain religious and political leaders for exacerbating intra-Muslim tensions. "Some of our [Arab] Knesset members are only interested in publicity. Everyone in the Knesset denounced the Palestinians for celebrating [after September 11]. Did they? No. How does it look when everyone else in the Knesset signed a letter of sadness to the Americans, but they refused to? I wish they would keep their big mouths shut instead of making trouble for the rest of us." Tarik heaps special criticism on the Israeli Islamic Movement. "Why let them operate freely? We [Israelis] should ban it. Throw them out of the Knesset." He singles out Islamic Movement Knesset member Abdulmalik Dehamshe. "He thinks Habashi is an Islamic martyr. He said he's even willing to be a shahid himself, to die protecting al-Aqsa. He's always stirring up trouble. He says he lives in 'Nazareth, Palestine.' Guys like him sit in the Knesset and call me a traitor for teaching my children to be loyal to Israel."

Palestinian Television broadcasts a children's program seen in Israel called *The Children's Club*. On the show, children surrounded by cartoon characters do the normal sorts of things, mostly singing and dancing, that appear on children's television throughout the world. On *The Children's Club*, however, the lyrics to the songs include (transliterated from Arabic here): "Let us drench the ground with our blood as shahids." Tarik understates when he says, "They're teaching children that Allah will be proud of them if they die trying to kill Jews. Turn on the radio and what do we hear? A sheik saying 'Send your boys to our [Palestinian] summer camp.' Do they teach soccer there? No, they teach them to shoot guns, that putting a bullet in a Jew's head gets them a place in heaven. I heard a [Palestinian] sheik on television saying, 'Blessed is he who puts a vest of explosives on himself or on his children.' My son showed me what he found on the Internet. Arafat's site [www.fatih.net]. It says the killing must continue until the Zionist state is demolished. And what message do Islamic Jihad and Hamas sites have for us [Arab Israelis]? Attack from within. They're asking us to join them, to destroy our lives, to destroy our country."

13

The Bedouin

Tribes, Tents, and Satellite Dishes

⟁ We are not an ethnic group. We are Arabs. Bedouin is a way of life. It is derived from the Arabic word badi, *and its root means "to begin." Originally all humans started out as Bedouin.* —Professor Ismael Abu-Saad, *founding director of the Bedouin Center at Ben-Gurion University of the Negev*

⟁ To be a Bedouin, why does a woman have to be miserable and live in the most humiliating conditions? A Bedouin woman who gets an education doesn't just get a degree. She breaks out of the tribe. She gets freedom of choice, independence for the first time in her life. —Sarab Abu Rabiya, *twenty-five, who has a master's degree from Ben-Gurion University and is a leader of the "quiet Bedouin women's revolution"*

Amal el-Sanna, like most of Israel's nearly two hundred thousand Bedouin, lives in the Negev, the rugged semiarid area that makes up over half the country. She is a descendant of fiercely independent semi-nomadic tribes, people who once roamed the Middle East unobstructed by borders or national allegiances. Although Bedouin are Muslim, most

278

consider their culture distinct. In fact, they often call themselves the People of the Desert, the "original Arabs." In her long, loose dress and white scarf, which obscures her hair and neck, Amal resembles other women in her dusty village, a disarray of homes surrounded by wandering sheep, camels, and goats. She grew up in a four-room white concrete and plaster house, where her mother always seemed to be preparing enormous quantities of food—delectable chicken and eggplant salads, handmade olive oil and yogurt—for her thirteen children and frequent visitors. An old Arabic saying describes the overwhelming hospitality: "A Bedouin will kill his last camel to feed his guests." A generator provides electricity for her eleven-year-old brother's computer, but modernity is a thin veneer. This is a world where extended families watch *Oprah, The Bold and the Beautiful,* and Egyptian soap operas brought in by satellite, yet spend most of the time in the tents in front of their homes. It's a world of poverty and polygamy, where wives squat on the ground washing clothes in plastic buckets while their shared husband chats on a cell phone. It's not unusual for a man to have four wives and thirty children. "We're a Third World people trying to live in a high-tech country," says Amal, twenty-nine, who is part of a growing group of literate, nonnomadic Bedouin. A community worker, she is trying to help her people grapple with a confusing, often traumatic, transition into the twenty-first century.

"People in our [el-Sanna] tribe cried when I was born. They were angry. I was the fifth girl, and they tried to convince my father to take another wife so he could have sons. He didn't take another wife. Instead, he gave me this name, Amal, which means hope, because he had hope he would have sons. My father wanted sons so much, I think that's why he treated me like a boy," confides Amal. "He let me be a shepherd, even thought it's a job for boys. I think he wanted to build my personality, to show me that girls could do something too. I got up at 6:30 every morning and rode a donkey and took the sheep and goats to the fields. Spending my childhood alone with nature, that's when I learned to dream."

Roaming the rocky hills, Amal dreamed of a good education. In her parents' time, if boys went to school, it usually was to learn to read the Koran. Girls stayed home. "My father knows good Arabic and Hebrew. Mother can't read or write; she never went to school. She's much more closed-minded about education than my father. But when I asked him to send me to a good school, a boarding school in Haifa, he wouldn't. He knew the tribe wouldn't permit it, that he would be criticized," she says, describing how Bedouin tribes are still tied tightly to traditions. Bedouin girls are under the strict supervision of fathers or older relatives and rarely go anywhere unescorted.

Her father's dream was realized when her mother later gave him six sons. They sent the eldest to a boarding school. "We [seven girls] always got the leftovers—leftover food, leftover clothes, leftover education," Amal complains. This is a world where some girls are kept out of high school, especially if it means riding to another village on a bus with boys. (One reason census figures for Bedouin are notoriously inaccurate is because when a Bedouin man is asked how many children he has, he sometimes gives the number of *walad,* sons. To arrive at the correct number, a census taker must know to ask about daughters.) Although every Israeli child is entitled to twelve years of free education, Negev Bedouin have Israel's highest dropout rates: over 50 percent of the boys don't complete high school; for girls, the number rises to nearly 70 percent. After their daughters turn thirteen, few fathers want them in school with boys, who could pose a threat to their daughters' virginity and their family's honor. After the fifth grade, most girls are forced to remain at home helping with their many siblings until their fathers arrange their marriages. Fathers, few of whom have finished high school, know that not many prospective husbands will pay a decent dowry for an educated bride.

Amal, however, wanted to go to high school. The closest one was a half hour away in Tel Sheva, built in 1967 in an attempt to urbanize Negev Bedouin. "The tribe said no girl can go to high school. My father told them, 'This is your rule, not mine. I'm going to send her.' He had a big fight with them. I was glad he had the courage to stand up to them," Amal says. "Once I started studying, the classes turned out to be terrible," a consequence of Bedouin schools' substandard facilities, grossly inadequate budgets, and desperate lack of certified Bedouin teachers. "The teachers were so bad, I knew more than some of them. The guy who was supposed to teach us English hardly knew it; he only had a high school diploma. I started becoming a troublemaker about then, and organized strikes. Keeping quiet about our frustrations didn't get us much. Look at the situation in the unrecognized villages."

She's referring to the remote encampments and shantytowns scattered over the Negev, where it's not uncommon to see a Bedouin girl balancing a water bucket on her head while her brother sits on a rock reading a book. Educational problems are especially acute for these children. "School" often is a tin or wooden shack, sometimes so overcrowded that children study in shifts. Afterward, some do homework by a campfire or in a tent by flashlight. Living far from paved roads, the closest high school is often a long walk or bus journey away. Their semipermanent "homes" receive no running water, sewage, electricity, or phone lines since the government considers them illegally built on state land. Because their roaming herds get in the way of military training and air force bases, kibbutz fields, towns and factories, and nature reserves, Israel's Ministerial Committee for the Advancement of Bedouin Affairs (affiliated with the Ministry of National Infrastructure) has been trying to convince the Bedouin to relocate to the seven towns and villages it has built, which have schools, clinics, and other social services.

Despite the hardships, roughly half the Negev Bedouin steadfastly refuse to leave their unrecognized tent and shack encampments. They're challenging the government, claiming they're living on lands where they've traditionally pitched their tents and grazed their animals. Under Israeli law, however, land must be formally registered and taxes must be paid, concepts that were unknown to most traditional Bedouin. (In most Middle Eastern countries, Bedouin have no land rights, only users' privileges.) Angry land disputes have been going on for decades, with Bedouin growing more alienated each time the state demolishes unlicensed buildings. In 2002, the government made moves to recognize seven of the encampments and to improve inadequate infrastructure in the towns. "Wherever Bedouin live, our big need is education," stresses Amal. "Ninety-nine percent of our women over forty are illiterate. We have to convince them that learning is a right they have, so they'll want all their children—including the girls—to be educated."

At age sixteen, even before she finished high school, Amal recruited her sisters and girlfriends to teach Bedouin women in her village to read and write. "First, I had to convince the husbands to let us hold classes in the village social hall because it's for 'men only.' They don't like their wives outside the house, so I told them we wanted to teach them to read the Koran. Learning the Koran is allowed because it's the message from God. Slowly, they gave their consent and started escorting the women to and from class. We have women in our classes who hardly ever leave their homes. They don't travel to town on their own. They can't read a street sign. That's why many neighborhoods go by numbers, not names. Well, I'm proud to say that my mother, who couldn't even read a word, is in the third grade."

They cautiously teach other subjects, from basic first aid—not to use toothpaste or camel dung to treat burns—to household chores. "Women don't know what a washing machine is," Amal continues. "They have to learn how to put clothes in the washing machine, to put meat in the refrigerator, and to organize a house. We don't want men to stop our classes, so we're careful not to teach ideas like asking men to help with the housework. We're a traditional society and we're still going through a very radical transformation. In other places in the world, it took centuries to make the transition from tribal tents to permanent homes. We were forced to do it overnight. When the government decided that we should live in villages, my mother went through a huge shift in lifestyle. She was used to living in a tent and her mother used to sew them. Grandma kept her veil on when she rode a horse. My mother was raised with cows and camels, sheep and goats. Women milked the animals and prepared all the food, sewed the clothes, wove the rugs, and helped men with the harvest. Each woman was like a whole factory and the men were there to help. Between the animals and the children, women were active partners with men. It's not like that these days," says Amal, who emphasizes that the drastic transition from nomadic life to permanent settlements has made women "regress into modernity," no longer able to herd flocks in the desert, where they aren't in danger of meeting male strangers. "Since we moved to villages and towns, women are no longer men's partners or helpers. They're no longer productive. They're unemployed prisoners in concrete desert houses, trapped behind four walls without land, sheep, or cows. They sit on mats making food on small fires. The only thing left for them to do is to get married and have children."

Amal sighs. "My mother and grandmother didn't learn in school, but they knew many beautiful stories and poems. When they brought water from the well, they used to sing 'I'm like a gazelle on the mountains.' It's about freedom."

Pressured by groups of Bedouin and Jewish activists and fearful of a growing Bedouin attraction to Islamic parties, the government slowly has been improving and building Bedouin schools and offering student scholarships. Amal recalls, "When my older sister received a scholarship to study at a teachers college in Beersheva, my father drove her to school and back every day because girls aren't allowed to go anywhere unescorted. People in our village were shocked. They couldn't understand why he'd send a daughter of marriageable age to school in the city. They made his life miserable. They called her a prostitute. They said they'd kill her if he didn't take her out of school. But my father was brave and let her finish." When Amal received a scholarship to study at Ben-Gurion University and live in a dormitory, her father faced an even worse predicament. A Bedouin girl living alone with no older relative to chaperone? He refused. When Amal threatened to go on a hunger strike, he relented. His intractable daughter became the first Bedouin woman student to live in the dorms. She stood out; there were only two other Bedouin women on campus. By 2003, there were 178 Bedouin women and 171 Bedouin men, largely thanks to a Jewish American philanthropist who funds the university's Center for Bedouin Studies and Development. Its founding director, Ismael Abu-Saad, lives in Amal's village. This son of an illiterate mother and a truck driver went on to become a professor of education. The Center offers Bedouin students tutoring in Hebrew and English as well as help overcoming culture shock, such as seeing lovers holding hands and female students challenging male professors and leading strikes. "In my village, everyone is surprised by how forward I am," says Amal. "Compared to the Jewish students, I'm not. I learned to take things from Jewish culture, to be open to other ideas. And how to nudge."

Nudging is a useful skill for Amal, who uses it to raise funds for projects ranging from a children's mobile library to summer camps for deaf children. Bedouin women now run several money-making projects. The Desert Embroidery started with only a handful of women from the el-Sanna tribe; today, more than two hundred women from all over the Negev make bags, wall hangings, and place mats for export. For quite a few women—those who have been abandoned, divorced, or widowed—embroidering is their main income. These women, from bickering tribes, work for the same cooperative, but not together, mostly from their homes. As part of the "quiet women's revolution," Amal trains Bedouin parasocial workers (high school graduates) to teach Bedouin women— and advises them to proceed cautiously before meeting their students. Bedouin from feuding tribes are uncomfortable sharing the same class-room. Some have trouble accepting a teacher from a rival tribe.

"*Hamula* [the tribe] is everything," explains Amal. The hamula are traditional networks of extended families, allegiances that govern the so-cial and political lives of most Arabs and Druze. Ask a Negev Bedouin where he's from and the answer is usually the name of the clan, not the village, scarcely surprising in a culture only a generation or two removed from nomadism. During elections, it's not unusual for a clan leader to approach each candidate and ask what he'll get in return for all the clan's votes. "Everything is loyalty to blood, loyalty to the clan, loyalty to the hamula. The hamula determines what man you can marry," adds Amal. According to Arab tribal tradition, a father who permits his daughter to marry outside the family is disgraced for not protecting the "purity of his daughter's womb." Flouting this tradition could even cost a woman her life. Amal learned this firsthand when she fell in love with a lawyer from a small tribe in a nearby village. "It was unacceptable that I would marry from outside our tribe. Everyone was very sad and tried to stop the mar-riage. My mother was afraid. All my uncles and brothers agreed to sup-port her. They said, 'We'll kill her. If she wants to marry a lawyer, she should marry her cousin.' One week before our wedding, someone burned my father's car." Undeterred, Amal married her first love and they moved to Beersheva, where she counsels women, many of whom were forced to marry relatives. More and more, some brave Bedouin women who have fallen in love with men from "inferior" tribes have run away with them, occasionally abroad.

The custom of marrying relatives, which long predates Islam, pre-serves the power of the tribe and persists among Muslim and Druze Is-raelis. Because tribal dynasties are determined by the male line, brothers commonly arrange for their children to marry each other. Marriages to cousins or uncles also ensure that dowries and inheritances remain within the family; however, they also mean birth defects, which are com-mon in nearly every Muslim and Druze community. The rates are espe-cially high among the Bedouin, about 70 percent of whom marry family members. Geneticists from Soroka Hospital in Beersheva train Bedouin high school graduates, Muslim clergy, and tribal leaders who then go to every Bedouin high school and community center to communicate the genetic dangers of marrying family members, but often the message is ignored. Many, perhaps most Bedouin would rather gamble on genetic risks than marry outside the family and thereby damage tribal honor, the "purity" of the family and the daughter. Bedouin counselors urge women to go to gynecologists and test for genetic disorders in fetuses.

"It's hard, because everyone always says *inshallah* [if God wills]," says a Bedouin counselor who works in a village health center and asked not to be identified. She is well aware that she is up against the prevalent fatalistic belief that Allah controls all that happens. A recent *fatwa*, a Muslim religious ruling, by a Jerusalem cleric allows women to have abortions, but only within four months of conception. "Family planning is another difficult topic," continues the counselor, who points out that the Bedouin birthrate is the highest in Israel and has grown more than tenfold since 1948. "People believe that God is generous, that Allah will provide, that 'a hundred children can be nourished by one dish.' Even so, more and more women ask us about IUDs or birth control pills. We know that some of them have to hide the pills from their husbands." Their husbands, she adds, want more children and often rely on the monthly government allowance that increases progressively with each child. A Bedouin family with ten children can receive more than $650 a month.

Traditionally, women gave birth at home; nowadays, about 60 percent of the mothers in the maternity ward at Soroka Medical Center in Beersheva are Bedouin. A few appear more often than every nine months; in fact, not long ago, medical personnel discovered that one patient had been in labor only three months earlier. Looking into it, they learned the woman was a Palestinian Bedouin, using a borrowed Israeli identity card. Soon afterward, computer records revealed another miracle in the maternity ward: a pregnant woman's blood type mysteriously had "changed" since the last time she was in labor. Such scams are only the "tip of the iceberg" according to hospital officials and police. Expectant women cross the nearby Palestinian borders from both the West Bank and Gaza. With identity cards borrowed from Israeli Bedouin kin, they can give birth in a modern Israeli hospital and also receive a $250 state maternity grant. As part of the arrangement, the actual Israeli Bedouin card owner becomes eligible for an additional monthly government check until the child turns eighteen.

Delivery room nurses sometimes recognize those fathers who are frequent visitors to the maternity ward. One sixty-seven-year-old sheik has six wives who have given him fifty-nine children. He married his youngest wife when she was fourteen; her father forced her to marry him. Nearly half of Bedouin are in polygamous relationships, which are becoming more, rather than less, popular. "Young men, especially those who earn salaries, want more wives," the counselor notes. "It is something like a status symbol." In February 2003, just before the Iraq War, one man drove his pickup truck to the Home Command in Beersheva to pick up twenty-two gas masks for his children and his two wives. Some men sneak wives in from Gaza, the West Bank, and Jordan. Some wives complain that their husbands don't have enough money for their children but somehow find money (a dowry is about $10,000) for a younger wife. Because Israeli law forbids polygamy, only one wife in a polygamous family can have an official marriage certificate. Men circumvent the rule by marrying their other "wives" in a ceremony presided over by a sheik; it is not illegal for a "husband" to have several girlfriends living in his house. The inequality between the legal wife and the other women (and the legitimate versus the illegitimate children) is not only built in, but sanctified.

"A lot of women are afraid to open their mouths to complain even if they are beaten. They don't want to have another wife take their place, or their husband to prefer the sons of the other wives." Many are afraid they will be pushed aside by a second, third, or fourth wife. If the husband marries a fifth wife, which is contrary to the laws of Islam, or if he simply wants to get rid of a wife, he can divorce her unofficially. Even after a "divorce," many women stay in his home and obey him, fearing they will be thrown out of the house and lose their children. "Many women think polygamy is legal in Israel, like it is in some other countries in the Middle East," says Amal. "They don't understand their legal rights, so we try to help them."

———————

At first glance, it's not evident that Rahat is, by some rankings, the poorest town in Israel. The unofficial capital of the Bedouin of the

Negev, Rahat has wide streets, streetlights, soccer fields, and basketball courts. There's a small shopping center with signs in Arabic and Cyrillic. Bargain prices attract Russian customers from Beersheva and from as far away as Ashkelon. The cell phone and auto parts stores and butcher do a brisk business. At an ultramodern science center, teenage boys and girls in headscarves attend extracurricular classes in biology, math, physics, and computer skills. Neighboring Kibbutz Shuval has been running bilingual kindergarten classes for years. Jewish and Bedouin children and parents often visit each others' homes and celebrate Jewish and Muslim holidays together. Nearly every multistory house in Rahat sits on about a quarter acre of land, has a satellite dish on top, a car and a tent in front. Behind the scenes, however, life here is another story.

When the first Bedouin theater group in Israel opened in Rahat in 2001, not many audience members ever had seen a live play. In fact, not many had been in mixed company; this is a town where many parents refuse to send their daughters to the coed high school, so they keep them at home. Since the first performance, the amateur actors, all young men, have continued to put on more plays that very subtly explore sensitive topics: polygamy, violence between tribes, the failing educational system, unemployment, crime, and drugs, problems that plague the inhabitants of Rahat, where about 65 percent of the residents live below the poverty line. At the bank on the 20th and 28th of each month, men wearing keffiyahs wait in long lines to pick up unemployment, disability, child, and old-age checks.

Before the government established Rahat in 1972, it tried learning from past mistakes it had made designing other Bedouin towns. Planners let families build their own homes in tribally homogeneous neighborhoods. Still, they failed, reports Ismael Abu-Saad, who volunteers at the Center for Bedouin Studies and Development at Ben-Gurion University and is a full-time professor developing educational, social, and medical programs to help alievate Bedouin problems, many of which he blames on the government's policy of forced urbanization. "Planners didn't understand that a Bedouin needs to be able to set up his tent or temporary shack and draw camel or goat milk. It's all part of the culture. You can't maintain such a culture in an urban environment. They didn't understand that Bedouin have flocks, sometimes multiple wives, many children, and don't like living in houses next to each other."

Forty-five-year-old Abu-Saad was born in a tent, the eldest of eleven children. He rode a donkey seven miles to the nearest school, which was in a shack. "We had one teacher for four classes. He also was the nurse and the janitor. First grade was the first row, second grade was the second row, third grade was the third row, and so on." Because local high schools were so bad, he was sent to a boarding school near Tel Aviv. The first Negev Bedouin to obtain a Ph.D., he has spent his professional career either teaching or setting up innovative educational projects such as the very successful Budding Scientists Program, which prepares Bedouin high school students for careers in physics, engineering, agriculture, and medicine. "Although Bedouin make up about a quarter of the Negev population—and our community is growing by 5.5 percent each year—we continue to be kept out of the Negev's planning process. Why are there over a hundred Jewish agricultural settlements in the Negev and not a single Bedouin one?"

Rahat, which has grown to about thirty-five thousand Bedouin and ten thousand sheep, is rife with clan rivalries and blood feuds. Under Bedouin law, for example, relatives of a murdered man can attack any male member of the murderer's family, all the way up to a fifth-degree male relative with absolutely no connection to the crime. Then there are the animosities between the Bedouin, originally from the Arabian Peninsula, who consider themselves the "desert elite" and who look down on the landless *fellaheen* (peasants), and Muslims who immigrated to the Negev in the nineteenth century from other areas of Palestine and the Nile valley and became their tenant sharecroppers. With pasture lands shrinking and high unemployment because of the second intifada, competition for scarce jobs is fierce: unskilled men are having trouble finding work in factories or construction or driving buses, trucks, and agricultural machinery.

As conditions worsen, conservative tribal elders are losing their authority. Juvenile delinquency, car thefts, vandalism and alcoholism, drug abuse—problems that used to be relatively rare among the Bedouin—are rampant. Bedouin men have been caught smuggling prostitutes, arms, and narcotics across the borders with the West Bank, Gaza, and Egypt. (There's a Bedouin saying, "God and the state exist up to Beersheva; south of Beersheva the desert knows no law.") "There was no such thing as a Bedouin junkie a decade ago," reports Abu-Saad. "The drug trade means making easy money and has created a new type of young Bedouin, a criminal." Some Bedouin whose fathers rode camels are driving Mercedes paid for with drug money.

As much as drugs, Abu-Saad worries about the surge toward religious fundamentalism, a worry shared by many other Israelis. Rahat has an Islamic mayor. The Islamic Movement and other militant anti-Israeli Islamic groups are also strong in the six other Bedouin towns and villages, where their members sit on town councils and fill a void by running preschools and recreation and antidrug programs and building mosques. In recent elections, more than half the Negev Bedouin voted for the Islamic Movement. Sheik Ra'ed Salah's radical northern movement is also making a concerted effort in the Negev. Such groups never were part of conservative Bedouin society until the past few years, according to Abu-Saad. "The Bedouin community has always been uncomplaining and patient. Since Israel was born, we Bedouin have been good, loyal Israelis. We volunteered for the army and voted for Zionist parties hoping that we would be treated fairly. What did we get in return? Neglect. That's why a peaceful community is becoming hostile. When people are desperate, they turn to religion, and some of them are becoming fanatics. We're seeing more Bedouin identifying with religious extremists."

It starts in the schools. With a serious shortage of certified Bedouin teachers for the exploding Bedouin population, the Ministry of Education has been sending Arabic-speaking teachers and principals from other parts of the country who volunteer to teach in Negev Bedouin schools. Some are Muslim fundamentalists who discourage Bedouin boys from volunteering for army service and bar Bedouin IDF recruiters from entering high schools. In 1998, a Bedouin leader of the Islamic Movement from Rahat issued a religious decree that Bedouin and Arab citizens were prohibited from serving in the IDF. The fatwa calls any Arab or Bedouin who does so a "heretic" who will be shunned by Muslims until he quits the army. In addition, members of the Islamic Movement, dominant on most Negev Bedouin town councils, make it hard for released soldiers to find jobs. Abu-Saad says that increasing numbers of Bedouin youth "do not believe in the state or in the government. They're alienated. Simply fed up with all the empty promises." Recent studies support him: 75 percent of Bedouin teenagers in the Negev would rather sit in jail than serve in the army if faced with that choice. Nearly 50 percent say that Israel has no right to exist. Only 17 percent say they identify themselves as Israelis. Of all the Arab Israelis surveyed in 2001, Negev Bedouin are the most frustrated, alienated, and radical.

Since the beginning of the state, Bedouin soldiers have excelled as skilled trackers in border patrol units, detecting terrorists who infiltrate across the borders and helping combat soldiers find their way. Most are northern Bedouin, the nearly seventy thousand who live in the Galilee and the Jezreel Valley, whose tribes once roamed the Syrian desert. Not only do they have very different backgrounds and speak different Arabic than Negev Bedouin; they are more prosperous and more urbanized. During the British Mandate, many purchased small farms, which they recorded in the Land Registry. They generally have closer ties to the state than the Negev Bedouin. In the struggle for independence, many northern Bedouin joined the Jewish forces and served on the front lines. Their sons and grandsons proudly continued this tradition, believing that army service is part of their Bedouin "blood pact" with the state. In the Galilee near Nazareth, there is a stone memorial honoring the many Bedouin soldiers who have died defending Israel.

When Sergeant Major Khalil Taher was killed in an explosion during his IDF duty on the Lebanese border in November 2000, the imam of the al-Jezera Mosque in the Old City of Acre refused to conduct the religious funeral service. Not one mosque official in Acre would announce Taher's death or read Koranic verses in his memory. When this Bedouin soldier's coffin was draped with an Israeli flag, most Muslims left the funeral. During the days of mourning, many Jews, but hardly any Arabs, made condolence calls on the family. The extended family are treated like outcasts by non-Bedouin Muslims of Acre. "Enough is enough," said Ahmed Taher, Khalil's brother, who, like all the males in the family, has served in the IDF. "Enough is enough. No one came to comfort us, people ignore us in the streets, at weddings no one will stand near us. We want to move out of Acre."

Other Bedouin soldiers have been refused burial in Muslim cemeteries because they died fighting for the "Zionist enemy," and their families also have been ostracized. Few Bedouin dare wear their army uniforms anymore when they visit their villages and towns. When their mothers wash their uniforms, they rarely hang them outside because Bedouin families have been threatened by their Israeli Muslim neighbors. During this intifada, their numbers have fallen to an all-time low.

"If the government continues to ignore our problems," warns Professor Abu-Saad, "the next intifada could come from the Bedouin."

14

The Druze

Between Modernity and Tradition

> ↩ *It doesn't matter what's on your head. What counts is what's in it.* —Fahmi Halabi, first Druze woman to become a village council member

The cherry orchards are empty. The tractors are parked. The café is closed. The mood is unusually somber. Weeping men in Israeli army uniforms stand by wives and daughters who wear traditional long dark dresses and diaphanous white headscarves and who look like Muslim Arabs. "He was first a soldier of Israel and then my son," a father says in Arabic, describing the well-known Druze readiness to sacrifice their lives defending the state. Nearby, more than fifty tombstones have the same sentences carved in Arabic and Hebrew: "Fell in the line of duty." As he leans over the nineteen-year-old's fresh grave, he takes comfort in knowing his son will return. This postcard-pretty village in the Upper Galilee nestled at the base of Mount Meron is typical of most Israeli Druze villages. However, the nine thousand Druze residents of Beit Jann have lost a higher proportion of their soldier-sons than any other place in Israel and tales of their courage in combat abound. Druze are famous for their fearlessness in the face of death. They believe in the immortality of every Druze soul, that they are brief sojourners in this world.

Nearly one million Druze live in four adjoining countries. Because their religion teaches that they must be loyal to the country in which they live, at times they've met at the barrel of a gun, wearing Israeli or Lebanese or Syrian or Jordanian uniforms. Occasionally, Druze even find themselves fighting deceased relatives: after a Druze dies, his or her soul enters the body of a newborn Druze of the same sex. This belief in next lifetimes can create some formidable dilemmas. "I can be an IDF soldier in this life, but I can be reborn as a Lebanese or Syrian and grow up to be a soldier," explains a Druze lieutenant. When his cousin served in the IDF he had a serious problem: he couldn't bear to be near tanks. He believed that, in a previous incarnation, he was a Syrian Druze soldier and an Israeli tank had crushed him to death. Reincarnation is a key tenet of the mysterious Druze religion.

In Daliat al-Carmel, the largest Druze village in Israel, atop the Carmel Mountains, the atmosphere also is subdued. The thirteen thousand residents are grieving over a twelve-year-old girl killed by a suicide bomber on a Haifa bus in April 2003. A stately sheik in a long black robe, white turban, and white beard oversees his crafts shop on the main street. Hanging from the walls are colorful weavings and wicker baskets made by local Druze women. This formidable-looking man is an *uqaal*, an enlightened religious knower, a watcher over the secrets of the religion. Only a select few are allowed to know the closely guarded teachings of the religion, which broke from Islam in eleventh-century Cairo. He divulges very little. Much of the religion is kept hidden from the outside world as well as from most Druze, who are allowed to know only a simplified version of the faith. However, his son, Fadel Nasralden, a twenty-eight-year-old Sylvester Stallone lookalike in a slick black leather jacket, is eager to talk. He too knows the inner meanings of the six holy books, but as a lapsed uqaal he is no longer bound to participate in the prayer services or follow all the exacting ethical codes. "I used to be very religious. Not anymore. There are a lot of rules. Strict rules. We can't drink. We can't swear. We can't smoke. Men can't talk with women. We can't go to discos. I want my sons to live in today's world," he says, answering his cell phone again. In this village near Haifa, where nearly every roof has a satellite dish, a cell phone is just about as exotic as a toothbrush. "Being Druze is more than our religion, it's our way of life," he adds. "We are forbidden from marrying non-Druze. And if someone wants to convert to our religion, they can't. You are born into it. If someone wants to convert out of our religion, they can't. That's why our communities have stayed together."

For almost a thousand years, Druze have practiced strict endogamy. Proselytizing is forbidden, so in theory no new members have been admitted since 1043. Marriages outside this ethnoreligious group are strictly forbidden. A Druze who marries a non-Druze is excommunicated and thrown out of the village. In 2001, Druze religious leaders in the Golan Heights demanded the expulsion of all primary and secondary school children who have one non-Druze parent. The Israeli Ministry of Education refused. Druze parents staged a strike and the children were transferred to other schools. A few months later, religious leaders pressed to have two popular high school biology teachers dismissed. Their sins: one has a Christian wife and the other has a Druze father and a Jewish mother. Druze even frown on marriage to a member of a rival hamula. As a Druze saying goes, "It's better to marry a poor relative than a wealthy stranger." More than a third of marriages are to close relatives, and in more conservative villages the rate rises to half. As a result, and as with the Bedouin, rates of birth defects and retardation among Druze children are high. "Until recently, everyone had an arranged marriage, within the hamula. We didn't know about genetic problems. Children had mental problems and bone problems," Fadel reports. "Now we're becoming more careful about who we marry." And they need to be; Druze are monogamous. Although divorce is now allowed, the couple are forbidden to see each other ever again.

The Israeli government officially designates the Druze as a separate religious community, which means they have their own religious courts, which oversee marriage, divorce, alimony, property, and other matters, and those courts, in accordance with Druze religious law, accord equality to men and women. A woman can initiate divorce proceedings and has the right to her own property; if a young mother dies, her children and property revert to a woman on her side of the family. However, like Muslims, Druze are strongly patrilineal and, like Islamic judges, Druze religious judges often rule in favor of men. A man can initiate divorce if his wife fails to bear children, especially sons. And if a widow remarries, her late husband's family frequently gets custody of her children.

As Fadel speaks, he moves toward the back of the shop. "When customers are curious about Druze heritage, I bring them here." Worn bur-
gundy-colored Persian carpets cover the spacious floor. There is no
furniture. "Each Sunday and Thursday night, religious Druze pray in a
room like this. It's called the *khalwa* [house of retreat]. When we pray,
we are separate from the women and don't face any special direction like
Mecca or Jerusalem. For us, prayer is a privilege, not a duty." A huge
Druze flag hangs on a far wall. Each of the five stripes represents the
traits of a Druze holy prophet. Red denotes bravery and courage; green,
land and nature; yellow, knowledge and englightenment; white, peace
and reconciliation; blue, tolerance, forgiveness, and fraternity. He moves
toward a five-sided Druze star, the symbol of the religion. "You see this
star everywhere Druze gather. It is very important that we always speak
the truth and keep our promises. And we must protect each other because all Druze are responsible for each other." There are no Druze religious splinter groups as in Judaism, Islam, and Christianity; however,
like other Israeli Jewish and Muslim communities, Druze are highly fac-
tionalized and politicized. They are divided along clan, village, and regional lines. Fadel draws attention to a picture of the Tomb of Prophet
Jethro, the holiest site for all Druze. Jethro is the biblical figure whom
Druze revere. Every April 25, many of Israel's one hundred thousand
Druze set out to visit the tomb five miles west of Tiberias near an extinct
volcano at the Sea of Galilee. "Prophet Jethro was Moses' father-in-law,"
elaborates Fadel. "Moses married his daughter Zippora. So, in a way,
we're connected to the Jews."

The Druze sect was founded by two Cairene preachers: a Persian
Afghani called Hamza ibn Ali and a Turk called Muhammad al-Darazi,
whose name ("tailor" in Arabic) is the likely source for the term
"Druze." They taught a belief in one God who has been revealed several
times in human form, starting with Adam, and that the ruler of the Fa-
timid Empire, Caliph al-Hakim, a Shiite Muslim with an Orthodox
Christian mother, was the most perfect revelation of God. Before Caliph
al-Hakim mysteriously vanished near Cairo in 1021 C.E. he ordered
his troops to destroy Jerusalem's Church of the Holy Sepulcher. After
descending to earth in human guise to found the Druze religion (a mix
of Judaism, Christian mysticism, Shiite Islam, Persian Zoroastrianism,

Gnosticism, Messianism, and Hindu-like reincarnation beliefs), he ascended to heaven. Druze believe that in a thousand years, al-Hakim will return to usher in the "Golden Age."

Persecuted by Muslims for their "heretical" beliefs, early Druze followers fled Egypt and settled in isolated, defensible mountain villages in what is now Syria, Lebanon, and northern Israel. For centuries, they were a maltreated minority in the Arab Middle East. Many Druze Israelis stress that they are a separate ethnoreligious group that became Arabized. In flawless Hebrew, Fadel emphasizes, "We speak Arabic, we eat the same foods, like the same music. A lot of us have names that could be Muslim or Christian, but we're not Arabs." Druze ethnic origins are unknown; they may be a mix of Persian, Kurdish, Turkish, and Crusaders, who often had Druze as guides and allies in battles against the Muslims. Some Druze, especially those from villages near Acre, the former Crusader capital, have fair complexions, light hair, and blue or green eyes.

Stepping outside the shop, Fadel surveys the scene. Even though Druze don't observe the Jewish Sabbath, few cars move. This is a typical Shabbat traffic jam. Since intifada II, Jews avoid outings to most Arab villages yet continue to visit picturesque Daliat al-Carmel, named after the surrounding vineyards (Daliat is Arabic for "vine") and known for its lively bazaar and scrumptious food. Under a Lucky Strike sign, Druze and Jewish soldiers eat take-out *shwarma* and *shishlik*. Druze are the only non-Jewish group of Israelis who perform compulsory military service. Many Druze men opt for military careers; their salaries and pensions often are the only support for their large extended families. Druze make up about one quarter of the Border Police and serve in elite IDF units.

In September 2000, more than three thousand Druze flocked to the western Galilee village of Abu Snan to honor Yosef Mishlab, the first Druze major general in the IDF. As Home Front Commander, one of his responsibilities was distributing gas masks. Why did so many Druze show up? "To demonstrate our pride in the highest-ranking officer in our history," according to Zeidan Atashi, a Druze commentator on Arab affairs for Israel Television and a former Knesset member. In his book *Druze and Jews in Israel: A Shared Destiny?* he describes the origins of the Druze "blood pact" with the Jews. In 1942, the Muslim Waqf, supported by the Arab Higher Committee headed by Hitler sympathizer Haj

Amin el-Husseini, the Mufti of Jerusalem, demanded control of Jethro's Tomb. Druze in Syria, Lebanon, and Mandatory Palestine were outraged and petitioned Muslim leaders as well as British officials. In 1945, British courts allowed Druze to retain control of the tomb, but the controversy caused an irreparable rift with Muslim nationalists. During the 1947–49 Arab-Israeli War, Druze were under great pressure to join in Muslim attacks on the Jews. Facing the choice of living as a minority in a Muslim state or living as a minority in a Jewish state, many Druze allied with and, in some cases, fought with the Jewish Hagana. (So did some Syrian Druze soldiers who defected and became Israeli.) Unlike most Palestinian Arabs, Druze did not become refugees and their villages and lands remained intact. (During the war, hundreds of Arab families who fled or were uprooted from their own villages found refuge in Druze villages.) In the mid-1950s, as Israel continued to face repeated Arab threats, Druze clan leaders appealed to then Defense Minister David Ben-Gurion to draft them. Today, a higher proportion of Druze than Jews serve in the IDF.

Druze have served in the Knesset and the cabinet and the UN. Druze in the Foreign Ministry served as ambassadors to Vietnam and Portugal. Druze are poets, yacht builders, and a veteran journalist was news director at Israel Television until 2003. Because they are so trusted and favored by the Jews, Muslims often resent them, especially Druze soldiers. When a group of Muslim swimmers in the Sea of Galilee spotted a Druze wearing a military dog tag, they beat him, saying he was "worse than a Jew because he speaks our language." In summer 2001, about one hundred Druze Israelis met in Amman, Jordan, with Jordanian, Lebanese, and Syrian Druze leaders who urged them to refuse to serve in the Israeli army. Druze Israeli leaders lashed out and told them to stop interfering, pointing out that there are hundreds of Arab Muslim and Christian volunteers in the Israeli army. Former Druze cabinet member Saleh Tarif accused controversial Arab Israeli Knesset member Azmi Bishara, who helped set up the conference, of making a "cynical and deliberate attempt to cause friction between Druze in [the rest of] the Middle East and Druze in Israel. Over 99 percent of us still feel like Israelis in every sense of the word."

Some Druze complain that when they're out of uniform, they don't feel very Israeli. Walid, a Druze teacher, was waiting at a bus stop on his way to report to army reserve duty when a suspicious police officer questioned him. "Jews look at us as Arabs and the Arabs call us the buddies of the Jews," he relates with unbridled resentment. "When I get my military call-up letter, I'm a Druze, but when we ask for more sewers, we're treated like Arabs." That discomforting encounter helped spur Walid's alienation. He now calls himself a Palestinian citizen of Israel and urges young Druze to identify with Arab Israelis and join their protests demanding more equitable government funding for their thirteen towns and villages. No longer do young Druze live complacently in isolated villages, he asserts. "We get around. I see the cars my Jewish friends drive. I've been to their nice homes in Tel Aviv and Haifa. At least they serve in the army. Those haredim, the government showers them with money. Do their boys shed their blood? My grandfather fought with the Jews in 1948. I fought in the last intifada and now I'm back in this one."

Another case of mistaken identity received attention in the Hebrew press, eliciting national outrage. After a spate of terror attacks near Haifa in 2001, a Druze couple pushing their baby stroller in the Grand Canyon Mall were assaulted verbally and physically by a group of Jews who mistook them for Arabs. The husband was an off-duty IDF soldier serving on the Golan Heights.

The twenty thousand Druze living on the Golan Heights keenly feel the dilemma of life in a region where borders are in flux and drawn with either a gun or a pen. After Syrian tanks invaded Israel during the 1967 War, Israel captured the strategically important Golan Heights, from which Syrian soldiers easily fired on Israeli kibbutzim. Muslim residents (except for Bedouin) fled to Syria; Druze remained in their four villages. Despite historic enmity against the Syrians, quite a few Golan Druze patriotically call themselves Syrian Arabs and wave Syrian flags. Those who openly show signs of loyalty to Israel realize that their relatives across the border may be treated as traitors (some six hundred thousand Druze live in Syria) and they too may suffer retribution if Israel returns the Golan Heights to Syria. Although flyers circulate with the warning "Death to the treacherous collaborators, wherever they are found," there are Golan Druze who have taken Israeli citizenship. A recent poll illustrates their paradox: when Druze high school students were asked where they wanted to live if Syria regains sovereignty, 75 percent said they want to remain Israeli. As a Druze teacher put it, "Why would I want to earn $72 a month in Syria when I make over $1,000 here?" Druze dislike this well-known joke: "Why does the Druze flag have an upper end and a lower end? The upper is to wave at the conqueror when he arrives and the lower end is to jab at his butt when he leaves."

It is not unusual to see photos of the president of Syria, Bashar Assad, displayed in the homes and shops of Golan Druze. Quite a few have relatives in Daliat al-Carmel, whose shops display Israeli flags and whose owners vote for Labor or Likud or the Communist parties. Daliat al-Carmel was founded 250 years ago by Druze mostly from Syria. Despite political differences, feelings of Druze kinship are strong; what happens in one part of the Druze community reverberates throughout. "The Druze are like a copper tray. If you hit it on one side the whole tray resounds," a popular maxim goes. "Wherever we live, however we vote, all Druze are brothers. We're good at adapting to changing conditions. Now we're trying to preserve our traditions and lead a modern life at the same time," Fadel continues. "It's not easy for guys like me, so just figure how it is for those girls." Near him, a Druze teenager, indistinguishable from secular Israeli Jews and Muslims with her makeup and tight Levi's, shows a girlfriend her mauve nail polish. "At their age, it's especially hard having feet in two cultures." On the corner, a lanky Druze soldier with a black beret and an M-16 chats with a Jewish female soldier. At the base and away from curious Druze eyes, they might date, even sleep together.

If seventeen-year-old Salwa is thinking about dating, no one must know. "I have a boyfriend, but we don't go out together. Our religion forbids it. When I want to have fun, I go to the [Haifa] mall with my girlfriends. And to the movies too. Boys and girls can be together, but it must be in the house and only if they're engaged." Right now, she's thinking about Brad Pitt, searching for a spot on her bedroom wall to tape up another poster of the movie star. Along with young Bedouin in the Negev and Islamic fundamentalists in Umm al-Fahm, this animated high school senior has a love affair going with television. "It's my life. I watch it at least two hours a day. Mostly American programs like *The Bold and the Beautiful*, because most Arabic programs are silly. And watching them is the best way to learn English." Salwa (not her real name) manages to speak excellent English and chew gum without entangling it in her braces. "I adore the movie channel. I just saw *Pretty Woman* again." Julia

Roberts as a lovable hooker who turns respectable is, of course, only a screen fantasy, but never more than to the Druze. In Druze culture, even the word "sex" is taboo. Volunteer sex educators who teach Druze high school girls gingerly substitute words like "family education," "hygiene," or "puberty." Pre- and extramarital sex are forbidden, considered prostitution. Druze women are forbidden to expose any part of the body that might arouse male passion. The honor of Druze women is so sacrosanct that they are not required to have photos on official Israeli documents; Druze religious judges waive the requirement because having her picture taken means shaming a woman's honor. "I will live at home until I marry. All of us do, that is not questioned," explains Salwa. In Druze villages, where stone houses are unlocked, there are few secrets. Is there any place to go where you shouldn't be? "Yes," she whispers. "To meet secretly, I hear that if you have a boyfriend, the community center is a good place." Such meetings are daring. Malicious gossip can cost a woman her life. If a woman is dishonored or raped, her relatives may take "appropriate" actions. Druze and Muslim women who have shamed their family become potential victims of family "honor killings."

Nearly everyone here knows the story of Ibtihaj Hassan. When she was a teenager, her family arranged her marriage with a local Druze man. After their divorce, she committed the transgression of moving away. But then she committed an unpardonable sin: she married outside the faith, a Bedouin. Years went by. Convinced by her younger brother that her family had forgiven her, she returned to Daliat al-Carmel. In the town square, in front of witnesses, her brother pulled out a knife. As he stabbed her in the stomach, some onlookers urged him on, cheering, "Hero, hero! You're a real man!" With the spilling of her blood, her brother publicly cleansed the tainted family name. That night Israel Television showed the video of a crowd around her corpse and several women flashed victory signs. "She came all the way to die here. It's not that we went after her and killed her at her place," her mother said. "I lived in shame for what she did to us. We Druze don't approve of a girl leaving home." The murder "served her right," added her cousin. "She disobeyed our rules and we were happy to finish her off. Any girl who does a thing like that has to die. Every dog will get what it deserves." After his arrest, her brother said that he agonized over the decision. "She's my sister—my flesh and blood—I'm a human being. I didn't want to kill her. I didn't want to be in this situation. They [community members] pushed me to make this decision. I know what they expect from me. If I do this, they look at me like a hero, a clean guy, a real man. If I don't kill my sister, the people would look at me like I am a small person." After the slaying, a hit list circulated through the village naming other women who had "misbehaved." Some men still believe in an ancient Arabic proverb: "Grass grows quickly over blood that has been shed honorably."

Then there's the story of twenty-eight-year-old Naim Asad, who told her family she wanted to leave Beit Jann. A woman who leaves her village unmarried can bring disgrace to the family. Her mother and older sister turned to a male neighbor for help in protecting the family honor. They asked him to hire a Palestinian hit man to murder Naim. The neighbor informed the police, who set up a sting operation and apprehended the two women. They were indicted in a Haifa court, charged with honor killing conspiracy.

Not long after that, Beit Jann awoke to another drama, more compelling than any Arabic soap opera picked up by their satellite dishes. Villagers discovered anonymous flyers in their mailboxes describing the local council chief's secret wild sex life with several married women from the village. "In our Druze culture, it's considered taboo," explained University of Haifa researcher Salim Bariq. "To accuse somebody of sleeping with someone is a very serious thing. Most serious of all is that they revealed the identities of the women who supposedly slept with the council chief. It's impossible to describe what this can do to the husbands and sons of these women. . . . Bloodshed is just a matter of time." The libeled man, Shafiq Asad, suspected that his longtime political rival, who narrowly lost the last election, was behind the defamatory flyer. The Asad clan declared war on the Qablan clan. Cherry trees were cut, grenades hurled, water tanks blown up, political rivals shot. Because nearly every male in a Druze village has served in the IDF, guns and ammunition are everywhere. At the last minute, a Druze spiritual leader intervened and called for a *sulha* (reconciliation meeting). The uneasy peace between the two clans might last—at least until the next election.

In Druze villages, it is not always customary for the loser of an election to embrace the victor. Right away, the loser often starts planning revenge and the winner starts persecuting his rivals. One woman from Beit Jann who is married to a man from a rival clan dreads each election because she's always accused of betrayal: her husband's side accuses her of voting for her parents' candidate; her parents accuse her of voting for her husband's candidate.

Druze religious law rules that a family must educate its female members. If there isn't enough money to educate both a daughter and a son, the daughter's education takes precedence because a son can always find work. Despite this progressive law, few Druze women above forty have high school diplomas. Not many of their conservative parents were willing to disregard a religious ban against mixed classes. These women tend to stay in their villages, selling homemade foods or crafts or tending small hill farms.

Women who work outside their villages, frequently in textile or food factories, often need a male relative as escort. "My girlfriends and I want to work, but not in factories," says Maisa Hamahdy. "We're a different generation. My sister is a nurse. And my friend just got into the Technion. She's going to be the first woman doctor here."

A transition to more modern ways is happening. When the first Druze woman dared get a driver's license in 1972, religious leaders condemned her, warning that her actions would lead to "rampant licentiousness." The head of the Israeli Druze community issued an edict forbidding all Druze women from driving. In 1992, another rebel from Daliat al-Carmel stunned her family when she came home with a driver's license. At first her father was adamant that she not use it. It took coaxing to change his mind. Although he bought her a car, he refuses to ride with her. Maisa says that few men will drive with a woman behind the wheel. Her mother also flouts the edict. A neighbor who only finished the sixth grade went even further. She caused a small earthquake when she became the first Israeli Druze woman to join a village council. "I really like what she said," recounts Maisa: "'It doesn't matter what's on your head. What counts is what's in it.'" Soon Maisa will enter nearby Haifa University. "When I heard that already over half the Druze students there are women, I was so happy."

Maisa heads through the center of Daliat al-Carmel, down a dirt lane to her part-time job. She enters a barbershop and walks through it to a converted bedroom where loud Arabic oud music is playing. "I prefer hard rock or Celine Dion," she says, as she joins nineteen other Druze women on an assembly line where they are soldering car alarm systems and making circuit boards. This is the national headquarters for Israel's first—and only—Druze high-tech company. "I know, it doesn't look high tech," her boss, Nisim Abu Hamad, says. His parents live upstairs; he grew up in this house with eleven brothers and sisters. "When customers see this place, they're surprised. Just getting customers is not easy. When I tell people I have a high-tech company in Daliat al-Carmel, they say, 'What? In that town with fast food?' They want to talk about eating, I want to talk business. Sometimes, I have to sit with them for hours, trying to change their ideas about Druze." A soft-spoken, good-humored man with beard and glasses and a degree in economics, Nisim is just back from comforting his wife, whose twelve-year-old cousin was among those killed on the Haifa bus.

He says he tries to use chutzpah he learned in the army to convince the government to create an industrial zone in the village. "With chutzpah, you get more results. Maybe I need more to get attention." Although Druze are known for their military prowess and are integral to the security of the country, Jewish towns get substantially more funding than Druze villages. "The young men especially are losing patience. Some are beginning to ask if all our sacrifices for the state are taken for granted." He quotes the line of a popular Druze poet: "The enemy bullet doesn't distinguish between Jews and Druze, so why does the government?"

Nisim started the company in 1994 with two of his brothers, a barber and an elementary school teacher. He has twenty-five employees now, he says with evident satisfaction. Most are female relatives. (Not many Druze women are allowed to be alone with unrelated males.) "Our company is trying hard to make it. I want to prove a Druze can do it. Druze lose time in the army. I lost three years. Yet, because of the army, I have this business. Before the army, I had no Jewish friends. It's difficult to make it in high tech as a Druze. To enter the market, I got a Jewish partner, a friend who is a colonel. His connections helped with the startup marketing." Nisim met him in the army during the first intifada. "They wanted to send me to Gaza. I was willing to serve, but not there. I can't bear to see fighting. I didn't want to pretend I had a medical problem, so I used my religion to help me. I told the officer, 'I'm a Druze and I believe in reincarnation. In my past life, I died fighting in Gaza.' It worked. I got transferred to the personnel office in Acre and got to live at home." He pauses. "Don't misunderstand me. One hundred percent, I believe in reincarnation. I am my father's brother."

15

The Christians

Uneasy in the Land of Jesus

*☉ Al-Aqsa a popular intifada? Arafat is behind it, and it
has only made our lives harder. We have lost our land, our
men, our freedom. I don't like Hamas. They are bad for us,
and we [Christians] are afraid of them. I do not understand
how anyone can go and blow himself up. —Nadia Yousef,
souvenir seller in Bethlehem*

*☉ Often I feel like a bridge between Jews and Muslims.
Christians have always lived between the two worlds. So,
maybe we're the ones who can connect them. —Michail
Fanous, executive director of Open House in Ramle*

Only a third of a square mile, the walled Old City in the heart of
Jerusalem is steeped in faith—and in blood. The two always have gone
together. The ringing church bells, chanting in synagogues, and muezzins
calling the faithful to prayer are reminders that here, religion and territory are inexorably intertwined. Over the centuries, a changing cast of
conquerors has destroyed synagogues, converted churches into mosques
and mosques into churches. Here, a group of teenagers, part of a Haifa
church youth group, follows the route many believe Jesus took as he car-

305

ried his cross on the way to his Crucifixion, the Via Dolorosa (Way of Sorrows). At a plaque marking one of the fourteen stations of the cross, they stop and recite fervent prayers in Arabic. Nearly 150,000 Israeli Arabs are Christians. Many are from families who have lived in the Holy Land since the early days of Christianity, some are descendants of Byzantine Christians, others of Crusaders. A microcosm of Christianity itself, Israeli Arab Christians are Greek Catholic, Roman Catholic (Latin), Armenian, Maronite, Melekite, Ethiopian Coptic, Episcopalian (Anglican), Baptist, Pentacostal, and a few other denominations.

Continuing their devotional walk along the labyrinth of cobblestone streets, past tourists following a man carrying a wooden cross rented from a Muslim entrepreneur, the teens enter a sunny plaza in the Christian Quarter. Elderly Franciscan friars in brown robes and sandals are reciting psalms. Dignified Ethiopian Coptic priests in white robes shuffle past Armenian Orthodox priests in black cloaks with purple sashes and triangular black hats. The teenagers seem more interested in flirting than watching the parade of Christianity until their group leader shepherds them inside a massive stone building, the Church of the Holy Sepulcher. Inside are the final five Stations of the Cross. (Catholics and Orthodox Christians believe Jesus was crucified, buried, and resurrected here.) In the cavernous church, overpowering aromas of incense waft through the air. It's so dark and noisy that they remove their sunglasses and headphones. A bearded Greek Orthodox priest hands them votive candles and leads them to a domed rotunda, the Fourteenth Station of the Cross, the empty tomb where they believe Jesus was laid to rest. Under a glass is a stone said to be the site of the Crucifixion. In the Latin/Roman Catholic tradition this is called Calvary; the Greek Orthodox call it Golgotha. The group strains to hear the priest because it is surrounded by other clerics reading the Gospel in a cacophony of competing chants, the many-layered music of Christian Jerusalem.

The music has been played at this site for more than seventeen centuries. After conquering Jerusalem in 306, Constantine the Great built the original Church of the Holy Sepulcher over what had previously been a Roman temple to Venus. As Jerusalem became a major pilgrimage center for Byzantine Eastern Orthodox Christians, the local Christian population grew. The Egyptians invaded in 1009 and under orders of

Caliph al-Hakim (whom the Druze revere) destroyed the building. The Crusaders conquered Jerusalem in 1099 and, along with destroying synagogues and mosques and slaughtering their occupants, rebuilt Constantine's church. In 1555, the Franciscans rebuilt the dilapidated shrine. The Greek Orthodox erected the present church in 1890 and still control major portions of it.

A dapper gentleman standing near the tombs of Godfrey of Bouillon and his brother Baldwin, French nobles of the First Crusade who ruled the "Kingdom of Jerusalem" from 1099 to 1118, presents his card to a visitor and explains that he is the Custodian and Door Keeper of the Church of the Holy Sepulcher. His family, the Nusseibehs, has held the key to the church ever since Saladin drove the Crusaders out of Jerusalem in 1187. "They need a Muslim to mediate between the Christians," he says with a chuckle. "They barely speak to each other." He's referring to the squabbling Greek Orthodox, Roman Catholic, Armenian Orthodox, Franciscan, Syrian Orthodox, Egyptian, and Ethiopian Coptic clerics who for centuries have been competing for control of the church, arguing how to worship, who can move a lamp, even whether a Franciscan monk has swept dirt into Armenian "space." Though, in theory, responsibility for every area of the church has been assigned, parts are in dreadful shape because of disagreements over who should fix what—repair implies ownership. Longtime rivals even have hit each other with heavy crosses. Unable to pay taxes to the Ottoman sultan in the sixteenth century, Ethiopian Copts lost "ownership" of their part of the church to their rivals, the Egyptian Copts, and live in huts on the roof.

Nothing better illustrates the conflict than the Easter season. During the Ceremony of the Holy Fire that marks the climax of the Orthodox Easter, about ten thousand Greek Orthodox, Roman Catholics, and Armenians jam inside the church. According to tradition, the Greek Orthodox patriarch enters the tomb of Jesus, which is then sealed, and a fire miraculously emits from the tomb. In 2002, a fracas broke out between Greek Orthodox and Armenian congregants over whose clergy should leave the tomb first. In past years, bloody fights have erupted with the rival Syrian Orthodox. Despite ongoing rivalries inside the church, outside, the Christians of the Holy Land face far more pressing problems.

On the Christian Quarter Road, lined with cluttered stalls and shops with sheep heads dangling from hooks, a balding merchant sits forlornly on a stool outside his small shop. It is packed with lovely olive wood statues of Mary and Jesus and silver rosaries. When he notices a stylish brunette in a business suit maneuvering around a donkey laden with figs, his face lights up. Naila, his former neighbor, is going to have lunch at her mother's house after work. He asks about her family. He's heard about the layoffs at Bank Hapoalim (Hebrew for the Workers Bank). Is her job still okay? So far, Naila answers with a sigh. "I was supposed to be promoted, but I'm still a teller. I guess I should be grateful." She makes her way past a man wearing a checkered keffiyah selling paintings of the Last Supper on velvet. Trying to entice some backpackers, he yells out "Special student discount," but they move on, uninterested in the plastic Jesus icons or bottles marked "Holy Land Water"—water that comes directly from a faucet. "*Salaam aleikum,*" Naila greets him and politely inquires about his health. He answers by describing his ailing businesses. The worst economic slump ever. He curses the intifada. She says nothing.

"Criticize the intifada to the wrong person and he may call you a collaborator," she confides when the Muslim merchant is out of earshot. She's willing to speak without self-censorship only if her name isn't used. For Christians, this intifada is different from the first one in 1987–91. "This is not our intifada. How many Christians shoot guns? Is there one Christian suicide bomber? It's called al-Aqsa intifada because it's Islamic and the people fighting it are waving the Koran. We're in a terrible position here." She motions toward a stall with Arabic newspapers and books. A few books have Osama bin Laden's picture on the cover. "Just months ago they were selling like candy. That scares me, but look at that wall." Naila translates the Arabic writing on it: " 'After Saturday comes Sunday.' Do you know what this means? It means 'After we are finished with the Jews, it's the Christians' turn.' " With muted anger, she continues, "They hate our religion. They call us infidel dogs. Heretics. They want us out."

To emphasize her point, she changes direction and stands in front of a store. It's shuttered shut with aluminum siding. "Like a lot of us, my uncle felt he had to act very nationalistic to prove he's a 'good' loyal

Palestinian. When they told him to strike, he closed his shop. And each time they told him to pay intifada 'taxes' [protection money to Muslim thugs] he paid. He finally got sick of it. And refused. And what did they do? They tried to burn it. He got fed up. He moved to Jaffa. And he was one of the last Christian shop owners. This is the Christian Quarter in name only. Everyone I grew up with has moved out. Now only my mother is left."

Her family is Greek Orthodox, which is the largest and richest Christian community in Israel and the rest of the Middle East. The Greek Orthodox patriarchate owns about 70 percent of the land of the Old City. In West Jerusalem alone, the Knesset, the Supreme Court, the Israel Museum, and official residences of the president and prime minister all sit on land owned by the Greek Orthodox Church. No one knows what will happen as leases come due in the next decade or two. The Greek Orthodox Church also owns some of Israel's choicest real estate in towns such as Nazareth, Haifa, Jaffa, and Ramle.

Stooping over a huge basket of olives, Naila samples some and hands a few shekels to a weathered-looking woman in an embroidered dress sitting on a doorstep. "My husband loves these," Naila remarks. "When we got married, I thought maybe to live near my mother. But to buy in East Jerusalem is hard. Even the most moderate Muslims are afraid to sell to Christians. People who sell to us or any Jews are called collaborators. Some are shot. Anyway, I'm glad we're living in West Jerusalem [which is predominantly Jewish]. Away from the disturbances, all the upheavals." Being largely urbanized, cosmopolitan, and in many cases closer to the Jews than the Muslims in education and income, Christians have been absorbed into Israeli Jewish society to a greater extent than Muslims. Most Arab Christian Israelis live in mixed Jewish-Arab towns such as Haifa, Jerusalem, and Jaffa that allow them (as well as moderate Muslims) a more Western lifestyle than traditional Arab villages. All-Arab Nazareth has Israel's largest Christian population.

With a twinge of bitterness, Naila comments that West Jerusalem has far superior facilities than East Jerusalem. "It's much less crowded. It has parks. Everything works better. We wanted a nice apartment. With our last name, we knew we'd have trouble finding a place. Which is why we got a Jewish realtor. I work with her sister in the bank. She advised me to wear a big cross when I met the landlord. That way he'll know we're 'good' Arabs. That's what it's like for us," she says, describing her overlapping identities. "We're caught in the middle. A lot of Muslims don't trust us because we're Christian. And a lot of Jews don't trust us because we're Arabs. They think all Arabs are terrorists."

Intermarriage between members of Israeli Christian denominations was once rare, but no longer. Naila has a "mixed marriage": her husband is Anglican. "The hardest part is coordinating Christmas calendars," she jokes. Her husband's family celebrates Christmas on December 25; her Greek Orthodox family celebrates Christmas on January 7. For her Armenian neighbors, some of them descendants of fourth-century pilgrims, Christmas is on January 19 (as it is for Ethiopian Copts). "Nothing is simple in the Middle East. Even going to church on Sunday. Everyone works." Sunday is the first day of the week in Israel; banks are open, as are Jewish schools and government offices. "Jews don't even know when it's Christmas or Easter. Here, they're just ordinary working days. When I take those days off, I always have to remind my boss why." Each Easter she and her husband worship in a sumptuous English-style garden outside the walls of the Old City, the Garden Tomb, where Protestants believe Jesus was crucified and buried. As it is in the rest of the world, Protestantism is a dynamic and proselytizing religion in Israel, though not among Israeli or Palestinian Muslims, who can be killed for converting to Christianity. Instead, efforts have borne fruit among Russian immigrants and Arab Christians, particularly the Greek Orthodox, many of whom feel neglected by the Church's exclusively Greek hierarchy; an all-Greek synod elects the patriarch, who is never an Arab. Partly as a result, centuries-old ethnic-national and political tensions between the Greek clerics and their Arab congregations are intensifying, and a number of congregants now call themselves "Arab" instead of "Greek" Orthodox.

As Naila approaches the old white stone house where she grew up, her spirits lift. She hears Arabic music the way it was. Her widowed mother is at the window, listening to the haunting sounds of the legendary Egyptian singer Umm Kulthum. The high-vaulted ceiling and blue mosaics on the floor make the large room seem more like a pasha's drawing room than a kitchen. Her mother inserts another CD into the player, this time *My Fair Lady*. "I just heard it at the Tel Aviv Opera House. Guess who played Eliza Doolittle? Mira Awad." A Christian Arab Israeli. Taking a plate of kibbe out of the microwave, she apologizes for serving leftovers. The class she teaches at a music academy in West Jerusalem ran late. "Do you mind waiting to eat? Your cousin called. Something happened."

Sitting in the sun-drenched courtyard under gnarled olive trees, Naila and her mother look relieved when they see Daoud (David). Out of breath and agitated, he describes the drive from his home in Bethlehem. First, there were the long waits at Israeli checkpoints. Then, as he drove his Subaru past a refugee camp, he placed a keffiyah on his dashboard so he wouldn't be mistaken for a Jew. Arab boys threw stones through his windshield anyway. "Luckily, I didn't get hurt this time. Remember when it used to take less than half an hour to get here? It took me almost two hours." Like all West Bank residents, he needed a hard-to-get permit to enter Jerusalem. He studies at Bethlehem University, the only Roman Catholic university in the Holy Land, which is partially funded by the Vatican as part of an effort to stem the Palestinian Christian emigration from the West Bank. Today, more than 70 percent of the students are Muslim. "Do you know what some of them want? To make a classroom into a mosque," he says ruefully. "My professors are afraid to say anything." Hamas runs the student government.

"Everyone knows what kind of Palestine they want," his aunt interrupts. "An Islamic Republic. Palestine ruled by the Koran." As talk turns to discrimination against Christians, Daoud looks conflicted. Even though he is a passionate Palestinian nationalist and admirer of former PLO spokeswoman and fellow Arab Christian Hanan Ashrawi, he hates Arafat for pushing the Islamization of the intifada. Since assuming control in 1995, Arafat has changed Bethlehem's demography by expanding municipal boundaries to include three refugee camps and encouraging thousands of Muslims to move in. In 1948, one mosque served the greater Bethlehem area; today there are more than ninety. Since Israel gave Arafat control over Bethlehem in 1995, hundreds of Arab Christian families have left town. The majority of Bethlehem's Christians were engaged in the tourist industry; since the second intifada destroyed tourism, most closed their shops, hotels, and restaurants. Many of those who haven't fled plan to. In 1990, Bethlehem was 60 percent Christian; today it is less than 20 percent. "What a wonderful Palestine you and Hanan are creating," admonishes his aunt. "Churches but no Christians."

During the 1948 War, about three quarters of Arab Christians stayed in Israel, but Daoud's parents were among those who fled to Jordanian-controlled Bethlehem. After the 1967 War, it came under Israeli occupation until, as part of the 1993 Oslo agreement, in 1995 Israel transferred it to the Palestinian Authority. "My parents wish it were still Israel," declares Daoud. They've applied for Israeli citizenship. So have other Arab Christians living in the West Bank and Gaza who can move to Israel either through family reunification or marriage with Israeli Arab Christians. Throughout the Middle East—Jordan, the Palestinian Authority, Lebanon, Syria, Iraq, and Egypt—there is an ongoing Christian exodus, mostly to South and North America. The exception is Israel, which is the only state in the Middle East where the number of Arab Christians has grown slightly.

In Jesus' time Nazareth was a tiny Galilee village of a few hundred Jews. Today it is Israel's largest Christian city. The renowned black-domed Basilica of the Annunciation can be seen from every approach to Jesus' hometown. The largest church in the Middle East, it is built on the spot where, according to Catholic tradition, the angel Gabriel announced to the Virgin Mary that she was carrying a son.

A cashier in a sweets shop on Casanova Street grows tense as he watches hundreds of bearded men stream into a green canvas tent-mosque next to the Basilica. Another fiery sermon by the young imam Sheik Nazim Abu Salim, who holds a degree in biochemistry from Ben-Gurion University, blasts from the loudspeakers: "Anyone who doesn't get on the Islam train is done for. Anyone who wants to be certain in his life and also after his death must convert to Islam. In the end, Islam will be the only religion left in the world." "The 'bearded ones' are in charge and they're pushing us out," the cashier mutters gloomily. "If Jesus were to come back, he'd be shocked. Sometimes I'm afraid to wear my cross."

The tent-mosque has been a source of friction between Christians and Muslims since late 1997. The municipality started building a public plaza on land next to the Basilica in preparation for an expected millennial flood of Christian tourists and for Pope John Paul II's visit. While demolishing an abandoned government school to clear the site, excavations uncovered a tomb said to be that of a nephew of Saladin. Hundreds of Islamic fundamentalists broke through the barriers around the construction area. Claiming that the land is Islamic holy ground, they presented blueprints for the largest mosque in the world, with minarets that would tower above the Basilica. They erected a temporary tent-mosque where incendiary sermons have been inflaming religious passions. "A mosque tied to the memory of Saladin rising right next to our church?" challenged an indignant Franciscan friar serving in the Basilica. "Can you imagine the call of the muezzin coming through loudspeakers from the minaret competing with our bells?"

The tug of war over Nazareth's identity intensified a year later. Campaigning on the mosque issue, the Islamic Movement won a majority of seats on the city council. However, the incumbent Arab Greek Orthodox mayor, who supports building the plaza, was reelected. He received death threats and was knifed by local fundamentalists. "I thought it was bad that shops with Christmas decorations were smashed. At Easter, it got even worse," reports Maryam, who teaches at the same Arab public high school she once attended. She was an eyewitness as religious passions in Jesus' hometown boiled over. "I was leaving Easter services at the Basilica with my husband and my son. We heard them [Muslim youth] shouting insults, screaming *Allahu Akbar* [Allah is great]. There were fights and many people were hurt. If your car had a cross on the mirror or a sticker of the Virgin, it was destroyed." During two days of rioting, churches were torched; more than sixty Christian-owned stores and two Muslim ones, both owned by supporters of the mayor, were vandalized. Nazareth's reputation for Muslim-Christian coexistence was left in tatters.

"Until this mosque business, no one I know cared if their neighbor was named George or Muhammad," Maryam continues. "My Muslim friends are open-minded in their thinking. We go together to concerts and films, to restaurants at the mall. We fight together for more government money for our roads that are choking with traffic, for our schools and for more playgrounds. Our sons play on the same soccer team. I'm trying to teach mine that we're all God's children. At school, my students never cared what family you come from, who is Muslim or Christian. Now I hear some say terrible things, like Christians are not real Arabs. That we worship idols. We believe Jesus is the Son of God; to them, that's blasphemy." When Maryam was born in 1962, Christians were still in the majority, as they had been for centuries. Today, largely because of a low birthrate among Christians—Muslim women have twice as many children—fewer than 30 percent of Nazareth's seventy thousand residents are Arab Christians. Moreover, a number of Christians are moving to Upper Nazareth, the adjoining Jewish town.

Maryam describes the scene in downtown Nazareth on the first anniversary of the intifada on September 29, 2001. Islamic Movement Knesset member Abdulmalik Dehamshe and other Arab lawmakers led roughly three thousand Islamic Movement supporters through the center of Nazareth. They were carrying green Islamic flags and pictures of al-Aqsa Mosque, yelling against the Israeli occupation, Christianity, and the United States for wanting to go after bin Laden. "The way things are going, Nazareth will become like Umm al-Fahm [half an hour's drive southeast]. Soon they won't even allow us to drink wine," Maryam laments. "Except maybe for the communion."

On the night of November 14, 2001, a group of men secretly broke ground for the mosque. The Israeli government, fearing interreligious violence would reerupt, ordered the illegal construction work halted. The Vatican issued a warning that "building the mosque will in effect put this holy place in a state of permanent siege." The leader of Nazareth's Islamic Movement responded, "The Vatican wants to control Nazareth. The mosque will go down in history as a symbol that marks the beginning of Muslim rule in Nazareth." The Holy See is caught in a delicate situation. It wants to preserve the holy site, but does not want to anger the Arab world. After heavy pressure from the Vatican, the Sharon government halted all construction work on the mosque, preferring a possible confrontation with Israeli Islamists to a row with the Catholic world. Most residents of Nazareth are fed up with the issue. The gaping hole where construction stopped resembles an open wound, waiting to be reopened or healed.

Above a coffee and spice shop overlooking the Islamic tent encampment and the Basilica are the offices of the influential Arabic-language newspaper *Al-Sinnara,* which has been covering the fault lines running through Nazareth and the rest of Israel since it started in 1983. Israel's Islamic Movement has tremendous freedom of action, observes the editor, Lutfi Mashour, who has written about its growing assertiveness. "What other group in Israel can bring over more than fifty thousand people to rallies like the ones Umm al-Fahm's Islamic Movement organizes?" Blunt and opinionated, this well-known Catholic journalist is unafraid to lash out at those Palestinians who celebrate after terrorist attacks or to criticize Jewish and Arab Muslim and Christian politicians (including fellow Nazarene and Knesset member Azmi Bishara). He believes that Arab Israelis will not be fully accepted by Jews without a durable peace between Palestinians and Jews.

The Mashours are middle class and Westernized, as are almost all Israeli Christian families. Christian Arabs are Israel's best-educated and most prosperous demographic group. In the early years of the state, they filled the gap created by the exodus of many Muslim Arab leaders. During the 1950s and 1960s, Christians made up about half of the Arab members of the Knesset, far exceeding their proportion of the Arab population. Even though Christians now make up only about 13 percent of Arab Israelis, they play a major role in Arab business, culture, and politics. Most speak fluent Hebrew and English and navigate easily between Middle Eastern and Western cultures.

Arab Israelis are "longing for moderation, looking for direction. I think, as many Arab intellectuals do, that reform in society should start at home first—how we treat our wives and daughters," Lufti asserts. He and his wife sent their two daughters to a Catholic college near relatives in North Carolina. They went on to get master's degrees at the London School of Economics. "To give my daughters a very good education is not doing them any favors. It's my duty." An ardent supporter of women's rights, he places a lot of hope in educated Arab Israeli women. In 2000, he helped his eldest daughter, Yara, launch a groundbreaking publication, the first women's magazine published by and for Arab Israeli women.

"I was really surprised by how much need there is for this kind of magazine. I never thought we'd sell so well," says Yara. She is the editor of *Lilac,* which is a cross between *Cosmo, People,* and the *National Catholic Reporter.* Although it is targeted to young, liberal Arab women, the magazine also sells well in the Koran Belt, in towns such as Umm al-Fahm. "Bedouin in Rahat read it. Druze too. Mostly women, but some men tell me they read it too." (She plans to sell *Lilac* in the West Bank, Jordan, Lebanon, and Egypt.) Very few vendors refuse to sell this glossy magazine, although its pages are splashed with photos of scantily clad foreign celebrities and lingerie models. "A lot of our readers are religious women. Yet we've gotten only a few complaints that some of the pictures are too risqué," concedes Yara. "No one gripes about the content. No women in the Middle East are as liberal as Lebanese and Israeli [Arabs]." Right on her computer screen she can choose photos of bone-thin Brazilian and French fashion models. By traditional Arab standards of beauty, they're underclothed and underfed.

Like any American women's magazine, *Lilac* is full of advice on makeup, manicures, pedicures, and plastic surgery. But it also tackles topics far more serious than thigh anxiety. "No Israeli magazine has really written about the issues that are important to Arab Israeli women," Yara comments. Writers explore sensitive subjects such as premarital sex, homosexuality, female circumcision, and surgical reconstruction of the hymen, a procedure some Arab women undergo before marriage to "restore" their virginity, to prevent "sullying" their family's honor. (Doctors also perform it on women who have been sexually molested.) Her cousin, the first woman Israeli Arab physician, writes an advice column that gingerly tackles subjects such as date rape. ("If you're brave enough, report it to the police. But if you think making it known could create a scandal that harms your reputation and might lead to acts that could be avoided"—a reference to family honor killings—"then I understand your decision not to file a complaint. But you must pay attention to your health.")

Yara's part-time staff of nearly forty includes both her mother (who writes editorials) and her father. In one of his monthly columns, "Confessions of a Man," he wrote frankly about why Arabs value sons more than daughters and that he doesn't mind not having a son. He likes to be called Abu Yara, which means "father of Yara," because he is proud of his first-born daughter. Traditionally, no Arab man would dare use the name of his daughter; the word Abu is attached only to the name of the first-born son.

"That's the way I was raised. I like running articles about independent career women, not just housewives," adds Yara. (More than twice as many Arab Christian women work outside the home as Muslim women.) She runs profiles about Muslim and Christian Arab Israeli women who tend to be like her: strong-willed, single-minded, and single. One of her father's favorites is about a Haifa nun, a school principal who candidly discusses gender issues in the Catholic Church. "I've never been prouder as a Christian than when I read it," he says. "What nuns like her are doing for Arabs—not only for Christians but for Muslims and Druze, not only in education and prayer but also as advisors—is a huge, huge contribution." With a laugh, Yara describes one of the first interviews *Lilac* ran, with the first Arab Israeli woman to earn her pilot's wings, who revealed her dream: to become El Al's first Arab woman pilot. When asked about marriage, the twenty-year-old from a nearby village said, "Marriage? I am not thinking about getting married now. First, I will take care of my career. I don't know any woman pilot who is married." About two years later, she gave up flying and married. Now Yara is editing a story about another Arab woman who has taken to the skies, an El Al stewardess.

Twenty-nine-year old Yara avows she is in no great hurry to marry—only when the "right guy" comes along, freethinking and fun-loving, who doesn't mind that she jets off to Paris to cover a Lebanese fashion show, works seven days a week, and manages to squeeze in workouts in the gym. Not long ago, her twenty-seven-year-old sister half-jokingly described their single status: "We're not over the hill, just off the map." Her sister finally found the right person. Her parents are thrilled to be planning a wedding to a local guy. Muslim Israeli women tend to marry young; Christian Arab Israeli women marry later—or not at all. Twelve percent of Christian Israeli women between twenty-five and fifty-nine are single, compared to 7 percent of Muslim women and 5 percent of Jewish women of the same age group. Quite a few single Arab Christian women voice the same complaint: there are not enough Christian men to go around. Most of the educated Christians who emigrate are young men, and those who stay tend to marry either younger women or Christian women from the West Bank. Yara's mother, a Greek Orthodox from Bethlehem, had a program on Israel Television. "My father interviewed her for an article. And right away, they fell in love."

Her mother, Vida, also an active career woman, runs the family's public relations agency, which once promoted Barak's campaign for Arab votes. The agency also plastered buses with lavender *Lilac* ads. Recently it won an award for its imaginative government antidrug radio campaign, which uses Arabic rap music. Vida is one of the few women members of the nearby Arab Business Club (ABC), a nonprofit organization that helps Israeli Arabs and Jews obtain business contacts in Jordan, and vice versa. ABC supports researchers such as a Bedouin biomedical engineer who is testing herbal extracts to treat diabetes and other diseases. It also awards scholarships to Arab Israeli students preparing for high-tech careers and gives financial advice to Arab Israeli entrepreneurs. Members are especially proud of Nazareth's first Arab high-tech incubator, which they got the Israeli government and Arab and Jewish Israeli investors to fund.

One of their successes is a brash college dropout with Bill Gates aspirations. Ayman Makouli started House Party, an Internet chatroom for other Arab Israeli teenagers, from his bedroom. "Thousands of kids met online," he says. "It became their virtual home, their own country. Online everyone's equal because they can't see each other." Ayman is from Kfar Yasif, a mostly Greek Orthodox village north of Acre, one of only six villages in Israel that still has a Christian majority. The son of an importer/exporter and a preschool teacher, he has been programming computers since age eleven. "I learned it from books and spent hours in front of the screen. I surfed NASA's website. I got a job doing Beta testing for ICQ." His bosses, three Jewish Israeli long-haired boy wonders all in their twenties, sold their Internet chat software to AOL for $407 million. "Not many Arabs lived the '90s Internet revolution. I did."

Ayman studied computer science at Haifa University but dropped out after a few semesters. "It was boring. A voice inside me said, 'Ayman, you're wasting your talents.' I wanted to be the youngest Arab high-tech millionaire. I went to Tel Aviv to meet venture capitalists. They said 'How much do you need?' At nineteen, I was offered $2 million. It was wow!" He partnered with a forty-five-year-old Jewish Israeli who already owned six high-tech firms. "I'm trying to prove that Arabs have brains, that we're not just construction workers and house painters. I want to inspire other kids. They need to understand that being economically strong is our only hope. I dream of Arab industrial parks. Imagine fifty Aymans with high-tech startups. It would be great for every Arab kid to surf the web and talk with the outside world. I aim to put free Internet in all schools, free email, free training so kids can write their own websites. We can create a quiet revolution. It will not happen overnight. One day we'll hear lots of eleven-year-olds say to their fathers, 'Your way of thinking has passed.' "

Ayman created the first Israeli Arab Internet news site, "Arabs48," which came online in 2001. The name refers to the Arabs who remained in Israel after the 1948 War. "This is the home on the Net for Israeli Arabs. We're building community and identity," asserts the twenty-two-year-old. Arabs48.com provides news, sports, business, weather, and culture. The dating service, job announcements, and opinion polls are especially popular. So are the chatrooms, where participants share spicy stories about Arab public figures. There are more serious postings as well: debates on corruption and power plays in the Palestinian Authority and whether Christians should volunteer for the Israeli Defense Forces.

According to an IDF spokesperson, a slightly increasing number of Israeli Arab Christians over age eighteen are either volunteering for the IDF or performing national service in schools and hospitals in their communities. In 2001, a young sergeant from Tur'an, a tranquil Galilee village where Jesus is said to have turned wine into water, became the first Christian soldier in the Israeli army to be killed in the intifada, shot in the head by a Palestinian sniper in Gaza. He and a number of other Arab Christians from this village enlisted after nearly one hundred men linked with radical clerics burst into a church during Good Friday Mass in 1997 chanting "Tur'an must be 100 percent Muslim." Christian-Muslim clashes continued for days. A Christian art student was stabbed to death. Rioters fire-bombed Christian homes. "The Muslims call us traitors now," said a soldier, a pastor's son, who keeps his army rifle close by during leave; the family kitchen was pockmarked with bullets. More and more, young Christians are unwilling to turn the other cheek. "We are not going to live in fear anymore. I think we realized that our future was more important than all the words of nationalism. You know the Muslims don't think of us as part of that nationalism, except when they need us. That's the truth. They talk about all this stuff against Israel and against occupation and collaboration. But they only care about fellow Muslims. We used to eat from the same plate, but now this village is torn apart. We [as Christians] have to do what is right for us now."

I've been living here, a minority all my life, an Anglican among Orthodox Christians, a Christian among Muslims, a Palestinian among Jews, a left-winger in a right-wing town," declares Michail Fanous, whose family has called Ramle home for seven centuries. Ramle is on the way from Tel Aviv to Jerusalem; the main road skirts it because few outsiders have any reason to visit this scruffy blue-collar Arab-Jewish town. So, why would an eligible forty-three-year-old bachelor, a rarity among Israeli Christian men, want to live here? Michail has been instrumental in transforming Ramle into a place where Jews and Arabs are business partners, live in the same buildings, and attend each other's weddings and funerals. He is the director of Open House, which is both an Arab preschool and a center for Jewish-Arab coexistence, wedged between a gas station and a trash-strewn lot. "It's not very beautiful, not very white, not very big," Michail admits. In the yard, toddlers play in a sandbox. In a former living room, children from poor families are learning Arabic and Hebrew songs. A former bedroom serves as a classroom for children getting a head start in math and computers. They wouldn't be doing so, but for Michail—and Dalia Landau.

Dalia Landau was an infant when her parents, Bulgarian Jews, escaped the Holocaust and arrived in Israel in late 1948, right in the middle of Israel's War of Independence. The government sent Dalia's family to live in an abandoned house in Ramle, where she spent a happy childhood and adolescence growing up, picking lemons from a tree that grew in the yard. Then, one morning after the 1967 War, Dalia, now a young woman, answered the doorbell to greet a well-dressed Muslim man standing at the gate. Warily, Bashir el-Kheiri introduced himself and informed Dalia that this was the first time in nineteen years that Palestinians like him were allowed to enter Israel. He was six in 1948, when the Israeli army expelled his family from the house. Dalia opened the door wide and showed him around his former home. Silently he walked through the spacious rooms, admired the high ceilings, the big windows. He recognized her bedroom; it had been his. Bashir gave her his address and invited Dalia to visit him in Ramallah in the West Bank. She had wondered about the former Arab owners who had left only months before her family moved in.

Dalia appeared unannounced at Bashir's house a few weeks later. She was the first Israeli his family had ever met; they were the first Palestinian Arab refugees Dalia had ever known. They viewed history very differently. For Dalia, 1948 was the War of Independence. For Bashir and his family, 1948 was the Nakba, the tragedy. Dalia does not deny Israeli responsibility for Ramle's refugees—in his biography, Yitzhak Rabin admitted his involvement in the forced evacuation of more than sixty

thousand Arabs from Lod and Ramle during the 1948 war—but con-
tends that, if the Arabs had accepted the 1947 UN Partition Plan, there
would have been no 1948 War and Bashir and his family would still be
living in the house. Dalia believes in a Palestinian state that will live in
peace next to Israel. Bashir believes in a Palestinian state instead of Israel.
He thinks all Jews who arrived after 1917 should be ousted. The encounter was difficult.

Although separated by a vast gulf created by wars, anger, and sorrow,
Bashir and his siblings continued to visit Dalia, sitting under the lemon
tree in the garden. Despite their political differences, their friendship
grew. The day they brought their blind, elderly father, he caressed the
stones of the house he had built. He asked Dalia if the lemon tree was
still alive, and when she took him to it, he broke down crying as he
hugged the tree he had planted. When he left, he was clutching the bunch
of lemons Dalia gave him. On sleepless nights, his wife saw him holding
a shriveled lemon.

Then, in 1969, after a grisly terror attack that killed two Israelis in a
West Jerusalem supermarket, Dalia read in a newspaper that Bashir had
been convicted of complicity in organizing it. She was horrified. She had
not known Bashir belonged to the extremist Popular Front for the Liberation of Palestine, and cut off all contact with him and his family. Every
time she passed the prison in Ramle where Bashir was serving his sentence, she felt betrayed.

After her parents' death, Dalia inherited the house, and its ghosts.
They would not let her stop thinking of Bashir, their common house, and
the vicious circle of pain-retaliation-pain-retaliation. In 1984, Bashir was
released after serving a fifteen-year sentence. Dalia and her husband, a
religious peace activist, decided to meet Bashir once again. Believing he
had paid his debt to society and hoping he had renounced terrorism,
Dalia told him she wanted to sell the house and give the money to his
family. Bashir welcomed the unexpected offer. But he suggested that, instead of selling it, she make it a day care center for Arab children of
Ramle. Dalia agreed and asked Michail Fanous to expand the idea, to
make it a house open to all Ramle's Muslims, Christians, and Jews. Open
House is the result.

With a Muslim clinical psychologist, Michail is training Jewish, Christian, and Muslim counselors who will work at the camp Open House

sponsors. Each summer, more than a hundred children hike, play soccer, and learn to challenge prejudice. Michail advises the counselors that in these volatile times, relations among the young campers will be strained at first, but then children forget the differences. "Explain to them that the mind is like a parachute: it doesn't work unless it's open." He recounts the story of a camp friendship. A Jewish girl asked her Moroccan-born mother if she could spend the night with her new Arab friend. Overnight with an Arab family? Her mother was shaken. It wasn't safe. The daughter convinced her mother to meet the other parent. Once the women started talking, they understood better why their daughters got along. "Most of the time we reach parents through their kids," Michail reports. "As they learn about each other, they see that if you don't talk, you can't make peace." These same mothers are now both participating in "From Conflict to Peace," one of the many Jewish-Arab workshops Open House runs.

Michail credits his late father, a pastor, for preparing him for this person-to-person work. "Every night as a kid I heard it at dinner: 'Christianity is one word: love.' I got sick of hearing it. I said to him, 'Hey father, I love you. I love food too. That doesn't mean I have to love that jerk next door. Do you really expect me to go to that right-wing Likudnik and say, "God bless you, Mordechai"?' And my father answered, 'This is what the love of Jesus is all about.' " His father wasn't so open-minded when Michail told him he wanted to attend a Jewish high school because the closest Arab school was too long a bus ride away. "My parents were afraid I might date a Jew. And the Jews were afraid that their daughters would date an Arab—it's the same all over Israel. There were only five other Arab kids. Whenever there was a terrorist attack the Jewish kids would blame us. One day a kid called me 'dirty Arab' and I beat him up right in front of the teacher. The principal told me I had to try to fit in. So I learned the Torah, even the history of Zionism. For a while my parents feared I was going to grow up a Jewish Zionist," he says with a laugh. The beefy boy with a shock of black curly hair became so popular that he was elected student body president.

The same appeal made Michail the only Arab ever elected to the Ramle City Council, where meetings are part Mad Hatter's Tea Party, part wrestling match. When the Likud mayor, a ramrod-straight former colonel, asked Michail to join his coalition, everyone was incredulous.

"Politically, we're totally opposite. I'm left and he's right. But then he said, 'As a Jew, I'm disturbed that Arab schools aren't as good as Jewish schools. I decided we should work together to end discrimination and get things done.'" And the unlikely duo have made an impact. Bedouin neighborhoods now have sewers, sidewalks, and streetlights; Michail has launched Arab Book Week and a series of innovative programs that have lowered Arab high school dropout rates.

When intifada II broke out, many Israelis lost hope in the possibility of genuine coexistence. In Ramle, Jewish rowdies ran through the streets shouting anti-Arab slogans and tried to burn an Arab school. Arabs tried to set fire to a synagogue. To ward off riots, Michail and the mayor told local Arab and Jewish leaders, "You will restrain your *shebab* [street toughs] and we will restrain ours." After that, violence was minimal. Still, with the ongoing trauma of terror attacks in other parts of Israel, people come to Open House disoriented and depressed, anxious and confused. At first, Michail was surprised that people came back. Now he's surprised that communication has improved. He leads a session evoking frank talk about what Jewish and Arab participants are feeling. A young Muslim describes taking the bus from Jaffa to his home in Ramle, fearing that if a bad news bulletin comes on the radio, Jews or police might assault him. A Jewish woman admits, "I get really paranoid when I'm driving my car and someone who looks Arab is driving next to me. I really hate this feeling. But I have it."

"Even these days, people are listening compassionately, not trying to score debating points or outshout each other. After the most agonizing sessions, they stay around and share jokes," observes Michail. "Ramle is a mirror of Israel: 80 percent Jews and a 20 percent mix of Arab Christians and Muslims. This town is a tough laboratory. If we can make coexistence work here, maybe it can work in other places. People sometimes ask me what it's like being a Christian Israeli. At Open House, often I feel like a bridge between Jews and Muslims. Christians have always lived between the two worlds. So maybe we're the ones who can connect them."

V The Sexual Revolution

16

Marriage, Polygamy, Adultery, and Divorce Israeli-style

-∂ *He who does not have a wife lives without joy, without blessing, without goodness.* —Talmud Yevamot 62b

-∂ *Where there are no children, there is no light in the house.* —Arabic saying

The couple stand outdoors under a huppa, or bridal canopy, a cloth spread across four poles. Israeli Jewish weddings usually are held outside, under the "canopy of heaven," recalling God's blessing to Abraham that his seed be as numerous as the stars. The rabbi explains that the huppa symbolizes the tents of the ancient Hebrews and the home the newlyweds will share. An Orthodox rabbi performs this ceremony, as is required by law for all Jewish marriages in Israel. Next to the Sabbath, marriage is the most sacred part of Jewish life. The ceremony is called *kiddushin*, Hebrew for "sanctification." It is a holy covenant between man and woman with God as the intermediary. Before the ceremony, the groom and two witnesses sign the *ketuba,* the world's first prenuptial agreement, dating back to 400 B.C.E., which spells out the husband's legal obligations to the wife should death or divorce part them. At the ceremony, the couple both drink twice from the same cup of wine. Then the rabbi reads from the hand-illustrated ketuba. The groom holds up a simple gold band, a symbol of eternity, and tells his bride, "With this ring you are sanctified to me according to the laws of Moses and Israel." He places the ring on the bride's right index finger, and after benedictions and blessings, they drink the second cup of wine and are married. The groom says, "You are set aside for me as my wife." The bride makes no parallel statement to her husband. The groom then stomps on a glass. Most believe this act recalls the destruction of the Holy Temple and is a stark reminder that life is not all joy.

As the ceremony ends, the guests shout *mazel tov* and the party begins. Once the rabbi is out of sight, the bride removes her shawl, revealing a strapless gown rented from a Haifa bridal salon. She and her new husband are in their early thirties and, shortly after meeting skiing on Mount Hermon, have been living together, typical of secular Israelis who are waiting longer to tie the knot. A female singer and the band perform an eclectic mix of Israeli Mizrahi music, tango, and European pop. The newlyweds dance. Then her father breaks in while the groom dances with his mother. The musical free-for-all, sumptuous buffet, and blend of wedding traditions reflect the families, a cross-ethnic multigenerational Jewish blend of Argentine, Polish, and Moroccan. Integration under the huppa is on the rise.

At another wedding at a two-star Jerusalem hotel, men in black hats escort an anxious twenty-year-old groom to a small room for the traditional veiling ceremony. The seventeen-year-old bride in a full-sleeved white gown with a high neck sits expectantly on a velvet chair surrounded by her mother and female relatives. The groom approaches, quickly glances at her face, and then gently pulls down the opaque white veil. This custom of veiling the bride-to-be has biblical roots. After Jacob thought he had married his beloved Rachel, he discovered that his father-in-law had tricked him: the woman under the veil was her elder sister, Leah. The veil also makes the bride *hekdesh:* literally, "set apart in holiness." The veil, which physically separates them, is a reminder that even as they unite in marriage, they will remain distinct individuals. Right now, though, they are semistrangers. Since the matchmaker introduced them, they have met a few times, always with relatives present. "They're not marrying because they're in love," confides one of the bride's older sisters. "When they're married, the love will come."

The friends and family who fill the hotel courtyard watch excitedly as the bride's parents slowly lead her to join her groom at the huppa, which in this case is a family heirloom, a prayer shawl. In the style of Abraham and Sarah's tent, the huppa is open on all sides to welcome guests. The flower-decked dais is packed with relatives; both families have been fruitful and multiplied. "No man without a wife, neither a woman without a husband, nor both of them without God," the ultra-Orthodox rabbi says, quoting Genesis. "Only by joining two souls is it possible to reach true fulfillment." The bride circles the groom seven times. Seven is a holy number: the world was created in seven days and Sabbath is the seventh day of the week; the expression "when a man takes a wife" appears seven times in the Torah. And just as Joshua circled Jericho seven times, inducing the walls to fall, the bride is capturing her groom's heart, causing walls between them to crumble. The seven blessings constitute most of the wedding liturgy. After the rabbi reads the ketuba, the newlyweds don't kiss. They don't touch. They have never touched.

After the ceremony, the bride and groom spend a few minutes alone in a "unity" room. In biblical times, this was when the marriage was physically consummated, verifying that the bride was a virgin. Nowadays, religious newlyweds simply eat. The couple have been fasting and praying since dawn to purify themselves spiritually for their life together. A wedding is considered a small Yom Kippur for the bride and groom. As they merge into a new, complete soul, all their past mistakes are forgiven. Before leaving the room, the new wife puts on a stylish wig. Now that she's married, other men must not see her hair uncovered. She enters the packed banquet hall, where women and men are separated by a line of plastic trees. Men eat and dance with men and women with women. An all-male band plays energetic klezmer music. The groom dances deliriously in circles with male friends, not with his bride. The bride's all-female party dances too. In a familiar Jewish wedding custom, men lift up the groom and women the bride, in two chairs. While they are held above the crowd, the newlyweds catch a glimpse of each other as they clasp opposite ends of a handkerchief. In this way, they avoid the taboo of touching each other in public. The food is kosher and copious, not lavish. According to custom, both sets of parents split the matchmaker fee: $1,000. They couldn't afford to buy an apartment for these newlyweds. They will have to rent.

Few of the wedding guests at Beit Daniel, the Center for Progressive Judaism, ever have entered a Reform synagogue or seen an "egalitarian" wedding, but this new type of Israeli marriage is growing more popular. The rabbi, also a new and unfamiliar type, reads from the ketuba; it is not the traditional Orthodox version written in Aramaic, with words largely unchanged for over two thousand years. The couple wrote their ketuba themselves in modern Hebrew, eliminating words about a man "buying his wife" and reflecting their twenty-first-century perspectives on marriage. In this ceremony, both bride and groom exchange rings, vows, and kisses.

According to the state, this marriage never took place. Because Israel's Orthodox religious establishment does not consider Reform Rabbi Meir Azari a real rabbi, this is not a real marriage. Afterward, the newlyweds will fly to nearby Cyprus to remarry in city hall.

"It's absurd. A civil marriage performed by a Greek Orthodox Christian clerk in Cyprus with a high school diploma is valid, but not ones I perform in Israel. Israel is the only country in the world that does not recognize me as a rabbi, and I was born here," complains Rabbi Azari, whose Sephardi family has lived in the Holy Land for more than six centuries. Despite the inconvenience of having to marry twice, guests ask for his card after each wedding. "To have people chasing a Reform rabbi to perform their wedding is amazing. When we opened in 1991, we had only about four weddings a year. Now, we have over five hundred." Beit Daniel probably is Israel's busiest synagogue. Weddings are booked a year in advance. Rabbi Azari officiates at about one hundred a year (including the 2003 marriage of Ehud Barak's daughter); he sends other couples to rabbis all over the country. These Reform and Conservative rabbis also are overwhelmed with requests to officiate at weddings. "Orthodox rabbinic control over Israeli marriages won't last much longer," predicts Rabbi Azari. In fact, the Knesset is under pressure to pass legislation to allow family courts to conduct civil marriages and divorces, which would solve the predicament of the tens of thousands of couples in which one partner is not Jewish.

Fewer Israelis register their weddings with the rabbinate than a decade ago, despite the gigantic surge in the population (primarily the more than one million former Soviet immigrants). Roughly one third of Israelis marry abroad in civil ceremonies and bypass the Chief Rabbinate altogether. Many are couples in which one partner is not Jewish; under Orthodox Jewish law, Jews are not allowed to marry non-Jews. For the first time in its modern history, Israel has an enormous population of non-Jews. Of the roughly three hundred thousand non-Jewish immigrants, mostly from the former Soviet Union, a few thousand are converting. Most are mothers who want to make life easier for their Israeli children. Immigrant soldiers are the largest group of male converts. Conversion courses now offer a bilingual Hebrew-Russian prayer book. "This is an historic chance to bring thousands of these immigrants into the fold," explains Rabbi Azari, who has a special interest in them: his Lithuanian-born wife was Israel's deputy ambassador to Russia and ambassador to Ukraine and Moldova. In 2002, the Supreme Court ruled that anyone undergoing a non-Orthodox conversion in Israel becomes a Jew. However, the convert still is not "Jewish enough" to have a legal marriage in Israel sanctioned by the Orthodox rabbinate.

To protest the Orthodox monopoly on weddings, one bold couple allowed an Israeli television program to broadcast the videos of their two weddings, which were held thousands of miles apart. Hundreds of friends and relatives attended their moving and deeply spiritual Jerusalem ceremony conducted by their Conservative Israeli rabbi. They didn't know anyone at their quick second wedding that an Elvis look-alike "pastor" performed in a gaudy Las Vegas chapel. The couple reminded television viewers that their outlandish civil ceremony was legal; the meaningful Jewish one wasn't. (Israeli Reform and Conservative rabbis may legally marry couples, but only *outside* Israel.) Another couple decided to skip the legal hassles of marrying in Israel and took their vows in a hot air balloon drifting over the Napa wine country. Others stay put and simply marry by proxy in Paraguay by letter. A number of Israelis are choosing to be "conscientious objectors"; they have "illegitimate" weddings in Israel performed by either a Conservative or Reform rabbi and refuse to have a civil ceremony abroad. Even though they consider themselves married, their official Israeli identity cards read "single."

Despite the new openness to nontraditional marriages, most secular Israelis still choose Orthodox rabbis. "My husband sees himself as an Israeli, not a Jew. He's a typical Sabra; he's been in a synagogue maybe twice in his life. After living together for over two years, we decided to get married. He said he wanted a 'real' rabbi. Orthodox, that's all most

Israelis know," says Rina, a jewelry designer who emigrated from the United States. "I agreed, but I had no idea what I was getting into." When she and her fiancé went to the Tel Aviv Orthodox Rabbinic Court, she learned about the many premarriage arrangements an Israeli Jewish couple are required to make. "If you don't meet the religious criteria, the rabbinical court won't allow you to wed. I couldn't believe all the red tape, the strict rules, the meetings." Prospective brides and grooms must prove they are single, Jewish, and eligible to be married. It is forbidden for a Cohen, a male descendant of the priestly Israelite tribe (often with family names such as Cohen, Katz, Kagan, Kaplan, Kahana, Azulai, or Adler), to marry a divorcée or convert. A *mamzer,* the illegitimate child of an adulterous woman or a woman whose husband did not give her a religious divorce, can marry only another mamzer or a convert.

"I had to go from office to office, trying to prove that I'm really Jewish. It didn't matter that I had a letter from my rabbi in New York. They wouldn't accept it because he was ordained in a Conservative seminary. So instead of needing two witnesses to attest that I'm Jewish, I also had to bring a blood relative. I didn't know what to do. I don't have any relatives here. An elderly friend agreed to come. He pretended to be my cousin and they were convinced. Thank God, he wore a kippa, because to them, a secular Jew is an oxymoron." Then Rina was sent to meet an Orthodox woman who gave her a crash course in *niddah,* laws of family purity that govern when a woman may have sex with her husband. No sex is allowed until seven "clean" days after the last day of bleeding. Rina was advised not to sleep in the same bed as her husband during her "unclean" time, that twin beds are preferable. She was assured that abstaining twelve days each month would be good for her marriage because it keeps romance alive. The ancient laws of niddah that prohibit sex with a menstruating woman also prescribe sex during a woman's most fertile time.

While sex fulfills the commandment of procreation, biblical laws also teach that intercourse, which is called "knowing," is an act of great holiness, a gift from God. Sex is as basic an obligation in marriage as food. Jewish texts, including the Torah, Talmud, and Mishna, are direct about ways to enhance sexuality. Some ancient laws of *onah* say that a woman's sexual passion is greater than a man's. To ensure a "peaceful tent," a husband must be attuned to his wife's sexual needs and "pay her a visit" whenever she desires it. A wife has the right to regular sex; the frequency depends on a man's occupation. Students of the Torah, for example, are obligated to perform their marital duty once a week and the preference is Friday night. To promote modesty, most rabbinical opinion holds that intercourse should take place only at night or in the dark. The Shulhan Aruch, the Code of Jewish Law, which regulates everyday behavior, also prescribes how and when a couple should have sex. During intercourse, a man is urged to think of the Bible or other holy scriptures. "He should have intercourse in the most chaste possible manner; he underneath and she above him is considered unchaste." Rabbinical opinions are divided about whether sex should take place clothed or naked and about other sexual positions. If a man has sexual intercourse standing, he is liable to convulsions; if sitting, to spasms. If the woman is above and he below, he will be subject to diarrhea. The Babylonian Talmud recounts a debate in which Rabbi Johanan ben Dahabai cautions that children will be born lame if their parents have intercourse in a non-missionary position; mute, if they kiss "that place"; deaf, if they converse during intercourse; and blind, if they look at "that place."

Rina recalls the Orthodox advisor asking when her menstrual cycle was due so she could make sure the wedding wasn't scheduled when she was bleeding. Under Jewish law, women are advised not to marry when they're menstruating because then they are not allowed contact with their husbands. "When I told her I have my period every thirty days, she said that it was impossible, women don't have such long cycles. I argued and said I was telling the truth. She warned me that if I got my period early, I'd have to change the wedding date." Some women ask their gynecologists to put them on birth control pills to assure they won't menstruate on their wedding night. Before the wedding, Rina was required to go to a ritual bath where an attendant would check her in intimate places to verify that there was no menstrual blood and then would give the bride a note to present to the rabbi who would marry them. "Well, wouldn't you know, the day before my wedding, I got my period. So of course, I didn't go to the mikvah. Why play that charade? Besides, I wouldn't want to get caught or pollute the waters for observant women. But no note, no wedding. I went to meet the rabbi anyway, even though

I was afraid he might call the wedding off. Luckily, he didn't even ask for the note. We had chosen a very cool Orthodox rabbi. Our wedding was wonderful. I just resent that I had to lie so much."

Israelis have a strong urge to merge. By age forty, more than 90 percent of Jewish Israelis have been married at least once. One reason is that most Israelis are child-obsessed. For all Israelis, life is fragile; it always has been a land where parents bury their young. Rina's husband revealed his feelings of vulnerability as he admitted his eagerness to have children: "I can get killed in a war or terrorist incident. I want to leave a child, a piece of me behind."

Israel is one of the few developed countries that actively encourages couples to have many children. Even before the Holocaust and the desire to replace 6 million murdered Jews, Zionists were conscious of their duty to be fruitful. Early state propaganda praised "heroine mothers" who did their demographic duty by producing soldiers to defend the young state. Ben-Gurion had strong feelings about the subject: "Increasing the Jewish birthrate is a vital need for the existence of Israel and a Jewish woman who does not bring at least four children into the world . . . is defrauding the Jewish mission." Israeli pro-natalism has only been increased by serious concerns about the Israeli Muslim birthrate and their demographic-democratic dilemma. To encourage this undeclared war of the wombs, the government offers economic incentives to large families and generous maternity benefits and paternity leaves. However, because benefits—twelve weeks of maternity leave with full pay from the National Insurance Institute, which can be extended up to one year unpaid by either parent—go to all Israelis, haredim and Muslims get the largest family subsidies.

Though neither family planning nor contraception is covered by National Health Insurance, every Israeli woman is entitled to free in vitro fertilization treatments; Israel has more IVF clinics per capita than any other country in the world. In fact, an Israeli physician, a Holocaust survivor, invented the drugs used in all fertility treatments for the past forty years. (He's responsible for more than a million births worldwide.) Or almost all fertility treatments; the arsenal of folk rituals used by religious Jewish women to become pregnant includes carrying red strings that have been wrapped around Rachel's Tomb, making pilgrimages to holy tombs on Mount Meron, and visiting the Israeli grave of Moroccan-born holy man Babi Sali. Others simply avoid eating radishes.

Adultery is the only sexual transgression forbidden by the Ten Commandments. The Jewish perspective, ancient and modern, is clear: adultery is wrong. The Israeli perspective has historically been a bit more tolerant. Israelis were baffled when the story of a U.S. military officer being court-martialed for committing adultery hit the news. Adultery a badge of shame? Doesn't an active libido make a good general? As one Israeli army official put it: If adultery were grounds for discharge, there might not be an army left. Outlawing adultery would threaten Israel's national security, journalist Amnon Dankner once wrote in *Ha'aretz*. "Everyone would submit his resignation. We'd be left with some religious soldiers—that's all. Think what we would have lost if Moshe Dayan had been fired—a chief of staff who won the Sinai War and a defense minister who won the Six-Day War."

The 1967 Six-Day War turned the charismatic general into an international hero. For most of the world, Israel meant Moshe Dayan, the sexy Sabra with the trademark black eye patch. People admired his devil-may-care personality. When the general was caught speeding, he told a policeman, "I have only one eye. Do you want me to look at the road or the speedometer?" Israel's most famous soldier also was the country's most famous adulterer. A senior officer once wrote to Prime Minister Ben-Gurion complaining that Dayan had sent him off to the front so that his wife would be available. When Dayan was chief of staff, one cuckolded husband found parts of Dayan's uniform in his living room, collected them, and sent them to Ben-Gurion. When Dayan's wife appealed to Ben-Gurion about her husband's roving eye, she was informed that the swashbuckling general's romantic trysts would not stand in his way; her husband was destined to become a national leader.

Dayan's only daughter, Yael, was a soldier in his army during the 1967 War. Afterward, they were students together at the Hebrew University, sharing classes and sometimes exam answers. She became his closest confidante. The activist chair of the Knesset Committee on the Status of Women (until the 2003 elections), Yael is disarmingly direct about her father's legendary bravado in bed. "Israelis not only tolerate adultery when men do it, it means point scoring. They admire macho values. Being disloyal to your wife can boost an officer's career." With little prompting, she adds in her deep, husky voice, "My father was a hero because he was naughty. He did things in his own way—from leading armies in victory to bedding third-rate women. He was restless, aloof, an unapologetic womanizer. My mother tolerated his infidelities with a martyr's patience." She pauses and searches in her purse for another cigarette. "He even had an affair with one of my closest girlfriends."

Israelis didn't seem concerned about philandering until the "Netanyahu affair." When Benjamin "Bibi" Netanyahu was running as the Likud Party's candidate for prime minister in 1993, someone made an anonymous call to his wife threatening to publish photographs revealing his sexual exploits with another woman. Israelis were staggered when Netanyahu went on national television and admitted he had cheated on his wife. The telegenic politician's public confession was a turning point: Israel had its first political sex scandal and, for the first time, adultery became a national issue. "Bibigate" was the Sabra version of Clinton. Adultery Israeli-style resembled adultery American-style as journalists tracked down some of Netanyahu's extramarital affairs, including an escapade with one of his advisors. Stories of the twice-divorced Netanyahu's tangled private life and his large sexual appetite did not hurt him with women voters or stop ultra-Orthodox rabbis from ordering their followers to vote for him. Macho values prevailed over family values. Netanyahu was elected prime minister.

It's no secret that extramarital affairs occur the world over. But the amorous ways of Israelis are somewhat different. Part of the reason is the IDF; chapter 2 pointed out that universal conscription takes most Israeli eighteen-year-old Jews and Druze men away from home with nothing but other soldiers—and their own exploding hormones—for company. The impact of Israel's extended military reserve obligation may be even greater. For example, in no other country are married men called into the reserves and required to spend about one month each year often away from their wives and families until they are in their early forties.

"My husband reacted to reserve duty as if it were a camp reunion, back with friends who've been in the same unit since they were eighteen. And the more gray in their hair, the more they brag or lie about their con-

quests," declares Avigail, a car insurance executive. "If Israel is machismo, then the army is machismo on steroids." She knows the
warrior-womanizer culture well. Sixteen years ago, she and Dov became
soldier-lovers. Soon after the army, they stood under the huppa. "When
Dov had to go on reserve duty, he didn't complain. At home on Shabbat
leave, he joked about all the fun I was free to have when he was away.
Sure. It's easy playing around with three kids at home. My 'jealous husband' never tried to get out of reserve duty, even when his friends did.
For him, it meant not having to invent clever excuses. When he was at
home, he did all the time. My aunt spotted him with a woman in his car.
Then there was an aerobics teacher. It's hard to be anonymous here. Finally, he ran out of stories." Even when Avigail threatened divorce, Dov
continued his philandering. Israelis rarely divorce over adultery alone.
"My mother pleaded with me to look the other way, not to break up the
family, at least wait until the children finish school. She's from another
generation. Nobody got divorced then. Without my father, she couldn't
have survived. Well, I earn more than Dov. We were among the first of
our friends to have a prenuptial agreement, so splitting the apartment
and the property wasn't such a nightmare. And me? I'm ready to meet
someone, but not to get married. Last night, I watched *Ha Bourganim*
[*Yuppies*, a weekly Israeli TV series], a shocking episode about Tel Aviv
couples who are into swinging, switching partners with friends. Israelis
always have had a *carpe diem,* I-don't-care attitude. Now with terrorists
blowing up bar mitzvahs and armed guards at funerals, people need new
outlets for the tensions. I hope swinging won't become one."

Shuli was at an ATM when she heard a man call her name. "I didn't
recognize him. Black hat. Black coat. A real haredi. He came up to me
and said, 'Don't you recognize me?' It took me a while. It was my old
boyfriend. We were together over a year and he was a real 'piece.' Now
he's got the haredi wife, the haredi children, the yeshiva, the whole scene.
He was a plumber, not very brilliant, but never did I think he was *that*
stupid. A few days later, he was at my door wearing the haredi costume.
He told me he wanted to talk. I guessed he wanted to convince me to become a 'real' Jew. Right away, I told him I hate the haredim and I didn't
want to hear his born-again religious brainwashing. He said it was not

religion he wanted to talk about. He sat down, wouldn't eat anything. My kitchen isn't kosher. I figured out what he wanted when he took off his coat. It really embarrasses me to say, but without his ugly clothes, he was the same gorgeous guy. We ended up in bed. It was great, like before. Afterwards, as I watched him pick up the black slacks off the floor and the black kippa, I asked him, 'How can you call yourself religious and do this to your wife?' He said we did nothing wrong, that nothing in the Torah forbids a married man from having sex with a single woman. Then I got angry and asked him straight, 'So it's okay if your wife has sex with an unmarried man?' He said no, that's not allowed, that's adultery. What a double standard. I told a few friends about this, and what did I hear? Stories about haredi women who sneak out of their neighborhood, change their clothes, and do it too."

Soon after celebrating her fifth wedding anniversary, Keren was leafing through one of her husband's books and noticed an inscription. It was a gift from his lover. Soon after she threw him out, she did what thousands of Israelis are doing. She went online with www.cupid.co.il, Israel's most popular online dating service. "I was surprised to see ads from married men looking for affairs. Some don't even bother using phony names. One ad I liked, he sounded great. When we met in a coffee shop, right away I saw his wedding ring. I stupidly hadn't asked him. He said he had a bad marriage, that she doesn't understand him, but that he would never leave her. I liked his honesty. One night, we went to hear Zubin Mehta. (The Israel Philharmonic has the largest subscription audience of any orchestra in the world.) And a couple spotted us. They were his wife's friends. I wanted to die. At intermission, he walked right up to them, put his arm around me and introduced me. I knew it would get back to her. I couldn't figure out how he could be so open about us. It took only a few calls to find out more. Because Israel is so small, it's easy to play detective. I learned he had had a long affair with a clothing designer. Apparently, his wife knew about it, but 'chose' not to know. She's very dependent on him and realizes that on her own, it's really difficult to find a provider," Keren says knowingly. "My life is just like that song by Yehudit Ravitz, 'Shabbat and Holidays.' It expresses what so many Israeli women go through, that we're always alone on weekends and holidays, while the 'perfect

husbands,' the 'great family men,' are with their wives and kids. He
made me no promises. Still, I had hopes—until I heard that he's remodel-
ing their house. So, I'm in love with the impossible. I know it. But tell me
and tell my girlfriends, where are the single men over thirty-five? Killed
in traffic accidents or wounded in wars. If they're single and not crippled,
they have a great time. There's a real shortage of men and a real surplus
of single women and widows. I hear Silicon Valley [in California] is full
of single Israeli men, so what am I supposed to do living in Herzliya? To
have someone here hugging me a few times a week, believe me, it's a lot
better than being alone."

In a carefully guarded house, a mother prepares omelets for her toddlers. The kitchen scene is chaotic. She lives with twenty children and a
dozen other mothers who fled here to escape their husbands' blows. Experts have observed a link between violence in the country and violence
in the family. Since intifada II, Israel's twelve battered women's shelters
report an upsurge in applicants and serious overcrowding, just as serious
cuts in government welfare services are going on because of the overwhelming cost of fighting terrorism. Jewish and Arab women's groups
alike lament that about one out of every seven Israeli women is a victim
of domestic abuse. Israeli women from all religious, ethnic, and economic backgrounds have bruised, burned, or battered bodies. Quite a
number of women seeking help in shelters are from the former Soviet
Union and Ethiopia. Their husbands, often unable to find jobs or cope
without Hebrew, direct their anger against them. Among Russian-
speaking men, a high rate of alcoholism contributes to the abuse. Accustomed to a strongly paternalistic culture, some once proud Ethiopian
men sometimes take out their frustrations on wives who adapt faster to
Israeli life. Customarily, Muslim women and fervently religious Jewish
women who live in conservative communities keep their marital difficulties shrouded in secrecy. Keeping the family together is their top priority.

Psychologist Debbie Gross had been working on a crisis hot line for
months before she realized that no calls came from religious Jewish
women. "When haredi women have problems, they turn to their rabbis
for help. And abuse they don't talk about. It's too much a disgrace. Without rabbinical approval, they would never call a hot line. Like Orthodox

women, they don't believe nonreligious women can understand their problems, because religious issues are usually involved." To meet their special needs, Debbie, an American-born Orthodox immigrant, solicited the help of sympathetic rabbis and launched the Crisis Center for Religious Women in Jerusalem. Each day, dozens of Orthodox and haredi women from all over Israel call the hot line, seeking anonymous help for crises ranging from battery to rape to depression. Since 1993, the center has helped more than seven thousand women. "A haredi mother who called couldn't get out of bed to care for her baby. She had never heard of postpartum depression," relates Debbie. "Our volunteer explained to her what it is and referred her to an appropriate doctor." Nearly two hundred volunteers offer counseling and referrals to therapists versed in Jewish law and rabbis specially trained to advise Orthodox and haredi women. They run workshops on family violence for women, children, and rabbis and their wives. One Friday a woman reported that her neighbor, a religious mother in her twenties, was preparing Sabbath dinner when her husband stormed into the kitchen, poured a pot of hot food on her, and hit her. The volunteer alerted the police, who arrested the husband.

Jewish and Arab women's leaders remark that just as the Israelis were taking a hard look at difficult family problems, the country was hit with its worst nightmare in two decades. The threat of terror attacks makes Israelis feel vulnerable, and tempted to rely on Valium. In 2002, mental health workers took a cue from services for Israeli women in crisis about how to treat the pervasive mental suffering. They set up twenty-four-hour emergency telephone lines and special gatherings for victims and witnesses of terrorism. The responses have been overwhelming. Israel has become a country of hot lines and support groups.

Israel's divorce system places all authority in the hands of the rabbinate, who base their rulings on traditional Jewish law. When that law was first codified more than two thousand years ago, the thinking behind it was very progressive. The husband couldn't just throw his wife out: divorce required the mutual consent of husband and wife. It still does, although most twenty-first-century Israelis find the law oppressive.

A family court lawyer, Yisraela Gratzyani, whom we met in her family's sukkah in chapter 12, is in Rabbinical District Court in the heart of secular Tel Aviv pleading a divorce case. Because the judges are all male Orthodox rabbis, the statuesque brunette is wearing her "court outfit," a dowdy below-the-knees suit with long sleeves. A male clerk disapprovingly eyes her uncovered cascading curls. "I'm not married," she says matter-of-factly. She opens her briefcase and prepares for a long wait. The Talmud requires that each *get*, or bill of divorce, be handwritten on parchment. To speed up this archaic system, Israelis who want to untie the knot can now submit divorce petitions by fax.

All Israeli Jewish divorces must go through the Rabbinical Court, even for non-Orthodox couples who marry abroad. There are no civil marriages or divorces in Israel. Divorce needs the consent of both parties. This consent, however, is not equal for men and women. If a woman refuses to consent to a divorce, rabbis may give the man permission to remarry even though he is not divorced. The Israeli Jewish divorce rate, which has risen to about 38 percent—still lower than the rate in either the United States or Western Europe—is higher for Ashkenazi than Mizrahi couples. Even though divorce is frowned on in ultra-Orthodox communities, their once very low divorce rate is creeping up.

A single line in Deuteronomy 24:1—"He writes a bill of divorce and puts it in her hand"—has created a thorny problem for Israeli Jewish women, because it means, in practice, that no Jewish woman can divorce her husband; she can only be divorced by him. "This is another messy divorce," explains Yisraela, whose client, a thirty-four-year-old chemist, is married to a businessman who refuses to grant her a divorce. "Her husband is blackmailing her. He won't give her a divorce unless she gives him the house her parents bought them as well as all her claims to alimony. It's outrageous. He's trying to screw her. To win the judges' sympathy, he's pretending to be religious. We're going to fight this," she vows. Most Israeli plaintiffs are not religious. To impress the judges, Yisraela instructed her client to wear a demure dress and the scarf of a married Orthodox woman. "I don't want this to drag on for years. She wants to get on with her life, remarry, and have children. So many women can't afford lawyers and their husbands won't give them a get unless they give up their custody rights or lawful property. I've seen women whose lives are in danger who can't get divorces. Our fossilized system ruins their lives. It's out of touch with reality."

It's a system that leaves tens of thousands of women in limbo, neither married nor divorced so long as their husbands refuse to grant them a get. But even they are in a less ambiguous situation than the *agunot,* or "chained wives," whose husbands have disappeared or deserted them or refused to give them a get even though the Chief Rabbinate has decided they should. An agunah's husband can go on with his life without paying alimony or child support. If he has children with an unmarried woman, under both civil and Jewish law, they are considered perfectly "kosher." However, if his wife has children with another man, she is an adulteress, and under Jewish law the children are illegitimate or *mamzerim* and cannot marry a Jew.

Yisraela's own mother was a victim of the religious courts, just as her Iraqi-born father was their beneficiary. "I was four [in 1974] when my mother wanted to divorce him. My father put her through a terrible battle for her freedom and it lasted until I was a teenager. In order for him to give her the get, he forced my grandparents to give him a lot of money. My mother had to waive all her rights, including alimony [in Jewish law, the husband must grant alimony], and agree to a ridiculously low amount of child support for the three of us. The divorce almost destroyed our lives. My father never gave her any money to raise us, he didn't even contact us." Yisraela and her two brothers grew up on their grandparents' moshav. When her grandfather died, her mother, a hairdresser, was so cash-strapped that she sent thirteen-year-old Yisraela to a free boarding school. Most of the children also were from poor Mizrahi and Sephardi families. "They were bright, innocent kids, but with soap opera lives. Neglect and broken homes. Because of the religious courts and impotency of the civil courts on this aspect of family law, a lot of these children, like me, were suffering. I don't want to see more go through what my family did." After her army service, Yisraela worked as a newspaper reporter to pay her way through Tel Aviv University, where about half her fellow law students were women. Almost half of Israeli judges are women and there are three women Supreme Court judges. Yisraela is quick to point out that despite these impressive advances, clerics allow no women judges on rabbinical, Islamic, Christian, or Druze courts— which control all Israeli marriages and divorces.

Yisraela's fighting spirit and acute sense of justice came from her mother's struggle with the religious courts; her grandmother inspired her to love Judaism and to be tolerant. "She taught me not to hate anyone, not even the rabbinical court judges. I've actually met a few enlightened ones who are helping women get divorces. There has been slow progress." Centuries ago, when Jews lived in insular communities, rabbis could order a husband to be shunned or beaten to compel him to grant a divorce. In secular, urbanized Israel, there is no such pressure. Today, only a handful of Israeli men who defy rabbinical court orders to grant their wives divorces are sent to prison. The Knesset has passed legislation that authorizes stricter punishments on recalcitrant husbands who are already in prison, including not allowing visitors and placing them in solitary confinement. Their credit cards, driver license, and professional licenses have been revoked. A few doctors and lawyers can no longer practice until they set their wives free. Rabbinical courts have located a few dozen missing men and convinced them to grant their wives divorces. More women are beginning to ask for prenuptial contracts to divide assets and to lower the potential for a blackmail situation where their husband can refuse them a get.

In 1987, 80 percent of couples submitted petitions to rabbinical courts. No longer. Over half of all couples seeking a divorce come to a mutual agreement; usually they have a lawyer draw up a divorce agreement so they don't have to wage war in front of Orthodox rabbis. Acknowledging this significant reversal, Yisraela stresses that "now that religious parties are losing their political power, I have hope that we'll see changes in our marriage and divorce laws soon. People are fed up. We must make civil marriages legal and end the religious monopoly over marriage and divorce. If Israeli men needed their wives' agreement to get divorced, this problem would have been solved long ago."

There's nothing like a traditional Islamic village wedding. Sounds of drums, tambourines, and singing reverberate through the streets. So do celebratory gunshots (though this practice is on the wane because there have been too many accidents). The cavalcade of cars—the bride's wedding party—arrives. Until recently, a bride usually arrived by Arabian stallion. A Toyota Corolla decorated with flowers and ribbons brings this bride and her family to the whitewashed two-story home where the groom's family lives and to which an annex has been built for the new couple. Resplendent in a flowing white chiffon gown, the bride alights. The bearded groom, wearing a new black suit, escorts her and her female relatives to his father's house and then heads to a field behind it. About three hundred men surround him, kissing him, shoving envelopes of money into his hand. They start clapping rhythmically and chanting: "Our groom is the best of youth, the best of youth is our groom. Our groom is Antar Abs [an Arab hero who rescues his lover after a raiding enemy kidnaps her from her desert tent]. Our groom is the sun of the dawn, he wasn't shy when he asked for the bride's hand."

Just as for Jews, all marriages and divorces for Muslims, as well as Druze and Christians, are controlled by religious courts. Muslim couples do not marry in mosques. The only requirement for a marriage is a simple all-male ceremony to sign the marriage contract, with a sheik or any man versed in Islamic tradition officiating. Timing can be important. Some people still believe that a contract signed when the moon is in the scorpion phase could lead to an unhappy marriage; if it is signed in sunlight, the bride may miscarry. Typically, the bride's father or a male representative and the groom clasp right hands in front of at least two male witnesses. The father says, "I give you my daughter, the adult virgin, in marriage according to the law of Allah and of The Prophet." After the groom agrees to accept her, he adds, "I hope in God she may prove a blessing." The sheik and the men recite the brief opening chapter of the Koran. All that is left is the marriage contract. The kitab is not only a legal contract between bride and groom, it also is a transaction between their families. It details what the groom will give the bride before the marriage is consummated and what he will give her afterward, frequently a house, money, or land. Sometimes a car and an education are included. The *mohar,* or bride payment, is based on her desirability and the "purity" of the family name and their other daughters. It also states how much he will pay if he decides to divorce her. With the signing of the kitab, the Islamic wedding contract, the marriage is legal.

Legal, but in Muslim families, not yet complete. It may take days, months, or years for the round of wedding parties to start, but no matter how long the interval, religious parents rarely allow their married daughter to spend much time alone with her husband. They look at it this way: should a problem arise and the marriage break up, the daughter may no longer be a virgin or she may have become pregnant. A death in the family may unexpectedly delay a wedding party. No wedding can be held within forty days of a relative's passing, and no family desires to fete an obviously pregnant bride. More liberal Muslim families allow the couple to be intimate after the signing ceremony.

Whether the couple is secular or fervently religious, every wedding deserves a huge feast, and for this one, the groom's father killed three sheep. Pungent aromas of grilling meats fill the air. His wife and women relatives prepared the traditional *mansaf,* enormous platters of steamed rice topped with succulent roast lamb and goat. The men are seated on cushions surrounding the platters, sharing the food, shaping the rice into balls and scooping up the meat with their right hands. (The left hand is considered unclean, as it was the traditional choice before the invention of toilet paper throughout the Middle East and much of Asia.) This is an alcohol-free Muslim wedding, but there is plenty of Coke and homemade tamarind juice. As the all-male, five-piece band launches into a high-spirited tune, a bouncy line of men weaves through the crowd, arms on each other's shoulders, spontaneously leaping, then squatting, with strong, staccato movements. They are performing the time-honored *debka* dance. Then the groom's brothers lift him high in the air.

The female guests can hear the infectious rhythms. They're celebrating on the roof of the house. As the drumming intensifies, clapping and ululating women swirl around the bride. Because no men are present, women have removed their headscarves and shapeless caftans, revealing stylish dresses. Using her white silk scarf as a prop, the bride's pregnant sister performs a graceful improvisational dance. The bride is the elder sister and should have married first, but she rejected her parents' first choice. Finally, relatives agreed on a suitable match: her second cousin. With this union, the hamula increases its size and retains its name and wealth. Without a house a man cannot get married, so marrying within the same family saves the dowry payment and keeps land and wealth within extended families. Despite genetic dangers, the ancient custom of marrying relatives prevalent among Bedouin remains widespread among other Muslim Israelis. An estimated 45 percent of all Muslim Israeli marriages are between relatives; 25 percent are between first-degree kin.

"None of my friends has an arranged marriage," says Samya, another new bride. "They met their husbands through friends, at clubs, at work, not through their parents. I've read newspaper stories of women who run away to marry men they love and then are killed by their families, but I don't know any. That's not in my world." Samya, scarcely the stereotypically passive Muslim wife, never has worn a long, embroidered caftan, hidden her hair with a scarf, or attended a traditional Islamic wedding. She reads the *New York Times* online, not the Koran. She first met Abdallah ("Servant of Allah") on a high school field trip and then again a few years later at the Hebrew University, where they both are students. "When we fell in love, it was months before our parents knew." Her parents live near Tamra, an all-Muslim Galilee town and Israel's cucumber-growing capital. Samya's father, a retired bus driver, asked a sheik to officiate at the signing ceremony at the house. It was less traditional because Samya was allowed to be in the room. Like most Muslim couples, they did not recite vows. Though few religious Muslims exchange rings, considering them a Jewish and Christian tradition, Samya and Abdallah did. She added clauses to her wedding contract that Abdallah will allow her to work and that they would live near Jerusalem, not with his parents. (The groom's family often adds an extension to their home for each son and his wife.) After the simple ceremony, the two families had tea and a ten-layer wedding cake. In the ensuing months, they went to unchaperoned movies and took walks on the beach. They were affectionate but also abstinent.

A round of parties began four months after the signing ritual. Samya's parents hosted a night of the henna party which resembled Moti and Adi's Algerian Jewish one (see chapter 10). Before the second henna celebration, at Abdallah's parents' home in Acre, Samya pasted fresh dough with daisies and coins on the front door to ensure a harmonious relationship with her mother-in-law. Finally, on the third night, Samya and Abdallah celebrated their long anticipated wedding party at a marble-and-gilt wedding hall near Acre, a place popular with Muslims and Christian Arab Israelis. In fact, it's difficult to tell the celebrations apart; the food, music, bands, photographer, and video crews are the same. The only obvious difference is that religious Muslims don't serve alcohol or eat pork and Christian Arab wedding ceremonies are held in churches.

Samya and Abdallah had a normal-size Arab wedding: almost nine hundred guests. How did their blue-collar parents manage to foot the bill? At every wedding, guests give cash; most deposit envelopes in a special box. Samya shows a video. She looked elegant, like a *Bride's Maga-*

zine model. As she and Abdallah took hesitant steps toward the head table, their path was strewn with flowers. Islamic clerics would not have approved of this event. It didn't begin with a recitation of Koranic verses, alcohol flowed freely, and women and men performed hip-swiveling dances to the band's pedal-to-the-metal pop. Instead of sticking to rich Arabic classical harmonies and folk tunes, the singer from Nazareth knew she was free to perform sensuous modern love songs. Because of the alcohol and mixed dancing, few religious relatives showed up. When the festivities ended, Samya and Abdallah spent the night at a four-star hotel in Haifa. Because the intifada killed tourism, it was almost empty. It was their first intimate night together.

A traditional Muslim bride can feel great anxiety on her wedding night, especially if relatives wait to see a bloody sheet. If she doesn't bleed, she can be handed back in disgrace to her family, who are thus deprived of a sizable dowry payment. Her humiliated male relatives may even murder her for dishonoring them. As an Algerian writer once put it, "Honor is buried in the vagina as if it were a treasure more precious than life." A twenty-two-year-old woman recently posted this on an Internet Islamic message board: "Although I am a virgin, I am terrified of what my wedding night holds because if there's no hymen (please Allah I hope there is), my family and my husband will doubt my virtue. Maybe I broke mine with a tampon." To guarantee bleeding or to compensate for lost hymens, some women resort to inserting sponges soaked in animal blood. Others ask their gynecologists to write a note certifying they are virgins. For those who are not, hymen restoration, a quick outpatient procedure performed a few days before a wedding reception, can save a woman's marriage and life. If the groom cannot achieve an erection on the wedding night, it is not unheard of for a concerned bride to rupture her own hymen, lest the marriage be considered invalid.

Attitudes toward sex, as reflected in Israeli Arabic-language media—Internet chatrooms, television talk shows, and *Lilac* magazine—are undergoing a tug of war, tradition versus modernity. While in single-sex company, nonreligious Israeli Muslims openly discuss sex as unselfconsciously as they discuss the latest restaurant or Egyptian movie. For observant Muslims and those returning to religion, and despite the teachings attributed to Muhammad that sex during marriage is to be enjoyed and foreplay to be encouraged, contemporary Israeli society seems overly promiscuous. It's difficult to avoid seeing Jewish men and women holding hands or kissing on beaches, buses, and billboards. The Islamic revival means embracing family life and a thirteen-centuries-old faith founded in what is now Saudi Arabia, which frowns on shameless Western behaviors.

Observant Jews and Muslims follow a prescribed, but quite different, lovemaking etiquette. The *Hadith,* a storehouse of originally oral religious traditions, offers guidance for much of Muslim life. On the wedding night, for example, a groom still is advised to wash the bride's feet and throw the water to the furthest corner so Allah will drive away seventy kinds of poverty, give seventy types of riches and blessings, and make the bride immune to mental illness. It is forbidden to have sexual intercourse with either the head or the rear end facing Mecca or standing up, like a donkey. A couple must not speak while making love lest they conceive a mute child. If a man is thinking of another woman while he makes love with his wife, and a boy is conceived, he may be stupid, effeminate, and desire sex with other men. Just as the Jewish Sabbath is an auspicious lovemaking time, for Muslims a boy conceived on Friday evening is destined to be an eloquent preacher. Having sexual intercourse on the first, middle, and last day of the (lunar) month, however, may lead to a miscarriage or cause a baby to become mad. If a couple makes love under direct sunlight and a child is conceived, he may face a life of poverty. A child must not see or hear his parents making love or he may become an adulterer. During the first week of marriage, a bride is advised to follow dietary restrictions. If she consumes vinegar, she never will be entirely clean of menstrual blood. Coriander causes heavy menstrual cycles and can exacerbate labor; eating a sour apple can make a womb "cool and barren." One of the worst Arabic curses is "May your womb shrivel up."

A couple feels great pressure to have children. As a beautiful ancient Arabic saying goes, "Where there are no children, there is no light in the house." In Arabic, which is a rich, poetic language, children are called the "staircase to paradise." When raised in extended families they are surrounded by love and attention. Sons are highly prized and customarily receive more pampering than daughters. In the hamula, a patrilineal and patriarchal system, it's a common belief that a family's fate is in the hands of its sons. During wedding festivities, friends and relatives wish the couple many sons. After a woman has her first son, she is often called by his name; for example, Umm Ahmad means Ahmad's mother. A father who has only daughters may be ridiculed and called Abu Banat, "father of daughters."

Nadia Hilou, a feminist bent on combating the widespread perception that Arab women are not equal to men, has four daughters. An Arab Christian social worker, she directs an Arab-Jewish early childhood center in an ultramodern building in a partly rundown Arab-Jewish section of Old Jaffa. Many mothers who bring their toddlers here for story hours, music, and playtime are newly religious Muslims and wear Islamic scarves. Nadia also runs a grassroots organization that helps Arab women tackle social problems such as coping with the constraints of male-dominated families. Traditional Muslim and Druze men feel apprehensive when this outspoken blonde with a master's degree from Tel Aviv University drives into their villages. One keffiyah-wearing man told her, "Nadia, I never would want to be married to you, but I'll listen to you." At home, she lives with an open-minded computer programmer who doesn't mind helping with housework when his wife is in the field.

Even though Nadia is Roman Catholic, she chose to marry in her husband's Greek Orthodox Church. Each of Israel's many Arab Christian denominations follows different marriage and divorce rules, and the Roman Catholic Church in Israel does not allow divorce. "I figured if ever, God forbid, I wanted a divorce, at least I would have a way out. A Roman Catholic living next to the Vatican can get a divorce, but not in the Holy Land," Nadia comments. At work, she is an expert at navigating cross-cultural divides. In Druze villages, she holds separate meetings for men and women. When the head of a Bedouin clan told this articulate activist that Bedouin women are "different," she bit her tongue and sweetly assured him that she had no intention of cutting women off from their traditions. When such men are out of earshot, she urges Arab women to press for changes and run for political office.

Living among the Christians, Muslims, and Jews of Jaffa has taught Nadia to understand "other mentalities." During the first week of intifada II, when riots erupted in Jaffa, she was on the streets trying to calm people. For educated Arab couples who live in mixed towns and can afford to live separately from the husband's parents, the power of the extended family and hamula is declining, but not in the all-Arab towns and villages where most Muslims live. "Most of these women are at home and they feel the control of the hamula. Only about 17 percent work. We're not happy with the figure, but at least it's up," says Nadia. "Because they have a lot of children and no income of their own, they're tied to the [husband's] extended family." In the hamula, where time-honored male values often still prevail, women must conform to accepted behaviors. A great dishonor befalls a man whose wife or daughter or sister is accused of the slightest sexual indiscretion. Even rumors can cause a family to be ostracized, daughters deemed unmarriageable, and sons taunted by the community. It is said that the "father of daughters does not sleep well."

Asked about the prominent politician from the Arab town of Taibe who said that he thought nothing of giving his wife "an occasional smack," Nadia pauses. "It does happen too often. But to think that all Arab women are abused or miserable, that's a very unfair stereotype. I know plenty of powerful Arab women who are the backbones of their families." On the other hand, for Arab women who have troubled marriages, the complex family structure makes life difficult. Even though the bride moves into the husband's extended family, her family remains responsible for her conduct. "If a woman is beaten, her parents say, 'Don't let inside problems outside. We will lose our good name. You can live with beatings, but we can't live with community shame.' Family is stronger than the individual. You can't break up the family. If a couple fights, there's a chain reaction. Everyone is intermarried. A woman's brother may be married to her husband's sister. If one brother fights with another, it's a mess, because people share the same land. For women in abusive marriages, it's hard to leave. They have no way to support themselves, trapped in a traditional society that legitimizes gender-based violence, husband against wife, brother against sister. For uneducated women, divorce rarely is a possibility."

Each year, an estimated one quarter of Arab Israeli wives are abused physically, and at least half have had this experience at least once in their marriage, according to research by Mohammed Al-Haj Yehiye, professor of social work at the Hebrew University. Although studies indicate wife beating is prevalent, Arabic-speaking social workers report difficulties convincing men and women that it is unacceptable. "Few other religions sanction a man's beating a disobedient wife, as does the Koran," wrote Judith Miller in *God Has Ninety-Nine Names*. A section in the Koran (Sura 4:34) has been interpreted to mean that men have "preeminence" over women, that they are "overseers" of women. The verse goes on to say that the husband of an insubordinate wife should first admonish her, then refuse to share her bed, and finally beat her. "The way Islam has been practiced in most Muslim societies for centuries has left millions of Muslim women with battered bodies, minds and souls," a Muslim expert on the religion told *Time* magazine's Lisa Beyer.

As director of Nazareth-based Women Against Violence, Aida Touma-Suliman does work few like to talk about. She and her staff travel to Arab high schools and community centers to discuss the problems of domestic violence and also offer support services to its victims. "You'd be surprised to know that a lot of Arab women don't know that sexual violence is against the law," Aida observes. Most abused women are afraid to lodge a complaint with the police. If a woman does, a male officer asks probing, intimate questions. (There are few female Arab investigators.) He may be a relative and advise her to return home and not shame the family. Sometimes an officer may accuse her of disobeying her husband. If a woman gets a restraining order issued against a violent spouse, his offended hamula may threaten her, even take her life.

In the recent past, battered women and girls had nowhere to turn. Now three Arabic-language hot lines help them and Women Against Violence runs a shelter in an undisclosed Arab village in the Galilee. "We have to keep the location secret," Aida remarks. "Word is getting out and women know how to contact us. We need much more space." The situation is particularly bad for rape victims. Under Islamic law, to prove rape, a woman must have four adult males of "impeccable" character who witnessed the penetration. Few women get to court; if they dare tell their families, likely they will not be believed, or worse, will be blamed or even killed. Women who come to rape centers are extremely worried about confidentiality. Some seek emotional support; others, a volunteer to bring them to a doctor to inspect if their hymen is broken.

Throughout the Islamic world, each year thousands of women are murdered by husbands or male relatives in the name of family honor—five thousand in 1998 according to a United Nations study. Of that, about 2,500 were women living in the West Bank, Gaza, and Jordan who were killed for "reasons of honor," according to Jordanian author Norma Khoury's eye-opening book *Honor Lost*. "Many families believe that once a woman tarnishes her image, it's just like breaking glass. It can't be fixed. And the only way to fix it is to kill her," bluntly states a female crime reporter for the *Jordan Times*, Rana Husseini, who crusades against honor killings. Under Jordanian law, a man who kills a female relative surprised in an act of adultery or fornication is not guilty of murder. Premarital sex is a criminal offense, regarded as equal to adultery, whereas a girl under eighteen who engages in consensual sex is deemed to have been raped. A woman cannot leave home without her family's permission. By law, an unwed mother is a criminal and her child is raised in an orphanage.

In Israeli courts, if there is enough evidence, convicted killers receive the maximum sentence, which under Israeli law is life. But in places where custom is as powerful as law, it is said that an unchaste woman is worse than a murderer; she affects not just one victim, but her family and the entire hamula. Honor is so valued that women have been slain because of flirting, dating without a father's permission, marriage against the family's wishes, or adultery. To get a loan excused, a debtor may blackmail a creditor by threatening to spread a rumor about the creditor's daughter. If a daughter has a sullied name, a family has little chance of getting a good match for her or a respectable bride payment. On occasion, men have accused mothers, wives, or sisters of illicit sex to inherit land or money. Adulterous men rarely are slain: killing a man could launch a blood feud that may last generations.

Nowadays, most Arab Muslim women live very different lives from their mothers'. They travel outside their towns and mingle with men on campuses and in cafés. Some conservative families react to these confusing behaviors with murder. In 2001, fourteen-year-old Nadine al-Wahidi, a Muslim student at a mostly Jewish high school in Ramle, was murdered by her uncle. Her crime was dressing and behaving like her Jewish friends. The names of her cousin and aunt also appeared on a hit list of "marked" women who were considered insufficiently modest. Twenty-two-year-old Samia Garoushi's name was on the hit list. She was visiting her parents' house when two male vigilantes entered and fatally shot her. As an unmarried woman living alone and working and studying in Haifa, she had stained the family honor. By planning a trip to Egypt, another young woman from a village in Galilee inadvertently broke an unwritten code that says "If you stray or people think you might stray, you die." Her transgression was not arranging for a male relative chaperone. Fearing that she might shame the family, her brother killed her.

Rudayena Jemael was sleeping in her home in all-Arab Taibe when someone shot her in the head. Police found no signs of forced entry. There was no robbery. They arrested her twenty-year-old son. His motive for killing her? After nineteen years living with the stigma of a divorcée, his thirty-seven-year-old mother wanted to remarry. The victim's former husband claimed his son was innocent. "It was all village gossip. Only Allah knows who murdered her." After serving his prison sentence, the victim's son threw a huge party. His grieving sister didn't celebrate. She could only say, "I despise these honor killings that Arab society supports."

"The police generally focus only on the killers and do not deal with the accomplices," complains Aida Touma-Suliman. Women too have been known to incite male relatives or even help plan murders. Because members of the family and community frequently collude to protect the murderer, police face formidable hurdles investigating honor killings. Police and Arab women's organizations are unable to gauge how many honor killings occur because usually they are hushed up, disguised as suicides, accidents, or disappearances.

In the 1950s, Israel banned polygamy mainly to affirm women's equality and as a reaction to a few Mizrahi Jews from Islamic countries who arrived with an "extra" wife, a practice some followed until the early twentieth century. In this practice, they, and not their Ashkenazi cousins who readily accepted an eleventh-century ban on polygamy, were closer to their biblical forebears. Abraham had a wife and a concubine. Jacob had two wives and two concubines. King David had at least eighteen wives (but committed adultery with the married Bathsheva), and King Solomon is reputed to have had one thousand wives. As with the biblical Hebrews, there are polygamous families in almost every Arab Muslim community, not only among the Bedouin. The Koran allows a man four wives, but under Israeli law only one of the wives in a polygamous family can have a legally recognized marriage agreement. Rather than face the ignominy of divorce, a number of Israeli Muslim women put up with a second, "unofficial" wife. "If you have one wife, it's no good. She takes you for granted," said a businessman who lives in a Galilee village. "I like having two wives. They're jealous. Always afraid I will love the other more, so they always compete to treat me better."

As Islamic fundamentalism grows, Israeli Arab men are bombarded with pro-polygamy arguments. In radio and television broadcasts, for example, clerics tell them that an additional wife or two helps maintain family unity; a man will not need mistresses or risk contracting AIDS from prostitutes or have to divorce an infertile wife. As Sheik al-Qaradhawi assured millions of al-Jazeera Television viewers, "Without polygamy, many women would die old maids, without experiencing the joys of motherhood. Maybe half a husband is better than none."

Banna Shoughry-Badarne, a Muslim lawyer with the Association for Civil Rights in Israel, complains that the Israeli government is not enforcing antipolygamy laws. "Bigamy is a crime punishable by up to five years in prison under state law. But the government doesn't enforce this law and allows Muslims to have multiple marriages because it considers marriage and divorce religious issues. By not enforcing the polygamy law, the state is encouraging Muslim men to violate women's rights."

Only recently have Israelis started talking about "blue marriages." Israeli Muslims bring in new and/or additional wives from the West Bank and Gaza, who then are entitled to Israeli health and other benefits. Conversely, Palestinian men leave unemployment and wives behind to marry Israeli Muslims, which can entitle them to "blue cards," jobs, and residency in Israel. "Blue marriages" also are demographic/political weapons, a surreptitious way to "return" Palestinians to their "homeland." The Interior Ministry charges that some 140,000 Palestinians illegally have received Israeli citizenship. For example, a Palestinian marries an Arab Israeli, brings in his children from a previous marriage, then fictitiously divorces the Israeli and brings in his Palestinian spouse. The government decided to tighten its policy of granting family reunification residency requests for Palestinians after a suicide bomber blew himself up in a Haifa restaurant, killing sixteen people and injuring forty-four others on March 31, 2002. It turned out that the bomber had Israeli citizenship because his Palestinian mother had married an Arab Israeli.

Muslim women tend to remain in bad marriages or let their husbands have another, unofficial wife rather than face life as a social pariah. Divorcées frequently move back with their parents, who sometimes hide their "shame" by keeping the woman in the house. Under Islamic law, no grounds are required of a husband to say the words "I divorce you" three times to his wife and the marriage is over; no other reason is needed. (The waiting period is three menstrual cycles to ascertain that she is not pregnant.) Without her husband's consent, it is difficult for a woman to get out of a marriage; mental or physical abuse seldom is grounds for her to seek divorce. A woman needs a compelling reason and often must agree to return all or part of her dowry. A woman can initiate divorce if her husband fails to have sex with her at least once in four months—a sexually frustrated wife is thought to be more easily tempted to commit adultery. All divorces must go through Islamic courts where judges, all of whom are male, often assume women are at fault. A woman's testimony is worth only half that of a man's. Fathers usually win custody of boys over the age of six and girls after puberty.

Women frequently go through long, humiliating court proceedings and rarely get child custody or enough financial support, complains Banna, a new mother and one of the few women lawyers who has studied how the Islamic courts work. "Only lawyers can advocate before Muslim courts and no Muslim women lawyers practice in this field, so we're at a severe disadvantage. And these decisions have a profound impact on our lives." Still, there has been progress. A Muslim woman can get out of an unhappy marriage without a husband's consent if her marriage contract stipulates that she has the right to divorce. And women are adding another clause: if their husbands take a second wife, they have the right to a divorce. In 2001, Muslim and Christian Arab women welcomed a major legislative achievement when they won the right (already enjoyed by Jewish and Druze women) to turn to civil courts to settle alimony and custody disputes. Banna celebrates this long-awaited breakthrough. No longer will mothers have to accept alimony decisions by religious judges who tell them how much they need to support their babies. "They don't know the price of pita or cheese because they've never bought them."

In Israel, couples fight, reconcile, marry, commit adultery, divorce, abuse one another. But from births to burials, life centers around family. Every spring, when the Galilee is ablaze with blood-red poppies, yellow daisies, and purple irises, Arab and Jewish families come out to enjoy the tranquil scene. "*Dir balak,*" a father says in Arabic, cautioning his children not to wade too deeply into the cool, emerald waters of the Sea of Galilee, which for the first time in years is full. During an impromptu game of dodge ball with his curly haired sons, a father shouts out "*Yoffe* [Great]" in Hebrew. A mother sets up a picnic while her daughter plays with a puppy. It's a relief to eat outside in the sun, far from restaurants that blow up. One Arabic expression used by Israelis of many backgrounds mirrors the bittersweet taste of their lives: *Yom asal, yom basal.* (Some days are honey, some days are onion.) Other than the occasional F-16 fighter plane, Hezballah and Hamas seem far away.

A couple sprawled on a blanket sit up suddenly. The husband hands his wife binoculars to watch thousands of white storks gliding through the sky, migrating from Africa to nest in Europe. The flight of the storks symbolizes an auspicious time, the arrival of spring and luck. At a moment like this, "it seems possible to dream," as a favorite Hebrew love song goes, "there is no war in the world."

17

Oy! Gay?

❧ Thou shalt not lie with mankind as with womankind; it is an abomination. —Leviticus 18:22

❧ Being gay and Muslim is not an oxymoron. —Faisal Alam, founder of al-Fatiha, an international group of gay and lesbian Muslims, on opening the Jerusalem chapter

An international television audience of nearly a billion watched a raven-haired Israeli beauty, Dana International, win the prestigious Eurovision Song Contest in 1998. The curvaceous twenty-seven-year-old singer, wearing a feather-bedecked vest over a slinky gown, accepted the prize once won by Abba and Celine Dion and proudly waved the Israeli flag. After her triumph, thousands of cheering Israelis spilled into Tel Aviv's streets, dancing and partying all night. Some were weeping for joy. Dana, a transsexual once known as Yaron Cohen, a former soldier and the son of working-class, religious Yemenite parents, brought new pride to Israel's estimated quarter of a million gays. On her triumphal visit to the Knesset, the gender-bending pop star was congratulated by Prime Minister Benjamin Netanyahu and kissed by Moshe Katsav, now President of Israel. In polls, 80 percent of Israelis called Dana "an appropriate representative of Israel."

A month later, more than fifteen thousand Israelis turned out for the country's first Gay Pride Parade. Men and women in flamboyant costumes, others in tank tops and shorts, gyrated down Tel Aviv's streets as Dana's hit song "Diva" blared from loudspeakers. People waved from balconies at floats carrying singers, dancing bare-chested men, and sequin-clad drag queens. Gay couples walked hand in hand. Heterosexual couples brought their children to show their support for the homosexual community's right to live openly and freely. At the finale in Rabin Square, Knesset members addressed the crowd as men openly kissed men and women kissed women. "Dana's victory and the parade were cataclysmic changes for our community. No one dreamed so many Israelis would feel safe to 'come out,' " recalls Mickey Gluzman, a professor of gay and comparative literature at Tel Aviv University. "Each year at the parade I can't believe my eyes: thousands more show up." Men wearing kippas carry signs reading "Gay, religious and proud" along with OrthoDykes, a group of Orthodox lesbians. Although religious Jews consider homosexuality an abomination, there are few protests. "Protests?" asks Mickey. "We're living with bombs on buses and security guards in our cafés and schools. So who cares if I live with my boyfriend?"

His lover runs a Tel Aviv café with an unmistakably heterosexual partner from his former tank unit. At outside tables, gays and straights gather to sip espresso and agonize over politics. One man reads the *Pink Time,* a monthly Israeli gay magazine with news, personal ads, and revealing photos of the Holy Land's homosexual hunks. Though Haifa and Jerusalem and eight other towns also have gay community centers, Tel Aviv is the undisputed center of Israeli gay life, with gay clubs, gay pubs, even gay soccer teams. No longer are homosexual themes in Israeli literature, music, film, or television unheard of. Many Israelis were glued to their televisions the night *Florentine,* a series, featured a coming-out scene. The popular 2003 romance film *Yossi and Jagger* was about two gay soldiers. In 2002, Israel had its first openly gay member of the Knesset, Tel Aviv University chemistry professor Uzi Even. State-run educational television has run programs for teens about the difficulties of being young and gay. Secular high school curricula are gay-friendly ("All people must be treated with respect and tolerance, even if their sexual orientation is different from the majority")—all in a country where religious politicians have tremendous power.

Israel has become an international gay rights trendsetter. Yael Dayan, the Knesset's chair for Lesbian and Gay Affairs until 2003, even had a rainbow flag in her office, and visitors didn't even wonder what country it represents. Since the Israeli Supreme Court decriminalized sodomy in 1988, justices have approved some of the world's most progressive gay rights legislation. Workplace discrimination against gays is outlawed. Unlike some armies—such as the U.S., with its "Don't ask, don't tell" policy—the IDF has dozens of high-ranking gay officers. The question of whether they should serve in the military has never been an issue in Israel. In 1993, Defense Minister Yitzhak Rabin decreed that gay soldiers be treated equally and also made it illegal for officers to ask soldiers about their sexual orientation. After a colonel died, the army awarded his same-sex partner a military widower's pension. Gay partners of Israeli diplomats and El Al staff receive the benefits of heterosexual spouses. Though there is no civil marriage in Israel even for heterosexual couples, both the Supreme Court and the military have ruled that homosexual couples are eligible for spousal and widower benefits. Israel's 1998 sexual harassment law, which is the strictest in the world, includes "sexual orientation" as an explicitly protected category.

"When it comes to protecting our rights, the laws are there. The problem is there are so many conservative people like my parents," says Michal Eden, a young Liza Minnelli look-alike who made history when she became Israel's first openly gay politician. When she was elected to the Tel Aviv City Council in 1998, her Yemenite and Moroccan-born parents didn't call to congratulate her, which was scarcely surprising, as they hadn't spoken to her since 1990. "I was twenty when I told my family I had a girlfriend. My mother and brothers and sisters stared at me without speaking. My father's face suddenly had a million wrinkles. He bit his nails and started pacing back and forth. He threatened that if I didn't change, I could never have any contact with my family. I pleaded, 'I can't give up my feelings. You have to let me be myself.' The defining moment in my life was when my family threw me out and my brother threatened to kill me. All I had was a backpack of clothes. I wandered from one friend's apartment to another, working at any job I could find. I was determined to live my life my own way. I went to college and found a partner and moved in with her. I've built a new family—the gay and lesbian community. More than Ashkenazim, Mizrahim still are hiding in closets, scared to come out and face rejection by their families. I know my parents may never talk to me again."

Describing his life in an affluent suburb of Beersheva, Shai, a fifty-five-year-old former archaeologist, looks pained. "Our friends thought we were the perfect family. For the first few years, I did too. Then, except for missing my kids, more and more I was glad to be away on [archaeological] digs. My wife complained we were having less sex. Was there someone else? What was I hiding from her? What could I say? That I was hiding from myself? I was confused." After seeing a television documentary about Tel Aviv's Independence Park, a well-known spot in Israel for hit-and-run homosexuality, Shai went to see for himself. "I saw all kinds of men, young, old, Russians, Arabs, and tourists meeting, talking, mostly looking for anonymous sex. I felt really uncomfortable there. As I was rushing away, a haredi came up and wanted to do it in the bushes. I asked, 'How can you? The Bible forbids homosexuality: "Man shall not lie down with man."' I'll never forget his answer: 'It's not a sin. We'll do it standing up.'

"Next time I was in Tel Aviv, I decided to go to a spa for a massage and soak in the hot pool. On the sunroof, I saw good-looking, athletic guys lying around naked. Dark-skinned, light-skinned, hairy, hairless, muscles. I tried reading a newspaper, but fantasies took over. That's when I discovered I wasn't the only married man 'like that.' My double life began. My wife no longer suspected I was seeing other women. She knew I wasn't attracted to her. She pushed me to go with her to a counselor. The more she pushed, the more I lied. I didn't want to destroy my family. During an argument, I lost it. I snapped back, 'You want therapy? Go find a therapy group for wives of homos.' That word hit her like a bomb. Neither of us knew what to do. We finally agreed not to tell our families why I got my own apartment. If my father found out, he'd sit *shiva* [mourn for the dead]. He grew up in Baghdad and used to say he was repulsed seeing Arabs holding hands, touching each other. My in-laws are liberal Ashkenazim, the kind who'd march in the Gay Pride Parade, but they're not liberal enough for this. Their daughter married a homo? When we got married [after the 1973 Yom Kippur War], no one knew anything about gays. At least no one said anything. If I had figured it out earlier, then what? No wife or kids? No seders or holidays together? So, in that way, I'm glad I'm not the 'new generation.' "

His college-age children know, but they don't want to know. "We never talk about it," continues Shai. For years, there was no one special in his life. Then he received an intriguing reply to his personal ad. "I liked his literary, graceful Hebrew. He's very cultured. I thought, he's younger, he lives in Haifa, so he won't have my hang-ups. Well, his are unbeliev-able. He grew up in Russia, where they used to put gays in labor camps." Until the breakup of the Soviet Union, a criminal law prohibited homo-sexuality; no one was allowed to be "deviant," so homosexuals were forced underground. Although the criminal law is off the books, homo-phobic attacks are rampant. Many immigrants to Israel have brought their homophobia with them: in the Israeli Russian media, homosexual-ity is a taboo subject. "He's been here ten years and hasn't loosened up. He's still afraid one of his friends or family or anyone in the Russian community might discover his 'terrible' secret. Maybe that's one reason he likes me. I can't even spell Tchaikovsky."

In our world, being gay is like eating pork on Yom Kippur," says Nurit, who lives in an Orthodox religious West Bank settlement near Jerusalem. Her tone alternates between anguished and angry as she describes what happened to her older brother soon after he was drafted. "My mother was cleaning his room and almost died of shock. She found male porn. My parents confronted him when he came home for Shabbat. I'll never forget that teary scene. They said being homosexual is against Judaism. He had the courage to speak up. 'Gay people aren't monsters. This is not something I chose, this is what I am.' They kept saying 'You'll never have children.' He tried to educate them that we live in the twenty-first cen-tury, that if he wants a family, gays in Tel Aviv and Haifa and Jerusalem are adopting. I didn't say anything. What I really wanted to say is, 'If you're so worried about having grandchildren, you'd better worry about me too.' "

She was a student at an Orthodox all-girls high school at the time and also grappling with her sexual identity. "The teachers always warned us not to have sex with guys. They never mentioned anything about homosexuals. The girls had no idea what lesbian meant. We used to walk around hugging and touching each other. It was considered a teenage girl thing to do. When I slept over at my girlfriends' houses, we experimented. I slept with two girls. We did quite a lot with each other, but we never talked about it. I had a very intense relationship with one. She told me, 'I wish you were a boy.' Sometimes I wondered, Why did God make me lesbian? Maybe God is testing me to overcome this. Some nights, I read the entire Book of Psalms and prayed 'my problem' would disappear.

"My brother was in much better shape than me. He was out to everyone in his unit and his commanders knew. They were totally supportive. Being gay doesn't clash with being a good soldier, so gays are accepted." Aware that she was struggling with her sexuality, her brother took her to Jerusalem's Cinemateque to see *Trembling Before God*, a groundbreaking, poignant American documentary about homosexual Orthodox and ultra-Orthodox Jewish men and women. "I cried and cried; my life was on that screen. Seeing religious lesbians who are hurting captured my sadness and answered questions. Can I still be Orthodox if I have lesbian sex? Can I be happy? Seeing that movie, I realized yes."

Nurit thought she was ready to come out to her parents. The timing couldn't have been worse. Life on the settlement had become unbearable, the area a war zone, and two of her childhood friends were killed in an ambush. "I decided not to tell my parents anything. It's hard enough saying goodbye to them in the morning, not knowing if it will be the last time." She carries a gun and drives a bulletproof car to Jerusalem, where she works as a geriatric nurse. "Whenever friends try to fix me up, I tell them I have a boyfriend. My classmates are married. Even one who is bisexual. I know, because we sleep together. If you're lesbian, you keep silent and go along with the program. In the Orthodox community, the number of gay men and women who marry is much, much higher than in the secular world. Growing up religious means we're raised to be wives, taught that fulfillment means bringing children into the world. Even if you're not religious, if you don't want children, you're not a real woman, not a real Israeli. In Israel, kids are everything, the center of life. On a deep psychological level, I think it's about continuing the Jewish people."

At a cozy Jerusalem restaurant run by lesbians for lesbians, a baby ("gaybe") boom is evident. At a large wooden table, a pregnant woman describes her Lamaze course. A child in a stroller calls one woman "Mom" and the other "Mommie." A recent study of lesbians age seventeen to twenty-four found most want to be mothers. "This is unique to Israeli society," according to Haifa University's social work professor Dr. Adital Ben-Ari. "In most Western countries, lesbian teens are often opposed to the traditional family structure. But in Israel, the idea of a family is so rooted that it also permeates the attitudes of lesbians." There are no statistics on same-sex parents, but a growing number of Israeli children have two mothers or two fathers or, sometimes, both. Tel Aviv, Jerusalem, and Haifa have matchmaking organizations for gay men and women who want to coparent a child. Because Israel's international adoption law allows anyone qualified to be a parent to adopt regardless of sexual orientation or gender, prospective parents travel to places such as Guatemala, Romania, Ukraine, and Vietnam. The Supreme Court made headlines in 2000 when it allowed a lesbian to adopt her partner's son, conceived by artificial insemination. The only Muslim Justice on the Supreme Court, Abd al-Rahman Zouabi, dissented from the majority opinion. The adoption order, he wrote, creates an "abnormal family unit." While gays called the ruling momentous, some outraged Orthodox Jews accused the Supreme Court of turning Israel into Sodom and Gomorrah.

In Arab culture, homosexuality remains "the love that dare not speak its name." "It's against our manly image," says Omar, a baker from an all-Muslim village near Umm al-Fahm, who lives near Haifa. His family does not know where. "When I was fifteen, my father saw some boys walking down the street holding hands. 'That's normal,' he told me. 'But if a man ever touches you in "that place," kick him hard in the balls and run.' That's all he ever said about homosexuals." All over the Middle East, it's common for male friends to embrace, put arms around each other's shoulders. What's not acceptable is a man showing a woman affection in public. "For me, it was great not to be pressured to be with girls. Boys hang out with boys. No one dates. By the time I was nineteen, I was renting [male porn] videos. Once, I was stupid and left one in the VCR. My mother discovered it and left it on my bed. Smashed. She was upset and frightened. I love her and we are close, very close. I told her, I am frightened too. When I admitted I'm attracted to boys, not girls, she didn't want to hear. She said it's just a 'condition' and I could get rid of it by practicing Islam. I went to the mosque, tried to pray at least once a day, and stopped drinking beer. Then I heard Sheik Salah call homosexuality a great crime, a perversion that brings Allah's anger and makes terrible things happen. I thought, 'I can't be the only gay Arab.' I went on the Internet and found many like me. I spend a lot of time reading men's stories on Arabic sites like QueerJihad and al-fatiha" (which means "the opening" in Arabic and is the title of the first chapter of the Koran). Omar is part of a growing new subculture of cybergay Muslims. They share secrets and discuss their conflicted feelings about being part of a culture that forbids same-sex relations.

When Omar was twenty-five, his mother told him her friends were asking when they would be invited to his wedding. " 'Even if I pray one hundred times a day, I can't change,' I told her. Men who are trapped in marriages, they beat their wives or drink or think about suicide. When she said 'A man without a family dies like a dog,' I reminded her about a man who lives not far away. When his wife's family heard rumors he was having sex with another man, they murdered him. I asked her, 'Do you want this to happen to me?' She warned me that if I don't change, I'll put my father in his grave and Allah will curse me. When my father found out, he went crazy. He said he couldn't accept that his only son would not marry, would not give him a grandson to carry on the family name. He yelled '*Inta luti!*' [You're a homo!] Being called a luti is tantamount to being condemned to death. I had dishonored our family's dignity. I had no choice. I had to leave. Because of me, he divorced my mother. He married another woman half her age. Already, she's given him a son."

Islam, like most Christian denominations and Orthodox Judaism, condemns homosexuality. Similar to the Bible, the Koran includes the story of Lot (Lut in Arabic), in which God punishes men in Sodom who have sex with men. In many Muslim countries, men caught engaging in homosexual acts can be jailed, tortured, or executed—all in the name of Islam. Islamic law has strict punishments for homosexual sodomy: "If the partners are married men, they may be burned to death or thrown to their deaths from a height. If they are unmarried, the sodomized partner can be executed (unless he is a minor) and the sodomizer lashed a hundred times." The different penalties reflect a cultural repugnance for a man who takes the "feminine" role. If an Arab takes the active sexual role (the penetrating partner), he can have sex and not even consider it gay. He just calls it "something men do," explains Omar. "I know married men who have sex and don't face the truth of their identity. There is also a line between sex and emotions. If you cross that line and a relationship develops, then you are gay and it means big trouble."

Walking in the area of downtown Jerusalem that is the favorite target for suicide bombers can be an act of courage or madness—or both. After an attack, cafés are empty, streets deserted. Even during red alerts, people like Omar and Nurit risk their lives to enter an office building with an enormous rainbow flag fluttering from its balcony. A Bedouin bartender, a reserve army officer, a Christian Arab Hebrew University student, a married haredi teacher are at a birthday party on the third floor. Joined together by the "otherness" that has alienated them from their families, they have made Jerusalem Open House (JOH), a unique community center for homosexuals, bisexuals, and transsexuals, their refuge. In the heart of the tormented Holy City, Israeli Jews and Arabs and Palestinians, secular and religious and antireligious, left-wing and right-wing share experiences. There's psychological counseling in Hebrew, Arabic, Russian, and English as well as groups for married gays, gay parents, and parents of gays. There are Purim parties and Passover seders and disco nights.

All too often, from outside comes a familiar fierce boom. Hagai El-Ad, the thirty-two-year-old executive director, can't count the times he's heard the sounds of death. "The windows shake. The wind carries the smell of the explosion. We rush to the balcony to see, call our terrified parents to say we're okay. Then we realize that someone from the office went downstairs to get pizza at Sbarro or make a Xerox. Horrified, we check to see if they're alive. It doesn't take long for our phone to ring. Is the teen group still meeting tonight? What about the Russian group? Is OrthoDykes meeting? In spite of the danger, people come. Nothing is cancelled. Ever. It's bizarre. No one dares venture downtown, except to JOH. We're crowded. Like one family, celebrating the fact we're all simply alive, able to see and feel and hug one another."

"This place is the oxygen we need," says David Ehrlich, a Jewish gay author who is taking a spoken Arabic-language class. Because of the suicide attacks, his nearby bookstore-restaurant, Tmol Shilshom (The Way Things Were), a favorite haunt of Israeli writers and gays, is nearing bankruptcy. He's had to lay off most of his staff, including his Arab chef and waiters. "At Open House we're trying to lead normal lives, pretending everything is fine. Outside it's a keg of explosives." Sounds of folk dancing and a choir emanate from other rooms. Some evenings, high school students screen original gay movies; on Fridays, men and women gather for Sabbath services. Panel discussions have titles ranging from "David and Jonathan, Ruth and Naomi: Just Good Friends or Same-Sex Lovers?" to "The Prose and Poetry of Same-Sex Love: Jewish and Islamic Perspectives." Steven Greenberg, the first openly gay Orthodox rabbi, calls the Arab-Jewish encounters at JOH an experiment in "cultural renewal. Roughly a thousand years ago, in cities like Baghdad and Granada, Jews and Muslims created vibrant, religiously complex and remarkably open cultures, which included a quiet toleration of same-sex love. Our traditions have very old and venerable resources of respect for difference. Our job is to rediscover them." Among the people in the library and lounge are a few men wearing knitted kippas and black hats. Fearful that word could get out and ruin their chances of a good match, most haredi members of Open House meet outside in secret places. A gay man who wants to remain in the haredi community has to do more than merely keep his sexual identity hidden; he also must marry.

Just like gay Arabs.

Hanin Maikey, one of JOH's few heterosexual staffers, is almost certainly the only person in the Middle East with the title Outreach Coordinator for Gay and Lesbian Arabs. Before leaving her Arab Christian family's village in the Galilee to study social work in Jerusalem, she'd never met an Arab homosexual. Roughly 10 percent of any population is homosexual, she says; that's why the gay club at the Hebrew University is called The Other Ten Percent.

Jerusalem, where one third of the population is Arab, is the best base for outreach, she says. In addition to writing Open House's Arabic publications and website, Hanin and Easau, a Bedouin bartender who works in Tel Aviv, run support groups for Arab men. "A lot have been thrown out of their parents' houses; they have despairing lives, cut off from their families. Some take drugs," she explains. Quite a few escape beatings or death by living clandestinely with Jewish and Arab friends, mostly in gay-tolerant Tel Aviv. Frequently, Hanin receives calls from men who don't dare come to meetings because they have wives and children. "On the phone, they talk and talk. They really need to get it out. They want to change their lives, but don't know how." She also runs a separate, much smaller group for Arab lesbians, mostly students at the Hebrew University. They insist on absolute discretion; known lesbians are marked women, usually forced to marry or else disowned or shunned by their families. Under Islamic law, single lesbians can receive one hundred lashes; married lesbians may be stoned. After a twenty-year-old told her family she was a lesbian, she was beaten badly. In desperation, she phoned JOH for help. After the families of two women from a village near Nazareth discovered their lesbian relationship, the women moved to Haifa. Relatives tracked them down and the women fled to Holland. "It's much worse for uneducated Arab lesbians," Hanin points out. "With no profession and no money, they have little choice but to marry."

JOH is making a special push to reach out to Palestinian homosexuals as well. "I get heartbreaking calls from Ramallah and Nablus, from doctors, from lawyers, whoever sees our Arabic website or ads. I get calls from men in Deheisha refugee camp. They'll never come out. They can't talk to anyone. I'm the only one they can turn to," says Hanin, who hears a startling array of stories every day. "I just got a call from a man in Bethlehem who's very nervous. His family is introducing him to a young lady. He doesn't know how to act so she'll accept [marry] him. Gays and lesbians have inner conflicts whether or not there's a war on."

Ezra, an Israeli Jew who works as a plumbing contractor, and Selim, a Palestinian Muslim who served time in prison for attacks during the first intifada, regularly attend JOH's events. They love going to restaurants, movies—and living together. They've been called "traitor," "Arab-lover," and "collaborator"; most Israelis and Palestinians alike consider it "sleeping with the enemy." Nevertheless, Ezra's family in Jerusalem treats Selim warmly (even though Mrs. Yizhak wishes her son had picked a "nice Jewish boy"). Selim works all over Jerusalem assisting Ezra with his plumbing business. Even though it's dangerous, Ezra and Selim travel past Israeli checkpoints to visit Selim's family in Ramallah. Although his parents treat Ezra like a family member, they hope one day their son will marry a woman. Sometimes they post an armed guard outside the door; few neighbors are open-minded about Jews or homosexuals. A forty-year-old man from Ramallah who was active in the gay community in Tel Aviv was assassinated under the pretext that he was a collaborator with Israel. A few Palestinian homosexuals even have asked for political asylum in Israel as a preferred alternative to arrest, beatings, and even the threat of murder. (Before this intifada, roughly five hundred Palestinian homosexuals were living in Israel along with thousands of other Palestinians who entered Israel freely as a refuge or in search of occasional sex, according to the Agudah, the Association of Gay Men, Lesbians, Bisexuals and Transgender in Israel.) Selim lives illegally in terror-wary West Jerusalem. When suspicious Israeli police stop the twenty-six-year-old, he pulls out a notarized document showing he's Ezra's long-time domestic partner. If police discover his criminal record, he produces a letter from Israeli security services stating that he's not a known security risk. He's trying to become an Israeli resident. He is not the first. The late Prime Minister Rabin granted resident rights to a gay Palestinian from Gaza who lives with his partner in Tel Aviv.

"In many ways Selim could be the poster boy for peace. During the first intifada he spent two years in jail for attacking Israelis. And now, he's in love with one," observes Hagai El-Ad, the astrophysicist who has been running JOH since it opened in 1999. "Despite the terrible political situation and few interactions between Jews and Arabs, our membership is swelling. What makes this place so unusual is not the sexual orientation of our visitors. It's that we're trying to create a different Jerusalem, open to all: gays and straights, Palestinians and Israelis, religious and secular."

On June 7, 2002 nearly four thousand people turned out for the Holy City's first gay march against hatred. Showing that the gay community in Jerusalem is a unique blend, an Arab and a Jew held a sign that read "Hummusexuality Is Not Tabouli." "The Israeli and Palestinian gay communities are coming out of the dark closet into the light," said one man carrying a rainbow flag. There was heavy police protection but not much opposition. One man blowing a shofar and calling for redemption was taken away by police. Some haredim held posters condemning the march as blasphemy, saying it would drive holiness out of the city. Jerusalem's ultra-Orthodox former deputy mayor Rabbi Haim Miller denounced the march: "It's a disgrace. Before, people with this perversion used to hide in shame. Today they go into streets and call it 'pride.'"

Passersby doing their Friday afternoon shopping who happened upon the march openly argued with one another. "What do they think this is, San Francisco? Amsterdam? There's a war going on," a woman said angrily. "I don't like them, but this is a democracy, so they have every right to march," another countered. They paraded through the streets of downtown Jerusalem, ending with a concert in Independence Park featuring a line-up of prominent gay Israeli singers and entertainers. For decades, the park has been a clandestine meeting place for Arab and Jewish gays and prostitutes; police regularly made arrests, noted one man. "Today was different. The police came to protect us, not to persecute us." To commemorate all the victims of the intifada, people released dozens and dozens of black balloons. A few drifted toward the Temple Mount.

18

Hookers and Hash in the Holy Land

⊘ When Israel has prostitutes and thieves, we'll be a state just like any other. —David Ben-Gurion

A taxi stops outside the four-star Tel Aviv hotel and a platinum blonde in a black spandex miniskirt and three-inch heels hops out. She pulls out her cell phone and in ungrammatical Hebrew with a thick Russian accent tells her client she is coming up. A few blocks away on Ben-Yehuda Street, a young man wearing a black kippa heads to an alley next to a discount appliance store. He bounds up an outside metal staircase to the second floor. A sign on the door reads "Health Club." The red-curtained reception room is filled with clouds of cigarette smoke. On a worn couch, scantily clad women watch a Russian soap opera. A badly bleached blonde leads him to a back room for a quick afternoon workout. It's difficult to keep a secret in Israel, but customers like him can be confident that these anonymous women won't gossip about them. At least not in Hebrew. There is no chance they will ever run into their wives, their children, their parents. They live in another world, the underbelly of Israel.

Politicians heading to Labor Party headquarters pass by upscale "massage parlors." Behind the Tel Aviv stock exchange, brokers, other businessmen, and even police can ease their tensions at a tantalizing array of high-priced strip clubs. At night, a car stops at a red light. A hard-looking woman rushes up, exposes her breasts, and bluntly states her price. On a dark beach near a high-tech area north of Tel Aviv, a vendor sells condoms and cigarettes and beer to hookers, their clients, and spectators alike. Israelis bring curious wives and friends as if they were at a drive-in movie, their car's headlights illuminating the strange outdoor shadow play. The women of the dunes are servicing an eclectic array of clients. Some men aren't interested in frolicking with women. The Israel Academy of Hebrew Language recently coined an official Hebrew word, *zoneh*, which means male prostitutes.

The Red Sea beach resort of Eilat puts out a glossy official entertainment guide. Alongside restaurant and scuba-diving ads are ones like this: "One-of-a-kind offer! Beautiful girls age 19 and up! $20 up to half an hour, taxis included—Visa and MasterCard are accepted." Ads for escort services, phone sex in Arabic, and large-breasted Russian bisexuals available for $50 an hour in a private apartment in Tel Aviv appear in prestigious Hebrew newspapers. Israel's shifting sexual scene is reflected in the latest music and TV sitcoms. Provocative billboards are visible from cemeteries and synagogues.

An estimated 700 massage parlor/brothels operate in the country, with 250 in Tel Aviv alone. The sex-for-sale trade is blatant and lucrative. It resembles a sexual supermarket, where Israelis easily can follow Oscar Wilde's advice: The only way to get rid of a temptation is to yield to it. On an Israeli television show, *Female Perspective,* during a discussion on illegal foreign prostitutes, a prominent lawyer bragged he does not know a man who isn't willing to go to one. Gossip columnists have spotted famous soccer players cavorting with call girls. According to police, about twenty-five thousand paid sexual transactions take place daily. To escape prying eyes in small towns and villages, married and single Arab Israelis make excursions to Haifa or Tel Aviv. So do men from straitlaced Jewish communities. Prostitutes claim that a fifth or more of their faithful customers are very religious Jews whom they identify by their black kippas and other traditional garb. Pious men, faithful to religious laws of purity, must abstain from sex with their wives on days when they are "unclean," at least twelve days of abstinence each month. Although the Seventh Commandment prohibits adultery, religious marriage laws are frequently interpreted as sanctioning sex with single women. Thursday afternoon, before preparations for the Sabbath, is the favorite time for some ultra-Orthodox Jews to travel to Tel Aviv for sex in secular Sin City. For most other haredim, prostitution is impure, a sacrilege. Driving by brothels, some of them have shouted, "You are going to burn!" In a wave of arson in 2000, a number of brothels and sex shops burned down. In an early-morning fire in a dingy brothel that served foreign workers, four prostitutes died, unable to escape their locked rooms. Two were Russian. The guilty man was not religious.

The brothel was in south Tel Aviv, Israel's seediest red-light district. The squalid area near the old Central Bus Station is home to down-in-the-gutter men, immigrants from the former Soviet Union who make up the majority of Israel's alcoholics. It's also a gathering place for sex-starved foreign workers, a prominent feature of Israeli life since the first intifada, which forced Israel to look somewhere other than Palestinians for blue-collar workers. As a result, Israel has one of the highest ratios of foreign-to-native workers in the Western world. About a quarter million illegal and legal "guest" workers live in the Promised Land; most either are single or have wives on other continents. These "shadow men"—lonely Romanian, Polish, Nigerian, and Turkish construction workers, Thai and Chinese agricultural workers—frequent sleazy massage parlors and cheap bars where male and female flesh is often for sale. Not surprisingly, the transmission rates for venereal disease and AIDS, once exceedingly low in Israel—far lower than in Western Europe or the United States—are skyrocketing. Even though the Ministry of Health checks known prostitutes for HIV every three months and some women carry results of their latest blood test in their purse, few drug-addicted streetwalkers bother to get tested. "If they don't want to wear condoms, I don't care. They're the ones who have to explain things to their wives," remarks a sixteen-year-old runaway from a drug rehabilitation center. "Foreign workers, I don't mind them. Money is money. And besides, a long time ago all the Jews once were foreign workers, or should I say slaves in Egypt. To be honest, I like to go with Israelis better. The foreigners, they can have the Russians." She shares a room with a girlfriend. It has a wide-screen television borrowed from their dealer.

Though prostitution in Israel is legal, running a brothel or living off the earnings of a prostitute is not. At spots like the Banana Club in Tel

Aviv, some rooms have hiding places under the velvet-covered beds in case of a raid; others have secret passageways behind mirrors for a quick escape. Israeli vice cops, understaffed and underfunded, often look the other way, more interested in tracking down drug dealers and much bigger players in organized crime. With suicide bombers stalking discos, pizza parlors, and bat mitzvah celebrations, police focus on capturing them rather than nabbing pimps. According to Efraim Ehrlich, commander of the Tel Aviv Vice Squad, "The policy . . . is not to arrest the pimps or the girls unless they break the rules and violate the guidelines of the state attorney. Everyone knows that prostitution exists and will always exist."

Hookers have been working in the Holy Land since before the days of Sodom and Gomorrah. Up until the 1990s, there were a few brothel-hotels scattered around the country. The sex workers were Israeli, often from poor Mizrahi families. Dalia was one of them. Now a sardonic pro, this suntanned Sabra in her late thirties says her life started a downward spiral when she fell for a big-talking small-time drug dealer in Jerusalem who drove a Mustang. She dropped out of high school and moved in with him, scandalizing her large, traditional Moroccan family. With her much older boyfriend, she made plans to get rich selling hash in Amsterdam. He went but never came back, leaving Dalia with a baby, a ruined reputation, and a mountain of debt. "Everyone needs money. I can make much more than any schoolteacher. Much more than $200 a day. It wasn't hard—until they came and took over." She stares daggers at the cutthroat competition, a leggy strawberry blonde strutting her wares on Tel Aviv's seaside promenade. A jogger passes and she smiles invitingly. He slows down and makes a U-turn. "They want the blondes, the exotic-looking ones, the Natashas, the Valentinas," Dalia grumbles. "These 'tourist' girls come here illegally and work for almost nothing. They're driving us [Israelis] out of business."

She's not mistaken. The Russian mafia or *Organizatsia* now controls most prostitution in Israel; police estimate at least 85 percent of the women have arrived illegally from the republics of the former Soviet Union. Ruthless men from the Russian-speaking underworld make a fortune out of these women's misfortune. For each $50 a customer pays, a "tourist" prostitute may get only $5. The math seems daunting—an Organizatsia hooker needs twenty clients to make $100 a day—but at home, she might need more than two months in a legitimate job to make the same $100. "Modern-day slavery" are the words Moshe Mizrahi, head of Israel's Fraud and International Crimes Division, uses to describe the situation in the brothels. "They're afraid of their pimps, they're afraid of the police. They can't explain how they arrived in Israel. They'll do anything to make money." "We don't have to worry about being deported," Dalia stresses. "We can say what we feel. If our pimps don't split the money fair, we complain. If they don't give us decent working conditions, we complain. Massage parlors don't want to hire us, they want the 'tourists.' We're too much trouble."

The trouble can turn deadly; owners of rival prostitution rings have had the walls of their mansions plastered with bullets. Brothel owners have been killed in drive-by shootings; others have been found decapitated. Rebellious prostitutes have disappeared.

Staggering profits are at stake. Some bosses earn up to $4,000 a day. A woman "purchased" for between $5,000 and $20,000, depending on her looks and the quality of her forged documents, can earn from $50,000 to $100,000 a year tax-free for her pimp, according to Yitzhak Tyler, commander of Haifa's Central Police Unit. It is such a profitable business that an official on Tel Aviv's police force reports that the mafia makes more from these women in a week than he has in his law-enforcement budget for the whole year. Trafficking in prostitution is a multimillion-dollar industry largely controlled by the mafia. Newly rich Russian speakers have been buying some luxury condominiums that line the coast between Tel Aviv and Haifa. "I certainly don't want to know the source of this money," says an Israeli real estate agent.

It started with the breakup of the Soviet Union. Criminals with phony papers hid among the massive wave of one million immigrants who came to Israel. The year 1994 was a watershed for the flesh trade: a KGB spy bribed an Israeli Ministry of the Interior official and, in return, dozens of top Russian mobsters "became Jews" and received "legal" citizenship. As well-known Russian Israeli activist Ida Nudel put it, "For $4,000 anyone can buy an Israeli passport in Ukraine through the mafia, and fly here direct, with all the documents showing Israeli citizenship." By spreading cash around, the mafia easily recruited local lieutenants among Israeli Russian-speaking immigrants. The brothel business took off, staffed with an endless supply of women desperate to escape the col-lapsed economies of the former Soviet Republics and Eastern Europe.

Sophisticated smugglers lure such women with promises of lucrative jobs around the world as models, masseurs, and dancers, with housing provided. The come-ons run in newspapers and appear on Ukrainian cable television. Each year, about three thousand women enter Israel ille-gally. Many fly into Ben-Gurion Airport bearing forged Israeli passports or stolen, borrowed, or bought identities of Jewish women in Russia and Ukraine, which entitles them to thousands of dollars worth of immigrant benefits. Police accused a fifty-one-year-old Russian Israeli, a profes-sional engineer, of working in a brothel. She later discovered that several women were using fake versions of her Israeli identity card. Others enter Israel posing as nuns or nannies. Some arrive on cruise ships from Cyprus and Odessa that dock in Haifa for a day. After touring, passen-gers return to the ship; prostitutes don't. A few women have been caught in the Red Sea swimming from Taba in Egypt to Eilat in Israel. Lately, the most frequented route is overland.

Natalia arrived in Israel this way. An unemployed single mother of a seven-year-old boy, she answered this newspaper ad: "18–30 year old women are invited to work abroad—great conditions." Compared to the $20 a month one can earn in Moldova, the $1,000 a month a "masseur" can make in Israel is astronomical. Natalia accepted a seven-month job. First she was treated to a holiday in Egypt. She flew to Cairo and was put on a minibus with ten other women with a police escort for the first part of the tour. Instead of seeing the Pyramids, they were taken on a long, harrowing trip through the Sinai Desert. Disembarking near the Israeli border, they were welcomed by a group of Bedouin who graciously served them tea and then raped them. When the Bedouin cut the barbed wire fence, the women climbed through. The Bedouin received $1,000 for every woman they smuggled. Natalia was put in a jeep and driven to a town somewhere in Israel; she didn't know the name. The next day, men arrived and examined all the women. A man "bought" Natalia and drove her to a midtown Tel Aviv apartment and put her to work with two other women from Moldova. He gave her $7 for each customer she slept with, out of the $50 the customer paid. Her pimp deducted the money Natalia owed him for her "Egyptian holiday" and his investment in bringing her to Israel. Within three months, police raided the brothel and arrested the three prostitutes. Natalia spoke before the Knesset Commission of Inquiry into Trafficking in Women in 2001. She also turned state's witness against the pimps and then was deported.

Neve Tirza Women's Prison in Ramle is packed with women who had expired tourist visas and forged identity cards indicating they were wives or daughters of Israelis. All are waiting to be deported to places like Ukraine, Azerbaijan, and Kazakhstan. Most of them came to Israel knowing they would be working in the sex industry; only a minority claim they were deceived about what awaited them. After working as a dancer-prostitute in a bar in Belgrade, Masha, age nineteen, returned to Ukraine and decided to become a "tourist" in Israel. "There is no work in Ukraine. I worked here in a call-girl brothel. The owner was a great guy and I don't want to hurt him. . . . Everything was great . . . we went swimming, we had days off—until one of the girls in the apartment called the police. She wanted to go home, so she turned us all in. They keep her separately because otherwise we would kill her."

Another woman, Tatiana, entered Israel on a tourist visa. She had been promised a job as a hotel maid in Eilat, with enough money to support her family. A man met her, but instead of taking her to work in the "hotel," he brought her to a brothel. After unsuccessful attempts to escape, a friend contacted someone in the Belarus Consulate who tipped off the police. Tatiana was brought to prison and found an anonymous note on her bunk threatening to kill her and punish her family if she testified. Although she was terrified—the traffickers knew her passport details and her family's address in Belarus—Tatiana testified in court against her captors. (Women who testify can receive housing and pocket money; some opt to remain in jail because they fear their pimps.) After the trial, Tatiana was deported to Belarus; her fate is unknown. A number of women who have talked to police have been hunted down in their home country and killed.

Few arrested prostitutes file charges or agree to testify against their pimps, which makes it hard for prosecutors to bring charges. When cases are brought to court, complains Tel Aviv District Attorney Miriam Rosenthal, judges are too lenient with the pimps. Others blame the Ministry of the Interior (until 2003 dominated by Shas politicians) for showing more interest in getting funding for their religious schools than deporting illegal sex workers. Members of the Israel Women's Network have demonstrated against "police laxity" and taken politicians on tours of brothels. They have set up shelters for women and encourage them to testify against their pimps and traffickers. A blistering June 2000 report by Amnesty International, which named Israel one of the international centers of trade in women mainly from the former Soviet Union, spurred Israeli justice officials into action. The next month, Israeli women's organizations pushed the Knesset to approve a bill making human trafficking a crime punishable by sixteen years in prison (twenty for trafficking in a minor).

Experts such as Hebrew University criminologist Menachem Amir believe that police allow brothels to operate in return for useful information from pimps concerning other underworld criminal activities. Brothels serve as a convenient cover for money laundering, counterfeiting, extortion, and drug trafficking. In 2002, police busted five major prostitution rings by pretending to be brokers interested in buying young women to work as prostitutes. The largest ring, made up of Russian speakers and young Bedouin from the same Negev clan, were smuggling sex workers into Israel via Egypt. In a 2003 crackdown on criminals controlling prostitution, police arrested seven brothel owners. Haifa Police Central Unit Commander Yitzhak Tyler says his officers are making a big push to eliminate the Soviet sex scene. The major problem, he reports, is that "every day more of these women find a new way to get into the country. Some have been deported two or three times and within a month their pimps have got them back again. In Russia, they earn only $40 a month. Here they're making $40 a day. They're not crying."

"We have deported blonde women and they came back as brunettes. We have deported brunettes, and they came back as blondes," adds a Tel Aviv police commander. "It is impossible to hermetically seal all of the transfer points. Last year, about two thousand travelers at Ben-Gurion Airport were denied entry, but the traffickers know we are looking for women who look like prostitutes, so the women arrive not looking like prostitutes. Anyone who thinks the phenomenon can be eliminated doesn't know what he's talking about."

Airport officials, preoccupied with figuring out which incoming passengers are potential terrorists, admit that they likely will remain unable to distinguish between call girls and nuns. A blonde presenting her passport was surrounded by police and interrogated for six hours. It was an embarrassing error; she was a celebrated Russian television journalist. Another blonde who told passport control she was entering Israel to visit her family was not allowed to stay. She actually was a medical student from St. Petersburg. She returned, but with hair dyed black. Obviously, blondes in Israel don't always have more fun.

Back in the early 1990s, when Jerusalem's then mayor Ehud Olmert complained about organized crime during a Knesset debate, the late Yosef Burg, then minister of police, retorted, "In Israel, nothing is organized. How is it that crime is organized?" At the time, few would have guessed how deep the tentacles of the Russian mafia would penetrate into the Holy Land. One Tel Aviv police officer says he fears these world-class criminals as much as Hamas. Prostitution is only the most visible part of the story. The Russian mafia, the world's "best" white-collar criminals, take full advantage of Israel's lax banking regulations, created to help new immigrants, to conceal the source of untold sums of dirty money. As Yossi Sedbon, head of the Israel Police Investigative Division, noted, "Israel is a promised land for money laundering. Millions come in and go out and you can't do anything about it."

Typically, it works like this: An immigrant or a Russian-born Israeli visiting the old country receives a bribe to take a suitcase full of criminal cash to Israel, much of it from the mafia's international cocaine and heroin business. Once in Israel, the courier gives it to a contact to deposit in an Israeli bank account. From there, the cash is transferred overseas electronically. Some money stays in Israel, where it is invested in legitimate and illegitimate businesses. Tel Aviv's posh answer to Madison Avenue, Kikar Hamedina, is lined with stores like Gucci and Ralph Lauren and is frequented by some well-heeled customers with shady connections in places like Uzbekistan and Ukraine. For years, Israel has been dubbed a "mobster's paradise." Tel Aviv police got a glimpse of it the day they opened the door of a nondescript downtown shop. They discovered a counterfeiting factory that produced fake identity cards, credit cards, check books, and other documents. Part of the scam was paying Russian "immigrants" to use bogus checks to open accounts. The immigrants gave power of attorney to the mobsters and disappeared from Israel.

Then the con artists deposited more counterfeit checks into the straw accounts. Using the money as collateral, they receive sizable bank loans. The ring managed to scam millions of dollars from Israeli banks. According to Tel Aviv Magistrate Court Judge Zion Kapah, if police hadn't busted the ring, it could have toppled the Israeli banking system.

Israelis had little contact with large-scale organized crime until the Russian mafia set up operations. However, they already were familiar with illicit drugs. After the 1967 Six-Day War, tens of thousands of young Westerners came to volunteer on kibbutzim. Rachel Biale, then a fifteen-year-old on Kibbutz Kfar Ruppin next to the Jordanian border, remembers it well. "We were living in a Godforsaken provincial place. It was so insular. Our government didn't even allow the Beatles to perform here because they were considered decadent and immoral. Suddenly, after the war, we were on the world map; everyone was fascinated by our David versus Goliath victory. Kids from California, from France and New Zealand came and taught us naïve kids about sex, drugs and rock and roll—the '60s culture. A few of my friends on the kibbutz had their first sexual discoveries with them." She describes kibbutz boys falling for what she calls "the myth" of the sexually liberated American and European women. Meanwhile, the male volunteers chased kibbutz girls, believing they had arrived in what *Playboy* referred to as "The Land of Milk and Honeys."

The 1967 War also opened up borders with the West Bank and Gaza. Israelis flocked in, some to buy cheap hashish from Arab dealers. By 1971, the Israeli government was distributing posters that read "About five million Egyptians take hash. In the Six-Day War, we all saw the quality of their soldiers. Don't delude yourself that there is no connection between the two." "Parents knew nothing about drugs then," Rachel maintains. "Now, all over Israel, parents worry."

The multibillion-dollar drug trade is a bizarre model of Middle Eastern economic cooperation. Jewish, Druze, and Bedouin Israeli smugglers have Palestinian, Egyptian, Jordanian, and Lebanese partners on the other side of Israel's porous borders. Lebanon is a major illicit drug-producing and transit country. Nearly one third of the Bekaa Valley, which is controlled by the Syrian military and Hezballah, is devoted to cannabis and opium poppy crops. Hidden laboratories in areas occupied by Syrian troops make heroin from morphine base arriving from Turkey,

Afghanistan, Pakistan, Iran, and Southeast Asia and cocaine from raw coca paste imported from South America.

Israel's 1982 invasion of Lebanon gave drug producers easy access to Israelis. A Lebanese farmer, for example, could sell a kilo (2.2 lbs.) of hashish for $300 to an Israeli soldier, who could easily resell it for a five-fold profit at home. In addition, thousands of Lebanese workers freely entered Israel daily, some even driving trucks filled with hashish. Right before Israel pulled out of Lebanon in 2000, two Israeli Jewish police from an anti-drug-smuggling unit were caught conveying top-secret information to Lebanese dealers about where their Lebanon Border Unit had set up ambushes and observation posts. For their services, the Israelis received hundreds of thousands of dollars. Dozens of other IDF soldiers and civilians also have been apprehended, mainly carrying drugs from dealers in Lebanon to dealers in Israel. A courier can make up to $10,000 for smuggling just two pounds of heroin into Israel, most of which is then sent on to Western Europe.

Even though Israel's eighteen-year occupation of southern Lebanon ended in 2000, the drug business is ongoing. With no buffer zone, Israeli Jewish and Arab buyers simply toss a wad of cash across the security fence and, in return, the Lebanese or Syrian seller throws over bags of hard drugs, aware that Israeli police and soldiers are focused on nailing terrorists. The largest source of funds for terrorism comes from the illegal drug trade. The Iranian sponsors of Hezballah follow an Islamic edict to distribute hard drugs as an ideological and destabilizing weapon against the "Small Satan." Mixing religion with narco-terrorism, they allow dealers on both sides of the border to keep smuggling drugs into Israel provided they also bring in weapons for Palestinians. In 2001, four Druze men, all former IDF soldiers, were arrested in Israel. Along with the cocaine and hashish, police discovered a cache of M-16s and bombs ready for delivery to Palestinians in the West Bank.

Smugglers are not deterred by the IDF checkpoints guarding the Israel-Gaza border against terrorists. The IDF can't find most tunnels used to smuggle drugs, arms, and explosives from Palestinians in Egypt to Palestinians in Gaza, in a town called Rafah. Tons of hashish and marijuana also move through Israel's unfenced and largely unguarded six-hundred-kilometer-long southern border with Egypt. The drugs and weapons are transported by a vast network of underground tunnels and desert drops, prearranged burial spots at the border, known to both Egyptian Bedouin and their partners, often Israeli Bedouin from the same clans who know the desert well. The Israeli Bedouin recover the hidden packages and make quick getaways in high-powered jeeps capable of outrunning police vehicles. Despite increased vigilance, for every ton of marijuana confiscated—fourteen in 2001—police estimate that another nine are getting through. Israeli users commonly complain the marijuana is full of sand, which has spurred some enterprising Israelis to grow their own cannabis. Next to a cooperative farm in the Negev, police recently found a large field that would have yielded nine tons of marijuana.

Israeli youth aren't just smoking hash and marijuana. Some have a passion for Ecstasy, a mildly hallucinogenic amphetamine known as the Hug Drug. In 2002 alone, in a series of stings, police confiscated tens of thousands of Ecstasy tablets from smugglers, students, and partygoers. And they're not just ingesting it. A few globe-trotting Israelis working in loose, efficient networks with trusted friends from school or the army have cornered part of the multimillion-dollar international market for this popular illicit drug. Israelis were among the first to identify its enormous profit potential. One of these little green or pink pills sells for up to $50 in clubs and campuses in the United States, Australia, and Japan and costs less than fifty cents to produce in clandestine labs in the Netherlands or Israel. Moreover, Ecstasy is easy to conceal and transport in large quantities. An Israeli movie about this adventurous trade was a breakaway success in 2001. In *Total Love,* a woman and her two lovers concoct a new aphrodisiac pill in their home lab in Tel Aviv. The twenty-somethings then journey from Israel peddling their daring pills to the rave set in Amsterdam and the Indian province of Goa. This story of backpacking Israeli wanderers and their quest for love captures a rising Israeli romance with drugs.

The Israel Anti-Drug Authority (IADA) reports that 12 percent of junior and senior high school kids, 20 percent of university students, and 9 percent of adults used illegal drugs in 2001. "Tel Aviv is now in the same league as Amsterdam or New York in terms of soft drugs," says IADA head Shlomo Gal.

Even though simple possession of Ecstasy, as of heroin and cocaine, is punishable by up to twenty years in prison, Israeli police tend to target the biggest dealers, leaving weekend users alone. At all-night rave parties, which go on from the shores of the Sea of Galilee to Eilat, enthralled young Israelis are dancing, touching, embracing, and kissing. Israel's world-famous rave scene is partly fueled by Ecstasy. One pill produces a euphoric high that can last up to six hours. "I've seen religious kids take their kippas off and dance. In the parking lots, I've seen cars with Likud stickers. Before the intifada, a lot more Arabs came," says Ori Heffetz, a Tel Aviv University physics graduate student who never has taken the pill. "If you were living with bombs going off, worrying about paying high tuition and being called for reserve duty and stuck in a tank, what would you take? I'm not surprised some kids are not popping Bayer aspirins."

One of his professors, Yoav Ben-Dov, writes about Israeli youth culture. His Tel Aviv apartment is filled with books he has authored and an impressive collection of the latest youth paraphernalia. "There's not much shame about using drugs in Israel anymore—it's out in the open," says Ben-Dov, who has the looks and easygoing manner of one of his students. He shows campaign literature from the Green Leaf Party, which nearly won a seat in the 2003 Knesset on the issue of drug legalization. "Israel's cannabis lobby is big. After marijuana and hashish, Ecstasy is the third most popular drug. It appears that adolescents take it. Students take it. People in their late twenties take it at parties and clubs." Ben-Dov displays an Ecstasy E-Z Test kit, which indicates whether a pill is a fake. Head shops on trendy Sheinkin Street in downtown Tel Aviv took it off the shelves when the government banned it in 2002. In the early 1990s, Ecstasy was a psychedelic drug for the artsy, secular Tel Aviv scene. Since then, a wider group of Israelis have been trying it, even some ultra-Orthodox Jews. "Some studies indicate that since haredi students easily can be caught smoking hash in yeshivas, they use Ecstasy pills because they're easy to hide." Ben-Dov holds up a homemade CD: "During Independence Day 2000, some twelve-year-old kids with a psychedelic world vision distributed this." He plays it. The music is "Hatikvah," the national anthem, set to druggy technoelectronic trance music created on a computer. The Green Leaf Party used it as background music in their TV election ads.

These two Israelis both are descendants of founders of the country. Ben-Dov's grandfather was a friend of Ben-Gurion's and his father was a general who built the bridges that let Israeli troops cross the Suez Canal in the 1973 War. Ori Heffetz's grandfather, an eighth-generation Jerusalemite, fought in the battle for Jerusalem during the War of Independence and captured Mount Herzl. He helped found the Israeli Air Force and started El Al Airlines. "My eighty-year-old grandfather also knew Ben-Gurion," says Ori. "When Ben-Gurion said we will have a normal country when we have prostitutes and thieves, people agreed. If Ben-Gurion could see Israel today, I wonder what he'd say."

What does Ori have to say? "We're always in the headlines. *The New York Times*. CNN. The BBC. We get more coverage than India. Than China. Than the entire continent of Africa. There's so much news about us, you'd think we're also a billion people, not six million. We're all the time on TV and front pages, so people think they know us. Unsmiling soldiers. Screaming settlers. Crying mourners. Bearded guys in black hats. Well, Israelis are much more than those photos. We complain about our teachers. Worry about exams. Flirt at parties. Wonder if we look good in our bathing suits. We curse at traffic jams and cut in line at the movies. We've got normal fears and dreams. Like young people everywhere, we want to find love and be loved. We're just normal people trying to live in this abnormal, tiny, beautiful country."

Epilogue Shalom/Salam

☞ A time for slaying and a time for healing . . . a time for war and a time for peace. —After Ecclesiastes 3

☞ I don't see why the Arabs and Jews don't settle this thing just like good Christians do. —Attributed to a U.S. congressman on the floor of the House of Representatives

Inspired by a line from the Book of Isaiah, "My people shall dwell in an oasis of peace," Father Bruno Hussar, a Dominican priest, started an ecumenical community for Jews, Christians, and Muslims on a rocky hilltop halfway between Jerusalem and Tel Aviv. Thirty years later, Neve Shalom/Wahat al-Salam—Hebrew and Arabic for "the Oasis of Peace"—is home to forty Jewish, Christian, and Muslim Arab Israeli families who coexist as equals and jointly run pioneering educational projects.

On the playground at the primary school, children shift effortlessly between Hebrew and Arabic. It's impossible to tell which are Jewish, Muslim, or Christian. When they fight, it's usually over a ball or a seat on the seesaw. In one class, children sit in pairs at computer screens learning common roots of both Semitic languages: In Hebrew, "peace" is *shalom;* in Arabic, *salaam.* In Arabic, "house" is *beyt;* in Hebrew, *beit.* The three hundred students, mostly bused in from neighboring towns, celebrate Muslim New Year, Passover, and Easter together. The only holiday they don't celebrate jointly is Israel Independence Day. That is the day Arabs call *al Nakba,* or "the Catastrophe," and Arab children quietly mourn.

The educational philosophy at this bilingual, bicultural school is that, to really understand and respect each other, people should know each other's languages, religions, traditions, and histories. This Jewish–Arab school is a model for a few others in Israel.

"Another TV camera. Another story about Arabs and Jews. They make a big deal that we play together," a girl on a swing says sarcastically. The children are comfortable mugging for American, German, and Japanese journalists who marvel that boys named Muhammad and Yossi can be best friends. Visiting dignitaries from archbishops to ambassadors, from Hillary Clinton to Jane Fonda, are guaranteed heartwarming photo ops: children gathered to light a Hanukkah menorah, a Christmas tree, and a Ramadan lantern. Children drawing doves, singing *A Time of Peace* in Hebrew and Arabic: "between the lightning, a rainbow will appear not just in the sky, but in our hearts and minds." The school and the tiny village sheltered by olive and cypress trees are symbols of hope, of Jews and Arabs living together. Or, more accurately, of how outsiders fantasize that Jews and Arabs *should* live together; for this reason, the village with two names is better known in North America and Western Europe than in Israel.

When the cameras disappear, how is this experiment in tolerance, diversity, and equality faring? Occasionally children play intifada, building imaginary roadblocks or throwing pinecones at each other. But instead of Arabs against Jews, it's usually girls versus boys or first against second graders. A few times teachers have caught them chanting "Death to the Jews" or "Death to the Arabs," and they encourage them to discuss their feelings. Children see Apache helicopters flying overhead to the West Bank and hear about suicide bombers blowing up buses. One anxious parent wanted to remove his daughter from the school, but she refused to stop coming. Since the start of the second intifada, no child has dropped out, and there is a waiting list of Arab and Jewish families who want to move into the village. "This place is not an oasis of peace, but neither is life," says a teacher who is pushing for more Arabic language and Palestinian history and culture in the curriculum. "The children give us hope to continue. We must be careful that the storm outside won't sweep us away. Our school is an alternative to what's happening down the hill."

After they complete eighth grade, the children go down the hill, there to attend either all-Jewish or all-Arab schools in nearby towns. "At my school, kids ask me if I'm afraid to live with Arabs," says fourteen-year-old Naomi. "I usually laugh and tell them that I was born among the Arabs, my best friend is an Arab, so why would I be afraid? But sometimes I get fed up having to defend my Arab friends all the time." After two Israeli reserve soldiers lost in Ramallah were lynched by a Palestinian mob, her Jewish classmates scoffed at her and said Arabs can't be trusted. When her neighbor Rami left the village to attend an all-Arab high school, he had a similar experience: "My friends don't understand the Jewish perspectives because they never get to know Jews. At home, we don't care much who's a Jew and who's an Arab. Living with Jews is not only possible, it's my reality." Nonetheless, after high school, the realities of the village's children diverge again: Rami and other Arab youth from the village go to university; Naomi and other Jews go to the army.

The army pushes the differences into sharp relief. These surfaced when two IDF transport helicopters crashed, killing seventy-three soldiers. One was Tom Kita'in, the son of the co-principal of the school. Weeping Arabs and Jews comforted each other as this twenty-one-year-old raised in the village was buried next to its founder, Father Bruno. But when Tom's family wanted to build a memorial to him, the Oasis of Peace divided into warring camps. Most Arabs and a few Jews argued that a peace village should not memorialize a soldier. Most Jews disagreed: just because they'd chosen to live with Arabs, must they give up the right to honor a child? "Once upon a time," said a grieving relative, "we didn't agree on our pasts, but we agreed on the future. Now we're told we must forget our pain and concentrate on the pain of the Palestinians." Abdessalam Najjar, one of the first Arab residents, recalls that comforting the family was "no problem for us, but when it came to memorializing him, that was a different story. The first response of the Jews from outside is how cruel we Palestinians are. The first response of the Palestinians from outside is that we Palestinians in the village are traitors for living with Jews. No one is satisfied with the outcome." At the basketball court where Tom once played, a simple metal plaque has these words in Hebrew: "In memory of Tom Kita'in, our child of peace who was killed in war. 5.3.1976–4.2.1997."

During this intifada, residents of Neve Shalom feel scared, depressed, and angry—just like everyone else in Israel. The atmosphere encourages villagers to confront each other about problems. Arguments can get brutal. On occasion, infighting gets so bad that Arabs and Jews meet in separate groups. Sometimes neighbors simply exchange nasty emails. When Tom's father accepted an invitation to light the national torch at the Independence Day celebration, some villagers criticized him for being insensitive to the Arab residents. Sometimes the bitterest disputes are between Jews and Jews and between Christian Arabs and Muslim Arabs. When asked if some Arabs outside the village consider him a traitor, former mayor of the village Anwar Daoud says, "I'm sure that they do. They don't accept me at all. They're against coexistence. I'm the enemy of them because I'm a friend of the Jews, because I am against their way of thinking. Conflict always is part of life here. And our experiment is facing a difficult test. Everything happening outside influences our life inside. There's no choice for us but to live together or die together. We need real dialogue."

That's why the villagers also established the School for Peace, which has workshops for Arab and Jewish Israelis and Palestinians. Groups that meet range from teens to university students to teachers. There also are dialogue groups for Bedouin and Jewish women school dropouts. There are others for social workers, psychologists, and lawyers. Initially participants are hesitant and conceal feelings: few Jews and Arabs have ever experienced three days of face-to-face encounters. Initial arguments are often over what language to speak: usually Arabs are more fluent in Hebrew than the Jews are in Arabic. Specially trained Jewish–Arab teams from the village coax participants to listen to each other's stories and pains. A typical line: "You first understand the Holocaust and then we can talk." A typical response: "You don't understand *al Nakba* [the Catastrophe], so how can we talk?" They challenge each other's interpretations of history. There are tough questions, accusations, and denials. Who is more humane? More unjust? Who is the victim? There are volatile exchanges about land, minority rights, and terrorism as well as negotiations about the future. People get angry, hurl ugly accusations, but since the School for Peace opened in 1979, there have been no fistfights. It's emotional, maddening, and exhausting work, says codirector of the school Nava Sonnenschein. "It starts as a cycle where there is no winner. Nobody wins until they realize they need to get out of the cycle.

As participants begin to see each other in new ways, the 'other' becomes human. Stereotypes slowly begin to break down. It takes time to build trust between the two sides. And it's so easy and fast to destroy."

The second intifada has destroyed a lot of trust. Because parents and principals are reluctant to let students go to the School for Peace, Arab–Jewish teams from the village visit high schools, helping teachers address the conflict in their classrooms and preparing students to attend live-in workshops. "Our programs are more necessary than ever," says Ahmad Hijazi, who attended the School for Peace with students from his Arab village and now is its codirector. "As hostilities come out, so does common humanity. Enemies become intimate." It's easy to look at everything in terms of black and white. People learn to see shades of gray, says Ronen, a high school student participant. "Whenever I heard about another terrorist attack, it made me hate Arabs more. Until our four days together, I'd never met Arabs. I met boys my age who like to play soccer and listen to music. I discovered that they aren't all murderers and terrorists." High school senior Yusef described his experience like this: "A person who aspires to peace needs an open mind, must be ready to make sacrifices and to trust the other side. When a bomb went off in Tel Aviv, some students in my high school were glad. Now I think it's not the right way." Is he optimistic about the future? "It's hard right now, but no Arabs or Jews are going to leave, so we have to find a way to live together." The School for Peace has been nominated for a Nobel Peace Prize five times.

Peace education was a growth industry before this intifada. Hundreds of coexistence organizations still provide a variety of encounters between Israeli Jews and Arabs, and others between Arab and Jewish Israelis and Palestinians. Unfortunately, the fastest-growing organization is a club that no one wants to join. Families Forum. Its more than five hundred members—half Israeli and half Palestinian from Gaza and the West Bank—share one thing: they're all bereaved parents. "We may not agree on what a just peace is, but we agree on one thing: we need a wise peace," says Yitzhak Frankenthal, an Orthodox Jew who founded the Israeli–Palestinian reconciliation group after his nineteen-year-old son was kidnapped and killed by men from Hamas. Consorting with the enemy?

"We've all paid the ultimate price. We don't want anyone else to suffer the pain we share. If we can sit down and talk, so can anyone."

The second intifada broke out only one week before a groundbreaking ceremony at the site of a proposed industrial park in Rafah, at the southern end of the Gaza Strip. Today, the land where it was to be built is barren, thousands of Israelis and Palestinians are dead, and both economies are in crisis. For the Palestinians of Gaza, with access to jobs in Israel now limited because of concerns about security, unemployment is almost 60 percent. Despair, if it could be measured, is much higher.

The industrial park near the Gaza airport was designed to create hundreds of jobs, to promote economic growth and coexistence. It was to have a vocational training center and about thirty Palestinian-run companies—from manufacturing car and aircraft parts to assembling semiconductor chips. To prepare, thirty Palestinians were set to attend entrepreneurial classes in Israel. Stef Wertheimer, the Israeli visionary behind the idea, had North American, European, and Asian governmental and private investors ready. Palestinian and Israeli officials—including President Arafat and then-Prime Ministers Netanyahu and Barak—backed the project. Contracts were signed.

After two years of planning, the only detail remaining to be negotiated concerned the joint coffee shop where Palestinians and Israelis could meet between the proposed twin industrial parks on either side of the border. "We hadn't decided what kind of coffee to serve," quips Wertheimer. Despite the bloodshed, he firmly believes that "helping the Palestinians to help themselves economically is the best thing for Israel. When you're sitting down for dinner and you've got food on your plate and the people around you don't, it's dangerous. Israel will be a lot safer if the people in our region have more food on their plates. I want them to be successful and afraid to lose something. If the region doesn't develop economically, it will continue being a breeding ground for terror." His formula is simple: wage trade, not war.

He knows something about war. Wertheimer arrived in Palestine in 1937 as a ten-year-old refugee from Nazi Germany. During the 1948 War of Independence, he was a close aide to General Yigal Allon. In 1952, he launched a business on his kitchen table, a modest metal-cutting-tools works. When Charles de Gaulle placed an embargo on the sale of all French weapons to Israel in 1967, Wertheimer graduated to jet engine blades, freeing the Israeli Air Force from depending on imports. The self-made maverick grew an empire called The Iscar Group, which exports carbide cutting tools used in the automotive, electronics, and aerospace industries all over the world. One of Israel's largest private industrial companies, it has annual export sales of $1 billion and is growing at almost 20 percent annually. His manufacturing empire is responsible for more than 10 percent of Israel's economic output.

When he talks, Israelis and Palestinians listen. "We've proved that Jews and Arabs can live and work together," says Wertheimer from his office at Tefen Industrial Park in the hills of the Galilee, overlooking the Mediterranean Sea and the Lebanon border only eight miles away. Jews, Muslims, Christians, and Druze from the area work at this gigantic complex where aspiring entrepreneurs grow export-oriented startups, all of which are required to be ecologically friendly. After four years of low rent and guidance, they must move on and stand on their own. The hundreds of acres of landscaped grounds have five museums, as well as art galleries and sculpture gardens for inspiration. Each year, thousands of Israeli youth from all backgrounds come, some to take practical technical training courses designed "to show them that they have creative ideas in their heads," as Wertheimer puts it. Among the 150,000 yearly visitors are mayors, diplomats, and businesspeople—including Turks, Palestinians, and Jordanians. At the Educational Center at his neighboring Lavon Industrial Park, Arabs and Jews live together and learn industrial entrepreneurship, managerial skills, and ways to develop export projects. One in five Israeli citizens is Arab, notes Wertheimer. "We can't have social harmony until the Arab minority is economically integrated into the majority. I want to see everyone working, exporting, and out of mischief." The magnate puts his millions where his mouth is, spending heavily on educational and technical training programs. Tefen, which opened in 1985, was so successful he opened two more parks in the Galilee and one in the Negev. These cooperative incubators, or what Wertheimer dubs "capitalistic kibbutzim," have launched 150 businesses and created about 10,000 jobs producing exports worth $900 million annually. Upcoming are two more industrial parks in the Galilee for Jewish and Arab entrepreneurs: one in Nazareth and another near Safed.

The empty lot in Gaza hasn't deterred him from trying other ideas to transform the region. He's exporting his economic know-how to a new park near Istanbul that he built with Turkish partners. In the works is another in Aqaba, Jordan's Red Sea port, with Jordanian partners. All his industrial parks are based on the same model—Tefen. He believes Israel's future, as that of other non–oil-producing countries in the Eastern Mediterranean, depends on exports. He's determined to see Turkey, Jordan, and the Palestinian Authority use their peoples' high literacy rates and Western outlook to become part of the global economy. "South Korea did it. So did Singapore. All with no natural resources except one—their peoples' creativity. Jordan is eager to transform itself. It has a forward-thinking king, only five million people. [Palestinians, the most highly educated Arabs, make up sixty percent of the population.] Once Jordan flourishes, it will prove an alternative to the oil story. The Middle East is an artificial map created after World War II—it's basically an oil map with little relevance to the twenty-first-century region. Oil is like hashish," he continues. "It's very dangerous, it makes you sluggish, prevents innovation, and creates unhappy people who don't work. The curse of oil created the Saddams, the bin Ladens. The oil-rich countries have too much money and no way to digest it. They didn't understand that they need to create more jobs for their peoples."

In 1960, the combined economies of all the Middle Eastern countries were greater than those of the "Asian Tigers"—the nickname that later would be given to South Korea, Taiwan, Hong Kong, Thailand, Singapore, and Malaysia. Today, the Middle East produces less than South Korea alone. In 2002, Arab experts published a report for the United Nations on the 22 countries of the Arab Middle East. These countries are home to 280 million people, 5 percent of the world's population, but contribute only 2 percent of the world's economic output. The thirty Arab scholars cited alarming evidence of decline. Labor productivity has slipped for 40 years. Arab economic growth per capita is lower than that of any other region except sub-Saharan Africa. Twenty percent live on $2.00 a day. Some 65 million Middle Easterners are illiterate, including half of all women. No other region has a higher proportion of young people, or a faster-growing population, which within 20 years could reach 450 million.

This man with a mission wants a prospering region, where people are not bitter, unemployed, and prone to extremism. "People who are busy meeting shipping deadlines and have something to lose don't fight about history. Jobs are cheaper than wars." That belief spurred him to devise a "mini–Marshall Plan" (after the scheme that helped rebuild post–World War II Europe) to set up hundreds of industries and training programs for Jordanians, Turks, and Palestinians. And also the Lebanese—"if they can push out the Syrians. Funds should go to projects, not politicians' pockets. And don't distribute fish, teach people how to fish," insists this seventy-six-year-old who has persuaded leaders of the United States, the European Union, and the World Bank to believe in his antidote to bloodshed.

There is a ticking clock for Israelis and their neighbors. "Sooner or later, people will find that good jobs are the answer. We have to make it sooner," says Stef Wertheimer.

Peace Child was founded in the spirit of Mahatma Gandhi's words:

> If we wish to create lasting peace,
> If we want to fight against war,
> We have to start with the children.

It uses theater as a tool for dialogue between Israeli teens who are from villages, cities, settlements, and kibbutzim and from the political right and political left. Two professional Israeli instructors—an Arab and a Jew—lead them in theatrical improvisations that explore subjects from fear of terrorism to hatred of military checkpoints to anger at the Palestinians who celebrate after suicide bombings. During reverse role-playing, Jews become Muslim demonstrators. Muslims play Jewish soldiers. Christians play Druze police. Children become parents. Through drama, they navigate areas dividing and uniting them. At the end of a year, students write and produce a play about issues they've explored.

The heart of the Galilee suddenly became one of the tensest areas in Israel when the second intifada broke out. Some Arab youth tried to set fires near Jewish communities and close some roads near the village of Sakhnin. Overwhelmed by unexpected demonstrations, unprepared Israeli police shot dead two young men from the village. Near the empty bed-and-breakfasts where Jewish tourists once stayed is the renamed central square: the Square of the Martyrs of the al-Aqsa Intifada.

Two years later, at a Jewish school outside the village about three hundred people, mostly strangers, filled the auditorium to watch an original Peace Child play. Parents brought video cameras. Women wore headscarves or miniskirts. Men wore keffiyahs or kippot. Jews and Muslims arrived from labs at nearby Medgenics, which uses genomics research to treat diseases ranging from cancer to kidney failure to AIDS. A carpenter, a taxi driver, a Bedouin mayor were in the audience. There were handshakes, hugs, and smiles. Grandmothers brought food for a postperformance feast.

Curtains opened, and forty teenagers performed while simultaneous Hebrew and Arabic translations flashed on a screen. "Why are you afraid to go into their villages?" a boy addressed his parents in Hebrew. "Is it harder to make peace than war? Why can't you deal with the conflict, instead of saying, look at all the happy Jews and Arabs at Home Depot?"

In Arabic, a fourteen-year-old imitated her father arguing with her at the dinner table: "You're wasting your time with these Jewish children. They hate us, we hate them."

Then she played herself answering him. "That's what you've been saying for over fifty years. You say there will be no peace. Well, we're going to find a different way. Solutions you haven't found."

When the lights went up, parents looked embarrassed. Puzzled. And proud.

Notes

1. One of the World's Most Volatile Neighborhoods

8   his Arab Israeli classmates: Israel's 1.2 million Arab citizens call themselves various names, which often reflect their political attitudes: Arab Israelis, Palestinian Israelis, Palestinian citizens of Israel, Palestinians who live in Israel, the "stand-tall generation." To avoid confusion, this book uses a neutral term: Arab Israelis. Because there are significant religious, historical, and cultural differences among Israel's various Arabic-speaking communities, in this book they frequently are called Muslim, Bedouin, Christian, or Druze. Israeli Muslims are a unique minority. They live in a Jewish state in a region that has twenty-two Arab states with 280 million Muslim citizens. Demographers predict that by 2020, the population of these states will grow to between 410 and 459 million.

9   present-day Israel: Hamas was formed in 1987 just after outbreak of the first intifada. Hamas spiritual leader Sheik Yassin has called PLO officials "pork eaters and wine drinkers." Hamas's explosive growth during the second intifada is due largely to the religious revival of traditional Islam among Palestinians and anger at widespread corruption among Palestinian Authority officials. In April 2002, Military Intelligence Major General Aharon Ze'evi told a Knesset committee that Arafat's net worth was an estimated $1.3 billion. On June 7, 2002 the Kuwaiti newspaper *Al-Watan* published photocopies of documents from Cairo indicating that Arafat had deposited $5.1 million into a private account he maintains in Egypt. The money, donated by Arab states in the Persian Gulf area to assist Palestinians, was diverted to cover the living expenses of Arafat's wife and daughter, who divide their time between Paris and Switzerland (Arabic translation by Middle East Media and Research Institute). Reports of Arafat's personal corruption and profligacy are not new. In 1990, the CIA estimated that Arafat and the PLO had between $8 billion and $14 billion worth of assets at its disposal. See *Jerusalem Post*, editorial, "Who Wants to Be a Billionaire?" August 14, 2002.

10   destruction of Israel: According to a poll of Palestinians in the West Bank
     and Gaza published June 12, 2002, 68.1 percent said they favor suicide at-
     tacks; 51.1 percent believe the goal of the intifada is to "liberate all of his-
     toric Palestine"—all the land between the Mediterranean and the Jordan
     River—rather than end Israel's occupation of the West Bank and Gaza Strip;
     78.9 percent of those polled support continuing the conflict. Poll by the
     Jerusalem Media and Communication Center, a Palestinian think tank,
     headed by Dr. Hassan al-Khatib, member of Arafat's cabinet. Cited in Amira
     Hass, "Most Palestinians Want to Liberate All of Historic Palestine,"
     Ha'aretz, June 13, 2002. According to an April 14, 2003 poll conducted
     jointly by The Hebrew University and the Palestinian Center for Policy Re-
     search in Ramallah, 71 percent of Palestinians favor a cease-fire with Israel,
     but 52 percent support continued attacks if there is none. Cited in Associ-
     ated Press, "Poll: 70% of Palestinians and 67% of Israelis Believe Peace
     Talks Will Resume Soon," *Jerusalem Post,* April 15, 2003.

10   and detonated: Israeli Magen David Adom ambulance medics who knew
     Wafa Idris and trained Palestinian Red Crescent medics believe she probably
     smuggled the powerful twenty-two-pound bomb to Jaffa Road in a PRC am-
     bulance. The al-Aqsa Martyrs Brigade claimed responsibility for the bomb-
     ing in which Idris killed an eighty-one-year-old Israeli and wounded 175
     others. At her funeral in al-Amari refugee camp near Ramallah on January
     31, 2002, thousands of Palestinians marched behind an empty coffin
     wrapped in Palestinian flags shouting "Wafa is a heroine" as masked men
     fired in the air. See Mohammed Assadi, "Palestinians Hail Woman Bomber
     as Heroine," Reuters, February 1, 2002.

10   caressed the smiling martyr: Michael Widlanski, "Virgin Video on Arafat's
     TV Promises Sexy After-life for 'Martyrs,' " Media Line, June 27, 2002.

10   "water running down their throats": In an interview with *Ha'aretz,* October
     26, 2001, Sheik Raid Salah, leader of the Northern Islamic Movement in Is-
     rael, probably the most important religious leader of Israel's Muslim citizens,
     was asked, "Do 70 virgins await a *shahid* [martyr] in paradise?" Sheik Salah
     replied: "On this matter, we have proof. It is written in the Koran and in the
     Sunna [the traditions about the life of Muhammad]. This matter is clear. The
     shahid receives from Allah six special things, including 70 virgins, no tor-
     ment in the grave, and the choice of 70 members of his family and his confi-
     dants to enter paradise with him." For more see Yotam Feldner, "72 Black
     Eyed Virgins: Muslims Debate the Rewards of Martyrs and Islamic Teach-
     ings on Violence and Martyrdom," report, Middle East Media Research In-
     stitute (MEMRI), www.memri.org. Copies available at memri@memri.org.

11   "says otherwise is a conspirator": Dr. Sadeq works in the Department of
     Psychiatry at Ein Shams University in Cairo; cited in Middle East Media Re-
     search Institute, MEMRI Special Dispatch No. 373, http://memri.org.

13   to stop would-be terrorists: Farqhat killed seven yeshiva/paramilitary stu-
     dents at Atzmona, an Israeli settlement in Gaza, on March 3, 2002. His
     mother's interview in Saudi-owned daily *Al-Sharq Al-Awsat,* translated by

Middle East Media Research Institute. Also see Daniel Williams, *Washington Post*, June 25, 2002, and "Suicide Bomber's Mother: 'Our Children Are in Heaven, Their Children Are in Hell,' " Associated Press, June 16, 2002.

Miriam Farqhat (who has taken the name Umm Nidal, "mother of the struggle") appeared on al-Jazeera on June 29, 2002 on a panel with Haled Mash'al, leader of the Hamas political wing, and Professor Sari Nusseibeh, PLO commissioner of Jerusalem, president of al-Quds, and a leading Palestinian moderate. Nusseibeh said to her: "When I hear the words of Umm Nidal, I recall the noble [Koranic] verse stating that 'Paradise lies under the feet of mothers.' All respect is due to this mother; it is due to every Palestinian mother and every female Palestinian who is a Jihad fighter on this land." The Arabic text is on the al-Jazeera website: http://www.aljazeera.net/programs/open_dialog/articles/2002/7/7-2-1.htm.

16 his southern Jerusalem neighborhood: Palestinians usually call Gilo a "Jewish settlement" built on occupied Arab lands that Israel captured after the 1967 War. Israelis consider Gilo a neighborhood of Jerusalem. Former Jerusalem municipal planner Israel Kimhi, now at the Jerusalem Institute for Israel Studies, says most of Gilo's land was legally purchased by Jews before World War II (much of it in the 1930s by lawyers Dov Yosef, later an advisor to David Ben-Gurion and government minister Zvi Schwartz, and Malka Shiff). In the 1948 War, the Jordanian government captured Gilo. From 1948 until Israel recaptured it during the 1967 War, Jewish landowners did not relinquish ownership of their land. Gilo is now home to some forty-five thousand Jews and several Arab families, many of whom built their houses during the Jordanian period.

17 The tactic worked: The PLO used this strategy in Lebanon starting in 1982, when they placed anti-aircraft guns on hospital roofs and positioned tanks next to apartments and schools. When Israelis returned fire, the PLO claimed Israel was "attacking hospitals and defenseless civilians." See Sayed Anwar, "Exiled Palestinian Militants Ran Two-Year Reign of Terror," *Washington Times*, May 14, 2002. Also Gil Sedan, "Palestinians Seek Christian Sympathy in Bethlehem," Jewish Telegraphic Agency, April 26, 2002. For more on Arab Christians of Beit Jala and Bethlehem, see chapter 15.

18 their political agendas: Arnon Reguler, "A Different Side of Beit Jala," *Kol Ha'Ir*, May 7, 2001. "A Call from Beit Jala" stated: "For seven months a few irresponsible armed men have been breaking into homes of quiet Christians and turning them into bases for shooting at Israeli positions and homes, even though they know that they are out of range of their weapons, with their only goal being to provoke Israel into bombing Beit Jala. In the last few months we've sent letters to the Palestinian Authority, we've appealed personally to Chairman Arafat and we've demanded that he issue orders to arrest those responsible, who claim to belong to Fatah, including Aataf Abayat, Ibrahim Abayat (both relatives of Hussein Abayat, a Tanzim activist killed by Israel at the beginning of the intifada) and Riad Amur, and those responsible for them, Kamal Hamid and Abdullah Abu Hadid. Despite our ap-

peals, the shooting has only intensified." The residents accuse the Palestinian Authority of giving tacit approval to the ethnic deportation of Christians from Beit Jala "in light of the lack of will on the part of those in authority to prevent the killing of our children and the destruction of our property and the deportation of Christian residents. We've become deported in our homeland by a group with no conscience known as the 'Taamra government.' " (The Taamra clansmen belong to the PA's Preventive Security and General Intelligence and the Tanzim of Bethlehem, commanded by Kamal Hamid.) "After corrupt Palestinian Authority officials have taken over church property, we decided to appeal once again to Chairman Arafat, to international institutions, to the EU and to the UN to put a stop to this tragedy, to protect us and to preserve the Christian presence in the city."

18 "living in a war zone": On October 17, 2000, Shimon Ohana, an eighteen-year-old border patrol soldier, was shot in the heart and throat and pronounced dead when he arrived at Hadassah Medical Center. Doctors operated, and after a month, Ohana awoke from a coma. Recovered, he has changed his name to Shimon Hadassah-Hai ("Hadassah lives"). According to a Jewish tradition, having a new name outsmarts the evil eye.

Gilo was shelled for eighteen months, which ended when Israeli troops occupied Beit Jala, Bethlehem, and other parts of the West Bank after the Passover massacre on March 27, 2002. There has been sporadic firing since.

During the IDF incursion into Bethlehem, some of the Tanzim gunmen shooting from Beit Jala were among the terrorists hiding in Bethlehem's Church of the Nativity. The internationally televised thirty-nine-day standoff with IDF troops was a public relations disaster for Israel. When Israel exiled thirteen of the hard-core Palestinian Muslim militants closely tied to Arafat, Palestinian Christians of Bethlehem and Beit Jala privately expressed relief. For almost two years the gunmen extorted and executed Palestinians they accused of collaborating with or doing business with Israelis. The gunmen preyed especially on prosperous Palestinian Christian businesspeople of Beit Jala and Bethlehem, demanding "protection money." In April 2002, Israeli authorities arrested Marwan Barghouti, commander of the Tanzim and the al-Aqsa Martyrs Brigade.

20 destroyed and rebuilt four times: Kibbutz Ramat Rachel overlooks Jerusalem and Bethlehem and the grave of the biblical Rachel (Ramat Rachel means "the hill of Rachel"). This strategically important kibbutz has a turbulent history. During the 1929 anti-Jewish riots the mufti (Muslim religious leader) of Jerusalem incited hundreds of Arabs to burn the kibbutz. Members rebuilt it. In 1936, more riots broke out and continued for three years. Several kibbutz members were killed and much of the kibbutz destroyed. Haj Amin al Husseini, the Grand Mufti of Jerusalem, spoke with Hitler on Berlin Radio in 1942 and said, "Kill the Jews—kill them with your hands, kill them with your teeth—this is well pleasing to Allah." During the 1948 War, the kibbutz members fought attacks until Jordanian and Egyptian soldiers killed some of them and many Israeli soldiers. At the end of British rule,

when Haganah and Palmach forces opened the road between Ramat Rachel and Jerusalem, forty members returned and rebuilt the kibbutz. During the 1967 War, Jordanian shells and bombs hit the kibbutz. After Israelis defeated the Jordanians and occupied the West Bank, members returned and rebuilt the kibbutz for the fourth time. Ramat Rachel has four hundred members today.

20 the "blood" of IDF soldiers: "Islamic Jihad Teaching Martyrdom in Four Summer Camps in Gaza," Israel Television Channel 2, July 20, 2001. At the "Paradise Camps," children undergo military training and view films about martyrs who killed Israelis. A teacher at one of the camps said, "We are teaching the children that suicide bombs make Israeli people frightened and we are allowed to do it. We teach them that a suicide bomber reaches the highest level of paradise." See also Amos Harel, " 'The PA Steals from Me, Hamas Takes Care of Me': Islamic Groups Are Gaining Popularity on the Street and Could Replace the PA," *Ha'aretz,* June 27, 2002.

20 medallions, plaques, and key chains: Sandro Contenta, "Pokémon Cards Passé as Traders Covet Militant Memorabilia," *Toronto Star,* June 17, 2002.

22 used in the gas chambers: The Hamas bomber attempted to release cyanide gas, according to Chief of Military Intelligence Major General Aharon Ze'evi, cited in *Ma'ariv,* June 8, 2002. See also Zvi Harel, "Hamas Commander Charged with Seder Night Bomb Attack: Sayad Planned Cyanide Attack," *Ha'aretz,* August 2, 2002.

2. Dating and Mating Israeli-style

26 only in 2002 enacted drinking laws: About 35 percent of Jews have a genetic mutation that may guard against alcoholism. A Columbia University study published in the September 2002 issue of *Alcoholism: Clinical and Experimental Research* shows that Israeli Jews with the ADH2*2 gene variant drink alcohol in smaller amounts and less frequently than most other people. It supports an earlier Hebrew University study that found that this gene, and not just religion, helps explain why Ashkenazi and Mizrahi Jews generally have fewer problems with alcohol than do the vast majority of Caucasians who lack the gene. See Judy Siegel-Itzkovich, "Ashkenazi Gene Linked to Lower Alcoholism," *Jerusalem Post,* September 17, 2002.

28 "someone related by law": Maya Levine, "Tongues Are No Longer Wagging," *Ha'aretz,* August 14, 2002.

28 "non-Jewish grandchildren": Israel is home to about three hundred thousand non-Jewish Russian-speaking citizens. In 2002, over 70 percent of the immigrants from the former Soviet Union were non-Jews.

31 going on beneath the sheets: Neri Livneh, "Let's Talk about Sex, Baby," *Ha'aretz,* April 21, 2000.

34 would singe birds overhead: Rabbi Yonatan Ben-Uziel lived in the first century B.C.E. The most outstanding of Hillel's eighty disciples, he translated the

books of the Prophets from Hebrew into Aramaic. During the 1500s, Rabbi Yitzchak Luria, the famous kabbalistic rabbi from Safed, is said to have identified this and other graves of *tsaddikim* scattered throughout the Galilee. During centuries of Turkish rule, some graves were neglected, others forgotten. In the 1950s, rabbis relocated many.

36 are mostly Mizrahim: Safed is one of the four holy Jewish cities, along with Jerusalem, Hebron, and Tiberias. Safed reached its zenith in the sixteenth century, when it became the recognized center of kabbalah and Rabbi Issac ben Solomon Luria ("the Ari") turned kabbalah into a mass movement. In the Talmud, the term kabbalah simply means "received doctrine" or "tradition." However, the word has come to mean esoteric teaching. Learned kabbalists believe it is impossible to reach or understand God through rational means. Everything is a symbol for God, the human soul, the Torah, nature, if one knows how to decipher its meanings. A prominent feature of kabbalah is the codes used to unlock these secrets. Kabbalists believe that because the Torah is holy, words and numbers in it also must be holy, and thus, once the keys are found, secrets in the text can be unraveled. Each letter in the Torah has a numerical value. Calculations based on these values reveal secrets of the universe. See Yael Chen, *101 Israeli Mystics: The Comprehensive Guide* (*Yediot Aharonot* and Hemed Books, 1999). Also see Yoram Bilu, "Good for What Ails You," *Ha'aretz*, September 17, 1999.

36 that age are unmarried: Israeli Central Bureau of Statistics data for 1999: 35 percent of the adult Jewish population in Israel are single, which is 1.123 million people; 30.1 percent of Jewish men ages 25 to 44 are single, as are 25 percent of women of that age, which is over half a million Israelis. According to the 2002 Central Bureau of Statistics, the Jewish population is continuing to grow at a slower pace than that of Muslim and Druze communities. The Christian birthrate is the lowest. The Jewish population grew by 1.4 percent in 2001, compared with 1.8 percent in 1997–2000 and 3.4 percent in 1990–95.

37 "back to traditional patterns": Abigail Radoszkowicz, "Jewish Mother's Job," *Jerusalem Post*, April 26, 2002. The Jewish marriage rate in Israel has fallen by 43 percent in the past twenty-five years. The Large Families Bill, which gave a monthly tax-free payment of NIS 700 for every child after a family's first four, was cut in 2003. Although ultra-Orthodox Jewish politicians initiated the bill, Arab Muslims also enjoy the benefits; they also usually have large families and are more than double the ultra-Orthodox population (20 percent versus 8 percent). The percentage of other Jews with five or more children is not significant. See also Yair Sheleg, "Come Forth, Marry and Multiply for a Strong Israel," *Ha'aretz*, July 10, 2002.

Abraham Rabinovich, "Census and Sensibilities," *Jerusalem Post*, May 25, 2000. The number of Jewish singles increased 9 percent from 1998 to 1999, while the growth rate that year was 1.8 percent. Had it not been for the Holocaust, according to demographer Della Pergola, world Jewry today would number 26 million to 32 million. Instead, the figure is 13 million, most of whom are in the United States (5.7 million) and Israel (5.1 million). He estimates that by 2020 the world Jewish population will be roughly what it is today.

39 weapons to the Palestinian Authority: On January 3, 2002, Israeli Navy Seals boarded the *Karine A* in the Red Sea 310 miles south of Eilat. The ship, purchased by the Palestinians, was laden with Iranian arms: Katyusha rockets, mortars, antitank missiles, mines, sniper rifles, and other munitions. Its captain was a senior member of Arafat's Fatah. Israelis found documents showing Arafat approved the $12 million cash arms payment to Iran.

41 Israeli women's groups: Larry Derfner, "Flirting with Disaster," *Jerusalem Post*, March 13, 1998. The 1998 Law against Sexual Harassment is one of the world's most progressive. It goes much further than U.S. and most European legislation, which relates solely to sexual harassment in the workplace. Israeli law recognizes sexual harassment anywhere, and between colleagues and equals as well as subordinates and superiors, and provides for imprisonment and fines. The law defines sexual harassment broadly: as sexual contact, repeated unwanted sexual speech, propositions, or innuendo, sexual blackmail, or debasing references to a person's gender. In cases involving minors or patients or where the harasser is in a position of direct authority over the victim, the conduct is prohibited even if consensual. The law defines sexual harassment as (1) using authority to get sexual favors, for instance, by threatening to fire a worker or refusing to promote her if she doesn't comply; (2) making repeated sexual advances even after being told that they're unwanted; (3) treating someone as a sexual object by commenting lasciviously on his or her body; (4) humiliating someone because of his or her sexual orientation (gay bashing).

41 "job if she didn't": Eeta Prince-Gibson, "Legislating Advances," *Jerusalem Post*, May 17, 2000.

43 "committed the crimes he did": Eeta Prince-Gibson, "Combating Sexual Harassment," *Hadassah Magazine* (August/September 2001).

44 it would do no good: Peter Hirschberg, "A Blind Eye to Sexual Harassment," *Jerusalem Report*, January 1995.

3. A People's Army

48 Middle East came to America: Shai Levinhar, twenty-nine, worked for the eSpeed subsidiary of the brokerage firm Cantor Fitzgerald, which lost seven hundred employees. He left a widow and ten-week-old son.

49 serve at least two years: In August 2002, Jewish women's service was extended to two years and women in combat units serve three years. Despite the universal draft, women constitute 32 percent of the Israeli army. (Women are 16 percent of U.S. armed forces.) More than 30 percent of Jewish women are not inducted into the IDF, either because they are ultra-Orthodox, Orthodox, married, pregnant, or for medical reasons or conscientious objec-

tion. The number has grown by 10 percent over the past decade, Brigadier General Avi Zamir, head of the Planning Division in the army's Personnel Directorate, told the Knesset State Control Committee and the Committee for the Advancement of Women on October 14, 2002. See also Leora Eren Frucht, "Women at War," *Jerusalem Post,* April 10, 2003.

Nearly half of draft-age Israelis are not required to serve. They include ultra-Orthodox Jewish men, Druze women, and Christian Arabs (but men and women are volunteering). Muslim Arabs are exempt, but Bedouin men volunteer (see chapter 13). One reason Muslim Arab Israelis aren't drafted is the complicated question of conflicting loyalties. By not serving, Israel's Arab citizens are not entitled to certain social benefits such as housing grants. There has been talk of a year of mandatory national service in which every eighteen-year-old Israeli, regardless of sex or religious belief, should be required to do work in neighborhood renewal, hospitals, care for elderly, tutoring disadvantaged children, and so on, similar to the national service Orthodox Jewish women can choose.

49   also volunteered: According to a May 2002 survey by Haifa University's National Security Research Center, there was a 50 percent increase in the level of motivation to serve in the army reserves compared with the year 2000; 73 percent preferred to serve in fighting units, compared to 59 percent in 2000.

51   government-subsidized yeshivas: In 2002, the Knesset passed the five-year Deferment Law for Yeshiva Students, which legalizes the practice of granting deferments to all male yeshiva students who study forty-five hours a week. The law allows them to leave the yeshiva for a year at age twenty-two to work. Then they must decide whether to declare Torah study as their "profession" or serve one year in civil service, and then they are permanently exempt from military service. The IDF has a special ultra-Orthodox single-sex, ultrakosher unit that meets their rigorous religious requirements, such as no contact with women soldiers and no work at roadblocks through which women pass. For more, see chapter 9.

52   more than 550 signatures: "We, reserve combat officers and soldiers of the Israel Defense Forces, who were raised upon the principles of Zionism, sacrifice and giving to the people of Israel and to the State of Israel, who have always served in the front lines, and who were the first to carry out any mission, light or heavy, in order to protect the State of Israel and strengthen it. We, combat officers and soldiers who have served the State of Israel for long weeks every year, in spite of the dear cost to our personal lives, have been on reserve duty all over the Occupied Territories, and were issued commands and directives that had nothing to do with the security of our country, and that had the sole purpose of perpetuating our control over the Palestinian people. We, whose eyes have seen the bloody toll this Occupation exacts from both sides. We, who sensed how the commands issued to us in the Territories, destroy all the values we had absorbed while growing up in this country.

"We, who understand now that the price of Occupation is the loss of IDF's human character and the corruption of the entire Israeli society. We, who know that the Territories are not Israel, and that all settlements are bound to be evacuated in the end. We hereby declare that we shall not continue to fight this War of the Settlements. We shall not continue to fight beyond the 1967 borders in order to dominate, expel, starve and humiliate an entire people. We hereby declare that we shall continue serving in the Israel Defense Forces in any mission that serves Israel's defense. The missions of occupation and oppression do not serve this purpose—and we shall take no part in them." www.couragetorefuse.com.

52 fought over the settlements: Khaled Abu Tomaeh, "60% of Israelis Say They Are Fighting for Their Survival," *Jerusalem Post,* October 4, 2002. Poll by Smith Research. In another October 2002 poll by the Palestinian Jerusalem Media and Communications Center, 64.3 percent of Palestinians support suicide bombings against Israeli civilians; only 9.4 percent said they strongly oppose suicide bombings; only 12.3 percent they would like to see these attacks stopped. More than 65 percent of Palestinians oppose the Oslo Accords; only 27 percent still support the agreements.

53 Entebbe that riveted the world: Masada, Hebrew for "mountain stronghold," is a fortress built by King Herod on a huge natural outcropping 1,400 feet above the Dead Sea. It is Israel's best-known martial landmark, the site of a dramatic episode in Jewish history. In 73 A.D., during the rebellion against Roman rule, 960 Jewish zealots—men, women, and children—held the fortress for three years and then killed themselves rather than surrender to 7,000 besieging Romans. Most Israelis grew up on the mythical narrative of a few brave Jews who fought the many until they committed mass suicide and on the slogan "Masada must not fall again." This national shrine is a powerful ingredient in Israeli identity and nationalism. See Nachman Ben-Yehuda, *The Masada Myth* (Madison: University of Wisconsin Press, 1995), and Yael Zerubavel, *Recovered Roots* (Chicago: University of Chicago Press, 1995).

57 launch the planned violence: In the Lebanese newspaper *Al Safir* on March 3, 2001, Palestinian Authority Communications Minister Imad al-Faluji said, "Whoever thinks that the Intifada broke out because of the despised Sharon's visit to the Al-Aqsa Mosque is wrong, even if this visit was the straw that broke the back of the Palestinian people. This Intifada was planned in advance, ever since President Arafat's return from the Camp David negotiations, where he turned the table upside down on President Clinton. [Arafat] remained steadfast and challenged [Clinton]. He rejected the American terms and he did it in the heart of the U.S."

See also the daily monitoring of Palestinian TV, radio, and newspapers before Sharon's visit to the Temple Mount by Itamar Marcus at Palestinian Media Watch. A PMW review (September 11, 2000) of official Palestine Broadcasting Corporation TV during July, August, and early September 2000 warned: "Broadcasts of violence and hate reached unprecedented levels this summer on Palestinian television, to a point where the atmosphere is one of the eve of outbreak of war."

58 lopsided prisoner exchanges: For example, in May 1985, after negotiating

with the Popular Front for the Liberation of Palestine, Israel released 1,150 imprisoned terrorists in exchange for three Israeli soldiers taken prisoner during the Lebanon War.

60   forces and special units: According to IDF personnel department, March 2003, 40 percent of combat soldiers are religious.

60   retreat from the West Bank and Gaza: The shaky 1981 cease-fire between Israel and the PLO in Lebanon fell apart in 1982 with the shooting of Israeli Ambassador to England Shlomo Argov and the PLO shelling of the Western Galilee from Lebanon. The Israeli government responded first with air and missile attacks and then with a full-scale invasion of southern Lebanon. "Operation Peace for Galilee" was Israel's longest, most controversial and divisive war. There was widespread opposition to it among soldiers and parents. In May 2000, Prime Minister Ehud Barak withdrew the troops from the security zone in southern Lebanon, hoping Israel would enjoy a period of "armed peace." Israeli military analysts, including Chief of Staff Moshe Ya'alon, maintain Hezballah and the Palestinians interpreted Israel's hasty retreat as a sign of weakness and encouraged the intifada, which erupted four months later. Hezballah leader Sheik Hassan Nasrallah compared Israeli society to a "spider web—fragile and easily destroyed," that despite their strong army and sophisticated economy, Israelis became weak and pampered. Israeli military analysts say the Palestinians' model for the second intifada was Lebanon, that Arafat and militia commanders applied the "spider web" theory to the intifada. They didn't anticipate that the killing of Israeli civilians would lead to hardening of Israeli attitudes toward Palestinians. See Leslie Slusser, Jewish Telegraphic Agency, September 20, 2002.

The IDF is very worried about the dangerous Syria-Iran-Palestinian axis, the military cooperation and joint support of terror. In Syria's military relationship with Saddam's Iraq, oil played a major role. There is an oil pipeline between Iraq and Syria and jointly owned storage depots on the Mediterranean coast. See Ze'ev Schiff, "Don't Underestimate Assad Jr.," *Ha'aretz,* August 3, 2002.

61   Hamas's manifesto: The Ten Principles of Faith
1. Hamas swears to conduct a holy war over Palestine against the Jews until Allah's victory is achieved.
2. The land must be cleansed of the filth and evil of the tyrannical conquerors.
3. Under the wings of Islam it is possible to have peaceful coexistence with other religious groups. But without Islamic rule over the Dome of the Rock, there can only be hatred, controversy, corruption, and repression.
4. By command of the Prophet, Muslims must fight the Jews and kill them wherever they are.
5. Hamas strives to set up an entity wherein Allah is the highest purpose, the Koran is its law, jihad [holy war waged on behalf of Islam as a religious duty] is its means, and dying for the sake of Allah is the noblest wish.

6. Palestine is a holy Islamic entity until the end of time. Therefore, it is nonnegotiable and no one can give up any part of it.

7. It is a personal, religious commandment for every Muslim to engage in jihad until the land is redeemed.

8. Hamas opposes any kind of international talks or negotiations as well as any possible peace arrangement. Sovereignty over the land is strictly a religious matter and conducting negotiation over it means giving up some measure of control by [Islam's] believers.

9. The Jews control the media and the world financial institutions. By means of revolution and war, and organizations such as the Masons, communists, capitalists, Zionists, Rotary, Lions, B'nai B'rith, and the like, they undermine human society as a whole in order to destroy it. By their evil corruption they try to gain domination of the world by such institutions as the United Nations and its Security Council. More details of their iniquity can be found in the *Protocols of the Elders of Zion.*

10. Hamas opposes any secular state the PLO would seek to create in Palestine, because by definition it would be anti-Islamic. On the other hand, if the PLO would adopt Islam and follow its flag, then all of [the PLO's] members would become freedom fighters who would light the fire to consume the enemy.

64   planning attacks inside Israel: Between 100,000 and 150,000 Palestinians and Jordanians live in Israel illegally. See Margo Dudkevitch, "A Woman's Place Is on the Border: Female Units Crop Up in West Bank," *Jerusalem Post,* October 12, 2001.

64   for smuggling arms or being turned into car bombs: On March 10, 2003, Red Crescent ambulance driver Isalam Jibril pleaded guilty in Israeli court to using his ambulance for transporting guns and suicide bombers' explosives belts to members of Fatah's al-Aqsa Martyrs' Brigade in Nablus and Ramallah. To disguise the contents of the ambulance, he transported his allegedly sick sister-in-law, her son, and a doctor to a hospital in Ramallah. IDF forces stopped him at a checkpoint outside Ramallah. From "Indictment for Use of Ambulances for Terrorist Activities," press release from IDF spokesperson's office, March 12, 2003.

67   pick up their guns and leave: Based on *Company Jasmine,* the first in-depth documentary of Women's Field Officer Training School, production notes, and interview with director Yael Katzir. Producer Dan Katzir (DanKatzir@earthlink.net) is one of Israel's leading young filmmakers.

68   a woman pilot on it: In July 2001, Eliahu Bakshi-Doron, then one of Israel's two chief rabbis, declared that the army's integration program violates halakha. A group of rabbis aligned with the right-wing national Zionist movement instructed their men to refuse to serve in units with women soldiers. Although most Israelis consider the rabbis' objections insulting and archaic, the army now allows Orthodox soldiers to serve in all-male units if they want. See Amos Harel, "Zionist Rabbis Prepare for Battle against Female

Fighters," *Ha'aretz,* July 2, 2000; Mary Curtis, "Rabbis Take Aim at Women in Ranks," *Los Angeles Times,* August 24, 2001.

68 suicide attacks inside Israel: "The Arafat Papers," *Sixty Minutes,* September 29, 2002. Lesley Stahl interviewed Colonels Ido Hecht and Miri Eisen, senior intelligence officers in the Israeli Army. Colonel Eisen oversees analysis of the documents the Israelis captured in Yasser Arafat's headquarters, documents they say show that Vice President Taha Yassin Ramadan personally directed the transfer of funds to families of suicide bombers. One handwritten letter signed by Ramadan says, "The intifada is a once-in-a-lifetime historic opportunity to build the Ba'ath organization and expand its organizational base" in the territories. The IDF has handwritten checks signed by Ramadan and documents signed by Arafat that show he was complicit in helping the Palestinian Liberation Front, headed by its Baghdad-based founder, Muhammad Zaidan (Abu Abbas) and his local representative, Rakad Salam, secretary of the Arab Liberation Front and the Iraqi Ba'ath Party in the West Bank and Gaza. Also see Micha Odenheimer, "Vicious Circles Closing," *Ha'aretz,* October 5, 2002. Thomas von der Osten-Sacken, coeditor of "Saddam's Last Battle?," says influential members of the PLO have had ties to Iraq since 1991, when the Palestinians decided to support Saddam. See Daniel Sobelman, "Iraqi VP Sent Checks for Intifada," *Ha'aretz,* October 10, 2002.

69 "flattened the area with a tank": Sharon Sadeh, "How Jenin Battle Became a 'Massacre,' " *The Guardian,* May 6, 2002. See also Richard Starr, "The Big Jenin Lie," *Weekly Standard,* May 8, 2002; "Urban Warfare in Jenin," *Azure,* Summer 2003.

70 "hasn't been occupied for nine years": Author's interview with Daniel Gordon. See also Gordon's "How the Times Distorted Jenin," *Jewish Journal of Los Angeles,* May 3, 2002.

70 committee investigating the massacre: The footage was shot by an Israeli Air Force remote-controlled unmanned aerial vehicle on a reconnaissance mission over the Jenin refugee camp on April 28, 2002. When Palestinian officials were shown the film of the mock funeral, they said they were filming a movie. IDF Colonel Miri Eisen showed it to an international press conference and said it was staged so Palestinians could "show as many casualties as possible were buried inside Jenin. They tried to falsify evidence in preparation for the UN committee by executing a fake ceremony, carrying the 'body' and filming the entire process." To view the IDF video: http://israelinsider. com/channels/diplomacy/articles/dip_0204.htm#.

71 if they had not been destroyed: Photos of Jenin before and after the April attack by Israel taken by Space Imaging's Ikonos satellite show most fighting and subsequent devastation were in a small area. According to IDF Intelligence Colonel Miri Eisen, 130 buildings were destroyed by the IDF, 10 percent of all buildings in the refugee camp. "We didn't want to level the whole area, but I don't think anyone in history [faced a battle where] every street and every house was booby-trapped," said Brigadier General Shmuel Yachin, acting director for research and development in the Ministry of De-

fense. "[The Palestinian militants] knew we would go toward the terrorist camp, so every few meters there was another booby trap or explosive." The UN report accused Israel of preventing medical and humanitarian aid workers from entering the camp. During the combat, Israel supplied food, oxygen canisters, and a generator to the Palestinian hospital and transferred eighty-three patients from that hospital to Israeli hospitals. Lieutenant Colonel Fuad Halhal, IDF civil administration officer in Jenin, presented documents and photographs at a conference at the Jaffee Center for Strategic Studies on Israel's media strategies showing Israelis met with International Red Cross and Red Crescent representatives, who denied the meetings took place. Ze'ev Schiff, "Back to Jenin," *Ha'aretz,* July 18, 2002.

A quarter of a million people live in the town of Jenin and surrounding areas, which was untouched. The Jenin camp, administered by the United Nations Relief and Works Agency for Palestine Refugees in the Near East (UNRWA), has 13,055 registered refugees. UNRWA helps only Palestinian refugees (the UN High Commissioner for Refugees serves the world's more than 21.8 million other refugees in 120 countries). UNRWA operates fifty-nine refugee camps in Gaza, the West Bank, Jordan, Lebanon, and Syria staffed by locally recruited Palestinians. According to UNRWA, its schools use the same curricula and textbooks as the host government schools. Palestinian Authority textbooks omit Israel on the maps of the Middle East. According to UN records, the United States finances more than a quarter of UNRWA's operating costs.

72 just 20 of their own: Arieh O'Sullivan, "IAF Whips U.S. Pilots in Exercise," *Jerusalem Post,* September 24, 1999. The exercise was between the IAF and the U.S. Navy Sixth Fleet, according to the American magazine *Air Force Monthly.* Israeli pilots "shot down" 220 American F-14s and FA-18s and lost just 20 of their own F-16s. The results were not officially released, to protect the reputations of the U.S. Navy pilots.

74 "rather than destroyed by Israeli nuclear retaliation": Harold Evans, "The Anti-Semitic Lies That Threaten All of Us," *Times of London,* June 28, 2002. Israel is in the atomic big league: the sixth-largest nuclear power after the United States, Russia, Britain, France, and China. Estimates are that Israel can produce at least 250 nuclear weapons. *Bulletin of Atomic Scientists* (September/October 1999).

74 "regardless of what the international community thinks": See the excellent cover story by David Horowitz, "Meanwhile, in Iran," in *Jerusalem Report,* April 7, 2003. According to Maj. Gen (res.) Yaakov Amidror, former head of Military Intelligence's research department, "Syria is the biggest chemical-weapons power in the Middle East." Syria also is a haven for the leaders of such Palestinian rejectionist terrorist groups as Islamic Jihad, Popular Front, Democratic Front, and Ahmad Jibril's PFLP-General Command.

During his February 2003 visit to a desert site two hundred miles south of Tehran, Mohammed Elbaradei, Egyptian head of the International Atomic Energy Agency, found centrifuges capable of producing weapons-grade uranium for nuclear bombs. His Iranian hosts acknowledged that by 2005, they plan to have five thousand fully operational centrifuges at the site. Members of his team went to another desert site two hundred miles southwest of Tehran, where Iranians had secretly built a heavy-water plant that enables them to produce plutonium in a nuclear reactor. The bottom line: Iranians have technologies to make nuclear devices with enriched uranium and with plutonium.

5. The Ashkenazim: Israel's "WASPS"

100   army captain Alfred Dreyfus: Alfred Dreyfus, a Jewish captain in the French army, was falsely accused of spying for the Prussians in 1894 and sentenced to life imprisonment. His court-martial created a violent upsurge in French anti-Semitism, resulting in not only Herzl's epiphany, but Émile Zola's famous "J'Accuse."

101   native language was Hebrew: For more, see Benjamin Harshav, *Language in the Time of Revolution* (Berkeley: University of California Press, 1993), Martin Gilbert, *Jerusalem in the Twentieth Century* (New York: Wiley, 1996), and Robert Alter, *Hebrew and Modernity* (Bloomington: Indiana University Press, 1994).

106   three-year membership procedure: According to a 2001 survey by Haifa University's Institute for the Research of the Kibbutz, three quarters of kibbutzim encourage members to work outside the kibbutz and outsiders often replace members. Almost 33 percent of kibbutzim have some sort of differential in their members' incomes, although only 6 percent pay actual salaries. Half the kibbutzim let members purchase private cars and one third allow members to extend their house at their own expense. Some kibbutzim aren't recruiting because veteran members want to divide the property and assets among themselves if their kibbutz dissolves. Some kibbutzim soon may be transformed into community settlements whose members own their own homes, don't share salaries with the kibbutz, and pay for basic services like health and education.

109   "to keep them out": Bernard Lewis, "The Revolt of Islam," *New Yorker*, November 29, 2001.

109   mostly by sea: The very limited legal immigration to Mandate Palestine was classified as Immigration-A or, in Hebrew, le-Aliyah Aleph. The much larger illegal immigration, Immigration-B, was termed le-Aliyah Bet. The organization running blockades and forging documents for immigrants from displaced persons camps all over Europe and the Mediterranean was the Mossad le-Aliyah Bet, the direct ancestor of Israel's security service, the legendary Mossad. Ian Black and Benny Morris, *Israel's Secret Wars* (New York: Grove Weidenfeld, 1991).

6. The Mizrahim: The Other Israelis

114 fleeing Yemen in 1949: From 1948 to 1949 about fifty thousand Jews were flown to Israel in over 430 flights, which was called "On Wings of Eagles" from the prophecy of redemption in Isaiah, "They shall Mount up with Wings of Eagles," and later was renamed Operation Magic Carpet.

115 modern Jewish history: Numerous Arab governments evicted the indigenous Jewish populations as part of a campaign of expulsion that was advocated by the political leadership of the Palestinian Arabs starting in the early 1940s. This leadership, led by Hajj Amin el-Hussayni, met and conspired with Hitler to annihilate the Jews of the Middle East and North Africa. During the Palestine Partition debate at the UN in November 1947, several Arab delegates (Egyptian, Iraqi, and Palestinian) issued violent threats against Mizrahi Jews. These threats were carried out after the 1947 partition vote, when hundreds of Jews were massacred in government-organized rioting, leaving thousands injured and millions of dollars in Jewish property destroyed. During the expulsions of the Jews, Iraq, Egypt, Libya, and Syria confiscated their property, which is worth tens of billions in today's dollars. Today, almost all of these ancient Jewish communities have disappeared: there are about two hundred Jews in Yemen, two hundred in Egypt, thirty in Iraq, one hundred in Syria, fifteen hundred in Tunisia, three thousand in Morocco. Iran, the largest surviving Mizrahi Jewish community outside Israel, has thirty thousand Jews. See www.jimena-justice.org (Jews Indigenous to the Middle East and North Africa).

116 their side locks cut off: Segev, *1949: The First Israelis,* 229.

116 "European cultural values": Ibid., 156.

118 cursed by Allah for their "disbelief": Jane Gerber, "My Heart Is in the East," pp. 143–45, *The Illustrated History of the Jewish People,* edited by Nicholas De Lange (New York: Harcourt Brace, 1997).

118 "protected peoples": Under Islamic law, both Jews and Christians were called *dhimmi,* "People of the Book," and were tolerated and allowed to practice their religion, but often subject to discrimination. They had to pay special taxes and wear dress to denote their inferiority and were prohibited from carrying weapons and riding horses or camels—noble steeds reserved for Muslims. As a sign of respect, synagogues had to be lower than mosques. The treatment of Jews fluctuated under different Islamic rulers: sometimes they prospered and were active in cultural and economic life; under others, they were persecuted. Over the centuries, Jews of the Islamic world often lived better than Jews in Christian Europe, where they were killed in crusades, inquisitions, pogroms, and the Holocaust. Nicholas De Lange, editor, *The Illustrated History of the Jewish People* (New York: Harcourt Brace, 1997), 147–48.

118 no origins in the Iberian Peninsula: Mizrahi Jews adopted the Sephardi liturgy. Prestate Israel ethnically was divided into Sephardi and Ashkenazi

communities. Under the Ottoman Empire, the Sephardi chief rabbi was the only officially recognized representative of all Jews in Palestine. But as the Ashkenazi pioneers arrived, the power of the largely religious Sephardim steadily declined. Sammy Smooha, *Israel: Pluralism and Conflict* (Berkeley: University of California Press, 1978), 61.

119   the world's 10.5 million Jews: Smooha estimates that non-Ashkenazim made up two thirds of the world's 1.5 million Jews in 1500, two fifths of the 2.5 million Jews in 1800, and by the end of the nineteenth century, only one tenth of the world's 10.5 million Jews. Smooha, *Israel: Pluralism and Conflict*, 49–51.

121   from Morocco in 1963: Jews have lived in Morocco since before the destruction of the Second Temple in 70 B.C.E. The community grew during the Spanish Inquisition, when Jews were expelled from Spain. Under Arab rule, Jewish cultural, commercial, and scholarly life in Morocco flourished; however, the notorious cramped *mellahs*, or ghettos, built in the thirteenth century to protect Jews from Muslim mob attacks, are a reminder of their second-class status. From 1438 to 1912, Jews under Muslim rule had the status of dhimmi, or protected vassals. Conditions improved in 1912, when the French Protectorate gave Jews equality and religious autonomy. During World War II, when the anti-Semitic French Vichy regime ruled Morocco, Sultan Muhammad V prevented the deportation of Jews. In 1948, when Arab armies attacked Israel, riots broke out against the three hundred thousand Jews. Waves of Jews emigrated, about 80 percent to Israel and 20 percent to France, Canada, and the United States. The 1967 War caused conditions to worsen and many of the remaining Jews fled.

126   and other university graduates: According to the Central Bureau of Statistics, only about a quarter of Israeli university graduates are Mizrahim, and Ashkenazim hold about double the number of white-collar jobs. A July 2000 Education Ministry study shows that 53 percent of all Israeli-born children of Ashkenazi origin have thirteen years or more of schooling, as opposed to only 23 percent of all Israeli-born children of Mizrahi origin. According to the 1999 report of the Israel Democracy Institute, Mizrahim make up 27 percent of lawyers, 26 percent of doctors, and 18 percent of Ph.D.s. The average Ashkenazi income is 1.5 times the average Mizrahi income.

7. The Russians: The New Exodus

132   the former Soviet Union: The thousands of "Mountain Jews" in Israel emigrated mostly from Muslim areas of the northern Caucasus: Dagestan, Azerbaijan, Chechnya, northern Ossetia, Kabarda. The oldest Jewish community in the former Soviet Union, they speak Judeo-Tat, a blend of an ancient Farsi dialect and Hebrew, a sort of "Persian Yiddish." Less educated than other immigrants of the former Soviet Union, they have higher unemployment

rates. Judith King, *Absorption of Immigrants from the Caucasus in the 1990s* (Jerusalem: Brookdale Institute, 1999).

134 at the central synagogue: Despite the fact that Ukraine was the site of some of the worst pogroms perpetrated under czarist rule, the idea of "Ukrainian Jewry" is new: Jews in parts of present-day Ukraine used to identify themselves as Russian, Polish Galician, Romanian, Bessarabian, Hungarian, Austrian, and Soviet Jews. During the civil war and struggle for an independent Ukraine following World War I, about one hundred thousand Jews were slaughtered. During World War II, the most notorious slaughter was outside Kiev at Babi Yar, where the Nazis massacred 33,771 Jews in a ravine on September 29, 1941. And, during the Holocaust, more than half the Jewish population of Ukraine perished. According to a 1999 Anti-Defamation League survey, 44 percent of Russians hold a wide range of anti-Semitic stereotypes; 58 percent believe that "Jews have too much power." Some leaders of illegal extremist organizations and their publications demand *zhids* (a derogatory word for Jews) either leave for Israel or be jailed.

135 nine years in a Moscow prison: When former KGB prisoner Anatoly (Natan) Sharansky arrived in Israel in 1986, he was a world hero. Ten years later, he started Israel's first Russian immigrant party, Yisrael ba-Aliyah (Israel with Immigration, which merged with Likud in 2003). He has held posts from minister of trade and industry to minister of housing to minister of diaspora affairs in several Israeli governments.

140 attracting Russian Christian converts: Since the 1990s Soviet immigration, Israel has some eighty Messianic congregations with over twenty thousand Messianic Christians. See Haim Shapiro, "Russian Olim Swell Ranks of Messianic Jews," *Jerusalem Post,* December 1, 1999.

140 just one Jewish grandparent: Nazi laws made anyone with one Jewish grandparent a non-Aryan and eligible for extermination. If being one eighth Jewish qualified one for the gas chamber, the argument goes, it should also qualify one for the automatic protection of the Jewish state born out of the ashes of the Holocaust. Hirsch Goodman, "Legislators Beware," *Jerusalem Post,* November 29, 1999.

141 tenuous Jewish links: According to a May 2000 poll by the International Fellowship of Christians and Jews, 41 percent of Israelis say the Law of Return should be more restrictive; 39 percent say it should not be changed.

141 "Will Israel still be a Jewish country": Herb Keinon, "Changing Faces," *Jerusalem Post,* November 25, 1999.

141 destroying the Jewishness of the state: Suzanne Zima, "Israel's Russian Revolution," *San Francisco Chronicle,* March 13, 2000.

141 "into Israel under false pretenses": Netty C. Gross, "Judaism? No Thanks," *Jerusalem Report,* November 25, 1997.

146 included all of Israel: "The Father of the Terrorist," German WDR television news program *Weltspiegel,* June 24, 2001. In the program, the bomber's family showed the letter signed by Arafat.

8. Out of Africa: Ethiopian Israelis in the Promised Land

150 biblical purity laws: Jewish villages are near rivers because ritual purification (the African version of a mikvah) is very important. Women moved into a "hut of blood" for seven days, during their menstruation, and then purified themselves in the river before entering the home. This ancient practice of nidda also applies to women for forty days after the birth of a boy and eighty days after a girl. It comes from Leviticus 15:19: "And if a woman have an issue and her issue in her flesh be blood, she shall be seven days in her menstrual separation: and whoever touches her shall be unclean until evening."

151 "come to Israel for": See Donna Rosenthal, "Israel: The New Exodus," *Atlantic,* May 1992.

154 scripture and liturgy writings: The Coptic Christian Bible and religious works also are written in Geez, which has not been spoken in centuries. Jews and Christians in northwestern Ethiopia speak Amharic or Tigrinya, also Semitic languages related to Hebrew. Like Coptic Christians and Muslims in Ethiopia, Jews eat only meat slaughtered by a member of their religion. Slaughter is done meticulously, according to the relevant biblical prescriptions governing the covenant between God and the believers (Exodus 29).

154 the blood of unwary victims: From author's visits to Ethiopian Jewish villages near Gondar. Also see Hagar Salamon, *The Hyena People: Ethiopian Jews in Christian Ethiopia* (Berkeley: University of California Press, 1999).

154 missionaries were converting Jews: An 1838 agreement between the Ethiopian emperor and the London Society for Promoting Christianity amongst the Jews stipulated these missionaries could proselytize among the Jews, but all converts must be baptized into the Ethiopian Coptic Church.

155 back to their homeland: Chief Rabbi Ovadia Yosef wrote, "The Falashas are undoubtedly of the Tribe of Dan and we are ordered to save them from assimilation and to quicken their immigration to Israel and to educate them in the spirit of the holy Torah, making them partners in the building up of our Holy Land." He concluded with a quote from Isaiah 11:11: "His redeemed one will return to Zion . . . and he will also bring back our brethren from Assyria, from Egypt, from Pathros [Upper Egypt] and Kush [Ethiopia]." This is only one of several biblical references indicating that Jews lived in Ethiopia (usually referred to in the Bible as Kush) at least as far back as the period of the first Exile at the end of the sixth century B.C.E. and possibly earlier. From author's interview with Rabbi Yosef on Kol Israel Radio, 1973.

160 vocational boarding schools: In 1984, the Likud government and the National Religious Party made a Coalition Agreement to send all Ethiopian children twelve years and older to religious boarding schools. The move, ostensibly on humanitarian grounds, was political. Although many kibbutzim wanted to take in Ethiopian immigrants, ultra-Orthodox Minister of Ab-

sorption Rabbi Yitzhak Peretz opposed it because kibbutzim "would force them into apostasy and crime." Shlomo Mula, leader of an Ethiopian immigrant group, charged that "Peretz uses immigrants from Ethiopia as ammunition in his fight against secular Israelis. They should consult us about whether to send our people to kibbutzim." The head of the kibbutz movement, Muki Tzur, called it "intolerable that Peretz, an anti-Zionist minister who doesn't understand the first thing about Zionism, should be in charge of our country's most vital part—the absorption of immigrants." Failing schools didn't have enough students, but with an influx of Ethiopian pupils, Orthodox politicians could demand more government funds. See Yossi Klein Halevi, "The Ethiopian Revolution," *Jerusalem Report,* September 24, 2001; Micha Odenheimer, "Malignant Neglect," *Jerusalem Report,* March 7, 1996.

160 put in low-level classes: The Joint Distribution Committee–Brookdale ran a study that asked teachers to predict the scores their Ethiopian students would get on math tests. The real scores of the Ethiopians were only about 10 percent below those of other children, but the teachers estimated they would be 30 percent below. There has been an overhaul: some boarding schools are preparing students for the matriculation exams, which are a prerequisite for college.

162 double the high school dropout rate: Among Ethiopian pupils who arrived in Israel during 1990–95, the dropout rate in grades 9–11 is 5.4 percent; among those who came in 1996–99, 16.5 percent; according to a 2001 report of the Adva Center, which studies equality and social justice in Israel. Forty-seven percent of those age 25–54 are unemployed. According to the National Insurance Institute, 90 percent of Ethiopian immigrants live below the poverty line.

165 "Destiny guided me": There were twenty-five Ethiopian officers in the IDF in 1992 and about two hundred in 2000. The IDF has made special efforts to promote talented Ethiopians into officers' positions, which is a fast way for upward mobility and social integration. For more on Bat Chen Yalu, see *Israel Air Force Magazine* (July 2000).

166 "spare parts for the Yemenites": Ethiopian Jews have strong regional identities and prejudices. In Israel, Jews from Tigre and Gondar provinces have had violent clashes. Villagers often call the usually more educated Jews from Addis Ababa snobs. The often squabbling community has its own racism. Many look down on the Jews from the Quara region, who are physically different, darker, and much poorer. Ethiopian Jews think of themselves as reddish brown and use the scathing word *kushi* to refer to the darker southern Ethiopians, whom many northern Ethiopians—Jews, Muslims, and Christians alike—consider racially inferior. From author's research in Ethiopia.

166 to marry an Ethiopian: When asked for their first choice among three equally qualified candidates for a job, 38 percent chose a Sabra, 22 percent chose an Ethiopian, and only 3 percent chose a Russian. The June 2000 poll was commissioned by the International Fellowship of Christians and Jews.

169 "I walked out": Even though a 1989 Supreme Court decision directed the rabbinate to register Ethiopian marriages without the conversion demand, only one Israeli rabbi will officiate at weddings of Ethiopians who haven't undergone "symbolic conversion" (ritual immersion in a mikvah).

169 accept Ethiopians as Jews: Under much pressure from the Ethiopian community, in 1985 Chief Rabbis Mordechai Eliahu and Avraham Shapira ruled that only uncircumcised men would have to undergo the symbolic circumcision. Some Orthodox groups such as the Habad-Lubavich still deny the Jewishness of Ethiopians and don't allow their children in their schools. In a similar case in the 1960s, the rabbinate told the Bnei Israel, the largest community of Jews from India, to undergo reconversion. After bitter protests, the rabbinate dropped the requirement.

9. The Haredim: Jewish-Jewish-Jewish

174 dangle them below their ears: Religious Jews wear peyot and beards following the biblical injunction in Leviticus 19:27: "You shall not round off the hair on your temples [sidelocks], neither shall you mar the corner of your beard."

174 "the sight of a woman's hair": Covering the head is not a biblical law. It is a custom observed by all ultra-Orthodox and many Orthodox Jews, symbolizing a "higher power" over their heads. Rabbi Ovadiah Yosef forbids married Mizrahi women from wearing wigs because they look "too natural."

175 a renaissance of newly religious Jews: Demographers predict that by 2023, Israelis will be 20 percent ultra-Orthodox. Ilene R. Prusher, "Jewish Scholars Toggle Torah and Technology," *Christian Science Monitor*, March 15, 2000, citing Boston University economist Eli Berman.

175 peeking out from under their shirts: The Bible commands Jews to wear visible fringes, tzitzit, in Numbers 15:37–41: "God told Moses: 'Speak to the Jewish people and instruct them to make for themselves fringes on the corners of their garments throughout the ages . . . thus you shall be reminded to observe all of my Commandments and to be holy to your God.' " Haredi and some Orthodox men and boys wear a little tallit, a simple four-cornered garment under their shirts, which has visible tzitzit. When men pray, they wear another larger ritual white shawl, tallit, which also has tzitzit.

175 Rabbi Schach's funeral in Bnei Brak: Many Mizrahi men attended Rabbi Schach's funeral because he was the first Ashkenazi rabbi to accept them in his yeshiva. Rabbi Yosef, spiritual leader of Shas, did not attend the funeral. He and Rabbi Schach cofounded Shas in 1984, but in the early 1990s the two had a falling out and Shas broke from Schach's influence. Tellingly, very few Hasidim attended the funeral. Lithuanian haredim have a traditional rivalry with the Hasidim. After the November 4, 2001 funeral, the Bnei Brak Names Committee changed the name of Herzl Street, one of the city's main

streets, to Rabbi Schach Street. "They have no shame," said Knesset member Yossi Paritzki (Shinui) on Israel Radio. "The city of Bnei Brak, thousands of whose citizens are supported by the Zionist society, changes the name of the street named after the founder of Zionism to the name of someone who hated Zionism."

176 traditions and extensive commentaries: Every synagogue has at least one Torah, a painstakingly handwritten parchment scroll. The T'nakh is composed of the Torah (the five books of Moses: Genesis, Exodus, Leviticus, Numbers, and Deuteronomy), Prophets (Joshua through Malachi), and Writing (Psalms through Chronicles II). The Talmud has two divisions: Mishnah, an interpretation of biblical law handed down over centuries as the Oral Tradition beginning in 515 B.C.E., and Gemarah, commentaries on the Mishnah by thousands of scholars over many centuries. The Talmud is a monumental storehouse of Jewish laws, traditions, and history. When Israelis say they are studying Torah, they may mean the entire body of Jewish teachings.

178 supplemented by charity: The average ultra-Orthodox family has 7.8 children (Jerusalem Statistical Yearbook). The government encourages high birthrates among Jews as a means of ensuring a demographic advantage vis-à-vis Israeli Arabs. Fifty-one percent of ultra-Orthodox Jews in Israel live below the poverty line, compared to 24 percent of Arab Israelis, according to the Ministry of Labor and Social Affairs December 2000 report and the Jerusalem Institute for Israel Studies. (Studies that broadly include "Arabs" are misleading: Christian Arabs have the highest income and education levels of all Israelis.)

179 "means God is everywhere": The Magen David, literally, the Shield of David, also called the Star of David, is the universally recognized symbol of Judaism today. However, it is relatively new. It is supposed to represent King David's shield or an emblem on it, but there is no historical evidence for that claim. Some attribute deep theological significance to the symbol, noting that the top triangle strives upward, toward God, while the lower triangle strives downward toward the real world. Some say its twelve sides represent the twelve Jewish tribes. The good luck symbol of intertwined equilateral triangles is common in the Middle East and North Africa. The Magen David became a popular symbol of Judaism when the Zionist movement adopted it as the emblem. However, the symbol was controversial, and when the modern State of Israel was founded, there was much debate whether to use it on the flag. See www.jewfaq.org/signs.htm.

179 specific ethical and moral laws: The 248 positive commandments correspond to the parts of the human body, the 365 negative commandments to the days of the solar year. Examples of positive commandments include visit the sick, be hospitable to guests, establish courts of justice, help each Jew have a proper wedding and burial if the family can't afford it. Examples of negative commandments are do not commit idolatry, blasphemy, incest, or robbery or eat flesh from a living animal.

182 "kosher" enough: The Bible separates animals into clean and unclean

(Leviticus 1:11–47). Jews eat only flesh of "clean" animals, mammals that chew the cud and have cloven hooves. This meat must be ritually slaughtered. Because eating blood is forbidden, meat is soaked and salted to withdraw blood. Fish with scales and fins may be eaten, but not shellfish, reptiles, insects, and certain birds. In several places, the Bible commands, "Thou shalt not seethe a kid in its mother's milk" (Exodus 34:26; Deuteronomy 14:21). From these lines came the ritual of separating meat and dairy foods and using separate utensils to prepare and serve them. Under a 1983 law, the state rabbinate has a monopoly over kashrut certification. Because ultra-Orthodox Ashkenazi Jews challenge the authority of the Orthodox Ashkenazi rabbinate, they often have their own certificates.

183 "call her by her first name": Ger, named after a village near Warsaw, was the largest Hasidic sect in prewar Poland. Its rabbis were respected Talmudists. After World War II, the Ger, like other haredim, were almost all annihilated. The First Lady of Israel, wife of Iranian-born President Moshe Katsav, grew up in a Ger family.

186 led the Lubavitchers/Habad: Like most other Hasidim, the Lubavitch get their name from their town of origin, in this case, the now Byelorussian town of Lubav, which means "love" in Russian. They also are called Habad, an acronym coined from the Hebrew words *hokmah, binah,* and *da'at,* for their central principles: wisdom, understanding, and knowledge.

187 Judaism's ten key institutions: Before private baths, these public baths were the only assurance of personal cleanliness. "You shall not approach a woman to uncover her nakedness when she is in her menstrual uncleanness," Leviticus 18:19. Family purity laws prohibit sexual relations during and for a differing number of days after a woman's menstrual period. Religious Mizrahi women follow the Shulhan Arukh, the code of Jewish law compiled by Sephardi Rabbi Yosef Karo (also spelled Caro) in the sixteenth century and wait ten to eleven days after menstruation before ritual immersion; religious Ashkenazi women wait twelve days. This difference is one reason Ashkenazi haredim frown on "mixed" marriages with Mizrahim.

188 day of "spiritual destruction": There are exceptions; for Habad/Lubavitch Hasidim, however, Independence Day is a religious holiday because they believe the birth of Israel in 1948 marked the beginning of the messianic redemption.

188 "a deadly poison which burns souls": Almost all members of the ultra-Orthodox Council of Torah Sages signed a rabbinical ruling warning against "the terrible dangers of computers, CD players, movies and the Internet." See Ilan Shahar, "Torah Sages Ban Internet Use," *Ha'aretz,* January 7, 2000.

192 few dare enter their haredi neighborhoods: The Nahal Haredi Unit, which started in 1998, gets about 160 recruits yearly. They spend two years in military service and another year in vocational training or studying for matriculation exams. *On the Fringe,* a 2000 Hebrew-language documentary by Noam Demsky, interviews soldiers in this haredi unit, many of whom are ostracized by their families and communities.

194 "never will I be able to erase them": Author's interviews with Drs. Ami Dolev and Laura Sacs, volunteers with Hilel, the Association for Jews Leaving ultra-Orthodoxy. There are no statistics on the number of newly secular Jews, but since Hilel started in 1991, the number of haredi youth they've helped and the number of haredi threats against them both have increased. After Hilel put up posters with its phone numbers in 2002, monthly calls doubled to one hundred. Hilel mostly helps eighteen- to twenty-three-year-olds; 85 percent are males in yeshivas where their parents can't monitor them or their phone calls. Girls are more closely tied to their families. See also Dalia Shehori, "The Yeshiva Boys Want to Know What's on the Outside," *Ha'aretz,* May 14, 2002.

10. The Orthodox: This Land Is Your Land? This Land Is My Land!

197 this Judean hills settlement: Alon Shvut is the largest of twelve settlements and three kibbutzim in Gush Etzion (the Etzion Bloc). It has grown from 11,000 residents in 1990 to 20,000 today. Each of the three attempts between 1927 and 1948 to settle the area ended in tragedy because of Arab attacks. Orthodox Ashkenazi and Yemenite Jews who built the first settlement in 1927 abandoned it after Arabs massacred the Jews of Hebron in 1929. During the British Mandate, Samuel Holtzman, a citrus farmer from Rehovot, purchased large tracts of land in the area, on which a second settlement, called Kfar Etzion, was built in 1935 and then destroyed by Arabs in 1937. ("Etzion" is a Hebraized version of the name Holtzman, "woodman"; "etz" is Hebrew for "wood" in honor of Holtzman.) Next, a group most of whom were Orthodox Jews set up four kibbutzim. Arabs attacked, killing 246 Jews and capturing 11 others, who were imprisoned in Jordan. Gush Etzion fell on May 13, 1948, one day before Israel declared its independence. See Ina Friedman, "Suburbia Under Siege," *Jerusalem Report,* March 26, 2001.

197 "Inca Jews": The B'nai Moshe, former Christians sometimes referred to as Inca Jews, have been practicing Judaism since the 1950s. They kept kosher, prayed with homemade Torah scrolls, wore homemade prayer shawls, used the sea as a ritual bath, and traveled to Lima to be circumcised. In 1989, a Jewish religious court converted a group on condition that they lead observant lives, which was impossible in Peru. In 1990, one hundred forty moved to the Elon Moreh religious settlement in the West Bank. After passing the rabbis' conversion examination, in 1991 a second group made aliyah. On November 23, 2001, three rabbis from the Chief Rabbinate of Israel flew to Peru and officially converted one hundred fifty more Inca Jews. In May 2002, the Israeli government flew them to Israel, where they joined three hundred other native Peruvians. This group moved to settlements in Gush Etzion, including Alon Shvut. From author interviews with members of

Gush Etzion and from Bryan Schwartz, "Peruvian Jews Given Glimmer of Hope to Make Aliyah," *Jewish Bulletin of Northern California*, October 26, 2001, and Jan Sedaka, Jewish Telegraphic Agency, November 26, 2002.

200 their national home: Author's interviews with the late Hebrew University professor Ehud Sprinzak, the leading expert on Israel's religious right. Also see his *Brother against Brother* (New York: Free Press, 1999) and *The Ascendance of Israel's Radical Right* (New York: Oxford University Press, 1991).

200 cash-strapped Palestinian owners: Nadav Shragai, "Some illegal outposts get reprieve after settlers buy disputed land," *Ha'aretz*, May 2, 2003.

202 dismantling many settlements: 2002 poll by the Hanoch Smith Institute of Jerusalem, commissioned by the Zionist Organization of America. See also Yossi Klein Halevi, "Terror Hardens the Israeli Right," *Los Angeles Times*, November 22, 2002.

211 stop the peace process: See Sprinzak, *Brother against Brother*, 244–86, for the background on Goldstein, Amir, and the countdown to the Rabin assassination.

211 tradition known as kabbalah: According to kabbalists, Lag b'Omer marks the day of death of Rabbi Shimon Bar Yohai in the second century. Just before his death, the Zohar says he expounded secrets of the Torah to his closest disciples. Actually, the Zohar, which means "splendor," was written by twelfth-century Spanish rabbi Moshe de Leon and contains Torah discussions by Rabbi Yohai and his disciples.

216 walk to a synagogue: Israelis do not formally belong to synagogues, almost all of which are funded by local religious councils. In contrast, most diaspora synagogues are funded by paid memberships and also serve as educational and social centers.

218 "inscribed for a blessing": Daniel Ben Simon, "Doing Things by Halves," *Ha'aretz*, June 16, 2000, review of *Eretz Shesu'a: Ha-im Milhemet Tarbut He Bilti Nimna'at?* (The divided people), by Eva Etzioni-Halevy (Arieh Nir-Modan Publishing, 2000).

11. The Non-Orthodox: War of the Cheeseburgers

222 Israel's public buildings: A 1999 study by the Louis Guttman Israel Institute for Applied Social Research found that 98 percent of Israelis put mezuzahs on their doorposts; 91 percent believe it is "very important" to conduct the Passover seder; nearly 90 percent keep a kosher home to some degree; and 71 percent fast on Yom Kippur.

222 bringing the holy into daily life: Shekel literally means "weight." When Sarah died, Abraham bought the Cave of Machpelah in Hebron from Ephron the Hittite as a family burial ground with four hundred shekels of silver. A Romanian Jewish poet, Neftali Imber, wrote a poem, "Hatikvah,"

which became the Zionist hymn. In English: "As long as deep in the heart/ The soul of a Jew yearns/And toward the East/An eye looks to Zion, Our hope is not yet lost/The age-old hope of two thousand years/To be a free people in our land/The land of Zion and Jerusalem." With music written by a Moldavian immigrant, Samuel Cohen, "Hatikvah" (The Hope) became Israel's national anthem. David Wolffsohn, a philosopher and historian, suggested that the Israeli flag be based on the tallit. He felt that the ritual "with which we wrap ourselves when we pray should be our national symbol of pride."

224   fifty thousand Sephardi Jews: Bulgaria's Jewish community, almost entirely Sephardic, dates back to the expulsion of Jews from Spain in 1492. Like many Bulgarian Jews, Sivan's father grew up speaking Ladino, the "Spanish Yiddish."

226   dying from cholera: One patient this ardent secular Zionist saved was a feverish haredi boy from Mea Sharim. Paradoxically, he later founded the tiny ultra-ultra-Orthodox anti-Zionist sect, Neturei Karta (Guardians of the City). His followers, who live nearby, don't recognize the "godless" state of Israel and hoist black flags on national holidays. Yasser Arafat appointed their leader, Rabbi Moshe Hirsch, to the Palestinian government.

232   "how they want to be Jewish": "Anglos," or English-speaking immigrants, established Israel's Reform and Conservative congregations in the 1960s. Instead of using the loaded word "Reform," in Israel it is called the Movement for Progressive Judaism (the Hebrew acronym is Telem). The Conservative movement in Israel is called Masorti, or "traditional." Many Reform and Conservative leaders say most Israeli Jews really are Reform or Conservative Jews—they just do not know it. The government gives more funding to Orthodox than to Reform and Conservative congregations.

234   where space is limited: In 1997, the Supreme Court ruled to end the Orthodox monopoly on burials. Most non-Orthodox burials are still on kibbutzim, which have a long tradition of secular burial but limited cemetery space. At a secular cemetery that opened in Beersheva in 1999, women can have equal status in the burial ritual. Orthodox organizations still control the burial of Jews. They do not permit Reform and Conservative rabbis to conduct funerals and do not allocate spaces in Jewish cemeteries for individuals they do not recognize as Jews.

240   forty years in the desert: Eating in the sukkah celebrates God's kindness to the Hebrews during the Exodus, following Leviticus 23:33–44: to "live in huts seven days so future generations may know I made the Israelite people live in huts when I brought them out of the land of Egypt."

240   God's omnipresence: The palm, which has taste but no aroma, symbolizes a Jew who knows Torah but doesn't practice kind deeds. The myrtle, with aroma but no taste, represents a Jew who does good deeds but doesn't know Torah. The willow, without taste or aroma, denotes a Jew who doesn't practice good deeds or know Torah. The etrog (citron), which has taste and aroma, represents the ideal person, immersed in Torah and good deeds. To-

gether the cluster of branches and etrog represents all Jews, learning and helping each other (Leviticus Rabba 30:12).

241 "simple wisdom, inspiration": Pp. 171–72 from Elie Wiesel, *Souls on Fire: Portraits and Legends of Hasidic Masters* (New York: Random House, 1972).

12. The Muslims: Abraham's Other Children

248 bumper stickers: In August 1986, and on the heels of the law banning Jewish Defense League leader's Meir Kahane's Kach Party (a move that was itself prompted by the Hebron massacre), the Knesset passed Israel's Penal Law 20, which makes incitement to racism a crime. *Touro International Law Review* 6 (1995).

249 Israel's Islamic population: Eighty percent of the world's Muslims are Sunni, a group that traces the leadership succession to Muhammad's four chief disciples. Most of the other 20 percent are Shiite, living largely in Iran and Iraq, who trace the succession to Muhammad's son-in-law.

249 rise to one in three: Of the 1.3 million non-Jewish Israelis, 82 percent are Muslim, 9 percent are Christian, and 9 percent are Druze, according to the Israel Central Bureau of Statistics, May 2003. Muslim Israelis have the highest birthrate (4.6 children per woman), nearly double that of Jewish Israelis (2.6 children). Bedouin are the fastest-growing segment of Israeli's Arab population. The population growth of Palestinians is even higher than that of Israeli Arabs, doubling every twenty years. Yair Sheleg, "A Very Moving Scenario," *Ha'aretz*, March 23, 2001. The median age of Israeli Jews is thirty years and that of Israeli Muslims is eighteen years, which means there are many more Muslim women of childbearing age. Eric Rozenman, "Israeli Arabs the Future of the Jewish State," *Middle East Quarterly* (September 1999).

249 UN-administered refugee camps: Almost 4 million registered Palestinian refugees live throughout the Middle East. Jordan has 1,650,000, the West Bank 608,000, Gaza 853,000, Syria 392,000, and Lebanon 383,000. The highest concentration, 81 percent, live in Gaza, which has the world's highest rate of natural population growth. Palestinian Academic Society for International Affairs, United Nations Relief and Works Agency, *New York Times*.

249 disoriented, poor, and mostly illiterate: About 95 percent of Arabs were illiterate in 1948. The number has plunged today.

250 hillside Mediterranean town: The golden-domed Bahai Shrine and its magnificent gardens are Haifa's most famous landmark. It is the headquarters for the world's 5 million Bahais, who believe all religions essentially are the same and that Moses, Buddha, Jesus, Muhammad, and Bahaula all were prophets.

252 "what kind of future it will be": In a survey seven months before the intifada broke out, more than 82 percent of Israeli Arabs said they preferred to be citizens of Israel than any other state in the world, and 75 percent expressed

satisfaction with their quality of life in Israel, virtually the same percentages as Israel's Jews. Survey by Sikkui, an Israeli organization in Jerusalem that tracks issues of Arab-Jewish equality. See Michael S. Arnold, "More Palestinian Than Israeli?" *Jerusalem Post,* May 21, 2000.

252 without problems for generations: Muslims revere the site as the cave of El Khader, the "green prophet" Elijah. Jews and Christians believe the cave sheltered Prophet Elijah from King Ahab. Jews pray for Elijah's return as the harbinger of the Messiah. Christian tradition suggests that the Holy Family rested here on their return from Egypt. For more on Arab-Jewish relations in Haifa, see Lily Galili and Ori Nir, "From King Faisal Square to Golani Brigade Street," *Ha'aretz,* November, 19, 2001.

254 governmental positions: The Ministry of Education spends nearly twice as much per Jewish child as per Arab child, and 28.3 percent of Arab Israelis live below the poverty line, compared to 14.4 percent of Jews, according to Sikkui, an Israeli organization that tracks issues of Arab-Jewish equality. The gap in government subsidies to Jewish and Arab municipalities slowly is narrowing. However, many Arab town councils are lax in imposing and collecting local taxes, which by national law are earmarked to pay for public services. According to estimates, only about 30–50 percent of municipal taxes are collected. Hertzl Fishman, "The Arabs of Israel," *Avar ve'Atid* (1996).

256 Oppenheim reported: Interview on *Jerusalem Online* television show, February 11, 2001. See also *American Journal of Human Genetics* (December 2000, November 2001).

256 either Israeli or Israeli Arab: Poll taken in 2000 by Givat Haviva's Institute for Peace Research.

257 a new Palestinian consciousness: Author's interview with Professor Sammy Smooha, Haifa University. See also Mark Tessler and Audra Grant, "Israel's Arab Citizens: The Continuing Struggle," *Annals of the American Academy of Political and Social Science* (January 1998).

259 Demographic forecasters say: Lily Galili and Ori Nir, "For the Jews, Acre's Arab Flavor Is Already Too Much," *Ha'aretz,* November 12, 2000.

260 "betraying us Palestinians": Druze men are conscripted. The Arab Israeli draft exemption is not spelled out by law and is up to the discretionary powers of the defense minister. The vast majority of Muslim and Christian Arabs do not serve in the IDF so they do not face a conflict of loyalties between Israel and their Arab brethren outside the borders.

260 "sigh in relief": Fatma Abdallah Mahmoud, "Accursed Forever and Ever," *Al-Akhbar,* April 29, 2002, translated by Middle East Media Research Institute, www.memri.org. The Egyptian government awarded a national prize to Ahmed Ragab for his April 20, 2001 column in *Al-Akhbar* thanking Hitler for massacring the Jews and taking "revenge in advance on behalf of the Palestinians against the most vile criminals on the face of the Earth. His revenge on them was not enough." In the Palestinian Authority newspaper *Al Hayat al Jadida* on April 13, 2001 a journalist wrote: "Six million Jews cremated in the Nazi Auschwitz camps is a lie for propaganda." See Yossi

Klein Halevi, "Dance of Death Overtakes the Arab World," *Los Angeles Times,* May 18, 2001.

260   Arabic-speaking teachers: Without knowing Hebrew, Arabs can't get into Israeli universities, read textbooks, or find well-paying jobs. Although Arabic is an official language in Israel, it's optional in Jewish elementary schools. Seventh- to tenth-graders are required to study it, but not all do. Citing pressure from Jewish parents, some principals don't employ Arab teachers. Many Arab teachers are reluctant to work in Jewish schools during these tense times and also because of discipline problems: Jewish students generally are more unruly than Arabs. See Ori Nir, "School Students 'Hostile' to Arabic," *Ha'aretz,* April 27, 2001.

261   solidarity with intifada II: May 15, 1948 is the day after the official declaration of Israel's independence according to the Gregorian calendar. Israeli Independence Day and other national holidays follow the Jewish calendar.

262   "the war zone that's called Israel": DAM stands for Da Arabian MCs. Interview by Richard Engel, "The World News Magazine," Public Radio International, March 28, 2002, and Gila Swirsky's report on DAM's performance at the Peace Rally at Jaffa Gate, Old City of Jerusalem on December 28, 2001. It was attended by Arab and Jewish Knesset members and groups including Peace Now, Coalition of Women for Peace, Bat Shalom, and Women in Black.

263   writes Isabel Kershner of *Jerusalem Report:* Isabel Kershner, "The Battle of Words," *Jerusalem Report,* December 17, 2001.

263   rushed to his defense: Knesset member Azmi Bishara was charged with giving support to terrorist organizations for two speeches he made—one to Israeli Arabs in Umm al-Fahm, the other to Syrian, Hezballah, and Palestinian "rejectionist" leaders in Syria—praising Hezballah's "determination, persistence, and heroism" in chasing Israel out of south Lebanon and calling it a lesson for Palestinians. Bishara's remarks were not much different from those made by several other Arab Knesset members. Three years earlier, Syrian president Hafez Assad received a group of Arab Israeli members, who, despite having sworn oaths of allegiance to Israel, wished Assad victory in further confrontations with Israel. In a November 2000 speech at Bir Zeit University in the West Bank, Knesset member Mohammed Barakeh stood with Hamas representatives and praised the al-Aqsa intifada and called on Arab Israelis to participate. According to one 2001 poll, almost 70 percent of Arab Israelis said they would support the Palestinians in an all-out confrontation with Israel. Poll cited in Jonathan Rosenblum, "The Threat from Within," *Jerusalem Post,* June 24, 2001.

264   certain roads in northern Israel: Michael Arnold, "Fear and Loathing in the Galilee," *Jerusalem Post,* October 15, 2000.

265   "good newspaper headlines" Aviv Lavie, "No Question Goes Unanswered," *Ha'aretz,* February 26, 2001.

265   Arab Israelis and Jews further apart: Ori Nir, "The Conquerors from Kafr Manda," *Ha'aretz,* June 18, 2001. Prime Minister Ehud Barak set up the Or

Judicial Commission of Inquiry on November 8, 2000 to investigate the clashes and, some charge, to win Arab votes for his reelection campaign. Commission members were Supreme Court Justice Theodore Or (chair), Tel Aviv University professor and former ambassador to Jordan and Egypt Shimon Shamir, and Nazareth district court judge Hashem Khatib.

266 launch terrorist attacks: From 2001 to 2003 there was a 2.5-fold increase in Arab Israelis involved in terrorist activities, according to the Shin Bet security service. Uzi Benziman, "The New Collaborators," *Ha'aretz,* April 6, 2003. There were 8 known cases of Arab Israelis aiding Palestinian terrorists in 2000, 25 in 2001, 35 in 2002. Editorial, *Jerusalem Post,* April 2, 2003. In February 2002, Shin Bet chief Avi Dichter said security services uncovered six separate incidents in which terror groups were being formed in Umm al-Fahm. The Shin Bet also suspect that some Islamic Movement activists have been accessories to Palestinian terror attacks in Israel. See Ori Nir, "A Change in Policy toward the Islamic Movement's Radical Wing," *Ha'aretz,* February 18, 2002; David Ratner, "Umm al-Fahm Terrorists Charged," *Ha'aretz,* September 24, 2001.

267 championed by the Arabs and Jews of the Israeli Communist Party: In 1989, Sheik Salah defeated Israeli Communist Party Mayor Hashem Mahameed, who became a Knesset member. In 1999, Prime Minister Barak appointed Mahameed to the Knesset's prestigious Foreign Affairs and Defense Committee. He also has made statements supporting Hezballah and has paid condolence calls on families of Palestinian suicide bombers.

268 "and it will be Islam": According to Islamic scholars, Muhammad appropriated the ancestor figure of Abraham and other key biblical characters, Jewish rituals, and numerous biblical tenets from ancient Hebrew monotheism and transformed it into Islam. After the many Jews of Medina and Mecca refused to accept Muhammad as The Prophet, he taught that Jews were evil and maliciously falsified their own Torah. Raphael Patai, *The Seed of Abraham: Jews and Arabs in Contact and Conflict* (Salt Lake City: University of Utah Press, 1986), 331.

269 problem among Israeli Muslim youth: Ori Nir, "Treatment Centers Show That Arab Youth and Alcohol Do Mix," *Ha'aretz,* August 9, 2001.

270 which means over all of Israel: Professor Eli Rekhess, who heads a program at Tel Aviv University that researches Arab Israelis. See his *Islamism across the Green Line: Relations among Islamist Movements in Israel, the West Bank and Gaza* (Washington Institute, August 1997), 14–18.

270 conflict is a religious war: Oil-rich rulers of the Persian Gulf emirates, including Kuwait, transfer money to Hamas and other religious Muslims in the West Bank and Gaza. Al-Jazeera is a regular platform for Hamas leaders. Israeli intelligence officials say that Iran helps fund Islamic Jihad, along with Hezballah, the Lebanese Shiite Muslim movement. See Danny Rubinstein, "Backing the Wrong Horse Again," *Ha'aretz,* August 6, 2001.

271 Come and kill him: Mohammed Draghmeh, "Palestinians Mark One Year Uprising," Associated Press, September 23, 2001.

271 Umm al-Fahm's Islamic Movement: David Ratner, "Umm al-Fahm Terrorists Charged," *Ha'aretz,* September 24, 2001.

271 move easily inside Israel: A bin Laden agent was arrested after a recruiting mission in Umm al-Fahm. Shin Bet sources said they are astonished by how easily Hamas has drafted Israeli Arabs. Amos Harel, "Bin Laden's Long Reach into Israel," *Ha'aretz,* September 14, 2001.

271 "to enter paradise with him": Jalal Bana, "Among the Believers," *Ha'aretz,* October 26, 2001.

271 $1,000 to each Palestinian: Abdallah Nimer Darwish, who leads the southern wing of the Islamic Movement, and Islamic Movement Knesset member Abdulmalik Dehamshe have ties with Hamas and have given contributions from Arab Israelis to the families of suicide bombers. Nadav Haetzni, "Another Ticking Bomb," *Ma'ariv,* February 1, 1998.

271 biographies of Muslim "martyrs": Yosef Algazy, "Always Suspect," *Ha'aretz,* October 15, 1999, and Rekhess, *Islamism across the Green Line,* 14–18.

272 victory over Judaism and Christianity: Islamic art historian Richard Ettinghausen argued that the Dome of the Rock was not merely a memorial to the ascension of the Prophet but that its extensive inscriptions indicate it is a victory monument commemorating triumph over Judaism and Christianity. Scholar Ignaz Goldziher argued that Abd al-Malik built the Dome of the Rock to divert the Mecca pilgrim trade to Jerusalem. Islamic scholar S. D. Goitein suggested that Abd al-Malik wanted to build a structure to match the magnificent churches of Jerusalem. The Arabic name for Jerusalem, al-Quds (the Holy), first appears in the late tenth century. Bernard Wasserstein, *Divided Jerusalem: The Struggle for the Holy City* (New Haven: Yale University Press, 2001). Also see Manfred Lehmann, "The Muslim Claim to Jerusalem," *Algemeiner Journal,* August 19, 1994.

272 actual location of al-Aqsa Mosque: Sura 12:1 of the Koran recounts Muhammad's dream of a night ride to heaven on al-Burak: "Glory to Him who took His servant by night from the Sacred Mosque to the furthest mosque." At the time the text was written (in about 621) there were no mosques in Jerusalem. The Sacred Mosque was in Mecca, but "the furthest mosque," according to Near East historian Daniel Pipes, "was a turn of phrase, not a place. Some early Muslims understood al-Aqsa metaphorically or as a place in heaven." Muhammad died in 632. The Arabs did not conquer Jerusalem until 638. Construction of the Dome of the Rock began in 688 by Caliph Abd al-Malik. The elaborate inscription in the Dome of the Rock, completed in 691, does not mention Muhammad's night journey, although Muhammad supposedly ascended from an exposed piece of rock at the site of the former Jewish Temple. According to Pipes, the interpretation of this Koranic verse as applying to Jerusalem was instigated for political reasons by the Damascus-based Umayyad dynasty, which lost control of Mecca. Twenty years later, the Caliph's son, Abd al-Malik, built al-Aqsa Mosque, claiming it also was once on the Temple Mount. The original

al-Aqsa Mosque was destroyed several times by earthquakes and rebuilt. Hershel Shanks, "How Israel Gave Away Judaism's Most Sacred Site," *Moment* (June 2002).

273 "only Allah knows": Jeff Jacoby, "A Mufti's Unending Vitriol," *Boston Globe*, August 23, 2001. According to Palestinian Media Watch, Mufti Sabri has called suicide bombings "legitimate means of confronting Israel." In June 2001, he preached, "Oh, Muslims, attack and you will gain one of two blessings: either victory or martyrdom. . . . The Muslim loves death and martyrdom." One week later, a Hamas bomber who studied in a mosque near Umm al-Fahm murdered twenty-one Israelis outside Tel Aviv's Dolphinarium disco.

273 "is not the western wall of the Temple": Jalal Bana, "Among the Believers," *Ha'aretz*, October 26, 2001.

274 Non-Muslims are not permitted: On July 19, 2001, Congressman Eric Cantor (R-Virginia) presented the Temple Mount Preservation Act to Congress, showing photos and other evidence from the Committee for the Prevention of the Destruction of Antiquities on the Temple Mount, a coalition of leading Israeli archaeologists and academics, led by Hebrew University archaeologist Dr. Eilat Mazar. Also see Nadav Shragai, "Knesset Examines Evidence of Temple Mount Work," *Ha'aretz*, July 17, 2001.

274 a week later to Israel: On March 2, 2001, Palestinian Authority Communications Chief Imad Falouji told a PLO rally in southern Lebanon that the intifada had nothing to do with Ariel Sharon's walk on the Temple Mount and was planned after the peace talks failed in July. Israel submitted a document to the Mitchell Committee report which notes in paragraph 173 that Palestinian Authority Security Chief Jibril Rajoub specifically had assured then Israeli Foreign Minister Ben-Ami that Sharon's visit to the Temple Mount would pose no problem. Isabel Kershner, "Jihad for Jerusalem," *Jerusalem Report*, June 7, 2001; Ranwa Yehia, "Recollection of Horror," *Al Ahram*, September 27, 2001.

275 to convert to Islam: Jalal Bana, "Among the Believers," *Ha'aretz*, October 26, 2001; Ori Nir, "Islamic Movement Blasts U.S. 'Crusade,' " *Ha'aretz*, October 16, 2001.

276 strike deep inside Israel: The number of cases in which Arab Israelis allegedly were involved in terrorism has more than tripled since the start of the intifada, according to the Shin Bet security service. It uncovered two incidents in 1999 in which Arab Israelis were allegedly involved; eight in 2000; twenty-five in 2001 (five cells in Umm al-Fahm); nineteen in the first five months of 2002. Shin Bet also suspects that some Islamic Movement activists have been accessories to Palestinian terror attacks in Israel. See Ori Nir, "Arab Israeli Involvement in Terrorism Has Tripled, Says Prime Minister's Office," *Ha'aretz*, June 4, 2002.

276 "life is better here": In a March 2000 survey of adult Arabs in Israel for the Institute for Peace Research at Givat Haviva, Dr. As'ad Ghanem and Professor Sammy Smooha of Haifa University found that almost two thirds

of the residents of Umm al-Fahm do not want to be annexed to a State of Palestine.

277 "lives in 'Nazareth, Palestine' ": Nina Gilbert, "Islamic Movement Knesset Member Abdul Malik Dehamshe," *Ha'aretz,* September 12, 2001. Abdul-malik Dehamshe spent time in an Israeli prison after being convicted of belonging to a terrorist organization. Before being elected to the Knesset, Dehamshe was an attorney for Hamas founder and spiritual leader Ahmad Yassin. See also Nadav Haetzni, "Another Ticking Bomb," *Ma'ariv,* February 1, 1998. In a September 1, 2000 interview on Palestinian TV, Dehamshe called agreements with Israel *hudna,* a temporary cease-fire until Israel is liquidated.

277 "Let us drench the ground with our blood as shahids": To view some 2003 Palestinian Authority Television children's programs go to: http://www. pmw.org.il.

A video that aired regularly after January 2003 shows a laughing girl, whose swing and rockinghorse suddenly catch fire. The implication: Israelis attack children at play. A father hands his son a stone to throw at Israelis. Israelis hide a bomb inside a soccer ball; it blows up when the boy kicks it. Actors depicting Israeli soldiers shoot an elderly man in the head and blow up a mother and her infant.

A children's music video broadcast in 2001 through at least April 21, 2003 shows children throwing stones at an Israeli soldier and at a window with the word "Israel" in Hebrew, a star of David, and an Israeli flag. They smash the glass, destroying the Jewish symbols and extinguishing the flames on a menorah (Jewish traditional candelabra).

13. The Bedouin: Tents, Tribes, and Satellite Dishes

278 unobstructed by borders: The problem of national allegiance became acute during the 1947–49 War of Independence when the Egyptian army invaded the Negev and some Bedouin helped them; others supported the new State of Israel. Tens of thousands of Bedouin were variously expelled by Egyptian and Israeli forces, with approximately twelve thousand Bedouin permitted by Israel to stay in the Negev, a population that has now increased more than tenfold. An additional seventy thousand Bedouin, mostly from different tribes, live in central and northern Israel, but they have different politics, histories, and allegiances.

280 lack of certified Bedouin teachers: In Negev Bedouin schools, 23 percent of the teachers lack professional qualifications and 40 percent are not Negev Bedouin. About 60 percent of Negev Bedouin children drop out of school, as compared to 40 percent in the rest of the Arab sector and 10 percent in the Jewish sector, according to the *Statistical Yearbook of the Negev Bedouin* (Beersheva: Ben-Gurion University, December 1999).

283 "And how to nudge": Philanthropist Robert Arnow, chairman emeritus of

Ben-Gurion University's board of governors, established the Center for Bedouin Studies and Development in 1998; it offers Bedouin full scholarships and is the major source of research material on Bedouin Israelis. According to a 1999 study by the center, only 10 percent of Negev Bedouin passed the high school matriculation exams, compared with 23 percent of other Israeli Arabs and 44 percent of Jews. For Negev Bedouin, there are two university graduates per one thousand, while the national average is eighty per one thousand.

285　birthrate is the highest in Israel: Data from interviews with Professor Yehuda Gradus, director, Negev Center for Regional Development.

286　until the child turns eighteen: Haim Shadmi and Anat Cygielman, "PA Women Pose as Bedouin to Give Birth in Israel," *Ha'aretz*, December 24, 2000.

286　more, rather than less, popular: Author's interviews with Professor Yehuda Gradus, director, Negev Center for Regional Development, and Professor Ismael Abu-Saad, director, Center for Bedouin Studies and Development. According to studies, about half of Bedouin women do not use birth control; 60 percent are married to relatives and 46 percent are in polygamous or common law marriages. Forty-eight percent of Bedouin women are victims of domestic abuse.

286　from Gaza, the West Bank, and Jordan: These legal and illegal marriages with Palestinian Bedouin from areas near Hebron and Gaza increase Israeli Bedouin ties to Palestinian nationalism. See Ori Nir, "There's a Limit Even to Bedouin Patience," *Ha'aretz*, March 21, 2002.

286　and lose their children: Dafna Lewy-Yanowitz, "The Quiet Revolution," *Ha'aretz*, August 27, 1999.

289　concerted effort in the Negev: Daniel Ben-Simon, "As Good as It Gets," *Ha'aretz*, January 24, 2000. See also Ori Nir, "There's a Limit Even to Bedouin Patience," *Ha'aretz*, March 21, 2002; Daniel Ben-Tal, "The Bedouin: A Traumatic Transition," *Ha'aretz*, August 8, 1999.

289　Negev Bedouin schools: There is a growing teacher shortage. According to studies by Professor Abu-Saad, over 65 percent of Bedouin are children and their numbers are increasing by 4.8 percent per year, one of the highest growth rates in the world.

289　for released soldiers to find jobs: Some Bedouin soldiers in the Negev have been caught selling guns to Israeli Arab and Jewish gangs and also to Palestinians. In 2002, two Negev Bedouin were arrested for alleged incitement and support of terrorist organizations during a Land Day demonstration at an unrecognized village near Beersheva. Some five thousand Arab Israelis (including non-Bedouin from other parts of Israel) waved Palestinian and Hezballah flags and called on Hezballah to attack Tel Aviv. See Jalal Bana and Aliza Arbeli, "Israeli Arabs Protest IDF Action in W. Bank," *Ha'aretz*, April 7, 2002.

290　frustrated, alienated, and radical: A 1997 survey by Ben-Gurion University sociologist Salman Albador. The Institute for Peace Research at Givat Haviva May 2001 survey of the adult Arab population in Israel confirms this: almost 50 percent of Bedouin say Israel has no right to exist at all, compared to 15.8 percent of the rest of the Arab Israeli population. There are significant differences in political outlook among non-Negev Bedouin, not shown in this poll.

290 "We want to move out of Acre": Sharon Gal, "Family of Slain Bedouin Soldier Requests New Home," *Ha'aretz*, December 13, 2000.

14. The Druze: Between Modernity and Tradition

293 all the exacting ethical codes: During the Lebanese civil war in the 1980s, Maronite Christians, fighting their long-time Druze rivals, reportedly got hold of Druze holy books, which are written in Arabic. Druze maintain that because only initiates of the religion can understand their scriptures' subtle inner meanings, no secrets were revealed.

294 in theory no new members: The three hundred thousand Druze of Lebanon are a notable exception. Lebanon's leading Druze political clan, the Jumblatts, are reported to have Kurdish roots. The Druze in Lebanon and Syria played pivotal roles in Arab struggles against French colonialism.

294 a Druze father and a Jewish mother: David Ratner, "In Druze Schools, Endogamy Is Everything," *Jerusalem Post*, September 2, 2001.

294 custody of her children: Ruth Sinai, "The Creeping Emancipation of Druze Women," *Ha'aretz*, July 5, 1998.

295 volcano at the Sea of Galilee: Jethro's tomb at the Horns of Hittin also is the site where Saladin's Muslim armies routed the Crusaders in 1187. The tomb is inside a mosque-like domed hall with hundreds of fine Persian carpets. Before entering, Druze remove their shoes and cover their heads.

296 usher in the "Golden Age": After al-Darazi's death, Hamza announced he was the true reincarnation of al-Hakim. All Druze are required to recognize al-Hakim's divinity. See Robert Breton Betts, *The Druze* (New Haven: Yale University Press, 1988), 8–19.

297 control of Jethro's Tomb: Mufti Haj Amin el-Husseini and other Muslim clerics and political leaders supported Hitler. At a meeting in Berlin on November 21, 1941, Husseini told Hitler that his plan to expel Germany's Jews to the Jewish portion of Palestine would create a powerful Jewish state, that a better solution was to "kill all the Jews." At the Nuremberg trials, Adolf Eichmann's deputy Dieter Wisliceny testified that "the Mufti was one of the initiators of the systematic extermination of European Jews and advised Eichmann and Himmler in executing this plan."

297 Ben-Gurion to draft them: Zeidan Atashi, *Jerusalem Letter: The Druze in Israel and the Question of Compulsory Military Service*, October 15, 2001, and *Druze and Jews in Israel: A Shared Destiny?* (Sussex, U.K.: Sussex Academic Press, 1997). A Knesset member in 1977–81 and 1984–88 from the Shinui Party, Atashi was the first non-Jewish Israeli to hold a diplomatic

post. He was a consul at the New York Israeli Consulate and later a member of Israel's United Nations delegation.

297 a higher proportion of Druze: Druze have been drafted since 1956. Eighty-three percent of Druze males are conscripted, compared to 80 percent of Jewish males, according to data by a subcommittee of the Knesset Foreign Affairs and Security Committee. See Dalia Shehori, "Druze, Circassians More Likely to Serve in IDF," *Ha'aretz*, December 2, 1999. However, the percentages change when different groups of Jewish soldiers are studied. Over 95 percent of eligible Ethiopian eighteen-year-old men serve in the army, a higher percentage than any other group of draftees.

297 "in every sense of the word": About fourteen thousand Druze live in Jordan. Jalal Bana, "Israeli Druze to Jumblatt: Stop Interfering," *Ha'aretz*, August 16, 2001.

298 wave Syrian flags: In 1925, Druze spearheaded the anti-French rebellion that led to Syria's independence. Even so, the late Hafez Assad and his son Bashar and their tiny but powerful Islamic sect, the Alawites, have blocked Druze from advancing in Syrian politics and the military.

301 naming other women: Suzanne Zima, "When Brothers Kill Sisters," *Montreal Gazette*, April 17, 1999.

301 "Bloodshed is just a matter of time": Sharon Gal, "Two Druze Women Charged with Honor Killing Conspiracy," *Ha'aretz*, July 9, 1999. See also Daniel Ben-Simon, "Trouble in Paradise," *Ha'aretz*, September 17, 1999.

15. The Christians: Uneasy in the Land of Jesus

305 souvenir seller in Bethlehem: Danielle Haas, "Muslim or Christian Palestinians," *San Francisco Chronicle*, June 8, 2003.

306 call it Golgotha: Golgotha is Hebrew for "skull," so named because of the Christian belief that Adam was buried here and that a drop of Jesus' blood fell on Adam's skull. Some archaeologists believe that under the church are signs of the original rock-cut tomb and also a small Jewish cemetery dating back to the First Temple period.

309 Israel's choicest real estate: Danny Rubinstein, "Sex in the Sepulcher," *Ha'aretz*, May 8, 2001.

309 Some are shot: While Jordan controlled the West Bank and East Jerusalem (1948–67) Christians were prohibited from acquiring property in East Jerusalem and compelled to close schools and businesses on Muslim holidays and to include Muslim teachings in Christian schools. In the Palestinian Authority selling land to Jews is a crime that carries the death penalty.

309 her husband is Anglican: The Anglican Church (British antecedent to U.S. Episcopalianism) was established in Jerusalem in 1841, during a time of fervor to bring Christianity to the Jews of Palestine. The first Anglican bishop was a former rabbi who converted to Christianity. A number of other "younger" churches—the Church of Scotland, the Baptists, the Seventh Day

Adventists, Pentecostals, the Church of Christ, Jehovah's Witnesses, and Mormons—also have congregations in Israel.

310 crucified and buried: In the late nineteenth century, British explorer General Charles "Chinese" Gordon concluded that Jesus couldn't have been entombed in the Holy Sepulcher, because according to Jewish custom, graves must be outside city walls. He theorized that a hill in East Jerusalem shaped like a skull was Golgotha, the place of "the skull." Nearby he found an ancient cave tomb. Protestants consider it the authentic tomb of Jesus.

310 congregants now call themselves "Arab": Danny Rubinstein, "Sex in the Sepulcher," *Ha'aretz,* May 8, 2001.

311 "Palestine ruled by the Koran": The official religion of the Palestinian Authority is Islam and laws reflect the Koranic Shari'a. Hamas, Hezballah, and Islamic Jihad advocate an Islamic Palestine. Most Palestinian churches do not teach the Old Testament, and passages considered unacceptable to Muslims have been eliminated from Arabic prayer books. References to Israel and Zion have been purged, as have psalms that exalt the God of Israel. Many Palestinian Christians are unaware that Jesus and Mary and the Apostles were Jews; they are taught that Jesus was a Palestinian Arab. Paul Merkley, *Christian Attitudes towards the State of Israel* (Montreal: McGill-Queens University Press, 2001).

311 encouraging thousands of Muslims: After the PLO assumed control of Bethlehem in 1995, Arafat tipped the demographic balance of sixty-five thousand by changing the municipal boundaries, adding thirty thousand Muslims from three neighboring refugee camps, bringing in a few thousand Bedouin of the Ta'amrah tribe and Muslims from Hebron. He fired the Bethlehem city council (nine Christians and two Muslims) and made it half Muslim. He appointed a Muslim from Hebron, Muhammed Rashad al-Jabari, to the governorship of Bethlehem. Muslims were appointed to top bureaucratic, political, and security posts. Yoram Ettinger, "The Islamization of Bethlehem by Arafat," *Jerusalem Cloakroom 117,* December 25, 2001.

312 the number of Arab Christians: Author's interviews with Professor Daphne Tsimhoni of the Hebrew University and author of *Christian Communities in Jerusalem and the West Bank since 1948* (New York: Praeger, 1993). Before the 1948 War, Christian Arabs made up 11 percent (139,000) of the total Arab population of 1945 Mandatory Palestine. After the war, the Christian Arab population shot to 21 percent, but since 1967, about four times more Arab Christians than Muslims have left the West Bank and Gaza. The Palestinian Authority does not publish data on Christian emigration, which is considered a "sensitive issue." Christian Palestinians living in North and South America far outnumber those remaining in the Palestinian Authority.

At the end of the nineteenth century, Christians made up 13 percent of the population of the Middle East; today, they are fewer than 1 percent. Israeli Christian Arabs, now 2.1 percent of the population, proportionally are one of the largest Christian minorities in the Middle East, according to Professor Tsimhoni. Non-Arab Christians (mostly former Soviets and Ethiopians) out-number Arab Israeli Christians.

312   she was carrying a son: The Basilica built by the Vatican in 1968 is the fifth on this spot and the largest Roman Catholic church in the Middle East. The first was built by the Judeo-Christian community in Roman times. The Basilica sits on the ruins of first-century Nazareth, the site of what some believe was Mary's (Miriam's) home, Joseph's carpentry shop, and the site of the Conception itself. The Greek Orthodox believe it happened at another site: the angel appeared to Mary as she was drawing water from a spring. On the site is Nazareth's Greek Orthodox Church of the Annunciation (which also is called the Church of the Archangel Gabriel).

313   serving in the Basilica: Vatican News Service, " 'Lebanization' Threatens Nazareth: Tensions Resulting from Plans to Build 'Largest Mosque in World,' " *Zenitm,* January 7, 2001.

313   left in tatters: Before the Pope's historic millennial visit, unsigned leaflets written in Arabic alerted Christians that if the Pope "dares" visit Nazareth, "we will burn down your homes with our own hands." They announced that all religious sites of the Holy Land are the "rightful property of Islam" and that "the cross must disappear and Islam take its place." "Islamic Extremists Threaten Christians in Nazareth," *Catholic World News,* December 20, 1999.

314   the adjoining Jewish town: About a quarter of Upper Nazareth's residents are immigrants from the former Soviet Union. Some are Russian Orthodox and worship in special services in Greek Orthodox churches in Nazareth, which are held on Saturday (Sunday is a workday). The majority of Orthodox Christians in Israel speak Russian, not Arabic, according to Greek Orthodox Patriarch Irineos. According to a 2002 Ministry of the Interior survey, 246,037 non-Jews have become Israeli citizens since 1988. Of these, 221,428 are former Soviets.

314   wanting to go after bin Laden: Jalal Bana and Ori Nir, "Israeli Arabs Commemorate a Year Since Riot," *Ha'aretz,* September 30, 2001.

314   "the beginning of Muslim rule": Laurie Copans, "Muslims Begin Construction of Mosque in Nazareth Despite Christian Protests," Associated Press, November 15, 2001. The Netanyahu government decided that Muslims could build a mosque on one third of the land, even though church leaders in the Holy Land complained that Israel was making excessive concessions to the Muslims. Barak's government agreed. In 2002, the Sharon government ordered work halted on the mosque.

318   still has a Christian majority: Kfar Yasif, Eilabun, Rama, and Jish are Galilee villages with Christian majorities. Fassuta and Mi'ilya (Greek Orthodox and Roman Catholic) are Israel's only entirely Christian villages.

319   hospitals in their communities: In 2000, Arab Israelis began volunteering for National Service for the first time. They work in schools, hospitals, and wel-

fare institutions in their communities. "Israeli Arabs Volunteer for National Service," *Ha'aretz,* January 20, 2000.

319 Palestinian sniper in Gaza: Margot Dudkevitch, "Palestinian Sniper Kills IDF Soldier in Gaza," *Jerusalem Post,* February 6, 2001.

319 "what is right for us now": Charles Sennott, *The Body and the Blood* (New York: Public Affairs, 2001), 277–79.

16. Marriage, Polygamy, Adultery, and Divorce Israeli-style

327 should death or divorce: The word *ketuba* literally means "that which is written." Written in Aramaic, the language of the Babylonian Jews, the ketuba is a legal contract. Because brides in the ancient world were considered property, the earliest marriage contracts were strictly commercial agreements. By the first century B.C.E., the ketuba was a legal contract in which the husband pledged to honor and support his wife and give her rights to her dowry and other property should he divorce her.

331 sanctioned by the Orthodox Rabbinate: Conversion is a highly political and incendiary issue. The Orthodox Rabbinate does not have the same power over conversion as it has over marriage and divorce. In 1989, the Supreme Court ruled that the Ministry of the Interior must recognize overseas non-Orthodox conversions and that these converts can become Israeli Jews according to the Law of Return. The Knesset recognizes that treating conversion like marriage and divorce will cause a serious rift with the diaspora Jews. In 1999, all three Jewish movements—Reform, Conservative, and Orthodox—started the Joint Institute for Jewish Studies to prepare people for conversion in Israel. The rabbinical courts approve these converts.

333 only at night or in the dark: Author's interviews with Rachel Biale, author of *Women and Jewish Law* (New York: Schocken Books, 1984). The times for conjugal duty prescribed in the Torah are: daily for men of independence; twice a week for laborers; once a week for ass drivers; once in thirty days for camel drivers; once in six months for sailors. The Talmud adds other times when a man should initiate sex with his wife: before he leaves on a journey and near her menstruation. *Iggeret Ha-Kodesh,* the Holy Letter, a popular thirteenth-century treatise by Nachmanides, influences Jewish attitudes toward sexuality: "Intercourse is holy and clean when done when it is proper and the time is right and the intention right. . . . For intercourse is called knowing . . . and this is its hidden meaning . . . if it were not an act of great holiness, intercourse would not have been called knowing."

333 "considered unchaste": Lesley Hazelton, *Israeli Women: The Reality Behind the Myths* (New York: Simon & Schuster, 1977), 116–17.

333 if they look at "that place": Author's interviews with David Biale, author of *Eros and the Jews* (New York: Basic Books, 1992).

334 "defrauding the Jewish mission": Hazelton, *Israeli Women: The Reality Be-*

hind the Myths. See "Cult of Fertility" chapter. Ben-Gurion quote from "How Can the Birthrate Be Increased?" *Ha'aretz,* December 8, 1967.

334 more IVF clinics per capita: A rabbinical concern is that a Jewish sperm donor's multiple progeny might marry and unwittingly commit brother-sister incest. Susan Kahn, *Rabbis and Reproduction: The Uses of New Reproductive Technologies among Ultra-Orthodox Jews in Israel* (Waltham, Mass.: Hadassah International Research Institute on Jewish Women at Brandeis University, August 1998).

334 a million births worldwide: Professor Bruno Lunenfeld of Sheba Medical Center developed Pergonal and its derivative drugs, which are the basis for all fertility treatments given to women in the past forty years. The first in vitro pregnancy in the world occurred as the result of fertility treatments he gave his Israeli patient in 1961. Serono, the Italian pharmaceutical company that manufactures Pergonal according to his research, has made billions of dollars in profits. He has made nothing. Neri Liveh, "The Good Father," *Ha'aretz Magazine,* May 31, 2002.

336 Israelis are somewhat different: There are no reliable research figures on the prevalence of extramarital affairs among Israelis. In a 1994 unpublished study on Israeli sexuality cited by Ronny Shtarkshall and Minah Zemach at Humboldt University, Berlin, over 35 percent of Israeli men and 25 percent of women reported having at least one extramarital affair.

338 sex with a single woman: The prohibition against a married man having sex with a married woman is derived from the biblical verse "Thou shalt not implant thy seed into thy neighbor's wife" (Leviticus 18:2). The Torah's injunction against adultery applies only to married women. Sexual intercourse between a married woman and a man other than her husband is adultery. In the Bible, the penalty for adultery is death. Even after the death penalty disappeared from Jewish law, the rabbis taught that an adulterous woman was *assur lebaal, assur laboel* (forbidden to her husband, forbidden to her lover). Although the laws forbidding adultery originally were to ensure the paternity of children, throughout Talmudic times rabbis taught that an unfaithful man cannot expect his wife to be faithful.

340 arrested the husband: Author's 2001 interviews with Debbie Gross. See also Emma Blijdenstein, "20 Calls a Day to Hotline for Religious Victims of Rape," *Ha'aretz,"* April 28, 2000.

341 "We're going to fight this": The Supreme Court can overrule the rabbis on alimony and child custody, but not on divorce. Even though the Supreme Court recently ruled that the rabbinical courts should apply Israeli civil laws in decisions about a married couple's common property, rabbinical courts continue to follow religious laws, which do not recognize "common property." Yisraela's client's husband preempted her by serving a petition regarding the property to the rabbinical court, so she will either end up with nothing or endure years of legal battles until she is eligible to appeal to the Supreme Court. If she had acted more quickly than her husband and served a petition to the civil court, she would have been eligible for half the prop-

erty, that is, if her husband agreed to give her a divorce. For more, see Jack Nusan Porter, editor, *Women in Chains: A Sourcebook on the Agunah* (Northvale, N.J.: Aronson, 1995), especially "The Rabbinical Ties That Bind," by Glen Frankel.

345 between first-degree kin: Ronny Shtarkshall and Minah Zemach, Humboldt University, Berlin, 1994, study on Israeli sexuality. Marriages between relatives keep wealth, especially land, within extended families. In reciprocal marriages, families exchange two pairs of their offspring, one male and one female from each family. These male-female pairs are often brother and sister or first cousins. This saves the dowry payments for both families and also creates double kinship lines. A second type of marriage is between first or second cousins, uncle and niece, or aunt and nephew.

347 "more precious than life": Raphael Patai, *The Arab Mind* (New York: Scribner, 1983), quoting Mouloud Feraoun, 125–26.

347 save a woman's marriage and life: Jan Goodwin, *Price of Honor: Muslim Women Lift the Veil of Silence on the Islamic World* (New York: Plume, 1994). Hymen restoration must be done a few days before the wedding because the procedure is temporary. Some girls are born either without a hymen or with one that does not bleed.

347 be considered invalid: Virginity is not required of men. Usually a groom's only premarital sexual experience is with prostitutes. *Wedding in Galilee,* a 1987 Arabic-language Israeli movie by Michel Khleifi, about a traditional Muslim Israeli village wedding, shows the pressure a bride feels to prove her virginity and the groom's to prove his virility in bed.

348 like a donkey: Geraldine Brooks, *Nine Parts of Desire: The Hidden World of Islamic Women* (New York: Anchor Books, 1995); see chapters 2 and 3 about insights into attitudes toward marriage and sex.

348 "cool and barren": These *hadith,* or anecdotal traditions, about the Prophet's life and sayings were compiled two centuries after Muhammad's death and are mainly from the book *Makarem al-Akhlaq.*

351 "beating a disobedient wife": Judith Miller, *God Has Ninety-nine Names* (New York: Simon & Schuster, 1996). A 2002 poll by the Society for the Advancement of the Palestinian Working Woman, in conjunction with the Palestinian Center for Public Opinion Polls, under the supervision of Dr. Nabil Kokali, found the following:

56.9 percent of Palestinians feel it is a husband's right to hit his wife if he thinks she hurt his manhood

47.1 percent feel that there is no need for intervention by social or law enforcement agencies in instances of husbands attacking wives, because that is a family problem

59.1 percent feel that it is a husband's right to prevent his wife from working outside the home

86 percent feel that Islamic traditions and customs retard women's advancement

68.5 percent feel that the Palestinian Authority (PA) should legislate firm punitive legislation for violence against women. (Cited in *Al-Ayyam*, women's supplement, "The Woman's Voice," October 3, 2002, translated by Palestinian Media Watch.)

351 told *Time* magazine's Lisa Beyer: Lisa Beyer, "The Women of Islam," *Time*, November 25, 2001, quoting Riffat Hassan, professor of religious studies at the University of Louisville.

351 hymen is broken: Arab women's organizations train police in the Arab community to help victims of sexual and physical violence. Under the Prevention of Domestic Violence Act of 1991 restraining orders can be issued against violent husbands. The husband's parental multistory home often has several married Arab couples, so if a restraining order is issued against a violent spouse, the wife remains living with his relatives, who may threaten her.

351 in the name of family honor: Douglas Jehl, "Arab Honor's Price: A Woman's Blood," *New York Times*, June 20, 1999. See also Norma Khouri, *Honor Lost* (New York: Atria Books, 2003), 196. In 1998 the United Nations conservatively estimated more than five thousand women are killed for reasons of honor yearly.

353 her brother killed her: Author's interviews with Aida Touma-Souliman.

353 "that Arab society supports": Walter Rogers, "Honor Killings: A Brutal Tribal Custom," CNN, December 7, 1995.

353 suicides, accidents, or disappearances: Arab women's organizations such as al-Badeel, the Coalition against the Crime of Family Honor, have documented over a dozen honor killings yearly since 1990. The numbers are inaccurate and low because families report many murdered women as "missing."

354 "better than none": Sheik Taysir al-Tamim, the head of the Palestinian Authority's Islamic courts, outlined pro-polygamy arguments in *Al-Quds* newspaper on March 8, 2001 and urged men to take additional wives.

354 married an Arab Israeli: Davan Maharaj, "Israeli Arabs Cut Off from West Bank Kin," *Los Angeles Times*, May 24, 2002. See also Haim Shapiro, "Yishai Freezes Arab Naturalization Requests," *Jerusalem Post*, May 13, 2002; Mazal Mualem, "Yishai Seeks to Cut Non-Jewish Citizenship," *Ha'aretz*, March 7, 2002; Mustafa Sabri, "The Blue Marriages," *Al Hayat*, February 2, 1998, www.alhayat-j.com.

355 tempted to commit adultery: Brooks, *Nine Parts of Desire*, 39.

17. Oy! Gay?

359 explicitly protected category: Amir Fink and Jacob Press, *Independence Park: The Lives of Gay Men in Israel* (Stanford: Stanford University Press, 1999), 9–10. See also Lee Walzer, *Between Sodom and Eden* (New York: Columbia University Press, 2000).

362 "I realized yes": When *Trembling Before God* debuted in Israel in 2001,

haredi families asked director Sandi Dubowski to show it to them. He went to their homes and showed it on a computer terminal hooked up to a VCR, because they don't have televisions or go to movies. For more on the film, see www.tremblingbeforeG-d.com. Also Naomi Grossman, "The Gay Orthodox Underground," *Moment* (April 2001).

363 "attitudes of lesbians": Leora Eren Frucht, "Happy and Gay Families," *Jerusalem Post,* October 12, 2000. In 1997, the Supreme Court decided single women and lesbians can obtain donations from a sperm bank just like married women. No longer do they have to undergo a psychiatric evaluation to determine if they are fit for motherhood.

364 the first chapter of the Koran: Michael Signorile, "Cyber Mecca," *Advocate,* March 14, 2000. For gay Muslim websites, see www.glas.org/ahbab; Queer Jihad.web.com; www.al-fatiha.net.

364 all in the name of Islam: In 2001, Egyptian police raided the Queen Boat, a gay disco on the Nile. Twenty-three men were sentenced to one to five years in prison, convicted of debauchery, contempt of Islam, falsely interpreting the Koran, and exploiting Islam to promote deviant ideas. Many considered the punishment lenient. *Al-Haqiqa* newspaper ran this headline on February 16, 2002: "Leading Egyptian Government Officials, Clerics and Scientists: 'Perverts [namely, homosexuals] Must Be Thrown Off Mountaintops, Killed, or Burned." Iran's penal law specifies execution for sodomy between consenting adults. A minor engaging in sodomy receives seventy-four lashes; lesbianism calls for one hundred and death on the fourth offense. In Saudi Arabia, Sudan, and the United Arab Emirates, similar laws mandate execution by stoning, hanging, or beheading. In April 2000, Saudi Arabia sentenced nine men to over twenty-four hundred lashes each and up to six years in prison for gay sex, according to Amnesty International.

364 "lashed a hundred times": Brooks, *Nine Parts of Desire,* 47.

367 lesbians may be stoned: Jewish law, as codified in the Mishnah Torah by Maimonides, is somewhat more nuanced: "Women are forbidden to be *mesolelot* with one another. This is the practice of the Land of Egypt, against which we have been warned, as it is said: 'Like the practice of the Land of Egypt etc. you shall not do.' The Sages said: 'What did they do? A man marries a man, a woman marries a woman, and a woman marries two men.' Although this practice is forbidden, no flogging is imposed, since there is no specific negative commandment against it, nor is there any intercourse at all. Consequently, [such women] are not forbidden to the priesthood on account of harlotry, nor is a woman prohibited to her husband on account of it, since there is no harlotry in it. However, a flogging for disobedience [*mardut*] should be given, since they have performed a forbidden act. A man should be strict with his wife in this matter, and should prevent women who are known to engage in this practice from visiting her, and prevent her from going to them."

18. Hookers and Hash in the Holy Land

371 in Tel Aviv alone: Baruch Kra, "Police: Brothels Run by Organized Crime," *Ha'aretz,* August 1, 2001.

372 Two were Russian: Lee Hockstader, "Arson Stalking Tel Aviv's Shadow Brothel District," *Washington Post,* August 25, 2000.

372 wives on other continents: Oil-rich Arab countries such as Saudi Arabia, Kuwait, and the United Arab Emirates have far higher ratios. "Relative to the Population, the Number of Foreign Workers in Israel Is the Highest in the Western World," *Yediot Aharonot,* August 24, 2000.

373 "will always exist": Martina Vandenberg, "Trafficking of Women to Israel and Forced Prostitution," The *Israel Women's Network* (November 1997), 29.

374 the situation in the brothels: Baruch Kra, "Police: Brothels Run by Organized Crime," *Ha'aretz,* August 1, 2001.

374 earn up to $4,000 a day: Vandenberg, "Trafficking of Women," 20.

374 budget for the whole year: Michael Specter, "Contraband Women," *New York Times,* January 11, 1998.

374 Israeli real estate agent: Tom Sawicki, "Mobsters' Paradise," *Jerusalem Report,* 1995.

374 "legal" citizenship: Robert Friedman, *Red Mafia* (Boston: Little, Brown, 2000), 277.

374 "showing Israeli citizenship": Gloria Deutsch, "Whatever Happened to Ida Nudel," *Jerusalem Post,* January 24, 2001.

375 enter Israel illegally: This estimate is from the Toda'ah Institute, an Israeli organization affiliated with the World Coalition against Trafficking in Women.

375 her Israeli identity card: Vandenberg, "Trafficking of Women," 13.

376 then was deported: Ruth Sinai, "Prostitute's Harrowing Testimony Sparks Argument between MKs," *Ha'aretz,* December 27, 2001. See also Aliza Arbeli, "Prostitutes Nabbed on Egyptian Border," *Ha'aretz,* April 4, 2002.

376 what awaited them: Ina Friedman, "Victoria's, and Israel's, Ugly Secret," *Jerusalem Report,* March 15, 2001.

376 "otherwise we would kill her": Vandenberg, "Trafficking of Women," 40.

376 her fate is unknown: Nina's and Tatiana's testimonies from *Israel: Human Rights Abuses of Women Trafficked from the Commonwealth of Independent States,* Amnesty International Report, May 2000.

377 into Israel via Egypt: Mazal Mualem, "Undercover Cops Bust Israel's Largest Prostitution Ring," *Ha'aretz,* May 20, 2002.

377 police arrested seven brothel owners: Roni Singer, "Police Sweep on Rishon Letzion Brothels," *Ha'aretz,* April 14, 2003.

377 "They're not crying": Barbara Gingold, "Red Plate Special," *Reporter* magazine (Spring 1998).

377 "doesn't know what he's talking about": Aryeh Dayan, "Price of a Woman," *Ha'aretz,* February 26, 2001.

378   "you can't do anything about it": "Police: Israel Has Become a Promised Land for Money Laundering," *Ha'aretz,* December 10, 1999.

379   the Israeli banking system: Amit Ben Areya and Amit Sharvit, "Counterfeit Ring Busted in TA," *Ha'aretz,* May 27, 2002. See also Tom Sawicki, "Mobster's Paradise" *Jerusalem Report* (1995).

379   "no connection between the two": Dr. Menacham Horovitz, "Drug Policies in Israel: From Utopia to Repression" (Institute of Criminology, Faculty of Law, Hebrew University of Jerusalem, 1997).

380   sent on to Western Europe: Sharon Gal, "IDF Officers Fingered in Drug Smuggling," *Ha'aretz,* November 9, 1999.

380   delivery to Palestinians in the West Bank: David Ratner and Amos Harel, "Four Members of Druze Family Held in Hezballah Arms Smuggling Case," *Ha'aretz,* October 30, 2001.

Bibliography

Ajami, Fouad. (1998). *The Dream Palace of the Arabs: A Generation's Odyssey.* New York: Pantheon Books

Alcalay, Ammiel (ed.). (1996). *Keys to the Garden: New Israeli Writing.* San Francisco: City Lights Books

Almog, Oz. (2000). *The Sabra: The Creation of the New Jew.* Berkeley: University of California Press

Alter, Robert. (1994). *Hebrew and Modernity.* Indianapolis: Indiana University Press

Armstrong, Karen. (1997). *Jerusalem: One City, Three Faiths.* New York: Ballantine Books

Ashkenazi, Michael; Weingrod, Alex (ed.). (1987). *Ethiopian Jews and Israel.* New Brunswick, N.J.: Transaction Books

Atashi, Zeidan. (1995). *The Druze and Jews in Israel: A Shared Destiny?* International Specialized Book Services

Ateek, Naim. (1999). *Justice and Only Justice: A Palestinian Theology of Liberation.* Maryknoll, N.Y.: Orbis Books

Avruch, Kevin; Zenner, Walter P. (eds.). (1997). *Critical Essays on Israeli Society, Religion, and Government.* Albany: State University of New York Press

Balint, Judy Lash. (2001). *Jerusalem Diaries: In Tense Times.* New York: Gefen Publishing

Ben-Ari, Eyal. (1998). *Mastering Soldiers: Conflict, Emotions, and the Enemy in an Israeli Military Unit.* New York: Berghahn Books

Benbassa, Esther; Rodrigue, Aron. (2000). *Sephardi Jewry: A History of the Judeo-Spanish Community, 14th–20th Centuries.* Berkeley: University of California Press

Ben-Eliezer, Uri. (1998). *The Making of Israeli Militarism.* Indianapolis: Indiana University Press

Ben-Rafael, Eliezer. (1997). *Crisis and Transformation: The Kibbutz at Century's End.* Albany: State University of New York Press

Benvenisti, Meron. (1996). *City of Stone: The Hidden History of Jerusalem.* Berkeley: University of California Press

439

————. (1989). *Conflicts and Contradictions: Israel, the Arabs, and the West Bank.* New York: Eshel Books

————. (1995). *Intimate Enemies: Jews and Arabs in a Shared Land.* Berkeley: University of California Press

————. (2000). *Sacred Landscape: The Buried History of the Holy Land Since 1948.* Berkeley: University of California Press

Ben-Yehuda, Nachman. (1995). *The Masada Myth: Collective Memory and Mythmaking in Israel.* Madison: The University of Wisconsin Press

Betts, Robert. (1978). *Christians in the Arab East: A Political Study.* Athens: Lycabettus Press

————. (1988). *The Druze.* New Haven, Conn.: Yale University Press

Biale, David (ed.). (2002). *Cultures of the Jews: A New History.* New York: Schocken Books

————. (1992). *Eros and the Jews: From Biblical Israel to Contemporary America.* New York: Basic Books

Biale, Rachel. (1984). *Women and Jewish Law: An Exploration of Women's Issues in Halakhic Sources.* New York: Schocken Books

Binur, Yoram. (1989). *My Enemy, My Self.* New York: Doubleday

Black, Ian; Morris, Benny. (1991). *Israel's Secret Wars.* New York: Grove Weidenfeld

Blady, Ken. (2000). *Jewish Communities in Exotic Places.* Northvale, N.J.: Jason Aronson

Blech, Rabbi Benjamin. (1999). *The Complete Idiot's Guide to Understanding Judaism.* New York: Alpha Books

Brooks, Geraldine. (1995). *Nine Parts of Desire: The Hidden World of Islamic Women.* New York: Anchor Books

Cahill, Thomas. (1998). *The Gifts of the Jews: How a Tribe of Desert Nomads Changed the Way Everyone Thinks and Feels.* New York: Doubleday

Caspi, Dan; Limor, Yehiel. (1999). *The In/Outsiders: Mass Media in Israel.* Cresskill, N.J.: Hampton Press

Chacour, Elias. (1984, rpt 2003). *Blood Brothers.* Grand Rapids, Mich.: Chosen Books

Chafets, Ze'ev. (1986). *Heroes and Hustlers, Hard Hats and Holy Men: Inside the New Israel.* New York: William Morrow and Company

Chertok, Haim. (1994). *Israeli Preoccupations: Dualities of a Confessional Citizen.* New York: Fordham University Press

Cheshin, Amir; Hutman, Bill; Melamed, Avi. (1999). *Separate and Unequal: The Inside Story of Israeli Rule in East Jerusalem.* Cambridge: Harvard University Press

Cohen, Asher; Susser, Bernard. (2000). *Israel and the Politics of Jewish Identity: The Secular-Religious Impasse.* Baltimore, Md.: The Johns Hopkins University Press

Cohen, Joseph. (1990). *Voices of Israel.* Albany: State University of New York Press

Crossan, John. (1994). *Jesus: A Revolutionary Biography.* New York: HarperCollins Publishers

Davidman, Lynn. (1991). *Tradition in a Rootless World: Women Turn to Orthodox Judaism.* Berkeley: University of California Press

Dayan, Moshe. (1976). *Moshe Dayan: Story of My Life.* New York: William Morrow and Company

Dayan, Yael. (1985). *My Father, His Daughter.* New York: Farrar, Straus & Giroux

De Lange, Nicholas (ed.). (1997). *The Illustrated History of the Jewish People.* New York: Harcourt Brace & Co.

Deshen, Shlomo. (1992). *Blind People: The Private and Public Life of Sightless Israelis.* Albany: State University of New York Press

Deshen, Shlomo; Shokeid, Moshe. (1974). *The Predicament of Homecoming: Cultural and Social Life of North African Immigrants in Israel.* Ithaca, N.Y.: Cornell University Press

Diamant, Anita; Cooper, Howard. (1991). *Living a Jewish Life: Jewish Traditions, Customs and Values for Today's Families.* New York: HarperCollins Publishers

Diqs, Isaak. (1967). *A Bedouin Boyhood.* New York: Universe Books

Domb, Risa (ed.). (1996). *New Women's Writing from Israel.* Portland, Ore.: Vallentine Mitchell

Donin, Rabbi Hayim Halevy. (1980). *To Pray as a Jew: A Guide to the Prayer Book and Synagogue Service.* New York: Basic Books

Dowty, Alan. (1998). *The Jewish State: A Century Later.* Berkeley: University of California Press

Dundes, Alan. (2002). *The Shabbat Elevator and Other Sabbath Subterfuges: An Unorthodox Essay on Circumventing Custom and Jewish Character.* Lanham, Md.: Rowman & Littlefield Publishers

Duran, Khalid. (2001). *Children of Abraham: An Introduction to Islam for Jews.* Hoboken, N.J.: Ktav Publishing

Eban, Abba. (1984). *Heritage: Civilization and the Jews.* New York: Summit Books

Elon, Amos. (1989). *Jerusalem: Battlegrounds of Memory.* New York: Kodansha Globe

———. (1991). *Jerusalem: City of Mirrors.* London: Fontana

———. (1981). *The Israelis: Founders and Sons.* New York: Penguin Books

Ezrahi, Yaron. (1997). *Rubber Bullets: Power and Conscience in Modern Israel.* New York: Farrar, Straus & Giroux

Ferguson, Kathy. (1995). *Kibbutz Journal: Reflections on Gender, Race and Militarism in Israel.* Pasadena, Calif.: Trilogy Books

Feuerverger, Grace. (2001). *Oasis of Dreams: Teaching and Learning Peace in a Jewish-Palestinian Village in Israel.* New York: Routledge Falmer

Fink, Amir; Press, Jacob. (1999). *Independence Park: The Lives of Gay Men in Israel.* Stanford, Calif.: Stanford University Press

Fishkoff, Sue. (2003). *The Rebbe's Army: Inside the World of Chabad-Lubavitch.* New York: Schocken

Frankel, Glenn. (1994). *Beyond the Promised Land: Jews and Arabs on a Hard Road to a New Israel.* New York: Simon & Schuster

Freedman, Marcia. (1990). *Exile in the Promised Land: A Memoir.* Ithaca, N.Y.: Firebrand Books

Freedman, Robert O. (1995). *Israel Under Rabin.* Boulder, Colo.: Westview Press

Friedman, Richard. (1987). *Who Wrote the Bible?* New York: Summit Books

Friedman, Robert I. (2000). *Red Mafia: How the Russian Mob Has Invaded America.* New York: Little, Brown & Company

Friedman, Thomas L. (1989). *From Beirut to Jerusalem.* New York: Anchor Books

Gal, Reuven. (1986). *A Portrait of the Israeli Soldier.* Westport, Conn.: Greenwood Press

Gaster, Theodor H. (1980). *The Holy and the Profane: Evolution of Jewish Folkways.* New York: William Morrow and Company

Gavron, Daniel. (2000). *The Kibbutz: Awakening from Utopia.* Lanham, Md.: Rowman & Littlefield Publishers

Gerber, Jane S. (1992). *The Jews of Spain: A History of the Sephardic Experience.* New York: Free Press

Gilbert, Martin. (1998). *Israel: A History.* New York: William Morrow and Company

———. (1996). *Jerusalem in the Twentieth Century.* New York: John Wiley & Sons

Gold, Dore. (2003). *Hatred's Kingdom: How Saudi Arabia Supports the New Global Terrorism.* Washington, D.C.: Regnery Publishing

Goldman, Ari L. (2000). *Being Jewish: The Spiritual and Cultural Practice of Judaism Today.* New York: Simon & Schuster

Goldscheider, Calvin. (1996). *Israel's Changing Society: Population, Ethnicity and Development.* Boulder, Colo.: Westview Press

Goodwin, Jan. (1994). *Price of Honor: Muslim Women Lift the Veil of Silence on the Islamic World.* New York: Plume Books

Gordis, Daniel. (2002). *If a Place Can Make You Cry: Dispatches from an Anxious State.* New York: Crown Publishers

Gorenberg, Gershom. (2000). *The End of Days: Fundamentalism and the Struggle for the Temple Mount.* New York: Free Press

Gorkin, Michael. (1991). *Days of Honey, Days of Onion: The Story of a Palestinian Family in Israel.* Boston: Beacon Press

Grossman, David. (1993). *Sleeping on a Wire: Conversations with Palestinians in Israel.* New York: Farrar, Straus & Giroux

———. (1988). *The Yellow Wind.* New York: Delta

Gruber, Ruth. (1987). *Rescue: The Exodus of the Ethiopian Jews.* New York: Atheneum

al-Haj, Majid. (1995). *Education, Empowerment, and Control: The Case of the Arabs in Israel.* Albany: State University of New York Press

Halevi, Yossi. (2001). *At the Entrance to the Garden of Eden: A Jew's Search for God with Christians and Muslims in the Holy Land.* New York: William Morrow & Company

Hareven, Shulamith. (1995). *The Vocabulary of Peace: Life, Culture, and Politics in the Middle East.* San Francisco: Mercury House

Harshav, Benjamin. (1993). *Language in the Time of Revolution.* Berkeley: University of California Press

Hazelton, Lesley. (1977). *Israeli Women: The Reality Behind the Myths.* New York: Simon & Schuster

Heikal, Mohamed. (1975). *The Road to Ramadan.* New York: Quadrangle/The New York Times Book Co.

Heilman, Samuel. (1992). *Defenders of the Faith: Inside Ultra-Orthodox Jewry.* Berkeley: University of California Press

Hertzberg, Arthur (ed.). (1961). *Judaism.* New York: George Braziller

Hertzberg, Arthur; Hirt-Manheimer, Aron. (1998). *Jews: The Essence and Character of a People.* New York: HarperCollins Publishers

Hertzog, Esther. (1999). *Immigrants & Bureaucrats: Ethiopians in an Israeli Absorption Center.* New York: Berghahn Books

Herzog, Chaim. (1996). *Living History: A Memoir.* New York: Pantheon Books

———. (1975). *The War of Atonement, October, 1973.* Boston: Little, Brown & Company

Herzog, Hanna. (1999). *Gendering Politics: Women in Israel.* Ann Arbor: The University of Michigan Press

Himelstein, Rabbi Dr. Shmuel. (1990). *The Jewish Primer: Questions and Answers on Jewish Faith and Culture.* New York: Facts on File

Hischberg, Peter. (1999). *The World of Shas.* New York: The American Jewish Committee

Holly, David C. (1995). *Exodus 1947.* Annapolis, Md.: Naval Institute Press

Horovitz, David. (2000). *A Little Too Close to God: The Thrills and Panic of a Life in Israel.* New York: Knopf

———. (ed.). (1996). *Shalom, Friend: The Life and Legacy of Yitzhak Rabin.* New York: Newmarket Press

Horowitz, Tamar (ed.). (1999). *Children of Perestroika in Israel.* Lanham, Md.: University Press of America

Isralowitz, Richard; Friedlander, Jonathan (eds.). (1999). *Transitions: Russians, Ethiopians and Bedouins in Israel's Negev Desert.* Brookfield, Vt.: Ashgate Publishing

Kaplan, Steven. (1992). *The Beta Israel (Falasha) in Ethiopia: From Earliest Times to the Twentieth Century.* New York: New York University Press

Kark, Ruth (ed.). (1990). *The Land That Became Israel: Studies in Historical Geography.* New Haven, Conn.: Yale University Press

Karpin, Michael; Friedman, Ina. (1998). *Murder in the Name of God: The Plot to Kill Yitzhak Rabin.* New York: Metropolitan Books

Karsh, Efraim; Karsh, Inari. (1999). *Empires of the Sand: The Struggle for Mastery in the Middle East 1789–1923.* Cambridge: Harvard University Press

Katriel, Tamar. (1991). *Communal Webs: Communication and Culture in Contemporary Israel.* Albany: State University of New York Press

———. (1986). *Talking Straight: Dugri Speech in Israeli Sabra Culture.* New York: Cambridge University Press

Kaufman, Shirley; Hasan-Rokem, Galit; Hess, Tamar (eds.). (1999). *The Defiant Muse: Hebrew Feminist Poems from Antiquity to the Present.* New York: The Feminist Press at the City University of New York

Kaye, Evelyn. (1987). *The Hole in the Sheet: A Modern Woman Looks at Orthodox and Hasidic Judaism.* Secaucus, N.J.: Lyle Stuart

Kessler, David. (1996). *The Falashas: A Short History of the Ethiopian Jews.* Portland, Ore.: Frank Cass

Khouri, Norma. (2003). *Honor Lost: Love and Death in Modern-Day Jordan.* New York: Atria

Kirsch, Jonathan. (1998). *Moses: A Life.* New York: Ballantine Books

———. (2001). *The Woman Who Laughed at God: The Untold History of the Jewish People.* New York: Viking Compass

Kishon, Ephraim. (1983). *My Family Right or Wrong.* England: Bachman & Turner

Landau, David. (1993). *Piety & Power: The World of Jewish Fundamentalism.* New York: Hill & Wang

Laslau, Wolf. (1979). *Falasha Anthology: Translated from Ethiopic Sources.* New Haven, Conn.: Yale University Press

Leiblich, Amia. (1989). *Transition to Adulthood During Military Service: The Israeli Case.* Albany: State University of New York Press

Levine, Donald N. (1965). *Wax and Gold: Tradition and Innovation in Ethiopian Culture.* Chicago: The University of Chicago Press

Lewis, Bernard. (1984). *The Jews of Islam.* Princeton, N.J.: Princeton University Press

———. (2000). *A Middle East Mosaic: Fragments of Life, Letters and History.* New York: Random House

———. (2002). *What Went Wrong? Western Impact and Middle Eastern Response.* New York: Oxford University Press

Lewis, Herbert S. (1989). *After the Eagles Landed: The Yemenites of Israel.* Prospect Heights, Ill.: Waveland Press

Lewittes, Mendell. (1994). *Jewish Marriage: Rabbinic Law, Legend, and Custom.* Northvale, N.J.: Jason Aronson

Liebman, Charles; Cohen, Steven M. (1990). *Two Worlds of Judaism: The Israeli and American Experiences.* New Haven, Conn.: Yale University Press

Liebman, Charles; Katz, Elihu (eds.). (1997). *The Jewishness of Israelis.* Albany: State University of New York Press

Linn, Ruth. (1996). *Conscience at War: The Israeli Soldier as a Moral Critic.* Albany: State University of New York Press

Lomsky-Feder, Edna; Ben-Ari, Eyal. (1999). *The Military and Militarism in Israeli Society.* Albany: State University of New York Press

Lowin, Joseph. (1995). *Hebrewspeak: An Insider's Guide to the Way Jews Think.* Northvale, N.J.: Jason Aronson

abu-Lughod, Lila. (1993). *Writing Women's Worlds: Bedouin Stories.* Berkeley: University of California Press

Meir, Avinoam. (1997). *As Nomadism Ends: The Israeli Bedouin of the Negev.* Boulder, Colo.: Westview Press

Melman, Yossi. (1992). *The New Israelis: An Intimate View of a Changing People.* New York: Birch Lane Press

Merkley, Paul. (2001). *Christian Attitudes Towards the State of Israel.* Montreal: McGill-Queen's University Press

Mernissi, Fatima. (1992). *Islam and Democracy: Fear of the Modern World.* New York: Addison-Wesley Publishing

———. (1991). *The Veil and the Male Elite: A Feminist Interpretation of Women's Rights in Islam.* New York: Addison-Wesley Publishing

Miller, Judith. (1996). *God Has Ninety-Nine Names: Reporting from a Militant Middle East.* New York: Simon & Schuster

Mishal, Shaul; Sela, Avraham. (2000). *The Palestinian Hamas: Vision, Violence, and Coexistence.* New York: Columbia University Press

Moore, Tracy (ed.). (1995). *Lesbiot: Israeli Lesbians Talk About Sexuality, Feminism, Judaism and Their Lives.* New York: Cassell

Nathan, Joan. (2001). *The Foods of Israel Today.* New York: Knopf

Ner-David, Haviva. (2000). *Life on the Fringes: A Feminist Journey Toward Traditional Rabbinic Ordination.* Needham, Mass.: JFL Books

Nuseibeh, Said. (1996). *The Dome of the Rock.* New York: Rizzoli

O'Brien, Conor Cruise. (1986). *The Siege: The Saga of Israel and Zionism.* New York: Simon & Schuster

Onolehmemhen, Durrenda Nash; Gessesse, Kebede. (1998). *The Black Jews of Ethiopia: The Last Exodus.* Lanham, Md.: The Scarecrow Press

Oren, Michael B. (2002). *Six Days of War: June 1967 and the Making of the Modern Middle East.* New York: Oxford University Press

Oz, Amos. (1983). *In the Land of Israel.* London: Fontana Paperbacks

———. (1994). *Israel, Palestine and Peace: Essays.* New York: Harcourt Brace

———. (1995). *Under This Blazing Sun.* New York: Cambridge University Press

Patai, Raphael. (1983). *The Arab Mind.* New York: Charles Scribner's Sons

———. (1986). *The Seed of Abraham: Jews and Arabs in Contact and Conflict.* Salt Lake City: University of Utah Press

Peri, Yoram (ed.). (2000). *The Assassination of Yitzhak Rabin.* Stanford, Calif.: Stanford University Press

Porter, Jack Nusan (ed.). (1995). *Women in Chains: A Sourcebook on the Agunah.* Northvale, N.J.: Jason Aronson

Quirin, James. (1992). *The Evolution of the Ethiopian Jews: A History of the Beta Israel (Falasha) to 1920.* Philadelphia: University of Pennsylvania Press

Rabin, Yitzhak. (1979). *The Rabin Memoirs.* Boston: Little, Brown & Company

Rabinyan, Dorit. (1995). *Persian Brides.* New York: George Braziller

Ragen, Naomi. (1989). *Jephte's Daughter.* New York: Warner Books

Raheb, Mitri. (1995). *I Am a Palestinian Christian.* Minneapolis: Fortress Press

Rapoport, Louis. (1986). *Redemption Song: The Story of Operation Moses.* New York: Harcourt Brace Jovanovich

Raviv, Dan; Melman, Yossi. (1990). *Every Spy a Prince: The Complete History of Israel's Intelligence Community.* Boston: Houghton Mifflin

Rekhess, Eli. (1997, August). *Islamism Across the Green Line: Relations Among Islamist Movements in Israel, the West Bank and Gaza.* Washington, D.C.: The Washington Institute for Near East Policy (research paper)

Rolef, Susan Hattis (ed.). (1987). *Political Dictionary of the State of Israel.* New York: Macmillan Publishing

Romann, Michael; Weingrod, Alex. (1991). *Living Together Separately: Arabs and Jews in Contemporary Jerusalem.* Princeton, N.J.: Princeton University Press

Rouhana, Nadim. (1997). *Palestinian Citizens in an Ethnic Jewish State: Identities in Conflict.* New Haven, Conn.: Yale University Press

Rubenstein, Danny. (1991). *The People of Nowhere: The Palestinian Vision of Home.* New York: Times Books

Sabar, Naama. (2000). *Kibbutzniks in the Diaspora.* Albany: State University of New York Press

Sachar, Howard M. (1994). *Farewell España: The World of the Sephardim Remembered.* New York: Knopf

Salamon, Hagar. (1999). *The Hyena People: Ethiopian Jews in Christian Ethiopia.* Berkeley: University of California Press

Schiff, Ze'ev. (1985). *A History of the Israeli Army: 1874 to the Present.* New York: Macmillan Publishing

Schiff, Ze'ev; Ya'ari, Ehud. (1989). *Intifada: The Palestinian Uprising—Israel's Third Front.* New York: Simon & Schuster

———. (1984). *Israel's Lebanon War.* New York: Simon & Schuster

Schlossberg, Eli W. (1996). *The World of Orthodox Judaism.* Northvale, N.J.: Jason Aronson

Segev, Samuel. (1998). *Crossing the Jordan: Israel's Hard Road to Peace.* New York: St. Martin's Press

Segev, Tom. (2002). *Elvis in Jerusalem: Post-Zionism and the Americanization of Israel.* New York: Metropolitan Books

———. (1986). *1949: The First Israelis.* New York: The Free Press. Reprinted Henry Holt, New York, 1998

———. (2001). *One Palestine, Complete: Jews and Arabs Under the British Mandate.* New York: Owl Books

———. (1993). *The Seventh Million: The Israelis and the Holocaust.* New York: Hill & Wang

Seidman, Naomi. (1997). *A Marriage Made in Heaven: The Sexual Politics of Hebrew and Yiddish.* Berkeley: University of California Press

Sennott, Charles. (2001). *The Body and the Blood: The Holy Land's Christians at the Turn of a New Millennium.* New York: Public Affairs

Sered, Susan. (2000). *What Makes Women Sick? Maternity, Modesty, and Militarism in Israeli Society.* Lebanon, N.H.: University Press of New England

Shahar, Lucy; Kurz, David. (1995). *Border Crossings: American Interactions with Israelis.* Yarmouth, Me.: Intercultural Press

Shammas, Anton. (1988). *Arabesques.* Berkeley: University of California Press

Sharfman, Daphna. (1993). *Living Without a Constitution: Civil Rights in Israel.* Armonk, N.Y.: M. E. Sharpe

abu-Sharif, Bassam; Mahnaimi, Uzi. (1995). *Best of Enemies.* Boston: Little, Brown & Company

Shendelman, Sara; Davis, Dr. Avram. (1998). *Traditions: The Complete Book of Prayers, Rituals, and Blessings for Every Jewish Home.* New York: Hyperion

Shipler, David K. (1987). *Arab and Jew: Wounded Spirits in a Promised Land.* New York: Penguin Books

Shulewitz, Malka Hillel (ed.). (1999). *The Forgotten Millions: The Modern Jewish Exodus from Arab Lands.* New York: Cassell

Siegel, Dina. (1998). *The Great Immigration: Russian Jews in Israel.* New York: Berghahn Books

Sinclair, Andrew. (1995). *Jerusalem: The Endless Crusade.* New York: Crown Publishers

Smooha, Sammy. (1989). *Arabs and Jews in Israel: Conflicting and Shared Attitudes in a Divided Society.* Boulder, Colo.: Westview Press

———. (1978). *Israel: Pluralism and Conflict.* Berkeley: University of California Press

Spiro, Melford E. (1979). *Gender and Culture: Kibbutz Women Revisited.* Durham, N.C.: Duke University Press

———. (1970). *Kibbutz: Venture in Utopia.* New York: Schocken Books

Sprinzak, Ehud. (1991). *The Ascendance of Israel's Radical Right.* New York: Oxford University Press

———. (1999). *Brother Against Brother: Violence and Extremism in Israeli Politics from Altalena to the Rabin Assassination.* New York: Free Press

Starr, Joyce R. (1990). *Kissing Through Glass: The Invisible Shield Between Americans and Israelis.* Chicago: Contemporary Books

Stevenson, William. (1976). *90 Minutes At Entebbe.* New York: Bantam Books

Stillman, Norman A. (1991). *The Jews of Arab Lands in Modern Times.* Philadelphia: The Jewish Publication Society

———. (1995). *Sephardi Responses to Modernity.* Luxemborg: Harwood Academic Publishers

Szulc, Tad. (1991). *The Secret Alliance: The Extraordinary Story of the Rescue of the Jews Since World War II.* New York: Farrar, Straus & Giroux

Tsimhoni, Daphne. (1993). *Christian Communities in Jerusalem and the West Bank since 1948: An Historical, Social, and Political Study.* Westport, Conn.: Greenwood Publishing

Unterman, Alan. (1997). *Dictionary of Jewish Lore and Legend.* London: Thames & Hudson

Urian, Dan; Karsh, Efraim, eds. (1999). *In Search of Identity: Jewish Aspects in Israeli Culture.* London: Frank Cass and Co.

Van Creveld, Martin. (1998). *The Sword and the Olive: A Critical History of the Israeli Defense Force.* New York: Public Affairs

Victor, Barbara. (1994). *A Voice of Reason: Hanan Ashrawi and Peace in the Middle East.* New York: Harcourt Brace Jovanovich

Viorst, Milton. (2002). *What Shall I Do With This People? Jews and the Fractious Politics of Judaism*. New York: The Free Press

Wagaw, Teshome G. (1993). *For Our Soul: Ethiopian Jews in Israel*. Detroit: Wayne State University Press

Waldman, Menachem. (1985). *The Jews of Ethiopia: The Beta Israel Community*. Jerusalem: Ami-Shav, the Center for Aid to Ethiopian Immigrants

Walzer, Lee. (2000). *Between Sodom and Eden: A Gay Journey Through Today's Changing Israel*. New York: Columbia University Press

Ware, Timothy. (1997). *The Orthodox Church*. New York: Penguin Books

Wasserstein, Bernard. (2001). *Divided Jerusalem: The Struggle for the Holy City*. New Haven, Conn.: Yale University Press

Westerby, Gerald. (1998). *In Hostile Territory: Business Secrets of a Mossad Combatant*. New York: Harper Business

Westheimer, Dr. Ruth; Kaplan, Dr. Steven. (1992). *Surviving Salvation: The Ethiopian Jewish Family in Transition*. New York: New York University Press

Wiesel, Elie. (1978). *A Jew Today*. New York: Vintage Books

———. (1982). *Somewhere a Master: Further Hasidic Portraits and Legends*. New York: Summit Books

———. (1972). *Souls on Fire: Portraits and Legends of Hasidic Masters*. New York: Random House

Wigoder, Geoffrey. (1991). *Dictionary of Jewish Biography*. Jerusalem: Simon & Schuster

Wolf, Aaron. (1989). *A Purity of Arms: An American in the Israeli Army*. New York: Doubleday

Ye'or, Bat. (1985). *The Dhimmi: Jews and Christians Under Islam*. Madison, N.J.: Fairleigh Dickinson University Press

Yiftachel, Oren; Meir, Avinoam (eds.). (1998). *Ethnic Frontiers and Peripheries: Landscapes of Development and Inequality in Israel*. Boulder, Colo.: Westview Press

Yilma, Shmuel. (1996). *From Falasha to Freedom: An Ethiopian Jew's Journey to Jerusalem*. New York: Gefen Publishing House

Yishai, Yael. (1997). *Between the Flag and the Banner: Women in Israeli Politics*. Albany: State University of New York Press

Yonay, Ehud. (1993). *No Margin for Error: The Making of the Israeli Air Force*. New York: Pantheon Books

Zerubavel, Yael. (1995). *Recovered Roots: Collective Memory and the Making of Israeli National Tradition*. Chicago: The University of Chicago Press

Newspapers/Online News

Ha'aretz: www.haaretz.com
Jerusalem Post: www.jpost.com
Globes: www.globes.co.il
Yediot Aharonot: www.ynet.co.il
Middle East Media Research Institute: www.memri.org [translates Arabic media]
The Media Line: www.themedialine.org
IsraelInsider.com

Magazines

Jerusalem Report
Israel Studies
Eretz
Moment
Hadassah
Midstream
Azure

Index

Abraham, 32–33, 59, 197, 200, 206, 208, 255, 268, 272, 329, 353
Abramov, Hani, 64–65
Acre, 250, 258–259, 262, 264, 290, 296
El-Ad, Hagai, 365, 368
Adalah (Legal Center for Arab Minority Rights in Israel), 263–265
Addis Ababa, Ethiopia, 148–150, 155
Adoption laws, 363
Adultery, 335–338, 352
Afghanistan, 115
Agmon, Shira, 31
Agnon, S. Y., 241
Agriculture, 105
Agudah (Association of Gay Men, Lesbians, Bisexuals and Transgender in Israel), 368
Agunot (chained wives), 342
Ahmadies, 252
AIDS (acquired immunodeficiency syndrome), 372
Air France hostage rescue (1976), 53
Alam, Faisal, 357
Algeria, 115, 121
ibn Ali, Hamza, 295
Alimony, 342, 355
Alliance Israelite Universelle, 154
Allon, Yigal, 390
Aloni, Shulamit, 42

Alon Shvut, 195–198, 201, 202
Alpha Omega Biomedical Engineering, 90–91
Amharic language, 158–160, 162
Amichai, Yehuda, 47, 108, 174
Amir, Geula, 210
Amir, Menachem, 377
Amir, Yigal, 56, 98, 210–211, 231
Amnesty International, 377
Andalusian Orchestra, 138
Anglican Church, 306, 310
Anis, Kamal, 69
Annan, Kofi, 18
Anthrax, 21
Antivirus products, 78
al-Aqsa Foundation, 273
al-Aqsa Mosque, Jerusalem, 51, 271–275
al-Aqsa Martyrs Brigade, 16, 64, 68
Arab Business Club (ABC), 317–318
Arab Israelis. *See* Bedouin; Christians; Muslim Israelis
Arab-Israeli War (1947–49), 297
Arab Legion, 198, 209
Arabs48.com, 318–319
Arafat, Yasser, 38, 40, 55–57, 68, 97, 146, 199, 205, 258, 272, 277, 311, 390
Arbib, Nitzan, 42–43, 59, 64
Armenian Orthodox Church, 306, 307

Arrow missile, 74
Ashkenazim, 2, 17, 27, 33, 36, 39, 58,
    92–94, 97–112, 114–116, 119,
    122, 123, 126, 127, 174,
    213–218, 341
Ashrawi, Hanan, 311
Asia Minor, 117
Assad, Bashar, 299
al-Assad, Hafez, 40, 263
Astrology, 35, 36
Atashi, Zeidan, 296
Atropine, 21
Auschwitz concentration camp, 55, 73
Austro-Hungarian Empire, 100
Avi-Zedek, Shani, 7, 8
Awad, Mira, 310
Ayalon, Moshe, 71
Azari, Rabbi Meir, 231, 232, 234,
    236, 330, 331
Azerbaijan, Jews of, 132, 376
Azrieli Towers, Tel Aviv, 65

Baal Shem Tov (Rabbi Yisrael Ben
    Eliezer), 185, 238
Babylonian Captivity, 117
Back Web Technologies, 77
Bakshi-Doron, Rabbi Eliahu, 232
Baniel, Eran, 38
Barak, Aharon, 236
Barak, Ehud, 56, 60, 84, 104, 144,
    199, 213, 265, 330, 390
Barak, Michal, 84, 330
Barakeh, Mohammed, 265
Barghouti, Marwan, 16
Bar Ilan Street, Jerusalem, 228
Bar-Ilan University, 98
Barkat, Eli, 75–78
Barkat, Nir, 75, 76, 78
Basilica of the Annunciation,
    Nazareth, 3, 312–314
Bathsheva, 352
Battered women, 339–340, 350–351
Bedouin, 3, 137, 144, 264, 278–291,
    349, 375, 381
Beersheva, 32, 33, 120, 124, 138, 206

Beit Daniel Synagogue, Tel Aviv, 231,
    330
Beit Jala, 17–18
Beit Jann, 292, 301
Belarus, 132, 133, 139, 376
Ben, Zehava, 122
Ben-Ami, Shlomo, 121
Ben-Ari, Adital, 363
Ben-Dov, Yoav, 239, 382
Ben-Eliahu, Eitan, 73
Ben-Eliazar, Benjamin, 121
Ben-Eliezer, Eli, 13, 14
Ben-Gurion, David, 24, 48, 61, 97,
    104, 110, 120, 133, 176, 187,
    198, 235, 297, 334, 335, 370,
    382, 383
Ben-Gurion University, 283
Ben-Yehuda, Eliezer, 101–102, 133,
    227
Ben-Yehuda Street, Jerusalem, 19,
    48
Bergen-Belsen concentration camp, 73
Berger, Orit, 8, 9
Berger, Raffi, 8, 9
Berihun, Shlomo, 163–164
Berl, Hila, 143–145
Betar (Zionist youth organization), 54
Bethlehem, 206, 208, 311, 312
Bethlehem University, 311
Betzalel, Avivit, 32–34
Beyer, Lisa, 351
Biale, Rachel, 23, 379
Bialik, Hayim Nahman, 130, 145, 233
Biblical Zoo, Jerusalem, 20
bin Laden, Osama, 69, 308, 314
Biotech, medtech. *See* Technology
Bird-plane collisions, 71–72
Birnbaum, Nathan, 100
Birth defects, 284–285, 294
Bishara, Azmi, 263–265, 297, 315
Blackhawk helicopter, 71
Black Panther Movement, 136
Blood riots, 165
Blue marriages, 354
Bnei Brak, 178

Border patrol, border police, 63–64, 290, 296
Boris II, King of Bulgaria, 224
Bosnia, 69
Bouskila, Meir, 120–124
Breslov Hasids, 241
BRM Technologies, 75–78
Bruce, James, 154
Buber, Martin, 104
Buenos Aires Israeli Embassy bombing (1992), 74
Buenos Aires Jewish Center bombing (1994), 74
Bugala, Galila, 8
Bulgaria, 118, 119, 224
Burg, Yosef, 378
Bush, George W., 275

C-4 explosives, 68
Café Caffit, Jerusalem, 19
Cairo, Egypt, 50
Calendar, Jewish, Christian, and Muslim, 222–223
Camp David II summit (2000), 56, 57, 274
Camus, Albert, 29
Castilian *reconquista,* 118
Cave of Machpelah, 208. *See also* Rachel's Tomb; Tomb of the Patriarchs
Cedar, Joseph, 200
Center for Jewish-Arab Economic Development, 89
Central Bus Station, Tel Aviv, 161–162
Centrino computer chip, 88, 125
Cervantes, 240
Chechnya, Jews of, 132
Check Point Software Technologies, 78–83
Chemical weapons, 73–74
Chernobyl, 133
Chinitz, David, 139
Christians, Arab, 1, 3, 17, 28, 37, 83, 252, 264, 276, 305–323

Church of the Holy Sepulcher, Jerusalem, 3, 306–307
Cisco Systems, 88
Clinton, Bill, 55, 56
Cocaine, 380, 381
Code of Ethics of the Israeli Soldier, 59
Cohabitation, 27–28
Columbia space shuttle, 73
Columbine Ventures, 92
Columbus, Christopher, 118–119
Committee on the Advancement of the Status of Women, 42
Communist Party (Hadash), 267
Company Jasmine (Women Field Officers School), 65–67
Computers. *See* Technology
Conservative Judaism, 218, 222, 231–236, 241, 330, 331
Contraception, 334
Coptic Christians, 153, 154, 167
Crisis Center for Religious Women, Jerusalem, 340
Crusaders, 12, 258, 275, 296, 306, 307
Custody, child, 355
Cyanide gas, 22
Cyprus, 109, 142, 330
Cyrus the Great, King of Persia, 117

Dagan, Oren, 18–19
Dalet, Beersheva, 120, 123
Daliat al-Carmel, 293, 296, 299, 300, 302, 303
DAM (Arabic rap singers), 261
Damascus, Syria, 50
Dan, lost tribe of, 153–155
Dankner, Amnon, 335
Daoud, Anwar, 388
al-Darazi, Muhammad, 295
Darvasi, Ariel, 92–94
Dating, 23–46
David, King, 124, 197, 203, 206, 208, 222, 223, 233, 235, 353
Dayan, Moshe, 42, 56, 187, 193, 335–336

Dayan, Yael, 42, 335–336, 359
Dead Sea Scrolls, 222
Declaration of Principles on Interim
  Self-Government Arrangements
  (1993), 38, 55
Defense spending, 56
Defoe, Daniel, 101
De Gaulle, Charles, 87, 391
Dehamshe, Abdulmalik, 277, 314
Della Pergola, Sergio, 37
Dharamsala, India, 238
Dhu Nuwas, 117
Diplomat Hotel, Jerusalem, 152
Divorce, 158, 286, 294, 337,
  340–343, 349–350, 355
DNA, 92, 93, 255
Dolphinarium, Tel Aviv, 146
Dome of the Rock, Jerusalem, 272
Domestic abuse, 339–340, 350–351
Dor, Dorit, 82, 83
Dotan computer chip, 88
Dreman, Solly, 7
Dreyfus, Alfred, 100
Driving behavior, 80
Drug trade, 288–289, 379–382
Druze, 1, 3, 28, 37, 47, 49, 264, 276,
  284, 292–304, 349
*Druze and the Jews in Israel: A Shared
  Destiny?* (Atashi), 296
Dugri, 83
Duvdevan IDF unit, 58

Eban, Abba, 83
Ecclesiastes, 34
Economy, 75, 87, 126
Ecstasy (drug), 381, 382
Eden, Michal, 359–360
Eden 2000 dating service, 36
Education, 126–127, 145–146, 160,
  161, 163, 187, 260–261,
  280–281, 288, 302, 323,
  385–389
Efrat, 199
Egypt, 50, 52, 72, 110, 115, 200, 257,
  260, 312, 380–381

Egyptian Jews, 39
Ehrlich, David, 365
Eidah HaHaredit, 188
Eilat, 24, 28, 29, 223, 371
Ein Harod, Kibbutz, 103–108, 140
Ein Hemed, Jerusalem, 12
El Al Airlines, 47, 149, 179, 223, 317,
  383
Elijah's cave, Haifa, 252
Elimelech, Etti, 67–68
Endogamy, Druze, 294
Entebbe, Uganda, 53
EPROM (Electrically Programmable
  Read-Only Memory) chip, 88
Erekat, Saeb, 69
Eshkol, Levi, 54, 104, 198, 209
Ethiopian Coptics, 306, 307
Ethiopian Israelis, 17, 56, 122, 144,
  148–169, 339
Even, Uzi, 358
Exodus (refugee boat), 109–110
Exodus (Uris novel and film), 104
Eyob, Batia, 162, 166
Ezra, Solomon, 148–150, 153,
  156–157, 161, 163, 165–169

F-16 Falcon, 71, 73, 157
Faitlovitch, Jacques, 155
Falash Mora, 166–167
al-Faluji, Imad, 57
Families Forum, 389
Family honor killings, 300–301, 316,
  351–353
Family planning, 285, 334
Fanous, Michail, 305, 319–323
Farhat, Mariam, 13
Farhat, Muhammad, 13
Farsi language, 33
Fatah, 16, 271
al-Fatiha (gay Muslim group), 357,
  364
Feingold, Noa, 67
Female Perspective (television show)
Feng Shui, 35
Fertile Crescent, 117

Fertility treatments, 334
Field Officers School for Women,
    Company Jasmine, 65–67
Figure skating, 147
Firewall computer software, 78–79,
    82
First Aliyah, 100
First Zionist Congress, Basel,
    Switzerland (1897), 100
Fisherman, Shraga, 219
Flag of Israel, 4, 222
Florentine (television series), 358
Food and Drug Administration (FDA),
    86
Forbes magazine, 79
Forbidden Marriages in the Holy Land
    (documentary), 38–39
Franciscans, 306, 307
Frankenthal, Yitzhak, 389–390
French Hill, Jerusalem, 11, 14, 15,
    63–64
Frohman, Dov, 88, 125

Gabriol, Solomon Ibn, 118
Gal, Shlomo, 381
Galel Zahal radio station, 40
Galilee, 37, 44, 119, 264, 290, 393
Galili, Nir, 42
Gallipoli campaign, 54
Gandhi, Mahatma, 393
Ganem, Assad, 261
Garoushi, Samia, 352–353
Gas masks, 21–22, 125, 130
Gates, Bill, 88
Gay men. *See* Homosexuality
Gay Pride Parade, Tel Aviv, 3, 358
Gaza Strip, 4, 18, 25, 47, 49, 52, 53,
    55, 57, 60, 61, 97, 199, 200, 204,
    205, 210, 249, 252, 257, 258,
    270, 271, 274, 285, 286, 303,
    304, 352, 380, 390
Gazi, Ayman, 8
GDP (gross domestic product), 81
Geffen, Aviv, 56, 57, 193
General Electric, 87

Generation of Discarded Kippot
    (Fisherman), 219
Genetic disorders, 284–285, 294
Georgia, 132
Gesher Theater, 130, 136
Ghana, 125
al-Ghoul, Muhammad, 9–10
Gillis, Dr., 205
Gillis, Ruth, 205
Gilo, Jerusalem, 16, 48
Givat HaShabahim (Hill of Illegal
    Entry), 64
Given Imaging, 86
Gluzman, Mickey, 358
God Has Ninety-Nine Names (Miller),
    351
Golan Heights, 50, 145, 257, 294,
    298–299
Golani Infantry Brigade, 54, 57
Goldstein, Baruch, 209–210
Goldstein, Shaul, 205–207
Goliath, 124, 206, 235
Goodman, Hirsch, 141
Gorbachev, Mikhail, 131
Gordon, Daniel, 69–70
Gratzyani, Gidi, 240–242
Gratzyani, Yisraela, 239–243,
    340–343
Greece, 118, 119
Greek Orthodox Church, 306, 307,
    309, 310
Greenberg, Steven, 366
Green Leaf Party, 382
Gross, Debbie, 339–340
Grossman, David, 187
Guidant, 92
Gulf War (1991), 24, 30, 72, 130, 230

Ha Am, Ahad, 180
HaAnafa Street, Jerusalem, 17, 18
Ha'aretz (newspaper), 41, 81, 202,
    251, 264–265
Habad House, Bangkok, 237–238
Habashi, Muhammad Shaker,
    275–277

Hadassah College of Technology, 199
Hadassah Hospital, Mount Scopus,
    11, 22, 164, 205
Hadith, 348
Haganah, 54, 62
Hagar, 33, 268
Haifa, 39, 60, 86–88, 102, 109, 110,
    223, 247–253, 255, 256, 293,
    303, 309, 354, 358, 363, 374
Haile Selassie, Emperor, 156
Ha'ir (newspaper), 31
al-Hakim, Caliph, 295–296, 307
Halabi, Fahmi, 292
HaLevi, Judah, 118
Halevy, Joseph, 154–155
Hamad, Nisim Abu, 303
Hamahdy, Maisa, 302–303
Hamas (Islamic Resistance
    Movement), 9, 13, 15, 22, 50, 60,
    61, 68, 74, 136, 256, 263,
    270–271, 275–276, 311
Hammoud, Suhad, 247, 256–265
Hanukkah, 53, 155, 222, 223
Haram al-Sharif. *See* Temple Mount
Harari, Michael, 152
Haredi Center for Technological
    Studies, Mea Sharim, 189–190
Haredim, 2, 28, 36, 51–52, 83, 107,
    123, 173–194, 196, 212, 217,
    225–233, 235–236, 253,
    328–329, 337–340, 341,
    371–372
Har Etzion Yeshiva, Alon Shvut, 196
Har Hotsfim, Jerusalem, 190
Harp, Ina, 146–147
Hashemi-Rafsanjani, Ali Akbar, 74
Hashish, 379–380, 382
Hasidism, 184–186, 219, 238
Hassan, Ibtihaj, 300–301
"Hatikvah" (Imber), 140, 187, 222,
    259–260, 382
Hauser, Emil, 226
Hebrew language, 1, 33, 83, 97, 98,
    101–102, 116, 130, 135–137,
    145, 159

Hebrew University, 11, 81, 91, 106,
    116, 138
    cafeteria bombing, 20
Hebron, 52, 206, 207–210, 243
Heffetz, Liron, 47–49, 61, 62
Heffetz, Ori, 24, 25, 237–238, 382,
    383
Heffetz, Reli, 61–62
Heffetz, Ronit, 23, 53, 62
Heffetz, Tamir, 48–49, 51, 52, 61,
    236–237
Herodion Palace, 203, 204
Heroin, 379–381
Herzl, Theodor, 54, 100, 187,
    208
Herzog, Chaim, 157
Hewlett-Packard, 77, 87
Hezballah (Islamic Party of Allah), 15,
    25, 60–61, 68, 73, 74, 251, 263,
    271, 379, 380
High tech. *See* Technology
Hijaz (the Arabian peninsula), 117
Hijazi, Ahmad, 389
Hilel (group for Haredi youth who
    want to become secular), 193
Hillel, Rabbi, 223
Hilou, Nadia, 349–350
Hitler, Adolf, 260
Holocaust, 22, 23, 80, 98, 108,
    109, 111, 112, 114, 119,
    155, 166, 174, 176, 204, 260,
    334
Homosexuality, 3, 41, 357–369
Honor killings, 300–301, 316,
    351–353
Honor Lost (Khoury), 352
Human genome, 92
Hunt, William Homan, 226
Huppa (wedding canopy), 12, 327,
    329
Hussar, Father Bruno, 385, 387
Hussein, King of Jordan, 20
Hussein, Saddam, 40, 51, 68, 72, 266,
    271
Husseini, Rana, 352

el-Husseini, Haj Amin, 296–297
Hussniya, Jabara, 269

Iberian Peninsula, 118
IBM Corporation, 77, 87
Iceland, 93
Iddan, Gavriel, 84–87
IDF. *See* Israeli Defense Forces (IDF)
IDgene Pharmaceuticals, 93
Imber, Naftali, 140
Independence Day, 4, 53, 188, 261,
    385, 388
Indian Israelis, 133
Inquisition, 118, 167
Intel, 2, 36, 75, 87–88, 106, 153,
    190–191
    Kiryat Gat, 125–126, 128–129
International, Dana (Yaron Cohen),
    357, 358
Internet, 75, 77–79, 87–89, 106, 145,
    188, 189, 254, 277, 318–319,
    338
In vitro fertilization, 334
Iran, 22, 39, 51, 60, 73, 74, 115, 121,
    125, 270
Iraq, 10, 22, 24, 30, 51, 68, 72, 73,
    110, 115, 271, 312
Iraqi Jews, 30, 115, 116
Iraq War (2003), 72
Isaac (Yitzhak) (of the Bible), 59, 197,
    208–210, 255, 272
Iscar Group, The, 391
Ishai, Eli, 121
Ishmael, 33, 209, 210, 255, 268
Ishran, Yosef, 202–203, 206
Islam, 117–118, 256, 267–272. *See
    also* Muslims
Islamic fundamentalism, 3, 253,
    270
Islamic Studies College, Umm
    al-Fahm, 270
Ismojik family, 99–100
Israel Anti-Drug Authority (IADA),
    381
Israeli Academy Awards, 200

Israeli Air Force (IAF), 48, 71–73,
    148, 149, 156, 157, 165, 383
Israeli Defense Forces (IDF), 2–3, 10,
    24, 27, 32, 40, 42–74, 164, 218,
    380
    Arab Christians in, 319
    basic training, 57–59
    Bedouin and, 289–291
    border patrol, 60–61, 63–64, 290,
        296
    chain of command in, 58
    Code of Ethics of the Israeli Soldier,
        59
    as cultural melting pot, 57–58
    discriminatory draft, 51
    dissenting reservists in, 52
    Druze in, 3, 292, 293, 296–298, 303
    Duvdevan unit, 58
    Education Corps, 59
    Field Officers School for Women,
        Company Jasmine, 65–67
    forerunner of, 54, 62
    gay officers in, 359, 362
    haredi men in, 192
    intelligence units, 81–82
    Jenin refugee camp and, 68–71
    military exemptions, 51, 56, 176,
        191–192, 230, 235
    Navy Seals, 39
    reserve duty, 49, 336–337
    roadblocks, 64
    uniforms, 67–68
    wars fought by, 50–52, 62, 198
    women in, 2–3, 41–46, 62–68
Israeli Islamic Movement, 265–266,
    269, 270, 273, 277, 289,
    313–315
Israeli Philharmonic, 137
Israeli Supreme Court, 42, 52, 63,
    192, 197, 228, 235–236, 264,
    342, 359, 363
Israel Television, 259–260, 263, 300
Israel Women's Network, 377
Italy, 118, 119
Izraeli, Dafna, 42

Jabotinsky, Vladimir, 133
Jacob (of the Bible), 198, 208, 328, 353
Jaffa, 100–101, 250, 264, 309, 349
Jaffa Street, Jerusalem, 19
al-Jazeera Television, 13, 251, 269
Jemael, Rudayena, 353
Jenin, 52, 266
Jenin refugee camp, 68–71
Jericho, 55, 329
Jerusalem, 57, 221–231, 234, 250, 257, 271–275, 305–311, 358, 363, 365–369
   al-Aqsa Mosque, 51, 271–275
   bus 32A bombing, 7–11, 13, 14, 16–17, 19
   Café Caffit, 19
   Church of the Holy Sepulcher, 3, 306–307
   French Hill, 11, 14, 15, 63–64
   Hebrew University, 11, 20, 81, 91, 106, 116, 138
   King George Street, 19
   Mahane Yehuda market, 13
   McDonald's, 228–229
   Moment Café, 12
   Old City of, 50, 75, 153, 173, 198, 204, 272, 305, 309
   Sbarro pizzeria, 270
   Temple Mount/Haram al-Sharif, 51, 57, 164, 197, 264, 271–275, 369
   Western Wall, 50, 153, 197, 198, 200, 221, 234, 272, 273
Jerusalem Open House (JOH), 365–368
Jethro (of the Bible), 59
Jewish Agency, 13
Jewish renaissance, 233
Jezreel Valley (God Will Sow Seeds), 103, 290
John, Elton, 55
John Paul II, Pope, 312
Jordan, 4, 20, 52, 72, 110, 198, 200, 203, 207, 209, 249, 257, 272, 286, 311, 312, 352, 392, 393

Jordan River, 204
Jordan Valley, 119, 192
Joshua (of the Bible), 329
Judea, 197, 198, 201, 203–204
Judean Desert, 11, 203

Kabbalah, 185, 211, 212, 230–231, 238
Kach Party, 209, 210
Kadouri, Rabbi Yitzhak, 123
Kafka, Franz, 241
Kagan, Helen, 226–227
Kahane, Rabbi Meir, 209
Kamir, Orit, 41
Karine-A (cargo ship), 39
Karissi, Tomer, 88
Kasparov, Garry, 145
Katreil, Tamar, 31
Katsav, Moshe, 121–122, 164, 357
Katyusha rockets, 25
Katz, Boris, 130–134, 142–143
Katz, Nevo, 199, 201
Katz, Shlomit, 197, 198, 202
Katz, Yaacov, 198, 201, 202
Katz, Yonit, 131, 142
Kazakhstan, Jews of, 132, 376
Keffiyahs (Arab male headdresses), 2
Kehati, Naomi, 113–114
Kershner, Isabel, 263
Kes/Kessim (Ethiopian religious leaders), 148, 169
Ketuba (marriage contract), 327–328, 330
el-Kheiri, Bashir, 320–321
Khleifi, Michel, 39
Khomeini, Ayatollah, 270
Khoury, Norma, 352
Kibbutz life, 103–108, 134
Kiddushin, 327
al-Kidwa, Nasser, 69
King George Street, Jerusalem, 19
Kippot (sing., *kippa*) (yarmulkes or skullcaps), 2
Kiryat Arba, 207, 209
Kiryat Gat, 124–129

Kiryat Malachi, 122
Kishinev pogrom (1903), 99, 100, 112
Kita'in, Tom, 387
Knesset, 39, 41, 42, 51, 66, 110, 122,
    132, 133, 140, 148, 180, 263,
    269, 270, 276–277, 315, 358
Kodak, 77
Kol Israel, the Voice of Israel radio, 98
Kollek, Teddy, 80
Kook, Abraham Isaac, 155
Koran, 10, 118, 255, 260, 267, 268,
    271, 273, 281, 311, 344, 351,
    353, 364
Kosher dietary laws, 29, 135, 179,
    182, 192, 212, 222, 228–229,
    241
Kotler, Gregory, 134–136, 139
Kotler, Marina, 136–137
Kotler, Talia, 136
Kramer, Shlomo, 82
Kriegel, Tamar, 233–235
Kulthum, Umm, 115, 310
Kurdish Jews, 13
Kuwait, 270

Labor Party, 98, 121–123, 144, 199,
    219, 251, 253, 299
Ladino language, 119, 240
Lag b'Omer, 53, 188, 202, 211–212,
    223, 251
Lalou, Adi Rosenfeld, 213–216, 218,
    346
Lalou, Liora, 215, 216
Lalou, Moti, 213–216, 218, 346
Landau, Dalia, 320–321
Larsen, Terje, 69
Lau, Rabbi Yisrael, 232, 238
Lavon Industrial Park, 391
Law of Return, 140–141, 263
Leah (of the Bible), 208, 328
Lebanon, 4, 22, 25, 60, 73, 74, 76,
    110, 115, 125, 147, 251, 259,
    260, 297, 312, 379–380
Lebanon War (1982–2000), 50, 168
Lesbians. *See* Homosexuality

Leshem, Yossi, 72
Levy, David, 121
Lewis, Bernard, 109
Libya, 115, 119, 124
Life expectancy, 3
Likud Party, 107, 122, 123, 144, 192,
    199, 253, 274, 299
Lilac (Arabic-language magazine),
    315–317, 347
Lithuanians, 175, 185, 186, 236. *See
    also* Haredim
Love March, Tel Aviv, 25
Lubavitch/Habad Hasidim, 185–186,
    188, 237–238
Lupolanski, Uri, 187

M2A capsule, 84–86
Maccabees, 53
Madonna, 55
Magen David Adom blood bank, 165
Mahane Yehuda market, Jerusalem,
    13
Maikey, Hanin, 366–367
Maimonides, Moses (Moshe ben
    Maimon), 36, 118, 123, 189,
    223, 233
Makor Rishon (newspaper), 31
Makouli, Ayman, 318
Malha Mall, Jerusalem, 20–21
al-Manar Hezballah Television, 251
Mandel, Kobi, 202–203, 206
Manitoba cell phone chip, 88
Mansour, Jumana, 250–252, 254, 255
Mansour, Yasser, 247–256
Marijuana, 380–382
Marriage, 327–334, 343–349
Marwani Mosque, Temple Mount,
    Jerusalem, 273
Marziano, Ahuva, 128
Masada, 53
Mashour, Lutfi, 314–316
Mashour, Vida, 317
Mashour, Yara, 315–317
Matchmakers, 36, 328, 329
Maternity benefits, 334

Matussevich, Konstantin, 141
Matza Restaurant, Haifa, 256, 354
Mayanot le Haskila (Many Springs for
    Education), 127
McDonald's, Jerusalem, 228–229
Mea Sharim, Jerusalem, 173–174, 225
Mecca, 252, 267, 268
Medical technology, 84–86, 89–94,
    196
Medina, 117, 118
Medinol, 86
Megiddo (Armageddon of the Bible),
    1, 86, 238
Meimad Party, 219
Meir, Golda, 54, 104, 116, 133, 136,
    187
Memorial Day, 50, 260
Menashe, Menasie, 148
Menelik I, King of Ethiopia, 153–154
Mengistu Haile Mariam, 156
Menstruation, 186–187, 332, 333,
    348
Meretz Party, 42, 253, 269
Merkava 4 tanks, 53
Meshulam, Mira, 224–227, 230,
    231
Meshulam, Sivan, 221–225, 227–230
Metulla, 25, 147
Michael, Sami, 113
Michal, daughter of King Saul, 233
Microsoft, 87–89
Mikvah (public ritual bath), 186–187,
    333
Military exemptions, 51, 176,
    191–192, 230, 235
Military service. *See* Israeli Defense
    Forces (IDF)
Miller, Alice, 63
Miller, Haim, 232–233, 368
Miller, Judith, 351
Mishlab, Yosef, 296
Mitchell Committee, 274
Mitzna, Amram, 121, 213, 250–251
Mixed-faith couples, 37–39
Mizrahi, Moshe, 374

Mizrahim, 2, 17, 28, 32, 33, 35, 36,
    58, 102, 107, 111, 113–129,
    213–217, 341
Modesty patrols, 2, 27, 225
Mofaz, Shaul, 121
Mohar (bride payment), 344
Mombassa, Kenya, hotel bombing, 27,
    36
Moment Café, Jerusalem, 12
Money laundering, 378–379
Mordechai, Yitzhak, 43–44, 121–123
Morocco, 115, 121, 127
Moses, 28, 110, 153, 176, 203, 252,
    295
Mossad, 156
Motorola, 87–89, 106, 133
Mouna, Amna Jawad (Sally), 15–16
Mount Herzl Military Cemetery,
    Jerusalem, 54
Mount Meron, 211–213, 292, 335
Mount Moriah, 59, 197
Mount Nebo, 203
Mount of Olives, 203
Mount of Remembrance, 54
Movement for a New Manhood, 43
Muhammad, Prophet, 117–118, 252,
    258, 267, 268, 271, 272, 347
Mukonen, Israela, 152
Mukonen, Malaku, 152
Muslim Israelis, 1, 3–4, 28, 247–277,
    343–349
Mysticism, Jewish, 35–36, 238–239

Nablus, 20, 50, 52, 68, 266, 270, 273,
    367
Nacht, Marius, 82
al-Naffar, Tamer, 261–262
Nagari, Shiri, 8
Nahariya, 275–276
Nahman, Rabbi, 241, 242
Al-Najah University, Islamic Law
    Faculty of, 270
Najjar, Abdessalam, 387
Nardi, Chen, 43
Nasdaq, 75–78

Nasralden, Fadel, 293–296, 299
Nasrallah, Hassan, 263
National anthem, 4, 140, 187, 222, 259–260, 382
National Council of Demographic Planning, 37
National Insurance, 124, 334
Navy Seals, 39
Nazareth, 89–91, 103, 108, 258, 309, 312–314, 391
Nazi gas chambers, 22, 55, 111
Nazim Abu Salim, Sheik, 312
Negev Desert, 3, 32, 48, 62, 66, 71, 72, 119, 120, 278, 280–281, 283, 284, 287–290, 299
Netanya, 111, 213, 239–240, 255
Netanyahu, Benjamin "Bibi," 144, 200, 213, 274, 336, 357, 390
Netherlands, 118
Neturei Karta (Guardians of the City), 227
Neve Shalom/Wahat al-Salam, 385–389
Neve Tirza Women's Prison, Ramle, 376
Nevo, Gil, 108
Nevo, Haya, 108–112
New Age Judaism, 239
New Israel Fund, 144
Newspapers, 31, 41, 81, 202, 251, 264–265, 314
New York stock exchanges, 76
Niddah (laws of family purity), 332
Nir, Ori, 265, 269
Nokia, 133
Non-Orthodox Jews, 221–243
North Africa, 115, 119, 120, 121, 127, 239
North American Conference on Ethiopian Jewry, 167
North Korea, 74
Novaris, 92
Nozich, Vadim, 143
Nuclear weapons, 73, 74
Nudel, Ida, 374

Nudelman, Yuli, 141
Numeri, President of Sudan, 157
Numerology, 35

Odessa pogrom, 112
Ohana, Yossi, 127–128
Old City of Jerusalem, 50, 75, 153, 173, 198, 204, 272, 305, 309
Olmert, Ehud, 378
Online relationships, dating services, 15–16, 338
Open House, Ramle, 320–323
Operation Magic Carpet, Yemen, 115
Operation Moses, 157
Operation Peace for Galilee, 50
Operation Solomon, 149–150, 157, 158, 164
Oppenheim, Ariella, 255–256
Organized crime, 378–379
Orthodox Jews, 2, 31, 68, 195–220, 330–333, 339–340
OrthoDykes, 358
Osirak nuclear reactor, Iraq, 73
Oslo Accords, 49, 55–57, 98, 203, 205, 209, 210, 254, 258, 312
Ottoman Empire, 100, 119, 215
Oz, Amos, 53, 187, 252

Pale of Settlement, 100
Palestine, 98, 100, 109, 110, 112, 117, 119, 140
Palestine Liberation Organization (PLO), 60, 74, 207, 209, 258, 260
Palestinian Authority, 13, 18, 39, 49, 68, 164, 200, 202, 203, 251, 258, 260, 274, 312, 392
Palestinian Islamic Jihad, 15, 20, 68, 146, 271
Palestinian Red Crescent, 10, 64
Palestinian state, proposed, 52, 53, 56–57, 200–202, 207, 252
Palmachim Air Force Base, 74
Paradise Camp, Gaza, 20
Park Hotel, Netanya, 22
Passover, 53, 134, 153, 222, 223, 237

Passover Massacre, 22, 49, 64
Passover Police, 229
Paternity leave, 334
Patriot missile, 65
Peace Child, 393–394
Peace Now, 205
Peleg, Anat, 97–99
Peleg, Israel, 97–99
Peleg, Ohad, 99
Peleg, Re'ut, 99, 101, 102
Pentium computer chip, 88
Peres, Chemie, 84
Peres, Shimon, 75, 84, 98, 104, 122, 144, 165, 213
Perestroika, 135, 145
Peruvian Indians, 197
Physicians, 137
Pinchaski, Gregory, 86
Pogroms, 99, 100, 112, 116
Poison gas, 21, 22
Polgat Textiles, 125, 129
Polish Jews, 98
Political parties
    Communist, 267
    Green Leaf, 382
    Kach, 209, 210
    Labor, 121–123, 144, 199, 219, 251, 253, 299
    Likud, 107, 122, 123, 144, 192, 199, 253, 274, 299
    Meimad, 219
    Meretz, 42, 253, 269
    Shas, 32, 35, 123, 142–143, 155, 213, 232, 236, 266, 376
    Shinui, 51, 145, 191, 192, 236
Polygamy, 3, 286, 353–355
Popular Front for the Liberation of Palestine, 321
Population, 1, 24
Proclamation of Independence, 235
Prostitution, 288, 370–378
Protestantism, 310
Protocols of the Elders of Zion, The, 260

Psychological stress, 21, 22, 340
Purim, 53, 155, 223

al-Qaeda, 22, 27, 36, 48, 271, 275
Qalqilyya, 65, 266
al-Qaradhawi, Sheik, 354
QueerJihad, 364
Quraish tribe, 117

Rabin, Yitzhak, 38, 54, 55, 74, 84, 97, 144, 209, 210, 213, 227, 253, 320, 359, 368
    assassination of, 56, 98, 188, 211, 220, 231, 254
Rabin, Yuval, 84
Rabiya, Sarab Abu, 278
Rachel (of the Bible), 261, 328
Rachel's Tomb, 197–198, 208, 335
Rachum, Ofir, 15–16
Radio talk shows, 31
Rafael, 85, 86
Rafah, 390
Rahat, 286–289
al-Rahman Zouabi, Abd, 363
Ramadan, 253, 267, 268
Ramallah, 55, 68, 143, 367, 387
Ramat Rachel, Kibbutz, 20, 80
Rambam Hospital, Haifa, 248
Ramle, 319–323
Ramon, Ilan, 73, 80
Rape, 42, 351, 352
Ravitz, Avraham, 141
Rebecca (of the Bible), 208
Red Sea, 1, 24
Reform Judaism, 218, 222, 231–236, 241, 330
Rehavi, Etti, 63
Rehovot, 214
Reincarnation, 3, 293, 304
Reserve duty, 49, 336–337
Rishon LeZion, 140
Rivlin, Ruby, 41
Robinson Crusoe (Defoe), 101
Roman Catholic Church, 306, 307, 349

Romania, 119, 125
Romeo and Juliet (Shakespeare), 38
Rosenfeld, Eli, 57–61
Rosenfeld, Melodie, 218
Rosenfeld, Sherman, 218–220
Rosenthal, Miriam, 376
Rosh Hashana, 35, 218, 222, 223, 232, 238, 239, 242
Rubin, Uzi, 74
Russia, czarist, 99, 100
Russian Israelis, 17, 56, 124–125, 130–147, 158, 331, 339
Russian language, 131, 132, 137
Russian mafia, 373–375, 378–379
Russian Orthodox Church, 139–140
Russo-Japanese War (1905), 54

Saad, Ismael Abu-, 278, 283, 287–289, 291
Sabbath (Shabbat) observance, 2, 107, 115, 180–181, 196, 223, 228, 229
Sabra (native-born Israeli), 26
Sabri, Akram, 272–273
Sadeq, Adel, 10–11
Safed, 34, 391
Sakhnin, 393–394
Saladin (Yusuf ibn Ayub), 275, 313
Salah, Sheik Ra'ed, 267, 269–271, 273–276, 289, 364
Samaria, 197, 198, 201, 203, 204
Same-sex parents, 362–363
Sandaka, Natan, 164
el-Sanna, Amal, 278–284, 286
Sarah (of the Bible), 33, 208, 329
Saudi Arabia, 51, 251, 260, 269, 270
Sbarro pizzeria, Jerusalem, 270
Schach, Rabbi Eliezar Menahem, 175–176
Schizophrenia, gene for, 92–93
Schneerson, Rabbi Menachem, 186
School for Peace, 388–389
Schwartof, Ilona, 146
Scud missiles, 22, 24, 25, 30, 130
Sderot, 204

Sea of Galilee, 1, 78, 356
Sedbon, Yossi, 378
Segev, Tom, 116
Sephardi dialect, 102
Sephardim, 118–119, 215, 217, 224, 240–241
September 11, 2001, 48, 86, 275
Settlements, 52–53, 195–207, 209, 210, 220
Sexual harassment legislation, 41–44, 359
Sexuality, 332–333, 347–348. *See also* Dating; Marriage
Shabbos goy, 225
Shabib 3 missile, 74
Shafir, Dorit, 11–12, 14
Shafir, Yael, 11–14
Shafir, Yair, 11, 14, 15
Shahab 5 missile, 74
Shaked, Rivka, 41
Shalom, Sivan, 121
Shalom Hotel, Jerusalem, 150
"Shalom-Salam" (Sheva), 239
Shalom Tower, Tel Aviv, 102
Shalon Chemical Industries, 125
Shamrock Group, 92
Shapira, Aaron, 55
Shapira, Dor, 55
Sharansky, Natan (Anatoly), 135, 151
Sharon, Ariel, 144–145, 200, 213, 220, 251, 265
visit to Temple Mount, 57, 164, 264, 274
Shas Party, 32, 35, 123, 142–143, 155, 213, 232, 236, 266, 376
Sheba, Queen of Ethiopia, 153
Shefayim, Kibbutz, 107
Shelef, Gil, 39–40
Shenkin Street, Tel Aviv, 33, 34
Sheva band, 239
Shevah-Mofet High School, Tel Aviv, 145–146
Shimon, Menberu, 160, 161
Shimon Bar Yochai, Rabbi, 211–213
Shinui Party, 51, 145, 191, 192, 236

Shoughry-Badarne, Banna, 354, 355
Shulhan Aruch (Code of Jewish Law),
    333
Shwed, Gil, 78–84
Sierra Leone, 69
"Silicon Wadi," 86
Simkovitz, Shani, 203–205
Sinai, 50, 257
Al-Sinnara (Arabic-language
    newspaper), 314
Six-Day War (1967), 50, 52, 72–73,
    87, 198, 200, 207, 209, 257, 298,
    312, 335, 379
Smallpox vaccinations, 21
Smooha, Sammy, 116–117, 119, 261
Soap operas, 3
Sofer, Nava Swersky, 92
Soldiers. *See* Israeli Defense Forces
    (IDF)
Soldiers' Letter, 52
Solomon, King, 28, 153–154, 157,
    353
Sonnenschein, Nava, 388–389
Soviet Union, 2, 17, 56, 124, 131,
    133–135, 138, 141–142
Springer, Jerry, 30
Stalin, Joseph, 135
Star of David, 4, 179, 222, 236, 259
Stein, Benjamin (pseudonym),
    175–177, 179, 181–185, 189,
    191
Stein, Leah (pseudonym), 184,
    185–188
Stein, Moshe (pseudonym), 173, 175
Stein, Sarah (pseudonym), 175,
    177–179, 181–186
Street of the Prophets, Jerusalem, 221,
    226
Street Under Fire (documentary), 17
Sudan, 157, 163, 165
Suez Campaign (1956), 50
Suicide bombings, 13, 20
    Ben-Yehuda Street, 48
    Dolphinarium, Tel Aviv, 146
    females and, 10, 64

French Hill, Jerusalem, 14, 64
Haifa bus, 248, 293, 303
Hebrew University cafeteria, 20
Jerusalem bus 32A, 7–11, 13, 14,
    16–17, 19
Matza Restaurant, Haifa, 256, 354
Moment Café, Jerusalem, 12
Nahariya, 275–276
Netanya market, 255
Number 18 bus, 136
Passover Massacre, Park Hotel, 22,
    49, 64
Rishon LeZion, 140
Sbarro pizzeria, Jerusalem, 270
    videos promoting, 10, 50
Sukkot (Feast of the Tabernacles),
    239–240
Sun Microsystems, 76
Sunni Muslims, 249
Suras, 271
Syria, 4, 22, 50–52, 60, 72–74, 110,
    115, 125, 145, 251, 257, 260,
    297–299, 312, 379

Tabjeh, Yossi, 164
Taher, Ahmed, 290
Taher, Khalil, 290
Taibe, 64
Tajikistan, Jews of, 132
Talking *dugri*, 83
Tal Law of 2002, 541
Talmud, 176, 177, 180–182, 185, 187,
    190, 233, 332, 341
Tanzim, 16–18, 64, 68, 271
Tarif, Saleh, 297
Tawil, Hussein Mohammed, 146
Technion, Israel Institute of
    Technology, Haifa, 83, 84, 89, 91,
    92, 102, 163, 190
Technology, 15, 75–94, 105–106,
    125–126, 128–129, 190–191,
    196, 318
Teddy Soccer Stadium, Jerusalem, 20
Tefen Industrial Park, 391, 392
Tekoa, 202–204

Tel Aviv, 3, 25, 33, 34, 65, 97, 99, 101,
102, 106, 114, 145–146,
161–162, 231, 262, 330, 342,
358, 363, 370–376, 378, 381,
382
Tel Aviv University, 106, 162, 262,
342
Tel Hai (Hill of Life), 54
Temple Mount/Haram al-Sharif,
Jerusalem, 51, 57, 164, 197, 264,
271–275, 369
Ten Commandments, 179, 180, 335
Third Egyptian Army, 50
Tibi, Ahmed, 258, 265
Tigrinya language, 159, 160
Time of Favor (film), 200–201
Tomb of the Patriarchs, Hebron, 198,
200, 207–210
Tomb of the Prophet Jethro, 295, 297
Torah, 34, 176, 177, 179, 187, 188,
190, 233, 260, 332, 338
Total Love (film), 381
Touma-Suliman, Aida, 351, 353
Trembling Before God (documentary),
362
Trumpeldor, Yosef, 54, 56, 133
Tu b'Shvat, 223
Tulkarm, 64, 266
Tunisia, 115, 121
Tunnel Road, 201
Tur'an, 319
Turkey, 72, 118, 119, 392, 393
Turkish Jews, 119
Tyler, Yitzhak, 374, 377
Tzur Shalem, 205

Ukraine, 130, 132, 133, 135, 139,
143, 374–376
Ultra-Orthodox Jews. *See* Haredim
Umm al-Fahm, 3, 265–268, 270, 271,
274–276, 299, 314, 315
United Nations, 70, 110, 392
Uris, Leon, 104
Uzbekistan, 132
Uziel, Rabbi Yonatan ben, 34–35

Vallis, Polena, 146
Vardi, Yossi, 75, 190
Vassa, Yossi, 148
Venereal disease, 372
Vesti (newspaper), 145
Vilna Gaon (Elijah Ben Solomon
Zalman), 185

Wafa news agency, 69
al-Wahidi, Nadine, 352
Waits, Tom, 39
Waqf (Muslim Religious Trust),
272–273, 296
War of Attrition (1968–70), 50
War of Independence (1947–48), 50,
62, 249, 320, 321, 383, 390
Warsaw Ghetto uprising, 72
Weapons, 86–87
Weitzman, Ezer, 63
Weizmann, Chaim, 103
Weizmann Institute, 35, 91, 92
Wertheimer, Stef, 390–393
West Bank (Gush Etzion), 4, 18, 42,
49, 50, 52, 53, 55, 57, 60, 61, 64,
65, 195–210, 249, 257, 258, 270,
271, 274, 285, 286, 352
Western Wall, Jerusalem, 50, 153,
197, 198, 200, 221, 234, 272,
273
Wiesel, Elie, 241
Wilde, Oscar, 371
Women Against Violence, 351
World Trade Center, New York
1993 bombing, 65
September 11 bombing, 48, 69, 275

Y chromosome, 255–256
Yadin, Yigal, 49
Yad VaShem Holocaust Memorial, 54
Yalu, Bat-Chen, 164–165
Yassin, Sheik Ahmad, 270
Yediot Aharonot (newspaper), 251
Yehoshua, A.B., 187
Yemeni Jews, 114–116
Yerushalayim (newspaper), 31

Yeshivot (religious academies), 31, 51

Yitzhak Rabin Synagogue, Rehovot, 220

Yokenam, 86

Yom Kippur, 35, 153, 222, 232

Yom Kippur War (1973), 50, 57, 62, 155–156, 230, 257, 382–383

Yonatan, Dalia, 17, 19–21

Yonatan, Gal, 17

Yonatan, Inbal, 17

Yonatan, Kobi, 16–22

Yonatan, Shani, 17

Yosef, Rabbi Ovadia, 143, 155, 174, 213, 215, 236

Yossi and Jagger (film), 358

Yossi Beilin–Abu Maazen plan, 199

Younis, Imad, 89–91

Yousef, Nadia, 305

Youth movements, 53–54

Yugoslavia, 118, 119

Zacharie, Liaura, 36–37

Zangen, David, 69–70

Zeidner, Moshe, 22

Zidkiyahu, Rahamin, 7, 8, 13

Zionism, 54, 100, 102, 116, 133, 187, 208

Zion Mule Corps, 54

Zippora (of the Bible), 295

Zisling, Aaron, 102–103, 105

Zisling, Ongy, 102–104

Zisling, Ori, 105–108

Zman (newspaper), 31

Zohar, 211, 212, 233

Zomet Institute, Alon Shvut, 196

Zuckerman, Roni, 72

Zyklon B, 22

About the Author

Donna Rosenthal's articles have appeared in publications including *The New York Times*, the *Los Angeles Times*, *The Washington Post*, *The New York Daily News*, *Newsweek*, and *The Atlantic*. She was a news producer at Israel Television, a reporter for Israel Radio and *The Jerusalem Post*, and a lecturer at The Hebrew University. She has reported from Iran, Lebanon, Egypt, and Jordan and was the first journalist to travel to the remote mountain villages of Ethiopia and introduce Israeli radio audiences to Jews praying in grass-hut synagogues to be able to go to Israel. A winner of two Lowell Thomas awards (for Best Investigative Reporting and Best Adventure Travel Writing), she has traveled to over sixty countries. She has a master's degree in International Relations (Middle East) from The London School of Economics. She may be reached through her website www.TheIsraelis.net.